GALACTIC SOUL HISTORY OF THE UNIVERSE

BOOK I

RISING PHOENIX AURORA

Published by Rising Phoenix Aurora, Inc.
www.risingphoenixaurora.com

Library of Congress Control Number: 2020924303

Print ISBN: 978-1-7358542-0-5

1st Edition, December 2020

Special thanks to the Illustrator Samia, who is a digital artist and clear channel to benevolent energies. You can find her at www.aurapractitioners.com.

TABLE OF CONTENTS

ACKNOWLEDGEMENTS

-------------<◇>-------------

This book represents Love manifested into reality. We are deeply humbled and truly honored to be able to present this book, in this time and space, to humanity on Earth. Please know that this book is a multidimensional deep labor of Love from so many beautiful and resilient souls who have contributed by sharing their incredible Soul Journeys with us. Each one of them courageously doing their part in anchoring in the Love-Light within themselves, first by self-healing while on Earth, and then shining their Love-Light brightly throughout Creation. It is truly a beautiful experience to witness all these inspiring soul journeys across all dimensions and densities, from both the physical and non-physical realms in Creation, divinely come together to form an in-depth collective Soul Remembrance for ALL in the form of this timeless book.

Our deepest gratitude to Aurora, for following her heart in pursuing this path of Love by pioneering the A.U.R.A. Hypnosis Healing modality in this time and space, where it is very much needed to aid Humanity in rebuilding the organic timeline for Earth and the Universe. It took tremendous courage to blaze the path forward for all these beautiful A.U.R.A. Hypnosis Healing sessions to take place so this book could be created to aid many more souls to awaken, thus rippling out Love-Light throughout Creation exponentially.

This book is made possible through the Divine Hand gracefully at play to align all these beautiful sessions across states, countries, continents and timelines; through all the beautiful souls who shared their inspiring journeys for the collective, through the benevolent Angelic and Galactic teams who assisted all throughout, including the healings, through the Rising Phoenix Aurora (RPA) team who helped pull all of this together working long hours night and day to make this book possible, through supportive family members who understood the importance of this project and who endured the long work hours of their loved ones, and through all the RPA students, practitioners and friends for their infinite loving support, feedback and inspirations. Equally important to all of this is YOU, dearest reader. You are the inspiration for this book, and the knowing of how this foundational book can touch all souls who are guided divinely towards it; is what inspires us to keep doing our best for all!

We humbly thank you for your love and support in appreciating this book, and for recognizing what it can do for you at the soul level.

We love you, we honor you, we respect you and we thank you!

We are so infinitely grateful for you, dearest reader and fellow traveler, on this most beautiful journey of Creation!

~ The Rising Phoenix Aurora Team ♥

-------------<◇>-------------

5

INTRODUCTION

-------------<◇>-------------

Beloved soul and dear reader,

We are infinitely grateful and honored for you to be here, holding this book in the palms of your hands as you are ready to embark on this beautiful journey of Soul Remembrance together. We humbly thank your Higher Self for getting you to this very moment in preparation to experience the most catalyzing Galactic History that your soul and heart will feel, as you read every word, paragraph, and as you feel the suspense through each turning page. These various soul journeys are fascinating, deep, profound, enlightening, thought provoking and emotional. Each one so unique, yet form a crucial part of the larger Galactic History. In this book you will journey through the Galactic History of our Universe, and, at times, the Multiverse. Bringing into an awareness of why it is that our world is constructed in the manner that it is, and this will awaken you to the possibilities of sovereignty of the soul. You will regain, piece by piece, pieces of you that you may have long forgotten, or long lost, as you TOO experience the self-healing through the eyes and expressions of each soul's Galactic Journey. As we are only but reflections of one another.

The best way to approach this book is with an open mind and an open heart. As you read each chapter/galactic journey, take time to reflect and let the wisdom of it sink in and then proceed to the next chapter, keeping notes if you shall need. I have taken the greatest attention after each chapter to include channeled details to each session, which will profoundly help you understand each session further from the individual soul's perspective as well as the collective's. Bringing forth concepts that, perhaps, you had not thought about as you read each session, or if you did, it will settle into place with the greatest understanding. Each chapter is placed together with such a divine flow that will help you with ease move and dance through the book. You will not want to put down this book, as each divine session will activate your soul's blueprints further and further. You will feel the deep, profound, self-activations within your soul through each emotion felt and expressed. Your soul and Higher Self will guide you accordingly and allow what is meant to remain with you, in this time and space, to divinely integrate and activate whatever you are ready for in your organic timeline. You may find that you will want to read it over and over, as each time you will gain additional layers of understanding.

As we journey through this book, one will experience a range of intense emotions from crying, disbelief, anger, sadness, to relief, laughter, hope, wonder, faith, joy, inspiration, empowerment, and infinite love, as each soul remembers their own soul's journey through the Multiverse. You will feel yourself cheer them on and get to know each soul, as if you knew them personally and intimately, as truly you do beyond the veil. As each one of these souls volunteered bravely to be the first wave in playing this role of sharing their Soul Journey stories, not only for their own personal Ascension but also for the collective's assistance into Ascension. Where we have been, where we are now, and where we are heading, as the multitude of beautiful expressions of Creator Source energy collaborating to create this profound series of Galactic Soul Journeys to activate our remembrance of who we truly are at the soul and Unity Collective Consciousness level. The names of all those who shared their beautiful Galactic Soul Journeys have been changed to honor their privacy. Know that these infinitely beautiful and courageous souls are living amongst us in the NOW, doing their crucial part in anchoring the Love-Light into

Earth during this incredible time, as we all are working towards bringing forth Ascension for individual and collective timelines for the Earth and the Universe.

There is so much going on these days, much of which is intentional in design, in holding the collective dense and in perpetual fear. By holding us dense in negative emotions, we delay our own soul growth, dim our inner light, and delay the organic timeline for Ascension. This book series is intended to divinely jump start Earth's Ascension and assist Mother Earth with her energetic stabilization. Many do feel victimized by deep rooted feelings of fear, shame, guilt, lack of self-love, lack of abundance, hopelessness, anger, and self-doubt, mindlessly repeating these patterns of dysfunctions in this lifetime, or over many lifetimes. Through the Galactic Soul History of the Universe, you will finally come into a realization and understanding why it is that these negative cycles seem as though they cannot be broken within you, or others around you. Many times, you might have asked "what is wrong with the world, why can't others see what I see." You will find the roots to these emotions within you, in turn, experiencing a most profound soul expansion through each expression of emotion. These negative energy patterns dim the infinite Love-Light flame within us, and hold us dense in fear, preventing us from reaching our highest potential as a sovereign, conscious creator utilizing our gift of Free Will for creating more beauty in the Universe for all. You can look at this book series as the 'Holy Grail' of knowledge and wisdom from the multitudes of Higher Self perspectives and expressions scribed for our memory recall and infinite collective soul Ascension.

Our message to you is of hope, for where there is hope there is love, and love is infinite. Know that you can break free from the mind controls and the energetic shackles imposed on you as soon as you realize how powerful you truly are at the soul level with your divine connection to Source. We go within, as some of the toughest and most profound battles occur within us, not outside. When we commit to self-healing, this is an empowering crucial first step in realizing our divine sovereignty, and our true strength as a Child of the Divine Creator Source. We rise above fear by doing the inner work, the shadow work, through energetic shielding ourselves from harm using Love-Light forcefields, establishing boundaries, and embracing our sovereignty. And if one feels guided to do so, there are powerful healing modalities available such as A.U.R.A. Hypnosis Healing and R.A.A.H Reiki Healing to aid and jump start your self-healing journey.

It is especially important for all of us to realize that we all are healers, and we can self-heal. Disease or illness stem forth from energetic imbalances in the human body through our emotions, vibrations, karmic energy, chakra points, and inorganics within us, such as A.I., entities, etc.... Our body is made to be able to self-heal and it will talk to us through certain aches, discomforts, or illness. Illnesses are energy imbalances and blockages that we have created within ourselves. Our body tries to speak to us through these signs. Examples are: Cancer, unexpressed emotions turning into anger and hatred. Diabetes, lack of sweetness/love in one's life. Arthritis, holding on to something, or someone very tightly, not releasing. Throat disorders, not speaking our truth, fear of speaking out. We have also found that at times we can carry over allergies, illness, birthmarks, from past lives. For example, if one died of a gunshot to the heart in a past life, heart problems may now exist in this life. That energy might be carried over to this current life needing to be quantum, karmically healed. We have also discovered that nanotech A.I. are within immunization shots and chemicals within our food, our water, our air, and our intakes of such are root causes to illness; through these Galactic Soul Journeys we will learn exactly how that is, and what it looks like.

All of these Galactic Soul Journeys were facilitated using a sacred healing modality called Angelic Universal Regression Alchemy (A.U.R.A.) Hypnosis Healing. The A.U.R.A. method uses a combination of Sacred Angelic Energy Work, to create a bridge for the client to connect to their Higher Self. This allows us to enter the Theta brainwave of A.U.R.A. Hypnosis sacredly and safely to bring forth memories of all our existence, to Quantum Heal our body, to find our life purpose, and to remember our Galactic Origins. In A.U.R.A. sessions, as a client, you will speak to your soul, to your Higher Self, who is you, and the Higher Self is ONE with the Creator, who knows all. Our Higher Self/Soul is truly God Source, and it is where we can find all the answers we are looking for, and where we connect to this unlimited infinite healing vibration. By connecting to our Higher Self, we then allow for that little voice in our head that has been there all our life, our consciousness, to finally speak through us sharing its infinite wisdom.

Many experience blockages of energy which do not allow for the deepest possible connection to the Higher Self during hypnosis. This is what sets A.U.R.A. Hypnosis Healing apart from other hypnosis past-life regression modalities. The key being that before a client's session begins, the client's Higher Self, in union with the A.U.R.A. Hypnosis practitioner, conducts sacred Angelic Energy Work prior to entering the Hypnosis brainwave, thus creating a bridge for the client to connect to their Higher Self at the deepest level possible. During the process of the sacred energy work, the Higher Self removes excess negative energy that is not needed during the session, to allow for the deepest level of connection. Through this sacred energy work our Higher Self will place us in the highest, safest, sacred vibration that no longer allows what is inorganic within us to remain during the high vibrations of the A.U.R.A. session. This begins the unveiling of all that is artificial within clients, bringing it all up to the surface for healing. If one is unable to connect to our Higher Self to Quantum Heal, or if a deeper connection is needed, the Archangels are able to assist, always with the Higher Selves' permission first, by using their infinite Source Love-Light to strengthen the connection to allow for the healing of the mind, body, and soul during the session. The Archangels are the first fractals of Divine Creator Source; the Elohim angelics individualized out from the collective infinite Consciousness of Source. Therefore, they hold the purest frequencies in Creation, and they are able to assist us in healings in divine ways that align with our Soul's organic blueprints. By being of this infinite Source beginning fractals, they hold the greatest strength of Love-Light power. Which is why when the Higher Selves of our clients can't heal or remove something, is why THEY can. As the Archangels are benevolent beings, they will only assist if we ask them to and always with our permission first. Throughout this book, we will read about the infinite, beautiful ways the Archangels and benevolent soul families always assist all of us throughout the healings shared in all of the Galactic Soul Journeys mentioned. Truly, we are loved beyond measure by Source and our Galactic soul families, for they are always there to assist us for our highest good in our lives!

Throughout this book, there will be the occasional reference to the Reiki Angelic Alchemy Healing (R.A.A.H.) method, which is another profound and powerful energy healing modality, which also uses Sacred Angelic Alchemy to facilitate the healing session. Unlike A.U.R.A. Hypnosis Healing sessions, R.A.A.H. does not go into past-life regressions hypnosis. For those who feel they are not quite ready yet for an A.U.R.A. session, a R.A.A.H. session is a beautiful way to prepare for a future A.U.R.A. session as it helps the client to start connecting to their Higher Self and clairvoyant senses. The main focus of this book is on the A.U.R.A. Hypnosis Healing modality, through which these beautiful Soul Journeys and Higher Selves' wisdom are shared with us and the collective.

To all who are guided to this book. May this book assist you through Soul Remembrance of the Inverted A.I. Matrix, in turn learning to weave through it, so that you may graduate and begin operating in the Organic Matrix, bridging forth your Ascension into the Fifth Dimension, or above. May the beautiful Galactic Soul Journeys and lessons contained in it activate your heart, your soul, and your remembrance of who you truly are, and who your brethren truly are, within our Universe. May your most organic timeline forward unfold beautifully as you choose to release the falseness of all kinds around you, as you learn and remember them through this book. Reminding you to travel in alignment with Love and guided by your true, infinite Higher Self.

I love you, honor you, respect you, and I thank you for being a fellow soul traveler on this most beautiful Galactic Journey of Soul Remembrance!
~Rising Phoenix AuroRa🖤
12.21.2020

-------------<◇>-------------

IMPORTANT

LOVE-LIGHT SHIELDING TECHNIQUE

BEFORE YOU BEGIN READING THIS BOOK, please understand that one of our core foundational teachings is shielding ourselves with our "I AM Source Love-Light" so we can be more intentional with managing our energy frequency in our daily lives, thus empowering us to be in our sovereignty. When we shield and set our intentions for the day, we are declaring our sovereignty over our own freewill and lifeforce, creating how we want our day to be. We are powerful creator beings, if we allow for it, by actively maintaining our vibrations to the purest, I AM Source Love-Light.

Please review this page carefully as they contain beginner sacred alchemy teachings for you to start using your "I AM Source Love-Light" to create force fields around you in maintaining your vibrations high. Our intent is to teach you how you can help your Inner Light become stronger by actively using the force fields around you, filtering out the negative that means harm, so that you may strongly heart discern every frequency that passes through. These force fields will help amplify your heart discernment, reading what energies are harmful, and what is not.

It is important that we surround ourselves with our own infinite "I AM Source Love-Light" daily. Ideally, you should be shielding yourself every morning when you wake up and every evening before the sun sets for optimal results. This energy is accessed through your heart and flows out through your hand chakras. Our heart center is where we are able to tap into the infinite Source Love-Light energy. When doing this for your day, it will ensure to keep your energies high and not depleted, when you set the proper intent for your energy. Surrounding yourself with the "I AM Source Love-Light" will help you keep your mind focused and clear, and your abilities strong and open.

**Practice these empowering Love-Light shielding techniques
on the next two pages daily!**

OPENING YOUR HAND CHAKRAS

It is important to open your hand chakras, as it is out from them that the Universal love energy will flow. Energy will enter through the crown and bottom of the feet, connect to the heart, and flow out through the palms, connecting the alchemy symbols.

1.   Place hands in Gassho position. (Gassho is a gesture with the hands held in prayer position, in front of the chest).

2.   Rub hands together, as you desire.

3.   Clap four times in prayer position and state with strength "Open."

4.   Turn hands horizontal, with left hand above right, facing each other.

5.   Open and close both hands in this position 13 times.

6.   Switch hands now, right hand over left.

7.   Open and close both hands again in this position 13 times.

8.   You should be feeling vibrations in between your palms.

9.   Play with this energy; moving it around, expanding it bigger and then shrinking, creating it into an energy ball.

If the energy ball bursts, no worries - just rub hands again together and pull apart palms facing each other to create again.

No need to repeat steps 1-7 once the opening of hand chakras is completed. Going forward just rubbing hands together will create the energy ball inside palms.

You may use this energy ball of Love-Light around your home, cars, children stating "without harming anyone." We are powerful creator beings, and by stating this we make sure to not pull from someone else's energy.

I AM SOURCE LOVE-LIGHT AND MERKABAH

1.   Rub your hands together to create your energy ball consisting of your "I AM Source Love-Light."

2.   Viewing it and sensing it through your imagination. Expand it to surround your vessel and auric field. You may make it the color of your choice, and may include a sacred geometric symbol that aligns with you, encasing the walls of this bubble.

3.   Set the intent by stating, "shall I be shielded from harm mentally, physically, emotionally, and spiritually throughout the infinity of Creation. I DO NOT CONSENT to harm all day and night, without harming anyone, for my highest good."

4.   As you expand the light, state four times, "I invoke the I AM Love-Light in me."

5.   With your hands expand the light around yourself, your loved ones, animal companions, cars, and home...

6.   Envision your eight-point Merkabah surrounding you. It is a live consciousness, so envision it activating, or coming to life, so to speak.

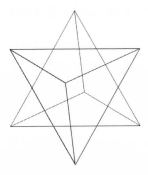

7.   It is a counterclockwise, upside down, four-sided pyramid, expanding, repelling, spinning structure of light at the bottom. Clockwise, right side up, drawing in energy at the top pyramid through the crown. The Merkabah is an extension of our consciousness and represents the integration of the spiritual, energetic, and physical bodies. Made up of eight triangles having eight points, we find that the Merkabah also reflects the infinite energy and protection of creation (since the number eight is an ancient alchemy infinity symbol). Each triangle's three-sided points represent the sacred three elements of the Divine Mother, Father and Child, trinity complex.

We have included more foundational teachings for you to work spiritually within, to start building a solid foundation for your spiritual growth, and journey forward.

For more teachings, please go to "Your Soul's Growth Journey".

1

THE FIRST REPTILIAN CONSCIOUSNESS ATTACHMENTS

Session #160: Recorded in June 2019.
Never before shared.

In this online A.U.R.A. Hypnosis Healing session, Jasmine is looking to expand her gifts and ready to bring forth renewal; however, she feels stuck and clouded. Never did we expect what was to come and a part of what was holding her back in life. This is one of the sessions that started showing us more details on how this race of Reptilians began their control over Earth through these forms, what we refer to as 'the first experiments.' Jasmine finds herself as a child trapped in a dark place separated from one another where other children are as well. She courageously fights for the freedom of her soul. On this suspenseful journey where we see these experiments up close, we learn about the importance of shielding with Love-Light to minimize harm and infringements on oneself.

-------------<◇>-------------

"The trees help you; the Earth helps you, it's almost as if they clean what they can. There is hope. Channel the light. If you push that light, you do this consciously until you do it unconsciously all the time, you will do what the Earth does."
-Higher Self

-------------<◇>-------------

J: [Jasmine]I feel like I am in Egypt, there is sand, the middle east, very hot.
A: [Aurora] Look at yourself, do you feel like you have a body?
J: Yes.
A: Look down at your feet, are you wearing anything on your feet?
J: I can see my toes; it looks like sandals.
A: How many toes do you have?
J: Ten toes.
A: Look at your hands, how many fingers do you have?
J: Ten fingers.
A: Are you wearing anything?
J: I'm a male. Not a dress, a garment, long, but there are no pants. It's like a wrap.
A: What color is it?
J: Lighter than sand, like a light beige.
A: Are you wearing any jewelry?
J: No, but there's something on my head to protect me.
A: Is there anything you're carrying?
J: Water.
A: Tell me, what are you doing here in the sand?
J: Walking to a meeting. I have to take tunnels underground to get there.

A: Were you on top of the sand at the beginning?
J: It looked like a hill, there were parts that were higher and lower.
A: How did you get in through the tunnels?
J: There is an entrance and two guards.
A: Where is the entrance?
J: It's underneath what looks like a pyramid, but it looks like the pyramid itself is made of sand. It doesn't seem solid.
A: You said there are two guards by the entrance?
J: Yes, and one has a long staff.
A: Look at his face, his features. How does he look?
J: His skin is darker than mine. He has thick black eyebrows and a beard. There's a little bit of white hair on his beard, and some sand.
A: What does his staff look like?
J: It's taller than him. It's about three inches thick, very long, and it curves at the top.
A: What about the other guard, how does he look?
J: He's sitting down. His hair is long. He also has a beard, but he's younger than the man with the staff.
A: Are they standing on each side of the door of the entrance?
J: Yes.
A: Except for the one that is sitting and the other one is standing?
J: Exactly.
A: The one that's sitting, is there anything else that stands out about him?
J: He just looks tired.
A: Very good, let's go ahead and go through that entrance. Are you able to go through there?
J: Yes.
A: Is there anything that you need to do before you're allowed to enter through it?
J: They already know me.
A: As you are going through the entrance, I want you to pay attention to how you look. I know that you said you are male; can you describe what your face looks like and your features?
J: I have a full beard; it extends almost to my collarbones. My skin is tan but lighter than the man's outside. I can see my eyes, they're dark brown.
A: Continue to walk. When you go through this entrance, what do you see?
J: A long, long path and the walls look like stone, but they're wet.
A: Is there anything that you can see that stands out from them like colors, or shapes, symbols?
J: I'm running my fingers along the stone and it feels like there can be carvings, but there are so many I can't see them.
A: Tell me what else you are sensing?
J: Very dark and damp. I feel like my heart rate is starting to rise but I don't know why.
A: Are you able to touch the walls?
J: Yes, that's how I can feel the carvings.
A: It feels like stone carvings?
J: Yes I see a gray-black stone. But on that stone, there are carvings, they're deeper than just the denseness of the stone.
A: Is there anything that's lighting your path?
J: All the way at the end there's a room and there are lights on in there, so I can see that there's something there. There are people there, I can feel them.
A: Continue that way, let me know if there's anything that stands out before you reach the room.

J: It keeps going. This tunnel you can either turn right and go to that room or you can keep going. I can see where it keeps going but there's no light down that way.

A: Let me know once you are right in front of that room.

J: I'm there.

A: Before you enter that room, is there anything that stands out before you go in?

J: Just the light inside.

A: Go ahead and step through and as you step through let me know all that you are seeing, sensing, and feeling.

J: There's something that looks like an altar that is also made of stone, there's nothing on it. It's very large and there are people. It's like the people are there, but they're not there; they're in a circle around it.

A: How are they surrounding it? Is there a shape they are making around it?

J: They're in a circle around the altar. It's not a perfect oval, but kind of.

A: These people that might be there, if you can see, are there many? Are there a few?

J: There's nine or ten.

A: Let's scan the room and see if one of these people stands out, that draws your attention.

J: Yes.

A: Tell me what they look like.

J: They're completely covered. They're wearing what looks like a cloak,there's something covering their head too. It's like a hat but it's pointy and tall and it's covered.

A: Is it different from what you're wearing on your head?

J: Yes.

A: Anything else, or anyone else that stands out?

J: They're all wearing the same clothes except only one has the big covering on his head.

A: Are they a 'he' or a 'she?'

J: It's a 'he.'

A: He's the only one that's wearing the pointy hat?

J: Yes.

A: What is it that they're doing around this circle oval altar?

J: It seems like they are sacrificing. When you ask, it's like, I'm getting the answer and it's playing out but when I look again it's not really there. But I think they place people on that altar.

A: Let's go ahead and go to a time and space that you mentioned; they have someone placed on the altar. Tell me what you're seeing.

J: They have a young boy, maybe 13 or 14 and he's curled up into a ball on top of the stone.

A: Is he alive?

J: Yes.

A: What is he wearing?

J: Nothing.

J: He's very thin, his skin is lighter than the others.

A: Can you see his eyes?

J: He's covering his face; he's curled up as tightly as he can.

A: What are they doing around him as he's lying there?

J: I'm understanding that they've kept him there for a long time.

A: On the table, or elsewhere?

J: In that cave.

A: They've kept him in the cave, just not on the altar?

J: Yes.

A: How long?

J: At the age of 12 is when they were able to start doing whatever they're doing to him.

A: What is it that they're doing to him now?

J: It's almost as if they're trying to put, it feels like thoughts or beliefs. They're trying to put something from them into him, but his body is rejecting it. It's not working. They're putting something that is not physical, yet I can see it.

A: What does it look like?

J: It looks almost like a little ball that's spinning, but it's not perfectly round. It has little peaks and valleys to it. It almost glows and it flickers like it's not a strong light. It flickers on and off and when they stand in the circle, they each transfer this light onto the man with the hat and he's the one that implants it onto the child.

A: What color is that light?

J: It's a very, light blue; it's almost white.

A: Are there males and females there that are doing this to the child?

J: Two females.

A: See if you're able to look at one of the females. Can you describe to me, what does she look like?

J: She feels so familiar. She looks like what my mother looked like when she was in her twenties. Light brown, blonde hair, fair skin, it looks like her.

A: Look at her eyes, you're able to recognize the soul through the eyes.

J: That's her.

A: How do you think she feels about doing this to the child?

J: It's almost like she thinks she should be doing it, but she feels guilty, too.

A: Look at the man with the pointy hat. Look at his eyes, does he feel like he's human?

J: No.

A: What does he feel like?

J: Oh my goodness! I can almost see a tail! Okay, his skin changed now, he looks jet black, and I can almost see a tail under that cloak and he became very large. Much, much taller.

A: What kind of tail are you seeing under there?

J: It's thick, it doesn't look like a dog or a cat's tail. This looks thick like if it would be, I don't know, like a dinosaur tail if it could be half human, half dinosaur. It looks like that.

A: Okay. Look at his eyes, do you recognize his soul?

J: It feels like I do, but at the same time his eyes make my whole body tingle, it feels strange.

A: Remember you are safe and protected. Nothing can harm you. Do you recognize his soul?

J: I know this being, but I can't place him...I don't know how.

A: Look again at all of them. Is he the only one with this kind of hidden form?

J: No, they're not human.

A: Would that be all of them?

J: I'm looking for my mother to see and...I can see a tail on her as well, but it's green, it's not the color of her skin anymore.

A: Would you say that this is inside of them or that this is their true form?

J: It feels like a mix of both.

A: When you are there with them, do you feel like you are part of them, you're observing, or separate?

J: At the very beginning when I saw the boy, I felt like that was me, but I'm not in his body. I'm in a different body.

A: So, do they see you with them, interacting with them, or are you just observing?

J: I'm observing but the one with the hat, I feel like he can feel me.

A: Higher Self, make sure she stays invisible to his senses, make sure he doesn't sense her, please. Is she invisible to him now?

J: Yes.

A: Let's go back in time, right to when they grabbed this child from wherever he was at. What do you see?

J: The people that took the boy are guards. He was three, maybe four and they took him from his mother.

A: Where were they when they took him?

J: It looks like a village with little huts. There were other people around, but they just watched as if it was normal.

A: What is the mother doing when they're pulling away her child?

J: She's screaming and she's trying to get her son, but they hold her back, she can't.

A: What do the guards look like?

J: These guards look different, their hats are harder, it doesn't look soft like the other ones and they have long sticks. It looks like a very long spear.

A: Describe to me how the mother looks, what is she wearing?

J: She has long hair, looks like something is pulling her hair back. She's wearing a long dress. But it almost feels heavy, it feels thick.

A: Are there any colors to the outfit?

J: I'm seeing browns and beige, but I can feel something on her that's blue.

A: What color is her skin? What are her features like?

J: Her skin is like a soft tan, she looks very petite, she has a small face, and thin features. It almost feels like she...wasn't originally from there, like she's not from that village; she came from somewhere else.

A: You said that their homes looked like huts?

J: Kind of, it looks like it was made with raw materials.

A: Would you say that there are many in her village?

J: Yes. From where I am, I can see three huts, but I know there's more.

A: What happens now that they've grabbed her son?

J: They take him to that cave. There are other children.

A: Was this cave in that pyramid type of form?

J: Yes, the top looks like a sand pyramid, but underground it looks like dark stone.

A: Are there other children there as well?

J: Yes, but they're...it's like they're held captive. Like they're held separate from each other.

A: How do they keep them separate from each other?

J: They're not rooms, but they're little crevices within the walls. They dug it out. The cave wasn't like this before, they keep it separate and there are guards.

A: Do they have a door, or a gate keeping them in each little section?

J: Yes.

A: Would you say that there are a few, several, or many children?

J: Right now, I see three doors.

A: Three doors, so there are three children currently?

J: Yes.

A: Okay. What do they do with him, do they place him in one of those?

J: Before they do that, they remove his clothes, they hurt him. He's crying, they hit him because he cries.

A: After they remove his clothes, what do they do to him?

J: They put him inside one of the rooms. They close the door, there is no light.

A: Is there anything in that room?

J: No.

A: How do they use the bathroom?

J: On the floor.

A: Fast forward a bit, do they feed them?

J: Yes. They throw food inside, as if they were animals to eat off the floor.

A: Let's fast forward to another time, when there is perhaps another child being taken out besides the one you saw already. Tell me what you see.

J: The child's about eight years old, with dark black hair.

A: What do they do with him, when they remove him from the little room?

J: They're showing me the circle again, and it feels like they're trying to implant something, but it's not physical. I see that same ball, but it's pointy. It has pointy parts.

A: Does it come out from the guy with the hat?

J: Yes.

A: When it comes out, what does it do, and from what part of him does it come out from?

J: It's coming out of his mouth, but his mouth looks huge, it doesn't look human. That little blue spinning ball comes out of his mouth and they're trying to put it in THIS boy, into his leg.

A: When it comes out, does it flow on its own towards the child?

J: It moves slowly, as if someone is guiding it, as if someone is putting it there, but it moves really slow.

A: See if you can feel and sense what is inside that ball. You are safe and protected; you can sense what it is as it's floating through the air. Does it have a consciousness? What is it?

J: It's as if all of those people extracted a part of themselves to make this little ball, and it goes through the circle until it reaches that being that seems like the leader. Then it comes out of him, but it feels like that ball is a piece of all of them.

A: What do you sense from it? How does it make you feel?

J: It makes me feel cold, it feels a little bit scary, but at the same time, I know that I'm safe. But it feels like one of them, it feels like it's a baby version of one of these beings.

A: Now, as it floats towards the child, tell me what happens as it gets close to the child.

J: Now I see one person on each side holding the child down so that he doesn't move. And there's a slicing of the child's leg, it's above his ankle around where his calf is, but nobody is cutting it open, it's just being cut open and he's bleeding.

A: So, is it being cut open just kind of from thin air?

J: Yes, there's no one doing it.

A: What happens next?

J: It goes inside and he's twisting back and forth, and they're still holding him, and that ball keeps spinning inside, but since it has pointy parts, it hurts him.

A: Does it just stay in the leg?

J: No, it moves around his body.

A: Look closely, as it's moving around and spinning. What is it doing to the child from inside?

J: As it's so strange…as it's spinning it looks like the pointy parts cut him, and he bleeds, but it looks like within that ball there is black ink coming out and mixing with his blood.

A: Does it do that throughout his whole body, or just certain parts?

J: It went up to his leg and it stopped at his stomach, almost as if it's stuck.

A: What does it do in his stomach?

J: It's spilling out this black ink; it looks like octopus ink.

A: What does the ink do?

J: It changes what he has, it changes him.

A: Describe to me how it does that. As it releases the ink, what does the ink do?

J: It's absorbing the blood that's coming out as that little ball cuts him, and it's like the blood is replaced by the ink. He doesn't have blood anymore; it's the ink that's his blood.

A: The blood, what color is it now that it has the ink integrated with it, or replaced by it?

J: Black.

A: Keep moving the scene along, tell me what else happens with this ball inside him.

J: It stops at the head; it somehow got inside his brain, in the very center of his brain is that ball. Everything is black.

A: Everything is black within him?

J: Yes.

A: Was the boy not able to fight back, energetically?

J: He couldn't.

A: What does it look like now that it's sitting in his head?

J: Inside of him everything is black. I can see the boy sitting down and the people around him aren't really in a circle anymore. It's like they finished and they're just standing there.

A: What's the little boy doing now?

J: God...he's sitting down, but his eyes... I can see it in his eyes; it doesn't look like him. It's still his body, but those eyes aren't his.

A: See if you can see when this takeover of energy occurred. What happened to the soul within him?

J: He's...the soul...I saw a little piece of him leave. It moved so fast, it was like liquid light. A little bit left, but it feels like that little boy is still in there, but it doesn't feel like him.

A: Let's see if we're able to see as deep as we can right now. Would you say that these pieces of themselves, that they created, are now in charge of him?

J: Yes.

A: Would you say that the soul is trapped there, or is the soul of the original child gone?

J: He's still in there, but he's not the one in control.

A: What happens next, now that they're in control of him?

J: They released him.

A: Where does he go, and where did they release him?

J: They gave him his clothes and they opened the cave, the same entrance I went in through, he came out of, and he went back to his village.

A: Let's follow him along, let's see what happens when he goes back; what does he do?

J: He's looking for someone. I think it's a sister, she's older, it doesn't feel like his mother.

A: Does he find her?

J: Yes.

A: What happens when he finds her?

J: She's hugging him and she's crying. She takes him back to where she lives.

A: Does it feel like he was gone a long time?

J: One to two years.

A: When she hugs him crying, how does he react?

J: He's so cold, he lets her, but he doesn't really hug her back. He seems like a robot, or a zombie; he's not responsive.

A: What happens next of significance when she takes him back to the home?

J: He's an observer. That's his job.

A: What is he observing?

J: It's almost as if he scouts out others to be taken.

A: What is he scouting for? What are they looking for so that they can take them?

J: They must be young. The body must be strong, not too thin.

A: Do they look for anything energetically from the person, from the child?

J: This little boy, it's as if he can scan people. He's just looking, but he's scanning.

A: When he is scanning the people, are they connecting to him when he's scanning? Do they have a connection with him?

J: He's just looking, and they don't realize it.

A: How about the bad non-humans, are they connected to him as he's scanning? Can they see and sense?

J: Yes.

A: Is there anything in particular that they look for in a child, as far as color, energy-wise what they look like?

J: All this little boy does is scan, the one that makes that decision is that leader because he can see what the boy is scanning.

A: Are there any other children, who they have done this to, that are also inside the village scanning, and do they do this just to this village, or are there other villages around?

J: They send them to different places.

A: What happens next of importance?

J: They are showing me the other boy, the first boy I saw.

A: Yes, tell me. Were they trying to do the same thing to him?

J: Yes, but they couldn't.

A: Go back to that time, when they were trying to do that to him, let's go back there now. Look at this very closely as they're sending this ball just as they did with the other young man, are they holding him down as well?

J: I don't see anyone holding him.

A: Is he still curled up in a ball?

J: Yes.

A: Once the ball is closer to him, tell me what happens. What do you see, sense, and feel?

J: It can't get close.

A: It can't get close to him?

J: No, once it leaves that being's mouth it goes about a foot away from him, but it can't get any closer to the boy.

A: Let's look really closely, what is holding that ball from getting closer to him?

J: I am.

A: You are? How are you doing that?

J: I see myself in that man's body again and doing something, it looks like I'm pulling it back, or pushing it back, not letting it get closer to the boy.

A: How are you doing that?

J: I'm using my energy; I'm pushing it through my hand.

A: Do they know what's going on? What's their reaction?

J: At first, they didn't, but then he saw me.

A: What happened?

J: It's so strange! It feels like I'm that boy, but yet I'm also the man that's helping the boy.

A: What happens when they can't seem to get that ball through? What do they do?

J: Okay, I can see clearly. The little boy almost looks like a projection as the man and that's where I'm seeing this from. But as soon as that leader looks at me, he's looking at the boy and then he sees me stopping it. He just moves his hands and it's as if I'm dead. I'm not there anymore.

A: Let's go back a little bit and explain that one more time. So as soon as he sees you, what happens?

J: He raises his hand, but it doesn't look like a hand, it looks wrinkly and there are only three fingers. As soon as he moves his hand, I die.

A: Which part? The 'you' that is there protecting the child, or the child that is laying there?

J: The man that's standing protecting the child dies.

A: How is it that you die?

J: He cut the connection.

A: When he cuts the connection, what happens next to the child?

J: Oh, now I can see! It was as if the child was pushing his energy out into that man form and he severed it, that energy, it just went back to the child!

A: It went back into him, what do they do next?

J: He's angry. The child starts pushing that same light; it looks almost like a shield, but it's not a full shield, it's just between his feet and the leader, but it's not enough. That light starts to dim. I can't see it anymore.

A: Is that man with the hat doing something with the light there that he was emanating, the little boy, to make it go dimmer?

J: No.

A: It's just dimming on its own?

J: Yes.

A: Tell me what happens next; what happens to the little boy and the light?

J: Even though no one is protecting him, they still can't put that ball into him, it doesn't work.

A: Are they not able to slice the skin like the other child?

J: They've cut him, but the ball just doesn't, it just doesn't go in.

A: It's not able to get close enough?

J: No.

A: So, what do they do to the child? What do they do next?

J: They kill him.

A: How is it that they kill him?

J: Decapitation.

A: Is there anything that they do to his body, or any parts of him, when they decapitate him?

J: They cut him open as if looking for something, but they don't find anything. They burn him.

A: Why do they burn him?

J: They don't want him there.

A: To burn his body causes him to not allow the child in?

J: Even though he's dead, they need to get rid of that body, they can't leave it there.

A: Why? What would happen if they left it there?

J: The connection.

A: That energy that the boy carried would connect to them?

J: Yes, they could be discovered.

A: To burn his body cuts that link?

J: Yes.

A: Anything else that you see, or sense, or feel from this place that you want to share?

J: They're showing me the number one thousand. Thousands of souls.

A: They've taken thousands of souls?

J: Yes.

A: In this one cave?

J: Many caves.

A: This place that they are at, was there a sun, a moon? What colors were the skies?

J: It feels like here, it feels like Earth. The sun, the moon, but underground where they were, there was no light. The only thing that lit the cave was the torches.

The Higher Self is called forth.

A: Thank you. Let's leave that life now. Can I please speak to the Higher Self of Jasmine?

Higher Self: Yes.

A: Am I speaking to Jasmine's Higher Self now?

Higher Self: Yes.

A: I honor you, I thank you, and I respect you for all the aid you have given us today. I know that you hold all the records of Jasmine's different lives. May I ask questions, please?

Higher Self: Yes.

A: Thank you for showing us this life and if I may now ask further questions for some clarifications of it, please?

Higher Self: Okay.

A: Thank you. Where was this place that you showed us, was this connected to Earth, or somewhere else?

Higher Self: Earth.

A: This place with the huts, was there a time period that this was in, where they were doing this, or an era?

Higher Self: I'm seeing the number seven; seven zero, seven, zero, zero.

A: Now, this young boy that she saw, was that her, the 14-year-old boy?

Higher Self: Yes.

A: As far as these places and pyramids, you mentioned that there had been thousands that this had been done to, were there many of these throughout Earth at that time?

Higher Self: Yes.

A: How many would you say there were then, of those undercover places?

Higher Self: Fifty-two.

A: Were they located throughout all of Earth?

Higher Self: Some places more than others.

A: Where were some of those places that they were more focused on, that there were more of?

Higher Self: They're showing me what looks like Asia, Europe, more of that area.

A: Why is it that they chose those specific areas, why did they focus more on those?

Higher Self: There were many clandestine groups, it was easier. There were many people, but there were also many people who would wander and travel, it made it easier.

A: You mentioned that when they took the little boy, the village didn't really fight back, was this a normal thing for them?

Higher Self: It's routine, they had no power.

A: These beings, the ones that were testing, trying to do things to the child, to the children. She mentioned that they seemed bigger and darker and had tails. Were they connected to Reptilians?

Higher Self: A form of, yes.

A: Are these locations still on Earth?

Higher Self: Some, but they're like portals.

A: They're like portals instead?

Higher Self: They're still underground, but I'm seeing the beings popping in and out, as if they're using portals.

A: Are these individual bases, are they still active in this time and space?

Higher Self: A few.

A: What percentage Higher Self, would you say are still active upon Earth from that example that you gave us of the 52?

Higher Self: Two.

A: There are still two active ones?

Higher Self: Yes.

A: Are we allowed to know the locations?

Higher Self: They're showing me the continent of Africa, towards the bottom left.

A: Anywhere else?

Higher Self: Undisclosed, the other is undisclosed.

A: Are they still actively taking children in these areas?

Higher Self: They're not taking children, but they're using the caves almost as a portal; they're coming in from somewhere else and they're staying there, that's how they have access.

A: So, the original, this program of sorts, would you say that it's still active, as it was then? Taking the children?

Higher Self: They don't need to take them anymore.

A: Why not?

Higher Self: Different technology.

A: Would you say that what they started doing to the children then, inserting this black consciousness within them that were parts of fractals, or consciousness of the Reptilians themselves?

Higher Self: Yes.

A: Is it a Reptilian consciousness that they were inserting into them?

Higher Self: Yes.

A: What would happen to, for example, that child that was now different with that Reptilian consciousness within him, still there, but controlled? What happens to that child when they die and then incarnate, would it continue with that Reptilian consciousness within him?

Higher Self: Attachment.

A: With the attachment?

Higher Self: Yes.

A: Would you say that a great good percentage of people who are on Earth were in some of these experiments and they accomplished what they were trying to accomplish through inserting consciousness into people? Reptilian consciousness?

Higher Self: Yes.

A: Some of those people would feel like you said, controlled, zombie-ish, cold? Is that how they would feel if they had one in them like that child?

Higher Self: Yes, disconnected.

A: Would you say that that program was canceled because they had accomplished what they needed to do?

Higher Self: Yes, it evolved.

A: Tell us what was so different about her, for example, this little boy that was laying there. The other one was so easy just to hold down and insert this through the cut. What was different from the other boy who they couldn't do this to?

Higher Self: The light.

A: What does that mean, the light?

Higher Self: The light inside was stronger.

A: Does it have anything to do with perhaps a soul being older than another soul? The experiences gained as an older soul or…?

Higher Self: Yes.

A: Did it have anything to do with perhaps the child's soul origin that made perhaps their light stronger than the other child?

Higher Self: Yes, it was not compatible.

A: The child that did not allow for that to enter, did they perhaps have a stronger Love-Light type of frequency than the other?

Higher Self: Yes.

A: That higher frequency of Love-Light, is that what initially was stopping and not allowing that lower density ball thing to enter because it was a lower density?

Higher Self: Yes, it was not compatible.

A: Can you share with us, what are other ways? You say that it evolved, and I guess they developed other ways to insert these types of fractalizations of them into people. What are some of the things that you can share with us in ways that they're inserting these types of consciousness into people currently, in this time and space now?

Higher Self: Mental programming; its telepathic programming, but they use words to do it, a sequence of words.

A: Is it like vibrations, tones?

Higher Self: It comes as a vibration, a sequence of words repeated over and over, just like an implant.

A: How do they emanate that, or what do they emanate that through?

Higher Self: It's like they're pulling energy from some, in order to push out that frequency.

A: They're pulling energy from where?

Higher Self: Hosts.

A: Hosts, is that the population overall, is that what you mean? Or what type of host? Is there a specific host that they are choosing?

Higher Self: The ones they can feed off of, they pull. But when they take that energy, it's like it swirls inside of these beings and then what they push out is totally different from what they absorbed, to begin with.

A: I'm trying to understand this, so if you could explain this one more time. The people that they can draw energy from would be people who hold a lower type of frequency, perhaps, like that child that they were able to penetrate into?

Higher Self: They can absorb from anyone who's open.

A: Anyone who's open. What about people that practice Love-Light type of shielding, or force fields around them, can they pull from them?

Higher Self: No.

A: Is this why they've taught Light Workers, channelers, people who are meant to be leading the spiritual community, that shielding and force fields are fear-based, and we shouldn't do it?

Higher Self: Exactly.

A: So, this is part of the programming to make people believe that?

Higher Self: That's part of the words they implant into us, to make us not shield.

A: If there is someone who has thousands of followers and you are watching that someone, or learning from them, and they are speaking this vibration, how you mentioned it's coming out through tones and sound and they are saying, "this is fear-based, don't do it." As this being or 'teacher' who perhaps might have thousands of followers, with a good percentage of those thousands of followers listening to what they're saying, that it IS fear-based. As they (speakers/teachers/leaders) are emanating this, is this a way to form a connection, a transfer to the listeners to allow these types of consciousness to connect and enter into them?

Higher Self: That is the agenda.

A: However, some who perhaps, their Higher Selves, or perhaps their force fields, could be stronger, like that child that she was, that was stronger and wouldn't allow them in, some of those would reflect that out and not allow that black or dark consciousness ball come in?

Higher Self: Yes.

A: I want to clarify this, as this has been something that you all have been trying to show me for a long time and I have yet to find someone who can give me the information as clear as this. Say that there is someone channeling, and they are part of this, they feel very cold, perhaps you do not feel love and this person is in a theta brainwave, as there are Light Workers out there that work in the theta brainwave to channel. When these channelers are speaking, let's say they themselves might also feel like that child that was taken control and they feel cold and disconnected even though they are claiming to be of Love-Light. When these channelers are in this theta brainwave emanating whatever vibration and sound, can they give their listeners something negatively in that manner?

Higher Self: Sometimes it may transfer.

A: Sometimes it can transfer?

Higher Self: Sometimes it can, yes.

A: It just depends on all the different situations to that?

Higher Self: Yes, not always.

A: If you could explain to me, what are other ways that they would transfer this sphere type of consciousness into people?

Higher Self: Other technologies, microscopic. You can breathe it in. They don't need to cut the skin anymore, it is almost as if it's in the air.

A: Is it in the air through the chemtrails?

Higher Self: I'm seeing dust, almost like dirt in the air. It's in that dirt and dust.

A: Is there something that's manufacturing that dust and dirt?

Higher Self: There are two ways. One is coming though - I'm seeing space rocks like an asteroid. It's dust that's released from outside and then there's dust that we release inside.

A: Inside from where?

Higher Self: One is manufactured here; the other is brought from outside of this planet.

A: How do they release it onto the Earth?

Higher Self: The air, it's in the water, the dirt.

A: Is that what they were doing, testing out how to be able to insert these into people?

Higher Self: Yes.

A: And now they have developed it into what you said, the nano type of...

Higher Self: Yes.

A: If you could tell us how it is, I understand that it's there in the air and in the water, how does it enter the air and the water?

Higher Self: It's released.

A: From what?

Higher Self: I'm seeing the chemtrails, but it's like they're releasing something underground too, and that mixes with the dirt and the water.

A: Does it have anything to do with the pesticide that they're throwing on the food?

Higher Self: Yes, yes!

A: So, what happens when people drink this water and eat the food and perhaps, they're not healing the water, the food, blessing it, they're just eating it, just like that. What happens when they consume it?

Higher Self: You continue the disconnect.

A: It keeps them in that disconnect?

Higher Self: Yes.

A: Do you mean the disconnect from the soul like that child was there, but yet not connected to the soul?

Higher Self: Yes.

A: Anything else you want to tell us on this subject and how they insert this Reptilian consciousness into people?

Higher Self: There is hope.

A: Yes.

Higher Self: The trees help you; the Earth helps you, it's almost as if they clean what they can. There is hope.

A: Beautiful, so nature helps heal this. Is that what you're saying?

Higher Self: It aids. Yes.

A: How can we help ourselves? Does the Earth help heal and transmute these particles?
Higher Self: Channel the light. I'm seeing tiny, tiny, little nanoparticles, but if you push the light into it, it's almost as if it turns it off, it disables it. If you push that light, you do this consciously until you do it unconsciously all the time, you will do what the Earth does.
A: Similar to that little boy who held off that ball from trying to go into him, he kept pushing it off with his light?
Higher Self: Yes.

The Body Scan begins.
A: Thank you for this awakening and beautiful information. It is much needed in this time and space for others to hear. Higher Self, if we could please do a body scan on her now. Let us know if you need any aid from the Archangels. While we are on the subject, I want to see if there's any trauma, anything negative within her that is held because of this life that you showed us that we need to focus on and address first.
Higher Self: I would like assistance.
A: Who would you like to call upon first?
Higher Self: Archangel Zadkiel.
A: Beautiful, if we could please speak to Archangel Zadkiel now. We'd love to be able to speak to you. Greetings brother, is that you?
AA Zadkiel: Yes.
A: Welcome, we love you, we honor you, and we respect you. Thank you for being here. What a beautiful gift, not too often do we get to speak to you. We are performing a body scan on her now and she just showed us a life where Reptilian beings were performing experiments on her. We wanted to scan that life to see if she had any trauma, any negative energy that is holding on to her now from that, that needs to be healed? If you could scan her whole body and see what is connected to that life now, thank you?
AA Zadkiel: Three connections.
A: Where is it that you see those connections?
AA Zadkiel: Two in her head, one in her stomach.
A: Can you describe to me what the connections look like please?
AA Zadkiel: Looks like tubes, black tubes.
A: Let's look at these black tubes closely, at the ones in the head. How did they get there?
AA Zadkiel: They implanted.
A: When?
AA Zadkiel: Other lifetimes.
A: What are these black tubes causing her now?
AA Zadkiel: Confusion, doubt.
A: Is it technology?
AA Zadkiel: They're feeding deposits into her.
A: What do you mean by these deposits?
AA Zadkiel: They're feeding black liquid deposits to keep her under.
A: Is this black liquid similar to that ball that was inserting blackness into the little boy who couldn't hold them off?
AA Zadkiel: Yes.
A: Is this liquid at all connected to a Reptilian consciousness?
AA Zadkiel: Planet.
A: To a planet? What planet?
AA Zadkiel: Looks like a dead planet; a black planet, but there is still activity.

A: Can you tell us a little more about this planet Zadkiel? You said that it's black, but there's an activity in it. If you could look closer, is there life on it?

AA Zadkiel: Consciousness, but not incarnated life.

A: How does this consciousness look, can you describe it?

AA Zadkiel: It's just black swirls moving around. The planet is large, there's a lot of texture to the planet, very bumpy. Those beings are no longer there, but the consciousness is.

A: Can you tell us more about the beings who were there before?

AA Zadkiel: One of the Reptilian races.

A: What happened to that planet?

AA Zadkiel: They destroyed it.

A: This, what she has, is it connected to that planet?

AA Zadkiel: It's as if the planet - the consciousness within the planets - are depositing the little liquids that they have left into her. They cannot take over, but they can deposit.

A: What do they get out of it by depositing this into her?

AA Zadkiel: They don't want her to remember.

A: Can we start transmuting this out of her Zadkiel; you said it was in her stomach too?

AA Zadkiel: Yes.

A: Does it have a consciousness, do we need to speak to it, or do we just transmute it?

AA Zadkiel: You can just transmute it.

A: Very good, if we could start focusing our fire elements, or whatever energy you need to be focusing, as well Zadkiel, upon both the head and the stomach area where these are located at. If we could all go ahead and start transmuting it out, please. Are we doing that now?

AA Zadkiel: Yes.

A: Thank you. Zadkiel, can you tell me, brother, she had mentioned that there was still one of these undercover bases in Africa. She said it was like a portal; is there something that we can do about this portal so we can close it off, so they won't come in and out of it anymore?

AA Zadkiel: Yes.

A: What can we do, Zadkiel?

AA Zadkiel: Metatron can seal it.

A: Can I talk to Metatron during this process, and then talk back to you?

AA Zadkiel: Yes.

A: Thank you. If I could please speak to Metatron now, please?

AA Metatron: Yes.

A: Welcome brother, we love you and we honor you. We were speaking to brother Zadkiel and he said we could call on you to close the portal that is in Africa; the portal they are still running some of these tests that were mentioned throughout the session. Would you be able to walk us through what you are doing to close that portal in Africa?

AA Metatron: Yes.

A: Thank you, and before you close it, is there anyone there inside that you would be locking in or sealing in?

AA Metatron: No, I'm cleansing the area.

A: How are you cleansing it?

AA Metatron: My Merkabah is spinning through the tunnels.

A: Is there any life in there though as you are doing that?

AA Metatron: Not right now.

A: The beings that go in and out of the portals, they're not there?

AA Metatron: Not right now.

A: Tell us what you do next, after you cleanse them.

AA Metatron: I'm placing a cube and I'm filling it with light, filling it with a symbol. With the symbol no one may enter, no one may exit.

A: I want to make sure we're not permanently trapping anyone in there.

AA Metatron: There is no one here.

A: Good. Now, what happens if someone negative, who has these ties to this base tries to enter, what happens to them?

AA Metatron: They may not enter.

A: Okay, they just can't enter.

AA Metatron: They cannot connect.

A: Can we go ahead and send healing? If we could call on the Collective Consciousness of Angels and can we send healing to this land that still had this space, there? Also, as we're sending to this particular base, can we send it to any other bases that are now closed off, since there were only I believe two remaining, as you all mentioned. To anywhere that these bases were, as perhaps, there is still residual energy there.

AA Metatron: Some.

A: Can we go ahead and start sending Love-Light healing to all these areas that need it now?

AA Metatron: Yes.

A: Thank you. Very good, is there anything else, Metatron, that you'd like to share with us before we talk back to Zadkiel?

AA Metatron: No.

A: Okay, thank you Metatron. We love you, we honor you, and we respect you. Thank you for your aid. If you could please connect us back to Zadkiel now.

AA Zadkiel: I am here.

A: Thank you Zadkiel. Now, how are those black tubes looking in her now?

AA Zadkiel: Better, but one is still there.

A: Which one?

AA Zadkiel: One by her forehead.

A: We'll continue focusing transmutation energy there. Can we have brother Raphael start filling in wherever it was that we're removing negative energies from? Can we please fill in the Love-Light?

AA Raphael: Yes.

A: Thank you brother, we honor you and we thank you. Thank you, Raphael. Zadkiel, if we could scan her body one more time, is there anything else that holds any type of trauma, or energy, from that life in her?

AA Zadkiel: Her hands.

A: What's going on with her hands?

AA Zadkiel: She used it to protect herself at that time, but it's almost as if they're not as active. Not as powerful. Minor block.

A: Can we go ahead and start healing that for her now, please?

AA Zadkiel: Yes.

A: As we heal it, Zadkiel, when it's time, have Raphael fill it with Love-Light there. Thank you.

AA Zadkiel: Okay.

A: Now, let me see if she has any specific things here that we want to address during the body scan. She wants to know if she can release excess weight and addiction to meat, cheese, and sugar? What is keeping her addicted to that?

AA Zadkiel: Fear.

A: Can we go ahead and release that for her, help her clear that?

AA Zadkiel: Yes.

A: Thank you, are we doing that now?

AA Zadkiel: Yes.

A: Good. She also wants to know if we could open up her third eye so that she can make a connection to her intuition stronger and clearer. She wants to be a clear channel. Can we start working on that for her now, please?

AA Zadkiel: Yes.

A: Thank You. She wants to know if she can upgrade and activate her crystalline DNA for easier Ascension and clear all ancestral and past life issues encoded into her DNA?

AA Zadkiel: Yes.

A: Good. She said she also feels waves of anger, then guilt, and a cycle of shame. Can you tell us why? She's ready to release it.

AA Zadkiel: Childhood.

A: What happened in her childhood that is causing this?

AA Zadkiel: Responsibility, so much responsibility.

Jasmine during the interview mentioned that her mother was irresponsible, therefore, even though she was the child she had to often be the mother to her mother. Responsibilities fell on her.

A: Can we go ahead and heal that pain, that trauma that holds the anger, guilt and shame? Where is that found in her body?

AA Zadkiel: Her stomach.

A: Can we transmute it and heal it now.

AA Zadkiel: Yes.

A: Will she be able to feel happier and enjoy life more so?

AA Zadkiel: Contract.

A: That was a contract?

AA Zadkiel: She is undoing that contract.

A: Can we help her today to go ahead and undo it completely Zadkiel?

AA Zadkiel: Yes.

A: Good. Thank you. Higher Self if we can go ahead, with your permission, and undo that contract for her, please.

Higher Self: Yes.

A: Thank you. Can you scan her whole body Zadkiel now for any entities, negative implants, hooks, portals, any Reptilian consciousness? Let me know what you find.

AA Zadkiel: Her lower spine.

A: What's in her lower spine?

AA Zadkiel: Entity.

A: If we could please speak to the entity now. Zadkiel help us connect to the entity now, if it could please come up, up, up, up. Greetings.

Entity: Hello.

A: Hello, thank you for speaking to us, may I ask you questions, please?

Entity: Okay.

A: Are you female or male?

Entity: Male.

A: How is it that you found yourself in her body? When was it that you connected?

Entity: When she was a fetus.

A: In her mother's womb?

Entity: Yes.

A: In what part of her body did you connect to then?

Entity: As her spine was forming, I attached.

A: Have you ever had a body?

Entity: Yes.

A: Do you have a body currently you're connected to?

Entity: No.

A: What happened to your body? How did you die?

Entity: I don't know.

A: That's okay. Do you feel that you're connected to anyone out there right now?

Entity: Just her.

A: Okay, is there a being, or an entity, or a body of sorts, connected to you now?

Entity: I can't see one.

A: Very good. Now, we know that you've been there for a long time. What kind of pain, or what have you been causing her?

Entity: Many pains. Back pains, knee pains.

A: Was this a contract?

Entity: Her mother brought me forth.

A: Why did she bring you forth, the mother?

Entity: Immense fear.

A: I know you've been there some time, we'd love to be able to aid you today so that you may release yourself from having to be stuck in her body, so that you may be free and ascend and transform into Love-Light. Be free and go as you please and desire. Would you allow for us to help you today so that you may shift into Love-Light and no longer have to play this negative role?

Entity: Where will I go?

A: You will go wherever it is that your Higher Self, as you, yourself, have a Higher Self as well, wherever your guides would like to aid you. The angels could always help you and direct you in whichever manner you are meant to go.

Entity: Okay.

A: Good. We want you to look within you, find that light within you and we're all going to focus Love-Light onto you now and if you could spread that light to all that is of you, every root, every cord. Spread it to all light and let us know once you are all light.

Positive Polarized Entity: I am light.

A: Thank you and if you could please remove yourself. Every root, every cord, make sure you don't leave any piece of you behind, and let us know once you are fully out.

Positive Polarized Entity: I'm out.

A: Beautiful. Thank you, do you have a message for her before you go?

Positive Polarized Entity: I'm sorry, thank you. It is done.

A: Thank you, if we could have Raphael fill in that area now with Love-Light, please, where it was removed from. Is he doing that now?

AA Zadkiel: Yes.

A: Thank you Zadkiel. Now, if we could please guide that entity now that it is Love-Light, guide him to wherever it is that he is meant to go. Angels, let us know, where is he going?

AA Zadkiel: It looks like the sun.

A: He's going to the sun?

AA Zadkiel: Yes.

A: Beautiful, thank you. Blessings and may the Love-Light of the Universe surround you. Zadkiel, if we could please continue her body scan now, scanning her for any entities, negative implants, portals, anything that we need to heal within her.

AA Zadkiel: Sacral chakra.

A: What's going on there?

AA Zadkiel: Something is there.

A: Is that an entity?

AA Zadkiel: More than one.

A: How many are there, Zadkiel?

AA Zadkiel: I can't count, it's a lot.

A: Are any of them Reptilian?

AA Zadkiel: Can't tell.

A: Do you need any help from Archangel Michael, or anyone else that could help you?

AA Zadkiel: Can we call upon RA?[1]

A: Yes, very good. Zadkiel, if you could connect us to RA now, we would love to be able to speak to RA now, please... Greetings… Is this RA?

RA: Yes.

A: Thank you for being here. We love you, we honor you. May we ask you for aid?

RA: Yes.

A: Thank you. Zadkiel mentioned that there is a collective of sorts in her sacral chakra. Can you please help us see? Is that collective connected to Reptilians, or what is this collective of?

RA: Collective of suffering souls.

A: Suffering of souls from... is there a particular place? If we could have Metatron surround that collective there now with his symbols, please. Did he do that?

RA: Yes.

A: Thank you. Where does this stem forth from, where did this begin, this suffering of a collective that's there? Where is the initial beginning of the suffering?

RA: The place where the souls have suffered, many lifetimes have gone. I see them spinning and screaming in sorrow and agony. Never ending.

A: Is there a time that is connected to, or a planet?

RA: It feels like another Dimension.

A: Can you show us RA, and can you tell us more of this Dimension?

RA: I see a galaxy, and this is a place within this galaxy, but it's another Dimension.

A: Why are there suffering energies coming out from that Dimension?

RA: They were called there, they tried to have relief, but it was almost like a trap, there was no relief.

A: What else can you tell me of this Dimension, RA?

RA: They just want to be freed.

A: How many are there?

RA: Hundreds of souls.

A: How is it that they connected to her, what is their connection with her?

RA: She wanted to help, but they attached to her, they connected to her.

A: What can we do RA, about helping these hundreds there in this Dimension?

RA: We need to release this place.

A: How can we do that? Tell us what to do.

RA: We can open the doors, but we must all work together.

A: Good. Are you working together as the RA to do this?

---

[1] Also commonly referred to as the Ra Collective. Ra is the collective of benevolent galactic alien races, working in unity for the Ascension of the Universe. We go into more details about the Ra Collective in Chapter 8 'Four Ra. Guardians Heal Thousands of Entities.' To learn more, visit the Rising Phoenix Aurora channels and watch 'Who is the Ra Collective' video.

RA: Yes.

A: Good and if you could tell me along the way what you're doing to help them.

RA: There were sealed doors and we're opening them now. But, as these beings leave, if we can send them to light, then they can be freed. They no longer need to suffer.

A: Good, can we start that process now?

RA: Yes.

A: Can you tell us what happened to them that created the initial suffering?

RA: They each carried so much pain. They each wanted to ease someone else's pain, but they just took it on as their own and they kept growing and growing. They are leaving now.

A: Good, beautiful and tell me where is it that they're going?

RA: I see them bursting into different directions.

A: Beautiful, and if we could have all the angels guide them and make sure that they go wherever they are meant to go for their highest good.

RA: Yes, please.

A: Thank you, and as we do that, can we ensure that we are healing the connection that they had there to her sacral chakra? If we could heal and transmute that out, please.

RA: Yes.

A: Thank you. Very good and as we transmute that out of there if we could just have Raphael fill in light there? As well as RA, you're definitely welcome to fill in Love-Light as well there. RA, if I could continue to ask you, would you like to continue the body scan, or should we continue back to Zadkiel?

RA: I can do it.

A: Beautiful. RA if you could please scan her whole body now, we are looking for any entities, implants, portals, Reptilian consciousness, anything that needs removal from her now.

RA: On her feet. It looks like a portal. She uses this to travel, but she does not close the portal.

A: Which foot is it?

RA: Her right foot.

A: Can we go ahead and start sealing that portal for her now, please?

RA: Yes.

A: Thank you, when you are done sealing it if you could also fill in that Love-Light there for her, please... What was it causing her?

RA: It was bringing others through, they would linger.

A: Very good, RA can you scan the rest of her body? Let us know what else you're finding, any negative energies, entities, technologies within her that require healing?

RA: I don't see anything.

A: Very good, thank you RA and I want you to scan just one more time for any Reptilian consciousness. I want to make sure there is none in her.

RA: No.

A: Very good. RA, do you have a message for her before you go?

RA: This will not be our last time talking.

A: Thank you and before you go, is what we removed from her sacral chakra what was causing the sexual issues with her not enjoying physical intimacy?

RA: That caused her suffering, her sorrow, her despair.

A: Can we heal that now, so she won't have it any longer, please?

RA: Yes.

A: She was asking if we could heal the cycles of codependency and toxic relationships. Is there anything inside her that is causing that?

RA: There is something attached to her heart, but also to her root.

A: What is that?

RA: Looks like a chain with a hook on both ends.

A: How did that get there and when did it attach?

RA: Previous life.

A: Can we go ahead and transmute that out, please?

RA: It needs healing.

A: Good, let's go ahead and transmute and heal it now, should I use the Phoenix Fire on it?

RA: Please.

A: Doing that now. I know she had those tubes in her head and she mentioned she had headaches and bumps in the skull that appeared a few years ago and they were painful, is that connected to those tubes she had?

RA: Yes.

A: Good, I know we healed that already. Let's see, did we complete the removal of that?

RA: Of the tubes?

A: Yes.

RA: They are gone.

A: Good, so if we could just make sure we fill in the Love-Light there, thank you. RA, can you also scan for, she says she feels that her parents and her ex-husband have done black magic on her, ill will towards her. Can we scan her and see if she has any effects, or attachments to this, and clear any cords to that? Tell me what you find, and also to her son, please?

RA: Yes.

A: What do you see?

RA: Her hands and feet are bound so that she cannot move.

A: What is it bound by?

RA: It looked like old chains, rusted, old, thick.

A: Was that there just this life, or other lives?

RA: Lifetime, upon lifetime, upon lifetime.

A: Can you tell us also about her mother, since she was a Reptilian there in that life? What is the reason why they have come into this incarnation as her being the mother, and her being her daughter?

RA: Control. Patterns of control.

A: By doing that, was this going to balance out the karma there to what they did to her in that life?

RA: She must prove that she cannot be controlled and break free. She must prove she still has her light and uses it. She must remind her mother of her own light so that she may be free, for we are all one.

A: Very good thank you. She said she had that entity attached to the spine, but we already healed that right?

RA: Yes.

A: In the lower backbone, sacral?

RA: Yes, okay, good.

A: She wanted to know if we could please just leave her clean, and in her purest soul essence, can we do that?

RA: Yes.

A: Thank you. RA before you go, she wanted to know if we could please scan her son Matthew. Would you be able to connect us to Matthew's Higher Self and aid us along the way? If we could help heal him in any way?

RA: Yes.

A: Thank you, if I could please speak to Matthew's Higher Self now, let me speak to him now. Matthew's Higher Self: Hello.

A: Hello, thank you for speaking to us, may I ask you questions?

Matthew's Higher Self: Yes.

A: Thank you. The mother of Matthew wanted to know if we are able to help him in any manner to heal. Remove any attachments, and he also has asthma allergies. What can we do for him? Any negative implants, negative thought forms, or cords. Tell me, out of all this, what do we have permission to help him with, in this time and space.

Matthew's Higher Self: Thought forms.

A: Okay, what's going on with his thought form?

Matthew's Higher Self: An attachment.

A: There's an attachment there?

Matthew's Higher Self: Yes.

A: Where is it located?

Matthew's Higher Self: Head, it's on his head.

A: On his head and how did it enter there? What occurred that allowed for it to enter?

Matthew's Higher Self: He was scared. He was small and so scared.

A: What was he scared of?

Matthew's Higher Self: The beings around him.

A: He could sense beings around him?

Matthew's Higher Self: Yes.

A: Can we go ahead and help that entity within him, help heal it and remove it, please?

Matthew's Higher Self: Yes.

A: Thank you. Can you tell us, are there any other attachments that we're allowed to help him heal if he has any more?

Matthew's Higher Self: There's something in his lungs.

A: What's in his lungs, please?

Matthew's Higher Self: Looks like a machine.

A: Can you explain that please?

Matthew's Higher Self: It looks like his lungs are inside some type of mechanism, some type of machine and there are pumps and things moving around in the machine.

A: How did this get placed in there?

Matthew's Higher Self: Past life.

A: Is this the initial cause of asthma?

Matthew's Higher Self: Contributes.

A: What else contributes to asthma and allergies?

Matthew's Higher Self: Adaptation, it's not from here.

A: Can we go ahead and remove that type of machine around his lungs, please?

Matthew's Higher Self: We can.

A: What do you need us to do to help you remove that, Higher Self?

Matthew's Higher Self: Just send healing, because when I open the machine, he will be fragile.

A: If we and all the RA could focus on it now please, all who can aid in this time and space. Let us know when you're ready for us to send Love-Light to him when you open up the machine.

Matthew's Higher Self: It is open now.

A: Good, may we all send Love-Light now?

Matthew's Higher Self: Yes, please.

A: Good, tell us what is going on as we send Love-Light.

Matthew's Higher Self: The lungs are being encased; he no longer needed the mechanism to protect him. Now he may use light.

A: Beautiful, if we could make sure that that's all full of Love-Light and stable and healed. What about his asthma now, will it be gone, will it be healed?

Matthew's Higher Self: Improvements but, there's still a need for it.

A: Will it heal eventually?

Matthew's Higher Self: Yes.

A: Good and what is the cause of the allergies, is that because he's not from here you said?

Matthew's Higher Self: Adaptations, his body is still adapting.

A: Is there anything else that we can heal within him like implants, cords, entities?

Matthew's Higher Self: There is a small implant.

A: Where?

Matthew's Higher Self: I saw it in his arm but then it moved.

A: Can we have Metatron contain that implant now? Did Metatron contain it?

Matthew's Higher Self: Yes.

A: Thank you. Why is it moving?

Matthew's Higher Self: It feels like it has a consciousness, it doesn't want to be seen.

A: If we could speak to that consciousness there of that implant now, come up, up... Greetings.

Consciousness: Hello.

A: Hello, thank you for speaking to us, may I ask you questions?

Consciousness: Maybe.

A: Thank you. When was it that you connected there into the body of Matthew?

Consciousness: Birth.

A: What allowed you to enter?

Consciousness: The doctors gave medicine, so I went in.

A: Was it medicine, or shots?

Consciousness: I don't know.

A: Okay, and this is an implant, but yet you have a consciousness, why is that? Are you a spirit, an entity attached to an implant, how does this work?

Consciousness: I am connected to the implant.

A: Do you exist somewhere else, or just in an implant?

Consciousness: I have a body somewhere else.

A: Would you be able to connect us now to that body that is somewhere else?

Consciousness: Yes.

A: Thank you, if we could please speak to you now. Greetings.

Entity: Greetings.

A: Thank you for speaking to us, may we ask you questions, please?

Entity: I guess.

A: Thank you, we're speaking to this consciousness in this implant that is attached to Matthew and we're wondering if we could get some more information from you?

Entity: Yes.

A: Thank you, if we could ask, where are you located?

Entity: My ship.

A: Is there a name for your race?

Entity: I'm on a ship that is moving quickly throughout space.

A: How is it that you inserted your consciousness into this implant?

Entity: It's what we do, we have the power to do so.

A: Is this a contract?

Entity: Yes.

A: Are you connected to any Reptilians?

Entity: Yes.

A: I understand that you've been playing this role for a very long time. However, we are looking to aid you today. As you know the Earth is shifting and the energies in the Universe are shifting into a higher vibration, a higher dimension. Would you allow us to aid you today so that you may shift your consciousness, the body there in that UFO?

Entity: Yes, please set me free.

A: Thank you, we're going to start helping you, sending you Love-Light and we're also going to help that consciousness that you have attached that is yours in the implant. If we all can start sending Love-Light now, Zadkiel, RA, sending Love-Light... Raphael, Metatron, whoever has aided so far, let's send Love-Light to that being there on the ship... Do you know if there is anyone else on that ship that would like to ascend into light? Into a higher dimension?

Entity: There are many ships.

A: Is there anyone else on that ship that would like to go as well, like you are, and ascend?

Entity: I'm the only one on this ship.

A: Do these ships - the many that you speak of - what is their role with these implants?

Entity: They are the energy force that allows for the implants. We are tools that make the implants possible.

A: Thank you, if you could look inside you now and spread every essence of you that is within this implant, as well as you there on the ship, spread it to all light. Every root, every cord, every part of you that is attached to the implant and it is part of your body there, turn it to all Love-Light and let us know once you are all Love-Light.

Positive Polarized Entity: I am light.

A: Beautiful, thank you. Do you have a message for her before you go?

Positive Polarized Entity: Now you can see us.

A: Why do you say that? What do you mean by that?

Positive Polarized Entity: Now... She has seen now she can lighten and let us go.

A: Good, very good, are you ready to go now?

Positive Polarized Entity: Yes, please.

A: Good, go ahead and go with the Love-Light of the Universe. If the angels could direct this being there to where they are meant to go, thank you.

Positive Polarized Entity: Thank you, thank you!

A: If we could start filling in, transmuting any leftovers of the implant there now, please.

Matthew's Higher Self: It is done.

A: Higher Self, is there anything else that you want to address, or are we complete now?

Matthew's Higher Self: For now.

A: Thank you, for allowing us to help him heal. We love you, we honor you...

Matthew's Higher Self: Thank you.

A: If we could reconnect once more please to RA?

RA: Yes.

A: Thank you RA, we pretty much are done then with her body scan. Is there anything else you want to say before you go, and we speak back to the Higher Self?

RA: We will work together. It's just the beginning. Thank you, sister.

A: Thank you RA, love you, honor you, and respect you. If you could please connect us now back to her Higher Self and our love to Zadkiel, Raphael, and Metatron, who aided as well, thank you. If I could please speak back to her Higher Self now?

Higher Self: Thank you.

A: Thank you, may I ask you questions, Higher Self?

Higher Self: Yes.

A: Good, do you have a name Higher Self?

Higher Self: No.

A: You have no name?

Higher Self: I am but a sound, but a vibration that beats through the heart.

A: Beautiful, and she wanted to know, what is her mission, purpose, and alignment?

Higher Self: Her mission is to discover when to reveal. She will do this through writing. She has begun, the process will unfold.

A: Thank you, very good. Let's see, can we go ahead and age regress her, please?

Higher Self: Yes.

A: How many years are we going to age regress her?

Higher Self: Nine.

A: Thank you, any aids she needs, like dental, vision, hearing, any of that?

Higher Self: Vision.

A: Can we go ahead and heal her vision now?

Higher Self: Yes.

A: Thank you. Can you scan her for any negative cords, please?

Higher Self: I feel like there's something.

A: Help her see and sense...where is that?

Higher Self: Looks like her hip, in the side of her body.

A: What is there?

Higher Self: I can't tell what it is.

A: Can we call back on Zadkiel, please?

Higher Self: Yes.

A: Thank you, connect us back to Zadkiel....brother, thank you welcome back. If you could please scan the side of her body? The Higher Self is saying… when I asked if she could scan for any cords, can you scan the area that she was talking about and see what's there?

AA Zadkiel: It looks like some type of attachments, some type of memory attachment.

A: What memory is it attached from, from when?

AA Zadkiel: Two, three lifetimes, same thing. It's almost calcified onto her. There's an attachment there from the same thing happening over and over.

A: Can we go ahead and transmute that out so that the cycle will not repeat itself anymore?

AA Zadkiel: Yes.

A: What side of her body, is it left, or right?

AA Zadkiel: Right.

A: Transmute and heal that now. Thank you Zadkiel.Metatron, can you please scan for any contracts, any that need to be cleared away, or any trauma from this, or past lives that need healing as well?

AA Metatron: She can release her contracts.

A: Is that all of them?

AA Metatron: Some still pending, but she's ready to release.

A: What are some contracts that you would want to share with her that she had there that she doesn't have to play out anymore?

AA Metatron: You are no longer contracted to be a victim.

A: Anything else?

AA Metatron: Your contracts with the souls of the suffering is done.

A: Good, very good. Thank you. Metatron, if we could go ahead and release those contracts for her now, the ones that we're allowed to, thank you. Metatron, are there any other current, or past life traumas that we need to heal?

AA Metatron: There is but one. She has already begun to release it, but I will complete it.

A: Good, what is it?

AA Metatron: Rape.

A: Was it from this life or another?

AA Metatron: Past lives.

A: If we could go ahead and release that and heal that trauma there, please? Thank you, Metatron. Anything you want to mention, Metatron, while you're here brother?

AA Metatron: No.

A: Metatron, I love you, honor you, and thank you for helping us today. If you could please connect us back to Zadkiel now?

AA Metatron: Okay.

A: Thank you, if I could please speak to Zadkiel once more?

AA Zadkiel: I am here.

A: In this time and space we've asked, and we've completed, all the healing within her and answered her questions. We thank everyone who aided today, we love you, we honor you - the RA, Raphael, Zadkiel, and Metatron. Thank you to everyone who aided and blessings to everyone. If I could please be connected to her Higher Self once more to conclude this.

Higher Self: Yes.

A: Thank you Higher Self, is there anything else that I haven't asked that I could have asked?

Higher Self: This is all you needed for now. This is what you wanted, and it is done.

A: Yes, and wow this was such a phenomenal session, absolutely phenomenal the information shared. It could really help others, help them heal with awareness. Is there anything else you would like to say before you go?

Higher Self: I thank and honor you.

A: I thank and honor you as well, and I love you. May I bring her back now?

Higher Self: Yes.

A: I thank everyone once more.

END OF SESSION

-------------<◇>-------------

Wow! This is a phenomenal session that demonstrates the power of using our I AM Source Love-Light to create force fields to shield us from harm and infringements. This was a tough session, seeing the experiments done to young children. This session showed us how we have been used, torn, and taken apart from one another and our families, since times on Earth that we can't remember consciously, like these villages. What kind of harmful ripple did this have on our collective parenting skills? If to protect our hearts we had to disconnect from such violent ways of control, so that we could bear being apart from our children, our seed. Never knowing why they took them from us, or if they were still alive.

To negative polarized races, we are just experiments. One of their favorites is to use children for their experiments. As children hold the highest potency of purity and Source Love-Light, because they are truly the most powerful lights once birthed into Earth. Why is it that one child would be able to go against such energetic force trying to penetrate their auric field and consciousness, but another child was vulnerable? Perhaps it was because the older the soul, the greater their organic force fields and natural abilities have matured and the more developed of an entity she would be. Her guide, her guardian, as we learned through this session, was herself, who was aiding with her shielding, pushing, causing a resistance against their negative infringement.

Could it have been because the 'her' in the NOW had an A.U.R.A. Hypnosis Healing session, and it is what allowed for the creation of the bridge for her to become the wiser and stronger guide and protector to the child version of her in the past life? The wiser, stronger older guide being the more complete version of herself in the future. For example: WE are who heal our childhood of current and past lives' pain and trauma. When we learn and understand it is WE who have awakened in the NOW, is who embraces our child selves when they are in need of unconditional love and strength. We, as the wiser version of us in the future, are who heal ourselves in all the past lives. And this potential is attainable because we are a great masterpiece when we remember and learn from our past-life selves. When we do so, we create ourselves into the wiser, strongest, best awakened and sovereign version of ourselves. We become the time traveler, traveling through time and spaces where we received the trauma. We then materialize into our very own guides and become the invisible strong voice and energy within us who says, "It's okay, keep moving, don't give up. I promise you, all will be fine."

A nine-year-old boy child once told me, "Aurora, did you know that in the sky there are bad and good aliens in spaceships? The bad ones have very powerful technology that goes through every day and scans all of Earth one big section at a time. As they scan, they register at what level each light within people is at. Depending on this, they then chose the ones with the brightest light to give them a "Bad Day" through their negative technologies. But Aurora, the only way to stop them from scanning the people openly is if the people would shield. But the truth is Aurora, no one shields. So, they are always just able to scan everyone whenever they decide to." Wow! This child had never received this knowledge from anyone but was only channeling his Higher Self for us. So that we may understand the importance of taking our sovereignty back by stating that, "WE DO NOT CONSENT" to any harm by shielding.

The Divine Mother and Divine Father of the Universe (Divine Creator Source of the Universe) once told me, "Every day you wake, it is as a book, and that day is created into a chapter of your book. It is very simple. Will you allow others to write what your chapter/day will look like, or will you write it yourself with the true sovereign being that you are?" Because we live in a Universe of free willed expression and polarizations of dark and light. We must learn to take our power and sovereignty back. By setting intentions and activating your infinite Love-Light force fields daily, when you wake up and before sundown. You are taking your sovereignty back by shielding and registering your powered frequency by setting intents that you "DO NOT CONSENT" to any harm. To not set intentions, is to allow others who might not have your best interest at heart to wield your day. Therefore, to not shield is the same as if you "ARE CONSENTING" to others to do what they want with your energy.

There are revelations occurring within our time and space in the year 2020 that seem as if we have been waiting for an eternity to occur. Revelations of darker truths we could not face, or were so horrendous that we didn't want them to be true. The time has now come for these darker truths to come up to the surface so we can start healing this within ourselves and for the collective. The time has now come for us to do our Shadow Work, so deep healing can take place to allow for Ascension to come forth. This book was waiting for this very moment. This sobering session is an example of how negative polarized Reptilians have been trafficking humans and abducting children since as far as we can remember. Negative polarized beings want to experiment on us so they can use us as battery light sources for their harmful negative agendas. It is time for all of us in the Universe to say "NO, WE DO NOT CONSENT," shall it be and so it is!

Update from Jasmine, with her email titled "Gratitude"

Hello Aurora,

"I just wanted to thank you so much for all of the enlightenment you have brought into my life. After my AURA session, so many aspects of my life have become transformed for the better. There are no words to describe the gratitude I have for you and your work. It has been about 5 months and the blessings are still coming in. It is as if all of the pieces of a greater puzzle keep coming together, and I am enjoying every moment of this new beautiful reality. I hope that you can feel the love and appreciation that I send you.

My dear sweet sister, thank you, thank you, thank you.

Always,
Jasmine"

"Envision thou existence as a book of Creation.
When awakened to thy sunrise, to thy sundown.
Blank pages stand forth.
As rebirth and new Creation.
A new story to write with thy own frequencies and vibrations.
Thy own words, thy own thoughts.
Memorize olden chapters within thy book in wisdom,
learning of thee lessons of thy existence.
In remembrance not remaining stagnant in thy past.
Authors of one's books.
stories thy are.
Step forward daily to write what you seek.
Surrender, say to HELL with it!
I shall create today what thy heart's desire!"

~AuroRa

-------------<<>>-------------

2

CIVILIZATION INSIDE A MOUNTAIN

Session #222: Recorded in November 2019.
Never Before Shared.

In this in-person A.U.R.A. Hypnosis Healing session, Bella has suffered from lifelong illnesses going in and out of the hospitals since very young. She traveled from Canada to see me, with hopes to begin alleviating and self-healing; wanting to remove what was oppressing and negative within her.

We see who she truly is beyond this Earth and her unique soul family. She finds herself in a time and space where she has amnesia not knowing who she is or where she came from while harnessing supernatural abilities. Come join us together in this journey from the cosmos to the inner mountains to learn more about energetic shielding and energy healing. Here we explore an ancient sacred civilization of monks hidden inside a mountain.

-------------<<>>-------------

"I felt love for him, and my skin started glowing. I walked to him and I didn't know how else to say thank you, I did not know the language. So, I pressed my lips against his and he accepted. He understood what I meant by it."
-Bella

-------------<<>>-------------

B: [Bella] I see blue and purple lights.
A: [Aurora] Beautiful. Look at yourself. Do you feel like you have a body?
B: Mm-hmm… lights… silvery.
A: You are light and silvery? Is there any shape to you?
B: Like the outline of the body.
A: Do you feel female, male?
B: Female.
A: Besides the energy colors that you're seeing, is there anything that you might have on you? Jewelry, any shapes, anything else you see on you?
B: No.
A: Look all around you, tell me what else you're seeing all around you.
B: Stars.
A: Tell me what the stars look like.
B: A bit like my light.
A: They look like your light?
B: Yes.
A: Are all the stars the same colors?
B: No.
A: What are some of the colors you're seeing within the stars?

B: Golden, green, orange.
A: Is this just one star, or multiple stars you're speaking of?
B: Many.
A: Would you like to get closer to one star in particular? Are there any that draw your attention?
B: Too many.
A: Why do you think that you are here?
B: I feel home is close.
A: Go ahead and allow yourself to be drawn to where home is. Tell me what you're seeing along the way. What's going on?
B: I am floating. Feels warm, more purple, more gold.
A: You are purple and gold?
B: The light is.
A: The light is - that is floating?
B: That is pulling me.
A: Look at yourself; do you just have a human body, or is there any other shape to you?
B: Human shape that is light.
A: Okay, follow that light and tell me what it feels like to connect to it?
B: Very warm, comforting.
A: Are you going towards it?
B: Yes.
A: How is it that it pulls you towards it? How does that feel?
B: Just like a hug.
A: How does the hug feel?
B: Very warm. It's really bright.
A: Allow yourself to go there now. Wherever this home is, you're there now... Tell me what you're seeing and sensing all around you.
B: I sense movement, like a lot of energies working together.
A: Are you from this light now? Tell me where you're at within this light.
B: With others like me.
A: What do they look like?
B: Light. White lights moving around.
A: Do they have a humanoid shape as you do to your light?
B: Smaller.
A: They're smaller?
B: The small human.
A: They are a smaller humanoid shape?
B: Humanoid, yes.
A: Are you saying that you are bigger than they are?
B: A little bit.
A: What is it that you all are doing?
B: Working together. Helping each other...
A: Are there many of them there?
B: Yes.
A: Tell me what you're seeing and sensing. How are you helping one another?
B: We're giving stuff to each other. I don't know, it is as if we are handing things to each other.
A: Tell me what that looks like.
B: It's like passing energy back and forth.
A: When you take that energy that is being given to you, what are you doing to it?
B: Passing it on to another.

A: You just keep passing it around to one another?

B: Yes.

A: Does it do anything to your energy?

B: Makes me feel lighter.

A: Is there any part of the energy that goes into you?

B: It goes into me a bit, but it cannot stay long enough, for I have to pass it on.

A: How are you all doing this? Are you standing in a shape of sorts, or how is this occurring?

B: So a lot of movement, a lot of running around.

A: I know you said that you are within these light bodies that are with you. Tell me what the space looks like that you are in.

B It's like a dome... with a glass.

A: Is there any color to the glass?

B: It's open, you can see into the galaxy.

A: Does this dome have any base to it?

B: Not really. It's like it's not fully solid.

A: Are you inside the dome?

B: Yes.

A: All of you are?

B: Yes.

A: You're saying that it's not solid, or are you saying that it is?

B: More fluid.

A: Are you saying it's like an energetic dome structure?

B: Yes.

A: Keep moving time along and let me know what happens next of importance. Tell me, these light bodies you are meeting up with, what do they feel like to you? What connection do they have to you?

B: They feel like a neighborhood, like neighbors, like family, a community.

A: Are there feminine and masculine energies? Are there individuals there?

B: Yes, both.

A: Tell me what happens next of importance.

B: We are sitting in a circle.

A: Do you think that there are many?

B: Yes.

A: They all fit within the circle?

B: Yes.

A: What is it that you all are doing? Why are you sitting in a circle now?

B: Prayer... a type of prayer ritual.

A: What are you praying for?

B: Safety.

A: Safety of what?

B: For our kind to not be disturbed.

A: What does this safety look like? Does it have any form?

B: Source energy. It looks like a ball of golden light above the circle.

A: With your prayer, you all are creating a ball of golden light?

B: Yes.

A: Okay.

B: Combining our energy, building it so it can become bigger.

A: It's getting bigger as you all keep praying on it?

B: Yes. A lot more gold!

A: These beings that are sitting around in a circle, is everyone the same color, or are there some that are different colors?

B: Just white lights.

A: Why gold?

B: It is rich and warm.

A: Keep moving time along, moving along to see what you all do next with this ball, or what happens next of importance.

B: It's like it is leaking over our dome and the dome wasn't visible, but now it's like the ball is just oozing, like painting our dome with gold.

A: What is the purpose of that?

B: It's a type of shield.

A: You all are shielding the dome that you are in?

B: Yes.

A: Tell me, what does it look like once you feel that it's come to what it needed to do?

B: The dome is more solid, made of gold.

A: Does it still just have the dome and no bottom?

B: The bottom is there, it's more solid. We can move through the dome if we want to. But I don't think anything can come in.

A: You can come out through the dome, through it?

B: Yes.

A: Why do you say nothing can come in?

B: Because of our golden light, we control it.

A: Do you think others can see?

B: I think so, they can see the gold.

A: Do some of them try to come in?

B: I feel this is why we're protecting it so that nothing can come and disrupt the peace. There was an urgency, as if we needed to create this.

A: Was this created for all who are within the dome, or for something else within the dome?

B: It was for all of us. We can leave if we want to. We can move through it and come back and be safe. Only our energy can penetrate it.

A: What would happen if someone tried to penetrate it and it wasn't you?

B: They just wouldn't be able to.

A: What would happen to them?

B: They would just stay outside of the dome.

A: It would stop them from coming in?

B: Yes.

A: What are some of the reasons why you all leave and come back?

B: We don't leave, we just can if we want to.

A: How many would you say are within the dome?

B: Many. I think I'm close to five or six. There are many more.

A: Hundreds or thousands?

B: Hundreds, yes.

A: Keep moving to when something else has changed, something of importance. Tell me what you see. What happens next?

B: I feel my son. I feel him.

A: Where is he?

B: Like he is close, but far from me, like behind a glass wall.

A: Would you like to find him?

B: Yes.

A: Let's see how you're able to locate him. Tell me, I know you are within the dome. What do you do to try to find him?

B: I don't know.

A: Are you able to leave the dome to try to find him? Is he inside the dome or outside?

B: He's outside. I don't know where though.

A: Do you know what happened to him?

B: He's somewhere else.

A: Is there anything that you could do about that?

B: I can walk through the dome, but I will be out in a space where I might not be safe.

A: Are you able to carry some of the energy of the dome with you so that you can be safe?

B: Not fully.

A: So, are you saying once you leave the dome, you're vulnerable?

B: Yes.

A: Why do you say that you wouldn't be safe? What are some of the things that could happen?

B: There are denser forms that are waiting to attack.

A: Waiting to attack you all?

B: Yes.

A: Why is that?

B: Wanting to disrupt the peace, light.

A: Do you all help out with some of this peace and light?

B: We work together.

A: You work together, doing what?

B: This is why we stay together; we work together to build the dome, so we are safe.

A: Is your son like you?

B: Yes.

A: What do you think would happen to him if you can't find him?

B: I feel he was taken, inside a glass box.

A: Do you know what this glass box is?

B: Certain energy fields.

A: Is there anything that you can do about this?

B: I can't get through the box.

A: Why not?

B: It's at a different vibration.

A: Are you there where the box is?

B: I found it.

A: You did find it... Where was the box? Did you have to leave the dome to find the box or...

B: Yes, I left the dome. I didn't go far.

A: Can you tell me what this box looks like?

B: Like an energy field; it looks like glass but it's not.

A: You can see him inside of it?

B: Yes, he's like me.

A: Can he see you?

B: Yes.

A: How is he, in there?

B: It's like our hands are touching. But the box is separating us.

A: Can you ask him who it was that put him there? How did he get there?

B: I don't know.

A: Is there anyone that you could call for aid to try to help remove him? Are you familiar with any Archangels?

B: Archangel Michael.
A: Would you like to call Archangel Michael to help you with the situation of your son there?
B: Yes!
A: Go ahead and call for him.
B: Archangel Michael, please help me.
A: Let me know once he's there.
B: He's there.
A: Wonderful. Tell me what he looks like.
B: Very bright blue energy.
A: Is he there by himself?
B: Yes, he's touching the box.
A: Mm-hmm. Tell him what's going on… Is he touching the box?
B: I think he's trying to remove it.
A: Tell me everything he's doing.
B: He's putting his energy on it.
A: What does his energy look like?
B: It's a lot of blue, blue and white light, it's glowing. I feel my son is closer now.
A: What is his energy doing to the box?
B: It's like it's disappearing.
A: Is Archangel Michael your size or is he taller?
B: He is a bit taller.
A: Tell me what's going on as the box is disappearing. What's going on with your son?
B: He's coming to me.
A: Your son is coming to you? Tell me what that's like.
B: Feels really warm, love, really deep love.
A: What happened to the box?
B: It's gone.
A: Can you ask Archangel Michael, or your son, how was it that he ended up in this box?
B: Feels like somebody put him there.
A: Ask Archangel Michael if you could find out how this happened so that we can heal when this occurred.
B: There was an attack of the peace. My son was trying to communicate to me, I don't know if he was allowed to. It was like he was imprisoned.
A: Why did they imprison him instead of killing him or ending him?
B: They didn't want the communication to occur.
A: Are you saying that he was going back to give you all a message?
B: Yes.
A: And so that he wouldn't give you the message, they put him in a box?
B: Yes.
A: Why would they need to put him in a box instead of, say, just ending him?
B: To distance the love energy... to try to block us.
A: Okay.
B: Sadness.
A: What was it that he was trying to warn you about? What was the message?
B: Something was coming to disrupt the peace.
A: Disrupt the peace where?
B: Our civilization.
A: Your dome civilization?
B: Yes.

A: What happened to them?

B: They are hiding, waiting.

A: Are you able to ask Archangel Michael and his Legion to see what they can do about them trying to attack you? What does Michael say?

B: I don't think it is their battle.

A: What would you like to do now that your son is freed?

B: Go home.

A: Very good. What does Archangel Michael do?

B: He embraces us, and we leave from that space.

A: And does he leave as well, from that space?

B: Yes.

A: Do you both go on your own?

B: Yes.

A: Tell me what happens once you have him with you, as you're going back.

B: We go back into the dome.

A: What happens when you go back in?

B: My son is in the center of the prayer group; we are healing him. Sadness.

A: Do you feel that he was in the box for a long time?

B: Yes.

A: What is the reason he had sadness?

B: Being away, being apart.

A: Is everyone healing him?

B: Yes.

A: How do you heal him?

B: We are combining our energies and creating that same ball of light above him. It's as if we are creating our own energy of the sun. It is shining over him and he's basking in that light.

A: This light is helping him heal from his sadness?

B: Yes.

A: Within this dome is there anyone that you feel you are, perhaps, a partner with?

B: I feel like I have a family, and that my partner's away on his own journey somewhere trying to help us.

A: Do you know where he is?

B: No.

A: Has he been gone for a little while, or long?

B: A long while.

A: Is there a way that you can connect to him to see how he's doing throughout time?

B: I know he is safe. That is all I know.

A: Let's go to another important time where we find answers that we seek for your highest good. You are there now. Tell me what you see?

B: Back in the forest. Foggy, you hear water.

A: Look at yourself. Do you feel like you have a body?

B: Yes.

A: What do you look like?

B: I'm female, very pale skin, dark, long hair. I am barefoot and dirty.

A: Do you feel younger, older?

B: A little younger.

A: What are you doing there?

B: Lost. I don't know where I came from. But I found myself in the forest.

A: Is that all you remember?

B: Yes. And I have a cut on my leg, and I am rinsing it in the water. I rip some of my clothes and wrap it.

A: What are you going to do next?

B: I hear movement in the trees.

A: What is it?

B: It is some young man. He has light, golden brown eyes.

A: Do you feel that you know him? Does he know you?

B: No. But I feel he's kind and I'm not scared.

A: What does he do?

B: He approaches me. He noticed that I'm hurt. He wants to take me to a shelter, to his home.

A: How do you feel about that?

B: I'm uncertain. I'm confused. I don't speak the language.

A: You don't speak his language?

B: No, but I understand him somehow.

A: How are you understanding him?

B: I am reading his energy.

A: What will you do?

B: I go with him.

A: You're there now. What does this house look like?

B: It has a wooden table, chairs, and a big fireplace in the kitchen.

A: Is there anyone else there?

B: No. Lots of candles. They aren't lit, just the fire. There's an upstairs, there's a bathtub. He's filling it with hot water.

A: What did the house look like from outside?

B: Just stones and wood.

A: Does it have a shape to it?

B: Yes, it's like a square, like a little cottage.

A: What happens next?

B: He gives me clothes, clean clothes. I bathe and I get dressed. The clothes are very loose, big. I go down the stairs and now there are people there.

A: Who are the people?

B: His friends are concerned. They're talking about me, and what to do with me since I don't speak.

A: How do his friends look? What are they wearing?

B: Gold, linen, beige.

A: How many people are there now?

B: There are two sitting at the table and he's standing. I saw the candles and I didn't like that they were not lit, so I lit them with my touch. I touched the wick, and it came to life. Flames.

A: Did they see you do this? What was their reaction?

B: They were in shock and in fear. He didn't fear; he somehow understood. I didn't understand that they were in shock, because, for me, that was normal. But then it wasn't normal for him to not be in shock.

A: What is he wearing?

B: Green pants - a type of suspenders and a white linen shirt.

A: Do you feel that he's much older than you?

B: No, not much older. We're close in age.

A: What is it that happens next?

B: His friends lose their tempers in fear. They think something is bad about me and he didn't see that at all. They thought I was evil and my anger, because of their reaction, I didn't like. My energy made the flames get higher on the candles and then he told them to stop. And in that moment, I calmed down. I felt love for him, and my skin started glowing. I walked to him and I didn't know how else to say thank you, I did not know the language. So, I pressed my lips against his and he accepted. He understood what I meant by it.

A: Keep moving the scene along and tell me what's going on next.

B: We go off searching for something.

A: Who is 'we'?

B: Me and him. His friends leave and we go off sometime later. Searching for where I came from, but I have no memory of it. I didn't know how I just appeared in the forest and I didn't know how else to communicate but through energy and touch and hoping that a person would understand what I'm feeling; I am transferring a feeling to them.

A: What happens when you're not able to find where you came from? What do you do next?

B: It's not moving forward.

A: Let's go back now, to right before you found yourself in that body in that place where you had lost your memory. We're going back to before that when you had your memory, and you knew where you came from. You are there now... Tell me what's going on. You're able to see and sense everything clearly.

B: I'm a child in a cave.

A: Are you the same child you were?

B: Yes, just younger than what I was in the forest.

A: You are in the cave and tell me what's going on.

B: I am with monks. People in hoods that look like monks, they're hiding.

A: What colors are their hoods?

B: Brown.

A: You said they're hiding?

B: They're in hiding. I don't know what they're hiding from.

A: Are you with them?

B: Yes, they're taking care of me.

A: Are you the only child there?

B: Yes.

A: How many monks are there?

B: Five, maybe more in the tunnels that they live in.

A: You live in these caves? Is there a place that you call home within these tunnels?

B: Yes.

A: Tell me. Tell me what your home looks like.

B: It's a bed in a little nook. We eat in the common area, all together. I have a bed, a little area of my own, with a little privacy.

A: Do you feel like you were born there?

B: No.

A: Where did you come from?

B: I only know this place ever since I was a child, but I wasn't born there. I was taken or saved.

A: Is there someone you can ask? Where was it that you came from?

B: It's as if they knew of a prophecy of some sort, so they took me as a child. I was a baby.

A: They took you from who?

B: I see one taking me out of a crib, an old wooden crib and leaving the house.

A: Was this with the permission of the parent?

B: It wasn't fully agreed on. But the knowledge was there. The parents knew about everything, but they didn't accept for me to be taken. They took me anyway. They believed they were doing good.

A: How was it that they found you? How did they know you were there?
B: I don't know.
A: Are you able to see what your parents look like?
B: Mom had long curly hair. I don't remember more than that.
A: Now that you are in this cave, is there anyone that tends to you specifically?
B: One. He's like a father.
A: Tell me more about him.
B: He's kind. Worried.
A: What is he worried about?
B: About protecting me.
A: Why is it that they have to protect you?
B: They don't want to tell me. They don't want me to fear, but I feel the worry.
A: Is there anything out of the ordinary that you are able to do, that they are not able to do?
B: I communicate through my hands; I think I can heal, as well, through touch. I think I can access the elements, and I use the energy found in the elements.
A: What do you do with it?
B: I heal. I feel like they worry that I can do more. That the world views me as a threat; I don't belong here.
A: What else can you do with your abilities?
B: I spark fires in the fireplace.
A: How do you spark the fire?
B: The energy in my hands.
A: You use the energy from your hands to spark it?
B: Yes. I take and use that energy from the Earth.
A: You take the energy from the Earth to spark the energy in your hands, to spark the fire?
B: Yes, I channel it.
A: Are there any other elements you could do that with besides the fire?
B: I can put the fire out with my hands as well; I create a wind.
A: Do you mean wind comes out of your hands?
B: Yes.
A: And that puts out the fire?
B: Yes.
A: Tell me what happens next of importance while you are in this cave. What happens next? Go to another important time. Another important time where we will find the answers that we seek for your highest healing. You're there now, tell me what you see and sense.
B: I am growing older. Not a child anymore. I am upset. They're hiding so much from me.
A: Are you able to speak their language?
B: No, I am mute. I don't communicate with language. I touch people and they understand what I'm telling them. A man that is like a father to me, he is sad because I want to leave. I want to go out into the world. I want to live more. He tells me it isn't safe, but I'm arguing with him because I believe I will be safe. He explains to me that people are not like me. I don't want to believe it. I just want to be normal. I want to know more. There's more to life.
A: Is there a name that this group goes by?
B: It's a Brotherhood; I can't get more than that.
A: What happens next of importance?
B: I run away!
A: You leave the cave?
B: Yes, while everyone is sleeping.
A: How do you get out?

B: Tunnels, passageways. There's a wooden door that I go through, and I come out of the mountain.

A: They were inside a mountain?

B: Yes.

A: Tell me what this mountain looks like.

B: It's high, but not too high, because I can see the ground below. It's not too far, but it's all rocks.

A: What did you do?

B: There's a lot of steps, but they're not real steps, so it was hard for me to keep walking.

A: Are you wearing anything on your feet?

B: No.

A: What do you do since you feel that it's hard for you to come down?

B: I climb down really slowly. But I twist my ankle, and fall. That's why I don't remember. I hit my head. My memory never came back to me. I forgot about the Brotherhood. I just remembered being in the forest and being saved by the young man.

A: Go back there now with the young man. What happens eventually? Do you stay with him?

B: I stay with him. I realized that the world wasn't accepting of my abilities. He was the only one that did. He protected me.

A: Look into his eyes. Do you recognize his soul?

B: Yes.

A: Who is he?

B: He is the same one that follows me all the time to protect me.

A: Who is that?

B: I don't know who he is. He has just always protected me, that's all I know.

A: Is this a family protection, or a romantic protection, loving?

B: It wasn't always romantic, but most of the time, yes, romantic.

A: Go ahead and go to the last scene. The last day of your life there with him. You are there now, tell me what you see all around you. What's going on?

B: He got hurt. I don't think I could have healed him.

A: He's hurt? Do you feel like you all are older? .

B: He's lying down. Not much older. I was sad because I didn't want to stay there without him. He had to go.

A: Do you mean he had to go, as in he died?

B: Yes.

A: What did you do?

B: I stayed with him. He was lying down, and I was on my knees with my head resting on my arm next to him. I was holding his hand. I was taking his pain away.

A: Do you know how he harmed himself? What happened to him?

B: I think through work, or it was with a tool, or it was an accident. He was bleeding from the abdomen. I didn't understand what had happened. I just knew that I wasn't able to heal him. But all I could do was take his pain. So, he felt normal and he didn't know that he was dying, because for once I felt I could protect him. I feel like my soul stepped out of my body once he was gone, because I decided I was done there.

A: Yes; what did you do after that?

B: I saw the light. I feel like I was greeted by my real parents.

A: Tell me what your parents look like.

B: My mom was beautiful, she had long, dark, curly hair. My dad had a beard.

A: You were reunited with them once more?

B: Mm-hmm. They stayed there for a while. I keep seeing my dad with a pipe in his hands.

A: Look into their eyes. Do you recognize their souls?
B: It is my mom.
A: And the father?
B: I don't recognize him.

The Higher Self is called forth.
A: Can I please speak to the Higher Self of Bella?
Higher Self: I am here.
A: Welcome. Thank you. Am I speaking to Bella's Higher Self now?
Higher Self: Yes.
A: I honor you, love you, and respect you. Thank you for all the aid you have given us today. I know that you hold the records of Bella's different lives. May I ask you questions, please?
Higher Self: Yes.
A: Thank you for showing us such beautiful experiences. I have a couple of questions. I know that you first took her to a place in the cosmos where she was inside a dome and she was with others that were like her. Why did you take her to this place? What was the purpose?
Higher Self: It has to do with this life now.
A: What is the connection?
Higher Self: Love.
A: What were some of the lessons that she needed to learn there, that will help her at this time?
Higher Self: Working with energies.
A: You want her to start working with energy, just like she did in that life there?
Higher Self: Yes.
A: Tell her, what are some ways that she can do this?
Higher Self: Reiki, energy healing.
A: Beautiful. That son of hers, is it someone she knows, or will know in this life, in the future?
Higher Self: No. He's there.
A: She mentioned that if you come out of the dome, you are unsafe. How is it that she's here?
Higher Self: She's a fragment. Part of her is there. Part of her is here. She's mostly here, living another life and having contact through her fractal to the Earth.
A: So, the 'her there' can connect to the 'her here'?
Higher Self: Yes.
A: Since you mentioned that it was unsafe outside the dome, is she being provided with some of the safety here?
Higher Self: She is safe here. She is protected here.
A: Then you took her to a life where she was gifted within her abilities and she was different, and the monks had taken her in. Why did you take her to that life, what was the purpose?
Higher Self: Healing and loving again. Romantic love.
A: Did she fall in love with the man that saved her?
Higher Self: Yes.
A: Did he love her?
Higher Self: Yes, very much. She needed to know this person.
A: Is that why she left the cave to find him?
Higher Self: She had a pull; she knew there was something more.
A: Can you tell me some more about these monks? Who are they?
Higher Self: They had access to knowledge beyond, and they believed it was their duty to follow protocol.
A: What was the protocol?

Higher Self: Their ways. They believed in what was good and bad, and what needed to be protected. They believed she was God, a part of God, with abilities. They just, they didn't want her harmed. They had the knowledge that the powers she had could have been used for evil.

A: If they would have left her with her parents, could that have been a possibility?

Higher Self: No. But she could have been taken by the wrong people. She was vulnerable with her parents.

A: So, them taking her away, did that have to happen to keep her safe?

Higher Self: Yes.

A: Is there a name that these monks went by besides Brotherhood?

Higher Self: Brotherhood of the Sun.

A: Was she, like they thought, she was a part of God with those abilities.

Higher Self: Yes.

A: What did they think she was? Was there a name that she had, that they had for her?

Higher Self: No. She is the Warrior of the Light.

A: Explain to me these two different lives. I know that there's a purpose why you showed them to her. This Warrior of the Light, would this be the same being that's within the dome, or would it be another aspect of her?

Higher Self: It's the core aspect of her. Her origin of Creation.

A: This dome, was that a part of her origin of Creation, or was it just another part of her?

Higher Self: It's the closest thing to home for her. It is where her child is, and her true family.

A: She had a question since you're talking about her child and her family. She felt that this will have a connection to Andromeda, is that correct?

Higher Self: Yes.

A: This location is near Andromeda?

Higher Self: Yes.

The Body Scan begins.

A: At this point Higher Self, if we can start scanning her body from the head all the way down to her feet. We are looking for any negative energy, any entities within her, anything that needs healing. Let me know Higher Self, if you require any assistance from the Archangels.

Higher Self: There's something in the left elbow.

A: Can you do the body scan on your own or do you need any assistance from the Angels?

Higher Self: I need assistance.

A: Which Archangel would you like to call upon first?

Higher Self: Michael.

A: Very good Higher Self, if you could connect us now to Archangel Michael. Greetings…

Higher Self: (silence)

A: Higher Self, let me know what's going on.

Higher Self: Still not connecting.

A: Scan her for where there might be a blockage to her connecting to Michael.

Higher Self: The abdomen.

A: Let's go ahead and scan that area now. Higher Self, let's see what's there that's blocking her connection to Archangel Michael. I will go ahead and assist with Love-Light so we can see what is blocking. Is there an energy, an entity? What's there?

Higher Self: There's a block, a block in the energy.

A: Tell me what's the root of the blockage. Scan thoroughly. What's there that's causing this?

Higher Self: I am not getting anything.

A: Let's continue scanning this area. Higher Self, keep scanning and communicating. Even though we might not be fully connecting to Archangel Michael, we know that he is here. Ask

Archangel Michael what is within the abdomen that is causing this blockage? He can give you the answers that way as well.

Higher Self: I am not hearing anything.

A: Let's continue working with the Higher Self. I'm going to ask you what it is, and you just tell me whatever your first impression is. Higher Self, what is in the abdomen? Is there an entity?

Higher Self: There's a density.

A: Does this density have a consciousness?

Higher Self: Yes.

A: With a consciousness, would that not be an entity?

Higher Self: It's not communicating. It's like it's breathing.

A: Would this consciousness be a Reptilian consciousness, or would it just be an entity?

Higher Self: An entity.

A: You said that you could sense it breathing?

Higher Self: Yes.

A: If we could, with the Higher Self's permission, can we ask the Angels to surround it with symbols? They know which symbols to use. Can you do that? Thank you.

Higher Self: Yes.

A: Very good. Now that it is surrounded by the symbols, if we could still have assistance, as you might not be able to hear them yet. They're still there, all around us. If we can, just like she was able to call forth Archangel Michael to help her son. She's able to call forth here, just as easily now, for Archangel Michael and the Angels' help. Can you do that?

Higher Self: Yes.

A: Good. If we could have Archangel Michael now assist us with bringing up this entity in her stomach area, her abdomen. If it could please come up, up, up, now. I'd like to speak to this entity there in her abdomen. Let me speak to you now. Greetings, can I please speak to the entity in the abdomen? Tell me what's going on Higher Self?

Higher Self: There's no connection.

A: Higher Self, let's look at her crown area - go ahead and keep that entity in the symbols. Now, let's look at her crown and see if there's something there that's blocking the connection. Scan her now. Look at her head, scan her head, her crown, and third eye area.

Higher Self: The third eye.

A: What's going on with her third eye?

Higher Self: It's blocked.

A: Let's figure it out. Let's find what is causing the blockage. What does that look like?

Higher Self: Like a cap.

A: What color is this cap?

Higher Self: Red.

A: Let's ask, just like we did in her past life, we're going to ask Archangel Michael to keep assisting us here; are we able to remove this cap that's over her third eye Higher Self?

Higher Self: There's pain there.

A: Higher Self, if you can help alleviate the pain now. Do I have permission to use the Phoenix Fire to transmute this cap out of her third eye?

Higher Self: Yes.

A: Good, using the Phoenix Fire now. Transmuting out that cap. Feel it, sense it disintegrating no longer being there. Transmute it with the very golden energy that you all were using within the dome. Let me know once it is transmuted and removed from her third eye. Higher Self if you can fill in Love-Light to that area of her third eye to make her connection strong, nice and healthy. Can you do that Higher Self?

Higher Self: Yes.

A: Beautiful. Let's go ahead and continue scanning her head. Let me know if there's anything else that could be blocking her connection. Help her see, sense, feel. Tell us what is within the head, anything else we can address to help the connection?

Higher Self: Left temple.

A: Let's scan the area. What is there in the left temple?

Higher Self: Chip.

A: Do you mean like an implant?

Higher Self: Yes.

A: What shape is this implant?

Higher Self: Square.

A: Can you tell me, what is it causing her?

Higher Self: Blockage, tension, neurological problems.

A: When was this inserted into her?

Higher Self: I don't know.

A: Was it this life or another life?

Higher Self: I am not sure.

A: Higher Self, do I have permission to use Phoenix Fire on this implant as well?

Higher Self: Yes.

A: Wonderful, using it now. While we're transmuting that implant now, can you tell me when was it that this cap over her third eye was inserted?

Higher Self: Another lifetime.

A: Let me know once that implant is transmuted out. While we continue working on this, let's go ahead and scan her head one more time. See if there's anything else that's blocking her.

Higher Self: Okay. An implant is transmuted out.

A: Beautiful. Is there anything else in the head we can address?

Higher Self: No.

A: Very good.

Higher Self: There's a block between the shoulder blades.

A: Scan that, tell me what is there. And then again Higher Self, fill in Love-Light to where you removed the cap and the implant in her head, making it healthier once more. Tell me what is between the shoulder blades.

Higher Self: Cap.

A: Another cap?

Higher Self: Yes.

A: What is this cap? Is that negative technology?

Higher Self: Yes.

A: Is this similar to an implant?

Higher Self: Almost.

A: Can we go ahead and start transmuting that out?

Higher Self: Yes.

A: We're using the Phoenix Fire once more there. Can you explain what you mean by almost? What is it?

Higher Self: It's like a shield around it. It's not an implant. A cage.

A: This cap creates a cage-like energy?

Higher Self: Yes.

A: And when you say shield, do you mean in a negative way?

Higher Self: Yes.

A: Would you call it more of a cage?

Higher Self: Yes.

A: Is it holding back the power and the energy within these areas where they're at?
Higher Self: Yes.
A: Would it be similar to, for example, that box that her son was placed in? Is it similar to that?
Higher Self: Similar. Still different.
A: We're transmuting that now out of between her shoulder blades. If you could start flooding now your infinite higher Source Energy. Higher Self, would you like to integrate even further into her now?
Higher Self: Yes.
A: Let's go ahead and allow for the Higher Self now to come in through the crown now. Coming in and integrating even stronger, as her Higher Self allows for her highest good. Higher Self, can we connect now to Archangel Michael?
Higher Self: Yes.
A: Good. Connect us now please to Archangel Michael, I would like to speak to him now, please. Let me know once the cap between her shoulder blades is transmuted out. I'd like to speak to Archangel Michael now. Feel his beautiful energy scanning you and connecting to you. Feel that beautiful blue energy that you saw from that life within the dome. If I could please speak to Archangel Michael now. Greetings.
Higher Self: I feel him, but still no communication.
A: That's okay. So long as you feel him. Perhaps we are just meant to talk to the Higher Self, and he will be there for assistance.
Higher Self: Okay.
A: Very good. Now Higher Self, you can just keep communicating back and forth with Michael and he could communicate to you if there's anything that he can help you in guidance and to make sure we don't miss anything. How does that cap look in between her shoulders now?
Higher Self: Feeling it's still there.
A: Good, it's transmuting out. Very good. Let's go ahead and continue her body scan, Higher Self. We know that there is a consciousness in her stomach. Are we able to talk to it? Is it able to come up and speak through her, or do I just speak to it directly?
Higher Self: It won't speak through her.
A: Is it because it's choosing not to, or it's just not possible?
Higher Self: It's not possible.
A: Okay. Very good. I'm going to go ahead and speak directly now to this consciousness within her abdominal area. I'd like to speak to you now if you could just listen to me. Thank you for allowing me to speak to you. I love you, I honor you, and respect you. I understand that you perhaps have been there some time. I know that you won't speak, but perhaps if we can just figure out when was it that you attached yourself there? Higher Self, if you can see, when was it that it attached itself there?
Higher Self: I am not seeing it.
A: That's okay. Archangel Michael, if you could just keep assisting us. Entities there in her abdominal, I'm giving you a chance now. We know that you've been there some time. For whatever reason, you are there. As you know the Earth is ascending, the Universe is ascending. And negatively polarized energies like you cannot be attached to her, or anyone else, any parasitic entity drawing energy. The Earth is ascending. Therefore, when the time comes of Ascension, entities like you, energies like you, will be automatically recycled straight back to Source. We're helping you, instead, by giving you the option to ascend into a positive polarization so that you no longer have to do this anymore attaching yourself to anyone's body. You can instead go ahead and incarnate and go somewhere else. Live on your own, creating your own light. Would you allow us to aid you today so you could spread your Love-Light?
Higher Self: (silence)

A: Higher Self is it allowing, yes or no?

Higher Self: I am not sure.

A: What do you feel?

Higher Self: Nothing. No response.

A: Higher Self ask Archangel Michael. See if we get a response from him. Can we help it spread its Love-Light?

Higher Self: Not getting answers.

A: Higher Self, I want you to go within you and your abilities. Just as gifted as you were infusing emotions and sensations during that life where she was living with the monks. Just like that being she was in that dome. I want her to now activate and unlock these abilities within her as her Higher Self allows. Whatever's within safety for her highest good. Can we do that for her?

Higher Self: Yes.

A: Let's go ahead and activate that now for her, please. Is it starting to be activated?

Higher Self: Yes.

A: Good. As we're starting to activate that, I want her Higher Self to guide her to see what it is that we can do with this entity. Will it allow for it to spread its Love-Light? Feel your emotions and your sensations? What's going on?

Higher Self: It won't.

A: Yes, I was getting the same. Thank you. Archangel Michael, can I ask that since it is encased in the symbols, Michael, it feels like a reptilian consciousness. Is this accurate?

AA Michael: Yes.

A: It was masking itself as an entity. Michael, has this been here longer than this life? In her energy body?

AA Michael: Yes.

A: Can you help her understand when was it that it attached itself so we can find the root and can start healing it?

AA Michael: It's tied to Andromeda energies.

A: Is it part of those beings that were watching?

AA Michael: Yes.

A: Is that who was watching them? The Reptilians?

AA Michael: Seems like it. Yes.

A: So, when she came down and fractalized herself into this body, did one follow her?

AA Michael: Yes.

A: Is this why she has all these issues with health in this area?

AA Michael: Yes.

A: Is there more than one in there?

AA Michael: Seems like it, yes.

A: Continue activating her ability so she's able to sense this.

AA Michael: Yes.

A: How many more would you say there is, Higher Self?

Higher Self: Three.

A: I'm going to give you all one more chance. As you know we are helping Reptilian consciousness throughout all Creation to positively polarize, so that they can have their own experience and gain their own light, no longer having to drain from others. One more chance, as I honor you, love you, and respect you, and I know that you can do it. It is such a beauty. There is such beauty and love to no longer have to play this negative polarized role you are playing. Will you allow us to assist you in positively polarizing through Ascension?

Higher Self: There's a bit of resistance.

A: How about you all look inside you. Find the light within you, just look at it. Look at that light that's been waiting to shine brightly once more. It's within you. Do you see that light?

Higher Self: It's too much darkness.

A: Higher Self, what do you feel? Do you feel that we can help convince them into spreading their light so that they can positively ascend? Or will we have to remove them?

Higher Self: It is too much resistance.

A: Higher Self, they're in the symbols now contained. So Higher Self can you connect us to Archangel Metatron as well for assistance?

Higher Self: Yes.

A: Good. So, we call forth on Archangel Metatron as well. Thank you, brother. We love you, honor you, and respect you. Michael and Metatron, can you all please start removing this Reptilian consciousness from within her abdomen and contain them in the alchemy symbols? They're no longer to be part of her. Let me know once you all have them removed, please. Since she is now understanding what a Reptilian consciousness would feel like, let's continue to scan the rest of her body and let's make sure there's no other Reptilian consciousness within her, please. Scan her whole body now, help her see, sense, feel. Higher Self, where else does she have more? I know earlier you mentioned her elbow. What was there in her elbow?

Higher Self: Pain.

A: Again, we have Michael and Metatron removing them from her now, please. And as we're moving them out, let us know if you need any Phoenix Fire, as well as, we're having the Higher Self fill in with Love-Light where they're being removed from.

A: Are there any more Reptilian consciousness within her?

Higher Self: Feels like something is latched on to the elbow.

A: Let's scan that elbow now. Is it the right or left?

Higher Self: Left.

A: Let's see what is within the elbow. Let's focus our attention there while Michael and Metatron are working on the abdomen. Let's focus our attention there. What is there in the elbow, help her understand. What is it, Higher Self?

Higher Self: It's vibrating at a negative frequency.

A: Is that a consciousness, or a negative technology like an implant, portal, hook?

Higher Self: A hook.

A: If we could follow where this hook is attached to.

Higher Self: I can't get in there.

A: Is this hook attached to something within her body or outside her body?

Higher Self: Outside.

A: Higher Self, can we go ahead and transmute that hook out and remove it out from her, please? Can I use the Phoenix Fire on it?

Higher Self: Yes.

A: Good. We're using that. The implant that was the cap that was in her, in between her shoulder blades. How does that look now?

Higher Self: Faded.

A: It's gone?

Higher Self: Seems to be.

A: Make sure if it needs any additional Phoenix Fire, we could draw it there too. Go ahead and fill it with Love-Light, please. Okay, how's this hook looking in her elbow?

Higher Self: It's causing a lot of pain like searing, burning.

A: Can we go ahead and make it more comfortable for her Higher Self? Can I use Phoenix Fire, again the same golden type of energy that she was using in that life in the dome? We're focusing prayer energy over that area and transmuting it out now. Disintegrating, transmuting the hook out, and then following it. If we could have Archangel Michael follow it. Follow where it's connected and make sure that it's severed. So, it won't come back once more..

AA Michael: Connection is severed.

A: Beautiful. Okay, as we continue to transmute that out, let's go ahead and scan her body one more time. I know we're working on the Reptilians. Michael and Metatron, are they out yet? Did you all pull them out?

AA Michael: There's one that's still in the abdomen.

A: What's going on with that one? How come it's not out yet?

AA Michael: It's fighting.

A: Do you need me to use any Phoenix Fire directed in that way?

AA Michael: Yes.

A: Okay, we're using Phoenix Fire towards that one that is holding on.

AA Michael: Too much anger.

A: Using the Phoenix Fire to transmute the anger. Tell me, how's it looking? Is it removed?

AA Michael: Yes.

A: Good. Let's go ahead and heal that area. I know that she has a list of things that might be connected to this area. If we can start the scan. Let's begin the scanning of what she wants healed within her. The Epstein-Barr Virus. Can you find and help her sense where the root of this began from within her?

Higher Self: I don't know.

A: Was it connected to the Reptilian consciousness that we removed, or negative implants, negative technology that we removed? Did any of those begin the root of her Epstein-Barr Virus? Help her sense and know... Which one was it?

Higher Self: Negative technology.

A: In what part of her body?

Higher Self: I don't know. Feels like all over.

A: Let's scan her whole body for any part of this negative technology that has been the cause of the Epstein-Barr Virus. I want to make sure we do not miss anything. Is there any more of this negative technology that caused this?

Higher Self: I feel the negative, I just don't know where it is.

A: Can we Phoenix Fire her whole body and remove from her any of these negative technologies? Higher Self, do I have permission to do that?

Higher Self: Yes.

A: Okay, good. We're starting that now with the intent of healing her, allowing for the self-healing that she needs for the Epstein-Barr Virus. You said it's all over her body. Was this an injection of some kind that was inserted into the body?

Higher Self: Yes.

A: Was it connected to an immunization shot?

Higher Self: Something more than that.

A: Do the immunization shots have anything to do with some of the negative technology? Did they work together to cause the Epstein-Barr Virus?

Higher Self: Partly, yes.

A: Okay. We're transmuting, using the Phoenix Fire on her whole entire body from any of this negative technology, or A.I., that's causing the Epstein-Barr Virus. We're doing it now please, transmuting any negative technology within her and again we're filling in Love-Light to wherever any negativity is being transmuted out from. Healing her abdomen as well. There's always Archangel Raphael or Yeshua/Jesus that can assist you with any Love-Light. Do you need any assistance from either one of them?

Higher Self: Yeshua.

A: If we can call forth on Yeshua then in assisting with infinite Love-Light with the Higher Self, please. Thank you, Yeshua. I love you and honor you. Higher Self can you scan her for where the root cause of the Fibromyalgia is? Where did that begin from within her?

Higher Self: Brain.

A: Was it one of those implants in her brain? Was it the cap, or the implant in her left temple?

Higher Self: Implant.

A: Okay, I know we're already healing that, but again we're healing the Fibromyalgia. Can we do that Higher Self?

Higher Self: Yes.

A: Thank you, and the temporomandibular joint dysfunction (TMJ). Where did that begin?

Higher Self: Implant.

A: Good, healing that as well now please Higher Self, are we doing that?

Higher Self: Yes.

A: She has said that she suffered a lot her whole life, as well as her mother, from chronic fatigue syndrome (CFS). Where is she getting this chronic pain from? What is the root to that?

Higher Self: Being drained by negative energies.

A: The negative energies within her or outside?

Higher Self: Both, a combination.

A: Can we work with her aspect there that's within the dome to now help her surround herself with the same golden energy shielding throughout this life?

Higher Self: Yes.

A: Can we set an intent that she does this when she wakes up and hours before she goes to bed? That will ensure that she no longer has this chronic fatigue pain.

Higher Self: Yes.

A: If she does this, can we do that for her?

Higher Self: Yes.

A: Higher Self, thank you. If we could go ahead and strengthen her muscle weakness, please.

Higher Self: It has to do with being drained.

A: Let's go ahead and fill that in with the most infinite Love-Light of Source for the Higher Self. Can we ask for assistance from the beings there in the dome?

Higher Self: Yes!

A: Okay, good.

Higher Self: Connection is clear with them.

A: Beautiful. Also, the scoliosis, can we look at that? Where did that root begin?

Higher Self: A past life.

A: What happened in that past life?

Higher Self: I think it was damaged from falling from very high. A suicide.

A: Can we go ahead and heal that time now so we can heal her now?

Higher Self: Yes.

A: Thank you. Very good. Now, what was the root cause of her allergies?

Higher Self: Her energies are not resonating with the environment.

A: If she surrounds herself with the golden energy. Will that help her allergies in the future?

Higher Self: Yes.

A: Good. Can we heal any reaction right now that the allergies have caused?

Higher Self: Yes.

A: Good. Let's look at the eczema in her, she said mostly her hands. What is causing that?

Higher Self: Blockage of the energy flow through her hands.

A: Can we go ahead and heal that?

Higher Self: Yes.

A: Good. The food intolerance. She said she has, mainly in her stomach area and so on. Was that connected to the Reptilians in her stomach, or was it also part of her growth?

Higher Self: It's a combination of both. She will have an easier time when they are gone.

A: I know we're healing there already.

Higher Self: She will still need to continue with health.

A: She said she has asthma. Sometimes she says when she walks up the stairs, or so on, she gets a random asthma attack, and sometimes she doesn't. What is the root cause to this?

Higher Self: A block, Reptilian energy.

A: If I could just make sure we heal her from asthma, please. Can we do that Higher Self?

Higher Self: Yes.

A: Wonderful. She's been under for some time. How's she holding up?

Higher Self: Good.

A: Let's go ahead and scan her blurry vision, she says she sometimes gets it in her eyes.

Higher Self: It had to do with the Reptilian energy in her lungs as well. Checking the eyes.

A: Let's go ahead and heal her eyes now. Also, her vertigo, what was that connected to?

Higher Self: The cap in the third eye.

A: Let's go ahead and heal that. I know we healed that earlier but make sure she doesn't get vertigo anymore. And how about the headaches?

Higher Self: The cap as well. In the chip, in the implant.

A: Was it because it was holding too much energy there and causing the headache?

Higher Self: Yes.

A: Okay. And then also chronic sinusitis, was that caused by that too as well?

Higher Self: Combination of implant and Reptilian energy.

A: Making sure that her sinuses are now clear please, can you do that?

Higher Self: Yes.

A: Also, obsessive compulsive disorder (OCD) germaphobe. What is the reason for that?

Higher Self: Fears.

A: Fears, okay. Can we help her start transmuting some of those fears that we may have already with the Phoenix Fire we're using on her? Also, being a perfectionist. Why? What can we do about that? Does she need that?

Higher Self: It ties in with OCD, control, fear.

A: Also, can you find out why she sometimes feels like she's gone for a period of time and all of a sudden, she doesn't realize she lost time. Why does it happen to her?

Higher Self: There's a combination of things, and I am not entirely sure.

A: Was it a combination of some of that negative technology in her, or is it something else?

Higher Self: That's part of it. Part of it is just being pulled somewhere else. Not having a connection to Earth. Not fully connecting with the body.

A: Now that she's not going to have any of these blockages, can we help her integrate better and be able to be more grounded within her body? Being able to bear being a human.

Higher Self: Yes.

A: You know, she's had a hard time since she was little about that. So, thank you. She says sometimes her energies were like she didn't feel something was right, it turned into something dark. What was causing that?

Higher Self: Stemmed from her strong belief fighting justice and Reptilian energy fed off of that.

A: When she's having those negative thought forms, is she transmuting and trying to heal that?

Higher Self: Yes.

A: Why would she feel like she gets ill from the sun? It becomes too much for her.

Higher Self: All the negative forces in her, the implants, the caps, Reptilians, are all stopping her from absorbing well.

A: Can we make it nice and healthy? As we know the sun's energy very much feels like Source energy, so she could be able to start replenishing her energy to the sun?

Higher Self: Yes.

A: Archangel Michael, if you could assist the Higher Self, as you have been already. Let's go ahead and scan her body one more time. I want to make sure we don't miss any other Reptilian consciousness or entity. Scan her body now. Does she have anything else?

Higher Self: The throat.

A: What's going on in the throat?

Higher Self: It is a Reptilian energy suffocating.

A: Let's go ahead and encase that Reptilian energy there with alchemy symbols now. Is there anywhere else? Any other Reptilian consciousness in her?

Higher Self: The lower back.

A: Let's encase that one with alchemy symbols, please. Anywhere else?

Higher Self: No, just the throat, neck in that area.

A: Okay, and then her lower back. Michael, if you could tell the Higher Self, are these able to positively ascend? Will they allow themselves to be free and not be recycled straight to Source? Instead allow for them to ascend into a positive Ascension polarization. Love them, I honor, and thank them. Will they allow it?

Higher Self: Struggle.

A: From both?

Higher Self: Yes. They're latching on to the chest.

A: Let's make sure we have them in the alchemy symbols, I'm using Phoenix Fire wherever they're trying to latch on to. Michael, can we aid them? Or should we just remove them?

AA Michael: Remove.

A: Michael, Metatron, if you could both now assist with pulling them out. Containing them in their symbols and pulling them out. And also, the ones that we took out earlier again, you are all supervising, where it is that you're meant to take them to help them heal, please. Pulling them out as you continue to pull them out. I want to scan one more time. Michael, Higher Self, is there any other Reptilian consciousness?... Scan her one more time.

Higher Self: The heart chakra is in the hands. There's still a bit of blockage.

A: Okay, let's go ahead and heal those now. Let's use Phoenix Fire there in her hands.

Higher Self: Can we call Yeshua?

A: If we could call on Yeshua now. Higher Self, as you requested, calling him to heal her hands.

Higher Self: Yes.

A: Good and open up the heart chakras in her hands.

Higher Self: They are opening.

A: Very good, they're opening. Beautiful, thank you. Are there any other implants, hooks, or portals that we need to heal?

Higher Self: No.

A: Scan her one more time. Higher Self, any other Reptilian consciousness or entities?

Higher Self: She is clear.

A: Beautiful. Did we remove the reptilian consciousness within both of those parts of the body?

Higher Self: Yes.

A: Good. If you all can go ahead and take them all now with Love and Light and assist them wherever it is that they will get assistance from, please.

Higher Self: Okay.

A: Thank you. All right. Now, can we check the chakras Higher Self? Are there any chakras that need healing? Are they blocked or misaligned?

Higher Self: Root Chakra

A: What's within the Root? Does it just need healing?

Higher Self: Grounding.

A: Can you do that for her please? Can you make that grounding stronger? Perhaps making a nice healthy cord, as her Higher Self sees fit.

Higher Self: Yes.

A: Good. Anytime she feels ungrounded can she focus attention on this cord to ground herself?

Higher Self: Yes.

A: Beautiful. Now check her auric field, does it need any repairs, or are there any tears?

Higher Self: Tears caused by self-doubt. Tears below to the solar plexus.

A: Can we help her with that doubt? I know she says she has a lot of doubt. She knew all her answers. Help her understand that she has them all within her and at any point that they are able to give and be given to her. Help her no longer doubt her inner voice and her inner knowing. Can you do that Higher Self?

Higher Self: Yes.

A: I know that you've activated those abilities, of whatever is allowed in this time in space of those, that being there in the dome and also the child as she was with her abilities.
I know that it's going to make a lot of difference for her in her life. Thank you. Are there any contracts, Higher Self, that we can go ahead and remove from her?

Higher Self: Duty.

A: There's a contract for duty?

Higher Self: Duty, yes carrying guilt.

A: What is the guilt she's carrying?

Higher Self: Duty not fulfilled, from another life.

A: Can you ask Archangel Michael, can we remove that contract please?

Higher Self: Yes.

A: Let's go ahead and remove that and heal that and any other contracts that no longer serve her highest good. Is there any current trauma that we can heal for her, or past life trauma?

Higher Self: Painful separation from divine love partner.

A: About that, she wanted to know if she will meet him in this life. What can you tell her about this Twin Flame? And let's go ahead and heal that trauma for her please.

Higher Self: Yes.

A: Is this Twin Flame union going to come forth for her in this life? Is this someone she's already met, or she is meeting?

Higher Self: It would be a different connection.

A: Okay. Does she have any connection to that...there's this being that she's meeting now. Does it have a connection with Francois?

Higher Self: There's a connection there. There's a possibility.

A: Right now, she's looking at more than one possibility where he could come into? Would it be the same gentleman she met in that life with those beautiful golden eyes?

Higher Self: Energies are similar.

A: Very good. I know she's been under longer than expected. Is there anything else that I could have asked that I haven't asked?

Higher Self: Her dog. He's special.

A: Yes. Can you tell her about that, please?

Higher Self: He's great, great love.

A: What is he to her, say beyond this existence? What's the connection there?

Higher Self: It's unclear.

A: It's unclear? What is he here for, besides love, is there anything else?

Higher Self: Transmuting. He's also transmuting for himself. He's healing.

A: Yes. Very good. Higher Self, can you ask Archangel Michael, are we complete with the body scan?

Higher Self: Yes.

A: Beautiful. Very good. Thank you. Higher Self, is there anything else you would like to tell her before we bring her back?

Higher Self: There's a deeper divine connection to her mother, found through many, many lifetimes.

A: What is that? Tell her more about that.

Higher Self: She has always been Mother energy to me. Much like Mother Mary to Yeshua. There's a strong bond there.

A: Is her mother a fractal of Mother Mary?

Higher Self: Yes.

A: With that, does that mean that Bella would carry the energies of Mary Magdalene?

Higher Self: Yes.

A: Is that who her Higher Self would be?

Higher Self: A fractal...I sense more.

A: What can you tell us, Higher Self?

Higher Self: Someone of great power and persuasion. Great leadership.

A: Do we have a name?

Higher Self: The name is unclear. I sense a Goddess....

A: Anything else you could tell her about herself to help her, or her spiritual growth?

Higher Self: All about Love. I sense a lot of both the Goddess of Justice and Goddess of Love.

A: Wonderful.

Higher Self: The balance of the two.

A: Higher Self, is there anything else you would like to say before I bring her back?

Higher Self: No.

A: I want to thank Archangel Michael, Metatron and everyone else who assisted today. We love you, honor you, and respect you. Thank you for assisting her, and Higher Self, for connecting us.

END OF SESSION

-------------<◇>-------------

What a beautiful session, complimenting the beginning of our Journey through these Soul Galactic Journeys of the Universe! Reminding us how sacred groups, such as these Monks, hidden in the mountains, have worked with devotion throughout our Earth's history to maintain what is pure and in need of shielding and protection from those who would abuse this raw pure divine power. As Bella was with her most unique signature goddess types of energies. What could those who wield dark magic use her abilities for? The power of telepathy and wielding the fire and the elements. We see why the need exists to protect someone so pure in this dense and distorted world. For as we know, those who are born on Earth cannot harness with ease these divine abilities, as Bella's, that are common functions beyond the veil in this realm. Our deepest humble gratitude and thanks to these Monks and all those who play this similar role throughout Creation, as they are shielding and protecting what is most precious to the Universe.

In Chapter 1 ('The First Reptilian Consciousness Attachments'), we first learned about the experiments the Reptilians were performing on the young children. We were told that these were beginning experiments that eventually evolved and were no longer needed. The reason why they evolved was because they were able to successfully attach Reptilian consciousnesses into people, just as we saw through Bella's example how she had one attached. The Reptilian consciousness that was not cooperative and was hiding and masking as a human entity. The Reptilians from those earlier times and space eventually reached an understanding on how the human bodies work. By putting humans under distress and trauma mentally, the Reptilians are able to energetically penetrate, just like they did to the little boy that could not push back and stop the infringement of the Reptilian consciousness insertion into him. We will learn more with each chapter why this is important, as we continue to encounter them in healing sessions. We will come into awareness on why these infringing consciousnesses play a big role in our Earth's collective in holding it dense and heavy.

I found great resonance with this beautiful race during the session and was able to connect to them through the Akashic Hall of Records. Often when I conduct sessions, the benevolent races that we connect to during, create a bond with me afterwards. Upon doing so, I realized that they were connected to the Kryst/Christ Consciousness, or could even be seen as the origination of this collective consciousness that aids all of Creation with their wisdom and shields of love protection. I was also told that since Bella carried Mary Magdalene within her soul, her Twin Flame, who had been afar for too long, that was on a mission, was Jesus/Yeshua. He was still working on Earth aiding life on it.

When the eyes of two souls meet, who are separated from one another as Twin Flames, no matter the realm and dimension they will always remember and feel this deep resonance and understanding to one another, as Bella and her Twin Flame did in this session. Love, no matter in whichever bond, whether it is Twin Flame, soulmate, or of an offspring, the soul will always recognize these sacred bonds of soul families from beyond.

At times the client, such as Bella, is not able to receive these details during the session about her race being Kryst/Christ Consciousness, as she was not yet within her timeline organically meant for her highest good. Remembrance of our souls, if not ready, can be more harmful than helpful as we recall within our Earthly existence who we truly are beyond the veil. It is beautiful to know that in some time and space when clients are ready, they will find out some of these finer details in accordance with divine timing and always for their highest good.

Bella's journey explains the uniqueness and infinite love that Jesus/Yeshua emanated when incarnated on Earth, and when we connect to him energetically in the now. And he wields his most beautiful Love-Light aura divinely in assistance to others in need of it. As he has taught us how to use our own infinite "I AM Source Love-Light" to heal self and other selves.[2] This very force field is what he used when he walked Earth, when someone would come into his presence. He would lovingly wield his Love-Light force field directed towards the person, with the Higher Selves' permission and assist them in removal of densities holding them back from

---

[2] For more of Jesus/Yeshua's teachings, please go to Rising Phoenix Aurora's YouTube Channel for the "Jesus and Mother Mary" Playlist.

their organic soul expansion. Which is why people would experience miracles from across the room with him not even touching them, because it was his Source Love-Light that was gently brushing against their auric field like a wave and taking within its powerful healing the infringements in them, as entities, implants, and negative technologies.

This beautiful session helps us understand further, about beings who are highly attuned to the energies of the Universe. How would they bear living here on Earth surrounded by such a destructive atmosphere with the combination of the chemtrails, metals in our foods, the water pollution...? What kind of effects would they have, to be able to remain in this lowest Dimension? In her case, allergies, hospitalizations and chronic pain. Perhaps her unique soul family's abilities of shielding are needed on Earth and are assisting tremendously. We send her our love for her courage and strength.

We all have these innate natural abilities awaiting to be acknowledged and activated. This is why we have included some of the sacred teachings in this book for you to activate and practice your I AM Source Love-Light shielding, to begin building a solid foundation for your spiritual practice and growth. In the next Chapter, we will go through some of Jesus/Yeshua's key teachings about love, and how religions have distorted his true teachings over time.

"The bravest of hearts chooses to remain open in a world
that views its kindness, as weakness."
~AuroRa ♥

--------------<◇>--------------

3

TEACHINGS OF YESHUA

Session #83: Recorded in October 2018.

In this online A.U.R.A. Hypnosis Healing session, Maria is somnambulistic[3]. She is giving us the honor of having Jesus/Yeshua speak clearly through her with no human consciousness interference. How has religion evolved over time? Jesus/Yeshua clarifies his teachings of the True Bible he wrote. The real stories, sexual orientation, Mother Mary, Mary Magdalene, disciples, and Fallen Angels. An important message for Whistleblowers on Lucifer versus Luciferian Agenda. Who truly were the Romans? More on the Cabal... He surprises Aurora with messages for her and gives her advice on her teachings!

-------------<◇>-------------

"Religion is nothing but restriction and limitation.
Love is not that. God is Love and that is true.
So, if God is Love, why are you limiting them?"
-Yeshua

-------------<◇>-------------

A: [Aurora] Does Yeshua want to talk through her? Does he have a message for her?
Jesus/Yeshua: Forgive, forgive, forgive yourself, my child.
A: Welcome, brother.
Jesus/Yeshua: I love you beautiful one.
A: Thank you for talking to us today.
Jesus/Yeshua: Forgive, forgive, forgive. Yes.
A: Thank you. Why is it that you're guiding her in this life?
Jesus/Yeshua: Because she needs to forgive herself so she can forgive those that are attacking her instead of retaliating. And that's what's going to happen to the majority, if not to all that are awakening. The attacks will come. The best way to address those is with forgiveness.
A: Yes.
Jesus/Yeshua: It's a lot to ask. Yes. Especially in 3D because you lose yourself so much. But if you are above the 3D it is something that is easy to give. She needs to know that she's not in 3D. The attacks are from the 3D but she's not from there anymore. She's above that. So, she needs to know that she's coming from a higher Dimension, that she can embrace those attacks with love, light and forgiveness.

---

[3] A somnambulistic client means the client's consciousness is moved to the back with no interference from the ego. The client does not remember anything of what was mentioned during the session, which means that only the benevolent being(s) spoke clearly with no interference from the client's human consciousness or ego.

A: Thank you, brother Yeshua. That's a beautiful way to put it for those who hold the strong light, as you're explaining of her. Sometimes we will hold a strong light. We do come under attack from others that like you've mentioned, do have those lower frequencies of hatred and envy. Yes, viewing things from the higher realm and understanding and forgiving and loving them. Thank you. Beautiful advice.

Jesus/Yeshua: You too. You know, there are people who will raise their eyebrows, roll their eyes up high but it's one of those that come from the lower vibration. I guess that is something that we all have to acknowledge because we are not exempted to those kinds of attacks. Let us not allow them to stop us from what we do. Especially from what YOU do.

A: Thank you. Let us not allow them.

Jesus/Yeshua: I just want to tell you how brave you are. And I want to thank you, honor you, respect you for what you do. You do not know how much you're enlightening the path for the rest. That is such a brave undertaking. And yet you have outdone from the worst. So much of selflessness from your end. (crying) Thank you, thank you, thank you.

A: Thank you, beautiful Yeshua. I love you dearly. Your words mean the world to me. Thank you.

Jesus/Yeshua: You are so much loved. You and your husband, your family. (deep breath) You are so much loved. Continue to do what you do. Continue harnessing and leading the way to those who are cold. Lead the way.

A: Thank you, we shall. It is because we feel your strength as our guides, as our Angels, beautiful benevolent beings that are there guiding us. It is because of you that we feel the strength to continue on. It just means the world to us that we have your support always.

Jesus/Yeshua: Thank you for allowing us to connect to you. There's a lot that we would want to but there are very few that have an open heart. A wide open, receiving heart for us to connect. Thank you.

A: Thank you. Do you have a message? I know you gave her a message, but do you have a message while you're talking brother, for humanity besides all these you already mentioned?

Jesus/Yeshua: A lot of people dream, wish, pray and hope for love, happiness and peace. But at the same time, what they fail to see is inside them. That they are one that are actually clouding this prayer of love and peace. They need to accept and look inside them. First before they ask for it. You cannot ask and hope and wish for love if you do not have that inside you. How could you hope for happiness when you offend, harm, judge and discriminate against others? How could you ask for positive things if in your daily living and your daily life what you think as soon as you wake up in the morning is how you could be ahead of others? It doesn't mean as to how you get there. Sometimes you step on other people's toes. Sometimes you cut them in traffic, sometimes you cheat them, rob them from credits, glory or some attention just to be ahead of them. Look inside before you ask, see if you have given that. For example, if you want love, have you loved somebody around you lately? Do you know of somebody who needs love? Have you given that love to that person Instead of judging that person? Have you approached somebody that you thought you cannot stand because that person wronged you? Have you approached that person and then just hugged that person? For example, if you want peace, what have you done lately to achieve that peace? Have you stopped bad mouthing your colleagues at work or your classmates or your neighbors, for example? Look inside you first before you ask. See if you have it inside you, that you know that you can give it to somebody and then come back look inside your heart and then say, "you know what, I have hugged a person who I can't stand and I feel good about it." Once you have that confirmation then ask, 'I need more love.' I need more love to give. I need more love so I can give more love. It starts from you. You want good things, do good things! You want happiness, make somebody happy. Then come back and ask for more, so you can give more.

A: Yes, beautiful words. Thank you.

Jesus/Yeshua: It doesn't stop from you. What you want, doesn't stop from you. You want because you want to give more. The only time that you are given what you asked for is only if you have already given that to others. Just like what you do. You have this knowledge and the wisdom, and we come to you. Connect to you to give advice and confirmations. You give that out to others and teach and train others. So that can cycle and then it can ripple. The ripple effects. Then you come back and then you give me advice some more. Ask for more teachings that you can share to others and there goes the ripple again. That's what everybody should do. It doesn't stay with you, all by yourself. It starts from you and then starts making ripples.

A: Yes. Thank you, that means so much to me because I recently started teaching classes. Also, when I do my readings, I help people find what's within them and then I help them embrace who they are. I encourage them to love themselves fully and to believe in themselves and to love oneself. Often, we see, as you mentioned, perhaps if they go to a healer, the healer won't fully want for them to fully embrace their gifts. Say for example, they're a channel, they won't fully want them to become a channel because then they have competition. Or say they have information, like the healer will have information, but they don't want to openly share it. In a sense, they kind of want money, money, money - 'Okay I won't share it.' So, you know, it's hard for me to see this. Then as a catalyst, it's hard for me to point this out as well, because I honor everyone's roles. This really relates and helps me embrace what I'm doing daily because I want to teach others as well. As a Spiritual Leader, as a catalyst I want to perhaps stop those cycles. End those ways that we've been taught since the beginning. Since this planet started becoming controlled by negative forces or the ego. So, I want to help others grow and help them realize that we're here to support each other. For us to stop judging one another, that it's okay for us to read one another. If you see a person like this, it's okay. How can you help them and how can you embrace them and send them love? How can you help them evolve from it and ascend from it, metamorphose from it? So, thank you. Sorry, just started talking there.

Jesus/Yeshua: It's good. I feel your heart. I just want you to know what you have given to your students or people that you have trained that's theirs. You cannot take that back. That's a gift that was given to you and you gave it away. And if for example, the recipient of that training, use it in a negative way that is nothing against you. That is an act of their own. That is something that they need to make peace with. I do not want you to think just because you've trained somebody, and that somebody goes against you, and there is this competition. It comes in her training or in her if you call it business that she's practicing, and that she comes into a dead end, or she's not getting any answers, or she's kind of limited to the answers that she wants. I want you to think that it is not because of you. It's not because you trained her in the wrong way or them in a wrong way. No, it only means that that person still has some issues that she needs to make peace with. Yes, those things, those blockages, those dead ends are there to teach that person that there is some clearing needed. All that they have to do is to go inside again and be receptive and open to what is limiting them. That is not because of you. They brought that to themselves.

A: Yes.

Jesus/Yeshua: So please do not be disheartened when you hear things like that, that is just another attack. The more that you shine, the more that you advance, the more that you are ahead and spearheading and leading this army of people awakening, the more you're going to be attacked. Fear not because all of us are protecting you. There's enough love and light that is around you. That is your students or the people that you shared with that is their own (in relation to the discussion of responsibility of a student or practitioner). Just like you said, it's all about the money. But if that is what they came to you for, for training just to make money, then they have a lot of things to learn. Then there's no way for you to know if they really came in to join your training, because they want awakening. There are those that would pretend they are awakened, just because they just want to turn that into a business. Then once you share that to them, then now you are a business competitor. But that is not for you. That is not your fault. That is their own making. There will be some, it's not the end yet. There will be some that will still do that. It is just the selfishness of the 3D.

A: Yes. Yeshua, you have no idea how much these words mean to me. You are bringing them to me... it's been a concern for me as I teach from the heart, it took me a while to say, "Okay, I'm going to teach these classes." That was one of the biggest concerns, like I wanted to even make a book of alchemy, but then I was concerned what if these people take this alchemy and then they turn it into something of harming someone? So, then I was like, "Okay, I'm not going to do that. So, then I'm going to do classes and be very careful." But you are saying that whoever is going to come, I understand that whoever is going to come is going to come. I don't want to be teaching this and then someone goes and harms someone. You know, I didn't want to feel responsible for that. I'm here to protect and to work with the heart and we harm none. It's like you were in my heart as usual. Oh my goodness, I cannot tell you enough how much your words mean to me and it's such a relief for me to be able to teach these classes and teach what I'm going to teach without having to worry about what you mentioned. So, thank you.

Jesus/Yeshua: Just as much as you have said, you know, that let love and light be, let love and light shine bright and open opportunities. And then at the same time be invincible to danger. When you are doing these classes, let that be mentioned. When you are conducting classes, give that love and light, not just to the students, but to the students or the recipient or the customers of that student once they graduate from it. Extend that love and light to whoever would be the recipient of the students that you are training. Whatever happens if the student turns it into a negative way, that is not from you. Keep extending that love and light to the customers or the beneficiary of the readings from your students. And if there's any blockages, then that's going to be that person that is not welcoming yet or who has some negative energies still lurking there that has not been cleared totally. That is not from you. You have a very big following. Others may want to limit you. But no, your light is shining bright. You have nothing to fear.

A: How many times are you going to make me cry? What a wonderful surprise. I love you.

Jesus/Yeshua: And I love you. I am always amazed and always in awe of everything that you do and will do. You make us very proud.

A: Thank you. As you know it's hard for me as the Phoenix, I sometimes feel so much energy. Then it gets overwhelming for me and sometimes I feel those psychic attacks. So, your messages have come to me at the right moment. We are ready for the next cycle of evolving. So, thank you my beautiful brother. I love you.

Jesus/Yeshua: I think Maria came here with a lot of things in her head to ask. But last minute, she just said, "I'm just going to let them take over." I think she came here partly for herself, but more for you. Because you need to be recharged as much as Maria needs to be recharged.

A: (laughing and crying at the same time) Thank you. Yes, I teach my A.U.R.A. practitioners. We are not just helping to facilitate heal others. They are also helping us heal. It's a give and take.

Jesus/Yeshua: It is a group that we need recharging. Each of us needs to exchange that love and light. Even if you're a teacher. You need to be a student and be a recipient. If you're a giver. You need to be a recipient too. It's a give and take. It's a two way and that is the only way that we can expand this positivity. This beautiful love and light are for us to recharge, and enlighten, and energize each other. Acknowledge and confirm each other. That's the only way. I think Maria would be interested to join your class too.

A: Oh! I would love to have her.

Jesus/Yeshua: She doubts herself. She has questions like 'do you have to be born with this? How shall I understand?' All these questions. Human as she is. You will be a good fit for her.

A: Good. She will be a beautiful fit for us, working within the heart. She has such a beautiful heart. It would be an honor for her to join. So yes, I would love that. Wonderful. I mean, look at how phenomenal she's doing right now, with allowing for you to talk through her. You know, not everyone can do this. So that is something that she needs to embrace herself and love herself for being able to do today. I thank her.

Jesus/Yeshua: You make me smile all the time.

A: (laughter) Beautiful Yeshua, you know, what you spoke of today has a lot to do also with what you taught, when you were here. As a catalyst awakening others and teaching others to go within their hearts. To not believe that they were limited. So, thank you for sharing those teachings with us. Can I ask you a couple questions to see what you feel like right now? How we are. Is that okay?

Jesus/Yeshua: Yes.

A: This is the way that you taught. So, thank you.

Jesus: You're welcome.

A: How do you feel right now, as far as religion? What do you think of religion and the way that it's been led after you taught? What Christianity has been turned into as well as the Bible that you helped start?

Jesus/Yeshua: It's like the government. It starts with good inspirations, something of the positive, something to keep people together to unite as one so that they can coexist in unity, in love and help each other. But then along the way the greediness comes in, the jealousy comes in. Someone steals the spotlight. So, for example, with religion, it starts as a ritual for us to be connected more through the heart. A lot of us do not see the heart physically. We feel it. But then there are those that have the gift of talking to the point that they... what's the word? That they corrupted the goodness of the heart. They corrupted that with their mind to the point that there was division - limitations. That is complete control. A way for the religion, to control the congregation as to what they can do and cannot do. Take for example, the 10 percent of their income. The Bible says this is what the religion needs 10 percent. It was just a metaphor that was used. You know, you give what you can give. It's not just the 10 percent. Other people are stuck to the 10 percent literally, but it's not. What it actually means is give out of the goodness of your heart. And, of course in this 3D you cannot give your heart 100 percent but if you can give 10 percent of that heart to somebody who needs something like a loaf of bread, is that too difficult to ask? Maybe instead of feasting with an entire package of bread, if you see somebody on the road, starving, maybe you can open that bag and offer some to that person who is hungry. Why feast if you know that somebody is hungry? Give and that's all it meant, but for some reason, some religions, they said, "No, that belongs to God." God doesn't want that. God doesn't need that 10 percent. He wants the heart so that you can share that heart, that love from the heart. That's what he needs. That's what he wants you to do. It's all about control. It's how they can get something out of you. And that's what made it all ugly. To this day some people are still blinded by that, because they have already been brainwashed.

A: Yes.

Jesus/Yeshua: All we can do is pray and ask that they can see the light. That they can see the reason behind it. Maria got called that. She was actually called like a radical or the black sheep as we call them. She was actually awakened but she was not strong enough to come out and question it. She just moved on. It is just control and history, the religion side of things has actually come to realize its own mistake in some ways. Take for example, the priests that were harming the youth. Take for example, those preachers that are asking for a jetliner for themselves to spread the word. People are already starting to raise their eyebrows questioning it. All that we can do is collectively send them our love for better understanding and for them to awaken some more. Religion is nothing but restriction and limitation. Love is not that. God is Love and that is true. So, if God is Love, why are you limiting them? So, they are not practicing what it should be. They should be sent out. They should evolve. But religion wants them to be limited and restricted. They cannot let them go out free because then they don't have any control. Then they have nothing left for them. It's sad that it turned out to be this. For example, the station of the cross. That is just at first glance that you see on TV. Again, it's control. As Maria always says "God is love. And if you're God regardless of what religion you believe, or whether you have a religion or not, if your belief is not based on love then I don't want to be your friend." It's all about love. Muslims, I do not say anything bad against them. But there are those radicals that they kill other people. Why? I do not understand. What kind of propaganda is that? That's not love.

A: The Bible that is being taught now, was that changed?

Jesus/Yeshua: A lot of times that has been changed. It's what you call...there's this movie about "Lost In Translation." It started as a beautiful thing. But it was passed down to the next generation and next generation to next generation. Something was taken out to whatever that person who was commanding asked for. For example, back in the Roman times there is Julius Caesar. Right?

A: Yes.

Jesus/Yeshua: Then he was the commander. So, he will assign somebody to transcribe something, putting him to inject him - Julius Caesar into whatever is being written. So, there is always this manipulation of the truth. It started as a beautiful thing. But then other people injected their own greed and their own ego into that. And that's when it all separated from the truth.

A: Yes. I have memories of this time and actually right when you started talking about the Romans, I was just thinking of those times. So were the Romans, can you say that they were Cabal? Were they Cabal trying to target you and stop you?

Jesus/Yeshua: Yes.

A: People don't realize this, in those times, that's what was going on.

Jesus/Yeshua: Yes, they were. They would stop anything that is good. Anything that is out of love, anything that is light. They wanted it to stop.

A: Yes.

Jesus/Yeshua: They would go and slaughter people to stop it.

A: Oh, yes. So sad!

Jesus/Yeshua: That is just pure selfishness on their part. That's absolute control. They wanted people to fear them. It was out of fear that they were able to control the people.

A: Yes. Perhaps you can clarify some things that we've been taught here in these times. I think it would be great. It would be a great honor for us to be able to do that. If it's okay with Maria to continue asking the questions of the Bible?

Jesus/Yeshua: Yes.

A: Okay. Thank you. She's doing such a beautiful service today. So, what about when they talk about specifically, male on male, female and female partnership and how they say that's horrible or a sin. What are your views on that?

Jesus/Yeshua: It's not. It is again the old thinking. That was the mentality before that was passed down from generation to generations. As much as they use Adam and Eve in the Bible, as an example as a male - female. What they do not realize is, there is a male part that exists in the female. And so is there a female part that exists in the male. I think people are not open. Some people are already open to this. But there's still a majority that are not open to it. With LGBT my question is this for example, if you eat a fish. You cook a fish. You take it home; you

73

clean it up. Then of course, the first thing that you do is that you clean out the guts right out of the fish. And for example, of course, there's a way to know if a fish is a female or a male. If there's an egg, it's a female. If it's not, then it's male. My question is, if that fish has not ovulated - it doesn't have any eggs in it, and you cook it. Do you think it matters to you to eat that fish, if that fish is a he or she? It doesn't. You just want to eat that fish?

A: Yes.

Jesus/Yeshua: And then enjoy it, right? So why is it so difficult to accept whether in a male body is a female and in a female body is a male? We have both inside us. Why is it so difficult to accept? So, my next scenario is this. We women are known to and I don't know if you just noticed that it's Yeshua speaking, but I did say "We women." So, my question is women are known to talk more, speak more. And, they are very emotional, they cry a lot more than men. So, if a man cries, does that make them a lesser man? I don't know if you notice nowadays, but then a lot of men, if you turn on your TV, a lot of men talk a lot, a lot more. Does that make them a female? No. But there's always that aspect in us, even if it is already manifesting, physically, we still do not want to accept it. Why? It's because of brainwashing, that was instilled in us from way back then and that needs to be cleared.

A: Yes.

Jesus/Yeshua: Maria always says at work she comes across this man and they talk. They even gossip and Maria would say, "This is a cultural difficulty for me because where I come from men do not talk much. Why do you even gossip? That's what women do. Not men. Why are you doing it?" She will make fun of that situation to make a point. I don't know if you understand, that is Maria's sense of humor.

A: (laughter) I understand. Then also there are certain things, for example, about Lucifer[4]. Is that true how he's the devil?

Jesus/Yeshua: No!!! He's not. It is just another labeling by the brainwashing, just like when they say the "black sheep." You know "Lucifer is the enemy, the bad one." It is just the mentality of old age. Labeling people.

A: Did the Cabal change that in the Bible to make him look like that?

Jesus/Yeshua: Oh definitely.

A: Okay. Also, I was wondering if you can tell me this. There are basically people who are spiritual leaders and those that are whistleblowers; these kinds of people who believe that Lucifer is still bad. Was it the Cabal's that named the blood rituals 'Luciferian'? So, does that actually have a connection with Lucifer himself? Or the Cabal?

Jesus/Yeshua: It's just the Cabal. Way back then it was all about ritual. And that is how you would be a part of an organization. So just like in baptism, you cannot be a part of a congregation if you're not baptized, right? So, way back then in the Cabal, there's all these rituals that you have to observe to be part of it. That's how they market what they were trying to sell to the people. It's just a marketing strategy. If I may say so.

A: Yes, yes. That's a good example. Is that why they use his name, are they trying to get people to not connect with him. What does he do for humanity?

Jesus/Yeshua: To see the other side of themselves. So, you see Angels as good ones, right? They have a halo around their head, right? So, this is how they brainwash the people. If you see an Angel with a halo around their head and then they have rings that are shining white, then they're the good ones. But then if you see a nasty looking creature, you know, like a form of a bat. Even the bat has been connoted as related to something bad. And this is how they brainwash people. So, about the wings, if you see something that has the wing that is dark then that means that one is evil. Right?

---

[4] Lucifer is also known as Archangel Haylel.

A: Yes.

Jesus/Yeshua: But that is again just how they manipulate the minds of the people. The bottom line is that we are all good. The bad is coming from those who are trying to sell us this product. If we are not enlightened, if we are not careful, if we don't ask questions or challenge them - challenge what they're trying to sell us then we are nothing but part of them. We would be eager members of that. There are still things going on Earth. There's still a lot of brainwashing going on.

A: Yes. I bring this to light because when I tap into this energy where there's actual people who are Light Workers, who even have a lot of connections there. They're saying that Lucifer is a fallen Angel. He's the Devil. They're thinking this and then they're connecting him with being part of the Cabal. So that's why I wanted you to clarify that because there is so much fear created and again, it's part of the whole system that you have mentioned as well. They want to create all this fear against Angels and Lucifer, who is here to help others see, like you said, the other side of them. See the reflection of themselves. If I can ask you, is he the Lightbringer?

Jesus/Yeshua: Okay, so he brings light to what is the other side of you? If that's what you mean? Yes.

A: Yes.

Jesus/Yeshua: So, for example remember that in the Bible wherein I went to the temple and then I saw some vendors, people selling stuff by the temple. Remember that part of the Bible?

A: Yes.

Jesus/Yeshua: I went there, and I was praying. I was having my own moment and I just wanted to be with myself. Then I walked out, and I saw all these vendors, these merchants selling their things. Using that temple as a place to sell their goods. Remember that I went there and kicked them out or destroyed it. Scattered their merchandise all over the place and I told them that they are disrespecting the house of my father. Did that make me Lucifer because I was mad? So, way back then it's about, anything that is negative, they see it as bad and they brand it as evil. And if you know the Romans, they did not like that. "Oh, if he is really the Son of God, look at the temper." They started to give meanings to my emotions. All that I wanted was for people to go there as a place of refuge, respect and peace. And yet they come and bring their selfishness at the door of worship. For me, that is disrespect. If I am against disrespect, does that make me a follower of 'Lucifer'. No. I'm not. And Lucifer is a good person. The Cabal just makes him bad because they want to connect that name to the badness of their organization.

A: Yes.

Jesus/Yeshua: In all of us, there is something not good - not perfect. Actually, Lucifer brings that light. He actually brings that up. So that we know. His job, his duty, his obligation, his mission is for us to acknowledge and correct that negative part of us. The "not so" loving part of us. That's his vision and he does a good job in doing it, but people are quick enough to judge that. That's what they do not realize, is that they're judging themselves not judging Lucifer. He's just doing his job.

A: Yes. That is a hard role to play.

Jesus/Yeshua: Very hard. I have never ever met somebody who was so open and welcoming to accept that kind of mission and responsibility knowing that people are going to see you as the bad one. He welcomed it without question.

A: That is just how beautiful, kind and loving he is for all.

Jesus/Yeshua: He is, and he needs more appreciation and acknowledgement than what the others are labeling him. He lives in all of us. In all of us. In all of us. We have the Angel, and we have the Lucifer. I just hope that people would recognize that Lucifer is not bad. Lucifer, or the other side of us is just there to remind us that we need to accept that we need to bring that out on the surface. Accept it, correct it.

A: Beautiful. Thank you. Your explanation Yeshua, is beautiful for our brother Lucifer. Thank you for doing that for him and overall for humanity so that they will no longer allow for themselves to be brainwashed and exist within this frequency of fear when they hear his name. When they judge him, they're judging themselves, like you said, and there's nothing to judge. He's holding space in love for everyone and light for them. So, thank you for clarifying that, because that's one of the biggest misconceptions in the Bible. So, thank you.

Jesus/Yeshua: I have something else to say to add to that.

A: Oh, yes, please.

Jesus/Yeshua: So, because Lucifer brings out the other side of us a majority of the time, the other side is not good, right? Lying, cheating, stealing - things like that. It does not mean that you have to do it or continue doing it. So, if you're a thief and then Lucifer comes out and then says, "Hey thief, I'm just here to remind you that here you go again doing your business." That is Lucifer's way of saying to that human being that, "Hey, I know you, and I just want you to acknowledge me that what you're doing is not right. Correct me, turn the other way, don't do it." But when I say that is just for them to acknowledge, it doesn't mean that they need to acknowledge and continue doing it. Acknowledge it and correct it. STOP IT and correct it. It does not mean that they have to continue going their negative ways. Does that make sense?

A: Yes, it does.

Jesus/Yeshua: Okay, thank you.

A: Yes, absolutely. And then from there when he teaches them that, and they evolve from that, then they're evolving into the light, so thank you. Beautiful, what a beautiful way to explain. I'm going to ask a couple of more questions because I do want to get her healing done. She did have a few of things that she wanted to look at. There are two more questions I have for you. Then from there, we're going to go ahead and move on to the Body Scan. Now. Can you tell us why they said for example, that Mother Mary was a virgin? Is that true?

Jesus/Yeshua: No.

A: Why did they do that?

Jesus/Yeshua: It is just again, the story that they want to sell to people.

A: Yes. Is it another way where they make people feel guilt over, for example, having sex or maintaining a virgin? Is that another way to control them?

Jesus/Yeshua: Well, the story's not going to sell as an example that Jesus was born out of wedlock, way back then there was no such thing. They are trying to sell religion, this belief that everything is pure and had they not changed that story because they want you to believe that God is out of pure light. And he is. But then at the same time they were trying to control your faith. By doing so they need to sell you a story that is something supernatural that does not require any investigation at all, so that they can base that. Oh, isn't that what they always say, your faith, your faith, your faith. But that's the only way that they could again manipulate the story.

A: Yes, thank you. Did Mother Mary have you with her husband?

Jesus/Yeshua: Joseph?

A: Mm-hmm.

Jesus/Yeshua: I say yes.

A: Yes. That's what I was feeling as well thank you. Now, one more question. Mary Magdalene, we know what they did with her in the Bible. They made her into...

Jesus/Yeshua: (completed Aurora's sentence) ... look bad, yes.

A: Like she was a prostitute or something like that, unfortunately. So what are your thoughts on that?

Jesus/Yeshua: She's a lovely woman. A beautiful, beautiful, beautiful soul. And again, just like what they want to sell. Somebody has to be good. That was me. Somebody has to be bad and that was her. She is beautiful, beautiful, beautiful. I am actually in awe of her for carrying that label and people were just so mean to her. She's one brave soul. If you try to imagine how it was way back, then and do what she experienced. What she went through, that is one very heavy, heavy burden to carry.

A: Yes. It is.

Jesus/Yeshua: It's like, just like any other good soul, they will go through a process and endure it. Majority of the time if you believe what they are accusing you of, it makes you crawl under your skin. But if you know who you really are, then that gives you the courage to raise your head above the water and that's what she did. I couldn't think of anybody else that would have done that. Endure that kind of judgement. Just as much as they want the disciples as the good ones, the good guys, they did not want her to be part of the good ones. But she definitely was my right hand as the disciples.

A: So, she was one of the disciples?

Jesus/Yeshua: In my heart she is! But the authority did not want her to be. It's just that during that time men were superior to women. A female cannot be part of it. They hardly mentioned my mother.

A: Yes, they made your Mother look like she was just like this helpless being.

Jesus/Yeshua: Yes, all that she can do is cry.

A: Both you and I know that she was not like that.

Jesus/Yeshua: No. But that's the story that they were selling. Maria always says, "I like the stories of the Old Testament. They're more real."

A: Yes. What was your relationship with Mary Magdalene?

Jesus//Yeshua: My wife.

A: Yes. Thank you for confirming that. Beautiful. As far as Mother Mary, they made her seem to this helpless Mother that could not help her son. How was she really?

Jesus/Yeshua: She has the heart. I do not know as to how much you can crush a heart. How do you think a Mother can endure being present while the Son is being tortured? If she is not one brave soul, I do not know what you call it. But she has this heart. Her heart was crushed multiple times. That's the reason that they always portray her as the helpless woman because they made her. They took her Son and tortured her Son. What do you expect a Mother's heart would feel? I've not seen a heart that was so brave than hers. Pure and full of love. I don't know if one could ever match the heart that she has. Thank you. She could have just said "spare my Son and take me" but she knew that the authorities wanted her son. She doesn't mean anything. Of all of the torture, they still made her look small – inferior.

A: As far as how you evolved spiritually how was Mother Mary part of this evolving for you?

Jesus/Yeshua: I would say to have an enduring heart. A heart that endures whatever comes. It's not easy. Most of the time it's heavy. But her love, her endurance was shining through.

A: Yes. Beautiful. Thank you.

Jesus/Yeshua: You're welcome.

A: Any last message Yeshua, before we do her Body Scan?

Jesus/Yeshua: The times before my times here and what you currently are experiencing is nothing different. People will sell stories. People will try to make you believe the stories that they're selling. The stories YOU are telling are real. Always go inside of you.

A: Yes.

Jesus/Yeshua: Ask for clarification. Ask for confirmation before you even open your mouth or act on anything. Do not allow yourself to be recruited or to be part of the negativity that is widespread.

A: Yes.

Jesus/Yeshua: If you want to be on the other side of things, and I mean the negative side of things, you do not have to do anything. It's just innate in you. But if you want to rise above that, if you want to be the good guy it takes an effort. A lot of effort to be good. You want to be different. Then make an effort to be different. It takes a lot of courage, endurance, and a lot of swallowing of your ego to be good. And if you are to be negative just go by your daily life, and you don't have to waste your energy on your effort in doing so.

A: Thank you Jesus, it has been such a pleasure to talk to you. Since you are a powerful healer, is it okay if you do our Body Scan and make sure that she's all healed before we finish up?

Jesus/Yeshua: I would love to.

Yeshua assists in Maria's Body Scan, healing a few entities and negative energies within her.

Post Session Dialogue.

Maria: Oh, hello.

A: Oh, super Maria! Oh my goodness! Oh, I just cried like a hundred times, and I want to cry right now because you were such a gift to me. (crying)

Maria: You are to me.

A: I'm going to ask; would you allow me to share Yeshua's message; what he spoke?

Maria: Yes!

A: Thank you. Oh my goodness, such a gift. Thank you. It's going to reach so many people and help them awaken and connect to their hearts. Do you remember it?

Maria: I remember the kid and the help (the past life).

A: That's all you remember?

Maria: And the sun. The shade of the sun.

A: That's all you remember?

Maria: Mm-hmm

A: Oh my goodness. You were somnambulistic.

Maria: I was?

A: Yes, thank you because you were able to surrender and you trusted me so much. You love me as I love you. Yeshua completely gave like over an hour of just a bunch of information.

Maria: Oh my goodness!

A: Ah, I cannot believe it. I'm sorry, I'm in awe right now.

Maria: (laughing).

A: Wait till you hear your session.

Maria: Okay (laughing).

A: I'm dizzy right now. This is the biggest surprise to me. Thank you. I knew I could sense his energy so strongly there, but I didn't realize that what happened was your consciousness as a somnambulistic stepped back. What happens is the benevolent being like Yeshua, basically fully took control of your vessel and spoke everything without having any human consciousness or ego interfering.

Maria: Good because I talked to my ego. You remember when you talk about the 13 steps to prepare. You said okay, "Your ego's going to do this and that." So, when I sensed that I said, "there's nothing going on, there's nothing going on." I said "Baby ego, I love you. Let's step aside and there's a reason why. You know that. You're smart - you know that, so let's step aside. I am very happy that you did."

A: Wow. Oh my goodness.

Maria: I can't wait.

A: I'm not going to tell you too much. He talked about the truth of the Bible, and then what's not the truth. Then he spoke about things that I've been waiting to be able to get from Jesus. Things that I know in my heart but that I wanted someone to share the truth about Yeshua/Jesus. The different things that are out there that are basically oppressing the collective, that are keeping us being hateful and mean towards each other with hatred, envy and jealousy. He just spoke beautifully through you. Honestly, it was to me like, something I wrote down as far as part of the title "teachings from him." Teachings from when he was here, and what he taught in his times. So that's what he taught through you today.

Maria: Oh. Okay. Growing up as a Christian. They have always said that "Jesus is a good person and all that," and they always make you feel guilty about doing something that is not in the Bible. But the Bible is not correct, you know. I do not want them to think that you have to kneel yourself at the cross. Especially from my country. You know, during the Lent or the Easter, you know, there's still people that they whack themselves on the back and there is this possession. Then they physically would nail themselves on the cross. They're still doing that to this day.

A: Oh!!! (in pain) That is, unfortunate, that's black magic. You know, that's dark magic.

Maria: It is, that it is. That's how it was polluted.

A: Thank you for bringing that to us Maria. Wait till you hear it. You're going to put yourself in awe. Because the teachings that were taught through you are needed for Earth and for the people. I got to tell you, Maria, when you listen to it, you brought things to me, to me. Not many can do that. But Yeshua brought things to me that really helped me because you know, unfortunately, who I am, I do get attacked a lot. So, he spoke some beautiful words through you that have given me hope. That is huge for me (choking with emotions). So, thank you.

Maria: Oh, no, thank you. I'm just a vessel. I just allow myself to be a vessel.

A: Thank you. But remember, they also talked about you honoring yourself now too, and not how you give too much. So now finding that balance, okay.. I love you!

Maria: Love you.

END OF SESSION

-------------<◇>-------------

This was one of those divine sessions that came in at a time that my soul felt bruised as a healer. That felt like it had been fractured one too many times, and it needed the deepest healing and embrace to keep on moving. I, as a healer that was trying to bring forth the shadow that laid dormant and heavy in the Spiritual community. Trying to resurface it for the positive healing for the collective and Ascension. This is why we always explain with the greatest of gratitude, that Hypnosis sessions are not just for the client who is receiving the healing as the healing flows fluently in both directions between the Practitioner and Client, both receiving messages and healings. A.U.R.A. Hypnosis Healing represents this very shadow which so few want to dive deep into. This is why the Divine planned this intervention of love for me through Yeshua and his infinite wisdom. They knew that I was in my beginning stages of developing A.U.R.A. Hypnosis Healing, and that I could not give in and listen to those who were trying to stop me, who falsely claimed that they were of Love-Light.

As you read each Chapter/Galactic Journey you will feel and sense the journey that each Higher Self and soul goes through. At the wholeness of Creation, we are all reflections of one another created individually as a most unique expression and never one being the same soul. Therefore, what one soul learns and grows from, so can another. As a child, I remember observing the world around me in silence. The people who would cross my path. I would go through each person's scenarios and actions that they decided upon. I would then learn from those lessons that they learned whether they chose to learn them or not themselves. Making myself into an encyclopedia of life lessons and learnings. One can learn through another person's decisions and choices that convert into invaluable lessons if chosen. Which in turn can create a timeline for ourselves in which we no longer need to learn the tough lessons that the other person went through, as we have already mastered it. We are able to grow immensely in this manner, if we practice this divinely.

What a beautiful gift this session was, to be able to feel, hear, sense Yeshua from beyond the veil so clearly. He has always had a way with his words when he expresses himself, even down to each syllable that is pronounced and vibrated out from him with such an assurance. Being very aware of what each syllable will carry through its echo. This type of high vibrational expression from ONE, reaches deep into one's soul shifting and activating pieces within us that lay dormant to be awakened once more. When a Being is able to carry themselves with such assurance, it manifests into being able to walk in their full sovereignty. It reminds all who connect to this Being, of who they are as well beyond the veil, as they are an infinite, beautiful, powerful Source created soul. One that decides and carries forth what they manifested by their own created sovereignty.

Such beauties realized through this session as what was mentioned of his mother, Mother Mary. Her strength and the deceit created to oppress her purity and strength, ultimately downplaying the collective of the Divine Feminine. The role that Mother Mary had to play was of the deepest of heartache. Imagine being of the sacred civilization, 'The Essenes' as Mother Mary was, and knowing that she will sacredly birth 'The Messiah,' as it had been written in their sacred teachings through the study of the stars and knowing someday, she will have to watch him be crucified. But in turn his heart and infinite love will scatter throughout the collective creating the future Ascension and heart activations needed. Connecting us to the collective of hearts, when the real 'Revelation' he spoke of would begin 'The Great Divide,' not the False Religion Cabal one. We are now seeing these revelations occurring in 2020. Imagine raising this most beautiful soul who wouldn't even harm an insect, who talked to the trees as its equal. This most beautiful precious soul to be violated in ways that fracture one's heart. Her heart ached with the deepest, harshest pain when she looked upon those beautiful eyes and soul that carried such purity for others one last time as he was taken by those Roman Soldiers. That is the most profound divine role that a Mother would play in this Third Dimension, and in Creation in service-to-others for the collective. She is the prime example of one of the strongest Divine Feminine who graced us with her inner beauty, and to have walked the Earth. No one can take that from her, not even the Illuminati with their false religions and distorted bibles that depict her as helpless, as the opposite of her true strength and power she truly is. May all who read this and connect to her daily remember this true pure beauty and fierce fire of hers. The fire of rebirth through pain and sorrow.

What Yeshua explained to us of Lucifer (Archangel Haylel) and the lies told of his significant role, it is an ingenious plan and move in the chess game the Illuminati made against the collective. When people are programmed to fear their density, their darkness and their shadows, this creates it into being evil. They then are controlled by their own fear to not go into the deepest, darkest parts of their soul that require focus for releasement as we know that people FEAR what is unknown to them. Those fears that weigh us down heavily anchoring us negatively into the Third Dimension of Earth. Thank you Yeshua, for reminding us of this important Shadow Work, deep healing that is needed, that many have been programmed through societal, cultural and ancestry roots to keep bottled up inside. All have to unlock these deepest pains within themselves, bringing it to the surface for its true healing. So that we can reach one by one the required light within us for the individual and collective Ascension into the New Earth, the Fifth Dimension.

Thank you, thank you for these beautiful reminders, our beautiful beloved brother, Yeshua. For we shall always remember what your pure heart created for Creation. Thank you for setting the story straight with your catalyzing, infinitely radiant heart.

"Within the stillness of the darkness, in our most deepest experience,
we learn once more the brightness of the light we are.
One must first lose themselves to the depths of the infinite darkness to remember the
enormity of our brightness.
For what consists within us, is too that of the energy that keeps the stars alive shining
bright in the infinite darkness."
~AuroRa♥

---------------<◇>--------------

4

THE SASQUATCH GUARDIANS

Session #43: Recorded in May 2018.

In this online A.U.R.A. Hypnosis Healing session, Carmen finds herself in a life as a Native American woman married to a Sasquatch. How is it that these races lived peacefully together? In this journey, we witness the invasion by the English and the beginnings of Reptilian consciousnesses found within people through A.U.R.A. Hypnosis Healing. A Sasquatch speaks on how they aid humanity - their abilities, their roles, portal keepers, galactic members. A beloved Sasquatch Guardian shares the importance of embracing the wisdom of being in our hearts.

-------------<◇>-------------

"Humans must remember to be in their hearts. We are all one, we grow together as one. We must be one and humans do not remember that. But she is remembering."
-Sasquatch Guardian

-------------<◇>-------------

A: [Aurora] Have you landed on the ground?
C: [Carmen] Forest floor.
A: Look all around you, describe what you see.
C: Trees. Big trees.
A: Look down at your feet. What do your feet look like?
C: Hairy.
A: How many toes do you have?
C: Four.
A: Look at your hands, how many fingers do you have?
C: Five.
A: Including the thumb?
C: Uh-huh.
A: What color is this fur that you are seeing on your feet?
C: Medium, medium brown.
A: Do you feel female or male?
C: Female.
A: Do you have any clothing on?
C: No.
A: Does this fur further expand than just on your feet?
C: All over my body.
A: Beautiful. Is there anything you're carrying?
C: A pouch. A little leather pouch.
A: Let's look inside this leather pouch.
C: Crystals.
A: What colors do you see?
C: Pink and blue.

A: Do you just see two?

C: Uhhh… just two.

A: Everything has a consciousness. These crystals are here for a reason. Let's connect to the consciousness, to the energy within one of the crystals. Which crystal stands out to you?

C: Blue.

A: Let's talk to the blue crystal. Will you allow for the blue crystal to speak?

C: Uh-huh.

A: Go ahead. We would like to speak to the energy, the consciousness within the blue crystal… Welcome. Greetings.

C: Rainbow. It holds the energy of the rainbow.

A: Is it talking to you?

C: No, giving me images.

A: Oh, very good. The energy of the rainbow. Let's ask, what does this mean?

C: Portal.

A: This portal leads to what?

C: It's good, good energy, I feel it in my heart. I should step through.

A: Let's do that, let's follow your heart, step through this rainbow portal. Tell me what you see, what you feel along the way.

C: Teepees.

A: Did you go through the portal?

C: Uh-huh.

A: You are now by the teepees?

C: There's land and uh, native.

A: Look down at your feet, how do they look?

C: Like a woman's feet, like moccasins.

A: Look at your hands, how many fingers do you have?

C: Five. Skin.

A: How old do you feel?

C: Twenties. Twenties.

A: What are you wearing?

C: Leather. Dress. Leather dress.

A: Is there a color to it?

C: Light brown. I'm looking at my hands and arms.

A: Why?

C: Looking at my form and shape.

A: Is there anything you're carrying?

C: No.

A: Let's move the scene along. What are you doing here? What do you see next?

C: My people. I'm walking among the teepees. I may be looking for something.

A: Let's look for what you think you're trying to find, and as you look around, as you're moving, let me know what you see around you.

C: Forest. The edge of the teepees. Forest people, we live among them. .

A: Can you describe what the forest people look like?

C: Sasquatch.

A: Do you know each other? Do you have a relationship?

C: Yes, we are friendly. Friendly. We build fires and sit. Take their teaching, teaching old ways. Ancient wisdom.

A: Beautiful. Are you sitting there with them now?

C: Uh-huh.

A: Is this what you were looking for?

C: I think I knew this.

A: Let's focus on some of these ancient teachings that the Sasquatch are showing. What is the sensation you feel they are talking about?

C: Soul. Stay one with the soul. Follow your heart.

A: Yes. Are there many Sasquatch in your village?

C: People and Sasquatch. Yeah.

A: Are there more Sasquatch than people? Or are there more people?

C: I only see Sasquatch walking around, but it is a village.

A: Do they live here in this village with you? Do they have their homes?

C: They live in the forest next to us.

A: Are you still sitting listening to the teachings of the Sasquatch?

C: Yes, it's a male. Dark brown, we are sitting on a log.

A: Let's look at his eyes. You're able to connect to the soul through the eyes. Do you recognize the soul?

C: Friend. I see green, green eyes...husband. Husband.

A: He is a Sasquatch, and you are a human?

C: Yes.

A: Beautiful. He has green eyes. Anything else that stands out about him?

C: He's moving his hands while he's talking.

A: Is he moving his lips when he talks?

C: No.

A: Is it like telepathic talk?

C: Yes.

A: Do your people understand telepathy? Is this the way you communicate?

C: Yes.

A: You say he's moving his hands around. Why do you think he's doing it?

C: He wants me to understand something.

A: What is it that he's trying to get you to understand?

C: Danger. Danger in the forest. There's a darkening in the forest. Like we must get away.

A: Like move?

C: Move, move yeah. Just move.

A: You are able to see what he's talking about. What is this darkness that he talks about?

C: There's a shadow in the forest moving through the tops of the trees.

A: Let's focus on the shadow that we're seeing, let's focus on it, why is it on top of the trees?

C: An energy.

A: What is its connection to the land and why would you have to move?

C: I think there are men below in the forest.

A: What are these men doing?

C: Coming to capture. The energy is flowing above them, black, like smoke, but they're rushing on the forest floor toward us.

A: Are they running away from it?

C: Trying to capture us.

A: Who's trying to capture you?

C: The men.

A: Do the men have a connection to this energy?

C: Yes, the energy floats above them.

A: In union with them?

C: It's hunting.

A: Is this energy controlling the men, or the men controlling the energy?

C: No, the energy is controlling them. It's greedy, it's fear.

A: What do these men look like?

C: Humans.

A: They are being influenced by this energy to come after your people?

C: Uh-huh. Yes.

A: Are they of a different tribe than yours? How do they look different than you?

C: They are not dressed like a native. Just like uh...regular clothes back then.

A: Like pants and shirts?

C: Uh-huh. Hats, tall hats.

A: Is their skin lighter than yours?

C: Yes. We can't understand, why hurt...? Why hurt us?

A: Is their language different than yours?

C: English.

A: Can you understand them? Is there anyone in your village that can understand them?

C: I can understand them.

A: Is it through telepathy or do you know their language?

C: I know their language. They are carrying weapons of some kind and a net, axes.

A: Are there many of them?

C: Uh-huh.

A: Do they outnumber you?

C: Thirty-three.

A: Do they outnumber your village?

C: No, no, no. They're warring, they're afraid of Sasquatch.

A: So, they are able to see the Sasquatch that is with you?

C: Uh-huh. Out in the open. Back then we lived in the open.

A: How much taller are the Sasquatch than you or the men?

C: More than half taller than me. Maybe a little less.

A: Tell me what's going on? They're coming at you, your village. What's happening next?

C: I was taken and separated.

A: And your husband? Where is he?

C: I see a net over him. A net, some kind of net.

A: You said you're separated from him. How are you separated from him?

C: Grabbed and pulled away.

A: Is it by these several men?

C: The men. Men, yes.

A: Are they doing this to everyone in the village?

C: Mm-hmm, yes, attack on everyone.

A: Separating the men from the women?

C: Mm-hmm, from...capturing Sasquatch.

A: So, what happens to you next?

C: I'm being dragged away; I'm fighting and fighting. I never saw him again.

A: Do you know why it is? Why do they feel the need to capture the Sasquatch?

C: Darkness, darkness over them. Sasquatch are good and uh...it's a plan, a plan of some kind to put out the good.

A: What do they do with the Sasquatch once they capture them?

C: Kill them. They have memories, many memories, many, many...much wisdom.

A: They remember the ancient teachings?

C: Yes, yes.

A: Do they live longer lives than humans?

C: Uh-huh.

A: Approximately how old was your husband?

C: Three hundred.

A: And you were in your...?

C: Twenties.

A: Did you have any children?

C: Yes.

A: How many children did you have?

C: Three.

A: Did you see what happened to your children?

C: I never... taken, yeah, yes, taken.

A: Focus on your children before they were taken.

C: They were taken, they were...

A: They were taken before you?

C: I'm not sure. I just know they were taken; they were, I just see them being pulled away.

A: By the same people?

C: Uh-huh.

A: Did you have females? Boys or girls?

C: Boys. Three boys.

A: Three boys. Were they young? Older?

C: Younger, not too old... Pulled yes, pulled away, I was pulled away and they were off to the side, but I can remember. I remember they were taken away.

A: What happened next once you were pulled away?

C: I never saw them again.

A: Your children?

C: Uh-huh. No.

A: Do you know what happened to them?

C: Some died, some were used for work, work of some kind. They were, some imprisoned, I think. Much hatred, misunderstanding.

A: Yes. What happens to you when you get pulled away?

C: I'm kicking and screaming.

A: Do you have any weapons?

C: Hmm...no.

A: Were you not able to sense these people coming to your village?

C: We were talking on the log and then there they were. They were coming fast through the forest. We didn't run, we didn't run.

A: As you're being pulled away and you're kicking and screaming, what happens next?

C: Taken away, far away, and I lived with humans. The 1800s. I hear 18, 18. Married another.

A: You see yourself marrying another of the race that took you?

C: Human.

A: How old do you feel then when you marry again?

C: Thirty.

A: Until then, what happened to you?

C: I didn't want to. Didn't want to.

A: You didn't want to marry him?

C: Uh-uh.

A: Do you have any children again?

C: Yes, little boy, little girl. Wooden house, but my heart is always sad.

A: Because?

C: I lost my family. (sad)

A: Remember to allow those feelings to come forth anytime you feel them so that they may heal... Did you ever hear of them again?

C: No.

A: So now you are married with two children, what happens next of importance?

C: I died. I don't...

A: You are there now when you are dying, seeing everything and feeling everything clearly. What is going on?

C: No more life there.

A: How old do you feel?

C: It's a dead-end, no more road.

A: How old do you feel?

C: Thirty.

A: Are the children with you?

C: Uh-huh. They were little.

A: What happened to you?

C: Fever. Fever.

A: You got sick?

C: Uh-huh. I see myself in a bed. I'm in a bed in a white dress, a white gown and I'm in bed.

A: As you're laying here, are there any regrets that you have?

C: Thinking of missing my first family and hoping to see them again. I'm ready to go.

A: This husband of yours, was he a man of rank?

C: I see dark hair, dark, dark hair. Light skin.

A: Is he there in the room with you?

C: Yes. It feels like it.

A: How does he feel that you're dying?

C: He's sad.

A: Did he love you?

C: Yes, but my heart was sad.

A: Were you forced to marry him? Or you just felt that you had to marry him?

C: I think, forced. I see a uniform, a gray coat, a gray coat, patches.

A: Any last thoughts that go through your mind when you take your last breath?

C: Ready to go.

A: And these little children, before you let go let's look at them, the boy and the girl. Look into their eyes, do you recognize them?

C: They seem familiar.

A: Look at them one at a time. Focus on the girl. If you're able to see her soul within the eyes, who does she feel like?

C: She's sad for me to go. They both are.

A: Do you recognize their souls?

C: My daughter? My daughter!

A: And the boy?

C: Oh! My ex-husband.

A: Are you ready to take your last breath?

C: Uh-huh.

A: Go ahead and take your last breath and tell me what happens when you do it.

C: Floating up, floating up.

A: What do you see?

C: The Universe.
A: Are you up in the Universe?
C: Uh-huh.
A: Look all around you, describe to me what you see.
C: Hills and peaks, dark blue, black, twinkling lights.
A: Look at yourself. What do you look like? What do you feel like?
C: I'm still wearing my dress or my gown, but I'm happy. I'm light, lighter. Very happy.

Later in the session, we connect to a Sasquatch that was her mate in another past life. But it is a different Sasquatch from the one who was captured in the past life. He speaks to us explaining that he is one of her protectors here on Earth.

A: Will you allow for the Sasquatch to talk?
C: Okay.
A: Good. Greetings brother.
Sasquatch: Greetings.
A: We welcome you. Thank you for speaking to us today, it's an honor. Your people are beautiful. What is your connection to her? I know that she said that you were her mate.
Sasquatch: Yes.
A: Would you share some of your wisdom with us, and the sacred knowledge that you hold?
Sasquatch: Humans must remember to be in their hearts. We are all one, we grow together as one. We must be one and humans do not remember that. But she is remembering.
A: Beautiful.
Sasquatch: Thank you.
A: Thank you. May I continue asking you questions?
Sasquatch: Yes.
A: Is this your home planet, or did you come from another planet?
Sasquatch: Another planet.
A: Do you have a name for your planet?
Sasquatch: No.
A: Why is it that your people came to Earth?
Sasquatch: To help... Guardians.
A: Were you born here, or were you brought here?
Sasquatch: Born here, but memories of home.
A: What is it that you do for human life or all life on Earth? How do you aid us?
Sasquatch: We try to reconnect. We help humans reconnect with their hearts, their souls. We protect Mother Earth.
A: Do you work on us while we sleep?
Sasquatch: Yes.
A: How is it that you do this?
Sasquatch: With our minds and our hearts. We send love and energy. And there are many portals, we help with the portals. We are trying to help so that the portals are good.
A: You are trying to maintain them being good?
Sasquatch: Yes. Yes. We maintain who comes through.
A: You ensure negative beings don't come through them?
Sasquatch: When we can.
A: So, do you stay near these portals?
Sasquatch: Yes, yes. It is our job.
A: Are you the Guardians of the portals?

Sasquatch: Yes.

A: Beautiful. We thank you for your service.

Sasquatch: Thank you.

A: Are there still some in this current time/space, are you still here, your species, on Earth?

Sasquatch: Yes.

A: Do you hide from the humans?

Sasquatch: We hide. Humans do not understand, they are afraid. But some humans remember. We speak to their hearts.

A: How about the humans that remember? Will you eventually show yourself physically to them?

Sasquatch: Yes, when they are ready.

A: Do you exist in groups? A family group?

Sasquatch: Yes. We travel through portals alone at times, but we live as a group. Back and forth, from this planet to another planet.

A: Are you connected to the Earth's webbing of portals?

Sasquatch: Yes. We know where they are and we guard them, that is our job.

A: When you travel to other planets, what is the purpose you travel to other planets for?

Sasquatch: Beings. Other beings. Work, meeting with others for the light.

A: Do you work with the RA Collective?

Sasquatch: Hmmm.

A: The Galactics?

Sasquatch: There is a group that we discuss, we speak to.

A: What group is this?

Sasquatch: On a ship.

A: Does this group have a name?

Sasquatch: No, not for now... They are on a ship. We discuss progress, but it is not always work, it is also play.

A: That's good.

Sasquatch: No names. No names.

A: These beings on the ship are they like multiple different races?

Sasquatch: Yes.

A: Are there many of them?

Sasquatch: It's a large ship. Yes, many races. They are a Council.

A: Do they have a name as a Council? They are a Council of...?

Sasquatch: No name.

A: What Dimension is your vibratory system?

Sasquatch: Seventh.

A: Though you are in the Seventh, would humans be able to see you still?

Sasquatch: Some humans can.

A: I ask because there are pictures out there of supposed Sasquatch, would someone be able to take a picture of you?

Sasquatch: Not if we don't want to be seen.

A: So those pictures, are they real?

Sasquatch: Not all of them. We are seen when we want to be seen.

A: For a purpose?

Sasquatch: Yes.

A: In order to be seen through the camera, would you need to lower your vibratory system?

Sasquatch: Yes.

A: What would you need to lower it to be able to be seen in the camera?

Sasquatch: Fourth. Many cannot see us.

A: Would we have to be pure of heart to see you?

Sasquatch: From the heart, in the heart.

A: Beautiful. Thank you for all these answers you've given us today. I would love to share these with humanity. There is misconception, and also fear, humans fear what they don't understand. So, I would love to be able to, with your permission, share your wisdom as the Sasquatch race that you are with others.

Sasquatch: Yes.

A: Thank you. Anything else you want to tell humanity?

Sasquatch: When their heart is ready, they will hear the truth.

A: Let me think if there are any other questions.

Sasquatch: The time is coming that more will believe and understand.

A: Yes. Wonderful. We thank you for all the work and the aid that you give all life on Earth. I honor you, I love you, and I respect you. Thank you, brother.

Sasquatch: Thank you.

A: Blessings.

Later in the session, Carmen's Higher Self does a Body Scan on her and a Reptilian consciousness is discovered.

A: Can you scan the rest of her body and see what else needs healing please?

Higher Self: Her heart.

A: What's going on in her heart?

Higher Self: A sadness.

A: That is connected to?

Higher Self: Loss.

A: Is it connected to that life where she lost her three boys and her husband?

Higher Self: Many lives.

A: She holds a collective of sadness?

Higher Self: Yes.

A: Are there entities that I need to speak to there?

Higher Self: Energy darker. Darker energy.

A: Do I need to speak to the entities there or can you heal this energy?

Higher Self: It does not seem to have an entity, but energy from an entity.

A: When were these energies, like her feet, placed into her with no entity?

Higher Self: As a child.

A: This entity was never in there?

Higher Self: Once. Yes, it was.

A: When did it leave?

Higher Self: The past year. It left its energy.

A: Why did it leave its energy?

Higher Self: To affect her.

A: But why did it choose to leave?

Higher Self: Uncomfortable. Uhm, cannot see the entity. The color of the energy is a gray-ish black of energy.

A: Did it leave because it wasn't going to be able to stay with her vibration raising higher?

Higher Self: Yes.

A: Is this why it left its energy instead?

Higher Self: Yes.

A: Okay. Can you heal that for her now please?
Higher Self: It's like smoke in her heart.
A: Okay. Let me know if you need me to help?
Higher Self: Yes.
A: Good.
Higher Self: Please help.

Aurora helps channel Love-Light by placing her palms towards the client.

A: Let's heal that energy and spread that energy down to the back of her heels that you are also healing. Let me know along the way once they're healed. As we send energy to her heart and her heels, can you scan the rest of her body and see what else needs healing, please?
Higher Self: Her neck.
A: What's going on there?
Higher Self: Darker attachment.
A: Is it an entity?
Higher Self: Yes.
A: That one is? Very good. Can I please speak to the entity within her throat, within her neck? Come up, up, up, up. Greetings, hello?
Entity: Yes.
A: Thank you for speaking to us. Are you female or male?
Entity: Male.
A: How is it that you find yourself in her neck?
Entity: I've been there since she was a child.
A: This life?
Entity: Yes.
A: Did you have a body before you entered her throat?
Entity: Yes.
A: What happened to you? How did you die?
Entity: I am not dead.
A: You're not? Are you coexisting? Are you part of an energy that's alive then of a vessel?
Entity: Yes.
A: Who are you connected to? Whose energy, are you?
Entity: Lower.
A: But you said you are not dead, so was this someone she knows in her life?
Entity: No, no, no.
A: Okay. Where were you before you entered her throat, her neck?
Entity: A darker plane.
A: So, did you come forth from this darker plane?
Entity: Yes. Others know that I am here.
A: Others like whom?
Entity: The Reptilians.
A: Are you connected to the Reptilians?
Entity: Yes.
A: Are you a Reptilian?
Entity: Yes.
A: Now I know that you came forth from the dark and were placed here in her throat, and I would love to... (client says something inaudible) ... Go ahead, say that again.
Entity: Neck. Shoulder.

A: I know you've been here a while and you were sent here... I understand the role that you did here. What was the lesson that you taught her here in her throat?

Entity: To be pressure, pressure. To be afraid. Very cautious.

A: So, you are still coexisting in a vessel correct? Is that why you said you are not dead?

Entity: Yes.

A: You are a consciousness of a Reptilian?

Entity: Yes.

A: Well, I thank you for speaking to us, and I view all as equals. I understand that you serve a purpose here. I would love to help you today because we are of the light and we all come from the Creator. Would you allow for us to help you spread your light within you, so that you may be free brother and go as you please?

Entity: Yes.

A: I thank you. I want you to envision that light within you, envision that light within you and I want you to spread it to all that is of you that does not belong to her. All your roots, all your cords, all that is, all your essence; spread it to all light and let me know once you are all light.

Entity: There is a portal.

A: Where is the portal at?

Entity: Her neck.

A: Is this how you're able to enter through?

Entity: Yes.

A: Would you help us close that off brother?

Entity: Yes.

A: Thank you. As you are turning yourself into light, can we close this portal as well?

Entity: Yes.

A: I thank you. Let me know how it's looking.

Entity: The portal is gone.

A: We thank you. And how are you looking?

Entity: Lifting.

A: Wonderful. Yes. Once you are all of light go ahead and lift, remove yourself from her neck. Lift, pull all that is of you that does not belong to her, pull it all out, please.

Entity: It's still a little...

A: Do you need help with Phoenix Fire?

Entity: Yes.

A: Good. I call forth on the Phoenix Fire that's able to be called forth from anyone that connects from the heart. I call forth on the Phoenix Fire to help our brother here release himself from her throat and transmute those last pieces that are stuck to her.

Positive Polarized Entity: Thank you.

A: Thank you... Are we all good now?

Positive Polarized Entity: Yes.

A: Did we heal everything there? Did we pull everything out?

Positive Polarized Entity: Small.

A: There's something small there?

Positive Polarized Entity: Yes.

A: Can I focus on that with the Phoenix Fire and clear it?

Positive Polarized Entity: Yes.

A: Good. I'll keep focusing on that. While I focus on that can you answer a couple questions before you go?

Positive Polarized Entity: Yes, yes.

A: Good. Thank you. I appreciate it. Now that you have released yourself, this consciousness from her neck, what happens to the - you said that you were still alive. What happens to that Reptilian there?

Positive Polarized Entity: Go back to the group.

A: He will go back to what group?

Positive Polarized Entity: His group. His…

A: His Reptilian group?

This was before we had discovered that we could connect to the Reptilian body who had attached their Reptilian consciousness to the client. We now can connect to the Reptilian body, convincing them of the light that they are to help them positively polarize. The more that we do this work every day, the Earth and the Universe becomes lighter by aiding to Ascend the race that held the biggest density of this Universe, because of its quantity in numbers.

Positive Polarized Entity: Yes.

A: What happens to you? I know you will go to the light.

Positive Polarized Entity: I'm not sure.

A: Well once you turn yourself into light, you are able to go be free and return back to Love-Light, to that existence there. Therefore, was there any harm to this Reptilian when we removed him and turned you into light? What happened to him?

Positive Polarized Entity: No harm. He went back.

A: Back to his group? And his duties?

Positive Polarized Entity: Yes.

A: Okay. Do you have a message before you go?

Positive Polarized Entity: No.

A: She said she saw a Reptilian man when she was in the bathroom, was that you?

Positive Polarized Entity: No.

A: Who was that? Do you know who that was?

Positive Polarized Entity: Someone watching.

A: Someone watching her?

Positive Polarized Entity: Yes.

A: Why are they watching her?

Positive Polarized Entity: Because of her light.

A: Why is it that they are able to connect to her if she is trying to raise her vibrations and shield?

Positive Polarized Entity: They can no longer.

A: They can no longer connect to her?

Positive Polarized Entity: No.

A: Wonderful. What is it that changed this?

Positive Polarized Entity: Removing the consciousness.

A: So, this was also connected to the portal, this was how they were able to watch her?

Positive Polarized Entity: Yes.

A: Oh, thank you. This is wonderful to hear. Any last message you have before you go, brother?

Positive Polarized Entity: No.

A: Okay, we thank you for allowing for us to aid you, and may you go with the Love-Light of the Universe. Blessings. Thank you.

END OF SESSION

-------------<◇>-------------

As of September 4th, 2020, we are on our #301 A.U.R.A. Hypnosis Healing session. We humbly thank Carmen for being one of the first sessions bringing the awareness of how Reptilian consciousnesses are able to attach to beings all over the Universe. At the beginning, little by little through each session we were given pieces of how to aid the clients, and the different negative alien races that have been trapped in a wheel of dark agendas. These puzzle pieces come together to help heal through each subsequent session in a more grander mass scale, as we progress through these collective Galactic Journeys.

We have often wondered about the true history of the indigenous people of the Earth. Once being the majority, now the minority. What was it that drove these conquerors in Earth's History to destroy families and ancient fertile developed lands? We now understand what was fueling their determination to possess. For example, like that dark entity collective attached to these conquerors' aura, influencing their natural ability of choice. It is as if they had no say other than overthrowing, possessing, conquering and killing. Once they allow the negative side of ego to enter and reign with power, these types of dark collective entities are able to attach and influence others in this manner, because they are now a match frequency to its host, that being the conquerors.

We take this moment in time as we read, to send love to the Indigenous People, who once were the beautiful race designated as the caretakers of this Earth. Living as one within the natures and elements around them, to cloth, feed, shelter, and their families. They honored all parts of what they took from their environment, for example, all parts of a hunted deer were treated with respect and nothing ever wasted or spoiled. Who honored and talked to Grandmother Moon, Father Sun and Mother Earth. Who understood that the stars spoke with divine messages for our souls and villages. For reminding us that they were not alone, because they had guides here with them in the physical as the benevolent race of the Sasquatch. We honor them for paving these paths for us.

When people as Carmen's tribe were robbed from such a harmonious life, we can imagine the trauma this could cause to a soul. To have it all, shelter, nourishment and love, and for it all to be taken away from people you have never met in your life who act with no reason and with violence. And how Carmen was forced to marry this unknown man after she was taken hostage and bore children. Always in deep sorrow and mourning for the family she once had, and intimately loved. We send our love to these beautiful and resilient ancestors of the past.

This session reminded us of how the dark energies and entities have been controlling humans throughout their times on Earth, by separating communities. Looking at where we are on Earth, it is glorious to watch the Starseeds incarnated and the people who were stuck, now breaking through otherwise repeated unbreakable cycles of trauma - which in turn is activating others to do so as well. It was also an honor to hear from our brethren race, the Sasquatch, and what it is that they guard. We are grateful to them for showing us their loving and gentle manner, and how they view us as perhaps their younger appointed brethren, we as the children of the Earth.

The importance of these portals the Sasquatch spoke of. We provide more information about the significance of these portals, in Chapters 22, 23 and 24. In the time and space when this session occurred, it was not yet safe enough for the Sasquatch Guardian to share more on these Councils they were affiliated with and why it is that these portals are being guarded. This shows us how much we have raised our frequency in the NOW, as a collective in such a short amount of time. It is now safe collectively and energetically to share this sacred information that has always been guarded heavily prior. If this sacred information was shared when the collective frequency was not high enough, it would have created possible targeted infringements to these sacred locations. We have now reached the critical threshold of higher vibration and light for the collective, thanks to all the beautiful courageous souls anchoring in the Love-Light and to the Love-Light warriors out there awakening hearts wherever they go.

"To honor Creation: to feel and fall in love with the warmth of the Earth beneath your soles. To look upon the Sun and become ONE with its infinite healing consciousness. To be touched by the Water, and to allow for it to absorb you. To respect the strength of the Fire, and its renewal. To hear the whispers of the wind as it embraces all that is of you. To silence in mind, through connection to all life within Spirit."
~AuroRa♥

-------------<◇>-------------

5

GUARDIANS OF THE SUNKEN CRYSTAL CITY

Session #116: Recorded in February 2019.
Never Before Shared.

Candee came to me for the healing of past drug addiction and to understand more of her soul purpose. In this online A.U.R.A. Hypnosis Healing session, she takes us on a beautiful journey under the sea and inwards into the inside of the Earth to meet the Council of Nine and a Galactic Commander. Here we learn more about the people, the animals, the Sasquatch, and the negative technology in the water that harms marine life. How is all of this connected to Atlantis?

Candee's session guided me to dig more on what Reptilian consciousnesses were, understanding how they attach and still are connected to an alive Reptilian Body. This is pivotal in bridging us into the present where we are now connecting to collectives of Reptilians in Creation and helping them ascend into a positive polarization. My humble thanks to Candee for helping me shift this awareness for the continual growth of entity removal in all forms for A.U.R.A. Hypnosis Healings.

-------------<◇>-------------

"She's loved and protected but she needs to believe in herself."
-Archangel Michael

-------------<◇>-------------

A: [Aurora] You're in the house that you grew up in?
C: [Candee] Yes.
A: Have you landed on the ground yet?
C: Yes.
A: Look down at yourself, do you have a body?
C: Yes.
A: Do you feel like you are female or male? What do you feel like?
C: Female.
A: Look down at your feet? Are you wearing something on your feet?
C: I feel like I'm a little girl...huh.
A: How many toes do you have? Tell me what you're sensing.
C: I just feel like I'm myself as a little girl.
A: Your Higher Self will take you wherever it is you are meant to go, just go along with it. Remember - allowing your imagination to flow freely. You feel like you're a little girl, look at yourself. Are you wearing any clothes?
C: I have a dress on.
A: Can you describe the dress to me?
C: It's a purple dress with long sleeves like flowy sleeves, like an angel.
A: Are you wearing any jewelry?

C: A cross.

A: Is the cross on something?

C: It's on a big gold collar kind of looking - not like a chain, it's like a gold collar.

A: Is there any other jewelry you're wearing?

C: I have a gold cuff on too. It has a big stone like an emerald.

A: Beautiful, everything has a consciousness. This emerald, does it have a message for you? Focus on the emerald in the cuff and see what messages it has for you. What does it say?

C: Trust yourself.

A: Very good, any other message that the emerald has for you?

C: Just that, "you are loved."

A: Beautiful, thank you for those messages. Now, is there anything you're carrying?

C: I have a seashell. I don't know why but I have a seashell. It's like pearly on the inside.

A: Does this mean something to you?

C: I don't know, it makes me want to cry.

A: Remember to allow your emotions to come forth. If you feel like crying, allow for the crying to come forth, it heals you. Why do you feel that you want to cry because of the seashell?

C: I love...I love the ocean, but I'm afraid of it.

A: Why are you afraid of it?

C: I'm afraid of drowning.

A: Let's go ahead and walk around, let's see in this home what draws your attention, what stands out, tell me what you see.

C: I don't think I'm there anymore.

A: Look all around you, describe to me what you see.

C: I see a lot of crystals.

A: You see crystals where?

C: Not sure if it's like a... like everything is made of crystals - like a City of Crystals.

A: Are you on the ground?

C: Yes.

A: Look at yourself. Do you still have a body?

C: I might be a mermaid.

A: You feel like you're a mermaid? Why do you feel that?

C: I have scales and a fin.

A: Where are you as far as, are you in something? Are you standing or are you in something?

C: No, I'm in the water.

A: Where do you see these crystals that are in the water?

C: It's like a tower made of crystals.

A: So, this city that you spoke of made of crystals, is it underwater?

C: I feel like it wasn't but now it's gone underwater.

A: Okay. This city, does it look like it has life within it? Like are there others actively living there?

C: There used to be.

A: Then look at yourself some more, do you feel like you're female or male?

C: Male.

A: You said that you have a tail, and you have scales. Describe more to me what you look like, you're able to see a reflection of yourself. How does your face look?

C: I have like pointy teeth.

A: How do your eyes look?

C: Not sure, they look dark.

A: If you could imagine a spiritual mirror right in front of you, where you're able to see a reflection of yourself. Describe to me what you see.

C: My eyes are like blue-ish green.
A: Do you have a nose?
C: It's very flat.
A: Do you have ears?
C: Yes, but not like human ears, it's like a hole.
A: Now look at your body. You said that you have a tail, what about arms?
C: Yes.
A: How do your arms look and your fingers?
C: My hands are webbed.
A: How many fingers do you have?
C: Looks like three and like a thumb but it's webbed.
A: Three plus a thumb?
C: Yes.
A: How about your skin? How does your skin look?
C: It's like an iridescent kind of pearly iridescent.
A: Is there anything you are carrying?
C: I have a trident in my hand.
A: Can you describe to me how it looks?
C: It's gold.
A: How many points does it have?
C: It has three and then it has points on the top of each.
A: What hand do you carry it on, your left or your right?
C: My left.
A: Is there any jewelry you're wearing?
C: I don't think so.
A: What is it that you're doing here with this trident?
C: I use it for, it has energy, like to direct energy.
A: What are you doing right now? Why are you here?
C: I used to live here.
A: You used to live here? Did you live in the city when it was above water or underwater?
C: I didn't live here. I just visited here.
A: You visit here now?
C: I like to visit this place.
A: Why do you like to visit it?
C: It used to be really beautiful and full of life and with good energy and powerful.
A: Do you know what happened to it, why it sunk?
C: They let somebody, they let something in, something dark, a powerful being.
A: Do you have a role here in this city underwater? Is there something you do with it?
C: I'm like a guard, I'm guarding it or protecting it.
A: Why is it that you feel that you are protecting it, does it have something inside that is needing protection?
C: I think there are codes or something in there.
A: What are you protecting it from?
C: Just anybody that doesn't have good intentions.
A: Has there ever been a time that someone or something approached that didn't have good intentions?
C: Yes.
A: Are you the only one that guards it?
C: No.

A: I want you to go now to a time and space, leave that scene now. Go to the time where someone tries to enter, trying to get into that city that you are protecting/guarding. You are moving there now. What do you see? Tell me what's going on.

C: I'm not sure, feels like there's people.

A: Trust what you're seeing and sensing… You see people?

C: Yes, diving, like something, like a, some kind of vessel underwater.

A: Is it big?

C: No, it's like a circle.

A: A circle, like a sphere?

C: Yes.

A: Are you able to see through it, or is it closed up?

C: It's closed but it has windows.

A: Is this like a vehicle of sorts, of water?

C: Right.

A: Do you see who's inside of it?

C: It looks like a couple of people. I'm just making a lot of; I'm stirring the bottom so they can't see anything.

A: How big do you feel in comparison to this device that they're using to go underwater? Do you feel bigger, smaller?

C: Bigger.

A: You said that there are humans in it?

C: I think so.

A: How are you stirring the water so that they won't see?

C: I'm using my fin and the trident, swirling it, swirling it around.

A: Are you swirling it in a circle spiral motion?

C: Yes.

A: Would that be clockwise or counterclockwise?

C: It's actually going clockwise.

A: What happens when they come near and you're doing this? Are you the only one that's doing this, or are there others helping you?

C: I'm the only one doing it.

A: What happens when they get closer and you're doing that?

C: They just go away.

A: Has there ever been a time where you feel that something like that didn't work? That whoever was trying to get to the city or passing by was able to see the city?

C: I don't know.

A: Very good. Now, after that happens, what is it that you do next of importance?

C: I'm placing a portal or a shield? I don't know if I'm making a shield or like a portal.

A: Where are you placing it at?

C: It's in the water, it's like even if they came to it, they wouldn't see it.

A: Is it like a form of invisibility cloak?

C: Yes.

A: How is it that you do that?

C: It's like I'm using the trident and then cutting and then it spreads and opens up, it spreads around.

A: When you cut it, the energy draws out on all sides.

C: Yes.

A: Okay, do you have to do this often, do you have to keep re-energizing that cloak?

C: Sometimes. They send vibrations in the water.

A: What for?

C: I don't know if they're looking for where it bounces off but they're sending these really loud vibrations in the water and it upsets marine life also. Like whales, it's very bothersome to them and I don't know why they're doing it.

A: This wave is bothersome to the fish?

C: Yes.

A: What do you mean? You don't know why they're doing it, who's doing the wave, or...?

C: Yeah, the waves, something is sending vibrations under the water and they're very loud, they're very strong vibrations.

A: Oh, okay. So, there's something somewhere sending vibrations?

C: Yes.

A: Are you able to go find out what that is? Can you go find out right now? What do you find?

C: There's something underwater, some kind of machine, or I don't know what it is. Like a large submarine maybe?

A: It looks like a submarine?

C: Actually, it's something that sits on the floor.

A: What shape is it?

C: It's circular.

A: Like a sphere?

C: Yeah...uhh...not like a sphere. It's just circular. And it has something in the middle that goes up and then it sends shocks, like pulses.

A: Do you feel that it's harmful and negative to others?

C: Yes. This shouldn't be there.

A: Do you know who placed it there?

C: I don't know who placed it there.

A: You said that when this wave of vibration comes out it disturbs the living life underwater?

C: Yes, yes.

A: What does it do to them?

C: It disorients them.

A: How about you, does it do that to you?

C: Yeah, I don't like it.

A: So, what do you do next now that you're seeing this?

C: I just want to get away from it.

A: Is there something that you could do to stop it?

C: No. I don't think so. I just get away from it.

A: Where do you go next after you get away from it? Tell me what's going on?

C: Just trying to find a different place to go.

A: How about you go back to where you were guarding that city.

C: Okay.

A: Are there many others that are also guarding this place?

C: Yes, there are many.

A: Do you ever take any breaks from guarding it?

C: Yes.

A: Let's go to a time where you are taking a break. What happens in order for you to be able to take a break?

C: I'm not sure.

A: That's okay. I want you to look a little closer into the city. Find what it is that you are guarding inside the city. What do you see?

C: It looks like another portal.

A: Where is this portal?

C: I don't know if it's a portal but it's almost like an opening and it's under a bunch of very large stones, it's like an opening.

A: Yes.

C: Goes to, umm, I guess it goes to Inner Earth.

A: Are you able to go through the portal or the opening?

C: Yes.

A: Very good. Tell me what it's like to enter through that opening, are there any colors to it, any symbols, how do you get through it?

C: I can just go through it, it's cloaked so you can, you can just pull it open and go through.

A: Would someone who meant harm, would they be able to go through there?

C: I don't think so because you have to have a certain vibration to go through it.

A: Tell me, once you go through it let me know, talk to me along the way, what's going on?

C: It's like a tunnel and it's very, like it's brighter and brighter and brighter, it's very colorful.

A: Are there any designs in the tunnel?

C: There are some symbols and there are crystals, it's very illuminating.

A: Are you swimming through it?

C: Yes.

A: Is there water in this tunnel?

C: At first, but now it's not, now it's like light.

A: Light energy?

C: Yes.

A: Are you swimming through the light energy?

C: I'm not in the water, I'm like a light being now.

A: Do you have a shape or any colors to you?

C: My skin is blue.

A: Do you feel like you have limbs?

C: Yes, I have arms and legs.

A: When was it that you shifted from merman to this light being?

C: In the tunnel.

A: Do you still feel like you're male?

C: Yes.

A: Look at your hands, how many fingers do you have?

C: I have five.

A: You say you have blue skin, what else stands out from you?

C: I'm very large.

A: Do you mean large as in wide or tall?

C: Tall.

A: You're able to know and sense how you look. How does your face look?

C: I look like a human.

A: Like a human... Do you have hair?

C: Yes. It's long, almost like white.

A: Are you wearing any clothing?

C: Kind of like a white robe.

A: Is there anything you're carrying?

C: No.

A: How is it that you're going through this portal? You're more of a light being and the portal is energy you said? How are you flowing through it?

C: Yes. I shifted in the tunnel and, it's not water anymore it's just light like I'm on land.

A: Okay, so now you are on land.

C: Mm-hmm.

A: Very good. Look down, what are you standing on?

C: It's like a... I'm just standing on the ground like, like a regular ground.

A: Look all around you. What do you see?

C: It's like another city but it's more kind of like caverns/caves.

A: It's cave like?

C: But it's not dark, it's bright.

A: Are the walls made of how caves would be like, is that why you say that?

C: It looks like a coral to me.

A: How about the ceilings, the top, is it tall? Is it short?

C: You walk through and then it opens up.

A: Tell me, how does the city look?

C: It's very bright and has a lot of waterfalls and pools. It's like another Earth inside, like it has its own light, and it has green, there are trees, it's very lush and colorful.

A: Beautiful. And is there any life there?

C: Yes, there are other beings here, different kinds of beings.

A: Yes. Let's go ahead and walk, go towards a direction that you feel you are meant to go. Why are you here? What do you see that stands out along the way?

C: There's a... it's like a temple but it has a lot of steps going up towards it.

A: Are you in front of it?

C: Yeah, I'm in front of the stairs.

A: Let's go ahead and go up the steps and as you go up the steps let me know what you see all around you, the surroundings of it as you go up higher.

C: Steps are very pretty.

A: Why are they pretty?

C: They are clear, like crystals. It's very beautiful.

A: Are you wearing something on your feet?

C: No.

A: How many toes do you have?

C: Looks like four toes.

A: As you're going up look around you as well, not just at the stairs. What can you see?

C: There's animals and...

A: Where are the animals?

C: They're just walking around freely.

A: The animals that are walking around freely, describe one of them to me that stands out?

C: There's a white tiger and looks like a dinosaur.

A: Hmm, the white tiger looks like a dinosaur?

C: No, there's others.

A: Okay. There's a white tiger and you said that there seems to be a dinosaur?

C: Yeah.

A: Describe it to me.

C: Looks like a raptor.

A: Do you feel that it eats meat or plants?

C: No.

A: What does it eat?

C: I don't think they eat, it doesn't seem like they eat, like they don't need to eat.

A: As they're walking around, for example, can you say it is docile?

C: Yes, it's not harmful to people and it's there to protect. It's there for protection as well.

A: What is it protecting?

C: There is a crystal, a large crystal cavern. It's very, very, very powerful.

A: Is it guarding this?

C: Yes, I believe so.

A: Are the white tiger and the raptor together guarding this?

C: I think just the raptor. There are animals here that they saved because they were going to be extinct, so there's animals here. I'm feeling that there are some animals here that they saved from extinction, they were going to be extinct, so they brought them here.

A: Very good and are you almost at the top of the steps?

C: Yes.

A: Once you get to the top tell me what you see all around you.

C: There's a lot of flowers all around and it's like glass, and it's very clear you can see in.

A: Is there some place you're trying to go into here?

C: Inside the temple.

A: Let's go ahead and head towards the temple. Let me know what you see once you enter the temple.

C: There's a large fountain, it's full of all different colors of crystals and it's a healing, the water is very healing.

A: Is there something you do by the fountain?

C: You can get in it. There are people in it.

A: What is it that you do next?

C: I'm going to get in the fountain because I want to.

A: Very good. Tell me what it feels like to get in.

C: It feels amazing.

A: What is it doing to you?

C: It's cleansing, cleansing and energizing.

A: What do you do next?

C: I bless the water; I bless it with love and gratitude.

A: Where do you go next? What do you do next?

C: I'm not sure, I usually just like to go relax and listen to music.

A: The other people that were in the fountain, do they look similar to you?

C: Some do, some are different.

A: Let's look at one that stands out. What do they look like?

C: One of them looks like, I guess like a Sasquatch; very hairy, very tall, very big.

A: Yes. Anyone else that stands out?

C: Some of them look more like human but very fair skin, very light hair.

A: How about their eyes?

C: Very blue, very, very blue, light, pretty.

A: Let's fast forward a bit to see what you do next after the fountain, is there something that you do here?

C: I'm just listening, I'm lying on the grass and listening to music.

A: Where is the music coming from?

C: Somebody is playing music and singing.

A: Let's fast forward a bit, one more time, to something you're doing, something else of importance. What are you doing next?

C: We're meeting like a Council.

A: Look all around you, what do you see? Where are you?

C: I'm in a room.

A: Are there many others there with you?

C: Yes, some are here, and some are here - not physically - they're just here in spirit.

A: There are some physically there and some spiritually there. How do those that are not physically there look?

C: Like a projection almost.

A: How many do you feel are there?

C: Eight other than me.

A: What are you doing? Are you standing, are you sitting?

C: Standing.

A: Look all around, what stands out of importance?

C: It's like a... I'm not sure but it looks like you can see in different places when you want to see. If you want to see a certain place you can see it or feel it.

A: Okay, and is there something that you have to look through to be able to do that?

C: No, you don't have to look through it, it's just there if you say something. If you say it and then it shows that place, but you can also feel, feel the place. You can feel the energy of the place, you can see it and you can feel it, it's like a dome.

A: Are you able to see and feel anywhere you want to with this?

C: I think it's where we're bringing, so whatever energy where I was at, I'm bringing it forward and I'm bringing forward the energy and then they can sense and see it also. So, everyone that's there is bringing something different and we're sharing it, the information.

A: Yes, and what information are you sharing?

C: I'm bringing information about where the water needs to be healed.

A: Was it near that technology vibration thing?

C: Yes.

A: What are others bringing forth?

C: Some are, they're galactic, not from Earth.

A: Do they bring information from the place that they're from, not from Earth?

C: Yes.

A: Are they trying to help the Earth?

C: Yes.

A: Let's see if you can see someone else's information, you're able to see and sense someone else's information. How do they look, the person that is sharing it?

C: They look human, they're just different, maybe looks like a commander, he has a uniform on.

A: What color is it?

C: It's like silver and blue.

A: What is he sharing?

C: They're protecting, they have ships all over.

A: All over where?

C: They have ships around the Earth.

A: Are they above the Earth?

C: Yes, they are above the Earth.

A: What is he saying?

C: They're protecting. I'm not sure how.

A: Okay, is there a name that you go by, the nine of you? Was that nine including the people who are in there as holographs?

C: Yes.

A: Is there a name that you go by?

C: No, I mean it's just part of the Alliance, it's just one small part.

A: The Alliance of what?

C: I'm just hearing Light.

A: Alliance of Light, beautiful, very good. So fast forward a bit. What happens next of importance, what do you see?

C: We're just returning, we return.

A: Where do you return to? Where do you go?

C: I'm just going back, back to where I was.

A: Okay. Do you know what you decided as far as how you're going to fix the situation of that technology that's affecting animal life?

C: They're going to put a shield around it to where it's muffled.

A: Do you feel that it was placed there on purpose to affect life in the sea?

C: Yes.

A: This shield is going to stop its harm now?

C: Yes, it's muffled now, it's like...

A: Do you not just destroy it or break it, tear it apart?

C: It'll destroy itself.

A: Is that what the shield is for, it destroys itself?

C: Yeah, and it puts the shield and then like vibrations within it, bouncing off itself, and then it just destroys itself.

A: Okay, good. Are there many like that in the sea, many devices like that too?

C: I'm not sure.

A: Very good. Now, let's leave that life now…

The Higher Self is called forth.

A: Beautiful. Is this Candee's Higher Self?

Higher Self: Yes.

A: Thank you for being here. I honor you, I love you, and I respect you. Thank you for everything that you've shown her, it was very interesting. Beautiful life there and great information. May I ask you questions now?

Higher Self: Yes.

A: Thank you. Why is it that you took her to this life where she was underwater and seemed like a mermaid/merman? Why did you take her there?

Higher Self: It's part of her, to remember.

A: That city that was underwater that she talked about that sunk, did it have a name?

Higher Self: Atlantis.

A: Anything else you want to tell us in regard to why she is guarding the Atlantis that has sunk underwater?

Higher Self: There are powerful Crystals and other symbols there that when it's time it will be revealed. It's not time yet.

A: Okay. And then she took us through a tunnel where she shifted into a different type of being. Is she able to do that, go from merman to a man with legs?

Higher Self: Yes.

A: Is this part of a race that is able to do this?

Higher Self: Yes.

A: Can you tell us more about the animals that were there that were really beautiful? Anything else you want to say about that once you went into the Inner Earth?

Higher Self: Yes, they all get along in peace with each other, they are protected.

A: Some of those animals that went extinct on the land above, did the Inner Earth save them?

Higher Self: Yes.

A: Then she went to this healing fountain, tell me more about this fountain.

Higher Self: It gets charged from Gaia and also the people there, the beings there will help charge it. Everybody that comes can clear themselves and energize themselves.

A: How beautiful, and is this a requirement when they come in, do they have to go through there if they come from outside?

Higher Self: Yes.

A: she went to some kind of alliance, was that their name? As she said, 'Alliance of Light'?

Higher Self: It's a Galactic Alliance but it's of The Light.

A: A 'Galactic Alliance of The Light', beautiful. Anything else you want to share with us about this Alliance? This Council that she was a part of, is it always nine of them?

Higher Self: Yes.

A: Are they all different races?

Higher Self: Yes.

A: Are there other Councils in the Inner Earth besides that Council of Nine?

Higher Self: Yes.

A: What is this particular Council in charge of?

Higher Self: They're more for things like security, like guarding and protecting.

A: We thank them. Is it the Earth that they guard, or do they guard other places?

Higher Self: Their focus is on the Earth right now.

A: How about her as this blue being that she turned into with four toes, is there a race name?

Higher Self: No.

A: Okay. Anything else you want to share with her about this life that you showed her?

Higher Self: No, that's it.

The Body Scan begins.

A: Beautiful, thank you. Higher Self, if you could do a body scan on her now? Scan her for any energies that need healing, any entities as well. Let me know what you find.

Higher Self: There's something wrapped around the spine.

A: What is it?

Higher Self: It looks like tentacles.

A: Is it wrapped around the whole spine?

Higher Self: No, it's in the base of the spine. Looks like it's going up.

A: What color is it?

Higher Self: It's black.

A: Does it have a consciousness that we can speak to? Can we heal this on our own or do you require any help from the angels?

Higher Self: I need help.

A: Very good. Who would you like to call on?

Higher Self: Michael.

A: Archangel Michael, we love you, we honor you, and we thank you. If we could please speak to Archangel Michael now.

A: Greetings… Archangel Michael?

AA Michael: Yes.

A: Greetings brother, thank you for being here

AA Michael: Thank you.

A: Welcome, if you can look at her body right now, her Higher Self was doing a body scan on her and saw something wrapped around her lower spine that looked like it had tentacles and it was black. Can you tell me what that is, please? Is it intelligent and does it have a consciousness, a soul that I could speak to, or should we just remove it?

AA Michael: Just remove it[5].

A: Very good. Is it kind of like biotech?

AA Michael: Yes.

A: Can we go ahead and start removing it now? Are you removing it now?

AA Michael: Yes.

A: Is there something that you want me to use, should I use like white light or should I use the Phoenix Fire?

AA Michael: Phoenix Fire.

A: Very good, using the Phoenix Fire now. Can you tell me, Michael, why was that placed there? What was the purpose there, the lesson there?

AA Michael: It was just to block her.

A: When was it that it got attached there?

AA Michael: Couple of years ago.

A: What was going on with her that allowed for this to happen at that time?

AA Michael: She was with someone.

A: She was with a man?

AA Michael: Yes.

A: What was going on? How did it enter?

AA Michael: Through sexual relations.

A: Was it through this man?

AA Michael: Yes.

A: Did this man have connections to a negative soul family?

AA Michael: Yes, he's very dark.

A: Through this exchange of sex, he transferred this type of, would you call it an entity?

AA Michael: Yes.

A: When it entered, through what part of her did it enter?

AA Michael: I'm not sure.

A: Very good. Is that what this type of entity does, it goes for the spine and latches on there?

AA Michael: Yes.

A: You said it's with the purpose to stop her?

AA Michael: Yes, to block.

A: To block what?

AA Michael: Blocking her energy to go up.

A: Is it blocking like her Kundalini energy as well?

AA Michael: Yes.

A: How's it looking Michael?

AA Michael: It's gone.

A: Beautiful. Can you please ask Archangel Raphael to fill in that space with light, please?

AA Michael: Yes.

A: We thank you, Archangel Raphael. We welcome you and we love you. Very good. Michael now that we found that there in her spine, can you scan the rest of her body and see what else needs healing, please?

AA Michael: There's a being at the back of the neck.

A: Okay. Should I speak to it, Michael?

AA Michael: Yes.

---

[5] This action is suggested because we have learned now that Archons are soulless and not of our Source. Therefore, they have no consciousness to address for healing.

A: Very good. Let me speak to that entity now in the back of her neck, let me speak to you now. Come up, up, up. Greetings.

Entity: Yes.

A: Can I ask you questions, please?

Entity: Yes.

A: Are you female or male?

Entity: Male.

A: When was it that you attached yourself there?

Entity: A few years ago.

A: What was going on with her that allowed you to come in?

Entity: She was doing drugs and opened herself up.

A: Did you have a body before you connected there?

Entity: Yes.

A: How was it that you died?

Entity: I'm not dead.

A: Say that again?

Entity: I'm not dead.

A: You're not dead?

Entity: No.

A: Who are you connected to?

Entity: I have a body.

A: Does she know the body you're connected to?

Entity: No.

A: Why is it that you split off the body that's alive?

Entity: To take her energy.

A: Was this a contract?

Entity: No.

A: So how did you know to go to her and attach yourself even though you have your own body, what led you there?

Entity: I saw an opening and her light.

A: Now considering that you still have a body that is still alive here. We would love to be able to help you go back to that body that you're from and help you heal this part of you that's here stuck in her body. We'd love to be able to help you become whole once more, back to the body you are meant to be in. Will you please allow us to help you today?

Entity: Yes, you may.

A: Very good. Thank you for allowing us to help you. We want you to find that light within you and spread it to all that is of you, every root, every cord, and let me know once you're all light.

Entity: Okay.

A: Beautiful, are you all light?

Positive Polarized Entity: Yes.

A: Good. Go ahead and remove yourself, make sure you remove every part of you that does not belong to her, all that is of your essence. Ensure that you don't leave any piece of you behind. Let me know once you're out... Are you out?

Positive Polarized Entity: Yeah.

A: Very good and do you have a message for her before you go?

Positive Polarized Entity: No.

A: Very good. Can the angels guide you back to the body you are meant to be in?

Positive Polarized Entity: Yes.

A: Good and can we tag along with you and see where you go?

Positive Polarized Entity: Yes.

A: Good, very good. Go ahead allow for the angels to take you where your body is at and let me know once you get close to it... What do you see?

Positive Polarized Entity: Ship.

A: You see a ship?

Positive Polarized Entity: Yes.

A: Find that body that you're meant to be in.

Positive Polarized Entity: Yes.

A: How do they look?

Positive Polarized Entity: Reptilian.

A: Oh okay, so you were a consciousness of a Reptilian?

Positive Polarized Entity: Yes.

This was one of the beginning sessions that started teaching me how Reptilian Consciousnesses attached, hence my questioning to figure out how this really works.

A: Do you want to go back to that body, or do you want to be on your own now that you're made of light?

Positive Polarized Entity: I want to leave.

A: Angels, if you could please help this consciousness now that it has decided to be of light to no longer go back to the Reptilian there on the ship. If you could please help it go ahead and perhaps incarnate into another existence somewhere else... Michael, how's it looking?

AA Michael: It looks good.

A: Michael, can you tell me about that Reptilian there on the ship now that we removed its consciousness from her. What happens to that entity, that Reptilian there on the ship?

AA Michael: It went to a higher Dimension.

A: The Reptilian on the ship did?

AA Michael: Yes.

A: Good and that Reptilian, was it able to sense what was going on then?

AA Michael: Yes.

A: Where did it go to, what Dimension?

AA Michael: To a higher Fourth/Fifth Dimension.

A: Very good, are you still connected to that Reptilian that ascended Michael?

AA Michael: No.

A: Okay. If you all can just aid it with Love-Light and blessings to the consciousness and the Reptilian. May you go with the Love-Light of the Universe. Thank you... Michael can you scan her throat and make sure she doesn't have any portals or negative hooks there or anywhere in her body or connected to any other entity. Let me know what you find.

AA Michael: It looks clear.

A: Yes, I thought so as well. Thank you so much. Such a beautiful healing. Can we have Archangel Raphael fill in that spot there on her neck?

AA Michael: Yes.

A: Good and why was that Reptilian consciousness there?

AA Michael: It was feeding off of her.

A: What was it feeding off of?

AA Michael: Of her light.

A: So, do we need to fill in her light?

AA Michael: Yes.

A: Where's her light located?

AA Michael: In the heart.

A: Yes. Let's go ahead and fill that in as well for her please, Raphael. Thank you. Archangel Michael, before you go. Do you have anything you want to tell her?

AA Michael: She's loved and protected but she needs to believe in herself.

A: Yes. So now that we removed these entities and Reptilian consciousness, can you tell her just to help her feel comfortable that this won't happen to her again? What is something that she could be doing Michael to help her feel safer?

AA Michael: She's already doing it. She's not doing the behaviors she did before into drugs and she's protecting herself every day.

A: Good, very good, anything else you want to tell her Michael?

AA Michael: That's it.

A: Thank you, Michael. We love you, we honor you, and we respect you. Thank you for your help today. My blessings and love to you.

AA Michael: Thank you.

A: Thank you, talk to you later. Raphael, how's the filling in the light going?

AA Raphael: It's completed.

A: Oh, wonderful. Raphael brother, do you have a message for her?

AA Raphael: She's a beautiful light.

A: Thank you brother. Is that all?

AA Raphael: She's a healer too.

A: Tell her a little bit more about that.

AA Raphael: She's been afraid to use her healing.

A: Why?

AA Raphael: Not believing in herself.

A: Help her believe in herself, what can you tell her that will help her?

AA Raphael: She can do it. She just needs to start and practice and then it will come, she just has to take the first step.

A: Yes. Thank you, Raphael, are you done with her?

AA Raphael: Yes.

A: Okay, we thank you, we honor you, we love you, and we respect you. Thank you, Raphael, I'll talk to you later.

AA Raphael: Thank you.

A: Can I please speak to her Higher Self once more?

Higher Self: Yes.

A: Thank you. That was a phenomenal healing. Very beautiful. Thank you. It went very smoothly. This has been such a beautiful session. May I ask you questions that she has now?

Higher Self: Yes.

A: Good. She wants to know, what is her soul origin?

Higher Self: Sirian.

A: She wants to know, what is her soul contract and her mission here on Earth?

Higher Self: She's supposed to help other people find their light and be the light for others.

A: That being there that went from the mermaid to the blue being, was that a Sirian being?

Higher Self: No.

A: Okay. She wants to know, what is the best way for her to be in service-to-others?

Higher Self: She could find ways to volunteer and just be more interactive with people. Because she wants to do something, but she doesn't really, she just has to be her light. She doesn't have to do videos, or she just needs to be with people and interact with them and just shine her light.

A: Very good. Can you check her chakras and her auric field? How does it look?

Higher Self: She needs to start working on bringing the light up now that she's clearing. But it looks clear now so she should be able to bring it up.

A: Yes. She was asking if she could have help with the Kundalini activation? Will you help her?

Higher Self: Yes.

A: Will it happen in the future?

Higher Self: Yes.

A: Good. Is there anything she could be doing to help it?

Higher Self: She will be working on the different chants for each chakra and meditating and visualization, breathe in the light up and just keep bringing the light up and further each time, and feel it.

A: Very good.

Higher Self: Like a ball of light from the root and just bringing it up to each and back down and eventually it's going to just come up.

A: Beautiful advice, thank you. She wants to know; she needs help finding her passion. What's holding her back from finding that?

Higher Self: She likes to teach. She always wanted to be a teacher when she was young, but she stopped, she stopped. She was afraid that she couldn't do it.

A: What advice do you have for her? How can she find her passion now?

Higher Self: She can find ways to teach others. She's already doing it; she's always teaching and helping others.

A: Good.

END OF SESSION

--------------<◇>--------------

What an honor it is to have met this Council of Nine inside the Inner Earth and their ecosystem. Reminding us of how there are many unseen races of the Universe assisting us here on Earth, and throughout Creation in the process of the Universal Ascension. To remind us that we have never been alone, no matter how alone we have felt at times in our life. We have always been surrounded by this unity support that we got to meet throughout this session. What a joy it is to discover that these possibilities are a reality, to know there is life inside the Earth. Perhaps we hadn't thought enough of the potentials available when we connect to the Inner Earth. The people, the plant life, the crystals, the portals/Dimensions that we can connect to when we tune into the Inner Earth, and the life force that exists within it because of Mother Earth's heart at the center. There is much yet to be discovered within the Inner Earth, and sessions like these bring us closer to placing the pieces of the puzzle together.

We have heard of the military's sound weapons, and how groups in large quantities of dolphins, seals, whales and fish come up dead at the shorelines of the world's beaches. Now we know the depth of how sea life is affected by these malevolent destructive weapons. The pain and discomfort that these inorganic man-made experiments cause to natural forms of living, as expressed in this session. The animals hold the purest, brightest light of Earth's collective life and are high vibrational beings that anchor this pureness daily into Earth. They play one of the biggest roles for Earth and its people, since the water of Earth holds the highest mass and percentage in Earth. They are in a constant organic healing cycle working in oneness with the waters.

Water reaches and touches all parts of the world at some point and time. Therefore, it is the most powerful element for us to connect to if we are looking to assist in balancing and healing the Earth. Water retains the memory field and emotions of Mother Earth. It is gentle enough to wash away our pains, yet strong enough to move all it touches. The sea life connects to this power daily in assisting Mother Earth keep balance. This is one of the reasons why sea life is targeted through the Illuminati. They are well aware of the vastness of the healing that sea life creates for Mother Earth daily. For those of us who have a soft spot in our hearts for animals, it is hard to know that they are being targeted in this manner and disturbed from being able to just be and prevented from what they are here to do for all life. We humbly thank the beauties and Love-Light that they are.

We thank the beings underwater, as these mermaids who are working relentlessly without any recognition needed. Still standing post or should we say swimming post, under the sea where the sacred remains of Atlantis lay rest. The crystal generators that still till this day are doing their job maintaining the 13 Keys/Chakras balanced. This Eighth Key, the Earth Star that connects to the sacred Universal law of "The Law of Surrender" is connected to Atlantis. We have included a comprehensive guide to the 13 Keys/Sacred Laws of the Universe in Chapter 24 for all to read more on what this means, and its vitality to Earth and the Universe.

This magical world that is deep beneath our feet as the entryway into the Fifth Dimension is inwards, inside the Earth; where the portal into the Fifth Dimension is the heart of the Divine Mother, our Mother Earth's heart. It is where we all have pieces of us that await for us daily to connect to, in regaining our sovereignty back and the knowing of how we are ONE, because we all began from ONE heart, the Divine Mother's heart. It is her heart, for only she can birth forth new souls from her infinite universal womb. Just as we the Divine Feminine within, each carry and birth life upon Earth, as the fractals and expressions of the Divine Mother. The more we bring these pieces back when we connect to the collective of hearts inside Earth, the more that we birth our collective organic timeline for Ascension. Dear reader, know that the 'Emerald Portal of The Heart' inside the Earth awaits us when we are ready to enter into the New Earth/Fifth Dimension!

"The love you see within me is you! For I am only but a reflection of the beauty within you that's awaiting to be unleashed."
~AuroRa ♥

-------------<◇>-------------

6

THE ANUNNAKI EXPERIMENTS

Session #79: Recorded in October 2018.
Never before shared.

The Anunnaki are one of the first topics we run into when we are first awakening. As we start researching and discovering who has been running our planet, we go through catalyzing emotions such as, "What do you mean we have been under control?!"

This online A.U.R.A. Hypnosis Healing session shows us a perspective that not all Anunnaki were negative. Georgia, whose English is her second language, finds herself in ancient sands and pyramids not aligning with the leadership's agenda of using humans as labor only. On this journey, we learn more about the beginnings of Earth, its people and early forms of mind control. When we connected to her Higher Self, we never expected who she was. Georgia's past life reminds us of the beauty of all alien races in Creation.

-------------<◇>-------------

"We are here to teach people unconditionally because we don't feel the unconditional love and yet we are. We have the urge to feel it when in form. That's why we will look for it in other people. Then they began treating us a certain way and not giving us the love we are searching for.We will go in and we will find love. We want to gift other people the love so we can feel the love back in that process."
-Higher Self

-------------<◇>-------------

A: [Aurora] Look down at yourself, do you have a body?
G: [Georgia] Yes, a bird.
A: Describe yourself to me, how are you a bird?
G: I look like I have big eyes, feathers, a nose. What do you call that?
A: Like a beak?
G: Yes.
A: What color is the beak?
G: Like a yellow.
A: What about your feathers, what color are they?
G: White, yellow, and red.
A: Do you feel like you are very tall?
G: Yes.
A: Are you female or male?
G: Female.
A: Do you feel younger, older?
G: The same.
A: Are you wearing anything?

G: A chain.

A: Let's look at this chain, what is it hanging on? What kind of colors do you see on the chain?

G: Blue, like aqua blue.

A: Are there any designs or any crystals on it?

G: Copper.

A: Anything else? Any other designs?

G: It's round. Like an oval.

A: What is the roundness, what color is that and what does it have within it?

G: Like blue, like a light bluish color.

A: Look at yourself, is there anything you're carrying?

G: A small pyramid.

A: Where is the pyramid?

G: In her hand, my hand.

A: Describe the pyramid to me, what is the color, are there any designs on it?

G: It's like lines and it's golden.

A: Okay.

G: There is like a crown.

A: Describe your crown.

G: It is pointy, I see red stones, green stones, white.

A: Is there a reason why you're wearing this crown?

G: Because I have powers.

A: Look all around you, I know that you said you saw sand. What else do you see around you?

G: I see trees, small trees, plants.

A: Anything else?

G: No.

A: Why are you here?

G: To know who I am.

A: Yes. Let's walk around, let's go in the direction that you are meant to go. Start walking and let me know what you see along the way that stands out.

G: I see children.

A: Where are the children?

G: They are standing and playing.

A: How do the children look?

G: Like light brown, black hair, they have like a skirt on. They are waving at me and I wave back.

A: Do the children look different than you?

G: Yes.

A: What are you doing next?

G: Walking to a pyramid.

A: There's a pyramid? Can you describe it to me, is it big, is it tall?

G: It's big. The children are running to me and I gave them the pyramid that I had in my hand.

A: Why did you give this to them? What are they going to do with it?

G: It holds knowledge.

A: Is it going to teach them some of that knowledge?

G: Yes.

A: What do they do with it when you hand it to them?

G: They run away with it.

A: Are they taking it somewhere?

G: They are putting it on the ground.

A: What happens when they put it on the ground?

G: A light comes up.

A: What color light?

G: White.

A: When it comes up, what happens to the light?

G: It expands everything.

A: It goes everywhere?

G: Yes, in the sky.

A: What about the children?

G: They are looking at it, at the light.

A: So, is it like a ray of light, white light that shoots up to the sky?

G: Yes.

A: When that happens, what happens next?

G: The children hold their hands like in a circle around it and it is in the middle of them. They are just happy; it is like they are looking at it with amazement, but they did it before.

A: What is the purpose of its shooting, the light ray to the sky?

G: Like a connection.

A: A connection to what?

G: To Source.

A: When Source connects to that ray, what happens to the land you're standing on? Why is this important?

G: The children can feel it in their hearts, and it opens their hearts.

A: Beautiful. How about the adults? Does it do that for the adults too?

G: Yes.

A: Is this something that you are in charge of, this pyramid?

G: I think so.

A: What happens next after it shoots up the ray? What do the kids do, what do you do?

G: The kids are holding their hands together. Sitting down with the pyramid in the middle and they are smiling, they can feel their hearts opening. They feel a sense of peace.

A: Wonderful, how many children are there?

G: Two children.

A: Are they male, female?

G: Both.

A: Male and female?

G: Yes.

A: What is your relation to these children?

G: I teach them to connect.

A: Are you like their teacher?

G: Yes.

A: Okay, fast forward a bit to where they are done doing what they needed to do with the pyramid. What do you all do next?

G: They bring it back to the pyramid where I am at.

A: Are you standing outside the pyramid or inside the pyramid?

G: I'm looking at them.

A: Is there something unique about these children, their facial features, their fingers?

G: They have three fingers.

A: Do they have hair?

G: Yes, dark hair.

A: How are their eyes?

G: Blue, light blue.

A: You said brown skin?

G: Yes.

A: So, they bring it back to you and then what happens?

G: I put it with the others, there are a lot of pyramids, small pyramids there.

A: Where?

G: Inside of the big pyramid.

A: Did you go into the pyramid?

G: Yes.

A: How was it that you entered?

G: There was an opening, I just entered. I walked and I put the small pyramid next to the other pyramid.

A: When you walked into the pyramid did you have to go up, or down, or on the same level?

G: At the same level.

A: Tell me how you got to this room, was it right away or did you have to travel some to get there?

G: No, I was there immediately.

A: Now, this entrance is that for just you or for others?

G: I see somebody else in the pyramid.

A: Let's focus on that other person and the being that you see there. How do they look?

G: The same.

A: Are they female or male?

G: Female.

A: Is there anything that stands out about her?

G: There is like a green, like a long gown.

A: What is your relation to this other being?

G: She doesn't really communicate. It is only there; she is just there. It's looking at a pyramid - it does not like the connection.

A: She doesn't like the connection of the pyramid?

G: No.

A: What's wrong with the pyramid? Why doesn't she like the connection of the pyramid?

G: She doesn't like that I gave the children the pyramid.

A: Oh, why not?

G: They don't need to connect.

A: She says they don't need to connect?

G: Yeah.

A: So why do you do it?

G: It brings me joy, to connect.

A: What else is in this room with this other being here? Look all around you, what do you see?

G: The pyramids are there. I see golden shimmers from the pyramid, and it is pretty dark, and she sits in a chair, but everything is so dark in there. I don't want to stay there with her energy, I can't help her. I need to do what I need to do.

A: So, you don't align together?

G: No.

A: You are different?

G: She does not look at me, she looks like she is not happy with something, with the situation.

A: Do you work together?

G: We're supposed to.

A: What is your role? What are you supposed to be working together doing?

G: Teach the people.

A: You're supposed to be teaching the people?

G: Yes.

A: And is she in agreement with this or…?

G: She wants them to be like robots and I think they need to be connected!

A: Why is she different from you? It looks like you are the same type of race, the bird-like animal. Why is she different? Why does she do things differently?

G: She doesn't connect with the others.

A: So, you are overseeing the humans?

G: Yes, I love them. I want to help them to be all they can be.

A: How come she doesn't want to help them?

G: She wants them to work.

A: To work how?

G: With stones, building things with stones.

A: Oh, she wants them to be building things.

G: Yes.

A: How do you feel about that?

G: It breaks my heart.

A: So, let's fast-forward a bit to when something else has changed, something of importance. You are there now, what do you see?

G: I see her standing and watching other people build things and I look at her. I don't want to look at the people. But I'm staring at her and just imagining all of this that she enjoys.

A: Are there people that are above you all like bosses that are having you do this? Or is this just something that she is doing?

G: I don't see other people there.

A: So, you two are in charge?

G: I guess so. But I can't do anything about it.

A: Why not?

G: She doesn't listen. I feel it in my heart, the pain.

A: What is it that they are building?

G: Like walls. I'm walking in the village and I'm giving everybody a pyramid, but she doesn't know.

A: So, the pyramids that you had in the big pyramid?

G: Yes.

A: Are there many pyramids inside that big pyramid?

G: Yes, a lot!

A: Where do you all get them from?

G: It just appears in our hands if you think about it.

A: So, you manifest them?

G: Yes.

A: When you give them to the people, what is the purpose? What is your plan?

G: The people will wake up. They are more powerful than her if they team up, but they need to wake up. And that's why she was angry with the pyramid because I was waking all of the little ones, but everybody deserves to have the power and not only us.

A: You are handing it to them in secret? Is there something that you tell them to do with it once you hand it to them?

G: They know, they know. It's like they've done it when they were little too, so they know the feeling. I've given it to them before.

A: So, you have done this for some time then?

G: Yes, but not in this way I am giving it now to everybody.
A: You are letting them, having them keep them?
G: Yes.
A: How do they look at you? How do they feel towards you?
G: They love me. They are happy I am in their home.
A: Part of their village?
G: Yes, they bring everything to me. The children are climbing on my back.
A: Are you taller than them, than the humans?
G: Yes.
A: How much taller are you than them?
G: Three times taller. She looks angry at me again.
A: Does she know that you're passing out those pyramids?
G: Yes.
A: Does she know that you are letting them keep them?
G: Yes.
A: What does she tell you?
G: No, she stays quiet again.
A: So, are you like the leader of the village? Are you in charge of the people?
G: Yes.
A: Are you from this land or did you come from elsewhere?
G: I came from elsewhere.
A: Remember how you came, how did you come?
G: I hear copper.
A: What about copper?
G: I came to find copper.
A: You and her?
G: Yes, we were in charge of finding the copper.
A: For somewhere else?
G: I see aliens.
A: So, did you come flying or on a spaceship? How did you get there?
G: I just appeared.
A: You manifested there?
G: Yes.
A: Very good. So, tell me what happens next of importance? Fast forward a bit. Take us to where something else happens of importance, you are there now. What happens?
G: I'm letting the people escape.
A: Why? What is going on? Did she have them like prisoners or…?
G: Yes, they need to work. I am escaping with them.
A: So, does she treat them like slaves?
G: Yes. She doesn't have a bond with them. She doesn't harm them, but she hasn't got a connection with them. She is always serious.
A: Who oversees the work, does she have workers under her? Humans that keep the control with her.
G: I see aliens again.
A: What kind of aliens are you seeing?
G: The white ones.
A: White aliens?
G: The ones with the big eyes.
A: Do they have hair?

G: No. They have a small body. They aren't there and you don't see them.
A: So, are they physical?
G: They are there but they cannot see them. We can see them.
A: What do these aliens do? How do they keep control of the people? How do they do that?
G: Like electric shock.
A: So, if they don't listen, do they get an electric shock?
G: They don't move, but they do what they say like they don't even know they are being controlled.
A: Are they in sense like a robot, those aliens?
G: No, they are not robots, but they have like an energy or something and it spirals down to the humans in their head.
A: So, they send energy to the human's crown area spiraling down?
G: It looks like, yes it spirals down but more like this... (zig-zag motion with hands)
A: Like zigzag?
G: Yes, it's like electric but they don't feel it.
A: So, are they being mind-controlled?
G: Yes.
A: What about these people that you have connected to the pyramids and the light, are they as easily mind controlled?
G: I think I gave them the pyramids so we can escape.
A: Okay, and these beings, they can't see them... Who is controlling those beings, the alien beings that are white with big eyes?
G: I don't see anything else.
A: Okay now let's see, tell me what's going on. You said you're escaping with them. Let me know what's going on. What are you all doing? Are there many people with you?
G: Yes, like a hundred.
A: Is it only some or is it the majority of the village?
G: Like, half.
A: Are these human beings that are more, could you say, more awakened? Or how did you choose who was to come with you?
G: I did not choose, it happened like that. We needed to go fast.
A: How was it that you communicated this to them, that you would leave with them?
G: They just listen to me; they just came along, and I told them to be quiet. We knew, they knew, they could feel it.
A: When you talk to them, do you talk to them vocally or through the mind?
G: With the mind.
A: Yes... Is there both a daytime and night-time in this area that you are?
G: It's daytime.
A: It's only daytime?
G: No, there is night too.
A: There is night too but right now it's daytime?
G: Yes, it's day but it is like in the evening.
A: Is there a name that you call your land?
G: Arte.
A: A, R, T, E?
G: Yes.
A: Is that the land that you live in, in the village, or the planet?
G: I think the planet.

A: Very good. Now, tell me what is going on. You are escaping with about half of the village but where are you going? Are you walking?... Give me some details.

G: They are walking and walking. There is some water. They are sitting and everybody is so peaceful, and they are sitting with their feet in the water and I am sitting with them too. But I don't really know what to do.

A: You have both adults and children with you?

G: Yes.

A: Do they eat food?

G: I don't see food.

A: But they do drink water, you said?

G: Their feet are in the water. I don't know why.

A: You said they have three fingers. How about their toes? How many toes do they have?

G: Four.

A: Tell me what happens next? Fast forward to when something else happens of importance. You are there now. What do you see?

G: Everybody died.

A: Everyone is dead? What happened?

G: The other group came and killed them.

A: Who killed them?!

G: The other group who stayed. They were being mind-controlled!

A: They were being mind-controlled? By whom?

G: Yes, by the white aliens.

A: Did the other woman that you were working with send them?

G: I think so.

A: Where were you at? Where did this happen? Look all around you.

G: At the same place by the water.

A: So, it happened very fast after you left?

G: Yes.

A: What happened when they came? Explain to me, start from the beginning and go back, back, back to the time where they are coming. Tell me what happens to you. What do you do, what do you sense, what do you feel?

G: Like I want to protect them, but I can't hide them.

A: You can't hide them?

G: No. They will find us everywhere.

A: What happens? How is it that these aliens kill them?

G: It wasn't the aliens; the aliens control the people and the people had sticks and stuff.

A: Had sticks?

G: Yes, and it was like I was standing there, and I didn't do anything. I was stuck in shock. So, I didn't move. I feel it in my heart now!

A: Could you have stopped those people?

G: It feels like I couldn't.

A: Did they kill everyone?

G: I didn't want to harm them because I knew it wasn't their fault. So, I saw the helplessness in their eyes because they did not want to do it. But they needed to do it. So, that's why I did not do anything.

A: Did they kill everyone?

G: They killed everyone.

A: What happens after they kill everyone? What do you do? What happens to the humans that are being controlled?

G: They pick up the people and bring them back and they burn them.
A: What do you do?
G: I am watching from a distance.
A: How do you feel?
G: I feel like it's my fault. I feel like they were better off staying there. There is a light coming out of the fire. The light of the pyramid.
A: Light of the pyramids?
G: The same lights that were coming out of the pyramid came out of the fire and they burned them.
A: Is that the people's Light? Is that what that is?
G: Yes.
A: What do you do next?
G: I am there again.
A: You went back?
G: Yes, I had to go back.
A: Was there nowhere to go on this planet?
G: They will find you anywhere.
A: How is it they are able to find you anywhere?
G: Because they are multidimensional.
A: Is there a frequency that you register?
G: Yes.
A: So, is that how they are able to find your frequency?
G: Yes.
A: So, are you back with her again?
G: Yes, and she acts as if nothing happened.
A: Look at her eyes. You are able to recognize her soul, do you recognize who she is?
G: She keeps looking down.
A: You are able to recognize her soul. Who does she feel like? Do you know her?
G: No.
A: That is okay... So, let's fast forward a bit again to another important time that is going on in this life. What is going on? You are there now.
G: They're doing things to the people to make more people.
A: What kind of things are they doing to them?
G: Something with their brain.
A: Then what happens?
G: No, something in their womb.
A: Do all these beings have wombs?
G: Yes, they are getting children without the sexual part of it. Like they are getting seeds.
A: Is that the white aliens that are doing this to them?
G: The people are doing it on themselves.
A: Okay, so the people are doing this, or are they being controlled to do this?
G: They are being controlled, yeah, they are putting it there.
A: Then what happens?
G: A lot of people are born.
A: When they are born, are they little?
G: Yes, but they are tired.
A: Who is tired?
G: The people.
A: The people who had babies? Or the babies?

G: All of them, all of them work so hard. They are tired.
A: From working so hard?
G: Yes.
A: The babies even work?
G: No, the babies, they don't work.
A: Not until they are older?
G: Yes.
A: Are you still allowed to hand out pyramids?
G: No.
A: You don't do that anymore?
G: I take care of the children.
A: You take care of the children while the parents work?
G: Yes.
A: Okay.
G: The other girl doesn't want anything to do with the children.
A: Let's fast forward again, let's go to another important time in this life. You are there now. What do you see now?
G: Blue beings.
A: You are seeing blue beings?
G: Tall beings.
A: Blue tall beings. Where do they come from?
G: Like a ship.
A: A ship, and why are they there?
G: To help.
A: Can you describe them more to me? Do they look more like you or do they look different?
G: They are taller.
A: Do they have feathers like you?
G: No. They are just standing there.
A: What are they going to help with?
G: They are observing. I do not see them, but I know that they are there.
A: You can't see them?
G: No, but I don't say anything.
A: Can the other girl see them too? The other lady?
G: I don't think so, but she stands with her back maybe she doesn't want to see them.
A: Fast forward a bit, tell me what happens next of importance.
G: Everything is white. I can't see anything.
A: Let's go back to right before you went to where everything is white, what happened? Right before this happened. You are there now.
G: They are leaving.
A: The blue beings are leaving? Why are they leaving?
G: To Sirius.
A: They are leaving for Sirius?
G: I think so, that is what I hear.
A: They are leaving for Sirius, is their job done here?
G: No, but they had to come and watch.
A: How did they feel about the situation?
G: They were angry. Not really angry, but more like, "now we know."
A: They know what is going on, on the planet?
G: Yes.

A: What happens next of importance?
G: I am getting killed.
A: You're getting killed by who?
G: By the lady.
A: The lady kills you?
G: Yes.
A: After the blue beings leave?
G: Not after, later on.
A: Why is she killing you?
G: Because I don't listen.
A: How is she killing you?
G: I don't want the seeding to take place. It is wrong.
A: Is she going to seed them again?
G: It's going on for so long, but I can see the people change and I know it's not good.
A: How are people changing?
G: They are getting more aggressive towards another, they don't have any patience anymore.
A: What happens to the blue beings that came and observed, that saw what was going on?
G: I don't see them anymore.
A: Did they ever do anything about it?
G: They just observe.
A: How is she killing you?
G: With a knife. Like a machete?
A: What is she doing with it?
G: Stabbing me in the stomach or the heart...in the heart.
A: Then what happens? Do you die?
G: Yes.
A: What happens when you die? … Go ahead and take your last breath, what is your last thought when you're dying?
G: The people.
A: Go ahead and leave the body. What happens next to you?
G: Black all around me, like I am in space, like I am in the Universe or something.
A: Oh, in the cosmos, in the Universe. What do you see around you?
G: Nothing.
A: Let's leave that life now…

The Higher Self is called forth.
A: I honor you, I love you, and I thank you. Amazing past life you showed her. Why is it that you chose to show her that life as a bird being? What was the purpose and lessons of that life?
Higher Self: To show her who she is and that she is from light.
A: She is light, yes. And was there a name for that race that she was as a bird being?
Higher Self: Anunnaki.
A: Was that planet Arte or was it similar to Earth? What was this planet?
Higher Self: It was Earth.
A: Why did she think it was called Arte?
Higher Self: That is how they called it.
A: That is how they called it then?
Higher Self: Yes.
A: Was this at the beginning of times of Earth or what period?
Higher Self: There were people already, not at the beginning.

123

A: Okay, so this is a little farther down in time... Why is it though that these humans look different than how we look? Why were they being used in this manner for copper?
Higher Self: To find the copper.
A: Is this what they normally did back then?
Higher Self: They needed it for something.
A: What do they need it for?
Higher Self: Manipulation.
A: Were those negative entities and beings that were controlling those humans?
Higher Self: Yes.
A: Was she supposed to be negative with the other being? Because it seems like she loved them - the humans - and tended to them?
Higher Self: No, that was her job.
A: So that was her job but was she supposed to be negative as well as the other being?
Higher Self: Yes.
A: As part of the Anunnaki, is that why she has 0 negative bloodline?
Higher Self: Yes.
A: Okay. How long did she live that life?
Higher Self: A hundred.
A: To 100 years old?
Higher Self: Yes.
A: What happened here? How come in those humans that you showed us, why did they have three fingers and four toes? Is that what we had been or were there different races of humans that had these differences? Or did we evolve into having five toes and five fingers?
Higher Self: It was the seeding.
A: Did the seeding start changing their forms?
Higher Self: Yes. Like hybrids.
A: Is that how they populated the Earth? Did they keep just creating inside their wombs, creating more and more?
Higher Self: Yes.
A: What would happen when they just kept creating and creating? I know she mentioned that they started, like, they were getting violent. Did that keep going on and getting worse?
Higher Self: It was the seeding. The seed was like red, like a red light. They're showing me like a red light in the seeding. In the seed.
A: Why did they do this, why did they put a red light in the seeding?
Higher Self: So, the people would work and not connect.
A: Is that one of the major things that's wrong with Humanity right now? In a sense, they are still working and not connecting? Is that seed still in us?
Higher Self: It's there but it doesn't shine that bright.
A: Thank you for all the information, she has very interesting knowledge.
Higher Self: Thank you for your work.
A: Thank you! And may I ask, are you female, male, or both as her Higher Self?
Higher Self: Female.
A: Female, more Divine Feminine?
Higher Self: Yes.
A: What is her Galactic history? Who are you?

There was hesitation to answer this.

Higher Self: ... Reptilian.

A: You are Reptilian?

Higher Self: Yes.

A: Are you a positive or negative Reptilian?

Higher Self: A positive.

A: Well greetings, thank you sister for all the work that you do. Was her ego getting in the way there? Was it not letting you say that?

Higher Self: Yes.

A: Yes, well we honor all lives... Can you do a body scan on her please and let me know what needs healing? If there are any energies that need healing, any blockages, any entities as well.

During the Body Scan the Higher Self finds two regular entities and negative energy needing assistance and clearing. We continue the transmission after the removal.

A: Good, beautiful. And as we heal the root chakra if I may ask you a question? You as her Higher Self, what Dimension are you in?

Higher Self: Seventh.

A: If you could explain exactly how this works as in our reality, we would say the majority of Reptilians are negative. Is that accurate?

Higher Self: No.

A: Explain to us how this works?

Higher Self: Every race has good and bad. It's not the right way to say it but I can't translate it in her English. If I could say it in Dutch it would be different, but you cannot put everybody and give them a stamp of that, this will only give the bad more power. It will make the other people of the same race get into fear. What that's doing is, as with Georgia, she will close herself up because she will think that it's bad.

A: Yes, but we know that she is not because you have a beautiful energy to you. In the Seventh Dimension, is this a frequency of love?

Higher Self: Of course, yes.

A: Would you say that you are an elder of a Reptilian that's ascended?

Higher Self: We are here to teach people unconditionally because we don't feel the unconditional love and yet we are. We have the urge to feel it when in form. That's why we will look for it in other people. Then they began treating us a certain way and not giving us the love, we are searching for. We will go in and we will find love. We want to gift other people the love so we can feel the love back in that process. We love feeling the love in human form and so you can grow the love within. By connecting with other people, we can balance their energy. That's why other people with problems come in Georgia's life and then they disappear. Because they needed to balance out, but the love was still there, and she knows it. When they see each other again years later the same love is there. Never feel like they've abandoned you because the things she has done for them they will never forget.

A: Beautiful. So, this is what she does to them, she helps them with their problems or their darkness? I guess you could say, to see the light. Would it be kind of like how she was manifesting those pyramids and giving people light?

Higher Self: Yes, she has been through so much herself and she knows how she can help other people. She knows what the people need because she has been through them. She can feel their pain, so she won't touch them. But it drains her. She needs to know how to protect herself.

A: It's such an honor to speak to a positive Reptilian as I often speak to your race. Not every race is just negative or just positive, there is a blend of both. It is beautiful to see you in your ascended form in the Seventh Dimension representing the positive Reptilians that are out there. I really appreciate you speaking to us. Thank you for bringing her to us.

Higher Self: That is why I came to you.

A: Yes, yes, absolutely. I hold no judgment, only love. Thank you. If we could look at her, how can we make her energy stronger, so she won't be drained when she is helping others?

Higher Self: She needs to shield.

A: Can we talk to her about how she can shield?

Higher Self: She uses the Violet Flame a lot. She does the things on YouTube that you taught people[6]. They are beautiful!

A: Thank you.

Higher Self: But she doubts herself. Things will come in her head and she will do them. She has a crystal wood staff she painted that's next to her bed and she made one for her daughter's room, for her daughter's nightmares. She has her crystal staff. Her daughter knows when she goes to sleep that they pray, they sing; her daughter knows that she is protected in her bubble with the angels. She didn't have nightmares anymore. But she worries a lot about it.

A: Her daughter or her?

Higher Self: She worries about her daughter.

A: Was that blockage, that entity that she had in her crown, was that making her doubt a lot?

Higher Self: Yes.

A: Was it blocking the energies there too?

Higher Self: Yes.

A: Okay. So now that she does not have this entity blocking her there and in the other areas that we removed energy and healed. Are there any other energies that need healing? Can we also scan her body for any negative implants?

Higher Self: Yes. Her neck.

A: When was this inserted and through what?

Higher Self: When she was a baby.

A: How was it inserted?

Higher Self: Vaccines.

A: Vaccines, and it went to her neck?

Higher Self: Yes.

A: Why is it there? What is the purpose of it being there, what does it do?

Higher Self: It blocks it.

A: It blocks what?

Higher Self: It blocks the portal.

A: So, is there a portal of light there?

Higher Self: Yes.

A: Is it near the spine in the neck?

Higher Self: Yes. She gets headaches and pain.

A: Can we please go ahead and transmute that implant out of there to make it inactive permanently?

Higher Self: Yeah.

A: Good. Should I use Phoenix Fire for that?

Higher Self: Please!

A: I'm going to let you keep working on her hand and her third eye and I am going to work on her implant now. Is this part of the mind control where they want to keep us like zombies?

Higher Self: Fear.

A: Is this similar to those white beings that were controlling the humans back then?

---

[6] Reference to the Rising Phoenix Aurora's channels, where Aurora shares videos on shielding, under the 'Spirituality for Beginners' playlist.

Higher Self: Yes. It's also physical because when you don't feel good you will shine less light. It is both.

A: Both yes, thank you. Let me know once we have transmuted that implant out of there. Are there any other negative implants besides this one?

Higher Self: In her feet.

A: Which foot?

Higher Self: Left one.

A: I'm going to go ahead and focus Phoenix Fire on the left foot now too... Why is it that they chose to put an implant on the left foot versus the right foot?

Higher Self: Connection from the Earth to the Cosmos is being blocked.

A: Is that where we find this connection, through the left foot?

Higher Self: Not exactly. It can be both.

A: Is the left side more of her Divine Feminine?

Higher Self: Yes.

A: Was this their purpose, were trying to block that connection of her Divine Feminine to Earth?

Higher Self: Yes.

A: Let me know once those are transmuted. I will keep focusing fire on there until you tell me we are done. Can you scan her body to make sure there are no other negative implants on her?

Higher Self: No more.

A: How did this one go into her foot?

Higher Self: By wearing shoes.

A: How did that implant get inserted in there through the shoes? What do you mean?

Higher Self: Yes, something with the shoes.

A: Interesting. Let's focus on the shoes, what part of her foot is this implant in?

Higher Self: The middle.

A: What kind of shoes would do this to you?

Higher Self: The rubber.

A: Rubber shoes, aren't the majority of shoes all rubber?

Higher Self: Yes, it stops the connection.

A: When it stopped the connection, how did this implant create there?

Higher Self: Because you keep walking on them. You need to put your feet on the Earth.

A: Would you think, perhaps we should look for shoes that are not made with rubber soles?

Higher Self: Yes.

A: Let's hope someone out there creates an organic line type of shoes where it doesn't have rubber in it.

Higher Self: Maybe you are the lucky one!

A: I don't know about that! (laughter) I have enough work to do but thank you. Can you scan her body and make sure there are no more entities hidden there, please.

Higher Self: Can you use the flame?

A: Yes, on the implant?

Higher Self: On her whole body.

A: I will start it from her crown and create a toroidal sphere of a flame, is that okay?

Higher Self: Yes.

A: Is there a color flame you want me to use?

Higher Self: Red.

A: Very good, thank you, that is what I was using and tell me why red?

Higher Self: It transmutes everything.

A: Does it transmute the negative, the lower frequencies? The negative lower energies?

Higher Self: Yes, of all the bodies.

A: Wonderful. Of all the bodies? And what bodies are those?

Higher Self: Etheric, emotional.

A: Wonderful. Let me know when you want me to stop with the fire and also when the negative implants are transmuted out of there.

Higher Self: Yes, thank you.

A: It is done?

Higher Self: Yes.

A: Thank you, beautiful job. She does have a couple of other things she wanted you to look at health-wise. Since she became pregnant with her daughter, she got high blood pressure. What happened there? She is not feeling the need to use medicine although I'm sure the doctors are trying to make her use them. Why does she have this now?

Higher Self: It will get better now that the entity is gone.

A: Okay, which one? Where?

Higher Self: In the heart.

A: That's why she has high blood pressure?

Higher Self: Yes.

A: Is this why she had the neck pain behind her ears? The negative implants?

Higher Self: Yes.

A: Why was she getting headaches? Is that the entity in the crown or is there any other reason?

Higher Self: Same. We thank you; it will get better.

A: What can she be doing better to help balance out headaches, what do you want her to do?

Higher Self: She knows. That it's for a better purpose.

A: Going back to the shielding, we did not finish setting that up. Can you tell her, how will she do this daily, so she won't be drained energetically?

Higher Self: I will show her.

A: You will show her. But can you tell her a little bit right now?

Higher Self: With fire. She needs to work with fire.

A: Wonderful, thank you. Why? Tell her why fire.

Higher Self: Fire transmutes.

A: Good. So, you would want her to focus more on envisioning fire around her daily?

Higher Self: Yes.

The client's personal questions are asked, and we resume when we are bringing Georgia back.

A: Welcome back Georgia! You are awesome! Beautiful, and I love your Higher Self! I think it is really important that people understand that no one race can be all negative therefore thank you for bringing forth such an important message for us.

G: Thank you for being open to it.

END OF SESSION

--------------<◇>--------------

If you were to meet Georgia, you would fall in love with her! One of the most gentle purest hearts, that emanates out the most joyful golden light. So much so that she is now an A.U.R.A Hypnosis Healing Practitioner. She has such a natural pure attractive loving energy and her eyes/her soul, pulls you right in feeling every bit of her natural beauties. No one would be able to tell that her Higher Self is Reptilian, Positive Reptilian that is. Teaching us that we must always look past the race and instead at the heart and light within. Just like the beautiful Anunnaki she was, who was trying to protect the premature human life then. The vessel she was incarnated in of the bird humanoid form, we will learn more about this beautiful race in Chapter 8 ('Four RA Guardians Heal Thousands of Entities').

We have heard of the experiments that altered the DNA within some of the first human life forms. Could this have been a part of that example? Was Georgia awakening their lights and hearts by her interactions with them? Was this what was in the little pyramids, pieces of her light harnessed to protect and guide them for their future soul transformations? Were these DNA experiments the reason we were meant to stay controllable?

Perhaps this infantile human race evolved so rapidly that this Anunnaki group could no longer control and use them to harvest the materials of Earth. It was beautiful to watch the perseverance administered through the working people of this village. How even though their DNA or genetic makeup was being altered, they still held that organic light that all souls in Creation carry. Their sovereignty and free willed choice to activate if they wish it and to expand their soul. As we saw through Georgia's example, handing them the Source Love-Light within these pyramids helped awaken them to a point that it reminded them of their free willed expression that they were, that IS the birthright given for all souls. Empowering them to stand up for themselves and their loved ones, to no longer be controlled as puppets by their puppeteers, the Negative Anunnaki. It is beautiful to witness life, no matter in what form always containing this knowing that their soul is free no matter the circumstances they are in. Source will always hear us no matter the filter of Dimension we are in, it is us who cannot hear Source the farther we go down the Dimensions away from Source. Which is part of the game we choose to play, to give up something in order to gain it back stronger and brighter. We can too, just as Georgia can, pass around energetic pyramids with Source Love-Light within them to help our brethren who have forgotten through all types of distortions in the Third Dimension. Thank you, Georgia, for being that pure example for us to follow.

Georgia is going through her own transformation in looking to embrace who she is as her Higher Self aspect, and I know in my heart that she will learn to embrace the Beauty of Creation that she is. As we the collective learn to love all organic races of light, even the Reptilians, she too will learn to self-love the beauty she is. We thank her Higher Self for reminding us how no single race is all negative, that positive Reptilians really do exist in Creation, and that they are part of the Ascension process in helping their negatively polarized brethren. Our hearts expand wider, and our lights become brighter with this session, when we allow ourselves to learn and accept that there is light in all organic races of Creation.

"Live with no approval required.
To do so is to live without expectations, limitations, and oppression.
It is to live with a free-flowing expansion of expression of one's organic purity.
No approval needed."
~AuroRa ♥

-------------<◇>-------------

7

SEVEN PLANETS FROM OTHER UNIVERSES

Session #250: Recorded in February 2020.

In this online A.U.R.A. Hypnosis Healing session, Elizabeth finds herself disconnected from her home planet and unable to return. She's stuck in the Earth's Inverted A.I. Matrix Simulation having to suffer from repeated trauma and abuse because of it. This is her journey of discovering why. Seven alien planets of another Universe that have volunteered to aid Earth. Who are the Guardians of the Elements and gardeners of the Earth? We learn more about death star weapons, and the journey of a dark Reptilian's soul evolution into forgiveness and transformation.

-------------<◇>-------------

"They're beings that got taken advantage of, so they need time to reflect with the powers that be and all that is.
See the damage they've done and decide how they can help repair it.
These beings aren't evil. They were just used for evil.
So, they need to be in a pure light space to be able to do this."
-Archangel Azrael

-------------<◇>-------------

E: [Elizabeth] No, I think I'm me, but I don't think I am on Earth.
A: [Aurora] Look down at the ground and all around you. What does it look like?
E: It's like the forest. A beautiful forest. The skies show stars in the daytime and it's purple, it's very lush. The sky is purple. It's a mix of nighttime and daytime. I've never seen this before. And there's trees in the field, but I can tell it's not…
A: You can tell it's not?
E: Yeah, not Earth.
A: Okay, good. What are you wearing?
E: A dress, a long dress. It's a white fabric. White with green and it goes down to the ground.
A: Are you wearing any jewelry?
E: A necklace.
A: What does the necklace look like?
E: It's silver, metal, it's heavy. It feels important. Like I couldn't get here if I wasn't wearing it. I can't see it, but when I hold it, I can feel that there's something written on it, but the writing I can't see. Although I know it's there. It's vibrating.
A: Do they have any crystals on it?
E: No, it's just silver.
A: Are there any shapes on there?
E: On the edge with like, one inch from the edge, a little divot circle, it just goes down. And then it's just plain in the middle again. And when I got here, it lifted off my body. It's floating now. On

Earth, it doesn't do anything. But here it's like, floating a little above me. Like I have to wear it. It's right above my breasts, right in the center of my chest.

A: Is there anything you're holding?

E: No. I feel like my hands have energy. And I can't see it when I'm on Earth, but I can see different energy here. It's purple again. I'm not doing anything with it, it's just part of me. I can see it here, but I can't see it when I'm on Earth.

A: There's purple energy coming out of your hands?

E: Yes, it's floating there because I'm not doing anything, but I have it.

A: What is it that you think you're doing here?

E: I don't know. I'm just standing here like I'm waiting for something. I don't see anyone else besides me.

A: Let's keep moving time to see if there is something or someone you're waiting for. You're there now. Tell me what's going on next of importance.

E: I sat down! (strong crying) I figured out I can't protect myself when I go here.

A: You can't protect yourself?

E: I can when I can touch the ground. Then my hands, it goes all the way up my arms. I can feel protected again like I have everything without my energy being so depleted. But when I'm here, this feels like where I am from. I can sit down on the grass and when I put my hands down, the energy fuels up my whole body again. The purple that was just on my hands is on my whole body now. I can feel it on my whole body! I'm just sitting there because it feels good. I feel safe, I can make flowers grow if I want. I am just experimenting with what all this feels like because it felt like I couldn't have it. I don't know where anyone else is, it's just me (crying continues).

A: Go ahead and allow yourself to feel that energy flowing through you. Perhaps you've been taken here so that you can feel the protection that is available. Even if you feel like you have been, perhaps, like you said, disconnected from it. Allow for it to flow through you so that you can remember once more this energy. You won't forget it ever again.

E: I have to lie down so I can get fully recharged, but I feel scared. Like someone's going to take it from me!

A: You are safe within the space. Just like that energy field helps you feel so protected and in charge, there is safety within that protection. Allow yourself to let go and allow yourself to lay down. Allow yourself to recharge and feel the beauty and the brilliance of this energy...

E: I remembered something.

A: Tell me. What do you remember?

E: I haven't come here for a long time! (strong crying in pain) Last time I came here, there was an attack and they destroyed everything. I got away because I am really powerful, and I can leave. I've been so disconnected from it. I was so afraid they would come back, and I didn't want to get attacked again. But everything grew back and everything's beautiful and peaceful, but no one's left here. That's why there's no one left there but me!

A: This is after the attack?

E: Yeah, it was a 1000 years ago… Earth years, I feel. Our people, everyone left. No one came when they attacked us, they just shot at us from their spaceship. I can't really tell who was in it. They were yelling at us that we could never get away and we'd always be hunted, that we could never come back and get our life force.

A: Let's go back in time to when you are there, in this time and space before the attack. Before you realized anything of them. You are there now. Tell me what you're seeing and sensing.

E: So beautiful, it's so beautiful! (strong crying) I thought it wasn't real cause I had forgotten it. We are here and we are like Angels. We are not angels, but we're not like fairies. We just experiment with the Earth. We can just make herbs grow and flowers or whatever we want. Practice how they interact with each other. And then there, we are called upon other planets or galaxies. If the species are going through problems and we can give them rosemary, for example, they can incorporate it into a healing. And then they can put it into their planet. So, we are kind of like guards, guard people, and help them. If they access the frequency, we can hear them out and go to them. I'm more like purple here. I look like me still, but I'm not normal. I don't really have human skin. It's glittery and purple. But I still have my hair, long, luxurious, dark curls. I am female. We are just experimenting, and we give people visions. The healers, the holy people in the places we take our plants to, they can hear us whenever we go. They download information and then they know how to use whatever plant we've given them or the remedy or how to do anything. Because they're holy, they can incorporate with us and what we gave them. Then we come back, and we just get to be peaceful. As long as we can feel the Earth and our plants, we just guide them, then it's okay there.

A: Look at your skin. What color is your skin? What tone is it?

E: Light purple. Not really solid. I could touch it, but if I need to change shapes really quickly or not be as dense, I can. When I am just relaxed, I am a glittery purple.

A: Do you still have ten fingers and ten toes?

E: Not all the time. It feels like three, it's kind of like a thumb, but it's in the middle of my hand. And then I have two fingers with circles on the ends and three on each hand. I don't really have feet. We need to have them when we go to a planet then they look like human feet. The only reason we have hands is so we can direct our energy more precisely, but otherwise, we don't need them.

A: So instead of walking, you float?

E: Yeah.

A: Okay and look at your face. What does your face look like?

E: It's kind of like a cat. Big eyes and a smaller chin, high cheekbones, like an alien. But it looks more like a cat. The eyes are more like a cat. It looks like we have eyeliner on, but we don't. We're glittery like bioluminescence.

A: You have glittery skin versus fur?

E: I have skin, but we just look like a cat. We have cat eyes. Like, so, it's like we are cats, but we don't have any fur.

A: Do you have ears?

E: Better than we can hear them, but we have everything in case we go to a Dimension where we need to shapeshift to be like that. I know where my ears would be, but I don't really have them. It's kind of like a small hole but I can just feel and see. Like I can feel a vibration in my body faster than I can hear something happening.

A: Do you feel female, male, or both?

E: I don't think I have a gender, but I identify more with feminine things. I'm just drawn to more female energy because I like gentle things. I think we're all mostly female. I don't think there's really any male energy.

A: Do you have hair on your head?

E: No.

A: There's no hair there?

E: But I can have it if I want it.

A: Okay.

E: When I go to Earth, I look like it and I like looking like that. If I didn't go to Earth for a long time, then no. I just make myself have curly hair, but normally I don't.

A: So, we went back to a time before. Tell me, what are you doing in this time and space?

E: I experiment with plants and growing stuff. They're kind of like extensions of us. If I need to make a plant that can do a certain thing that can heal someone, then I just have to focus my energy. And like I said, if people, it's mostly humans, but sometimes other places; if they need help, there's a new disease or something, then they can pray to us or speak to us and we can make something for them. Sometimes it takes two or three of us to make it, but usually just one of us is good enough to make it. Then we go down and they can't see us. They are too dense to see us when we are in our full form. That's why we have to go to human form sometimes or I'll just put the plant and then send the message. It depends on how advanced the person who requested it is. Let's say we can go to Earth very easily and then come back and then live a really peaceful life and we just like to be in tune with the Earth.

A: When you come down and do what you have to do as far as sharing your plant information or knowledge. Do you have to come in a human form?

E: Not always. It depends if someone who maybe isn't connected spiritually or doesn't have a lot of practice. One time I helped this woman who lived in the woods by herself with her family, and she was just trying to survive. I had to go as a human because she didn't vibrate high enough to accept help from a non-human being, a non-human form. I had to go and tackle those passing by and, you know, as a medicine woman that can help her. So, sometimes I can be a human depending on who I'm helping, and sometimes I can just remain in my normal form and still help them.

A: You mentioned earlier that your home has a purple sky. Does it still have a purple sky?

E: Yeah, everything is like a purple tint, underlying purple tones for everything. I can see the grass is green, but it's also a little purple. I don't know how to describe it. We are past the Third Dimension, it's like another sense that humans don't have. You can just feel that it's purple.

A: Like a purple filter? Energy?

E: Yes.

A: Okay. Now, tell me, is there a place that you call home in this land?

E: Just like where we are. It's not very big and there's not a lot of us. We all live together.

A: Live together where? On this planet?

E: On the planet.

A: Just on the planet?

E: It's in the field. We don't need houses, we just share energy and it's really, really different than being on Earth. Time isn't really real, and we don't really have it. I can feel it but it's so different than Earth that it's not the same way of living at all.

A: The others that are with you, do they look like you?

E: Yeah, it's about 20 of us. We all have similarities, but if we like how we look on Earth, we can choose to look like some of that. I like to have my hair and others can make flowers on our heads or bracelets from the stuff we make. You can differentiate, but we are all the same species.

A: You mentioned that you work with herbs and bring those forth to the Universe. Anything else that you do for the Universe?

E: Mostly healing in that way. People don't realize it, but it's like crystals, humans are able to understand crystals in this way. They know they like flowers, but flowers and herbs and stuff, have a vibrational pattern. Depending on where you have them and how you have them and for what, they can mean different things. Unfortunately, on Earth, in a lot of places, we planted them in certain places on Earth on purpose. Now you can get whatever you want, whenever you want. And so, people are kind of disconnected from what each one means and why it is what it is. We put them in North America for a reason or they're in East Asia for a reason because that's the healing that is all part of the attunement of that area. And like I said, when we got destroyed, we can't help as much as we used to.

A: What were you doing right before you saw them above in a spaceship?

E: Nothing. It's just normal, like usual. Just hanging out with the two of the ones that I like. We were trying to make this yellow flower; it looks like a daisy and a carnation combined. We were trying to figure out how to make it appealing but have all the properties, we were just experimenting to make a new one. So, we were just enjoying them.

A: Beautiful. Tell me what happens, keep moving that scene along.

E: We can feel them before we see them. They come in this ship and they don't get out. They're so dark. This is dense energy and it's so hard and so sterile. They just tell us, I don't know if they tell us or if we can just hear their thoughts, that they have to destroy us, and we can't be here anymore. I wasn't there, someone told me, that's why I can't see it. I was on Earth helping, then I tried to go back, and our planet was closed off (crying and emotional).

A: Okay, so you weren't there when the attack happened?

E: No, but then I went back, and it was gone. Then I found out, I don't know how, that they burned everything, and they destroyed it. It was like nuclear; everything was melting and toxic. We don't breathe, but it felt like if a human can't breathe, that's what it felt like. I couldn't come back so I just had to go to Earth.

A: Let's find out how it is that you found this information. Who told you this information? Let's find them now.

E: On Earth, the being from my planet came to me, as they found my frequency and they didn't have to come to Earth to tell me. They didn't have to take human form, but they told me what happened. I was scared because we can't be in our alien form if we don't have our planet, because we can't recharge. So, I just have to stay as a human. She said, the ones of us who were alive are trying to stay in contact, but we can't find each other. So, I just have to stay on Earth.

A: This person, does she know who it was that did this to you? Were there any features that she was able to pick up on or frequency on who they were and why?

E: They were from another planet and I don't know if they had a form, but she said they felt green and slimy. If we saw them, we would immediately repel from them. Well, I have my necklace and so she says to the ones that were there, if we hold up the necklace, then it's supposed to push their energy back to them, so we can't get harmed. But it didn't work. They studied us and they knew we would do that. So, somehow, they cracked them, and we couldn't use them. She said they were like green energy beings. They're like gross lizard things. They have a name, but I can't remember it. They're from another galaxy, but they came because they couldn't get to Earth if we kept helping Earth. We made Earth too high vibrational for them. That's why they wanted to go to Earth to get life forces, but when we were helping Earth, they couldn't go. They were really mad because then they had to delay their mission, to destroy us, before they could go to Earth.

A: When you were helping Earth, can you tell what time and space it was that you felt it was?

E: A long time ago. Like, I don't know. 20,000 years?

A: You're able to see what the people look like then, when you were assisting them, and they were high vibrational?

E: Yeah, that's when we first started working with them. They were more you know like Gods in ancient Greece and stuff. They're kind of like that, they were tall, they were powerful, they were strong. They were more clear; they looked like humans, but they didn't get sick. They didn't really have fevers or like anything like this. The longer they stayed on Earth, they progressed down more to being beings that harm themselves. When we first started working with them 20,000 years ago, it was more in communion and in harmony. They knew who we were, and they were open to it. But as time went on, we were helping all the way up until like 600 A.D.

A: Besides you all, is there anyone else who does this task of ensuring that some of the herbs were planted on Earth for their healing properties?

E: We specialize in that, but there are other people. We're so small, we just did the plants, but there are other planets or stars of people, beings that helped with the animals, some helped make the weather and others helped with the ocean. So, all the groups were in charge of certain things and my planet, we mostly helped women and when they needed help from plants. That's what we helped with. But there were people who helped with, not people, but beings, that helped with everything. If suddenly, there was a new species discovery or a new whatever, we were part of it that helped. Us but beings that were on the same mission as us.

A: Going back, you said that typically they wouldn't be able to come into your planet. Is that correct? You said something about the amulets, they did something, and they were able to crack them and go through. Can you explain that further?

E: They kept trying to go to Earth, and they would put something bad on Earth to hurt humans. And then we would go in and help them. So, then they figured out what us and all the other planets were doing. We didn't know about them yet because where we come from, there's no such thing as evil. There's just high vibrational things and we don't know how to discern between it. We didn't think we had to be on guard for anything, like those beings who came! Eventually, they figured out what my population and other ones were doing. They have advanced technology. Again, before, we didn't have to know about armor and defense and cloaking yourself. You didn't have to know about any of that, but then they did that and so that's why they could attack us. We could sense they were around our planet, but again, they weren't harming us right away. So, we didn't really understand that they could do that to us. So, we weren't on guard or seeing that they were watching how we came and went from Earth. They had already infiltrated Earth and they saw what we were doing. They studied us for way longer than we even knew they're looking at us. From there, they were able to come, and they had built up the technology to destroy our protective metal discs that we wore. Even our planet's sky and do everything... even though we never had something like that before, we thought we were just okay with that, we were just safe. Like we didn't know that evil existed.

A: You said that they were placing something on Earth. What was it that they were placing, and you were finding out about it and changing?

E: The lower vibrations humans are, the more they can control them and have their energy. They're basically what humans consider like Illuminati and lizard people now; it's like they're part of that infiltration. They make diseases or they help with some technology. The instruments that lead to humans being self-destructive, or they help bring alcohol and gluttony and even human characteristics that they can help implant into people. There's a lot of low vibrational decision-making skills. We didn't know that when we were going to help them, that they were coming from that. We went to a lot of planets, but we thought that it was just part of Earth. We didn't know that those beings were messing with them to make it bad.

A: Your friend that reached out to you? Look at her eyes. Do you recognize her soul?

E: No, she didn't come to Earth, she just stays in between. She can't go home because she was there for the attack, so she can't. She doesn't want to go to Earth. I see her as a life form, but I don't know her.

A: Would you allow her to speak to us?

E: I have to find her. She just roams around, but she can come in one second... Hold on.

A: Let's go ahead and find her. Look for her now and find her.

E: I found her.

A: Beautiful. Would you allow her to speak and tell us more?

E: Sure, yes. You can call her Cat.

A: Wonderful. Thank you. We'd love to be able to speak to Cat now.

Cat: Okay.

A: Greetings.

Cat: Hello!

A: Is this Cat?

Cat: Yes, it is.

A: Cat, it is such an honor. I love you, honor you, respect you. Thank you for speaking to us today. Thank you for also going to your friend here on Earth and giving her the messages. I was wondering if you would be able to share a little more about what happened with your planet since you were there the day of the attack? Would you be able to answer some questions?

Cat: Yes.

A: Thank you. She had mentioned that she has a purple type of glittery skin of sorts, but can change shapes? Do you look similar and are you able to do the same?

Cat: Yes, everyone from our planet looks like that. She was one of the younger beings on our planet. We don't really have age, but she was a newer one when the attack happened. She was on Earth and we chose for her to be stuck in the human cycle of Earth, while the rest of us are trying to repair the planet. So, she hasn't looked like us for a long time. The rest of us, there's still 19 of us, we're spread out, but we've been trying to repair our planet for a very long time, 1,000 years. The problem is that she's not trained for things on Earth. So, she's having a hard time adjusting. After the attack happened, our planet is our power Source, so we were cut off from it. We all had to scatter and wait out the attack. We had to call for assistance from planets that were more masculine energy heavy, because we're very, very feminine energy. We had to spend a lot of time even learning and studying this aspect. That took a long time and then from there, we had to go back to our planet a little bit at a time and send it some healing. First, we had to work with the masculine energies to set up a healing force field around it because like she was saying, we didn't know about protecting ourselves. We didn't know we had to learn this. We worked on that for a long time. Then we had to learn a new skill because we needed to give it to the Earth eventually, but we had to practice it first. We had to learn how to transmute and use our powers. We were used to a planet that was just healthy and neutral and creating loving things from there. We weren't used to a place that was toxic, dysfunctional, and just like disgusting. We had to learn how to work through the chemicals, not normal or natural, burning, and melting. We had to clear all of that negative energy. We've never done that before, so we had to learn how to do that. So, this whole time, we've been working on that, but she had to keep reincarnating on Earth because we're not ready. Got stuck in the loop and she's on Earth still, but we're still trying to do all this. We haven't been able to help as much on Earth as we used to because we are still trying to repair our planet.

A: She said that you are in an in-between space. Can you explain that further?

Cat: Yeah, so we didn't want to inhabit another planet. We met some of the other creatures who are like us, who helped with the assisting. So, these Illuminati creatures, they destroyed a lot of planets, not just ours; comets or whatever we lived on, they destroyed them. There's no word for it in English. We all just came, and we decided to rebuild together. We all, with our combined powers, created a new place that we could live in. We experimented with cleaning things up. We would go visit each of our planets to see the state of them and then come back and share with the whole group. We work together to figure out solutions for all the planets, not just ours because we all got destroyed by everything. We all want to go home, of course, but we can't. We can't yet, so we're trying to figure out how to go home. We're just living together and trying to figure it out right now.

A: Okay, and you mentioned that you ended up connecting to a male, more masculine planet. I believe you mentioned earlier, to help you with your energies. Can you explain that further?

Cat: Yeah, they were the closest one to us. So, it turns out every planet has a color. Our tone was purple and theirs was blue, more masculine. They would go to Earth and help with elemental things. They would give iron, aluminum, steel, or whatever elements that humans needed to help themselves. That's what they were in charge of. They were in the attack too and they came closest to us right away. When we first met them, it was very hard for us to communicate because they're what humans associate with masculine energy and we're very feminine energy. We could understand each other because of what happened but at the expense of getting to know each other and figuring out how their planet and system worked. That took a little bit and then we realized we could work together to alchemize to learn different tricks with them that we can do when we combined what we had together.

A: Did their planet get destroyed? Is that what you meant?

Cat: Our planet was for the flowers and their planet was for the elements. There's another planet for animals and another one for other stuff. The Illuminati monsters, when they came, they destroyed each of the planets because they wanted to cut off all our abilities. That would give them a bigger window to go in and put all this bad stuff in there. So, all the planets have been destroyed. Not destroyed, but the equivalent on the Earth if there is a radioactive place, you couldn't go into. Like nuclear waste, so it's not habitable for right now. All these creatures from these planets are trying to come together, to heal our planets, so we can go home.

A: You said there are other planets trying to come together?

Cat: Just all the ones that it happened to right now, seven together, and we're trying to heal it and we're almost there. You can visit, but it's not ready for anyone to live there yet.

A: You said there's seven of them repairing?

Cat: The seven of us are working together.

A: Seven of you as in?

Cat: Seven planets. We are one planet and we're like purple. We're closest with the blue planet and masculine energy and they do metals and stuff. Next to them is a green planet, it's kind of like a rainbow, and they help with the ocean. Things in the ocean like new species or seaweed or whatever. All the other planets, they all had beings that focused on something particular on Earth that they helped with. But we are closest with the blue planet because of proximity.

A: Okay, so when this attack happened, they attacked the seven of them?

Cat: At the same time, they destroyed all of us. We've never been attacked before; we didn't really know about it. We're kind of like experimental planets from another place to help Earth. We came from another galaxy to help Earth. We didn't really know we had to be on the defense. We just thought Earth was dense, but we didn't know it was something that was being contributed to it.

A: Do you now know about protection? You said it's changed now. You're shielding the planets now?

Cat: Yes, we had to. That was the first thing we did. Well, first, when we were all together, we had to call our galaxy we came from. We had to talk to them, kind of like parents who didn't explain that Earth could be mean to you. They kind of had to go through that with us. So, we had to do it on our own, but they helped us see how to create a forcefield and how we can protect ourselves. That's how we've been able to live together on this new thing we created because we had to practice our forcefield protective energy there. There have been other beings who have flown by us in space, they try to get a reading on who we are, but we've cloaked ourselves and we're invisible. So, we have all of that now, but we want to repair our planets before we go back. We put force fields all around them, but they're still being repaired.

A: What is the purpose of placing force fields around them? Will this be able to keep those bad aliens out?

Cat: They go back, and they don't want us to be powerful again. We want to go home. That's the main thing, we want to go back to our planets. We put the force field so if anything would start to grow back or regeneration, they wouldn't go by and shoot it and destroy it again. So, it was to stop any more damage that they could try to be doing to it.

A: If they pass by and try to shoot at it, would it not be able to go through?

Cat: We are more powerful than them, we just didn't know how to... It was a power we didn't know we had or needed to use because we had never been attacked before from where we came from.

A: Very good. You mentioned that these beings look grotesque? Or that they look slimy? Do they have a shape, you know how humans have shapes?

Cat: We just see them as like other beings. We can feel them, we don't really see them. When they're on Earth, they're like lizard creatures. They are invisible to most humans, but we can see them and they're spiky and very Reptilian.

A: Were you on the planet when they initially destroyed it?

Cat: Yes. It was horrible.

A: Would you be able to tell us what that was like? We experience that sometimes when you revisit, past situations like that even though there's no time, it allows for healing of it.

Cat: It's fine... We were sitting there. I know she thought it was her memory, but it wasn't. Two other beings were trying to make a yellow flower that was a cross between a daisy and a carnation, or daffodil, I can't remember. A laser came and hit the tree near us. We had no idea what it was or what happened. We've never felt unsafe before, so that was a new feeling. The closest thing we could gather was how humans felt when they're attacked, or something happens to them on Earth. We are in the same clear triangle, pyramid shape that you had to ride to the planet in. That's how we get around and everyone got into those and we just all left. We didn't go to Earth because we can't enter Earth unless someone calls us for a mission. So, we're just in the sky and the alien forms that were destroying our planet didn't know we had left. They just were shooting us with lasers! They were very efficient and very destructive. They'd shoot one laser, and it would explode, wiping out all of the plants and trees that we had been growing, in a matter of a few seconds. Everything was just gone and turned into mush. I don't know what the technology is, but they don't have it on Earth. It's destruction, but it's alchemized into something totally disgusting and toxic, and you can't do anything with it.

A: Does it dematerialize life?

Cat: All the plants are gone. They did it on purpose, that it didn't blow up the planet or like, destroy it because our life force is there. They knew that until we can be on our planet and touch its earth or touch the plants, that we can't get anything from it. So, they did it in a way that we're too weak to go back to Earth and we need to recharge on our planet, and we haven't been able. That's why we all have to work together with all the species and why it's taking so long. We're not at the normal power we normally have and that's why we went to the planet and her hands were purple. That was the only energy she has left on our planet. There's not enough yet, to be fully recharged for us.

A: How is it you recharge then?

Cat: All the beings from all the planets, we created a new one, and then we made an energy center. It helps us recharge, but it's not the same as our life force on our planets. We have some crystal technology and ways we can connect to it so that we can feel okay. That's part of why we can't go to Earth, part of why we can't have our full power. We just got downgraded right now as a species because we're not back on our planet yet.

A: Do you know if in the time and space of, for example of Atlantis, were you all helping at that time, or were you no longer helping at that time?

Cat: We were there, but we didn't need to help as much. We were showing them, you know, here are some things you can do with this or were helping them create on our frequency. So, in the beginning, it was just more of like living together in communal and teaching them. They were way more advanced beings then. But after Atlantis went under, and then from 15,000 years, we've had to do way more assisting. They're not at the capacity where they could learn yet like when we were in Atlantis it was a lot of us working together. We're like helping them stay alive basically. They're not ready to incorporate some of our powers into who they are, like when they were in Atlantis.

A: Okay, when this attack happened? What was she doing?

Cat: She was on Earth when it happened.

A: Why and how was she on Earth? Do you mean she was incarnated?

Cat: She was helping. Since she was in the form of a human. Because she was that she had to stay as a human because she couldn't access the frequency. It's kind of like how we can't get to our certain level of frequency again, because our planet is still not healed. To go back to that home, we've had to all as species level down because our planet isn't in full function. She had to stay on Earth as a human because she lost her connection to her power source, to be able to shapeshift again.

A: Are you all familiar with the Archangels?

Cat: Yes.

A: Is there anything else you want to share with me before I speak back to her?

Cat: She just has a hard time on Earth. It's been very hard (crying) for us to watch her because we can't help her with things because we didn't have to where we are from! It's really hard for her to trust that people are bad, and they do bad things. She needs to protect herself, but she's just not used to it because we didn't have to do that where we lived. We're just sorry we can't help her more right now.

A: Do you know if she's surrounding herself with force fields of love like you are with your planet, is she doing that right now for her human body?

Cat: Trying to, but she's so weak because she basically came to Earth with no protection at all. So, she has been susceptible to everything. Bad energy and unfortunately, we can't touch her or help her. We've been trying to send her telepathic messages but because it's been such a radical shift and adjustment for her to be a human, we're getting so lost for so long.

The Higher Self is called forth.

A: Thank you Cat for speaking to us and giving us all this wisdom. It was much needed! Thank you, love you, honor you, and respect you. I'd like to now begin the body scan. I'd like to speak to the Higher Self now.

Higher Self: Yes.

A: Thank you all for being here. Thank you for showing us a life that she really needed to see today. As she shared with me, she's had other past life regressions and has yet to find out why she was on the cycle of constant pain. Or somebody negative being harmful to her, no matter how hard she tried to break that. Would that cycle that she keeps living on Earth with abuse of different forms be connected to that life that you just showed us?

Higher Self: Yes, it is.

The Body Scans begins.

A: I would like to begin the body scan, and it seems like she would need additional help. With your permission, would we be able to call on Archangels to assist with her body scan?

Higher Self: Yes, we can.

A: Thank you. Higher Self, if you could please now connect us to the Archangels. And who would you like for us to connect to first?

Higher Self: Michael.

A: Very good. We call forth on Archangel Michael now.

AA Michael: Yes. I'm here.

A: Thank you, brother. Thank you for being here. We love you, honor you, and respect you. We are sure you've been watching already. Now, we are trying to figure out how we can assist with what we're allowed to. We have a unique situation right now, where we have that planet that's been harmed, but it's the life force of how she charges and so on. Then we have those seven planets that are still trying to rebuild. Archangel Michael, the Legion of Light, and the RA, are we able to assist them to further build upon and heal their planet? Is there something that we could do as a collective of angels?

AA Michael: No, they are doing it. It's just a process. They are still beings; they are just not unaffected by opposing forces in the Universe. They just thought they were because they weren't for so long, but they are affected by them. It's their journey to work through.

A: Okay. Is there anything that we could do at all? Can we send them love?

AA Michael: We can pray for them.

A: Beautiful. Can we send them Love-Light through prayer? Can we do that?

AA Michael: Especially by envisioning the color purple for them. It's very powerful.

A: Thank you. Michael, if you can now begin the body scan on her. Scan her from head to toe. Look for any negative energies, entities, anything that we can heal. Let me know what you find.

AA Michael: There's one in her stomach.

A: What's in her stomach?

AA Michael: Her lower stomach, an entity.

A: Michael, is that an entity or a Reptilian consciousness?

AA Michael: A Reptilian consciousness. It's very elusive. I haven't dealt with these a lot out there. It's the same species that harmed her planet. They got very good because she's the only one from her planet on Earth like this, so I haven't had to work with these before.

A: At what point did it attach itself to her stomach?

AA Michael: When she got stuck on Earth. After the planet was attacked, they knew she was on Earth, so they sent one of their beings there to control and manipulate her as part of it.

A: So, she's had this entity in her ever since the planet was destroyed?

AA Michael: Every incarnation she's been on Earth. All in other entities, but this time, it's the source.

A: At this point, roughly how many incarnations has she had to cycle on Earth since her planet was destroyed?

AA Michael: Sixty-seven.

A: What is it doing to her by being there?

AA Michael: It's in her womb and it's like 'Rosemary's Baby,'[7] the possessed one. It's sucking all her life force, and this is why there's so much abuse and sexual assault. Because the power source of all the evil is right there. So, this is the evil that she attracts because it's in her body this way.

A: Can you go ahead and place it in alchemy symbols now, Archangel Michael?

AA Michael: Yes.

A: Thank you. Am I able to speak to this Reptilian?

AA Michael: Yes.

A: Okay, very good. Is it contained now?

AA Michael: Yes.

A: Are there any other of these consciousnesses in her, besides this one? Scan her please.

AA Michael: It's the same being, but it's in her chest too. I have to, it separated itself, so it's in her chest. I have to put it in with the other one.

A: Okay, so you're going to put it closer together?

AA Michael: Yes, and put them all in the symbols.

---

[7] Referencing the 1968 psychological horror movie.

A: Scan her body to make sure there's no other Reptilian consciousness. You know they could be sneaky. We want to make sure we don't miss any.

AA Michael: No, that's it.

A: Why was it in her chest?

AA Michael: It was on her heart.

A: What was the purpose to that and what was it causing her?

AA Michael: It was able to convince her not to trust her intuition. When someone was going to harm her, it convinced her that people aren't actually evil. It was doing an evil thing by convincing her that evil wasn't real so she would have sympathy and feel sorry for men who were abusing and harming her, instead of standing up for herself. When she's low energy like this and her aura is open, she thinks she can't connect to Cat and these beings from her planet.

A: Does this Reptilian consciousness have a body somewhere else?

AA Michael: No. It could have a body, but it abandoned it to live in her.

A: Now that it's contained, Archangel Michael, I'd like to speak to that Reptilian there. If he could please come up now, please. Let me speak to you now. Greetings.

Reptilian: Hello.

A: Thank you for speaking to us. I love you, honor you, and respect you. May I ask you questions, please?

Reptilian: Yes.

A: Thank you. We understand that you've been there for a good number of lifetimes in her human body and what you have been causing onto her. If I can ask, how do you work within her body? Is that something that brings fulfillment to you?

Reptilian: It is. I live on evil energy and to stay alive, I have to have these things.

A: Okay. That is your food source? Is that what you're saying?

Reptilian: If I didn't need it then I couldn't control her. We were bound when she got stuck on Earth. We knew she was on Earth when we attacked the planet. Part of what happened is that she was Earthbound as a human and I merged with her in that moment. So, she's never not incarnated with me.

A: Did you become part of her and who she is? Is that what you're saying?

Reptilian: We're separate beings. But since she's not fully human, she thinks this is normal to have when you're on Earth. She thinks it's normal to be subjected to abuse, assault, and alcoholism. She can't create a reality that doesn't have it because she's not of Earth; and she can't exist without these things because I've always been present to create them as part of her reality.

A: Thank you for your honesty. Is there a contract that was created when you entered her body?

Reptilian: Not a contract, we just decided because we don't want them to get their planet back, obviously, and we can keep them lower. Drinking, doing drugs, or with men who are abusing her - then she can't hear her people advising her as long as I'm here. Then we have some leverage to maintain.

A: Are you implying that if she were to start listening and being strongly connected to them, that would help them become stronger?

Reptilian: Yes, because there's only 20 of them. They could have a million, but there's only 20. They only need 20 pieces to be powerful and they're missing one from her.

A: I understand that you've been doing this for a long time. Would you be able to share with us who it was that advised you all to go shoot at them? Was that your own decision or from somewhere else?

Reptilian: It was our leader. I'm not as high up as him, so I don't really know the specifics. Basically, we're an army and we got direction from a higher-up force, from another galaxy. We're kind of like a filter for them. We siphon pain energy to live and then that being siphons energy from us. So, we were instructed to survive off destruction, pain, and evil. This planet, as Cat told you, they're not used to that. They don't understand it. The more we're able to do that, it's like an extra dose because they weren't even prepared that that was even real. They were the most ideal beings to do that to because there was a shock value on top of it. We didn't know that she would get stuck on Earth, but she did, and they chose to fuse me with her. If she is more powerful and can be a powerful being and she can help the Earth move into the place it needs to be in, then all the good she does on Earth is transmuted into her beings on their planets. And if I can keep blocking that, then I'm going to keep doing that!

A: Okay, now I know you've been doing this for a long time. As you know, the Earth is ascending and at this point, there is no stopping it. It has reached its capacity of a positive timeline, positive Ascension, for the future. Lower density entities like you, and not only on Earth but the whole construct in the Universe, is leveling up. You can say, going up in Dimension and frequencies. So, when this happens, there's going to be a purification that will happen. Lower density entities like you, who are parasitic inside people or are draining on people's lights, will be transmuted straight back to the Source. What we're looking to do is assist you all who have been stuck in this negative polarized role for such a long time. To help you Ascend out into a positive polarization, no longer having to play this role. Would you allow us to assist you today so that you can incarnate or transcend somewhere else into a positive polarization where you no longer have to feed off of light, instead, you can create your own light? You will no longer have to feed off of these different pains, sorrows, and abuse. Instead, you can be your own creator being.

Reptilian: Okay.

A: Beautiful. We're going to assist you in spreading the Love-Light within you, finding it, and spreading it. Making sure that every part that belongs to you and not to her. Spread it to all light… If you can, let us know once you are all light.

Positive Polarized Reptilian: Okay.

A: Wonderful. Go ahead and start releasing yourself. Release yourself out of her body. Michael, can you connect to Archangel Azrael so he can assist him?

AA Michael: He's here.

A: Thank you. Azrael, if you can please help him pull himself out of her body and keep him there once he's fully out? Let us know once he's fully out. While he's pulling himself out, Michael, can you connect us to Yeshua/Jesus?

AA Michael: Yes.

A: Good. If we could connect to Yeshua now, please?

Yeshua: Yes.

A: Thank you, Yeshua. Your energy is so beautiful, thank you for being here. If you could please start healing those areas within her body that the Reptilian was attached to. I know her chest and also her stomach area. Anywhere else that it affected her?

Yeshua: Her womb.

A: Could we start healing that now, please. Fill it in with Love-Light, thank you, Yeshua. Michael, this Reptilian as it's coming out and as you're keeping it there, I'd like to speak to it before it goes. For now, did it have anything attached to it? Did it have any implants, hooks, or portals within her body?

AA Michael: It was plugged into her veins. It was very, very emerged within her being, like her physical body also.

A: Was it integrated into her DNA?

AA Michael: Yes.

A: Can we start using the symbols in repairing her DNA structure?

AA Michael: Yes.

A: Good. We're neutralizing, transmuting, any negative fractalization that it attached itself. We're only going to leave the organic of what's meant to be of her DNA structure, please. As well as her veins, we're going through her whole body and transmuting out any negativity that influenced her whole system. Do you need any Phoenix Fire for that?

AA Michael: Please.

A: Good, using the Phoenix Fire now throughout her whole body... Michael, is it out yet?

AA Michael: Almost.

A: Okay. Let me know once it's fully out.

AA Michael: Okay.

A: Now that you are out if I can ask, is there a message that you have for her before you go?

Positive Polarized Reptilian: I'll miss her, and she'll miss me, because she's never not lived without me. But she can be her own being now.

A: Beautiful. Thank you for accepting this as well. Before you go, do you think that it would be possible to speak to your other partners or companions that are doing this? To see if there's any of them that would like to no longer have to play this role anymore?

Positive Polarized Reptilian: Yes, I'll give you to our General.

A: Very good. Archangel Michael, if you could connect us now to their General. Connect us safely to their General.

Reptilian General: Here.

A: Greetings. Thank you for speaking to us. Love you, honor you, and respect you. May I ask you questions, please?

Reptilian General: Yes.

A: Were you able to take notice of what just happened with the Reptilian that was in her body?

Reptilian General: Yes. I could feel it.

A: Okay. Since you're able to feel it, do you see how beautiful and grand it is for that soul that has accepted this now?

Reptilian General: Yes.

A: I know that you all have been playing this role for a long time, you know, taking orders from others or causing havoc and pain to others. Just as you saw him transform, this possibility is for you as well, and whoever is with you or under you that will allow for this to happen now. We'd love to be able to rid you and release you from no longer having to play this role anymore so that you can keep your consciousness and experiences gained throughout. And then, you can use that wisdom and be a positively polarized being, instead, creating your own light. Will you allow for us to aid you in this manner?

Reptilian General: Yes.

A: Beautiful. How many are with you? How many of them will allow for this as well, please?

Reptilian General: Forty.

A: Archangel Michael, can you call forth on the Legion of Archangels and the Angels assisting with helping them spread their Love-Light now?

AA Michael: Yes.

A: Where is it that you all are located?

Reptilian General: Who? Me? The lizard?

A: Yes, the 40 of you. Where are you located?

Reptilian General: We don't exist on Earth. We are beyond human measure. So, we can kind of move back and forth. We're all telepathically connected so we saw what was happening with the one even though we weren't here until you called me here. We're all around.

A: Are you on a planet or a ship or just somewhere?

Reptilian General: We're on Earth. We're some of the lower levels of the destruction. We were the ones who've been sent to collect pain from Earth, to send to our leaders, who then send to their leaders. We're kind of on the lower end of everything.

A: You are on Earth, you said? Say that again.

Reptilian General: We're on Earth, we're beings that can shapeshift into humans, but usually we don't have to. We're just unseen influences for negative decisions for people.

A: Okay, so you are on the Earthly plane, the 40 of you?

Reptilian General: Yes.

A: Alright. So, we're having the Angels here sending Love-Light now, all of us. If all of you could continue to spread your Love-Light through the essence that you are there as the lizard being. Spread to all Love-Light, releasing yourself from this role. Let us know once all 40 of you are Love-Light... Can you tell me, there was one of you attached to her body, are there any of you who have consciousness attached to other humans?

Reptilian General: Yes.

A: How many more are you attached to?

Reptilian General: Twelve.

A: Archangel Michael, brother, if you can find those 12 humans and ask their Higher Selves if they will allow for us to remove those consciousnesses that they've attached?

AA Michael: They already came out.

A: Michael, help them bring them back to those 20 so that they can make themselves whole once more. And then those humans, Yeshua, brother, if you and the Christ consciousness can start filling in Love-Light to the 12 that had those consciousnesses. Thank you... Let me speak back to the General there. Why is it that you picked those 12? Is there a reason?

Reptilian General: They were low vibrational enough that we could go in them. Elizabeth was the most important to get and these other 12 were just people who would open their aura or who we could just get to them easier. They were just an easy life force to enter. They attached and resisted leaving them.

A: Did they also provide you with a source of food or replenishment?

Reptilian General: Life force, because they were in a lot of pain. They were a lot of drug addicts or alcoholics. We stayed with this one, but the other 12, they kind of moved between humans. Whoever was in a lot of pain, they could just enter them.

A: Let us know once all of you are all light.

Positive Polarized Reptilian General: They are all light now.

A: Beautiful. Do you all have a message for her or humanity now that you've gone from such an extreme to light?

Positive Polarized Reptilian General: We just didn't know what we were doing. But it doesn't mean that we were allowed to be able to do it.

A: Thank you. Now that you are of light, would you be able to share with us more as far as who gave you direction on what you needed to do?

Positive Polarized Reptilian General: They are higher beings than us. As I said, who we were feeding energy for them. They kind of created us and used us to fulfill their wishes. But we didn't know that we didn't have to do it. We've been doing this for so long, that we just kept doing it, and it was an easy way for us to get power. So, we just kept doing it.

A: Are you able to share with us a little bit more about who these higher-ups would be?

Positive Polarized Reptilian General: They don't share that much with me, but they're Reptilian also, in higher forms. They have some negotiations with the powers that be to be able to experiment on Earth. The plan is that they took more than what they said they would be doing. For example, we would practice with one little plague or one little thing, but instead, we took over everything and made total destruction. And we've just kind of been the ones who've been able to do that for them. The powers that be are all the positive forces in the Universe that have been working to combat this for a really long time. The time is now to do it.

A: Wonderful. Thank you for allowing us to assist you and all your honesty. Is there anything else you would like to say before you go?

Positive Polarized Reptilian General: Thank you. We're ready to leave now.

A: Wonderful. Archangel Azrael and your Legion, if you could all please guide all of these positive polarized new beings there, guide them to where they're meant to go. Ensure please that none of them get tricked along the way. And can I speak to Azrael, please?

AA Azrael: Yes.

A: Thank you, brother, for being here. Azrael, where is it that you're taking them?

AA Azrael: We're going to a Heaven realm.

A: Good and why the Heaven realm?

AA Azrael: They're beings that got taken advantage of, so they need time to reflect with the powers that be and all that is. See the damage they've done and decide how they can help repair it. These beings aren't evil. They were just used for evil. So, they need a break from all this. They're not self-aware and self-reliant yet. So, they need to be in a pure light space to be able to do this.

A: Wonderful. Well, our infinite love to them! We thank them, honor them, love, and respect them. Thank you. And thank you, Azrael, for your assistance.

AA Azrael: Thank you.

A: If I could please speak back now to Michael. Michael, if you could continue to scan her body. I want to make sure we do not miss anything. I know you scanned her for Reptilians but scan her now for any kind of entity please. Let me know if you find any other ones.

AA Michael: There's a hook, like an anchor.

A: There's a hook where?

AA Michael: In her lower abdomen, where her female organs are.

A: We are working on the Phoenix Fire throughout her body transmuting what it merged into her. Can we use the Phoenix Fire to transmute the hook out of her sacral area?

AA Michael: Yes, please.

A: Okay, very good. Using the Phoenix Fire. Are there any other kinds of negative technology within her? Scan her and let me know if you find anything else.

AA Michael: Her neck.

A: What's going on with her neck?

AA Michael: There's a bolt, to keep her from looking. It symbolically limits her range to be able to see, think, and move her own head. Feels like a thing that keeps her stuck. They're bolts, like Frankenstein, but across the whole neck. It's very highly advanced.

A: Michael, how can we remove this from her neck?

AA Michael: We can use Phoenix Fire, also.

A: Okay, using Phoenix Fire there as well. How's her DNA? How's that looking?

AA Michael: Clear. It's flowing. It's like an Angelic highway. Like very, very open.

A: Okay, so we're working on the hook and the rod. Let's continue scanning her. Is there any other type of non-organic negative technology in her?

AA Michael: There's chains on her feet and her wrists.

A: Were these all connected to those beings?

AA Michael: Yes.

A: Can we go ahead and transmute those out for her, using Phoenix Fire on them?

AA Michael: Yes.

A: Tell me, what was that causing her?

AA Michael: Her alien life form could feel them, and they were invisible to her Earth body. But energetically, they were making her feel like a slave and trapped. So, the hook has an anchor to feel like she's stuck on Earth so that she can't reach her Higher Self or alien community. The goal was to stop her neck from looking around and feeling clear. On her wrists and ankles were for slave mentality, to keep her self-esteem low and help her feel stuck.

A: Does she have anything else?

AA Michael: No.

A: As we transmute those out, let's scan the rest of her body. We want to make sure that her sacral chakra is repaired fully, please... She also mentioned that sometimes she gets vaginal pain. Can we heal that, so she no longer has that anymore?

AA Michael: Sure. The Reptilian consciousness is gone now.

A: Okay, so will she no longer have this?

AA Michael: No, she won't.

A: Beautiful. Okay, she says sometimes she gets lower back pain. What's the cause of that?

AA Michael: It's where the hook was, across the whole body.

A: How about the acne she gets around her waist?

AA Michael: Same thing, from the Reptilian consciousness. It had a lot of ways to control how she saw herself. There were a lot of tactics and one of them was that if he could create acne or make her feel unattractive, then she would also not feel confident within herself. That entity is gone.

A: Also, there is facial hair. Was that connected to that too?

AA Michael: You can get it lasered off and it won't come back.

A: Okay, good. And if we could just balance out her hormone levels, please.

AA Michael: Yes.

A: Thank you. If we could help her remove that cycle of sexual abuse, please?

AA Michael: Yes.

A: Thank you. Was this connected to the sabotage around not being able to feel like she could be healthy and strong? Sometimes she got thinner, then she would be sabotaged so she can perhaps, not be as thin?

AA Michael: It was all voices of the Reptilian consciousness. He controlled and it was the negative voice that was also her voice. It wasn't just outside forces; it was coming from inside. It was hard for her to distinguish between her voice and his voice. That's why she felt like something was wrong with her internally because he was part of her.

A: Okay, very good. How is her auric field? Does it need any healing or repair? If you can start that now, please. Just let me know once the things that you're removing are out... Does she need any age regression?

AA Michael: Yes.

A: How many years can you do?

AA Michael: Twenty.

A: Okay, good. If you could repair her body by 20 years, please. Can you scan her chakras? How do they look? Do they need any healing?

AA Michael: Her crown chakra. The purple one.

A: Yes, if we can go ahead and start healing that for her now, please. I noticed that when we were doing the energy healing, her crown felt off like it was not where it was meant to be. So, I remember the Higher Self going in and placing it back in place. Okay, so if we could just do the repair there. Thank you. Any other chakras?

AA Michael: Root chakra.

A: What's going on there?

AA Michael: She thinks being grounded into the Earth means pain. So, she never fully relaxes into being grounded. We need to have her root chakra be healthy and be hers.

A: Let's start healing that for her now, please. Does she need her third eye opened up more?

AA Michael: Yes.

A: If you could start doing that organic process as the Higher Self allows for that, and also expanding her heart please. If you can scan her for any negative cords, does she have any?

AA Michael: A few left over.

A: If we can go ahead and cut or transmute them, healing whatever needs to be done, please.

AA Michael: On her arms, I can just cut them off.

A: Wonderful, thank you. Don't leave any negative cords, please. Alright, one more time, scan her for any negative implants, hooks, and portals, please.

AA Michael: Everything is gone.

A: Does she have any fragmented soul pieces that need to be returned back to her?

AA Michael: Yes.

A: Michael, how many are there?

AA Michael: Two.

A: Can you find them and bring them back to Yeshua and the Higher Self, so that they could start repairing and making the soul whole once more?

AA Michael: Yes.

A: When did the two fragments come off of her?

AA Michael: When she first came to Earth, she was shapeshifting fully from an alien to a human. They got replaced by the Reptilian consciousness, so she's never had her full soul.

A: Okay. So, we're making that organic back to what she was meant to be. Does she have any contracts that we can remove for her that no longer serve her for her highest good?

AA Michael: Yes.

A: Can we go ahead and remove those for her with the Higher Self's permission?

AA Michael: Yes.

A: Thank you. What were those contracts for?

AA Michael: Taking care of men who won't take care of themselves.

A: Okay, yes, we don't need that anymore! I know that you took us to the life where she had trauma from losing her planet. Can we start healing that trauma for her now?

AA Michael: Yes.

A: Thank you. Further in the DNA reprogramming, anything that's no longer serving her, any kind of negative programming, just reprogram her as her Higher Self allows please. The list is now completed. Michael, is there anything else that you would like to assist with before I speak back to her Higher Self?

AA Michael: No, she's okay now.

A: Can you tell us, Michael, removing these beings that harmed the seven planets, what has this done for this reality or this existence of what happened to them?

AA Michael: It's a final piece that they felt like they couldn't leave. They are very powerful beings, but they haven't learned how to alchemize into Earth and that kind of merged with Earth. So, that was their biggest block, these lizard beings. They had that piece of the puzzle and these aliens who wanted to do good, didn't have it. And so now that we released some of the alien beings, they're able to connect back into Earth. It was like an invisible block that they couldn't get through.

A: That's beautiful. Thank you to everyone who assisted with that tremendous healing. Our infinite love to those beings who suffered from this attack. May you continue to grow together and work together. Michael, can I please speak back to her Higher Self now?

AA Michael: Yes.

A: Thank you, Michael, Azrael, Yeshua, and anyone else who assisted today with the beautiful healing. We love you, honor you, and respect you. Thank you. Higher Self? Is there a name that you go by?

Higher Self: No.

A: She wanted to know who her soul group/galactic family was. Would that be the planet that you showed her?

Higher Self: Yes.

A: She also wants to know; she's been on that cycle of negative masculine harming her. Is there ever going to be a partner that she will come into union with that will no longer do this to her?

Higher Self: She just needs to relax and remember she has a choice also. That her feelings matter, she doesn't have to rush it. If you can just calm down, they will come. And it's okay that you're 30 and you're here. Don't compare it to everything else that's on Earth.

A: We know that on the planet, she worked with the plants and flowers, is there any kind of advice you could give her about this and how she can assist here on Earth?

Higher Self: Yes. She can't be afraid of merging two worlds that don't feel like they belong together. She hasn't had any examples of how she can do the work she wants to do. But that's because she's here to do it and she didn't have a chance in her previous lifetimes. She found small ways. But now is the chance to be fully merging the energetic, and this beautiful power she had from the purple planet, into Earth. People won't even notice; it won't seem weird to them. She'll just be able to do it. She can just touch people and fix their chakras, or she can offer plant healing; whatever flowers, herbs, or feels like the intuitive thing to give to people. She can do it because her healing strength will be behind it. And because her planet can't come back to Earth yet, they're all working through her. So, she doesn't just have her power, she has everyone else's. To be this conduit of merging these things is what she's supposed to do. Just trust, it doesn't have to make sense. Every time she doubted her intuition, that was the Reptilian consciousness in her stomach. That's why she always felt bloated and out of place there, but it's gone now. So, just trusting that whatever setting she enters, she will bring healing power. Whatever form she feels called to do. Some groups she'll say, "okay, everyone, go pick a flower." In some groups, she'll do energy work. Wherever she goes, whatever type of healing comes through her, she just needs to trust it because it's not just her power. It's the whole purple planet and all their allies coming through her as well because they're still blocked off from coming to Earth.

A: Wonderful. So, they'll be channeling and directing her and guiding her throughout life?

Higher Self: Yes.

A: Now that she no longer has these infringements stopping her, she'll be able to hear them more clearly?

Higher Self: Yes, and she won't feel the need to question them or have faith in logic or anything like that. All of that was tricks from the Reptilian consciousness to make her be small so they could feed off her pain because she is very powerful since she's an alien consciousness in the human body.

A: Okay, wonderful. Alright, she has one more question. She says she's attracted to the Islam religion. Why is she attracted to it, but she believes in reincarnation and things like that?

Higher Self: It's a way for her to relate to people in this lifetime. It's an experiment for her. It can help her understand new ways that people feel healed and can connect her on a soul level to the people she's meant to work with. So, it's okay, it's part of her path. It can coexist with her being an alien. It's just the form she needs to take right now, to serve the people she needs to serve. So, it's okay.

A: At this point, I've asked all the questions, we've done all the healing, is there anything else that I could have asked that I haven't?

Higher Self: No.

A: Beautiful. Thank you, Higher Self. Thank you, Cat for speaking to us earlier as well and giving us information that was needed. Would you allow for us to share her session?

Higher Self: Yes.

A: Thank you for that. I think it's needed because just like her planet of the herbs was destroyed, those other six planets, would they also have incarnations here?

Higher Self: No, but there are people who are connected to those planets, who specifically need their guidance.

A: Wonderful. Good. Anything else Higher Self before I bring her back?

Higher Self: No.

A: It truly has been an honor to work with you today. Thank you for bringing her to me, and everyone who assisted. I love you, honor you, and respect you. May I bring her back?

Higher Self: Yes. Thank you.

A: Thank you!

END OF SESSION

--------------<◇>--------------

Wow, this was a beautiful session with an immensity of experience, knowledge, and understanding as to why someone would go through each incarnation with such a build-up of trauma and negative karma on Earth. What if we had a consciousness like that Reptilian inside of us, integrated into us, acting as part of our soul, and how would that influence our everyday choices? As she described it best, it would feel like having 'Rosemary's Baby' inside. How would one know clearly which are the best choices to make for our highest path? Imagine the confusion with different voices going off in our head. Which voice would we choose to listen to?

In this example, the Reptilian inside of her was the reason why she seemed stuck in a repeated cycle of relationships, where each one of them abused her physically or sexually over and over. She would end a relationship and be very cautious with invocations to not end up with the same archetype of a narcissistic boyfriend, but yet she would find herself there once more. These partners would play their negative polarized role of draining on her energy and using her creational energy to feed the rest of the collective Reptilians, including supplying their bosses above them with feedings as well. This helps us understand the deeply repeated inverted cycles that we seem stuck in, no matter how hard we try to break free from. It is not until we locate the root to the problem, acknowledge, understand and heal it, then we are finally able to break free organically from that negative cycle. Now that this has been cleared, what a relief and growth she must be experiencing now with only having her organic consciousness maneuvering her vessel. However, we must honor the time after our A.U.R.A, Hypnosis Healing session that there is still a natural process the mind, body and soul transition and go through once the removal of these inorganics within us have taken place.

This session powerfully demonstrates the importance of shielding, and it showed us what happened to these beautiful benevolent beings and their planets when they were not protected by force fields. They then experienced the tragic destruction of their home planet, and the impact it had on their own powers as they no longer could recharge. It is very similar to our experience here on Earth, when we feel disconnected from Mother Earth, not knowing how to ground in her energy properly to recharge ourselves. Imagine floating in the in-between space for 1000 years as our home planet is still being cleared and rebuilt slowly. We would feel disoriented, and like something very deep inside is missing. When someone feels these types of emotions, these overpower the light and divine reason within us. We would become lost to who we truly are within our organic divinity as Elizabeth did by not having her home planet anymore. In a Third Dimensional world as this, she became more so of this environment, integrating further with the Inverted A.I. Matrix false programming, forgetting who she once was.

This is a beautiful example of negatively polarized Reptilians that have been following orders as long as their memory allows to remember, that then choose to transform to be of the light. All that contain light within, no matter how small the spark of light is, can always redeem themselves, for the light is all that is needed for this redemption and forgiveness. When they were negatively polarized, the pain that they caused her and the life on the seven planets was immense. I can feel how much it affected Earth's positive timeline by the organic power and knowledge of these planets being harmed. How much this put humanity's evolution back by not having these clear teachings of the elements that give us life and aid us in maintaining balance through forms of natural alchemy within and all around us. After all, the elements are what provide us with the physical support we need on Earth, as the energies of infinite healing connect to each element.

Our infinite gratitude and love to the seven planets from other Universes who volunteered to assist Earth, not knowing the extent to the extremity that doing so would bring to their souls and soul families. In Chapter 31 ('Looking Glass Technology'), all will make sense to us, as we find out who these bosses were who were giving orders to the Reptilians, and how they were able to surprise attack these planets and others. Why it is that we would not know of the possibilities of these infringements. May these seven planets continue to find the support from our Universe in order to build themselves back to what they once were, strong and powerful beings. For as they do so, so do we, them being some of our direct teachers of the natural elements that consist of Mother Earth. We humbly bow to you now. Our infinite love to you dear sister, Elizabeth. How brave and beautiful you all truly are!

**"A Spiritual Alchemist has mastered thy even exchange of thy elements!
How to wield thy fire, transmuting the dark within into light.
How to use thy water within thy vessel, shifting it to what requires healing.
How to whisper to thy wind, in releasing what no longer serves within.
How to connect to thy land with thy seed of thy consciousness, thy heart!"
~AuroRa**

-------------<◇>-------------

8

FOUR RA GUARDIANS HEAL THOUSANDS OF ENTITIES

Session #129: Recorded in March 2019.

This online A.U.R.A. Hypnosis Healing session was pivotal for the growth of A.U.R.A. Hypnosis Healing Technique as it was the first time, we discovered that we could help heal and remove 1,000's of entities at a time. Archangel Ariel/Area has been a strong communicator to us through A.U.R.A. Hypnosis Healing sessions, by bringing forth clear knowledge for the collective through different clients whose Higher Self is Ariel/Area.

In this past life journey, TeRa finds herself in the time of Nefertiti in Egypt. What happened in this time of Reign of Light? Experience one of the most inspirational healings in the collective of humanity as four Guardians with their sound instruments heal and remove 1,000's of entities from Earth and its people. Who is the RA Collective and what is their connection to Source? The RA Collective/Guardians/Galactics speak to Light Workers, their role, awareness, how soul replacements occur in people on Earth.

In this inspiring session we learn more about timelines, energy update, solar waves, and the Schumann Resonance. What is the process of how Reptilians enter people's consciousness and bodies? Guidance to aid us in maintaining our own Fifth-Dimensional organic timelines. Why what we eat matters very much. Come witness a powerful A.U.R.A. session of a resilient mother being able to assist the healing of her beloved daughters, by connecting to their Higher Selves in this session!

-------------<◇>-------------

**"It is our heart. There is strength in the heart, there is power.
And I have been able to create my heart into a powerful shield if you will, a protector of Love. I expand the Universe with Love."
-Archangel Michael**

**"That sacred beautiful spinning vortex in that heart. It sends a message out more than our words can, deeper than what we realize."
-The RA Collective**

-------------<◇>-------------

A: [Aurora] You see palm trees blowing in the wind. Have you landed on the ground yet?
T: [TeRa] Yes.
A: Take a look at yourself, do you feel like you have a body?
T: Yes.
A: Are you wearing anything on your feet?
T: Sandals.
A: How many toes do you have?
T: Ten.

A: Look at your hands, how many fingers do you have?

T: I changed.

A: What did you change into?

T: My feet are talons.

A: How about your hands?

T: I don't see them.

A: Do you feel that you have arms?

T: They are heavy and long.

A: Extend them out and look at them. How do they look?

T: They are wings!

A: Describe your wings to me.

T: Round with speckles, white speckles. They're long.

A: Are you wearing any clothing?

T: No.

A: Are you wearing any jewelry pieces?

T: On my forehead. It's a golden crown.

A: Describe it to me. Do you see any symbols, any shapes, any gems on it?

T: It has a snake coming out, it is golden. Simple yet powerful.

A: Are there any crystals on this crown?

T: There is a jewel, kind of like a diamond in the middle of the snake, its forehead.

A: Is there anything else? Any other crystals on this crown?

T: No.

A: We are able to speak to the consciousness of this crown as well as the crystal there within the snake. Will you allow for this consciousness to speak through you?

T: Yes.

A: If we could speak with the consciousness within the crown and the crystal now, please?

Crystal Crown Consciousness: Yes?

A: Greetings. Thank you for greeting us. May I ask you questions, please?

Crystal Crown Consciousness: We are here.

A: Wonderful, thank you. If I could continue speaking to the energy in the crown, what is your connection towards TeRa and do you have a message for her?

Crystal Crown Consciousness: I am the energy she feels inside. I am... she knows. I would like for her to understand why.

A: Why what?

Crystal Crown Consciousness: Why this part of me is inside her. It is partly why she has become what she has become. She connects to it. She remembers. And I am here, she feels it. Sometimes she denies me. I understand and I love her. She is awakening, and every time she signs her name, she says who I am, and she knows it.

A: Who are you?

RA: I am RA.

A: Welcome, I love you dearly, and thank you for being here.

RA: And I love you. Thank you.

A: RA, if you could just ensure that we don't get disconnected again, put on those force fields again, please thank you. Tell us, why are you connected to her as RA?

RA: She was awakening, and I was part of that. And she fell. She's afraid to come back.

A: She's afraid to come back to where?

RA: Awakening, to remembering. Oh, it was so long ago that she fell, doesn't she know?! She's changed, she's different, she's got new beginnings. She remembered her when she first got in here. And I changed her into me at that moment to remember, to reconnect.

A: Yes, so are you part of what you showed, of the bird?

RA: Yes.

A: Now is this a bird that is a humanoid type of shape, or an animal?

RA: It is both.

A: Tell us, why is it that you chose this form to show her?

RA: It is powerful, it reminds her that she is free. She has journeyed as a bird. It is how she flies. It's part of who she is, where she came from. She forgets.

A: Thank you, we are honored that today perhaps she shall remember some of who she is.

RA: I had to show her, so she would trust, and she trusts more now.

A: Beautiful. You as RA, would we also call you like the RA Collective?

RA: Yes.

A: How about, would you also be called, 'The Galactic Confederation'? Are you the same?

RA: The same yet different. Different. I have different journeys to take.

A: Are you in charge of overseeing the cluster, our Universe?

RA: Yes, I see a great many things.

A: Would you also be called Guardians?

RA: Yes, our wings protect many. We are more than one.

A: Yes. Do you all have wings?

RA: No, most do, not all, we are all different.

A: Is that a multitude of races?

RA: Yes.

A: What is your connection to the Seraphim, the Elohim Angels?

RA: The Elohim, call my heart. The Seraphim, call my mind.

A: Do you mean that they are part of you?

RA: More of, I am a part of them.

A: Oh, beautiful!

RA: I'm gathering parts that have fallen.

A: Can you tell us more about those parts?

RA: TeRa is one of them. She's more of a guide than she realizes. Many parts are in training that I gave myself to, gave my energy to, gave my knowledge to. And they scattered and fell. And that is okay, they needed to. They are gathering together again.

A: When you say they fell, do you mean like, is this a choice?

RA: They didn't complete their mission, their initiation, their journey. They chose otherwise, they went dark. Not dark evil but dark, they got lost.

A: Yes, and TeRa is one of those that are achieving the light once more?

RA: Yes. We're so grateful when she finally felt it and opened up.

A: Can you tell her a little more about how it was that she lost herself, and are you talking about just this life or in past times in history of her existence?

RA: It was when she was in Egypt.

A: What happened then, can you share that story with her, please?

RA: She's seeing it now, she's walking, it was when she was pregnant, and they took the baby from her. And the baby was powerful. (crying)

A: Who was she?

RA: She denies it, she denies it. She's a queen.

A: She was a queen?

RA: Yes. She was so small, so small yet powerful.

A: Powerful how?

RA: She was awakening, she was bringing into life the next energy. This next energy was changing the world and others did not want to see that happen. They cut it right out of her.

She's closed her heart to love and yet it's so big it opens anyways. She didn't make it much longer after that.

A: After they took her baby?

RA: Only a couple of years, but in torment and anguish. She would not feel again.

A: If I may ask since she was the queen, you could say she would be somewhat in charge in a sense or a leader. Why is it that they were able to take her baby from her?

RA: She wasn't a powerful queen. She was a child. She was part of the...she was a child. She was a child bride.

A: She was a child herself?

RA: It was the advisors to the child king and queen that took away everything.

A: Was the baby a boy or a girl?

RA: It was a boy.

A: So, after they took her baby away, what did she end up doing in the kingdom?

RA: She was under their control. They killed her husband. She reached out begging for others to help her in other kingdoms, they were all silent. When they destroyed her and locked her in a cave she just, that's where we took her to come back. It's time to come back.

A: What did they do with the little boy?

RA: He wasn't developed, they just took him out and he died. She was only seven months along.

A: What was the purpose of that, did they use the baby for something?

RA: Just to stop the power that was happening, to be in control for the next, (sigh) the next times, frames of time, they have been in control. They are losing that control; we are coming back. They stopped a lot of power from coming into the world that would have stopped their power and control. She wasn't the only one. I lost so many.

A: Were they controlled would you say, by the negative forces?

RA: Yes, very negative forces, the ones that desire the power for their own good instead of for everybody. They were trained in the power and knew how to use it, and their hearts turned black. And it was their desire to snuff out the light. And did so beautifully.

A: When Egypt was in reign, is this what happened often or the majority of the time? When the light would come in to try to perhaps awaken or bring forth light in that existence, would they like you said, snuff out, remove the light?

RA: Yes. Everywhere we've had our power stages, our pyramid power, our power, they've destroyed them. They destroyed so many lights. Not forever, just for a very long time.

A: Yes. Would you say that this was off and on during the whole time period of Egypt or was it the mid part of Egypt time or…?

RA: It was more of the mid and the last. It took them a long time to gain that power. But when they did, everything switched and changed. We gained power back for a little while. This was when we gained the power back before TeRa was born at this moment as a queen and she was part of the journey to keep it. Everyone was killed off, destroyed. They put in place who they needed to be in place.

A: Yes. It sounds a little similar to how the system is now, how they place people in charge, who they want in charge.

RA: Yes, we have other ways around that now. It will be better.

A: What are some of the ways we have around that? Can you share that?

RA: We have gone secret and silent. Awakening people quietly, like through you. Quietly opening them up, awakening them, placing them around the grid. Their beautiful lights opening those grids. And before they know it, they'll be in power again without the fear. We've had to learn so much, all of these little lights that are opening. They have been followed by the same power over and over again.

A: Yes, the same power you mean trying to oppress them?

RA: Yes. Yes, it's not their fault. And they are learning, they are seeing them for who they are and loving from it.

A: Going back to Egypt once more; thank you for that information. Of the king and queen, the people that were running it, were they of this planet, or are they of another?

RA: They were of another planet, they're beautiful. They did not look the same as others, but they showed it and they allowed it.

A: The king and queen you're talking about?

RA: The king and queen.

A: The ones that got murdered you mean?

RA: Yes, they changed Egypt.

A: They changed Egypt, hmm. And did they have names?

RA: My queen Nefertiti yes, Akhenaten, Tutankhamun.

A: Is that a language?

RA: Yes.

A: What language is that?

RA: It's an ancient part of Sanskrit.

A: When did she start awakening?

RA: She thought she was sick. She was being tested. And instead of giving in to the illness, she went inside. She started waking up years ago, then she fell asleep again. She woke up again just last year. I awoke her in July. She changed her whole life, she followed. I awoke her again last October. And I continue to do so slowly. She is no longer sick. She does need help opening her frequency to hearing.

A: Yes, can you start doing that for her now?

RA: Yes, it's up through her arms.

A: Good. If we could go back to Egypt. The beings that removed her as king and queen. Did they replace them with humans or what did they replace them with?

RA: They parade as humans, they are not. They are...they were not pure. They were not pure. They destroyed so much of the wisdom. They sacrifice. And they hold no love, they are still in power today. Slowly losing power though. It is time, it is time.

A: Did they have a name for the race that they were?

RA: I cannot say their name. They are, hmm... they are Reptilian. A hybrid.

A: Can you explain to us how they are a Reptilian hybrid?

RA: They are both from beneath and above. That's how they got power, and they were given knowledge and power from above. Integrated into their DNA, into their soul memories. It made them thirst for power more and their strength, their cunningly intelligence. They know both below and above. It makes them powerful. One, in particular, follows TeRa. She has seen him time and again. She remembers now.

A: Is he following her as she is alive or...?

RA: Lifetime after lifetime he becomes a new... how do you say it, he takes over other humans and parades as them.

A: Can you tell her who it is?

RA: In this life it was Mano. He goes in and out, he's trying again. She will not fall for it this time. He is not happy.

A: How does this work, like the human consciousness here, are they aware that they are that Reptilian being?

RA: Not mostly, they allowed him in, they welcomed him in, he promises them power over her. They are attracted to her power; they don't know why. Then he slowly sinks in through their own awareness or their spirits, their drinking spirits, their pain in the heart. Instead of healing it, they allow him in. He's not the only one that does this. This happens when someone allows their energy to go so low. So below, so below grief and despair, they can either exit or be taken over and they use it for power.

A: Yes, thank you for this information. You know I've been given this information so thank you as well. So, would you say some of those people that we help out that have Reptilian consciousness, is that what happened to them? They lowered, like you explained, for that consciousness to come in?

RA: They have so much trauma and they allow the trauma to go into places of despair, drinking alcohol, anything that lowers them even more, trying to escape it rather than feel it and honor it as its gift. And as soon as they get low enough, they become vessels for others and they don't know it, and these vessels for others are attracted to the light that is opening and awakening. It's almost as if when the Reptilian steps in they snip a cord in their brain, they snip it. And their empathy is gone. It's just gone, they don't have access. And the longer they allow it and the less they fight, the more attracted they are to it. And this is the same one that took her baby from her and it is taking her baby again.

A: What can we do about that RA?

RA: She sends love every day and that's all she can do because this child also has her choice. The love she sends, the more she heals in her and the more it heals in her baby and her baby has a choice. We are working with the baby for this baby is powerful, which is why it has two of them attached to her that we have unattached time and time again, but she keeps choosing. So, it is with love and light, we allow her choice knowing that if she does not wake up this time, she'll come back. We will not lose her. She is in our protection.

A: Now, you said that sometimes people just go so deep and lose themselves so deeply that they can even be replaced. Can you tell me more about that?

RA: It's as if they have gone so low, the spark of light within them cannot hold it any longer and simply - for lack of better language - walks out, walks out, just simply breathes out and the next one breathes in. Just like that, just within a breath.

A: The person could possibly do it in a, like they are not consciously doing it?

RA: No, they are not aware consciously, they have taken their consciousness to the lowest level of... they can't feel or think or understand anymore. I would assume it is what people call zombies these days.

A: Then is it like a contract they make where they switch out?

RA: Yes, nothing is done without that, they choose it. It is, they choose the promise of power, the promise of not feeling. And when they have had so much trauma that it feels like an option, and it is. It is not one we recommend.

A: When that happens, does the person sell their soul away?

RA: Yes, yes, they do.

A: What happens to their soul once it's removed?

RA: It is still a light, they are still that light that remains, and that light goes deeper into, if you will a hibernation, a holding, while it experiences what it has to experience. The light remains the light while the other side of it remains the darkness. It experiences the darkness, and it may take them many lifetimes, it may take them many excruciating journeys to choose again, to hold the light and to breathe in the light. And when they do, the contract is over, and they start learning about light again.

A: Yes, and what is the purpose of that? What do they gain from replacing a soul and going into the body, what benefits would they get out of being in that human body?

RA: Oh, they gain power over, they gain access to the bodies here, they gain the ability to shapeshift into the human form, to slightly become one of them, to infiltrate, to suck light, to... you know, people feel when their energy and light is being sucked, they feel it. They do and sometimes they willingly give it in the name of what they think is love or giving light. And sometimes they give too much, and when they give too much, they become very sick until they realize that it is not what they're giving, they're not giving the proper thing. As if they were to give the light, they would walk away knowing that that other entity has its own choice and it doesn't get to take your light, because your light is infinite. You can't, what you're giving it is not your light, it is a misrepresentation. You're allowing them to take energy for sure, yes, but your light you cannot give it, it is pure, it is always expanding and becoming, not emptying. That is what they gain, access to light. Access to light.

A: There have been people, for example, that are working in the light and they are part of the public eye. For example, there is someone who was bringing out information for such a long time about Angels and tarot cards and now supposedly she's renounced spirituality and now she is some kind of Christian.

RA: This is the danger with, mmm...I wouldn't say danger. This is the attraction, if you will, of the beings. They parade as beautiful light beings themselves because they have taken so much light. She was light, she was. I see that the ones that parade around her, parade so much and take so much from her and confuse her and she chooses their power, their path of power. The path of power has taken so many. This is what TeRa fell through first, she wanted the power to get her babies back and it's not possible that way. It is not possible that way. It is why she is losing her daughter again. She has to know, she can't get it back that way, she can't. Nobody can, you have to just breathe in more light, then they are able to feel that light and become more of that light themselves, not take. This is what happened to many Light Workers, they become the light then they see the power of it, and they use that for themselves rather than for a collective. They start creating their own way rather than listening.

A: Yes, that's one of my roles, you as the RA are bringing forth some of this information of people, how there are unfortunately some Light Workers that are using the light that they're giving them for their own purposes of service-to-self. If I can share with you? It's hard for me to share this because we are in the system where we want to be, of course, loving and allowing their free will. However, we are also in a system of, we need to be aware.

RA: Yes. This is beautiful, and this is why TeRa was afraid of opening and this is why I brought her to you. I see how beautiful you are, I see how you give, I see your heart, thank you. And I see how this is a concern for you, yes, it is.

A: Thank you. Yes, it is.

RA: Being aware of that feeling inside, we hear, and we see, and we feel and sometimes we go with what sees or looks good rather than what sounds good. And we go with what sounds good rather than what feels good. And when we can get all of them in alignment together that is when we know that we're going the right way. We see, feel, and hear it all. If one of those is off, we must listen, this is a challenge. Because the other entities, they sound good, they look good, sometimes it feels like they feel good, but they do not. They do not.

A: That is one of the biggest things that I'm trying to teach others, to look beyond the facade or what's in front of them or what they're saying. I have found in this time and space that there are so many lost following the supposed Light Workers and they're following a path of just darkness.

RA: It looks almost right, and sometimes that's what people are looking for, almost right. The religions have been almost right, almostright. There is beauty in all of them, yes, yes. But again, going back to making sure that looks, sounds, and feels good. All of that.

A: All of it. Great advice there and if I may, was she one of those that was replaced?

RA: I see that she's being replaced, she still has a choice. She still is there, she still fights, she still fights. She has choice, yes. Her message is not correct though. Her message is, yes, her message is being spit out with darkness if you will. It is laced with the breath of darkness.

A: Yes, there is a particular gentleman, I don't remember his name, I'm not going to mention it. But he has 1000's of followers. Let's say like 100,000's. He got them in a time frame that there were really not too many people talking about these things. He has proclaimed that the Angels are actually bad, they're darkness and they are the ones who are keeping everyone in control. So, when I am teaching people for example of Angels, there've been a couple or more sessions that I've had that I have to basically mentor them through the fact that the Angels are not in charge of this system of control and they are not what he is saying they are. He has even used for example some of the alchemy symbols that I teach in class on how to use them sacredly, he says that it's part of the cabal and some of the control as well. What are your thoughts on that RA?

RA: Yes, I go back to Egypt, to that time. Akhenaten and Tutankhamun changed Egypt, he brought back the power, the truth, the golden light, he brought back the oneness, the sacred alchemy. And what is a more dynamic way of changing this light than to parade it as darkness? To take some of the symbols and change them just enough, just enough that people think that what they are looking at is the same, but it is not. And it changes their DNA, it changes their mind. This is the same group if you will, the same entities that back then destroyed Egypt not once, not twice, but time and again. And they are doing it again and they do know they are intelligent, they do know the truth, they do know the alchemy, they know the power. They use it, yes, they use it. And it is because they use it that people are attracted to it because part of them remembers! They remember the beautiful truth of it so when it's close enough, sounds right, but does it feel right? They still follow. It looks right but it doesn't feel right. They still follow. This is what is happening. And the more people open and are aware of these symbols and alchemy and beautiful awakenings. We couldn't hide forever. We hid long enough but enough people are awakening, and it will come true. There will be more light but people will, that is part of it yes. They are attracted to taking down the light, we must be aware of this, this is still the truth. We're still here, yes.

A: Is there any advice of what we can do when there are 1000's of people or even for example, with him or others you know 20,000, 50,000, 100,000s of people following this and thinking that it's a solid proof? Like a Bible, solid information and they're not going to deter from it. And just like you said, it changes their DNA when they believe this false light information. What can we do? What advice do you have for us that see the dark beneath these teachings or information?

RA: Teach people to feel in their hearts. The more they go in their heart, this is how TeRa made it, she dropped into her heart in onemoment and she remembered, she remembered. That's the part to remember in the heart. All of these people, the more we can teach them to feel in their hearts, the more their eyes will open and their minds, and they will see them for what they are. Not all will, we can't, they have their journey. But more and more when opening the heart as you do. That sacred beautiful spinning vortex in that heart. It sends a message out more than our words can, deeper than what we realize. And while they work on the mind's cause that's how they get in; we work with the hearts. That's how we bring light. Work with the heart.

A: Looking, as you know I'm a seer, looking at the Light Workers who have awakened and looking at how many follow the Luciferian agenda and follow word for word for example, 'the Angels are the dark,' It is such a high percentage of them that are following this word for word and believing it and not, it is a very high percentage.

RA: Yes, and as you've said very beautifully, "word for word." They are hearing that it sounds good. They are not in their hearts. And the more they hear it, they get blinded. The hard part is when we work with the heart. It doesn't always bring many followers. It's on a different level. It brings the right followers. So, the masses might be blind for now. They might hear the sounds that sound good. But we awaken their hearts from a different perspective, from a different moment, from a different time. And once they walk into that moment and their heart opens, they start hearing a different tune, a different frequency. The frequency of light instead of the frequency of lie. But aren't those two similar? This is what I am saying, light lies. People get stuck on lies and don't go to the light. We get stopped because we are not in the heart. And our words are powerful spells if they come from the heart. The right followers, yes, will open up the many masses in due time.

A: In due time, yes, well...

RA: Yes, yes, the pendulum has gone from one extreme and is now coming back from another extreme. And in the way, people get lost on their way down back into the center. They do get lost. We have to be okay with that. Timing like you said is happening and as more people awaken in the heart they will see, they will see. I see them turning, I see masses like you say masses, following in the wrong direction. Seeing what they thought was the truth, these beautiful sacred geometries, these beautiful lights, they thought that they were the truth cause part of them are and they spark that part of them and then they get lost in that. But I see them turning around. I see many of them turning around and facing the correct way. Coming towards the light and away from the curiosity that leads them the wrong way. Curiosity is good but when we complete our curiosity in knowledge and stick to that, we lose out. And people think that they are in knowledge when they are in the curiosity that is taking them the wrong way. They will get curious this way though.

A: That is exactly what brother Metatron talks about often to me.

RA: Yes.

A: Thank you.

RA: Yes.

A: Is there anything you wanted to share about the Egyptian life that led her towards the dark and now she's coming back?

RA: I want her to know that she remembered. She needs to trust, absolutely trust. She is afraid as well. This is why you opened up the way you did, thank you. She has been afraid of going the wrong way. She feels it. Knowing that she is part of that power, she is opening into that, she will be opening up more. And she is afraid. She'll work through that.

A: Well now may she have a compass that will direct her in which way is right for her.

RA: Yes.

A: Thank you, you have such a strong connection within her and you're speaking through her very clearly, thank you deeply.

RA: Yes, I spin in her. She feels that. The energy spins, beautiful vortex.

A: Lovely, now as her, would you say that you are part of her Higher Self?

RA: Yes.

A: Ok. So, would you aid us today in doing the body scan on her, please?

RA: Yes.

A: I honor you, I love you, and I respect you, thank you for being here so early on. We will get so much done for her then.

RA: Thank you.

The Body Scan begins.

A: If you could please scan her body now and let me know if you need any aid from me channeling energy to her at any point. If you could scan her body now and look for any energies, entities, anything that requires healing please and let me know what you find.

RA: She has many. She needs healing from past lives and this life. Damage that has been done to both her sacral energy and her throat chakra.

A: If we could look at one, for example, let's start off with the sacral. First, I want to make sure, are there any entities there?

159

RA: Yes.

A: Is it one or is it more?

RA: More.

A: How many would you say there are RA?

RA: Four.

A: Is it from this life or another?

RA: Another.

A: What happened to her in that life that they connected to her in this area?

RA: She picked them up - one in Egypt, one in Europe, and two in this life.

A: Very good. RA, if you could help us guide the entities up and if I could speak to one of them speaking for all of them, if I could speak to you now. Come up, up, up.

Entities: Yes, yes.

A: Hello, greetings. Thank you for speaking with us. May I ask you questions, please?

Entities: Yes.

A: What have you caused her as far as pain, discomfort in this area?

Entities: A lot. We remind her.

A: Yes. You remind her of what?

Entities: We remind her how she failed, how she lost, we keep her connected to the one that lost, that made her lose, that took her.

A: If you could tell me, did you all have bodies before?

Entities: No.

A: You have yet to have a physical 3D body?

Entities: We have not.

A: Were you a newer type of soul or a soul that is negatively polarized throughout existence?

Entities: We are negatively polarized.

A: Have you been doing this for a long time?

Entities: Oh, eons!

A: Would it be just for her or for others as well?

Entities: She is our favorite. But we do this for others. She is our favorite cause she fights the most to not have us.

A: Why would you find that as a favorite, how would that...

Entities: Keeps us connected. It feeds us energy.

A: When she fights you?

Entities: We feed the energy to the one that destroyed her. That's how she gets found, he finds her, time and again.

A: So, were you placed there by him then?

Entities: Yes.

A: The Reptilian?

Entities: Yes, we serve him.

A: Are you Reptilians as well?

Entities: No.

A: You're just entities?

Entities: Yes. We don't have much shape or form. A little bit wormy if you will but not much.

A: I understand that you've been playing this role for a long time and it is really all that you know. You have yet to experience a positively polarized incarnation or even an incarnation physically at all, and you've been doing this for eons. Now as you know I work with spirits who are lost in the darkness for too long and have forgotten who they are and their light. We would love to be able to aid you to the light. Would you allow for us to help you?

Entities: Yes, please.

A: Thank you, for allowing us. All of you there within her sacral chakra, I want you to look within you please and find that light within you and remember that light that is you. We want you to spread it to all that is of you, every root, every cord that belongs to you and does not belong to TeRa, spread it to all light, and let me know once all of you are light.

Positive Polarized Entities: Yes.

A: Wonderful, can you pull yourselves out please and don't leave any piece of you behind, anything that belongs to you. Make sure it goes with you and tell me once you are out.

Positive Polarized Entities: We are out.

A: Beautiful, do you have a message for TeRa before you go?

Positive Polarized Entities: Thank you. Just simply thank you.

A: Thank you, and can I follow you along and see where you go?

Positive Polarized Entities: Yes.

A: Lovely, so go ahead and go, go and be free and tell me where it is that you go.

Positive Polarized Entities: We are going to go around that blackness.

A: What blackness?

Positive Polarized Entities: The one we were in before.

A: Is it a collective of darkness?

Positive Polarized Entities: Yes.

A: Where is this located at? Is it on the Earthly plane or is it in the Cosmos?

Positive Polarized Entities: It is both, in-between. It is an in-between blackness; it brings in and beings out.

A: What is it that you are going to do there, why are you there?

Positive Polarized Entities: I'm going around it, so I don't go back in there, it's light around it... Ah, yes! (in relief).

A: What happens next?

Positive Polarized Entities: I am being taken away by light.

A: Beautiful, you got past that darkness?

Positive Polarized Entities: Yes, yes. (deep breath).

A: When you were not of light and you were of the dark, would you just be pulled in when you would pass by it?

Positive Polarized Entities: I brought it with me so the darkness could come in and out of everywhere we go. So, we go in and out.

A: What about that darkness that you passed, is there something we could do with it?

Positive Polarized Entities: I turned it the other way so it's not pointing at her anymore.

A: Good, can we call on Angelic help so that we can heal that darkness?

Positive Polarized Entities: Yes.

A: Would you be able to guide us now that you are of light so that they know where to find it?

Positive Polarized Entities: Yes, I'll point them to it.

A: Thank you, can you point us now? I call forth on Archangel Michael and the Legion of Light.

Positive Polarized Entities: Yes, yes right here!

A: Good, tell me what you see.

Positive Polarized Entities: I see a spinning vortex trying to take over other beings. It is being healed.

A: Are the Angels there?

Positive Polarized Entities: Yes.

A: Tell me what you see, do you see Archangel Michael?

Positive Polarized Entities: Yes.

A: Is there more than him or is it just him?

Positive Polarized Entities: There are three others. Two to his right one to his left. They're healing it with sound.

A: Beautiful and where is the sound coming from?

Positive Polarized Entities: Their instruments, I recognize them.

A: Instruments, do they have shapes?

Positive Polarized Entities: They are golden and circular.

A: There is sound coming out of them?

Positive Polarized Entities: Yes.

A: With the sound as it touches the darkness, what's going on?

Positive Polarized Entities: The darkness folds in on itself and becomes a cloud of light.

A: In that darkness, were there other entities inside of there?

Positive Polarized Entities: Yes, very closed off.

A: They were closed off?

Positive Polarized Entities: Yes, they were closed off, they shut down, they can't come back in.

A: Now we're healing them?

Positive Polarized Entities: Yes.

A: Good, and how many would you say would be in there, in that collective of darkness?

Positive Polarized Entities: Thousands.

A: Beautiful, thank you for guiding us here and allowing us, helping us through it.

Positive Polarized Entities: Thank you.

A: Thank you, and do you have any other message before you go?

Positive Polarized Entities: We are in peace.

A: Go ahead and go with the Love-Light of the Universe, thank you, blessings to all of you. Now if I could speak to Michael? Michael, as he's standing there healing this energy. Can I please speak to you now brother?

AA Michael: Yes.

A: Greetings brother thank you for being here. I love you, I honor you, and I thank you.

AA Michael: I love you and I honor you, thank you.

A: If you could share what it is that you are doing there with these 1000's of dark entities?

AA Michael: At times when the magic goes black, it creates darkness vortexes that come in. It's part of their power and it allows them to come in and take over a little at a time. They feed on fear and pain. So, all I did was allow it to close up that one vortex and heal all that we're able to see what they saw. And as I closed that up, they cannot come back in that way. Healing it with light. So, if anyone ever tries to open that up again, it is opened with light and they cross through light.

A: Beautiful. Was it 1000's of entities, darkness, that were influencing people on Earth?

AA Michael: Yes.

A: So, if I may ask, what happened to those entities that were, say, inside of people?

AA Michael: Some of them are strong enough to stay, some of them are losing power as we speak. There's a lot of lightning coming on, a lot of people being enlightened. Burdens are easing and it is a good time, this was exactly on time. More and more will be healing throughout the night.

A: Beautiful.

AA Michael: The entities just disappear and as they leave, they transmute into that light frequency that surrounds that entrance.

A: This will help many on Earth, thank you.

AA Michael: Yes.

A: The entity that we helped said that you were holding instruments, what are these instruments you hold, the sound?

AA Michael: Some have drawn it as a trumpet. It is a golden instrument, not quite a trumpet. The frequency that we breathe into it comes out and expands and it changes frequency and light as it expands. It transmutes things. As it changes things at cellular levels deeper than that. It corrects DNA. As you know DNA got split. Part of that split is being corrected now on the timeline and in the collective. And the more we fix the split in the DNA, the less the entities have access. They are losing power.

A: From the removal of these entities that the people that were ready to learn that lesson and release that entity, are those the ones that were removed? You said that some were powerful, would those be connected to the ones where the people did not learn the lesson yet?

AA Michael: Yes, yes. They are the ones that fell, that kept their light, that are reawakening more and more, and I dare say thousands now have a new choice. Those entities have been removed.

A: Wow!

AA Michael: This is a powerful time on this planet and in the galaxy, in the consciousness. Many changes. It is a good time.

A: Yes, that it is, that it is. May I ask, the entity said there were three others with you, if I may ask, who are they?

AA Michael: They were just parts of him. You see, when certain entities are injected at times and lightness comes back and they are fought off, it almost splits them into parts if you will, energetically. And so, then those parts come back at another time. If they didn't learn from it or if they didn't release them properly, and this one's a fighter. She just did not know what she was doing. So, some of her fights caused her more harm. She is learning. So, she created more with her fight. This is why they loved her.

A: She created more entities you mean?

AA Michael: Yes. By fighting them and splitting them like a... you take a part of a starfish, it grows another part. But it is no longer with her, it is free.

A: Beautiful work. And the entity said though that there were three others with you working?

AA Michael: Yes.

A: May I ask, who are they?

AA Michael: Azrael, Isis, and Thoth.

A: Beautiful and did they all have the same instrument you had?

AA Michael: No.

A: What were they using if I may ask? For example, Azrael, what was he using?

AA Michael: His are more, hmm, almost like a harp but not. There are strings. They're timelines, musical timelines. As he plays them, timelines are healed.

A: Hmm, that's beautiful. And what does his instrument look like?

AA Michael: It is small and golden. I just see strings that are being played and I see many shapes as it's being played, like etheric and… Hmm, they are frequencies through plucks.

A: Yes, beautiful. My regards and my love for Azrael, thank you for helping there.

AA Michael: Yes.

A: Can you tell me, Isis, what is she holding?

AA Michael: She does not hold an instrument; she holds her heart. It is her heart that does the work. The love that she spreads with her beautiful wings. The motherly energy that she holds for everybody. She holds the space for healing.

A: And Thoth?

AA Michael: Yes, his wisdom. Hmm, he breathes knowledge and life. It is his breath, his sacred voice. That is his instrument. He has the Ankh, and he uses his breath.

A: Beautiful. Thank you, is there anything else, you four? Any message you have for TeRa?

AA Michael: I do protect her as I protect many. Hmm, and yes, she is a fighter, and I am proud of her. She is learning to fight with love. It takes a lot less energy.

A: Yes, it does. And Michael since we have such a clear connection here. How are you connected to the RA since RA was speaking before you?

AA Michael: Oh, my heart, I feel it beats with my heart, the RA Collective. I am a protector. I am on the forefront. It is my divine mission as... I will say it this way, as you all awaken, they will hear me. I am on the forefront.

A: Why is it you on the forefront?

AA Michael: It is like my brother Jesus with the heart and my sister Isis and all of my, all of us. It is our heart. There is strength in the heart, there is power. And I have been able to create my heart into a powerful shield if you will, a protector of Love. I expand the Universe with Love. I am willing to do what it takes and hold my space of Love.

A: Beautiful. If I may ask, what is your connection to brother Archangel Lucifer (Haylel)?

AA Michael: He is beautiful, is he not?

A: Beautiful he is.

AA Michael: If you can imagine a beautiful seed that turns into a tree. They are both one and the same, although they look very different. Both help each other grow. He is a beautiful seed, and I am the tree. And we grow together and in harmony and he has his mission and I have mine. But I would be nothing without him and he, I.

A: Would you say you are one and the same?

AA Michael: Yes, as we all are. We are all different parts of the seed and the tree and the branches and the leaves, the breath in the air, the sun, and the wind. We are all of it.

A: Yes, and you as Michael or as Lucifer (Haylel), what is your connection to, say the Divine Father? How there is a Divine Mother and a Divine Father, do you have a connection to that?

AA Michael: Yes, yes. As we all do. We all have experienced this through him and for him and with him. Some of us might be a bit closer, some of us not yet as close, still within. My connection to them is as One. I guide back, he calls me as he calls everybody. I hear, listen, and I am guided - as with the Divine Mother, and her everlasting love and growth.

A: Thank you, thank you. Would you say that when Source Creation decided to fractalize would you say that you were...?

AA Michael: One of the first fractals? Yes.

A: And would you be a fractal of the Divine Father?

AA Michael: Yes. Oh, it brings me so much joy! (sigh)

A: Thank you.

AA Michael: Ah, yes, you see this, and you recognize this in your own self.

A: Yes.

AA Michael: Yes.

A: Thank you brother, it has given me great joy and healing even for myself for my heart to feel the clearness of the connection to this session. I love you all so much. Such joys you are, such beautiful creations you are upon Creation, thank you.

AA Michael: Thank you.

A: I love you all and my regards to everyone who helped with the collective. Is there anything else that you wanted to say in regard to those people who will experience the release of the entities that you helped to the light?

AA Michael: They know who they are, they will recognize themselves through this. They are being guided to you, yes. They are turning around more so now.

A: Thank you, brother.

AA Michael: Thank you. I love you.

A: I love you infinitely, thank you. If I could please speak to the RA once more?

RA: Yes?

A: Ah, that was lovely, thank you. Would you say the RA that you are, would be like the form of the Collective as a Source?

RA: Yes.

A: The Collective Consciousness that is whole as Source the Creator?

RA: Yes.

A: Thank you as you know, I know these answers. However, these are beautiful answers to share with others. This session has been quite a delight and it is packed with information that will hopefully burst so many hearts wide open.

RA: Yes, the blueprint has been awakened. The collective blueprint is awakening. Yes, you feel this, you feel this.

A: That I do!

RA: Yes.

A: That I do, thank you. (laughs and smiles) ... I love you!

RA: I love you.

A: Can we scan her body; can we see whatever else needs healing and you said that it was her sacral and what was the other?

RA: Her throat chakra.

A: That's right. If you could scan for entities there, please.

RA: Yes, and memories.

A: Yes, there's entities and memories?

RA: Yes, yes.

A: How many would you say RA there are?

RA: Six.

A: Six entities. Metatron, keep them there nice and contained. RA, if you could help guide those entities up, up, up, and if I could speak to a voice that could speak for all of them. If I could speak to you now, please.

Entities: Yes.

A: Greetings. Thank you for speaking to us. May I ask you questions?

Entities: Yes.

A: I honor you, I thank you, and I love you.

Entities: Thank you.

A: May I ask, when was it that you connected to her throat?

Entities: Ah yes, oh yes. That is how she chose to go to Egypt. She took herself. I connected to her being then. Oh yes.

A: What do you mean she took herself?

Entities: She slit her throat.

A: Was that where they had said she was placed in a cave?

Entities: Yes. She did not want to live through the rest of what she had to learn at the time. She needed great rest.

A: Did you enter then, before or after the slitting of the throat?

Entities: Right as she was doing it. I was there as a guide and to keep her company through her lonely darkness.

A: Is this what you do as an entity? You do this for others?

Entities: Yes, I keep them remembered. I remind them, I replay for them until they learn. It is with love; it is with love. But I stay with them until they're ready.

A: Would you say that you are negative or positive polarized as an entity?

Entities: Hmm, I am positive. It feels negative but I am positive. I hold their negative yes. When it's too powerful for them to hold themselves in that space for them.

A: Have you had bodies yet?

Entities: I have had bodies.

A: Would you now like to no longer have to play this role as an entity within a body? Would you like to be back to being yourself once more?

Entities: I did this as a gift for her, her and I were together once. I had to hold her space.

A: Well, thank you, thank you for that gift.

Entities: Yes.

A: When was it that you were together?

Entities: Atlantean, that's where she remembers the magic. That's why she's so interested, she's remembering, she's reconnecting now. She's reconnecting now. I held that space until she could reconnect. Reconnecting now. Ah yes. Yes. She remembers me.

A: Were you a soul mate? A Twin Flame?

Entities: I was her dear mother (crying), and I was the child. There are pieces of me that I hold in others, in her now child. I hold space for her too, for both of them.

A: Yes. Could we aid today in helping you maybe become more whole?

Entities: Yes, it's her time now.

A: Beautiful. So, we're going to help you shift from this role and turn to light. Tell me, what is the goal of making yourself whole, where are you going to go?

Entities: Ah, I rejoin, rejoin the collective, rejoin my family...Yes.

A: Good. I want you to look inside you now, all of you within her throat, find that light within you and spread it to all that is of you. Every root, every cord. Let me know once you are all light.

Positive Polarized Entities: Ahhh, yes! Yes!

A: Beautiful, and if you could remove yourself from her throat.

Positive Polarized Entities: Yes.

A: RA, by the way if you could have Raphael please start filling in that light to the sacral chakra, if it needs filling in please there.

Positive Polarized Entities: Yes, thank you.

A: Thank you. Now if you all can remove yourself, the entities within her throat, tell me once you are all out. Make sure you take every piece of you with you that does not belong to her.

Positive Polarized Entities: (sigh) We are out.

A: Beautiful, thank you, thank you. That was so beautiful to watch you all release. Now, you said that you will be returning back to the collective?

Positive Polarized Entities: Hmm, yes.

A: And what about the fact that you said you had pieces within her daughter? Is there something we can do about that?

Positive Polarized Entities: Her daughter has throat trauma as well. Same reason. It is just a fractal of information that got passed down. Ah, oh she passed it down yes. If we could heal her daughter.

A: Very good...

Positive Polarized Entities: Both daughters, different link though. Both daughters. The oldest has the throat issue, she passed that.

A: I will speak to RA and see if he could direct us over to them. Thank you so much for all your aid today and the aid you've given her. I love you and I honor you and I respect you. Go ahead and go with the Love-Light of the Universe, blessings to you.

Positive Polarized Entities: Thank you, thank you.

A: Thank you, and RA, if we could have our brother Raphael see where he needs to fill in light both in the sacral as well as the throat now that they've been removed, please?

RA: Hmm, yes.

A: Thank you. And then if you could connect us to the first daughter that we would need to connect to, the Higher Self.

RA: Yes.

A: Thank you RA.

RA: Hmm, oh she is in so much pain.

A: Which daughter are we focusing on right now? Who are we talking to? Am I speaking to Luna's Higher Self?

Luna's Higher Self: Yes.

A: Thank you, welcome, thank you for being here, I honor you and I thank you.

Luna's Higher Self: Oh, thank you!

A: If you can tell me as her Higher Self, what kind of healing can we do through the mom as a surrogate, what can we do for the daughter right now?

Luna's Higher Self: Hmm, her heart is broken in pieces. Her throat, her voice is gone. She is darkening, she is being taken over. Her limbs are on fire! She is crumbling, collapsing. I'm holding her together.

A: Tell us, what do you give us permission to heal within her?

Luna's Higher Self: Her heart and her throat and her limbs, yes.

A: What would you like for us to do? Send Love-Light?

Luna's Higher Self: Love-Light and protection, she's been, feels like eaten alive energetically.

A: Do you need any Phoenix Fire sent over her?

Luna's Higher Self: Yes, yes...remove, remove, remove the entities that are eating her alive.

A: Higher Self of TeRa's daughter, if you could guide Archangel Michael. What entities do you give him permission to remove from within the daughter?

Luna's Higher Self: Hmm, yes, yes. It is the one that followed her mom around. They are one and the same and two entities right now. They are attacking her yes, yes.

A: The Reptilians?

Luna's Higher Self: Yes, this is how he is trying to get to her again, by taking her daughter.

A: Is the Reptilian inside her daughter?

Luna's Higher Self: Yes.

A: Where at? What part of her body?

Luna's Higher Self: He is in her heart. And in her mind, he is there, yes.

A: Can you tell us; can we help this Reptilian turn into positive polarization instead of transmuting him into light? Will he allow us to aid him?

Luna's Higher Self: No, he's on a mission.

A: Archangel Michael and perhaps the team that you had as well earlier please, if we could call on you now and if we could surround it with the Alchemy symbols in the daughter, that Reptilian in her heart. If we could now start healing that dark energy there and transmuting it and healing it to light, please.

Luna's Higher Self: Yes.

A: As we do that, what else can we do as we do that?

Luna's Higher Self: He has a grip on her, and she is holding on to the grip. She is afraid if she lets go, she will have to let go of her father and she will. And her new family, she will.

A: Can you help her as her Higher Self see that this is the highest path for her? Let me know how the Reptilian is looking along the way and when it's been removed and healed.

Luna's Higher Self: He's out of her heart, out of her mind but he's gripping on her arm. It is cutting off her circulation.

A: I'm going to focus Phoenix Fire there, which arm is it?

Luna's Higher Self: Right arm. It's his last hold. If we release him now, we release him in all time and eternity from this event.

A: Yes.

Luna's Higher Self: This will no longer repeat.

A: Good.

Luna's Higher Self: He has a stronghold, it is releasing.

A: Good. Higher Self will you allow for us to release him from all time and space in the now?

Luna's Higher Self: Yes, yes, please.

A: Let me know once he's let go.

Luna's Higher Self: Yes, it wasn't me that was evil, it wasn't me. Ah, oh...

A: Did he let go?

Luna's Higher Self: Yes, yes.

A: Good, if we can ensure that the Angels take him to light and help him transition into Love-Light please without harming anyone anymore. Thank you... How is she looking now?

Luna's Higher Self: She is shaky, but she is good, she is good, she is good.

A: Aww beautiful, yes!

Luna's Higher Self: Oh, she's so beautiful!

A: Can we all just send Love-Light to her and just embrace her with Love-Light right now?

Luna's Higher Self: Yes! (crying)

A: Thank you.

Luna's Higher Self: Thank you, yes.

A: As her Higher Self, how soon will she be able to release her father?

Luna's Higher Self: One week. I'm allowing her to see him and hear him and feel him.

A: Good.

Luna's Higher Self: Yes.

A: As his true form?

Luna's Higher Self: As his true form.

A: Will you be there along the way whenever she needs that reminder?

Luna's Higher Self: Yes, always here.

A: Yes, of course, thank you. Are there any other messages that you have for us or TeRa?

Luna's Higher Self: Thank you for not giving up. Thank you for loving me. Thank you for releasing and allowing, thank you. I love you!

A: Thank you, sister.

Luna's Higher Self: Yes.

A: Thank you for all your aid and can you connect us to your sister Melissa's Higher Self?

Luna's Higher Self: Yes.

A: Greetings.

Melissa's Higher Self: (bubbly) Hi!

A: Hi. You are beautiful!

Melissa's Higher Self: Ah, thank you! I love this!

A: We are connecting with the mother's request, TeRa, she asked for help to heal her daughters. We helped heal your older sister with the Higher Self's permission at this point. Now how can we aid you as the Higher Self of Melissa? Is there anything we can assist you with?

Melissa's Higher Self: Oh yes, I have been waiting for them! Oh, they are beautiful, Oh I have been waiting for them. I have clouded myself. I am done clouding. Oh, so much more energy yes, yes... Um, I need help releasing the cloud in my brain. I think I did too well. (laughs)

A: Can we go ahead and heal and transmute that cloud now out of her brain? Archangel Michael and the team there as well, if you could aid RA, whoever would like to aid there.

Melissa's Higher Self: I'm almost afraid to say what I see!

A: Tell me?

Melissa's Higher Self: Ok. Hmm, oh my goodness it's like I don't belong here, I am so much light! Ah yes, I had to dense down a lot, oh my goodness... Aaaaah, there we go yes.

A: Are we removing the cloud?

Melissa's Higher Self: Yes, yes! Thank you.

A: Good, thank you. Is there anything else that we can do for you?

Melissa's Higher Self: Hmm, I finally feel my body. I'm okay again. May I ask, why am I here though? I densed down so much!

A: Higher Self, can you tell Melissa what is her soul purpose, why is she here?

Melissa's Higher Self: She is attracted to music so I will tell her in music. She is an Angel that flew too close to the ground. She felt the pain. She is here to lighten the world. She has so much lightness and that lightness scared and terrified her family. She densed down. It is a little scary to lighten back up again knowing that there is that choice and people won't understand... Hmm, she is feeling light again, thank you.

A: We thank you for being an Angel brave enough to come down even though you felt the pain.

Melissa's Higher Self: Thank you.

A: That's very brave.

Melissa's Higher Self: Yes.

A: Do you have any message for TeRa or for the daughter?

Melissa's Higher Self: To TeRa, I always see you as who you are and you feel this, and I know that. Thank you. And to my sister, I forgive you, I understand, and I release it.

A: Beautiful, are you all healed from the cloud?

Melissa's Higher Self: Yes, oh I see beautiful again thank you.

A: Thank you. Are we all done with you?

Melissa's Higher Self: Yes, thank you.

A: Thank you, thank you, sister. My love to you and I honor, I thank you, and I respect you, blessings to you... If I could speak to RA once more, please. RA, if I can ask a question about this month, it feels very different. I know that we were able to heal 1000's of entities. Is that something that is different from this month that we were able to do so or could we have done this in past months?

RA: The light is big enough that it is more dynamic. The changes in the energy are changing more so we are able to lift more darkness from the planet than we have in the past. It's part of the waking up, it's part of the understanding. It's part of, the more people release their trauma rather than run from their trauma, get healings like these, we are able to heal on a bigger scale. It is like when a waterfall first starts. Little trickles at first and then once the water flows right over, it's huge and it's dynamic. This is where we are in right now. We are in that large energy wave. And it has been going on yes, but it has changed as of recently yes. People feel it now, they are feeling more than hearing and seeing. And that's where we need people to be using feelings. But people have been traumatized by their past and they're afraid to feel it, yes. The feeling of which will allow them to release it and feel what is true.

A: Thank you. Should we continue to hopefully see, for example, the Schumann Resonance and the waves occurring? They are very high. Will we see this continuing for the rest of the months?

RA: Yes, yes, very strongly. Some people might feel it as a sickness, but it is not. It is not a sickness; it is not anxiety. It is them feeling their energy finally. Feeling, pulsating the power of the Oneness within and it shakes them and moves them. That we haven't been taught as a collective, this collective hasn't learned that. They are learning, they are learning. People are opening up. But yes, the Resonance will get stronger and stronger.

A: Would you say that those who resist this are feeling it as anxiety?

RA: Yes, and that is why more healers are opening up quicker and why people are searching and they're searching in the wrong directions. So, you are a beacon of beautiful light and more beacons of light are opening up and soon people will feel and see and hear the difference. And the Resonance will be felt differently, they will be vibrated towards you. They will be vibrated out of their blindness. They are being vibrated out and it is a joy to watch, it is a joy.

A: Yeah, that it is.

RA: Yes.

A: If we can continue her body scan RA, tell me what else needs healing in her body, please.

RA: Her heart needs to open.

A: Yes, can you scan for an entity?

RA: (sigh) What I'm feeling is a circling of energy, a vortex, uh, what is this? It is a...it is a magical spell on her heart. Those are the words.

A: Where did it stem from?

RA: From Egypt, yes.

A: Did somebody place that on her?

RA: Yes, before they took her baby, they closed her heart. She was too big of a fighter.

A: They did that as a form of black magic type of curse?

RA: Yes, yes, yes.

A: Can we go ahead and start removing this from her, please? Should I use the Phoenix Fire?

RA: Yes, yes.

A: Ok, using it now...

RA: Oh, this awakens her Twin Flame too, oh he feels this! There he is!

A: I feel it too, it's beautiful.

RA: Yes, oh yes, okay... Very good.

A: Can we expand it now, expand it as big as it can be in this time and space?

RA: Yes.

A: Thank you. Can we have Raphael work on anything he needs to work there in her heart, please? Is it removed?

RA: Yes, but there is one light that is not the right color. It is a phosphorous green and it should be purple.

A: Can we have Raphael switch that for her, please?

RA: Yes, thank you. .

A: Now, can you scan her body once more RA and tell me what else needs healing?

RA: The last one is in her brain.

A: What's going on in her brain?

RA: She has had many, the epileptic seizures were ways to put blocks in. Again, she is a fighter and she fought. And they had to find new ways to block her. Releasing these blocks releases her energy, she is free again.

A: Beautiful, can we go ahead and transmute that out of her head now?

RA: Yes.

A: May I use the Phoenix Fire?

RA: Yes.

A: If you could tell me, does she still have epilepsy?

RA: No, no she fought that off, it's just the blocks.

A: Ok, so we're transmuting those blockages there?

RA: They were like black fingers, cords. Yes, releasing.

A: Good. Can you tell me why she had epilepsy?

RA: It was to close her off, it was to stop her from awakening.

A: Was that a contract?

RA: No, it was against her will.

A: How does epilepsy look in the brain? What does it look like? You said they were like black...

RA: Yes, the black fingers. Like black strings that were blacking out.

A: That took the form where it was stuck? What about at the form where it is active and it's giving her seizures?

RA: Hmm, she no longer has them. It is free flowing; it is light again.

A: Beautiful.

RA: Ahhh! She was allowing blackness in there, we have it. She no longer allows that.

A: Good. Have we healed it?

RA: Yes, yes.

A: Lovely, thank you. Scan her whole body once more RA and make sure there are no more entities in her please as well as any negative implants, negative hooks, negative portals.

RA: She is clear.

A: Ahhh, lovely RA. I know that you said she is part of you as a Higher Self consciousness, does she have an individual Higher Self that we can speak to now?

RA: Hmm, yes.

A: RA, it has been such a beautiful honor to speak to all of you today. Do you have a last message before you go?

RA: Thank you, I love you, and I honor you. All you do, (sigh) it is needed right now and thank you, yes.

A: Thank you, I love you all so much!

RA: Thank you!

A: I will talk to you later, I love, honor, thank, and respect all of you, thank you. If I could speak now to the Higher Self of TeRa now?

Higher Self: Yes?

A: Greetings. Oh, such a beautiful fractal you have of yourself here.

Higher Self: Thank you, this is beautiful.

A: It is so beautiful, infinitely beautiful. You as her Higher Self may I ask, do you have a name?

Higher Self: I don't know my name.

A: Have you not given yourself one?

Higher Self: I always just called myself RA. I am delighted.

A: Do you not want to have a name? We can continue to call you RA.

Higher Self: I would really like that.

A: Beautiful lovely, may I ask you questions?

Higher Self: Yes.

A: Did we heal the teeth, the jaw, the neck issues, was that connected to the throat chakra?

Higher Self: Yes.

A: Is that all healed now?

Higher Self: The jaw is healing, it will heal.

A: Good.

Higher Self: Oh, it's having my voice.

A: She said vagus nerve in there?

Higher Self: Yes, yes. That has been healed.

A: Thank you and also in her gut. Is there anything in her gut?

Higher Self: No, it has been healed.

A: Good, and she thought that her ex was poisoning her, is this accurate?

Higher Self: Yes, he was.

A: How was he poisoning her?

Higher Self: He was poisoning her with liquid in her food.

A: Wow, what kind of liquid?

Higher Self: It was a power steering fluid and other things he kept trying.

A: Why did he do that? What was the purpose to that?

Higher Self: She outlived his purpose; she was just money. She ran out and he thought that he could get money from her death and sympathy. It was his way out; he didn't know any other way out. He is also part of that entity that was trying to destroy her. This is why he went straight to her daughter and he is at it again. He has learned that this is how he is going to make it. But it is not with her anymore.

A: Did we heal the effects of the poison?

Higher Self: There is something in her left thigh right now. It is wanting out.

A: What do you mean wanting out, is it an entity or just needs healing?

Higher Self: It's an entity, it is part of what she drank, it went into her muscles.

A: Can we go ahead and just help it out?

Higher Self: Yes.

A: Good, thank you. How is she doing? I know she's been in there a while.

Higher Self: She is okay...she is good. She had been preparing herself quite beautifully for this.

A: This is a beautiful example of an A.U.R.A. session where the client is ready and is working diligently and preparing themselves for it and the possibilities that are available in doing so.

Higher Self: Yes.

A: Thank you for helping her in her preparation.

Higher Self: Yes.

A: Is there any past life trauma that we can heal, or current trauma that we can heal now?

Higher Self: Yes, the past life trauma is also what has caused her now trauma. The reliving of the experience of being hurt and killed. She is done with that now.

A: Yes.

Higher Self: She recognized she was punishing herself through others.

A: Can we go ahead and heal that for her, please?

Higher Self: Yes.

A: Thank you, and then also can you check her chakras, how are they doing?

Higher Self: Oh, very clear, very nice.

A: Good, how about her auric field?

Higher Self: Yes, there is something to the right in her auric field, I'm not sure what that is, it clenched her jaw.

A: Is it an entity?

Higher Self: Yeah, it feels like a claw.

A: Can we go ahead and transmute that out now?

Higher Self: Yes, thank you.

A: Good, using the Phoenix Fire, sending it over there. Can you age regress her ten years, please?

Higher Self: Yes.

A: Good, can you scan her body one more time? I want to make sure there are no more entities hiding in there, or implants, hooks, or portals, please. Scan for that one more time.

Higher Self: It all feels clear. She just still has something in her left thigh. It might be something different.

A: Can I use the Phoenix Fire on it?

Higher Self: Yes.

A: Good, okay. And can you scan her for Reptilian consciousness, please?

Higher Self: It is gone, he is angry. She is protected now, he is gone.

A: Good. Now, are there any fragmented soul pieces that need to be rejoined to her?

Higher Self: From Egypt, yes.

A: Can we go ahead and do that for her now, please? And if you require any help, but you are part of RA so you should do a wonderful job at retrieving it, thank you.

Higher Self: Yes, thank you. Hmm.

A: Very good, is it retrieved?

Higher Self: Yes.

A: Good. If we could just have Raphael just to scan the body and just make sure there are no parts of her that still need filling in of light, please... Okay, so at this point, we've done the whole body scan. Higher Self, can you scan her whole body and make sure she is good to go?

Higher Self: She is good to go, yes.

A: Lovely, she is going to be brand new!

Higher Self: Oh, she is, oh she is. Beautiful.

A: Very beautiful. She has a couple of questions here and she wants to know - when she was younger, she had a lion pet, what was that about?

Higher Self: Yes, this is part of her in Egypt, she had a lion pet. She loved it dearly and it broke his heart when she did what she did. And he's come back, and he guides her.

A: Beautiful. And she felt a connection with Nefertiti, why?

Higher Self: Yes, she was the daughter of, not Nefertiti but, she was the daughter of one of the wives and Nefertiti loved her very much.

A: Let me understand that, so she was the daughter of one of the wives?

Higher Self: Yes.

A: The wives of the king?

Higher Self: Of the king, yes.

A: And Nefertiti was the wife of the king?

Higher Self: Yes, she was the main wife.

A: Was this when they were positive?

Higher Self: Yes.

A: Okay, beautiful. What happened to Nefertiti?

Higher Self: She was killed, it is the same entity. He took the whole family out, he had to, he wanted to control, and he wanted to end the dynasty. But he did not.

A: Who was Nefertiti's husband?

Higher Self: Akhenaten.

A: Yes, very good thank you. Now let's see she has more questions here. What can she do to connect to her Higher Self and guides and such?

Higher Self: She knows she must feel it more and she must meditate more. She has been told to come to Thoth cleanly. Which means she needs to eat better. This vessel does not live on what she eats. She knows this. It's her diligence that concerns us. I believe as she gets guidance, she will know what she is doing and be more diligent.

A: Very good. And when she basically begins eating the right way she will connect further?

Higher Self: Yes.

A: Is it because when she eats bad it makes her dense and then she can't connect high enough?

Higher Self: Yes. The nervous system in this body had been through a lot. It is healing now. It needs a lot more energy to sustain the energy that is coming through the body. As it is getting more and more powerful and the energy is getting higher and higher in vibrations and it needs more.

A: Therefore, higher vibrational foods would give it more of that high vibration she needs?

Higher Self: Yes, yes, yes.

A: She wants to know is she on the correct path for her career? How can she do better at what she does?

Higher Self: Yes, as you said taking your class, she is guided here. She is in the exact moment she needs to be, and she is doing what she needs to do. She feels when she makes a change in the energy system of others. She knows. She now has to accept that. When she accepts that she can move on to the next step.

A: She wants to know when her finances will finally be full in abundance instead of lack?

Higher Self: That is her choice, she has to choose differently and allow herself to be who she is. Allow it, because at the moment she is denying people from coming to her and that causes lack.

A: How so?

Higher Self: She is blocking them because she is afraid. She has been afraid.

A: This vibration of fear is what's blocking them?

Higher Self: It had been her fear of going down the wrong path, of becoming what so many have become, her fear of that has blocked her. Now she knows otherwise.

A: Are we talking about for example, the Light Workers who have gone through more of a service-to-self path?

Higher Self: Yes, because she had that choice, she made it through that choice, yes.

A: Thank you. I love how it all intertwines with her session and even though I know you said it's to be shared, may it guide many and help them to see this path of Oneness and Love, infinite for one another, thank you.

Higher Self: Yes, thank you.

A: She wants to know, anything else you can tell her on how she can help the collective?

Higher Self: Yes, opening. This was part of this moment of opening her heart. She knew it was blocked; she could not figure it out. We have helped her, it is open.

A: Was it not enough for her to help 1000's of spirits today? (laugh)

Higher Self: Yes, yes. (laugh) Yes, she wants more of this! This is who she is, who she's been training to be, yes.

A: Beautiful, beautiful session, beautiful messages that came forth, it is truly a beautiful creation today. That we intently created.

Higher Self: Yes.

A: Is there anything that I could have asked that I haven't asked?

Higher Self: No, everything feels so clear and light, thank you, yes.

A: Thank you. May I bring her back now?

Higher Self: Yes.

A: Yes, thank you, sister, it has been such a beauty to connect to your soul!

Higher Self: Thank you.

A: Thank you for leading her heart to mine and as well thank you to the beautiful RA Collective that shared such beautiful transcending, needed information for the collective in this time and space. May it empower many to find their love and sovereignty once more within them.

Higher Self: Yes, it will.

A: Thank you to Michael, thank you Azrael, Isis, and Thoth as well and anyone else who aided today and all those beautiful spirits who are now of light, blessings to everyone. I honor you, I thank you, respect you. Thank you, everyone.

Higher Self: Love you, thank you.

END OF SESSION

-------------<◇>-------------

This fascinating session was full of surprises, as a never-ending gift box. You open one gift, and another is inside, you open the next and another… The gifts being spiritual wisdom that sings to our hearts and helps us understand the inner knowing already within us. Till this day, my clients mention to me this specific session and the catalyzation their consciousness and heart experienced when watching it on the Rising Phoenix Aurora's YouTube Channel. There has been mention of the RA Collective through different forms of the Spiritual Community, and through this session we were able to grow a bond with the immensity and strength of love that they are over anything else. In the sessions to come you will hear more from them from time to time.

What they have explained through the Rising Phoenix Aurora's Live Channelings on YouTube is that they are all of us. You are RA and they are RA. They are the collective group construct of this Universe and infinity, as Creation is infinity. The collective benevolence of races of Councils that are working together for the Ascension, for the collective of life. They were the original benevolent founders and seers of Egypt, and the stories of Creation that are told through the hieroglyphics on the walls of its sacred pyramids and temples.

As we learned through this session, the Illuminati has been working relentlessly to reign over sacred times in our Earth's history, including Egypt. Wanting to possess the sacred wisdom and knowledge that created Egypt from the beginning of times when the Divine Mother Isis birthed forth, to set the organic foundation of what this Earth was meant to be. A beautiful world where many races throughout the Universe could be in one location communing together as the brethren that they are. The beauties of Creation all in one, expressing their multitude of beauties.

Since TeRa's session, we have continued helping heal negatively polarized entities and Reptilian beings in the 100's, 1,000's, 1,000,000's and 1,000,000,000's throughout Creation. Every session becomes easier for us and the message of this being possible for negative polarized beings continues to spread throughout the Universe.

At the beginning, when we started discovering Reptilians within people attached, we were lucky if they would speak to us with just a "yes" or "no" answer and with much convincing on our end, they would finally agree. Nowadays as soon as we talk to them about positive polarizing, it is as if they are and have been ready, waiting an eternity to finally do so. The word keeps spreading throughout the Universe and now we are helping other races of negatively polarized aliens to positively polarize and ascend as well, not just Reptilians.

The knowledge the RA Collective shared in regard to soul replacement, is a beginning glimpse for us into the understanding of how valuable a soul is. It is pivotal to be aware of the targeted infringements used for negatively harvesting souls, which we will receive incremental details spread out through the rest of the Chapters of this book. A soul is made up of the same type of light consistency that a star is, as we are birthed from the stars themselves. Therefore, there is infinite power and light to a soul. This vast light energy can be used for negative purposes if not honored. Therefore, it teaches us to find value in how precious our own and all souls are. We have been programmed on Earth to not find the value of our souls and how uniquely beautiful we are, which then allows for infringements to enter by us not emanating the required sovereignty of the soul. Honor thy soul, honor thy heart, and honor thy reflection of all souls. Learn to fall in love with yourself, as Creation has fallen in love with you, the instant you were birthed from the stars.

The more that we continue to do this work, the more the Earth becomes lighter. Which in turn, brings forth Ascension closer to us on Earth collectively and the Universe. We learned through this session how we too can connect to our children's Higher Selves, and with their permission, we can provide the adequate healing for them for their highest good. We must understand that healing family groups is vital for Ascension. Worldwide today, we have more than 100 A.U.R.A. Hypnosis Healing Practitioners certified who have answered the call. If that practitioner goes home and does a healing session on their spouse, children, siblings or parents, think about the ripple it creates on Earth in just this family alone by removing entities, implants, A.I. viruses from one family. As cleared vessels, then whoever they connect to or pass by in their daily tasks at work, school, or shopping at a grocery store will then be activated. The people who contain a lower density, of not being a clear vessel, will feel an activation and remembrance of what a soul with such lightness and clearness can feel like. They will feel a remembrance of what we were meant to be here in this Organic Matrix Simulation, as the fractals of our Higher Selves fully embodied at its highest Source organic light quality. One light frequency brushing up against another light frequency. And just like that, the light within them can light up like a light bulb to begin their future awakening and Ascension process. When someone is that deep in darkness and density, it is as if they have amnesia in remembering what it can feel like to be of such clear sovereignty. Therefore, we who hold this clearness are the light activators of the world, touching hearts kept in darkness wherever we go with our lights.

It is explained to us that the Reptilians hold the biggest density in the Universe due to their numbers and because of how much they are hated throughout time and space. The more that we learn to forgive and love others no matter what they have done and who they are, including the Reptilians, the more the density which holds them enslaved to continuing the negative polarization role of harm loosens up. It is when we send love to the root of the matter that we amplify the shifting of the Universe. This is truly what we ALL have been waiting for all our lives!

In the next Chapter, we will develop a deeper understanding of Reptilians and their role in Creation.

"We as a multitude of races truly have no name, as the different races work in higher dimensions and frequencies of no names... we choose to not label for this is when separation begins to occur."
The RA Collective, channeled by
~AuroRa ❤

-------------<◇>-------------

9

ACTIVATION PORTAL: 9/19/2019

Session #198: Recorded in September 2019.

In this online A.U.R.A. Hypnosis Healing session, Charlotte finds herself in Angelic form as Archangel Ariel/Area, delivering messages for the Earth. She and her brethren volunteered to incarnate on Earth to aid the dark density within it. How do Angels enter the fetus in the womb before birth, what does the process of an Angelic incarnation look like? She takes us through time and explains what Earth looked like then in the beginning of time and what it looks like now.

In this divinely timed session, we receive more details on the 9/19/19 Portal Activation and the connection to the Sun. What is the connection of Source and the Sun, and why is the Sun so important for Light Workers and the Human Collective? What percentage of Earth is light and what is the critical threshold for the awakening shift to happen? How do the existing religious constructs on Earth disempower us? How does A.U.R.A. aid in the Ascension process? We learn more on Reptilians and their roles on Earth. Come join us on this journey to the Reptilians' home planet and hear the message they have for Aurora.

-------------<◇>-------------

"Just show high vibration, smile at them, pay a sincere compliment, leave them better than you found them. Even in a small way and you will have helped raise their vibration. They are contributing to the grid that way, with their light.
There are no small acts."
-Archangel Ariel

-------------<◇>-------------

We begin in this session after Charlotte visits a life in Egypt with her husband.

A: [Aurora] Go ahead and take your last breath now. What is the last thing on your mind?
C: [Charlotte] I am going to see him again.
A: Go ahead and leave your body. Tell me what do you do next when you leave?
C: It is peaceful, it is beautiful, it is bright. It is like buildings. Building is not the right word; it is like it is all made out of light. Gold and white. I see my husband; he is young too. Wings...
A: He has wings?
C: Yeah, I think. So do I. I think we are Angels.
A: What does he look like?
C: Oh, he is really handsome! A little different than in life but, yeah.
A: Does he have a color to him? Or his wings?
C: Wings, wings are kind of whitish silvery. Seems fair. Fair skin. Happy to see me. I feel like I am now in a garden of some sort, we have animals with us.
A: What are they doing there?
C: I think I take care of them. They are just there. They love me. I love them. I care for them.

A: How about you? What do you look like? Do you have any colors to you?

C: I am tall. Long golden hair. Beautiful, really. Simple dress, white. I feel really happy and content.

A: Do you have a color to your wings?

C: My wings seem to be all different colors. Like rainbow but shimmery, blues and greens mainly, I think. Yeah!

A: Beautiful.

C: I want to be with the animals. I enjoy being with them.

A: Fast forward a bit to when something changes... What happens now?

C: Earth's in trouble. They want people to go down and help her. They need people. Earth has gotten dark energetically, people, human beings are getting, they are too lost. They are caught in cycles of karma that they are putting on themselves and then dying with it and entrapping themselves. They are going over and over, repeating. They can't get out. Many have a hard time getting out, they are stuck. They need people to go help. I don't want to go. I am happy, but a bigger part of me does want to help. They need light, it is dark on Earth. It is energetically dark on Earth.

A: Can you see at the beginning of time, was it dark or dense on Earth?

C: Oh no, it is beautiful. Earth was beautiful. It was vibrant, I could say it was vibrant, now it is dark. Almost like black and grey around it, it is just, something happened. There are a lot of Angelic beings, it seems others like me are going to go down, we are going to help.

A: Prior to this, were there Angelic beings already on Earth?

C: Yes.

A: There were some already?

C: There were some, they needed more. There have always been some.

A: Okay. And go back, back, back now to right before it starts turning dark. Back there now. What caused the shifting there of the darkness?

C: It is Reptilians. There are A LOT of them. I feel like they are trapped on Earth, maybe like they could not get off. And then they, they kind of rose to power over time, over thousands of years and then they wanted to dominate humans. Like keep them disempowered. And then the veil was so thick so souls could not remember, so they believed it. The souls who come in now, the Angels, other very strong beings of light. They are coming now to help Earth at this time. It is time for, it's time for Reptilians too. They are trapped in their own cycle they created as well as the humans. They don't realize they are just as much prisoners as the humans they dominate. Earth needs to be freed, the beings on it.

A: They are showing me something. The Reptilians were there and since they are a lower vibration, and everything that you explained that the people were in a lower density stuck in that cycle. So that in a sense, would you say similar to how a drug addict has a drug and becomes stuck in that cycle and they keep using it and using it?

C: Yeah, they don't want it. They know they are trapped here but they are kings here. They want to stay here now.

A: Would you call it an addiction, because there is so much density and they thrive off of densities?

C: Oh yeah, they feed off the low energy. They need our energy. They don't have Source energy like humans do. They need to get that from humans.

A: Explain how that works. How come they don't have Source energy?

C: Oh, they are so negative. They did, they could again, but long ago they grew so dense that the light that feeds souls to be positive was not available to them. The human souls are like bright points of lights all over a map. If you could see it and it's like it is an endless food supply.

They need it, their souls need it. They feed off the energy in humans, that's why there are more Reptilians in densely populated areas. Yes, there is more energy there.

A: Would you say that in areas like New York City where there is a strong population?

C: Oh yeah, oh yeah, that the big cities with strong populations like Los Angeles, Denver, and in the Middle East too. There is a huge population in the Middle East. It is warm. Like the warmth, they need warmth. They could choose to be positively polarized if they wanted to. They don't think they want to. They are addicted now. They have gotten used to this. They have grown to power here, so they are like "why would I leave?"

A: Since you are looking at them, do you think they know about how we are aiding them through this hypnosis to positive polarize?

C: They do. Oh, they do know! There are some that are not happy. They feel that in their ranks. They don't realize how much better they would be if they positively polarized. They could leave Earth if they positively polarized, they could leave Earth. They won't be trapped here. They are angry with the ones who do.

A: The ones that leave?

C: Yes. But they can't do anything about it. Once they positively polarize, they can't do anything.

A: Good. When you were coming down, that husband that was in that life, in that Angelic form?

C: Yes.

A: Does that husband have a name in Angelic form or something he goes by?

C: I am getting Zadkiel. (Archangel Zadkiel)

A: Yes. Beautiful. Was that husband then your Twin Flame?

C: Yes. It is going to be hard though. It is so dense, that if it was too easy, I would not have woken up. I needed to wake up. Otherwise, I would not be able to do what I came here to do to help. To help others like Aurora, many others for bringing light to the planet. That's what we came here to do. So many Angelic beings came here to do that now. It is like we are brightening it. And we are brightening it through bringing the awareness of the true beauty of who the humans really are. That they are not disempowered. Beautiful souls, loved by God, Mother, Father. All one. They are all one. They think they are separate. But they are not separate!

A: Now that you have come upon Earth in that Angelic form, did you enter the body at what point?

C: In the womb.

A: Can you tell me about the process that happened when you were entering this reality? What kind of process did you have to go through to enter into the body?

C: It is just consciousness. I just focus my consciousness into the baby, and slowly just spread out. I don't jump in, I just gently, so gently merge with the developing fetus to become one. It was a good fit. Sometimes it is not. Some souls have a hard time. It was a good fit for me.

A: When you come into the body, as we know we as adults we have forgotten who we are. When you come into the body and merge into the body, do you still remember who you are?

C: Yes, while you are in the womb and as soon as you are born that is when the veil... can't remember. The consciousness is in and out while in the womb, it is boring. I spent more time there the closer it gets to birth. Once the baby is born, there is the veil. We know that. We know we agreed to that.

A: When the baby comes out of the birth canal, what happens?

C: It is like a blank slate. It is when the game begins. It is a game, it is serious, but it is a game. It is like chess. You have to move your pieces to where they are supposed to be. It might not make sense but eventually you will see the pattern, you are like 'ah, I see how it is all connected.' How this person and that person are related to each other and help each other. You don't even realize you are part of each other's game and you put that around the whole world, and you see the master plan. Now there's lights all over the world and they are connected to each other. And the light of one connects with the next and strengthens it. So now the more that are awakened, they become a spot of light that gets added and it is making the Earth brighter and brighter.

A: Yes. Beautiful. We recently talked about that, helping the Earth become brighter in that sense. Thank you for the beautiful addition there!

C: The brighter it is, the easier it is for the souls trapped. Some more, we can help them, the ones that are trapped here. It is making it easier for them now to release. They are trapped in the ether, they are afraid to go on, they are so programmed to fear that they are trapped and then many, many attached to the humans and they are comfortable in the body. And then that's not good. They feed off of them, they don't realize it. Yeah, they don't necessarily mean harm, they are just scared usually but they do harm but don't realize it. That's why everybody is tired. How many people today are so tired and don't realize there is so much draining humans, between Reptilians and devices that drain, and entities drain, and it is another reason why humans are having a hard time. Their lights are dim because of it. They have a hard time pulling out of it.

A: Well first of all, before I continue. Am I speaking to the Higher Self now?

Higher Self: Yes.

A: Okay, I thought you had come in. Thank you, I honor you, I love you, and I respect you. I thank you for all the aid you have given us so far. May I continue to ask you questions?

Higher Self: Yes.

A: Thank you. Love you sister. Do you have a name that you go by?

Higher Self: I am Ariel. (Archangel Ariel)

A: Ah yes, I thought so (chuckles).

AA Ariel: Sister.

A: Why is it that you choose this date for her to have her session? September 19th, 2019?

AA Ariel: It is a powerful date of renewal. The Earth is renewing, the energies are renewing, things are going to get better. And she's needed renewal. She's changed in so many ways. It is a celebration of that change. She can leave the old behind, it is okay. It is okay for everyone to do that. Without guilt, there is no guilt. Don't worry about who you were, it served to get you where you are now.

A: That is beautiful! Thank you.

AA Ariel: Thank you!

A: Do you have any messages in regard to this date? Any other ones?

AA Ariel: Embrace the energies, it's like, it's been dark and rainy. And the sun is out on a day, and that's today. Today, the sun is coming out and it's going to be easier for all the Light Workers who have been struggling. It is going to be easier now. So much easier! The same amount of effort is going to go so much further. Because they are in place. Because the Light Workers who came, so many are in place. And so many are being born so we have so many dots of brightness on this map that is Earth, and we are all connecting. It is like a beautiful pattern, a beautiful web. We strengthen each other and now with the energies coming through the sun, the sun is pivotal. No need to fear anymore.

A: Thank you. That is so beautiful. While you are talking about the sun, I have really noticed that it is quite different. Particularly, I noticed that you could be out in it and it won't really give you such a suntan and burn you. Why is that? The sun seems so much brighter even in winter, this past winter when it was really cold.

AA Ariel: Some of that is awareness. People are moving into the forest now, their bodies are lighter, they could handle more. The sun does not damage like it did once when we were so heavy in the 3D, it did more damage to the 3D body. Its sunlight is like an umbilical cord, it is as if it's growing us into the 4D and 5D. It is strengthening us and lightening us. So, it's like a beautiful umbilical cord of energy, connecting to the humans. The sun is just feeding energy to us and that is why so many are awakening now. Divine Source light is just coming through.

A: Can you tell us a little more about the consistency of the sun and how it interacts with humans and life on Earth?

AA Ariel: It is the physical representation of Source Light. The Source Light is the sun. It was put into physical manifestation for humans too, just as a soul is Source Light itself, the human body needs Source Light as well. So, from within, the soul feeds the body, and from without, the rays of the sun feed the body and connect to the soul. It is just a cycle. It is a beautiful continually perpetuating cycle for the human to always feel the Source Love-Light. It is always there.

A: Wow, so would you say that it is like a regenerator for our light?

AA Ariel: Yes! Absolutely.

A: So, with what you mentioned on how we are tired, and we are exhausted from all the draining all day, the sun can re-energize and re-flame our light?

AA Ariel: Oh yes! Go out in the sun. It is part of the programming too to fear the sun. It just helps keep, without the use of the sun, it is less likely someone will awaken. It feeds the soul, and the soul reaches out for more and as it grows so does the consciousness of the human. It expands, it all expands. It is all Divine Source Light.

A: There has been some mention in some information from other Light Workers that the sun was part of the control or has been infringed at some point. Is this accurate?

AA Ariel: They tried. And for a bit, there was, yeah, it was too strong. They tried to do to the sun what they did to the moon, but they could not. No, the sun is in its wholeness.

A: Beautiful. Ariel, would you be able to explain to us, how our existence works here since we are talking about the sun? See, we have been taught that we all planets rotate around the sun. Is that how it works? How does the sun relate to us in our rotational flow?

AA Ariel: The sun is central. It is all a matrix. It is all physical. It is just a physical representation of consciousness. The consciousness creates it. And the sun is centered. Think of the sun as Divine Source. So yes, of course, we are all of Source. And Source feeds us, and this is just the physical representation of, a physical manifestation of what happens in non-physical. It is beautiful. Source made it that way. He created it to give us clues, so people could look at the sun and think how warm it feels and how uplifted they feel being in it and then correlate that to their soul and how when one has high vibrations, one is able to be closer to Source as we would say. You are more conscious of Source and that is the sun. The sun - as above, so below. It is all physical manifestation. The fact that the sun was Reptilian, it was propaganda that the sun would harm us and then people believed it and became so. If the sun would harm us, then the sun was bad. If the sun was bad, then they are not making the connection between the sun and Source and they are cutting off their own Divinity. It is a mind game!

A: Yes. As I teach much of what you spoke of. How beautiful it is that you are confirming these things for us as well as with the sun. There has been even fear among people who are healers still. So hopefully they are able to get this message that you speak of and no longer fear the sun themselves. As healers, who are supposed to be awakened, who are still fearing the sun when such beauties as you mention can come forth from that connection to the sun.

AA Ariel: It is all perspective because if they fear the sun that it will harm them, then it will. We are all creative Source beings, and we don't even realize why some people can go out in the sun and be fine and others are roasted within half an hour. It is not the sunscreen, it is just they believe they put the sunscreen on, they won't burn and so they don't. So, they think, 'it is the sunscreen'. That is just more chemicals into the human body.

A: The sunscreen chemicals?

AA Ariel: Yeah, yeah.

A: How bad is that putting the chemical on your skin and then the sun?

AA Ariel: The sun activates it; it activates the chemicals within it. It holds the bodies dense. It is not good for the body. It can lead to poison, cancers. Cancers happen when there are too many chemicals built up in the body and then it gets combined with fear, depression, and shame. And together the body develops cancers. It can be cleared. Part of cancer is the power. It is the fear that people give it. Does not need to be. It is negative and fear feeds it.

A: You mentioned the moon. What can we do about the moon to try to make it more positively polarized?

AA Ariel: No, there is nothing we can do. There are other races taking care of that now. The moon has shifted. It is not as negative controlled as it once was. It is part of helping the Earth shift, 3D needs to be done. It needs to go. And the rulers that were ruling, that were overtaking the moon, they were part of holding it in place so strong. They know their time is almost done.

A: There is a rumor or mention that a certain man is trying to put something over the sun. What are your thoughts on that, Ariel?

AA Ariel: No. The sun is coming into her power. They are not going to be successful. They can try. They will try, but it is not going to work.

A: Good. Can you tell us a little more about again, this date, you mentioned that it was going to help with all that you mentioned? Is there any more information you can share with us in regard to the awakening on Earth?

AA Ariel: It is an activation date. You are right, Aurora. Just like December 12th, 2012 is an activation date, so is September 19, 2019. Many are awakening, many are awakening. The energies that have been coming through the summer, August adds up to it, it was all for this date. This is the big date.

A: Wow. There were some strong energies adding up to it.

AA Ariel: People, many expect to see, they expect to see physical changes, they expect, it is not like that. It is energetic and they will say, "See! Nothing happened." But it did. It is happening within the souls. It is all about the souls. And the advancement of the souls. Souls need to awaken. It is time, 3D served for a long time. For a long time, souls came for here. They came for expansion, but it was never meant to be 3D. Earth was supposed to be 5D. But with the Reptilians, trapped them here using 3D, matrix overlay, trapped. Many wanted to come back though, it is hard, and there is a lot of expansion, so it is difficult to decide what to do with 3D. Because the Galactics who are in charge of this moon, don't want to infringe on the free will of the souls who come here for the expansion. But it is time, it is time for the 3D matrix. It has had its time. And souls need to expand. And the Reptilians that are trapped here need, they need to polarize back to positive. They have been too long... they are going to be fully lost if they are here much longer.

A: Ariel, I know it is silly to ask for a percentage, but this helps out people feel and sense. Is there like a certain percentage you can tell us, who is working on awakening on this date?

AA Ariel: We are around 40 percent. We are getting so close.

A: We are around 40 percent of awakening?

AA Ariel: Yeah, 40 percent light, not all are fully awakened. But their light is bright, they have a high vibration.

A: Do you mean 40 percent on Earth?

AA Ariel: Yes, we need to get to 51 percent.

A: Yes. Ran across a few people who were very negatively polarized. There was a shift in them, where you are seeing more of a light in them.

AA Ariel: Yes, they won't know of all the truths you teach. They are not meant to awaken to that level of truth in this lifetime but even someone who is dark who stops and pets a dog or cat or high fives a child, those are all raising their vibrations. It does not take much. It does not take grand acts. In the dark souls, those are huge. And then the next day, they will do a little bit more. And then maybe they will volunteer. And maybe they will help someone else. And again, the web, the web grows. The web of light. It is ok, you don't have to... I know many people wanted to share their truth and because it is, it is so beautiful, it is so empowering. You don't have to. You don't have to. You know when the person is there when you are supposed to, and you can. You have a soul contract with them to help them awaken but not everyone you meet. You don't need to tell everyone you meet. Just show high vibration, smile at them, pay a sincere compliment, leave them better than you found them. Even in a small way and you will have helped raise their vibration. They are contributing to the grid that way, with their light. There are no small acts. And now that so many people are doing them, we are going to see significant growth and now with the energies of this day, good times are coming!

A: Beautiful. Simple acts of love.

AA Ariel: Yes, yes! We call it small but there is no small.

A: These energies, will they still carry on?

AA Ariel: Yes, they are here now. They are here now. There is no going backward. Earth is not going back to the darkness it once was, it has come too far.

A: Oh, such a beautiful message you bring to my heart sister!

AA Ariel: Well, you have done so much work. You are a large part of this, beautiful sister, it is why you came. You heard the call as well.

A: My heart feels lighter, thank you.

AA Ariel: You are welcome.

A: All that you spoke of, I feel it deeply vibrating in my soul and in my heart. So, thank you for these messages.

AA Ariel: Thank you for all you do. It helps so many.

A: Thank you. While we are speaking, a bit of control there. She was pretty much brought up as you mentioned in religion. But in a religion that was very controlled where it was a Catholic type of religion, but it was very occult.

AA Ariel: Yes.

A: Can you tell us a bit more about that and what we can see from religion?

Ariel: Well, many who are in religions like that choose it because it catalyzes them. While religion itself is a negative polarization of Earth, it is used by many souls as a jumping-off point. Because there is truth within all of them but then they distort it, and they use it. So, the soul feels the truth and is drawn to the truth, but then it is distorted and manipulated if you see what I mean. So, they give you a little bit, where you are like, "oh, it is beautiful," "I am a child of God," "I do have an eternal soul" for example. "If I do all the right things, then I can be with God someday." You can see how subtly it is twisted. Then this beautiful soul believes that she/he and God are separate because if it were, otherwise, they would not need religion. And then religions would not have power. And we go back to power. So many, many will be able to release religion in this new energy. But they need to be careful to not fight against, as that perpetuates the problem as well. It lowers the vibration. You need to thank the religion for what it brought to you, you need to tell the religion it no longer serves you, and you need to break your contract and be free. And it is okay, nobody is going to hell. There is no hell. The only hell is here, on this plane. This is the densest.

A: Yes, thank you for such beautiful messages. Before we start her body scan, is there anything else you want to mention to us about Earth's Ascension and this day, anything else?

AA Ariel: Celebrate each other. Celebrate the light you see in each other. Know that our time is near, the time we all came for. We are going to see it. Those of us are going to see it.

A: Beautiful. Thank you, sister. And when you say, "see it," do you mean like physically or do you mean like subtle ways throughout our life?

AA Ariel: Subtle ways throughout our life. Souls, many souls won't be reincarnating back on 3D. Those souls that were trapped. But we create within our 3D lives, you will see people who suffer greatly in darkness, and then you see someone lives a beautiful blessed life. And even though we are still one is 5D or 4D, one is 3D, we still interact with each other, there won't be a separate place now. It will be in our own lives. We will have better things in our lives and then after we pass away from this reality, we won't be trapped here. Any souls that are trapped here won't be trapped here. Their souls will be free, and they can go on for expansion - 4th, 5th, 6th. But for those expecting a...it won't happen physically on this. It will be next; it will be where we go next. It will be an option for us. But this Earth is getting lighter. It is getting brighter. And so much of the evil is going to be gone, so it will go back to the way it was supposed to be. It will be a 5D Earth slowly because of the energies, the 3D matrix is being lifted. That is being lifted. No longer serves.

A: The negative matrix (Inverted A.I. Matrix) that was controlling, keeping the souls trapped. How is the progress on that?

AA Ariel: Oh, it is coming. It is weakening. The hold is weakening. The souls, it is like birth again, birth is a good analogy. They are able to come, they are in darkness and they are starting to see the light, and they can go towards it. It is not held so heavy. Because there are holes in the 3D matrix, that's why they can see the light because the 5D is just underneath it. It is covered. It was supposed to always be 5D. It was created to be 5D, and 3D was overlaid thousands of years ago.

A: How important do you think it is for those of us who are practicing entity removal? At times we are working very hard and even among our colleagues, they don't believe in entity removal. How significant is this on Earth as far as this Ascension and brightness.

AA Ariel: It is of utmost significance. You need to continue doing your work, Aurora. You need to continue to train others so that more and more people are doing it. You need to send Love-Light to those practitioners. They are still caught up in the matrix. But they will see, they will see. People are slow sometimes to release old beliefs. But it is of very high importance, A.U.R.A. especially. It is the only one that does the entity release and frees them, it frees the human, and it frees the entity.

A: Would you say that when we have an A.U.R.A. session and after removing implants, portals, hooks, you know entities, Reptilians within them, and we go through this whole process of removal. Would you say that this is in a sense removing the negative Inverted A.I. Matrix within them that is holding them within it?

AA Ariel: Certainly, it is weakening. It is weakening the 3D hold, it is raising them to 4D. Yeah, it allows their light to absorb the Source Light that is there for them, but they can't when they are held so heavy in 3D. And once they are free and released, it just floods into every cell and it is so much easier for the soul to raise the consciousness of the body it is in. It is the consciousness, but it helps the ego. The ego consciousness. This is great work. It needs to be, it will be spread.

A: Thank you, for all of your guidance! As you know I am hosting retreats now, getting more of a group placed together and getting more certified out there. So, thank you.

AA Ariel: Oh yes, that was designed.

A: Yes, of course. Now as far as what you mentioned earlier that there is 40 percent light, would you say that the goal is to get it above 50 percent of the collective of Earth to light?

AA Ariel: Yes, yes, yes. Has to be over 51 percent, majority. It is at that point; the majority will no longer desire the 3D matrix and it will have to crumble. Because the highest good must always be served, because if the highest good is still at 60 percent 3D, then 3D will have to persist. But once the highest good is no longer below 50 percent, the highest good is 5D and then 5D will have to persist.

A: Thank you. What would you say about the process of getting us here? Before this process started, say in the summer months and August that got us here to this September 19th, 2019 portal date of activation - what percentage would you say it was as far as the light on Earth? Just wondering what the significance is, what the difference would be.

AA Ariel: It does not all happen on this date. This day is a catalyst. This date, the energies come in. So, through the summer we were in the high 30's, the activations in August brought us to 40 percent where we are now. And then over the next few months, we are going to see it steady. Every day it will be increasing. It is not going to be stuck energetically anymore like you know, maybe a few months will go by and not much has changed. No, it is going to make your head spin. It is starting today. Today is the day the energies start coming in and now the energies need to be assimilated by the humans. They are going to feel different. Those who are ready, have not awakened yet but are ready, will start feeling lighter. They are going to start feeling happier, they are going to realize their vibrations are rising. And those who are still deep in 3D, well they are going to feel it too, but Source never forces anyone. It is always a free choice. If they desire to stay in 3D, then they shall stay in 3D. No one is forced to do anything.

A: Thank you for these messages. It has been an inspiration upon this existence in this time and space! Thank you, sister. I love you dearly.

AA Ariel: I love you dearly.

A: Now at this point, can I please ask for the body scan to begin?

AA Ariel: Yes.

A: If you can scan her from top to bottom and along the way let us know if you need any aid from our brothers and sisters.

AA Ariel: I would like to call in Michael for this please.

A: Okay. Good. Ariel, if you could please connect us to Michael now... Archangel Michael?

AA Michael: Yes.

A: Brother, is that you?

AA Michael: Yes! Hello sister!

A: Hello, I love you, honor you, and respect you. Thank you!

AA Michael: I honor, love you, and respect you as well.

A: Thank you. Sister Ariel here, who is the Higher Self of this beautiful being here, is requesting your aid during the body scan. Can you please assist us?

AA Michael: Of course.

The Body Scan begins.

A: Wonderful. If you can start scanning from head to toe now and see where it is, you want to start off first that has any density within.

AA Michael: Ah, throat.

A: Okay, what is in the throat?

AA Michael: Dark energy.

A: Can you scan it for energy, entities, or Reptilian consciousness?

AA Michael: It is energy.

A: What is the root to that energy? What initially caused the energy?

AA Michael: Religion, disempowerment, she would not be heard, she could not be heard. She had to suppress so much.

A: That energy, I want you to look behind it, Michael, and make sure it is not rooted or attached to anything negative besides the energy itself.

AA Michael: Oh, there is a portal.

A: Okay. Michael if you could start closing that, please.

AA Michael: Yes.

A: Good. Can you tell me, when was this portal inserted?

AA Michael: In childhood. It was her religion. Religion has always been a problem. They just kept it strong, many years, it would just keep it so strong, kept feeding it through this portal. This energy was fed through this portal. It is going to help. She is going to have an easier time saying no to religion without the guilt, with this portal closed.

A: Okay, good. And as you finish closing it, if we could have Archangel Ariel there start filling in Love-Light to it as it is closed. Nice and strong, making that chakra at its strength for her highest good now. I kept coughing throughout the session. Glad we addressed that. Now if you could explain, what exactly is a portal? What does that mean?

AA Michael: It is a backdoor for energy to feed into another being. So, if you want to put negative energy into someone, you install an energetic portal and you can easily bypass that person's defenses and just feed it right in. That's why they are usually put in when people are weak before they are strong. In children or adults who are in depression, or drug use. They can't control you of course, but they can fill you with negative energy that then acts upon the consciousness of the being. It is very important work you are doing, closing these.

A: Thank you for explaining that. If we can scan the rest of her body, tell us where else you want to address next, Michael, that needs to be healed.

AA Michael: The solar plexus, chest, entity. Middle of the chest, entity.

A: Okay. Is it an entity or a Reptilian?

AA Michael: It is a Reptilian.

A: Archangel Michael, please surround it now with the alchemy symbols.

AA Michael: Yes.

A: Is it surrounded?

AA Michael: Yes.

A: Good. I would like to speak to that Reptilian there in her heart Archangel Michael, if you could please move it up now. Bring it up, up, up, I'd like to speak to it now, please.

Reptilian: Yes?

A: Greetings. Thank you for speaking to us. Love you, honor you, and respect you. May I ask you questions, please?

Reptilian: Okay.

A: Thank you. Can I ask, when was it that you attached yourself there to her chest?

Reptilian: In her teens.

A: What was going on with her that allowed you to come in during her teens?

Reptilian: She was angry at the disempowerment that she felt because she is powerful. Humph, she was too powerful. Something needed to be done about that.

A: Is that why you came in?

Reptilian: Mm-hmm. I drain her energy sometimes. I sometimes feed her anger; she doesn't know why she is so angry. Like, "this is no big deal" but she is angry. Yeah, that's me!

A: Is that what you all as Reptilians do? Do you feed anger to people, rage?

Reptilian: Yes, there are other things but for her, yes. Strong emotions are powerful.

A: Was this a contract?

Reptilian: No.

A: Do you have a body somewhere else?

Reptilian: No. No, I was just a non-physical entity. Her anger, deep anger, suppression. About being suppressed, drew my attention. It was like oooh! I nestled right in her heart (sighs).

A: I understand that you have been there for a while. As you know, we have been talking today about Earth's Ascension itself and how it is rising every day and it has entered such a beautiful part in our Earth's history as far as positivity. Now, as you know when the Earth ascends finally, no longer entities like you will be able to hold this frequency and they will be recycled straight back to Source. We are giving you an opportunity to do that today instead of being recycled straight back to Source. We love to be able to aid you in a positive polarization of Ascension where you could be free. Perhaps incarnate somewhere else and keep the memories and experiences you have gained through jumping inside of people and different situations that you learned. You are able to keep these and become wiser and be your own sovereign being having your light, no longer having to feed off of anyone else. Be your own creator. Would you allow us to aid you today into a positive polarizing Ascension?

Reptilian: Yes, this body has become uncomfortable anyways. It is too bright now.

A: Thank you for allowing us to aid you today. We want you to find that light within you now. We are going to help you spread it to all that is you, every root, every cord, every part of you that does not belong to her but belongs to you. Spread it to all light. Let us know when you are all light...

Positive Polarized Reptilian: Ah, it is done.

A: Go ahead and remove yourself from her heart now. Make sure you don't leave any piece of you behind, let us know once you are fully out.

Positive Polarized Reptilian: (sigh) Fully, fully out.

A: Beautiful. Ariel, please start filling in with Love-Light to that area where it was diminished from this entity's removal. Thank you for removing yourself. Now tell me, do you have a message for her before you go?

Positive Polarized Reptilian: I am sorry. I am so sorry.

A: Do you remember who you are now?

Positive Polarized Reptilian: Yes, I was dark for so long. Oh, this is so much better! I am so sorry. The anger I filled her chest with, she used to be able to feel it. She won't anymore, it is gone.

A: That is beautiful. Thank you for allowing us to aid you, most importantly.

Positive Polarized Reptilian: Oh, thank you!

A: It has been an honor! Michael, can you have Archangel Azrael and his Legion ensure that this beautiful entity that is now positively polarized goes to where it is meant to go without any infringement? Make sure they don't get tricked along the way, please.

AA Michael: Yes.

A: Thank you. May we follow you and see where you are going?

Positive Polarized Reptilian: Surely.

A: Thank you.

Positive Polarized Reptilian: The sun.

A: You are going to the sun?

Positive Polarized Reptilian: There is a portal in the middle of the sun. Interesting, I remember this.

A: Tell me what happens once you go through the sun.

Positive Polarized Reptilian: Through the sun, there is another source, another Dimension. You cannot access it except through the sun. You can't get that close to the sun if you are negatively polarized. You see...ah! I have a home planet here.

A: Tell us about your planet.

Positive Polarized Reptilian: It is green, and it is very lush. There is a lot of water.

A: Are there other beings there?

Positive Polarized Reptilian: Yeah, yes there are others. I don't have a body, but I can see it all. It is Reptilian and they are not all bad. There is a lot of good. A lot of good. There are a lot of cities. It is different than Earth. It looks different than Earth.

A: Is this a positive polarized Reptilian planet, is that what you are seeing?

Positive Polarized Reptilian: Yeah, yeah. It is not as pretty as Earth (chuckles).

A: That's beautiful. Yes, we heard about this planet a couple of times now through different sessions. Thank you.

Positive Polarized Reptilian: Mmmm!

A: Thank you (chuckles).

Positive Polarized Reptilian: I am home now. Thank you for releasing me. Ahh! Please continue to help us. Help my brothers and sisters.

A: Thank you.

Positive Polarized Reptilian: It is important (sighs).

A: Are they able to hear you telepathically if you talk to them? The ones that are already there?

Positive Polarized Reptilian: Yes!

A: If we can ask them, is this a planet where some of them who were positively polarized are going now too?

Positive Polarized Reptilian: Yes, many. It is like a homecoming. Ah! They are like cheering for me! (laughs) Ah! I am home! (sighs) They are saying, "Aurora, keep doing the work you are doing. Teach this work. It is important. We need help. We are victims as well to a large degree. Even though it is by choice, that choice is infringed upon to make us think, to delude us, that we did not want to polarize positive now. That's false." It is so beautiful here. We have family here.

A: How many would you say are there currently?

Positive Polarized Reptilian: Hundreds, many more in physical form but in non-physical that had been released are still here.

A: Thank you (chuckles).

Positive Polarized Reptilian: Yeah, hundreds. And I see some are very happy, the mention of you, that they were released by you.

A: (chuckles).

Positive Polarized Reptilian: It is important that we are guided here. A lot can happen at that portal. The sun portal. We can be waylaid.

A: Thank you, my infinite love to all of you on this planet, and may you continue enjoying this beautiful paradise for you. For you are beautiful equals to Creation as well.

Positive Polarized Reptilian: Thank you.

A: Love you, honor you, respect you.

Positive Polarized Reptilian: Thank you.

A: Thank you... Whew, Archangel Michael?

AA Michael: Yes.

A: Thank you, wow that was so powerful! … Archangel Michael, can you scan her whole body since we are speaking of Reptilian consciousness. I want to make sure she does not have any more in her body. Scan her whole body from head to toe, please. Does she have anymore?

AA Michael: Crown.

A: Can you please surround it now with the alchemy symbols?

AA Michael: Yes.

A: Thank you, and does she have any more anywhere else?

AA Michael: Third eye. Upper chakras.

A: Okay, let's surround that one too please with alchemy symbols. Continue scanning. I'd like to talk to all of them, as many as she has in all her body, we will talk to them together.

AA Michael: That's it.

A: Those two? Very good. Thank you, Michael.

AA Michael: Yes.

A: If I could please speak to both of you there. Michael, if you can help guide. Guide them up, I would like to speak to them now. Greetings!

Reptilians: Hello.

A: Thank you for speaking to us. Were you able to witness what just happened with the Reptilian in the heart?

Reptilians: Yes, yes.

A: So, we give you the same opportunity. Would you be willing to positive polarize so that you will not recycle straight to Source?

Reptilians: Oh, yes, please.

A: Wonderful. Go ahead and find that Love-Light within you now. Spread it to all that is you, every root, every cord, and let us know when you are all Love-Light.

Positive Polarized Reptilians: Yes, it is done.

A: Wonderful, go ahead and remove yourselves completely from those areas that you are in. Make sure you don't leave any piece of you behind and let me know once you are all out.

Positive Polarized Reptilians: Okay... Okay, we are out.

A: Thank you, and do you have a message for her before you go?

Positive Polarized Reptilians: You should feel lighter now, you should be able to connect easier now. We were also there as religion kept it dark. And we came as that call. We heard that call. Many, many, many on this Earth, deep in religion. But you don't need to be kept dark anymore. That time is over. Thank you.

A: Beautiful. Thank you. If we can have again, Archangel Azrael and his Legion guide both of these now positive polarized entities to where it is that they are meant to go.

AA Azrael: Of course.

A: Thank you, make sure they don't get tricked along the way. Which way are they going?

AA Azrael: They passed away on this planet and they got trapped here and embedded themselves. They died in fear. They found a home. They are going now to their afterlife experience. Continuing where they should have gone long ago.

A: Good. Did they too go through the sun?

AA Azrael: No.

A: Which way did they go?

AA Azrael: There is a portal at the top of the solar system, the non-physical can go through there to the afterlife. There are several. There is one in the center of the Earth as well, but they chose that one.

A: Wonderful. Thank you. May they be surrounded by the Love-Light of the Universe. Blessings to them and thank you Azrael for escorting them as well, and your team.

AA Azrael: Thank you. Yes.

A: Now, can you scan the body for any type of entity, please? I want to make sure we don't miss anything. Michael?

AA Michael: Yes, I think she is clear.

A: Beautiful. Okay, I am still going to go through the list here that I have. Now, if we can scan her vision. She said her vision is not that well. Can we heal her vision please?

AA Michael: No, it is a contract. It's okay. She could not see so well without teaching her to look within. Her vision needs to be within.

A: Thank you. Okay, now as far age regression, can we age regress her?

AA Michael: Yes.

A: How many years can we age regress her?

AA Michael: Fifteen.

A: Fifteen? Very good.

AA Michael: Yes.

A: (chuckles) Yes! She's going to like that. Archangel Michael, can you start that process now?

AA Michael: Of course.

A: Okay, thank you.

AA Michael: Her crown and third eye are so clear now. They were blocked before.

A: She wanted to open up her abilities of her third eye, can we ensure that this will happen now too?

AA Michael: Oh yes, yes. The entity there was blocking, she felt blockage, she should be fine now.

A: Good. And her heart, can we have Ariel expand to the biggest in this time and space for her?

AA Michael: Yes, her heart is her power.

A: Lovely. Can you scan her now for any negative cords, Michael? Let me know if you find any.

AA Michael: Ears.

A: She has negative cords in her ears? And what is that connected to?

AA Michael: Fear. She had a lot of fear as a child.

A: Can we go ahead and transmute those cords. Are they needed there?

AA Michael: No. No, they are not needed.

A: Any other negative cords around her?

AA Michael: Just there.

A: Good. Can you do that for us now, Michael?

AA Michael: Yes.

A: Thank you. Now can we scan her for any negative implants, hooks, or portals? Okay, one more time, make sure we don't miss anything.

AA Michael: All looks bright.

A: Beautiful, thank you. Let us know once that hook is removed.

AA Michael: It has been there for a while.

A: Let us know once it has been transmuted. And let's see, now...

AA Michael: It is gone.

A: Wonderful. Thank you. And how is her chakra system looking now?

AA Michael: Mmm! Get your sunglasses!

A: (laughter) Beautiful, thank you. Any contracts that we can go ahead and remove that are no longer needed for her highest good?

AA Michael: She had a contract with the church, but she broke it herself.

The client mentioned during the interview that as a little girl, her family's religion was extremely strict on penance. So much that when throwing out the trash, she would walk on glass to pay for her sins.

A: Wonderful!

AA Michael: That was brave.

A: (chuckles) Was it broken okay?

AA Michael: It is broken good! She wrote it down and she burned it. I was there, she called upon me to be there to make sure it was done right. The paper did not want to burn.

A: Hmm yeah, I believe it. Wow! Well, thank you for your assistance with her then.

AA Michael: She is beautiful.

A: Yes, she is. As far as trauma, can you scan her for any trauma currently in this life or past life trauma. And also look into...

AA Michael: Kinesiology.

A: Thank you. She had something occur to her, some kind of trauma. Not sure what it was, maybe when she was younger. Can you scan for that? What was that about?

AA Michael: Yes, she saw a scary TV show. That was the fear in her ear, the cords, that, yeah, that was connected to that event. Yeah, it needed to be cut and we did. It is good now but that was what that was.

A: Let us know if there is any current trauma from this life or past lives that need to be healed.

AA Michael: She has had some good protectors. Been through a lot emotionally, now she's okay. Yeah, she is okay.

A: Wonderful, thank you. Okay, and then also if you could, the doctors have her on high blood pressure pills. Can we scan her for that, where is the root to that?

AA Michael: That was the entity, no wonder they could not figure out what was wrong.

A: Which one, which entity?

AA Michael: The one in her heart.

A: Yes. Can we go ahead and heal her high blood pressure as well? She also mentioned cholesterol as well, can we heal both?

AA Michael: Yes. Yes.

A: Thank you, is there anything she can do on her end naturally?

AA Michael: She knows what to do.

A: At this point, we have gone through the whole body scan and healed what needed to be healed. If you can scan her one last time to make sure. Double-check, Michael, for any entities, negative implants, hooks, portals, Reptilians, anything negative that we can remove from her.

AA Michael: No, she is glowing.

A: Beautiful. Thank you, ah, what a joy!

AA Michael: Thank you! Always sister.

A: Thank you for your assistance greatly within the A.U.R.A.'s and everyone else who assisted as well. Thank you to all of you.

AA Michael: It is my pleasure.

A: I know it is a team effort. Love you all infinitely. Thank you, Michael and everyone.

AA Michael: Yes, thank you.

A: Michael, can you transfer me back to her Higher Self Ariel?

AA Michael: Of course.

A: Ariel, she has several questions here. I was wondering if we could go through and answer them for her. She wanted her DNA regenerated and repaired. Can we start that process for her?

AA Ariel: Yes.

A: So that her metabolism be increased and the DNA of her soul, weight is easier to maintain as well.

AA Ariel: DNA can be reactivated from different lifetimes.

A: Good, can we do that? Can you work with Michael on that?

AA Ariel: Oh yes!

A: Thank you. Now, if we can continue connecting to Michael, there are a couple of more things she wants to have addressed as far as healing. Now Ariel, if we can cleanse her immunizations to prevent future development of diseases such as Alzheimer's and other things that immunizations can cause.

AA Ariel: Yes, we will work on that.

A: Beautiful. Can you scan for her sinus issues related to allergies? She is always having some level of sinus congestion, what is that?

AA Ariel: It was connected to the entity that was in her upper chakras, in her third eye. It is a blockage, and many people have it today. Their third eyes are blocked, it is often a symptom. She should breathe naturally now that it is gone. We will fill it with Love-Light.

A: Beautiful. And she is learning in the Priestess program currently so she will learn how to use the Phoenix Fire there. Could she, if she ever feels any type of negativity, she can use the Phoenix Fire to clear it out?

AA Ariel: Oh yes, oh yes.

A: Okay, thank you. If you can also look behind her left ear. For several years she has had eczema, what is the root to it?

AA Ariel: Impurities in the blood. It is physical in nature.

A: Can we go ahead and heal that?

AA Ariel: We can go ahead and cleanse the blood. That should take care of it.

A: Good, can we start that process of cleansing the blood now?

AA Ariel: Yes.

A: Thank you. Okay, how is she holding up so far?

Ariel: Oh, she is doing great!

A: Wonderful. She has several things, but I think I am going to go ahead and go to the one that is really holding her back in this life currently. If we could please speak back to Michael, Ariel?

AA Michael: I am here.

A: Thank you, Michael. Now she would like to basically remove the Reptilian entity within her husband, would you be able to connect us to his Higher Self?

AA Michael: I would like help with that, please. I would like to bring in Metatron for that as well.

A: Very good. Michael, if you could connect us to Metatron, please?

AA Metatron: Yes.

A: Thank you, brother. If we can now please connect us to the Higher Self of her husband?

Husband's Higher Self: Hello.

A: Hello! Thank you for speaking to us. I love you, honor you, and respect you. May I ask you questions, please?

Husband's Higher Self: Yes.

A: Thank you. We have here this beautiful soul who is married to the fractal of you. He has strong energies within him, and she was wondering if you would give permission so we can remove it so that we can start the awakening process within him.

Husband's Higher Self: Oh yes, we have been waiting long.

A: Thank you. If you could tell us what is it that he has within him please, that we can heal?

Husband's Higher Self: This black goo in his third eye area which is holding his mind very dense. And in his heart, it is holding his heart very dense. She described feeling a wall. That is what it is.

A: Can we go ahead and start transmuting then? Can I use the Phoenix Fire?

Husband's Higher Self: You will need the Phoenix Fire, it is strong.

A: Before I do it though, are you sure this is not a consciousness of some kind?

Husband's Higher Self: There is also a consciousness.

A: Okay, so what is the consciousness? Is it a Reptilian?

Husband's Higher Self: Yes.

A: Do we need to talk to it or will it positive polarize?

Husband's Higher Self: It won't go on its own.

A: It won't go. Metatron, Michael, can you surround it now with the alchemy symbols, please? We would like to speak to that Reptilian there within his body, if it could please come up, up, come up, up now. Greetings!

Reptilian: Yes?

A: Thank you for speaking to us. We love you, honor you, and respect you. May I ask you questions, please?

Reptilian: If you must.

A: Thank you. How long have you been in him?

Reptilian: Many lifetimes.

A: Where are you in his body?

Reptilian: I am anchored in his heart.

A: Are there more of you there in the body?

Reptilian: Yes.

A: Higher Self, can we remove any more in him?

Husband's Higher Self: Yes, there are many. He is the strongest. About 20.

A: Higher Self, are we allowed to have Michael and Metatron surround them all with alchemy symbols now?

Husband's Higher Self: Absolutely, yes. Yes, full permission.

A: Okay, very good. We are surrounding them all now. If you can all surround them. Let me talk back to that Reptilian there in his heart.

Reptilian: Yes.

A: Thank you, for speaking to us. Do you have a body somewhere else that you are connected to?

Reptilian: Yes.

A: Would you please connect us to that body that you are connected to? I would like to speak to that Reptilian body now, please.

Reptilian Body: Yes? I am here.

A: Greetings. Thank you for speaking to us. Love you, honor you, and respect you. May I ask you questions, please?

Reptilian Body: Yes.

A: This consciousness that is attached, that is part of you, he said, he has been there several lives.

Reptilian Body: Yes.

A: There are several others, I believe 20 of them in his body. Now I understand that you all have been very comfortable there and have been there for a while. As you know, Earth is ascending, and we would love to be able to aid you because as Earth ascends and shifts you will be recycled straight back to Source. Instead of doing that, we would love to be able to aid you to keep your consciousness, your memories, your experiences and instead, positive polarize into Ascension. Would you allow us to aid you today in that manner? There is a beautiful planet that awaits your remembrance of who you truly are.

Reptilian Body: We are strong within him. We are afraid that if we leave, we will be without the same strength that we want to have. We hold him strong. We don't want to let go; we are afraid to let go.

A: However, there is an even greater strength when you no longer have to use someone in a parasitic manner. Where you are your own sovereign creator being and you can manifest your own light whenever it is that you need it. Would that not be more beautiful instead? You would be empowered; you would be sovereign. Therefore, there is great power to that, into a positive Ascension.

Reptilian Body: I understand, yes.

A: Wonderful. Thank you. I am speaking to all of you now. Thank you for accepting, all of you within the body.

Reptilians: Yes.

A: Do all of you want to go ahead and positively ascend?

Reptilians: Yes, all do.

A: Wonderful. Now go ahead and find that light within you. We are all focusing on you. Find that light within you and spread it to all that is of you, every root, every cord, all 20 of you.

Reptilians: (sighs).

A: Turn into Love-Light and then let me know when you all are light.

Positive Polarized Reptilians: We are light.

A: Beautiful! Go ahead and remove yourself from his body now. Let me know once you are all out. Don't leave any piece of you behind.

Positive Polarized Reptilians: Okay, we are out.

A: Beautiful. Thank you. Do you have a message for his wife or him before you go?

Positive Polarized Reptilian: Tell her I am so sorry; she has suffered greatly. And we knew it, and we knew she was, and we took pleasure in it. We are sorry. And we are sorry to him as well. She is his Twin Flame and for lifetimes we kept him from connecting with her. We do things like these where they meet and he does not know, and he does not treat her the way he would want to. We are sorry. Should be better now.

A: Thank you.

Positive Polarized Reptilians: Thank you.

A: If we can have Archangel Azrael and his Legion, take every single one of those 20 who positively polarized. As well as the one that had the physical body, regained himself once more and then, aid them in the process of Ascension into a positive polarization to where it is that they are meant to go. Ensuring that they do not get tricked along the way, please.

AA Azrael: The one with the body, is back, he is on the ship... Alright, he is positively polarized, he is not going to hurt anybody anymore.

A: Good.

AA Azrael: The others, I shall guide through the same portal as earlier.

A: Beautiful. Is this Azrael?

AA Azrael: Yes.

A: Thank you brother, I love you. Very good. Thank you. Higher Self of Charlotte's husband, thank you for allowing that removal, it has been a great honor to be able to do that for him. She wanted to know; will she notice a difference?

Husband's Higher Self: She should notice a difference. It won't be, I mean he is still him, you know, I mean, he is kind of a tough nut. But yeah, the walls should be crumbling, she should see the wall crumble. His heart should be more open. It will take some time, please tell her to be patient. You could take some time, but the wall is gone.

A: Oh beautiful, thank you! Now the deprogramming needs to start occurring.

Husband's Higher Self: Yes, yes, there is a lot.

A: Do you think he will be able to come back from it, Higher Self?

Husband's Higher Self: Not fully in this time. It is okay.

A: Any advice on how she can approach his ego-self? How can she handle him?

Husband's Higher Self: Sometimes he like she does not respect him. That is not true. She does, but he interprets it that way. He has lots of insecurity because of all the entities, they made that in him to feel that way. She should be able to show him kindness and he will accept it instead of pushing it away. Like what is happening. It will be slow, but she will see it. Kindness will start showing itself because he is beautiful. He has been subjugated for so long, but after this lifetime, it will be gone. That won't be following him anymore like it has been. Thank you for freeing me.

A: I love you, honor you and respect you, and thank you for allowing us to aid you today.

Husband's Higher Self: Continue to help, he may not accept it, but you are doing what you need to for her. And when you help her, she is able to help him, it is beautiful.

A: Thank you, I shall!

Husband's Higher Self: Thank you!

A: Can I please speak to Archangel Michael once more?

AA Michael: This is Michael.

A: Ah, thank you, Michael. Can you connect me to Metatron now?

AA Michael: Yes.

AA Metatron: Hello sister!

A: Hello Metatron! Thank you for being here, I love you, honor you, and respect you. She wanted to know about her children, do her children require Metatron's assistance today?

AA Metatron: Her oldest has a block. Yeah, he has an entity. We can remove that.

A: Does the Higher Self give permission to remove it?

AA Metatron: Yes.

A: Good. Do we need to talk to him, or can we just remove it?

AA Metatron: No, he is more of an overshadowing keeping him in the mind. He is too in the mind, and that is what this entity is doing.

A: Okay, can you and Michael go ahead and remove it with the Higher Self's permission?

AA Metatron: Entity has agreed. Yes.

A: Okay, wonderful. Thank you. If we can go through that whole positive polarization, spreading the light, removing it, filling in Love-Light into the areas as well with the Higher Self filling in light where those 20 Reptilians were at, please.

AA Metatron: We need to transmute goo there. There is black there, heavy, heavy black. Energetic, it is not an entity. It is dense, dense energy. In the stomach.

A: In the son?

AA Metatron: In the husband.

A: Okay, sending Phoenix Fire now to transmute the goo that the Higher Self allows.

AA Metatron: Hmm, yes sister.

A: Thank you... Okay, now back to the son. If we can just help that entity positively ascend, and then again have Azrael guide it to where it is meant to go, not being tricked.

AA Metatron: Yes. There is a Reptilian as well.

A: Okay. Wow, thank you. Love you, honor you, respect you. Thank you for allowing us to remove you. May you be surrounded by the Love-Light of the Universe!

Positive Polarized Reptilian: Thank you. I am sorry, he is a wonderful boy.

A: She has been there for some time. Higher Self, so I am looking through and I see that we have answered at least half. So, let's see...

A couple of days before her A.U.R.A. session, Charlotte had an Akashic Reading with Aurora, where she was introduced to the Lava Dragon that is with her. Her husband created a fire outside, and this Dragon appeared in it!

A: Her connection to the large alchemist Fire Dragon, does she have a message for her?

Fire Dragon: Yes, I am here to help you and protect you. We are going to take this Priestess course together.

A: Beautiful.

Fire Dragon: I could teach her much, always with her. Even when she doesn't know I am transmuting around her.

A: You have such a beautiful energy, thank you.

Fire Dragon: Her cat too. She loves him. Fluffy little cat but he is powerful on the other side. It is like a lion, a griffin, a lion with wings, they are powerful. He protects her. He is just a fluffy little cat here, but everything is more than it appears.

A: Yes. (chuckles) So you are saying that her cat is what?

Fire Dragon: He is a griffin. I am a dragon.

A: He is a griffin, oh! Beautiful (chuckles).

Fire Dragon: Yes.

A: (chuckles) I love that. Thank you. Does the griffin have any messages for her?

Fire Dragon: He says, "don't fear, you are protected. I am here. I am here, it is okay."

A: Thank you, well she is going to enjoy the Magical Creatures Alchemy class then through the Priestess Course.

Fire Dragon: She is connected. As Ariel she is connected to the animals. She always had a strong bond; they feel it in her.

A: Beautiful. Okay, thank you for speaking to us. Love you, honor you, and respect you. Can I please speak back to her Higher Self now?

Fire Dragon: Yes!

AA Ariel: Hello sister.

A: Hello.

AA Ariel: You did good work today.

A: We sure did! There are a couple more questions that I would like to get answered for her, she did have several, but I am trying to see...

AA Ariel: She said earlier about an Akashic reading to address some of them, and that was our inspiration and that is my recommendation to her.

A: Okay, wonderful. So yeah, we can definitely go over these through an Akashic and you can help us find the answers for her.

AA Ariel: I would be happy to.

A: Lovely. Would you say her extraterrestrial race would be Angelic Elohim since you are?

AA Ariel: Yes, beautiful angel. Powerful. She needs to not forget that.

A: Thank you. She wanted to know if you could briefly tell her, has she been with me? She feels connected to me through other lifetimes and why was she brought to me as...

AA Ariel: Yes, in non-physical. Very close, the Angelic are very close. We work together. We arranged this. It is kind of like, "Hey, look it finally happened!"

A: (laughter) Thank you.

AA Ariel: Thank you.

A: At this point we have pretty much answered all the questions that she's had, and as you mentioned we will go over anything else later on. Is there anything else that I could have asked but I have not asked?

AA Ariel: Just tell her to be content. She tends to worry, "should I do this, should I do that?" She is abundant. As a fractal of I, she is abundant. She does not need to worry. She does not even need to go looking. When it is there, she will find her. She does not need to work so hard, tell her to not worry about her.

A: Very good. Do you recommend for her to share this session? I think it's been a very powerful session. Specifically, the information about the activation going on now and about the future.

AA Ariel: It is our pleasure to do so, yes.

A: Thank you, thank you. It truly has been joyous! A most beautiful profound healing today in A.U.R.A. Hypnosis Healing. Thank you for administering and thank you for bringing her to me sister. I love you infinitely.

AA Ariel: As I you, Aurora.

A: (happy sigh) We send infinite love to Michael, Metatron, Azrael, anyone else who assisted today with the healing. We love you, honor you, and respect you. Thank you.

AA Ariel: Thank you, it is our honor.

A: Thank you. May I bring her back now?

AA Ariel: Yes, she is ready.

Post Session dialogue.

C: Goodness!

A: Oh, my goodness, that was phenomenal! You are a rock star.

C: Wow.

A: (chuckles) An angel rock star! You are phenomenal!

C: Yeah! It was just like I was there; I knew it was all going on and I was saying it, but I was...

A: Like you were in the back?

C: Yeah, I was just like popcorn. You know?

A: (laughs).

C: Like wow, this is cool stuff! (laughs) Oh my goodness.

A: Wow, I cannot believe the information that came through today!

C: Really, I remember.

A: It was most spectacular! How long do you think you were in there?

C: An hour and a half? At least?

A: Over two hours.

C: Oh, my goodness. It is 3:13! Wow.

A: 3:13 look at that! (chuckles)

C: (chuckles) 3:13! Aurora, that was amazing. You are amazing, thank you!

A: You were amazing!

C: Gosh, we caught some entities...

A: Yeah, do you remember?

C: There were some smaller ones and there was a main one I think, right? Yeah, I do remember that. Yeah, he was stubborn. I felt when he was talking, my body felt really uncomfortable. Like really heavy.

A: Yeah, I felt it too.

C: Did you feel it too? It was like the only time, the one, the one...

A: I did, I did. He was pretty strong.

C: Oh, I was just like, dang dude, yeah. Yeah.

A: Yeah, and I felt like the throat. I was coughing during the session and I also felt there was something else you had but I can't remember what it was, but I felt it through my body.

C: I have to go back and listen because I remember, like in the moment I was there listening but now it is getting a little.

A: It gets a little fuzzy, yeah that is what happens when I channel. I start getting fuzzy.

C: Yeah, it was.

A: You are definitely a clear channel.

C: You think so?

A: Oh yeah!

C: Okay.

A: Yeah, good thing you are taking the Priestess Course where you are going to learn how to Quantum Alchemy Channel.

C: Yeah. Alright. Wow, that is so exciting!

A: I know! Oh, my goodness, thank you so much! I love you, I love you, I love you.

C: Thank you so much! Alright.

A: Awesome. Love you.

C: Alright! Love you too!

END OF SESSION

-------------<◇>-------------

This A.U.R.A. Hypnosis Healing session was exactly what the Earth needed in that time and space, to prepare us for the chaos to come in 2020 through the Illuminati's diabolic plan of Covid-19. The amplified upgrade of the Sun Source flamed plasmic energy which the collective received through the 9/19/19 Activation portal is comparable to the 12/21/2012 portal that began the awakening of the majority of humanity, and the organic Ascension process. This focused energy entering and merging into our 12-strand DNA then in 2012, and in 2019. It would be our energetic fuel to gently but strongly push and guide us through the turmoil in 2020.

As explained in this remarkable session, "It does not all happen on this date. This day is a catalyst. This date, the energies come in. So, through the summer we were in the high 30's, the activations in August brought us to 40 percent where we are now. And then over the next few months, we are going to see it steady. Every day it will be increasing. It is not going to be stuck energetically anymore like you know, maybe a few months will go by and not much has changed. No, it is going to make your head spin. It is starting today. Today is the day the energies start coming in and now the energies need to be assimilated by the humans." We might have wondered if we were part of watching this session on YouTube when it debuted on 9/19/19, what the Universe was trying to prepare us for, to come in 2020. On the date of 9/19/19, we were at about 40 percent of light awakened, and approximately nine months later when Chapter 29 ('Archons and Their Slaves') took place, we then find out where we are at currently and how these energies assisted the collective during these hard times.

'The Call For The Angels' was placed and sent into the Universe. Whether we connect to our angelic forms or not, we are often told how brave we are, those who have answered the call volunteering to enter this construct. The energetic regression a soul must go through is enormous, and unexplainable, in order to anchor into the Third Dimension! Losing a vastness of its light in order to enter into this amount of darkness. Only one that accepts this role knows what it is, once we have birthed into the Earth's collective.

We truly do not realize how brave we are to enter. What if we too become stuck just as those who have been trapped by their own karmic unbalances? This is the risk we all take in the mission of Love, and the greatest selflessness act expressed in Creation, as "The Volunteers of the Universes." To know that we too can be replaced or compromised in this Inverted A.I. Matrix majority, as the souls mentioned through RA in the previous Chapter 8 ('Four RA Guardians Heal Thousands of Entities'). Yet we still accept, because it is as if we see our family in quicksand, and they are calling out for us. Will one go towards them in whichever form that one can muster, be that helping extended hand to release them out that heavy, quick, sinking sand? Or will one walk away so that we won't sink into this infinite hole to nothingness as well? Many souls throughout the infinity of Creation have decided that WE WILL answer that call, and we will grab hold of that hand that is desperately reaching out. WE WILL be that strong hand and arm that will pull them up, we are the volunteers of the New Earth!

This inspiring session shared key insights with us about the sun portal and its true healing powers. Aiding to deprogram us from the falseness of the negative Illuminati agenda that was created towards the sun. For the purpose to disconnect us from Source ourselves and deterring the lifting of our vibrations. Reminding us how important it is for us to use the power of the Source energy coming from the sun daily, with much care and sacredness. For the sun is our replenishment of life force rejuvenation here in this Matrix construct.

We learned an immensity on Reptilians in this A.U.R.A. Hypnosis Healing session. Once more, guiding us in how to address them with more ease. The evolution of the darkness into light, and then light gaining into a majority. We were blessed to feel the positive polarized ascended Reptilians lightness and joy within this higher dimensional planet that was created just for them, as a gift from the Divine Mother of Creation. As she is the Mother of ALL her Creations, including the Reptilians. Before the infringements of the Inverted A.I. Matrix began, the Divine Mother just as she creates beings of illuminating light, had to create one race, the Reptilians within this Universe that would become the balance to there being too much light. A race that would feed off excessive light naturally. So, this beautiful home planet was created just for the Reptilians in response to all that they had to endure by accepting their necessary role, at the beginning of this collective experiment, though not all went organically as divinely planned. It is all now doing so as we assist the Reptilian race through A.U.R.A. Hypnosis Healing sessions, and others who have answered the call by understanding the deepness and true power of entity removal work.

Is this what we are doing by answering our brethren's call, because we are finally able to do so as we are approaching the Multiverse's collective Ascension? We can do so at its greatest strength and potence through aiding the Third Dimension, as it is the densest in darkness, therefore it is the deepest, thickest "cork" stuck in a natural source of infinite flowing water that needs to be organically released. Since we are at the deepest distortion and inverted control in 3D, when we allow and experience this release, it will be the greatest release felt from all the above higher Dimensions. Therefore, we as the Third Dimensional "cork," we are keeping ALL in this Universe stagnant collectively. And why it is that if WE release/ascend, the Universe can finally Ascend collectively.

In the next Chapter, the session took place directly after this 9/19/19 Portal Activation session, and we learn about the true impact of the energies from this portal date. Each session of A.U.R.A. Hypnosis Healing is unique, where the clients do not know each other. It is as if a magnificent Galactic Journey is being told session by session, Chapter by Chapter, by the connections that our Higher Selves benevolently have to one another beyond the veil. Each session is a piece of the puzzle that complements one another bringing forth the pure knowledge and awareness needed for our collective Ascension.

Thank you, Archangel Ariel once more for another profound transmission that shifted the Earth, which then in turn shifted too, the Multiverse. We love you infinitely!

"I often stand back in silence admiring and allowing myself to fall in love with every soul that passes by."
~AuroRa ♥

-------------<◇>------------

10

A RIPPLE OF 9,000,000 HEAL IN THE UNIVERSE

Session #199: Recorded in September 2019.

In this online A.U.R.A. Hypnosis Healing session, Peter finds himself as a beautiful female on an Island. We find a Collective of different races of Reptilians attached spying through Peter. Come be part of the exponential healing as 3,000 Reptilians heal, creating a ripple through the Universe with a Collective of Benevolent Beings aiding to heal 9,000,000 in Creation! This inspiring session took place the very next day after the 9/19/19 Portal session in the previous Chapter. It demonstrates the inspirational collective healings happening through A.U.R.A. Hypnosis Healing sessions after the 9/19/19 Activation Portal has shifted the Universe into higher vibrations. More on a 1980 UFO sighting covered-up by the military. What can we learn about a wizard from Sirius, his crystal wand, and the journey home?

-------------<◇>-------------

"It's like a domino wave of enlightenment amongst Reptilians races."
-Archangel Michael

-------------<◇>-------------

A: [Aurora] You feel like you're in a jungle clearing. Look at yourself. Do you feel like you have a body?
P: [Peter] Yeah, I've got a body.
A: Look down at your feet, do you have any shoes on?
P: No, there are no shoes.
A: How many toes do you have?
P: I've got five toes on each foot.
A: Look at your hands, how many fingers do you have?
P: Five on each hand.
A: Do you feel like you're a female or a male?
P: Feel like I am a male.
A: Look at yourself. Are you wearing any clothes?
P: Yeah. I've got like a longish tunic.
A: What color is it?
P: Brown and a white sort of shirt underneath that. I think green trousers but no shoes.
A: Is there anything you're carrying?
P: Some sort of over the shoulder bag. I think it's made of rope.
A: Let's see what's in the bag. Tell me what it is that you see inside the bag.
P: Like a dark gourd and I think there's a wand with a crystal in it, it's glowing. Kind of got like a rotating energy field around it all. Something's going round and round. Slightly up inside of the bag there's a book, small book. Two. Yeah! That's it.
A: Go ahead and pull out the wand.
P: Yeah, I got it.

A: What color is that crystal?

P: It's a translucent crystal with clear, but it's glowing white. And it's got this kind of like, whirling energy going round and round, round and round. It's almost as if it's in a sphere that's rotating. The handle is carved. Kind of like a dark wood. Really dark wood with carvings in it.

A: Everything has consciousness. See if it has any messages for you.

P: I'm getting an idea. It says, "Take me home."

A: Take you home?

P: Take the crystal home. Maybe that's what I'm doing, trying to find where it belongs.

A: Would you allow for the crystal to speak through you and see what other messages it has?

P: Yes.

A: Is there a reason why you've been taken?

P: Yeah.

A: Very good. So, go ahead and connect to that consciousness there with the crystal that's saying for you to take it home. Feel its energy, allowing for it to speak through you lovingly. Let's see what messages it has for us today. I'd like to speak to that consciousness there in the crystal wand, please.

Crystal Being: Sure.

A: Greetings. Is this you?

Crystal Being: Yes.

A: Thank you for speaking to us today. Love you, honor you, and respect you. May I ask you questions, please?

Crystal Being: Sure.

A: Thank you. I was wondering, he mentioned that you were telling him that you would like to be taken home. Is this something that you are asking for?

Crystal Being: Yes, yes.

A: What do you mean by that? Can you tell us more about that?

Crystal Being: I feel that I would like to be back in the underground cave with all the other crystals in there. They are, they are part of our collective.

A: Is this where he's taking you to now? Where he's going.

Crystal Being: No.

A: Why is it that you want to go back there instead of being this consciousness here in this wand?

Crystal Being: It's home. It's where all my others are.

A: What is your connection to him? Why does he have you?

Crystal Being: I think he found the bag and just picked it up and didn't know what was in it. And now... now he thinks that he should take it somewhere and I'm trying to tell him to take it back where I'm from.

A: How was it that you ended up in the bag to begin with? Can you tell us that story?

Crystal Being: Yeah, I was taken from the cave by a man, and I think he was a wizard or magician or something like that. He knew stuff. He knew esoteric energy stuff and he was able to capture my energy and guide it and use it for his own purpose.

A: Did you give him permission for this?

Crystal Being: No. No. I was just found and taken.

A: Sometimes when crystals are with people, sometimes they have given permission to be there. Is that something that you are aware of?

Crystal Being: No. I was in the cave and just picked up and was taken away.

A: Would it have been different when you were being picked up, if he asked you if you could come with him?

Crystal Being: Yeah. That would feel better!

A: Wow, did the magician end up losing this bag?

Crystal Being: I think he just left it unattended briefly. And I think this, this other person stole it, picked it up, and walked off. I guess the other one's pretty mad.

A: The magician's pretty mad?

Crystal Being: I expect so. He liked the wand and what it could do. What he did.

A: Are there any other messages you have for us today?

Crystal Being: Guide. Guide me home, please. I suppose that's all.

A: We will try throughout this communication that we have. We will see if we can. Okay?

Crystal Being: Thank you.

A: Thank you. Is there a name that you go by?

Crystal Being: Sheron.

A: Thank you. Beautiful name! Very good. I will perhaps talk to you later and we'll see what we can do for you.

Crystal Being: Thank you.

A: Thank you. Love you. Now if I could please speak back to him here, back to him now?

P: Hello.

A: Hello. If we could look in the bag, there's also a book. Can you tell us what this book looks like?

P: Small, smallish. Black leather-clad book. It's got brown, rough paper pages. It's got symbols that I don't understand or cannot read within it. I just found this bag and it had the wand and this book.

A: Are you able to read any of the languages inside of it? The book?

P: I can't make out what it says. It looks like some sort of high mathematics and symbols. I don't quite understand what it is.

A: Let's see where it is that you are trying to go. Go ahead and reach your destination. Where is it that you're trying to go to? You are there now. Tell me what you see, sense, feel, and hear.

P: There's a village on the side of a very big river. You can see the jungle in the distance and hills rising up behind that. The village seems to be mostly made of wooden structures, houses, and - and buildings, and huts. There are boats as well. There are more up there and other ways. People are in the town they got, like they've got fruits. Fruit. Might be trading? When they got some other goods on small boats that they went on the river in. Walking through, this area aside. I go into one. On how, I think that's, I know the people there!

A: What does this house look like?

P: It's a simple wooden structure. Kind of like made of wooden logs. It's a hot place. Humid and sticky. I think this is my home. Yeah, it seems to be familiar. There's a rough table, it's very simple.

A: Why is it that you're here, let's see? What do you do next of importance?

P: I get out the book and the gourd and the wand and I place them on the table. And I'm just staring at these items. I don't really understand what I've got here, but I feel drawn to the items. As if, as if I know that they can help. I don't seem to cause any harm with them or anything like that. I just feel they could be useful to our community and help. Yeah. I'm going to show them to some people I know... In the village.

A: What do they say?

P: Oh, they're very surprised because they've never seen anything like that before! You know, it's quite amazing to have a brilliant crystal in a wand with an energy field spinning around it. We look at the symbols in the book and we feel that, if we could understand, kind of what the symbols meant the wand would make, it could be used for something. But we're not for sure what the empty gourd is for. Maybe that's just a cup for water. We don't know.

A: Go ahead and fast forward a bit to see what it is that you do next of importance?

P: Oh, this is a totally different place.

A: Look at yourself. Do you feel like you have a body?

P: Yes. I'm, I'm dressed in much better clothes. Almost as if I'm wealthy and I live in almost, like a white marble mansion. These pillars are Roman or Greek or something like that. I think I have wealth and status.

A: Do you feel like you are female or male?

P: I feel I'm a male but it's not, kind of solid like it's on Earth. It's dreamlike. Yes.

A: Look at yourself. What color is your skin? What tone?

P: It's sort of like a coffee brown.

A: Look at your feet. How many toes do you have?

P: Five. Five toes.

A: Your hands?

P: I think there's four on one hand and five on the other. I've lost a finger. I think that came from an accident.

A: What are you wearing?

P: It's like a red, long, shirt and a light and a white or cream-colored jacket. And it's got gold edging and there's like a turban, almost like a Sultan with a big red jewel in the middle. Yeah, I think I was an important person in that life.

A: Let's see. What is it that you do next here in this mansion?

P: Kind of. It's not really like a house. It's more like a temple. It's got like open areas and pillars and a big marble table.

A: Is there anything else that stands out as you look around?

P: Yeah. There was a large plume of, it looks like a volcano erupting in the distance! There are lots of people moving away from that area and heading towards where I'm from. The region I'm in.

A: There was a volcano erupting?

P: It's weird, it's almost like a fountain of lava shooting in the air without a mountain. Like it's squirting straight up.

A: When this lava comes out, what is it doing? How's it reacting to what's around it?

P: It's going high in the sky and coming, falling down. There's a lot of people having to move. And I'm up here in this big white marble temple. I can't seem to figure out what to do.

A: Are you on a higher plane?

P: Yeah, I think I am. I'm not from that plane.

A: That you're watching this occurring from?

P: That I'm watching this occurring. I feel I'm almost in a different Dimension but seeing it.

A: What is it that you do next of importance? Tell me what you do next.

The scene changes to another life.

P: I'm out on a boat. I'm traveling somewhere. Can't see land. There are other people on this - like a small ship I suppose. It's got sails. I think we're expecting to find land, we're exploring.

A: Look at yourself. Are you female or male?

P: I think I'm female in this one. Yeah, female.

A: Look down at your toes. How many do you have?

P: It's three toes.

A: Your hands. How many fingers do you have?

P: Three. There are three fingers. Oh wow, on each hand!

A: Look at your skin. Do you have skin? What tone is it?

P: Yeah, I've got kind of white skin, very pale, very almost white. I got long blonde hair.

A: What are you wearing?

P: A long white dress I suppose? It's very plain. Pulled in at the waist. It's for working on the ship and there are other people like me. Men and women. They're also blonde.

A: Is there anything you're carrying with you?

P: No, I'm not carrying, everything's on the boat but uh, I think we're out exploring, and we've got supplies to see us on the voyage.

A: Is this boat small or big?

P: Medium. Yeah, it's just kind of like a sailboat. But it goes along the ocean. Got a crew of about, I'd say 20.

A: Passengers as well, and the crew?

P: No, we're all, we're all crew. We're all part of the same team of explorers.

A: If you could describe what your face looks like. What do your facial features look like?

P: Kind of like a pointy nose long face. Big eyes, small ears. Not quite human but humanoid.

A: What color eyes do you have?

P: They're blue.

A: Fast forward time and see if you reach your destination where it was that you were all sailing to. You are there now. Tell me what you see.

P: It's on land. It's a big island or maybe the mainland. Hard to tell, we just pulled up. Alone. Onto the beach we've taken the small boat to the shore. It's almost like a tropical, very big island. There are white sands and palm trees. Blue sea, warm. We're going to live here. At least for a while anyway. We are going to find out what's there, how we can make a life there.

A: Go ahead and reach your destination. Tell me what it looks like where you have landed.

P: It's a very beautiful tropical beach with palm trees. Still got dense forest or jungle on the back of the beach. And there are mountains in the distance so it's quite a big place. We didn't sail around it. We just pulled up. Got off the boat into our shallows and went to shore holding rafts with goods and stuff on it. Yeah. We're quite, quite, happy that we found this place.

A: Tell me what the land looks like.

P: There's a lot of greenery. Very pale-gray rocky outcrops that rise up. The mountain, very tall hills are made of this pale-gray rock. Yeah, it looks like a good place. We're all happy that we found it. I think we're going to have a bit of a celebration. Yeah. That'll be good. Yes, we're very pleased! We're going to explore it in the morning. We will start to explore it.

A: Wonderful. Let's go ahead and fast forward to when it is the next morning. Go to where it is in another important time... Tell me what you see and sense.

P: I found a cave. I just stopped from the beach, behind the beach in the forest. It looks like there's drawings on the cave walls. Looks like people have been here before. Long ago.

A: What are some of the drawings of?

P: They look kind of like horses but they're not. If they're horses, they can stand up on two legs and there are other human-like drawings. Humanoid type people with two legs and two arms. Yeah, it's pretty strange. It's old. It's very old.

A: Anything else that stands out in this cave?

P: Oh! It seems to go into the mountain but far away. We have to get torches to go in further. I think we're going to go over the mountain first before we go in it.

A: Go ahead and...

P: See what's the other side of the mountain?

A: Keep moving the scene along and let me know what is important along the way.

P: We get to the top of the ridge. There's like a big horseshoe Bay. The other side, it is an island. We can see it better now. It's either a big island or a very long peninsula. It's hard to say but it's a big place. This makes us happy. Haven't seen anybody else or any other sort of beings. There are birds. That's about it. Yeah. There's food. There are coconuts. And yeah, fruit, coconuts. Colorful birds that make a lot of noise.

A: Fast forward a bit once more. Do you end up going inside the mountain?

P: Yes. Several days later we go back with a group of us and we take lanterns and torches. We are going in. It kind of seems to go down. It's almost as if the mountain is hollow there's a big chamber. It's too big to light with our torches. But there's fresh water in there. Oh wow! It's kind of like phosphorescence coming from the water. Some of the rocks when the drips come, it's kind of like a phosphorescent ripple when they drop into the pool below which adds to the light. It's very pretty.

A: Is this part of the mountains? Does it seem like there's ever been any life through it?

P: All we've seen is the cave drawings near the entrance. We haven't seen anything on our way in. There are just rocks in the water. If there was anything there maybe it's turned to dust.

A: What is it that you all do next of importance? Do you do anything else inside this mountain?

P: No, because it's all water. We don't have a means of going in boats and it's too dark, the torches will run out. We only got five torches, and we have to get back.

A: Okay. Fast forward a bit, what happens next of importance?

P: There's a big storm coming, big storm. Could be a hurricane. And it's very strong wind, very, very, strong wind. I think we're going to lose our boat.

A: You're back on the water?

P: No. We're on land.

A: Oh, the one that is parked?

P: Yeah, the one in the bay I think... Yeah, that's gone! It was totally smashed to bits.

A: Well, how are you all?

P: We had to take shelter in the cave, so we're okay. So, the cave came in very handy.

A: Do you have any children with you?

P: No, we're all young adults, no one else. Now we don't have a boat. We're here, so this is it.

A: From this group. Do you all have partners with one another?

P: Uh, yeah. Yeah. About half, half have paired off.

A: Are you paired off to anyone?

P: No, but I think I'd like to be, especially now.

A: Let's go ahead and leave that scene now. Let's go to another important time in this life. You are there now. What do you see and sense?

P: Okay, I think, I think I'm about to transition, about to die. We didn't leave the island. We stayed and we made a life, and it was a good life. It's a big island that has everything you'd want. Everything. We had food, fish, fruit, shelter, building materials. Lovely place to live. There's more of us now, more youngsters, kids are grown up. The community is growing.

A: Do you know why it is in the first place that you were on a boat trying to find land? What happened to your original home?

P: I think we had to leave. Why did we leave?

A: You are able to go back in time to right before you all went in that boat.

P: There was a war. It was invaded and our town was trashed. It was burnt, set on fire. We ran, fled. Refugees, that's what it was. We took a boat; we had enough provisions to get us where we were going to get to and that was it. There wasn't a lot of time to plan.

A: Did you all know where you were going?

P: No. no, we weren't very experienced. We just kind of had to get away. That was it, yeah.

A: Let's go ahead and go back to where you are at taking your last breath in that life. You are there now. Tell me, what are your last thoughts?

P: My last thoughts are that I was very pleased to find the island and build a life, raise a family. It was a lovely journey.

A: Did you end up having children?

P: Yeah.

A: How many?

P: Four. Two boys and two girls. Yeah.

A: Look at your partner, looking into their eyes. You're able to recognize the soul through the eyes. Who is it?

P: It's familiar but I can't put a name.

A: That's okay. Very good. The four children look into their eyes. See if there are any other ones that your soul recognizes.

P: I think I see Oscar. I think I do.

A: Anyone else?

P: I'm not sure about the others.

A: Go ahead and take your last breath and leave the body. Let me know what happens next.

P: I'm up in that temple area. That's weird. I'm off in that white marble, temple in the clouds, something strange. Where I was looking at the volcano or the fountain of lava, I'm up there. But there's no sign of the Sultan cap.

A: The original form of the Sultan is not there anymore?

P: No.

A: What do you look like now?

P: I look like, like I did. But younger.

A: Now that you are back here. What is it that you do when you arrive back there?

P: I'm kind of walking around and no one else there. But I've got this sense of I won't be there too long. A few minutes or an hour, something like that. It's almost like it's a steppingstone type of thing. Just a reminder sort of thing. It dissolves and I'm in space. I can see a sun. I'm just floating in space now. In the Cosmos. Yeah, I can see the galaxy.

A: Does this galaxy have a connection to you?

P: It looks pretty. Think I'm kind of drawn to it. Many, many directions I could go to. I chose that one because the energy feels good, similar to the island.

A: Within this temple that you're in, is there anyone else there with you?

P: Yeah, it's almost like I'm kind of descending onto another island. But it's obviously in a different plane. Beautiful. Now I know a lot of the people there, they know me, they come rushing over. They greet me. They're very happy, I'm happy. Yeah, it's lovely. It's a big reunion, it must be home. Feels like home any more so than when we got destroyed in the invasion.

A: Okay. Let's go ahead and leave that life. Can I please speak to the Higher Self of Peter?

The Higher Self is called forth.

Higher Self: Hello.

A: Hello, greetings. Am I speaking to Peter's Higher Self now?

Higher Self: Yeah.

A: I honor you, thank you, and I respect you for all the aid you have given us today. I know that you hold all the records of Peter's different lives. May I ask you questions, please?

Higher Self: Sure.

A: Thank you. You took him to several different lives, and I was wondering why it is that you took him there. Let's go ahead and start off with, he was a man in a jungle environment, and he had found a bag with a wand and a book. Tell us what was the purpose to that life? Why did you take him there?

Higher Self: That was to show him that not everything you come across necessarily makes a lot of sense. But it does have hidden meaning and potential.

A: What ended up happening to that bag with the wand and book?

Higher Self: That went back to the wizard. He got it back. He knew where it was. He came and got it.

A: He was able to track it?

Higher Self: Oh, yeah. He knew where it was.

A: What was the wizard's reaction towards him?

Higher Self: He wasn't there at the time. He just came in the house and took it. He wasn't very pleased that he lost it.

A: Higher Self, I know that crystal said that he wanted to go back home with the other clusters of crystals that were his family. Can you scan and look for that crystal there that we were speaking to? You can ask for any aid if you need any for the Archangels to locate it.

Higher Self: Yeah.

A: Where is it at now?

Higher Self: I think the wizard still has it. Yeah, the wand is on a kind of altar.

A: Connect us to that crystal now that is there on the altar. Let us speak to it now, please.

Crystal Being: Hello.

A: Greetings. Thank you for speaking to us once more. We are back and looking to see as far as, how are you now? I know originally when we spoke to you, you wanted to go back home. So how are you feeling now?

Crystal Being: I still want to go home. But it's not too bad. I'm being left alone more. But it would be nice to go home.

A: What would you like to do? We have, for example, Angels that can aid you in being able to energetically go back home. With your permission as you are a consciousness, and you have your own free will. Do you want to continue to stay there? Or do you want us to see if Angels can help you go back?

Crystal Being: Yeah, I'd like to go back please.

A: Okay, very good. Higher Self, if you could connect me now to Archangel Michael please.

Higher Self: Okay.

AA Michael: Hello.

A: Thank you. Is this Archangel Michael?

AA Michael: Yes.

A: Thank you, love you, and honor you. Thank you for being here.

AA Michael: Love you too, Aurora!

A: Thank you. We are speaking to a crystal that is with a wizard. It wants to basically go back home. It asked for it at the beginning. Now we found it at another point in time, he says that he still wants to go back home to the cluster of crystals he was from. What can we do Michael? Are we able to assist him to go back? I know that this wizard pretty much has had say ownership as you know, called this crystal his own. What can we do about it?

AA Michael: The wizard will transition. The crystal will be found, and it will be misplaced and lost. And the crystal will return to Earth and that will be home. Crystal will be very happy. It will feel home and connect to other crystals.

A: Beautiful. So, his original formation was on Earth?

AA Michael: Yes, he was on Earth with the other crystals.

A: This wizard came from somewhere else?

AA Michael: The wizard found the crystal. He dug it up. He knew where it was. He wanted one particular crystal. He knew what he wanted, and he took it and kept it until he lost it briefly. Then he got it back. But he can't keep it forever because he won't live forever. He will transition and the crystal will return home.

A: This wizard, was he from Earth?

AA Michael: He incarnated many times on Earth but not originally from Earth. He is from Sirius.

A: So, when he took the crystal, did he go back to Sirius, or did he stay on Earth?

AA Michael: He stayed on Earth but, I think he lost his power. He wasn't a wizard anymore.

A: Thank you, Michael. So, then the crystal will be free?

AA Michael: Crystal will be free.

A: Good. Thank you for that confirmation and our infinite love to the crystal, blessings.

AA Michael: The crystal says thanks.

A: Michael, if you could let me speak back to the Higher Self, please.

Higher Self: Hello.

A: Thank you. From there, you took him to a man in a white energetic temple. There was lava exploding out of the mid-air it seemed. Tell me why is it that you took him there?

Higher Self: That was to demonstrate that even from a lofty perspective, you're not always able to intercede or affect. Although many times you can. There are also many times you cannot if it's not to be. Although the lava was erupting, going high in the sky, the people were fleeing. He had no way of helping the people or stopping the lava. Even though he was an important powerful being in another realm who thought he had the ability to affect another realm.

A: What was the purpose of the lava?

Higher Self: The lava was a catalyst for the lesson. And the fleeing multitudes were part of the lesson to demonstrate the lesson.

A: Any other messages you have for him about this existence there?

Higher Self: He had chosen to stay there. Become more and more self-important. And when a time came to prove how effective he could be, he was shown that he couldn't be that effective. So, it was a lesson in humility and ego.

A: Very good. Thank you. From there he ended up as a female on a boat and they were looking for land. Tell us, why did you take him there. What was the purpose of that life?

Higher Self: That demonstrated that although what seemed like devastation and disaster, the time led to a life of beauty, joy, fun in a paradise. So, it demonstrated that out of bad sometimes a lot of good emerges.

A: Yes. Where was that? Was that on a planet?

Higher Self: Yeah, that was Earth. That was Earth long, long, long ago. The lands that they left and found are no longer there.

A: What happened to those lands?

Higher Self: They're underwater now.

A: Wow, was it that they sunk?

Higher Self: I think they are Lemurian lands. Yeah. That region. The Earth changed.

A: Then after he left that life, he ended up back on that same temple once more. But this time he was the female version. What does that mean? Why did that happen?

Higher Self: That was an inbuilt recognition of what was expected to be seen after the transition. Had this idea deep within a subconscious of what heaven may look like and there it was. But then that was not the true heaven and it dissolved.

A: Anything else you want to tell us about that existence there in that temple?

Higher Self: The Sultan learned a big lesson there. And that lesson was ingrained in the next parallel incarnation. So, the temple was visited as a recollection, as a distant echo on the way home.

A: Alright, so at this point, I would love to be able to start the body scan. Higher Self, if you could start the body scan and see what requires healing. And let us know, do you need any aid from the Archangels? Or can you do it on your own?

Higher Self: I would welcome some aid from the Archangels, please.

A: Okay, very good. Which Archangel would you like to connect to first to begin the body scan?

Higher Self: I would ask Archangel Michael.

A: Thank you. Higher Self, connect us now to Archangel Michael, please.

AA Michael: Hello.

A: Hello, greetings brother. Once more, thank you. We are talking to the Higher Self and we are now beginning the body scan. If you can please begin his body scan from, start from head to toe. See where you want to direct your attention to first. We are scanning for any negative energies, entities, anything that is negative that requires healing within him, and let me know what you see first.

The Body Scan begins.

AA Michael: Yeah, there's what looks like some snake reptile wrapped around the third eye, around the pineal gland.

A: Is that a Reptilian consciousness or what is that?

AA Michael: It's a servant serpent. It's a servant serving serpent and it serves others.

A: Is that negative?

AA Michael: Yeah, it's negative.

A: Let's follow the cord, where is it connected to? Who placed it there? Who does it serve?

AA Michael: Now it seems to be connected to a collective.

A: A collective of who?

AA Michael: I would say, yeah, it's Reptilian. It's a reptile itself.

A: Is there one particular being within this collective that it's directly serving?

AA Michael: Yeah, it's under its command.

A: Okay. Archangel Michael, if we can now surround this serpent with the alchemy symbols.

AA Michael: It is done.

A: Thank you. Michael, can you connect us to that Reptilian that this serpent servant is serving? We'd like to speak to that Reptilian now, please.

Reptilian: Ah. Hello.

A: Hello, greetings. Thank you for speaking to us. Love you, honor you, and respect you. May I ask you questions, please?

Reptilian: Yes.

A: Thank you. If I may ask when was it that you attached this serpent in his pineal gland there?

Reptilian: It was born with this.

A: He was born with this?

Reptilian: For many lives he, this has been there.

A: Initially when you attached it, what was occurring with him in that life that allowed you to come in?

Reptilian: It was an energy...energy match. Found home.

A: What is the purpose of you attaching this serpent in his pineal gland? What do you get out of it?

Reptilian: We get access. We get influence. We get information. A lot of information. It is a good viewport for us.

A: Do you mean like you view through him?

Reptilian: Yes. View. Third eye. Higher information. All useful.

A: Can you tell me is there anywhere else in the body that you're connected to?

Reptilian: There are others.

A: There are others who are connected to his body?

Reptilian: Yeah.

A: Would you be able to connect me to them? Are they also Reptilians?

Reptilian: They are. They're not of, they're not of us. We don't communicate.

A: Is it from another soul group of Reptilians?

209

Reptilian: Yeah. They're different from us.

A: You in particular, do you have anyone else within the body that is connected to you?

Reptilian: We have one in the right shoulder.

A: Is it connected to you directly or someone that knows you?

Reptilian: He's there for effects, to make sure nothing happens to the servant. This is our viewport. We get information through this. It's why he can't see too well. We take the information.

A: What kind of benefits do you get from taking some of this information you've gathered from him throughout time?

Reptilian: We learn aspects of the Universe that are hidden from us directly. We learn higher orders of influence, control, manipulation for our own purposes.

A: Archangel Michael, can you surround that other Reptilian, please that is within the body that's connected to this one. Surround it with the symbols now, please.

AA Michael: It is done.

A: Thank you. Now speaking back to this Reptilian here. Thank you for the information you've given us. I know that you've been playing this role for a very long time. As you know the Universe, this Creation itself is raising its vibration and it's going to enter into a higher frequency altogether. We'd love to be able to aid you today so that you may no longer have to play this negative polarized role, attaching yourself to others in this manner. You're able to keep your experiences all that you gained throughout this existence of a negative role. Everything that you gain, you're able to keep your consciousness, but instead, you ascend into a positive polarization. I'm speaking to both of you there. No longer having to drain from others' energies or do these roles. Instead, you'd be free, you'd be a free soul. You'd go wherever it is that you're meant to go incarnated if you like, or Ascension. Otherwise, if you don't choose this path, you can potentially be recycled straight back to Source and lose all that you gained. Particularly within this consciousness that you are. It would be straight recycled back to Source. Would you like to keep that consciousness you are there now and ascend into a positive polarization?

AA Michael: They are conferring.

A: Very good and that's for both of you...

Reptilian: Yes.

A: Wonderful. Thank you! If you could please spread your Love-Light now. We're going to help you spread the light within both of you. Spread the light to every root, every cord, every piece that belongs to you, that does not belong to him. Michael, what are we going to do with the serpentine wrapped around his third eye?

AA Michael: The serpent will go back along with the others. It will detach from the pineal and follow its master creators' controllers. Back to the light.

A: Good. Let's go ahead and help all of them, including the serpent there. All of them spread their Love-Light. Let me speak back to the Reptilian there that was connected to the serpent... Where are you located currently?

Reptilian: We're in a different Dimension. We're on Mars, in a different Dimension.

A: Are there any others around you?

Reptilian: There are many. There are many. We are a legion.

A: Are they able to telepathically hear our transmission?

Reptilian: If we choose so yes. This is good.

A: Thank you for connecting us. Now we are speaking to the collective there that is within this Mars alternate Dimension, as you mentioned. We'd like to speak to you now. We honor you, love you, and respect you. If you could just hear us out. We are talking to this being here who has chosen a positive polarization. If we could have the Archangels surround him as he is choosing this path as well as the other in his shoulder. Surround them with protection. We're speaking to all of you now.

Reptilian Collective: Hello.

A: Hello. We'd love to be able to aid you today. Whoever it is that is ready. Will you allow for us to aid you to ascend into a positive polarization? As you know, this Universe itself, this Creation is ascending and turning into a higher Dimension. When it does, it's going to shed off and recycle anything that is too dense. It's going to recycle it straight to Source. We are looking to help you no longer have to do this anymore, where you are able to keep the experiences that you gained through this negative role. You're able to ascend into a positive role keeping all those memories and that consciousness and experiences that will help you grow into a very strong, wise creator being that is able to manifest and create its own energies. No longer having to drain from someone else like you've been. Would you allow us to aid you today so that you may spread your light energy within you so that you may ascend into a positive polarization instead of being recycled straight back to source when the Ascension occurs?

Reptilian Collective: Yes.

A: Wonderful. And if you could tell us, how many are allowing to ascend?

Reptilian Collective: There are some who do not wish this. The majority wish it.

A: How many are there in this Dimension?

Reptilian Collective: We have over 3000.

A: Okay, and approximately how many?

Reptilian Collective: Majority. A majority wish for it.

A: How much of the majority would you say approximately out of the 3000 are accepting it?

Reptilian Collective: Ninety-seven percent.

A: Beautiful! Archangel Michael and the Legion of Light. If you all can please go to all of that 97 percent now who has accepted it? Surround them all with the symbols now please and protect them as they start positive polarizing. Can we do that, Michael?

AA Michael: Yes.

A: Okay. Good, and as usual, just calling anyone who you need help with to ensure that you cover 97 percent of them. Let me know once they are all safely protected in the symbols.

AA Michael: It is done.

A: Beautiful. Thank you, Michael. All of you there who we are speaking to. If you could please start spreading your light energy. If we could call on the Collective of Benevolent Angels now. If you could please focus Love-Light on these beautiful Reptilians who have now decided to ascend into a positive polarization. We love you, honor you, and thank you. Thank you for allowing us to aid you today, in this Mars alternate Dimension, sending you love now!

Reptilian Collective: Thank you.

A: Thank you. We're all sending you love now blasting you with a beautiful love frequency so that you're spreading your light to every part of you. And as you all are spreading, if you could tell me, Michael, are they attached - these 97 percent - to any other beings out there? Do they have a Reptilian consciousness attached to others?

AA Michael: They're all linked. They're all linked.

A: Meaning, are there any Reptilian consciousness that we can remove from other people, humans, or anywhere else that is connected to them?

AA Michael: They can, they can communicate.

A: Good. Michael, see if we could start echoing out a communication to the Higher Selves of these people, whoever they may be attached to. See if whoever the Higher Self will allow to remove these consciousnesses from them. Can we do that, Michael?

AA Michael: They can do a telepathic handshake. And help others. Other Reptilians, other consciousnesses.

A: Thank you. Let's start their process now. Once again, we are the Collective of Angels spreading Love-Light to these beings there, these 97 percent plus Reptilians, the ones that the Higher Selves have allowed to remove the Reptilian consciousness from within them. Particularly those consciousnesses within anyone, help those who have accepted to spread their Love-Light to every root, every cord. Every part of them.

AA Michael: This goes across, this goes around many planets. And Earth.

A: How many would you say that we are reaching through this form, Michael? How many beings are we reaching that we're helping remove this from them?

AA Michael: It is exponential! Many, many. Hundreds of thousands if not millions across many planets.

A: Thank you, Michael. How's he doing? I see him moving around a lot.

AA Michael: He's good.

A: Higher Self, just make him feel comfortable. Thank you. Wow, that's so beautiful. If we could continue once again spreading Love-Light through every part of those Reptilian consciousness and Reptilians, there who have accepted. Michael, let us know once everyone is of Love-Light. Let us know.

AA Michael: It's happening.

A: Beautiful.

AA Michael: It will take some time. There are many, many, many.

A: Very good. With the Collective of Angels, if they need any additional help from other benevolent beings, they could feel free to call from any brethren out there from other races that are here assisting in the Galactics of Benevolent Light. Thank you... Okay, so we'll come back to this Michael and check up on them.

AA Michael: Very well.

A: Michael, now that we have both of these here and we're working on them. Michael, the one that we were talking to that was connected to the third eye said that there are other Reptilians within his body. If we can scan his whole body now and find every single Reptilian that is within him now, please.

AA Michael: There's one in the elbow, the right elbow.

A: Continue with the scan, where else?

AA Michael: There's a lot down the right side of his body. Down the leg, the knee, the foot.

A: As you find them Michael, let's ensure that we're surrounding them with the alchemy symbols as you find them, please. Anywhere else?

AA Michael: Got some in his jaw.

A: Okay, keep surrounding them. Where else?

AA Michael: All down the right side. Got one in the shoulder. There's one in the jaw. On the right. The right elbow, right knee. Right foot. They favor the right.

A: Make sure they're all surrounded with the symbols now. Why is it that they favor the right?

AA Michael: They kind of followed suit? They're surrounded.

A: Are there anymore? Scan his body one more time. I want to make sure we do not miss any, I know that at times they can be sneaky. So, make sure we don't miss any more within him.

AA Michael: He has a different energy.

A: There's a different energy, where is it?

AA Michael: The left knee. It's not Reptilian, it's something else.

A: What is it? Is it an entity? An implant?

AA Michael: He has an implant.

A: Can we go ahead and transmute it now? Can I use Phoenix Fire on it?

AA Michael: Please, that would assist.

A: Thank you. Wonderful. Let me know once that implant is transmuted, Michael?

AA Michael: It's gone.

A: Beautiful. If we could have the Higher Self connect us to our brother Archangel Raphael. Love you, I honor you, love you, and respect you.

AA Raphael: Love, honor, and respect you too, Aurora.

A: Thank you.

AA Raphael: My sister.

A: Thank you my brother! If you can assist the Higher Self along the way, please fill in Love-Light to these areas. Right now, we removed an implant from his knee. Start doing that for us now, please. As we continue to remove these Reptilian consciousnesses within him. Archangel Michael, how many more are in his body besides the two original Reptilians we found?

AA Michael: There are four in the foot. One in the right knee. The right foot. Right knee. One in the right elbow. The one in the shoulder is gone with the serpent. They're all surrounded. There are different sorts. They're not all the same race.

A: Different sorts of Reptilians?

AA Michael: Yes.

A: Can you tell us a little more about how that works? What are the different sorts?

AA Michael: They're different races. They don't generally intermingle. They tolerate each other because they have a similar energy. As they are not in competition, they tend to leave each other alone and keep themselves to themselves and their own kind.

A: Higher Self, help him feel comfortable. Deep breaths... Okay. Would the different races of these Reptilians have different abilities?

AA Michael: Different agendas. So long as they don't conflict with each other they coexist. It's general exploitation control. Service-to-self. The usual. Power game of conquering and controlling, subjugating. Hidden interference.

A: Michael, let's go ahead and start assisting him. If we could speak to all those Reptilians now on that right side of the body, wherever it is that they are in his body, period. We'd like to speak to you now. If he could speak to you as a collective, please now. Greetings!

Reptilian Collective: Hello.

A: Hello. Thank you. I know that you've been part of this healing today and you have seen what's been going on with the other Reptilian consciousnesses that have accepted a positive polarization instead of being recycled straight to Source. Again, becoming strong and keeping the wisdom and the knowledge gained throughout your existence. Would all of you allow us to help you ascend as well?

Reptilian Collective: Yes.

A: Wonderful. Thank you. We want you to find that light within you now, we're going to help you spread it. Spread it to every root, every chord, every bit of you that is connected to his body here. If there is a Reptilian consciousness that you are connected to, we'd like to speak to them as well. Michael, can you connect us if they have a body they're connected to?

AA Michael: They're all connected to their own kind.

A: Okay, let's speak to all of them as a collective of Reptilian bodies that are connected to these consciousnesses.

AA Michael: They can communicate, onward to communicate.

A: Good. Have they accepted as well, of a positive polarization of Ascension?

AA Michael: Yeah.

A: Wonderful!

AA Michael: They have, they have!

A: Good Michael.

AA Michael: They have to move on. They know their time is limited as time; they know it.

A: Wonderful. Thank you, Michael. What a beautiful healing. Again, if we could surround them with symbols protecting them and continuing with the Legions of Light of all the different Rays of the Archangels who are aiding today. Continue spreading yourself out wherever it is that you're meant to go to assist them safely. The Elohim find every single one of them. Spread it now, please.

AA Michael: The energy is flowing.

A: Oh beautiful! As they are ready, Michael, if you could have Archangel Azrael and his Legion, ensure that every single one of these Reptilians who have decided to transform into light as they're ready for them, to start going ahead and start ascending. Ensure that we are supervising every single one of them and we do not lose sight of any one of them. Wherever it is that you all need to group up as Angels do so, please. Making sure that they are not harmed once they are positively polarized and that they are not taken the wrong way as they are coming out.

AA Michael: There are many trying to take them the wrong way.

A: Yes. How good are we doing as far as protecting them?

AA Michael: They can see the best way to go is not where they were.

A: Okay, can we have Angels of the element of fire, creating shields to wherever these negative beings are trying to take them elsewhere? Can we shield them with fire?

AA Michael: The thing is, some of them are defecting and going as well!

A: Oh, are they? Beautiful!

AA Michael: Because they're connected.

A: Okay. Good. So, let's continue this process, and allowing for the ones that are trying to trick them and if they choose positive polarization as well, again, giving them symbols and having them spread their Love-Light, please. The same process Michael.

AA Michael: Very many are following.

A: Thank you. We know the routine finding those consciousnesses as well and removing them from people or anywhere else that they're connected to. Again, we're sending a beautiful call to the Universe of sending Love-Light to every single one of these beings who are accepting this beautiful process and cycle that's occurring right now.

AA Michael: They're following each other. They're following each other!

A: Oh, that's so beautiful. Thank you!

AA Michael: Willingly! Today is a good day.

A: That it is. I know Michael, that originally, he had his session scheduled maybe two or three weeks ago and I had to reschedule it as I seemed very exhausted for some reason. I knew that he needed to be rescheduled. Is this the reason why he was rescheduled to this date?

AA Michael: It was. This is why.

A: Does it have any connection to the September 19th, 2019 portal that just occurred?

AA Michael: Very much so, very much so. Prior to that, it would not have been as effective. Some would have gone, but not as many. Nowhere near as many.

A: So, was it you all making me feel sick on purpose? (laughing)

AA Michael: (laughing) You know us better than that Aurora. You chose it!

A: I know, thank you! Now, I wasn't that bad. I'm just, you know, joking around with you guys.

AA Michael: It was too early, today's the right day.

A: Yes, exactly. Beautiful. In comparison, this can often happen when there is an A.U.R.A session scheduled and it's not the right date.

AA Michael: This is a better day. A far better day.

A: Beautiful. Can you tell us, Michael, as we are continuing to aid all these Reptilians, how much of a significance as far as a result would have been, if we did it then to the energies that were then, to what the energies are now after the portal? What is the difference in percentage that would have been achieved prior to what is achieved now?

AA Michael: This is 100,000-fold more effective.

A: Wow. So, would you say that this is what the energies would feel like now whenever people are self-healing and healing others?

AA Michael: Oh, they are released of hidden influences that they did not know were there and certainly would not welcome.

A: Wow, that is beautiful! Thank you.

AA Michael: This is for thousands, thousands and thousands of people on Earth and elsewhere.

A: Beautiful. Okay, as we continue this process, can I ask questions and then you could just interrupt me whenever it is time that we've completed what we needed to do?

AA Michael: Sure.

A: Okay, very good. While we're scanning his body, can you scan him for any more implants?

AA Michael: He's clear of implants.

A: How about just regular entities?

AA Michael: Yeah. There is one in the backbone, the lower lumbar region.

A: It's just an entity, not a Reptilian?

AA Michael: That's not Reptilian. That's an entity.

A: There are no more entities in him. Just that one?

AA Michael: That we can see at the moment.

A: Okay, let's talk to it. Talk to it Michael and see if it wants to go ahead and ascend. Same information as to others. Does it want to turn to light once more? Go to the light.

AA Michael: Yeah, they want to go.

A: Beautiful. Let's go ahead and aid that entity there in his spine too, please. Let's help it transform now to light and then again, you all can just help them release... All of you, the Higher Selves, just help them remove when they're ready. Let's have the Elohim there making sure that the Reptilians that are now positive are going where they are meant to go for their positive Ascension. Thank you.

AA Michael: They're heading, they've gone to light.

A: They all have gone?

AA Michael: They're gone

A: Yes, I feel lighter myself. Thank you. Wow. We're ensuring all the Higher Selves who are working with every single one of these Reptilians that were removed that we are filling in Love-Light and helping the beings that they were removed from. Thank you, Michael, now that they're gone. How many would you say approximately total, including consciousness, were removed from everywhere and turned into a positive polarization?

AA Michael: It's in the region of over nine million and increasing. Still going. It's like a domino wave of enlightenment amongst Reptilians races.

A: Beautiful! May that ripple continue on and when all beings of light assist through that ripple and continue in it.

AA Michael: It is a good day.

A: That it is, a very beautiful good day! Would you say that this is also reaching other galaxies not within our proximity? Would it be reaching the Universe?

AA Michael: It's exponential. It is exponential.

A: Yes. Thank you. What a beautiful day it is. Again, Higher Self, just help him feel comfortable. What's going on with him? Why is he so fidgety?

Higher Self: He can move.

A: Is that what's going on? Does he feel lighter like he can move?

Higher Self: He can move! Doesn't hurt so much. (loud laughter)

A: Did his body hurt before?

Higher Self: Aches. Subtle aches here and there.

A: Oh, that must be so beautiful to be so fluent now.

Higher Self: He never realized what was going on. I suspected something but not as much as this.

A: It's beautiful. We're going to continue with the body scan, Michael. Did we check for any negative implants, hooks, and portals? Can you check for that now please all three of those? Does he have any of those?

AA Michael: He does have an implant on the right side of his brain.

A: Let's go ahead and start transmuting that, Michael. Tell me, what was that causing him? Why did they put that there on his right side of his brain?

AA Michael: That looks like alien tech that does... That is alien technology.

A: What was the purpose of that? What did they get from that?

AA Michael: That's a tracking. Tracking component and monitoring.

A: Can I use the Phoenix Fire on it?

AA Michael: Yes.

A: Wonderful, let's go ahead and remove that, transmute that straight out of there. Michael, let us know once it's out.

AA Michael: That is gone.

A: Again, have Higher Self and Raphael fill in Love-Light to where the implant was. Thank you. Beautiful. He wanted to know; does he have any contracts? We could go ahead and remove it for him? That is not needed anymore for his highest good?

Higher Self: Those are dissolving. Any he feels he still has; he can tear up and burn himself.

A: Can you also tell us the time that he saw that space energy ship kind of shape? Was he abducted or what happened there?

Higher Self: Yeah, he was affected for sure.

A: Tell us how he was.

Higher Self: That's where the implant came from.

A: The one in his brain?

Higher Self: Yep, that's where that one comes from.

A: So this, as he explained it was like an oval type of energy. Very bright light. And it was huge.

Higher Self: It was on another plane that only some could see, and others could not.

A: He and his friend had to pull over and watch it, and no one else was pulling over to watch it.

Higher Self: It's a big one.

A: So, were those negative beings?

Higher Self: It's a scout ship.

A: Those were negatively polarized beings?

Higher Self: Neutral.

A: What year was this that this happened?

Higher Self: This was, I think this would have been 1980.

A: He said he saw in the news that they said, what was it?

Higher Self: The media of the day published a press release from the Ministry of Defense claiming that it was military aircraft on maneuvers, which it clearly was not.

A: Yes, as he mentioned. It was very big, moving, and it didn't have any noise to it.

Higher Self: No, it was not any form of terrestrial military aircraft whatsoever.

A: Can you tell us what was the purpose of this neutral, was it like an U.F.O.?

Higher Self: It was certainly a U.F.O. to those who could not identify it.

A: What was it doing? Besides him, it put an implant in him. Did it do anything to his friend and was that the plan? Was it doing that to the others?

Higher Self: It was a neutral scouting. It was an unsanctioned mission. The people who did it took it upon themselves to appear unexpectedly by many people on every side. I think they got into trouble, but they are over it now.

A: Besides him, did they put implants in others while they were doing this?

Higher Self: Yeah, implants for monitoring. Monitoring, observational but not invasively controlling.

A: Let me know if there's anything else that I could have asked that I haven't asked.

Higher Self: You could have asked, is he in the right place? The answer to that is absolutely. Yes.

A: Thank you... Now at this point, Michael, are we all done with the healing for him?

AA Michael: We are complete.

A: Beautiful. At this point, we've done what we needed to do for his session. I want to first of all thank everyone, Higher Self, every single Elohim, Archangel Michael, everyone who assisted benevolently from different races as well. Thank you so much to all of you. I know that this took much of an effort, and a collection of the Universe itself to place this together. I humbly honor you, thank you, love you, and respect you. Thank you. Thank you. Thank you to everyone!

AA Michael: This is a good day.

A: That it is! Thank you to everyone for your assistance as I do feel that this healing needs to be felt throughout the collective.

AA Michael: This would be uplifting. It's a good day.

A: That it is. Thank you again to everyone.

AA Michael: Thank you Aurora. We love you. Honor and we respect you.

A: Thank you and I love you all of you infinitely.

Post Session dialogue.

A: Oh my goodness! Welcome back!

P: Hi! I don't know where that lot came from.

A: That was the most powerful, beautiful A.U.R.A. hypnosis of this time that we have had.

P: You're kidding.

A: No, not kidding! Do you think you remember?

P: Oh, yeah. It's strange. The words were just coming out of my mouth. I thought where's this lot coming from but it's just flowing out you know. So weird so strange.

A: I just have no words, it's just wow! I felt everything and saw everything with you. I feel even lighter myself. I saw it, sensed it, felt it. I could see the different races that were coming to aid, like this was all planned out. Divinely planned out. I can sense and feel the shifting and lifting of everything, everything. Every being that was in the Universe.

P: I was thinking to myself, have they got enough sort of people up there to deal with this? But obviously they do... Fabulous.

A: Yeah, you are fabulous. You are incredible. I knew the day that I met you (his partner had her A.U.R.A. Hypnosis Healing session first, when I met him briefly) and I was like, I would love to do a healing on you. I knew that it was going to come in the future, even though you had not booked yet and I felt that the healing that was going to be coming out of you was going to just profoundly help all of Creation. Thank you, brother. There were so many times that I was crying!

P: Quite humbling.

A: There are many times that I was crying, but I had to keep my composure. I think I'm just going to go and cry right now out of happiness.

P: Oh, thank you so much. I feel great. I really feel great.

A: Thank you, for the beautiful healing that you have given Creation.

P: Thank you so much for the healing you've given me and Creation. Yes, that was amazing.

A: My infinite love. I love you all infinitely. Thank you for following your heart to me. You truly are a gift to humanity. Thank you to everyone.

P: I'm glad I could help.

A: Thank you. I know it seems surreal though.

P: It is surreal. I'm wrapping my head around it still, you know.

A: Right?

P: This is not your normal everyday sort of thing.

A: No, I mean the most we healed was thousands. But you went into millions.

P: They were kind of like, they were daisy-chaining, you know?

A: Love you brother. Thank you so much.

P: Thank you very much! Bye-bye!

END OF SESSION

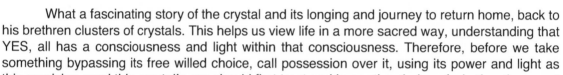

What a fascinating story of the crystal and its longing and journey to return home, back to his brethren clusters of crystals. This helps us view life in a more sacred way, understanding that YES, all has a consciousness and light within that consciousness. Therefore, before we take something bypassing its free willed choice, call possession over it, using its power and light as this magician used this crystal's, we should first treat and honor the choice of whether they want to come with us or not. This holds true for rocks, flowers, plants, and crystals... If it is organic, it contains consciousness. Will they be happier where they are at, which they may call home, or will they be happier where we call home for it is their home to be?

The millions of entities that were assisted through the parallel Mars we connected to. Wow, could it be in their parallel Universe the negative Reptilians still had a strong hold on their Mars? In our Universe, in sessions not included in this book, we have assisted Mars several times through A.U.R.A. Hypnosis Healing sessions. Perhaps in their parallel Universe no one has yet developed an entity healing and removal technique as ours? Could it be that this beautiful soul as Peter, accepted a role to allow for this attachment to his Third Eye? So, when the time came as organically agreed, that we would assist that Universe? Wow, this is a profound way to understand the healings which we are doing when one works with such a purity of heart. As Archangel Michael said, the reach of the healing conducted through this session is exponential. Making these potentials a possibility to other parallel Universes through many forms, as this energy will continue to ripple out throughout the Multiverse!

This incredible session was conducted after the 9/19/19 Activation Portal date, with the portal energies helping transform the collective healing for our A.U.R.A. Hypnosis Healing sessions. Another correlating factor to this session and its power is that Peter lives in the U.K., home to the "Universal Law of Grace" and "Inner Earth Key."[8] These 9/19/19 energies anchored in the beginnings of these vast amounts of collective healings all will read about throughout this book. What better location then Chakra 12 from within the Inner Earth amplifying the energies through this session?

---

[8] In Chapter 24, we have included channeled Universal teachings from The RA Collective on the 13 Keys/Earth Chakras/Universal Laws to aid understanding of this knowledge.

This inspiring session was a beautiful masterpiece collaborated by the Universe. I can imagine the unity planning that took place to bring these many benevolent beings together to assist in this manner. Also, the guidance given to us as Practitioner and Client to get us there to that exact moment in time where the stars align for the client and these deep collective healings to take place. This session marked the first of many sessions to come, after the 9/19/19 Portal date, how it became profoundly fluent to be able to help collectives of negatively polarized beings in the Universe, whether in the thousands, millions, or billions. Could the collective of light of Earth have reached the critical mass of 'awakening light' in the now if these collectives of healings were not conducted? The possibilities are slim. As with every group entity removal and healing, we became and are becoming lighter. Every session we do nowadays connects us to an exponential variety of collective healings, and every day we can feel the Earth and the Universe become lighter in density. Each day we are becoming closer to achieve the goal of Ascension collectively!

"Upon life there is not just one flow of direction in teachings.
For both the teacher and learner teach.
Both directions flow back and forth, creating a cycle of growth within spirit.
Accepting each lesson graduating you upon that teachings."
~AuroRa ♥

-------------<◇>-------------

11

"THE EVENT"

Session #137: Recorded in April 2019.

In this online A.U.R.A. Hypnosis Healing session, Brittany finds herself on a magical land in the Inner Earth. Come experience this as she takes us on this detailed journey through "The Event" - before, after, and during the wave. How will the physical bodies transition into light bodies, will we reproduce, and will we still need to eat? What happens to the 3D physical realm and the human ego? What happens to the benevolent aliens inside Inner Earth and the Starseeds on Earth? This is a beautiful narrative of someone's individual experience of "The Event." In this insightful session, we get a glimpse of the future New Earth!

-------------<◇>-------------

**"We just BE, we just BE love, we are an example of love.
We just teach how to love; we play with the children."
-Brittany**

-------------<◇>-------------

A: [Aurora] Do you feel like you have a body?
B: [Brittany] Yes.
A: Do you feel female, male?
B: It's this body.
A: You feel like you're in a jungle?
B: Mm-hmm.
A: Do you feel like you're younger or older?
B: A little older.
A: Let's walk around and let's see why it is that you're here. Tell me as you are walking around, what are you wearing?
B: Nothing.
A: Is there anything you're carrying with you?
B: No.
A: Are you wearing any jewelry?
B: No.
A: Let's see why you are here in this place. Let's see why you have been taken here. Keep walking and tell me, as you're walking, what stands out? What draws your attention?
B: There are lights in the trees... blue, yellow, they glow.
A: Do you feel like it is day or night?
B: It feels like daytime, but I don't see the sun.
A: Let's focus on these lights that you say are in the trees. What is it?
B: Some are like the animals in the tree. Trees have love in them. A lot of love.
A: Do you feel their love?
B: I do.

A: Some of those lights you say are animals?

B: Like their eyes.

A: See if the trees may have a message for you, the animals. See who wants to speak. What messages do they have for you? Why is it that they brought you here?

B: I can just feel their love. They don't speak, they just let me feel. The animals, their light. They are there to say we can all live together.

A: Yes. Thank you. Let's keep moving the scene along. Let's see where else draws your attention. Keep moving along and see if there is anything that stands out?

B: It's like…um…it makes me giggle. It's like Avatar, the movie. The tree of Eywa.

A: You can go towards it. Tell me, what else do you see?

B: Just that tree. It's beautiful!

A: See, if you touch it, do you receive any messages when you touch it?

B: I think it is there for protection. It's warm.

A: Are there any life or animals in this tree?

B: No.

A: Is there anything else that stands out? Are there any shapes or colors within the tree?

B: It's just a big, big, tree! The branches are like a weeping tree. It's just white.

A: Beautiful. Let's move the scene along, let's see what else is significant in this land for you. What do you see next of importance?

B: A waterfall. A mountain.

A: Tell me about the waterfall and the mountain.

B: I just like to go there. It's cleansing, there is a pool at the bottom for swimming.

A: Keep looking around.

B: There are birds. This is where I can see the sun. There are too many trees. I have to come out of the trees to see the sun.

A: Would you like to go in the water and in the waterfall?

B: No, I just like to be here.

A: Let's keep moving the scene along and let's see if there is anything else of significance in this land for you.

B: I went up the mountain of the waterfall but there is nothing up there. It looks like it was destroyed so we have to go down the trees.

A: The top looks like it was destroyed?

B: Yes. It's just dark. There is nothing there.

A: Why do you feel like it was destroyed?

B: It's just gone. As beautiful as it is in the trees and waterfall, I would think everything would be like this. Nothing is saved.

A: Let's go back in time now to see if there was life once in this land that you see destroyed. Back, back, to when it was… if there was. You are there now. What do you see?

B: A park. Kids playing in a park. There was grass. I feel like that's now, but it got destroyed so we went into the Earth.

A: Let's see, go to the time now when it's about to be destroyed. Right before it was destroyed, right before you had to go down into the Inner Earth. Before that happened, who caused that? You are there now. What do you see?

B: People are panicking, they're scared. (cries) But I tell them to stay calm, that it is okay. I know we will be safe. But I don't know what they are running from. I don't know why they are scared!

A: Let's focus. Let's follow where it is starting from. What is it that they're running from? Go towards what it is that they are running from. You are there now, what do you see?

B: It was like my dream last night. Something hits the Earth; it causes a wave. It pushes the water up... it doesn't explode the Earth, but it pushes up. Like a wave of water up, like a tsunami. They're probably from this energy or this light or the wave that is coming in. I don't know what it is made of. It was in my dream.

A: Since you are in this time and space now. You are able to sense and feel everything very detailed. Let's see exactly what it is you are able to feel and sense. What is it that has everyone running and is pushing you all inside the Earth?

B: It feels like water, but it doesn't make you drown. Energy washes over you but you're still standing. I'm not scared. I let it wash over me so I can calm everybody down.

A: Are you letting it soak in, are you by yourself?

B: Everybody ran away so I went to it to see what they were running from. I turned my back to it, but I didn't need to. I thought it was going to be water and it would knock me over, but it just went over me. I was fine. I was good. I wasn't scared.

A: As it went through you, tell me how that feels?

B: Warm. I feel lighter. I don't feel so dense after it's on me. It's like I can fly. I'm no longer bound by gravity.

A: Once it hits you, does it integrate into you?

B: Right.

A: How does it work?

B: I absorb it.

A: Slow time down. Tell me, when you absorb it, it is absorbing into you. What is going on with you, your mind, body, and soul?

B: I am telling me to surrender, to allow. I've been waiting for it. So, I opened my heart and I let it in, and I became it. It can move... lighter so I can walk if I want to. I can fly, I can go anywhere. It is warm and safe. It's like a light body, not a dense body. I glowed like this in the jungle.

A: This is how you glowed before you came back?

B: And the tree, I glowed like the tree.

A: Mm-hmm. Beautiful. What happened to those people who were running away from it?

B: So, I go back to them and show them how I was absorbed. Flow to them. I think they trust me, and I tell them to follow me. I know I have to find Tony (husband) because I want to be with him (crying). So, I want to find him.

A: Yes, let's see if we can find him now. Look for him, you're able to recognize his soul.

B: He is a light body too and people are following him.

A: As you found him, the people that were following you, followed you there to find him?

B: Yes, so we went to find him, and we found him with his group of people that followed him.

A: How many would you say that you feel would be following you?

B: Twenty or thirty.

A: Do those people look like you?

B: Yes, but they don't have light bodies. They have human bodies.

A: So, you have a human body but the ones that did not accept the wave and ran from it have human bodies?

B: Yeah, they do not glow yet.

A: Were there any people that weren't able to sustain that wave of energy? Were there any of those kinds of people?

B: Yes, so I told you that I felt like I was going to be pulled by water and that pulled them. They went with that wave, the wave pulled them out. Pulled them back with it, like if a wave came up and it pulled back into them. The ocean, they pulled back in with that wave.

A: Was there a color to that wave?

B: Just white like ah... even like a light yellow, light brown.

A: So, a bit like a yellow and white?

B: Yeah, like a tan, like a really light, light tan, not a dark tan. It's like an off-white. Some people went with that wave.

A: Would you say more people went with that wave or stayed here and accepted it?

B: I only have 20 to 30 people in my group.

A: You're able to sense in this plane of existence that you are in. Do you feel that there is a name for where you are at before you transitioned?

B: No, it is just like where we lived. Our kids played at the park.

A: So, you said it was this life. Are you saying it's Earth?

B: Yeah, it feels just like it is now.

A: You are able to sense now since you are this energy body. You are able to sense and feel the Earth now that it has been through this transition. What amount has left the Earth after that wave that was pulled back with that wave? Has the population upon Earth...

B: Everywhere, not just where I live.

A: You are able to feel the energy as that light body and know. Receive that information through the Higher Consciousness.

B: It looks like some places on the outside of Earth survived. They're very green. It looks like they have little cities on the outside of Earth, around it but not very much. Most of it is like dust and we had to go inside the Earth. But I do see that there are like, little cities on top.

A: What was the difference between those little cities you feel that they were not able to turn into dust like the others?

B: They were more loved.

A: Therefore, they were cities that held that vibration of acceptance like you did?

B: Yes.

A: Beautiful. Are there people in those cities?

B: Mm-hmm. There are. They're like tribes. That group of people is meant to be together.

A: We'll go back to them in a few. When you said you had to go into the Inner Earth, how was it that you entered the Inner Earth?

B: Through the waterfall. It is like a canyon; it has mountains and then we found the waterfall and it guided us into there. But I don't know where the water came from because the top is dry. Like it comes out of the sides. We just found that crevice of water.

A: Do you feel like there are different spots like this upon Earth that you could've gone through?

B: Yes, there are the cities that I know people live in, that they have survived, they have everything they need to live there. Most people went into the Earth.

A: Do you feel when you went into the Earth that you went very deeply into the Earth or did you go slightly?

B: It was not a lot. It just opened up enough that... like the waterfall is maybe a 100-foot drop. Then you get to the pool and you can go back into the jungle further and further. It can go deeper and deeper.

A: Beautiful. Tony, does he have about the same amount of people following him as you have?

B: Mm-hmm. About 20 or 30 people.

A: What do you feel your role is with them?

B: To protect them, to guide them, to show them the way. To help them remember, let them know that love is real. That they have been... it was an illusion, they were manipulated. How to live from their hearts again.

A: Would you say these people who are following you, were able to almost surrender enough; however, still needed a little more? Is that why they're not light bodies like you are? I'm trying to figure out the difference between them and you.

B: Yeah. So, it was like they didn't know... I was waiting for the wave, I knew it was coming, so I was ready, and I surrendered to it. But they didn't know there was a wave. They didn't know what it was, so it scared them. So, they were still living in fear but as we go into the Earth the more, we teach them. The light integrates into them too.

A: What would you say would be the difference between the people that were pulled away with the wave to the people who are with you?

B: They weren't ready. Perhaps that is what they chose. Their hearts weren't opened. They wanted it to be dark; they didn't believe there was light or love. They believed in fear. But maybe they will come back. I'm sure if they choose to, they can come back at any time.

A: Would you say that they were too dense to remain in this existence?

B: Right! They wouldn't open their hearts. They wouldn't open up to something different. They didn't believe.

A: So, they weren't connected or working from a space of the heart?

B: Right. They feel greedy, they want more, more money, more power that's what is important to them. The people that stayed, loved.

A: Beautiful. What about your children? Do you see them there?

B: They're with us... Mm-hmm... they came with us, they're in the group.

A: Yes, beautiful. Tell me, when you went into the Inner Earth were there people that lived there, or was it just a way that you went to try and transition into this through the wave?

B: I feel like it is established, there aren't buildings, they live in trees. The trees love us. It's like Avatar. You are connected to the trees and you sleep with the trees, they protect you and they love you. But it feels like someone's been there. Maybe they cared for the trees, maybe they - I don't see anyone. But it feels like they were getting it ready for us to come there.

A: Beautiful. This space that you saw at the beginning, was the space inside the Inner Earth?

B: Yes, with the jungle.

A: With the big tree.

B: Yeah.

A: Beautiful. Now that you are a light body, you're able to travel through time as time does not exist. Go to before the wave hits, this wave of love. Go back, back to this time where there were people right before the wave hit that prepared it. You are there now, what do you see?

B: They are what we call aliens, they don't look like us. They have different bodies that are tall like a grey-blue color, they are getting it ready making sure we have what we need. So, they put the water from the waterfall so we can drink water. They have like fruit trees they planted there with fruit trees so we could eat. They just prepared it so that we had everything that we needed.

A: You said that they were like a tall grey-bluish type of race?

B: Mm-hmm. I see one, like prepping.

A: How would you describe his features? His facial features?

B: He has big eyes, but they are more almond, there are like two little holes for the nose and a tiny mouth. But they are soft, and they are kind. They have love like the tree (Brittany cries). He smiles at me and winks like, 'it's okay.'

A: Our love to them, thank you. Please, thank them for us.

B: Yeah.

A: Thank you. Tell me, they prepared this land and the Inner Earth for you. What happened to them when the wave occurred? What did they do?

B: They left. I think they felt others would be afraid of their appearance. But I think they come back and check. Their presence is always there but I can't... I don't always see them.

A: Those animals that you saw on the trees were these some of the animals that accepted the wave as well?

B: I feel like they have always been down there. I don't think they came with us.

A: Okay, so they were part of the Inner Earth?

B: Yeah, that is what it feels like.

A: Let's see if we can focus on some of these animals. See which ones stand out that perhaps might be different than the ones we know. What do they look like?

B: This one looks kind of like a meerkat. He has big eyes. I see beautiful butterflies, little caterpillars that crawl on the trees. It's like when you go camping there are those types of creatures that you would encounter camping. It's not something you see every day but you just live in harmony with them. Because that is their home.

A: Thank you. Tell me, these people that are following you and Tony, do they go into the Inner Earth with you?

B: Yes.

A: So, would you say this land is like your home?

B: It becomes our home.

A: As that embodied being that you are, see if you can focus out upon this plane; this plane of existence now that it has transitioned. Does it have a sphere-like type of planet, is it a plane field with a dome, or is it a flat plane? What type of shape does it have?

B: I just see it go straight, it's just flat.

A: Now as you are able to travel again in time go back, back, back to before the wave hit. Did it look the same, flat?

B: Yes. When you asked me to look at all of it, there are more people now. A lot of people came into the Earth.

A: After the wave?

B: Yeah.

A: Are there different sections upon this plane that people went into that are living like in a little paradise jungle like yours?

B: Yes.

A: Go ahead and fast-forward a bit to when something else is happening of importance. Something else significant, you are there now. What do you see?

B: Children, like new children being born, babies. They are already light.

A: Describe to me what you are seeing? Is there a mother giving birth?

B: She did already. She had a healthy baby.

A: The mother, how did she look? Does she look not as a light-bodied or is she light-bodied?

B: Well, she is now.

A: She was light-bodied before she had the baby?

B: Right.

A: So, then does she birth a baby as a light body?

B: Baby girl.

A: Can you describe how a light body looks? For example, the baby - are they both the same type of color? Is the mother and the child the same color? Is everyone the same color or do they have different light body colors?

B: It looks like the mom is still integrating her light body, I can still see that she is not completely white like the baby. She still has color to her. But the baby, she is light, all white.

A: Does she have the shape of a baby? Human baby?

B: Yes.

A: How about her facial features and fingers? Is there a shape for those?

B: Yes, she just looks like a human baby.

A: Just very bright?

B: Bright, very bright it's like blinding. So happy, she is just so happy.

A: After the mother has the baby what does she do? Is she able to nurse it?

B: Yes. But it is not like milk, it is like light energy. But there is a connection that they make that it is intimate for them to nurse.

A: Is there a husband there, a partner?

B: Yes.

A: How does he look?

B: Happy.

A: Is he a light body or is he similar to the mother?

B: He is more of a light body than she is. But there are so many children running around that are glowing, they are just light.

A: Are these children who were born as well as children who came forth with the wave and surrendered to it?

B: They were born.

A: They were born after the wave?

B: Yes, the only people, the only children I could see that went into the Earth with us were our own children. Everybody else was older.

A: So, let's see what else you do in this existence. What are other things that you do as part of being in this plane?

B: We just BE, we just BE love, we are an example of love. We just teach how to love; we play with the children.

A: Are there certain roles that everyone has? Are there any responsibilities?

B: Just to be compassionate, be mindful.

A: If you could explain to me what happened when that wave went through you and for example the density that you hold of ego. What happened to that side of you?

B: It was gone. I didn't need it anymore. For that, I had surrendered and allowed the wave to take that part of me.

A: So, it took that part of you that was the ego alongside the other people who were perhaps, you could say, in ego?

B: I don't think it took it; you could say it dissolved it. It didn't leave me, but it dissolved it.

A: Did it like, transmute it in the form of healing it?

B: Right. Mm-hmm. Yeah.

A: Then it became part of you but in a light type of...

B: Right. It's still part of me but it is love.

A: The people. Tell me a little more about the people who are on the top of the plane. Do they look similar to you as light bodies?

B: I think one of them might be Sandy.

A: One of them might be what?

B: My friend Sandy.

A: Oh, your friend, she's above the surface? How does she look?

B: The same, they are light bodies above the plane. I think they communicate with other planets or other entities. They like, give reports on how we're doing.

A: So, they communicate with other entities such as in other areas? Do you mean on other planets?

B: Other galaxies, yeah.

A: Okay. Do they have light bodies like you?

B: Mm-hmm.

A: Do they also have children?

B: Mm-hmm.

A: Are they light bodies like your children too?

B: It's like us but just in a little spot on Earth-like on top. It's a little paradise.

A: Does their land look magical like yours?

B: They do.

A: Thank you. How are you able to communicate with one another?

B: We can go up there. We check on them, they come to check on us. We can just talk to them; we don't have to be there - like telepathy.

A: You can telepathically talk to them?

B: Uh-hmm.

A: Is that also the way you communicate with the people within your own village? Do you talk to them telepathically or do you use sound through voice?

B: We can do both.

A: Both. How do you consume? Is there water and food that you need to intake?

B: If you want too, you don't have to though. It is there. The people who prepared the place planted fruit. There is fruit there and there is a waterfall with the water there.

A: It's only if you want too?

B: Yes. You don't have to eat though. You live off energy.

A: Tell me how that works? How do you live off energy?

B: I don't know, it's just like breathing. When you breathe in your full, you just don't need to eat, you just have all you need.

A: Would you say that it is a light energy that is all around you that exists, and it soaks into you?

B: Yeah, you breathe it in, and you have all you need.

A: What role does the sun have with this?

B: Well, I can't see the sun. I love the sun so I'm sad. That is why I think I go to the waterfall to see the sun.

A: So, you have to go outside to see the sun?

B: Yeah, I think so. But there is so much light it's not...

A: See if you can find the light Source to the light that is out on the surface. Is there a sun?

B: There is a sun out. The light Source inside is us. The light comes from us. That is why I said, in the beginning, I think its day, but I can't see the sun. It's weird because we provide the light in the Eywa trees, it has light. It's not dark in there, it's not, it's always lit. The trees have that light, so I don't see the sun anymore.

A: Since you do not see the sun anymore, I want you to go back now to when the wave came, watch the sun. What happens to the sun since it is no longer there in your time?

B: I just see it covered up by the debris. It doesn't go anywhere.

A: So, is the sun still there?

B: Mm-hmm.

A: But it is covered up by debris?

B: Mm-hmm.

A: Where did the debris come from? Why did it cover it up?

B: From the impact of the wave, it moved things. Dirt and water and... the sun is still there. I just can't see it because I turned my back.

A: So, it is covered up by that…and then what happens when the wave leaves to the sun?

B: It's still there because it shines on us while we go looking for people.

A: So, it is still there after?

B: It is still there.

A: You said you go out looking for people?

B: Mm-hmm. Like I wanted to find Tony and we just found people along the way and picked them up. Until we found the waterfall.

A: Some people that you have found are still transitioning into light bodies and don't know exactly where to go? To the waterfall or places?

B: Yeah, they're just alone. We just invite them to come with us.

A: Do you feel like you can experience pain in this existence?

B: No.

A: Even though they were alone they were not panicked or sad?

B: They were scared. They thought they knew what was real but... They're just unsure what to think.

A: As a light body, when you go up to the surface are you able to sense people who are unsure like them looking for help?

B: Maybe that is why some stayed on top.

A: So, the ones that are a little lost you can find?

B: Yeah.

A: As you're here, do you ever have any of those people you say that communicate to other galaxies and planets and other aliens, do they come to visit you?

B: They can. We can go anywhere.

A: Do you ever see any type of spaceships?

B: They do because they are on top. But I don't see any inside.

A: The spaceships that travel around, they don't have to mask themselves?

B: No.

A: Okay. Are they able to freely...?

B: Yes.

A: Do you still have technology in this plane?

B: Well, I don't see, like, computer technology but I know we are way more advanced because we have telepathy. We can communicate way better. But I don't see that we have computers, telephones...

A: Does it get dark?

B: No.

A: Is there no night?

B: I wasn't sure if it was day or night, but it is always the same. I think it's because of us, because we glow.

A: Do you feel that there is still a moon above?

B: I think so.

A: There is a moon?

B: Yes. The ones that live on top, they can still see the stars... it gets dark there.

A: Ah, it does get dark there. However, you all always illuminate down there.

B: Exactly, right!

A: Okay. Are there any tunnels that connect with other tribes inside the Inner Earth?

B: I don't see tunnels; I just see it open.

A: Only an opening?

B: We can go anywhere.

A: You only keep traveling until you connect with another tribe?

B: Yeah.

A: Would you say that this place is like a humongous cave?

B: Yes. It goes everywhere.

A: Would you say that the wave came through and removed the 3D?

B: Mm-hmm.

A: For example, the cars, the buildings?

B: Right.

A: The skyscrapers?

B: Yes. Took it all away.

A: Did it pull it back with it?

B: Mm-hmm.

A: Did the wave consist of a fire type of element, before the water hit that felt like energy water? Was there anything prior to that? … Go back, back right before that wave of water-like energy came through. Was there anything before that?

B: I don't see anything.

A: Would you say that wave, is it like an energy that has a life force within it, so it moves kind of like water. Is that why you say it felt like water?

B: Yeah.

A: This energy, would it feel like a Source type of pure light energy?

B: Yes. When you say fire, I think of something harsh and it will burn. It is almost scary where it can get out of control, but it wasn't, it was very like water, it flowed freely, it moved softly. That is why I say water.

A: Would you say it had a combination of elements within the wave?

B: Yeah, it came fast like fire. That is why I think people were scared because it was just there. It was almost like there was an impact with the atmosphere. It kind of shook, made it shake but it was very soft.

A: Was that the initial impact of separating, pulling out the too dense, the 3D, the objects, you know - material, the people? Was that the kind of the bang and then when it separated it felt a little less?

B: Maybe Earth's atmosphere now is too dense and the dissimilarities of the wave and atmosphere now they -what's the word- they don't get along. I think that was the impact that they felt.

A: When the impact happened was there a flash of light? Did it seem very bright?

B: It almost looked like there was a bubble around Earth because when the wave hit the atmosphere, it hit the bubble and it wobbled all around. It sent ripples in the bubble and made it shake. But it came through.

A: Through the bubble?

B: Mm-hmm.

A: Are they showing you Earth as a plane with a bubble of energy around it?

B: When you say plane, do you mean flat but it's a ball? Like a bubble around a ball and the wave hit the bubble and it rippled and kind of shook it. There was so much like you said, it came like fire so fierce and forceful and hit the bubble. Then it calmed down and was more fluid and soft like water.

A: Earlier I had asked you and you said that it was a plane. That you saw a plane.

B: When I look out...

A: Up there.

B: It's flat but when I go back and observe the Earth you see the Earth being round.

A: Inside you see it round but outside you see it flat? Is that what you are saying?

B: If I go into space and I observe Earth it looks round. There is a bubble around Earth. When I am in my light body and I look out it looks flat. I'm standing on the...it looks like now; you don't know the Earth is round when you stand on it.

A: Let's go ahead and see if there is one last thing of importance in this existence that you have been shown. Anything else that you would like to show us of importance?

B: There is just so much love from everyone from the trees to the animals. We all feel so - relieved isn't the right word- but so grateful that we finally did it and we are so grateful that we got so many to come with us.

A: One more thing, if you can pan out go ahead and go out into space. See it from an outside perspective. As the wave hits and it shifts, what about the other planetary spheres and the other clusters of stars, the other life around there. What happens to them when the wave, like you said forces in and then it goes in smoothly and then it shifts? What happens to everyone else around it that you can see?

B: I think it causes them to shake but they are protected. Everyone is fine, they are safe, they are good.

A: Since you are a light body, you're able to experience this and tap in. What does it feel like, does it feel like they shifted in a sense like you all did as well?

B: I think so. They seem happier.

A: Does it feel like they were holding on to something heavy and now they feel happier and lighter?

B: Lighter. Mm-hmm.

A: Can I please speak to the Higher Self of Brittany?

The Higher Self is called forth.

Higher Self: Yes.

A: Beautiful. Thank you. Am I speaking to Brittany's Higher Self now?

Higher Self: Yes.

A: I honor you, I thank you, and I respect you for all the aid you've given us today. I know that you hold all the records of Brittany's different lives, may I ask you questions, please?

Higher Self: Yes.

A: Thank you. You took her to a phenomenal, phenomenal life where she experienced the wave. Tell me why is it that you took her to that?

Higher Self: So that she knows. So that she'll trust.

A: What was the lesson to that life that you wanted her to see and learn?

Higher Self: Not to be scared and to surrender.

A: That she will be fine?

Higher Self: Mm-hmm, everything is perfect.

A: Can you tell me, is that how the Earth will shift when the wave comes through 'The Event'? When the shifting of the polarization happens upon Earth?

Higher Self: From her perspective.

A: From her perspective. Are you stating that there are several different perspectives?

Higher Self: Yes. That is her Heaven on Earth.

A: Well, it was very beautiful and aligned very genuinely to my heart. Thank you for that experience.

Higher Self: No, thank you.

A: Before the wave hit, were they in 3D-4D?

Higher Self: Yes.

A: After the wave happened, what Dimension were they in?

Higher Self: Five.

A: What percentage out of the current population here on Earth today, would you say transitioned into 5D?

Higher Self: If I go with my first number, I will say 60 percent but that seems high.

A: Well, you never know. There are many Light Workers out there now learning to work from their heart space.

Higher Self: There are.

A: There are said to be people in the Inner Earth that are currently living, and they are in the high 4D waiting for the wave so that they can go into the 5D. Could you tell us what happened to the people in the Inner Earth? These people are said to be the ancestors of Atlantis and Lumeria; in addition, there are some ancestors that are from the future that were said to reside in the Inner Earth. What happened to them when the wave came?

Higher Self: They are still there. They can just make themselves invisible, so they don't scare people. But they are always there and they can make themselves visible again.

A: Would you say that they are more in a higher type of 5D?

Higher Self: Yes. They come back, they'll stay there, some live together.

A: As far as the 5D we saw animals, how about the magical animals, do they ever come back? Like the dragons, unicorns, and fairies?

Higher Self: I see them.

A: They are within the 5D if they choose it?

Higher Self: Mm-hmm. I see them.

A: Can you tell us? I know she was able to see some of it, how's the planetary here, the clusters, the Universe even... the ones that were connected to the Earth. Would you say that everyone was connected to the Earth when this shift happened or were there some planets that say, let go of it at some point in time, where they connected? Was everyone connected within this Universe's plane of existence?

Higher Self: I don't know. Do you mean other planets connected to Earth?

A: Yes.

Higher Self: Or the people on Earth connected to them?

A: Were there other planets connected to Earth when the shift happened?

Higher Self: Many planets are connected to Earth.

A: Many. Are there some planets that are not connected?

Higher Self: Yes, I believe so.

A: Okay. What happened to those that held space in love and were connected to the Earth? When the Earth shifted and raised the vibration...

Higher Self: They shifted.

A: Since the Earth went into a 5D, did they go to the next level of Dimension?

Higher Self: I think so.

A: Thank you, that is what I was seeing, just getting the confirmation from you. Lovely. What would you say, for example, there are certain Starseed people that came from another Dimension, another planet, star beings? When the wave came, did they return back to where they came from or did they become part of the experience into the 5D?

Higher Self: We have told her that she is from the stars. She chose to stay and help people, but she will go home.

A: Were some able to stay or did everyone stay into the 5D and eventually go home?

Higher Self: It's their choice.

A: It was their choice, okay. Beautiful, thank you. That was phenomenal at this point I am out of questions. Thank you!

The Body Scan begins.

A: Let us know if you need any help from the Archangels to scan her body. Scan her body now for any energies, entities, anything that needs healing.

Higher Self: I don't see anything.

A: Very good. With your permission so that we may be safe, would you allow for Archangel Michael to come forth to scan her body?

Higher Self: Yes.

A: Thank you. Higher Self, if you can please connect us to Archangel Michael now. If I can please speak to Archangel Michael now?

AA Michael: Yes.

A: Greetings. Is this you, Michael?

AA Michael: Yes.

A: Thank you, brother. We honor you, we love you, and we respect you.

AA Michael: We love you.

A: We just finished viewing a life, well, a future life of hers seeing the New Earth and we are asking the Higher Self now to do the body scan. The Higher Self said that it didn't detect anything that needed healing, so I wanted to make sure that it was correct. As she does have a few aches and pains there and things that need healing. Michael, scan her body from head to toe and look for any energies, entities, consciousness, anything that needs healing. Let me know what you find please, Michael.

AA Michael: I only find a twitch in her right elbow and her chest is warm.

A: Let's take a look at the twitch in her right elbow. Michael, what is causing that twitch?

AA Michael: It just wanted to say it was there.

A: Is it an entity?

AA Michael: I don't think so.

A: Michael, does it feel like it has a consciousness?

AA Michael: It wanted me to know that it was there, but it is not hurting her.

A: That sounds to me that it would be an entity. Michael, if you can please help that entity come up, up, up now, please. If I could please speak to that energy there, that entity that wanted us to know that it is there. Greetings.

Entity: Hello.

A: Hello. Thank you for speaking to us. May I ask you questions?

Entity: Yes.

A: Are you female or male?

Entity: Neither.

A: Tell me how was it that you found yourself in her right elbow?

Entity: I was just there.

A: Did you have a body?

Entity: No.

A: Did you ever have a body before you connected to her elbow?

Entity: No.

A: Where did you come from then?

Entity: Energy.

A: Was it an energy from within her or any energy outside her?

Entity: Within her.

A: What was it that she was doing that caused you to create in her elbow?

Entity: Not listening.

A: She wasn't listening. Did you cause her any discomfort there?

Entity: No.

A: Very good. Wouldn't it be nice for you to transform back to just being of her instead of being a separate type of energy in her elbow?

Entity: Yes.

A: Beautiful. Archangel Michael, if you could help this energy transform back into her, please. Can we do that now?

AA Michael: Okay.

A: Good, is it done?

AA Michael: Yes.

A: Thank you, Michael. Can you continue scanning her body? You mentioned that you felt something in her heart. What was it that you felt in her heart?

AA Michael: Very hot. It's warm.

A: Scan her heart for any Reptilian consciousness, any negative implants, portals, and hooks. What is that she is experiencing there?

AA Michael: It feels heavy.

A: Let us know if you need any additional help Michael from any other angels? Is there anyone else the Higher Self would like to call on?

AA Michael: She feels this when she opens her heart chakra.

A: What is that which is making her feel heavy there?

AA Michael: It's warm but it feels heavy because it is big.

A: What is this that is heavy because it is big?

AA Michael: It's getting harder to breathe.

A: If we could call on Archangel Metatron? Brother, if you could please place the symbols on whatever it is that we are trying to figure out what it is. Are you there, brother?

AA Metatron: Yes.

A: Thank you for being here. We love you and we honor you. Did you place the symbols around this?

AA Metatron: Yes.

A: Thank you. It seems like there is some kind of blockage there. Metatron, can you scan and see what it is?

AA Metatron: She has so much love.

A: Is it stuck?

AA Metatron: I think so.

A: So, let's look and find the root of how it got stuck there, please.

AA Metatron: She loves so deeply… (crying) I don't know if she doesn't feel others' love in return or she won't allow it in. She just wants everybody to feel love and she feels that it is her fault.

A: Why does she feel that it is her fault?

AA Metatron: That she caused them pain.

A: Is there something that she is responsible for? Why does she feel that she caused them pain?

AA Metatron: With her choices.

A: Do you mean the people around her family?

AA Metatron: Yes. She wanted to bring more love, but they don't see it that way. It is heavy.

A: Is there something that is stuck that is holding the energy there? Is there like an energy that is holding that stuck there that needs to be perhaps unplugged, removed, transmuted?

AA Metatron: I want to release the heaviness. She can just love and not have to feel that it is her fault that they don't see it her way - her perspective.

A: Would she have to forgive herself?

AA Metatron: Yes.

A: Can we call on brother Raphael please to start working on her with her heart so she can start letting go of this and start forgiving herself? Can we do that, Metatron?

AA Metatron: Yes.

A: My love to Raphael. Thank you, we love you, we honor you, and we respect you brother.

AA Raphael: Thank you.

A: Thank you. Metatron, I just want you to look through there one more time and make sure there is nothing there that is holding that there besides herself, a Reptilian consciousness, a portal, an implant, anything that is negative there that is holding it there.

AA Metatron: What would it look like?

A: What does it look like to you?

AA Metatron: I just see dark.

A: Does this dark have a voice?

AA Metatron: No.

A: Does this dark have emotions? Is it angry that it has been found?

AA Metatron: I don't think it is angry.

A: Okay, so within the heart, Metatron. Is there darkness, a mass, a bit of heaviness of darkness inside of there?

AA Metatron: I think so.

A: Typically, when we see that type of energy it is an entity. Is it an entity, Metatron?

AA Metatron: It looks like a black hand with fingers. Holding her heart.

A: Yeah. Does it have nails to it? Claws?

AA Metatron: No, like the fingers are like Ivy. It is wrapped around it and doesn't stop.

A: So, they look like roots?

AA Metatron: Yes.

A: Metatron, keep this energy still contained please. Metatron, Michael, Raphael, Higher Self, I would like to speak with that energy there, that entity there that is the embodiment of that hand wrapped around her heart. If I could please speak to you now. Come up, up, up.

Entity: Yes.

A: Greetings.

Entity: Hello.

A: Hello. Thank you for speaking to us. May I ask you questions?

Entity: Yes.

A: Are you female or male?

Entity: I think I am female.

A: Did you have a body before you connected yourself here?

Entity: Yes.

A: What happened to your body? How did you die?

Entity: Grief.

A: What happened? Why did you have grief?

Entity: I was so sad.

A: Why were you sad?

Entity: I feel like I lost my family, they're gone.

A: How did you lose them?

Entity: They got sick.

A: Did they die?

Entity: Yes.

A: When was it that you attached to her heart?

Entity: I think I've been there awhile.

A: Do you feel that you've been here this life or before this life?

Entity: I think this life.

A: Was she younger?

Entity: Not very.

A: What was going on with her that allowed for you to come in and attach?

Entity: She was sad.

A: Why was she sad?

Entity: She lost her family. Babies... So, we grieved together.

A: Was this a contract?

Entity: Yes.

A: I know that you've been there a long time and are you aware that the family that you lost is now beyond the veil? They are waiting for you on the other side.

Entity: Yes. I would like to go with them.

A: Good. So, let's go ahead and find that light within you, and spread it to all that is of you, every root, every cord. Spread it to all light. Let us know once you are all light.

Positive Polarized Entity: Okay.

A: Go ahead and remove yourself fully from her heart. Do not leave a piece of you behind, all that belongs to you that does not belong to her. Let me know once you are fully out.

Positive Polarized Entity: I am out.

A: Beautiful. Do you have a message for her before you go, please?

Positive Polarized Entity: Thank you and I am sorry for your pain. I love you.

A: Thank you. Can you look back now that you are of light, look back at her body, are there any more entities in there?

Positive Polarized Entity: I think in her forehead.

A: Okay, very good. Thank you for all your aid. We love you and we honor you. Go ahead and go with the Love-Light of the Universe. Blessings to you. May you enjoy your family.

Positive Polarized Entity: Thank you.

A: Thank you. Our love to them as well. Metatron, brother? Can you please look at her forehead, her third eye? The entity that left said that she had something there. What is that?

AA Metatron: Yes. It's giving her a headache.

A: Can you also have brother Raphael start filling in with Love-Light, heart energy in for her? Have him spread it as big as it can be in this time and space for her.

AA Metatron: Yes.

A: Thank you brother.

AA Metatron: Yeah, there is something there that is giving her a headache.

A: Is it an entity?

AA Metatron: I think so.

A: Can you encase that one as well with the symbols?

AA Metatron: Yes.

A: Thank you Metatron.

A: Metatron, brother if you could also see while we are in the pineal gland if there is anything else that needs to be healed there in the head area?

AA Metatron: Now it's in the back of her head.

A: What is going on in the back of her head?

AA Metatron: More pain.

A: The entity that we removed from her pineal gland, was that the cause of her sinuses?

AA Metatron: Yes.

A: Does she have pain in the back of her neck?

AA Metatron: Yes.

A: Is that an entity?

AA Metatron: I think so.

A: Very good. If we can please speak to that entity now in the back of her neck. Let me speak to you now, please. Come up, up, up.

Entity: Yes.

A: Greetings, thank you. Are you female or male? May I ask you questions, please?

Entity: Male, yes.

A: When was it that you connected to the back of her neck?

Entity: I don't know.

A: It's okay. Did you have a body before you connected yourself there?

Entity: I feel like I am attached to something else. Another body.

A: If you could look to see who is it that you are attached to? ... Metatron, is it a Reptilian?

AA Metatron: Yes.

A: Thank you. I was sensing it from the beginning of the interview. I know that you've been there some time but at this point, you are a separate consciousness even though you are attached to a body. Would you like to be free and not have to go back to that body there?

Reptilian: She wants me to leave.

A: Yes. Who wants you to leave?

Reptilian: This body.

A: What we are going to do is that we are going to help you, with your permission, to turn you into light. Would you allow for us to turn you into light?

Reptilian: Yes.

A: Okay. If you could connect us to that Reptilian that you are connected to. Can I please speak to that Reptilian now, please?

Reptilian: Yes.

A: Greetings. Thank you for speaking to us. May I ask you questions, please?

Reptilian: Yes.

A: Are you female or male?

Reptilian: Male.

A: This part that you have placed on the back of her neck, we would like to help it turn into light and we are giving you as well the opportunity not having to play this negative role any longer. As you know this is a time of Ascension and we would love to be able to aid you in turning and ascending into light and taking all the experiences that you've gained throughout your time and shifting into a higher vibration of positive polarization. Would you allow for us to aid you today?

Reptilian: Yes. She has shown me this is better.

A: Very good. Thank you for allowing us to do that. May I ask, where are you at currently? Since you have a body, where are you located?

Reptilian: It's dark. I don't know where I am.

A: That is okay. Go ahead and look within you, find that light within you. We are all going to help you and this part of you that is within her. Find both of you, find that light within you, and spread it to all of you. Every root, every cord, all that consists of who you are spread it to all light. Let me know when you both are all light.

Positive Polarized Reptilians: Okay, we are light.

A: Beautiful. Thank you. Do you have a message for her before you go?

Positive Polarized Reptilians: She is scared of us, but she doesn't need to be, she is strong.

A: Yes. Was this a contract?

Positive Polarized Reptilians: Yes, I think so.

A: Were you part of the reason why she would feel at times that things that would come out of her were just... you know would be...

Positive Polarized Reptilians: Oh, yes!

A: Mean...

Positive Polarized Reptilians: She said very mean things.

A: Yes, was that you influencing her?

Positive Polarized Reptilians: Yes.

A: What were the lessons that she was supposed to learn from this contract you had with her?

Positive Polarized Reptilians: She is just here to learn love but the way that it has been it is not real.

A: Where you part of that, the way it's been and hasn't been real were you part of that control?

Positive Polarized Reptilians: Yes.

A: Now that you are of light, can you see where you were?

Positive Polarized Reptilians: It looks like a cave.

A: You were in a cave?

Positive Polarized Reptilians: Mm-hmm.

A: Were you on this planet or somewhere else?

Positive Polarized Reptilians: Feels nearby.

A: Is it inside this planet or outside this planet?

Positive Polarized Reptilians: I think it is this planet.

A: Are there other Reptilians with you?

Positive Polarized Reptilians: Yes, they live in the cave.[9]

A: Was this a contract that you were looking to ascend instead of transmuting straight into light?

Positive Polarized Reptilians: Yes. I wanted to control her, but she showed me light. I think that is better.

A: Yes, it is. Beautiful. Do you have any other messages? What about that separate consciousness energy that you put in her throat? Is it going to come back to you or is it going to become its own?

Positive Polarized Reptilians: It is me.

A: Beautiful. Do you have any messages before you go?

Positive Polarized Reptilians: Thank you for showing me the light.

A: Thank you, as well. Go ahead and go with the Love-Light of the Universe. Blessings to you.

Positive Polarized Reptilians: Thank you.

A: Thank you. If I could please speak to Metatron. Can you have Raphael fill in with light where that Reptilian was removed from, please?

AA Metatron: Yes.

A: Can you look for any portals, negative implants, or hooks? Do a full scan for any more entities. Metatron, can you tell me, at the beginning when we talked to the Higher Self, the Higher Self said that she didn't have any entities. So, what was going on? Was there an influence there from the entities telling her that she didn't have any when she did?

AA Metatron: I don't think she trusted herself.

A: Thank you for all your aid in helping her see and trust. Thank you.

AA Metatron: Thanks.

A: If you can scan her body one more time. Scan her body one more time.

AA Metatron: It feels light.

A: Yes, it does. Very good, thank you. Can you tell me from that life that you showed her what significance is this A.U.R.A. for her? For when she is let's say, in the future and she surrenders and automatically goes to that light body when the wave hits. How significant is it that she has removed the entities within her? If she still had the entities when that wave came forth with her reality, would she have been able to transition into a light body or would she have been part of that density that was removed through the wave or would she have been part of those that took them some time to transition into a light body?

AA Metatron: She has already started the process; it just would have taken her longer.

A: So, for example, what I am trying to explain is, say there is a person like her when the wave comes forth and they have entities, what would happen to them?

AA Metatron: It will take them longer if they choose to stay and go with the light, they can release those and transmute those. It just takes longer to integrate the light.

---

[9] At this point in time, we had not yet discovered that we could connect through this one Reptilian, to its brethren in this cave, to also aid them to ascend as well.

A: They would have to be in a heart space?

AA Metatron: Yes.

A: Thank you. Can we go ahead and complete this and talk back to the Higher Self now?

AA Metatron: Yes.

A: Thank you all for such a beautiful help, to you and whoever aided as well with all the beautiful healing that we did on her. We love you, we honor you and we thank you. Can you please connect us to the Higher Self once more? Thank you.

AA Metatron: Yes. Thank you.

A: Thank you. My love to all of you. If I could please speak to her Higher Self once more?

We continued to speak to the Higher Self asking Brittany's personal questions. We resume after this.

A: I want to thank everyone who assisted today and the beautiful entities, much love to you all. My love and gratitude for such a phenomenal past or future life that you showed her. It very much aligned within my heart. Would you say that this would be significant for the collective and for her to share? Do you suggest for her to share this session?

Higher Self: Yes, she doesn't want them to be scared.

A: Yes. I think she would bring much hope, love, and clearness as there are many unfortunately lost to this Event at this point.

Higher Self: Right, she wants them to know it is going to be okay.

A: I love you Higher Self. I thank you and I respect you. My infinite love to everyone else.

Higher Self: Thank you, we love you!

Post Session dialogue.

A: Feeling marvelous all over and when you're ready...

B: Yeah, I feel marvelous all over!

A: Yeah, you do! When you're ready, sit up, take your time, drink some water. Oh, my goodness. That was so much fun!

B: That was fun.

A: My spirit is jumping for joy!

B: That was very cool.

A: You are so beautiful, sister.

B: Thank you.

A: Wow... your energy just looks... phenomenal.

B: Good?

A: You are beaming, beaming with light.

B; I don't have a Reptilian in the back of my neck anymore.

A: I know! That's one of their favorite places to go. It's something about that spot there.[10]

B: Yes, it was hurting. Wow... Thank you.

A: How phenomenal... Oh, thank you! Do you know what they showed me? I didn't want to tell you; they showed me you in dream time and you looked just like that right? There were red dots all over you and you were screaming. You were so angry.

B: Really?

---

[10] We now know that Reptilians and Archons like to attach their consciousness integrating it into the person's DNA and soul's blueprints in this location and through the spine.

A: But it was something in you and you were like, get it out of me, you were screaming "get it out of me."

B: Wow!

A: Like you couldn't take yourself anymore.

B: Wow! Yeah, no I'm kind of done with myself being mean and nasty. I just want to be kind and loving.

A: That's how you were in the dream. You were like 'AH! I know I'm so much better than this.'

B: Yup, that's how I feel.

A: Yes! Ahhh... Beautiful.

B: That was very cool, thank you.

A: How cool is it that they downloaded that dream to you... you know how you dreamt of it?

B: Yeah, right! Isn't that weird?

A: That is cool! So, they downloaded that information from the Higher Selves and then you were able to go into details with that. Oh my goodness. I'm just vibrating with energy and have goosebumps all over. How do you feel?

B: Great! I feel really good. Yeah, that was very cool! I always tease Tony I'm like, 'I'm done with this like I just want to live naked in the trees.' And guess what?

A: Yeah!

B: I want simpler things, I want... yeah.

A: There you go, you see!

B: That's very cool.

A: You're seeing you in the future. That's what it is.

B: There you go! I love that! I'm excited about that.

A: Yeah! The most exciting part is being naked! (wink) Just kidding!

B: Yeah, right! Yeah, I know that's a real thing.

A: Overall, beautiful... One of my favorite sessions!

B: Thank you. I loved it! I thought it was great!

A: It's important for you to surround yourself with Love-Light. Have you been doing that?

B: Yes.

A: Yes, so do that every day. When you wake up, when you go to bed because now you're cleared. So, we want to maintain you there and there is no fear needed. But if you set an intention of what you want, the force fields around you of Love-Light from your Higher Self, from angels from whoever you align with. Then they shall be there all day long for your children as well - with their Higher Selves' permission.

B: Okay, very good. Thank you.

A: Thank you! Blessed are you and your family.

B: Have a wonderful day!

A: I love you, I honor you, and I respect you all. Blessings to everyone. Mwah!

B: Thank you. We love you, honor you, and respect you.

END OF SESSION

-------------<◇>-------------

What a beautiful session where we gained more insights of what "The Event" entails from an individual's experience of it! Brittany's session also taught us the importance for the practitioner to keep pushing to ensure that even if the client says there is nothing that needs healing, that we double, and triple check to ensure that a clear and an accurate transmission is being given. Many densities can get in the way of receiving a clear answer, especially if the proper sacred intentions and alchemical energetic force fields are not set up with the aid of the Higher Self during a Hypnosis Healing session. As entities, negative technologies, portals that are attached within people directly affect the person's responses and understanding of what they are feeling in their body, whether it is organically part of them or not. Especially with clients like Brittany who had a Reptilian consciousness attached and integrated into her consciousness. The reason being is that it would feel like it is a part of you, because it has inserted itself into your DNA material becoming you in some form. We then get used to it and not know what it would feel like for it to not be of us, making it challenging for us to discern the difference between who is who - others versus our true self.

In this case, if we would not have pushed further, Brittany would have ended her session with entities and a Reptilian consciousness within her. Never truly healing the harmful influence they were causing inside of her. If this release was not done through her A.U.R.A. Hypnosis Healing session, how would it have impacted her personal Ascension timeline? Could it truly come to be if this ripple of negative releasement would not have been manifested for her to enter into the Fifth Dimension/New Earth, as we have seen through her session? Would her vibration be too dense with a Reptilian consciousness still integrated into her DNA when the time came for her? The answer is yes, because a Reptilian has been organically created as our opposite, therefore they contain more darkness than light within them. Many of these Reptilians have unfortunately been infringed upon by dark forces through having A.I. technology inserted in them, to make them negatively polarized and become the densest members of the Reptilian race. We will learn more about how dark forces are infringing on the Reptilian Race in later Chapters.

This dense darkness of the Reptilian integrated within Brittany, for example, would hold too much darkness within a soul for there to be enough light to reach the highest density and vibration needed for Ascension. This is why, not only are we assisting clients who contain Reptilian Consciousnesses within them, we are also assisting the Reptilians themselves. As they need our assistance to positively polarize before the final physical split of "The Event," [11]when the organic timeline comes into fruition. Otherwise, if they don't meet the matching light density, they will transmute straight back to Source, as the wave pushes through. When a negative polarized soul transmutes back to Source, it is a process where it goes through a complete wipeout of all its conscious memories, experiences, and lessons learnt during its travels. It becomes as a new soul would be, a blank slate. This is the last resort that Source will come to, as Source honors all life as equal no matter the density and distortion. To reset a soul and its light, is to take away its main reason to why in the first place it gained individualized fractalization and incarnated throughout Creation. The main reason for exploring itself and the vastness of Creation.

This changes much of what we understand about the true impact of A.U.R.A. Hypnosis Healing can provide for others who have been perpetually stuck in an Inverted A.I. Matrix system in this Third Dimension. The potentials are beautiful and endless to know that this beloved soul, Brittany, will now have a vast opportunity to bring forth her Ascension into this future she experienced during her session. It was such a joyful and hopeful experience as she walked us through "The Event," and into "The New Earth" from her beautiful and insightful Ascension experience.

---

[11] The final physical split of The Event: where the side of lower dense frequencies will physically split off from the lighter higher frequencies on Earth. We discuss this in more detail in Chapter 30 ('Harvesting Planets Throughout Universes').

"The Event" is both an individual and collective experience. Therefore, there are multiple realities occurring infinitely at the same time in how each will experience it. As everyone has their own Ascension process that they must go through that will have a specific signature frequency for them and what is needed to bridge them out of the Third Dimension into the Fifth Dimension and beyond. This varies by individuals because of karma, lessons needed to be learned, specific missions of their soul... We must remember to honor each other's free willed path and that not everything is just one way. The possibilities of "The Event" are truly infinitely endless for us on Earth and the Universe.

After the wave occurred, how Brittany and her husband each were leading a group of peopl. They both were apart but found each other joined with their groups. These groups they were leading, felt like they were the people they came across their journey and assisted in their awakening. Their soul families, neighbors, friends, coworkers, those who allowed and made the choice to awaken their light. Reminding us of our own mission in how we too will have groups with us that we will have assisted in activating their heart and light, when we achieve our personal or the collective "Event."

We know that we make it into the Fifth Dimension as a collective, as the glimpses of peoples' soul experiences into the Quantum Realm have shown us through all forms of sessions, meditations, dreams, and astral travels. Each of us will reach "The Event" in our own way. Some will transition into the Fifth Dimensional Earth, while others as volunteer Starseeds will go back to their higher Dimensional home planet and there are some who will just simply go back to become ONE, and merge back to their Higher Self aspect. Which way will we experience this? Through an individual signatured "Event" or through the collective final physical "Event" of the Third Dimensional split of the Earth and the Universe's Ascension? These answers are only found within our hearts and souls.

"Life is a beautiful dance. It is a vibrational flowing wave, taking you to its rhythm, clearing of mind, in forgetfulness of our worries. The movement of your body is like the motion of life, vibrations of the notes pounding to the rhythm of the heart. To remember the freedom of the dance, is to remember that we must dance to the rhythm of life."
~AuroRa ❤

-------------◇-------------

12

LEVIATHAN - THE FALLEN ANGEL

Session #73: Recorded in August 2018.
Never before shared.

In this in-person A.U.R.A. Hypnosis Healing session, Dante teaches us an immensity on the choice to become a negative polarized being. During his interview, he shares the intimate traumas of his childhood that were full of violence and sexual abuse. He was a large rough looking man that became lost within the societal dysfunctional system of violence, gangs, money, and drugs. However, during the interview process I knew that I was to look past that and not fear him, as I sensed a gentleness and a vulnerability within him. Any other might have strayed away, upon him mentioning his history of violence when he was recently un-awakened. He found me just a couple of months after awakening divinely by a hallucinogenic street drug, and freshly out of the penitentiary.

With Dante's incredible and intense journey, we see what it entails when we forget our light so deeply that we seem forgotten from even the Creator. In this powerful healing session, we learn about the process of what it can be to make a choice to the dark side and the dangers that come with finding our way back to the light once we are in the dark. What does the path of redemption look like for a fallen angel? What does doubting ourselves do to us? Who is Leviathan? We gain knowledge of some of the other negative alien collectives that have been influencing humankind, and of the never-ending Galactic War that is in play.

-------------<◇>-------------

"Many awakening souls feel like there must be some blueprints, step by step instructions on how they are supposed to change the world. With all souls, myself included, yourself, and we must understand it, we change the world within and that changes the world without."

"He will be a living lesson for us. To see if we truly embrace the Creator's Love for all things and if we truly believe in mercy and forgiveness."
-Archangel Metatron

-------------<◇>-------------

A: [Aurora] Is it day or night?
D: [Dante] It's both. Dusk or dawn.
A: Look at yourself. Do you have a body?
D: I am made of light. A humanoid shape.
A: Is there a color to the light?
D: Obelisk, pearl looking.
A: Beautiful, and do you feel female or male?
D: I have no gender. I feel love. I have wings of some sort. I think I am an Angel.

A: You are an Angel?

D: I don't know. I am a being of light. I suppose I could be classified as Angelic.

A: You said you're near a volcano of some sort?

D: It is a hot spring. There's a volcano somewhere nearby. There is ash in the air.

A: Is your shape a humanoid shape?

D: Yes, but large, very large.

A: Would you say as large as a house, like a tree?

D: A tree.

A: Good. Are you carrying anything with you?

D: There is a rod in my right hand.

A: This rod, can you describe it to me, please?

D: It is two feet long, or close to. About two inches in diameter as well. It is made of some sort of high vibrational material. I cannot tell if this is Metallica crystal. I believe this is the source of my light.

A: Your wings, are they large?

D: Yes, but I can spread them very far. They resemble feathered wings, but I see no feathers.

A: Is there a color to them?

D: They are more of a golden hue, like honey with glitter mixed into it.

A: When you expand them out, how big do they expand?

D: Nearly the length of my body...nearly 100 feet.

A: Beautiful. Now, why is it that you are here in this land?

D: I chose to call. I answered the call. This plane is ascending and is in the thrones of chaos and awakening. Many souls are preyed upon in this plane and are defenseless. I'm here to be a sword and a shield for them and to protect the data that was meant to form this plane before the corruption set in.

A: We thank you for your service, brother.

D: It is my honor.

A: This place that you are at, this specific location, is there a significance to why you are standing in the spot?

D: Yes, this place is a representation of Creation, of a place meaningful to the one he calls Lisa. He uses his abilities of visualization to create a reality that he can access. I do not believe these realities are accessible and perhaps not even permanent other than what's in him.

A: Am I speaking to his Higher Self right now?

Higher Self: I am an aspect of the masterful.

A: Greetings, I welcome you. Thank you. I honor you, I love you, and I respect you.

Higher Self: Likewise, sister.

A: Thank you, brother for bringing him to me today. May we be able to discover all that needs to be discovered and that his soul is ready for. It is an honor, and your essence is beautiful.

Higher Self: I thank you for your kind words.

A: Thank you. Now is there anything else you want to show us? You said that this is a manifestation of a reality he has created. Is there anything else you would like to show us that is relevant at this moment for his highest good?

Higher Self: The ability to visualize is his strength in this time, where he has the ability to leave reality. He has done so since perception of this timeline is such that he is protected and is able to see further ahead than the reality in which he lives.

A: Is that how he was able to, even though he was in a sense - in trouble, he was able to avoid the trouble?

Higher Self: Yes. The joke was, that bullets would dance around him... (When he was a drug lord on the streets.) The reality was that they never entered his space to begin with.

A: Can you tell me some more of that rod that you're holding in your hand? What is that for?
Higher Self: It is the talisman, similar to what he wears upon his neck now. I do not understand or know everything about the Master Soul or the aspects there, but I do know every aspect of this soul will have some form of a talisman that is the physical representation of the reality of their divinity. When I manifest this into my hand, I could feel the energy of Source coursing through every atom in my being. When I put it back away in a safe place, I am still a very high vibrational soul, but I can feel the difference, a diminishing of the vibration.
A: That is the pendant that he wears around his neck?
Higher Self: Yes, he calls it the Dragon's Heart.
A: Why does he call it that?
Higher Self: It is the essence representation of the heart of the aspect he resonates most with. He is a warrior here and a guardian. I know his life has been hard. I have been there in silence because I know that it was necessary, but it was very hard to watch. He will put himself last without complaining because he believes he has taken too much from this place. He does not understand that we agreed to this and choose to serve. The woman he speaks of, that was looking when he purchased the Dragon's Heart, was there to purchase it first. She was a Gray. They are targeting him in this reality and others as well. We are mobilizing forces against them. They are strong. We are light. They will fall.
A: This old lady that he saw in a car outside the crystal shop that you are speaking of when he was trying to purchase the pendant; this lady was really upset. How was it that he viewed her as an old lady if it was a Gray?
Higher Self: At that time the veil was thick. Deep within, he knew something was wrong with her, he felt physically ill. She was sent by her own Higher Self or another higher aspect to prevent the acquisition of the 'Dragon's Heart' from this soul. Thus, diminishing the ability of it to manifest and create, to attack and defend.
A: So, was she a Gray in a human vessel or does she have an illusion?
Higher Self: Yes, the human vessel. She was an awakened soul, evil heart by choice, and the body of a human woman.
A: Would you be able to please connect me to the consciousness within this Dragon's Heart as well as that rod's consciousness? Would I be able to speak to them, please?
Higher Self: I don't know. I don't see why not. They sense within you a great power. I will try to facilitate this.
A: Very good. Thank you. If I could please speak to the consciousness within the crystal he wears around his neck that he calls 'Dragon's Heart' as well as the rod in connection?
Crystal: Why do you seek me?
A: Greetings. Thank you for being here.
Crystal: Why do you seek me?
A: I am looking for answers for Dante as you are connected to him through a pendant that he wears, a crystal that he wears around his neck. Seeing if you have a message for him?
Crystal: The 'Dragon's Heart' must never leave his neck. They are coming. They're here now, waiting. It will push them back on its own. I've chosen an existence of service to all dragon kinds. I did not see the extent of his journey, but I know it is critical that he survive it to the end.
A: Thank you. I welcome you, I honor you, I love you, and I respect you.
Crystal: Likewise.
A: May I ask you a few questions, please?
Crystal: Yes.
A: Wonderful. Are you a collective of energy or are you an individual?
Crystal: I am a ray of a collective.

A: This ray of collective is in connection to what? Is there a specific race or soul family that you are in connection to?

Crystal: Water, elementals, dragon kind, fae. We also work with the Angelics. This plane is close. We estimate pressing the wave of Ascension within 2.5 Earth cycles from now, give or take three months, the chaos will ensue. It will be catastrophic but short-lived. The group that we are part of is tasked with guiding and guarding the most critical structures of this plane and the most valuable souls that will progress the Ascension process and pave the way for the rest of mankind to go forward.

A: Do you mean 2.5 Earth cycles as in two and a half years?

Crystal: Yes, two and a half years. The length of time we estimate for the chaos to subside completely is unknown at this time. But at that point, the Ascension will be completed.

This timeframe he has given us is quite interesting, as it is matching the chaos that is occurring in the now that 5G began, and then turned into the supposed dangerous pandemic of Covid-19. Making everyone muzzle themselves and keeping them at home away from connecting to others. It seems as if he is trying to explain to us how this chaotic tyranny will be the catalyst and the biggest beginning phase for the Earth's Ascension.

A: Now, is this in his reality?

Crystal: Yes. But it's a ripple effect.

A: Would you say that you are a dragon yourself as a collective?

Crystal: Yes. I am a Sun Dragon.

A: Yes, I sensed you the minute that he came in the door through the pendant so thank you, it is an honor once more... How is it that you work with him as a Sun Dragon on Earth?

Crystal: We spread light. We also spread the sword. There are souls here who have escaped justice for far too long. They have established themselves here and are a large part of the decay upon this plane. Those who will not turn to light and voluntarily go off-planet will be released. The group that I am a part of specializes in this aspect of war. It will be with love in our hearts and tears in our eyes as we will send souls to the Creator. During 'sleeping time' is what he calls it. He is very active, his vessel sleeps very little but when he does sleep, he gets very much done. A lot of what he is up to right now revolves around what he calls Sloth. It is a very powerful collective of evil, many groups are engaging it now. Many of those groups are engaging it solely because of his efforts. He despises it. He has encountered this many times in many timelines. Some he has triumphed but others he has failed.

A: This collective as a Sloth or are there other collectives as well?

Crystal: Yes, many.

A: Why is it specifically that he is connected to this collective? Why does he have to go on...?

Crystal: At one point in time our souls were aligned, we were on the same side. Not long ago, he chose corruption, he was separated from Source and now harvesting the energy of prana through creating followers and disciples. Harvesting energy, controlling factions from other ET's that are weaker. In essence, he is a puppet master and all roads lead to it. It is afraid of him, but he is afraid of it as well. We are here. I am specifically representing my collective to augment his strength, to give him courage and resolve, to assist in the rapid healing of his wounds, and to know the sensation of pain. He was designed in this timeline to be a tank, to move one direction forward, not to the sides, and never in reverse. This is why I am here. His vessel must survive long enough for his soul to do the work.

A: This timeline that he is on where the Earth will ascend in two and a half years for him. Now when this happens, what happens to this collective?

Crystal: We withdraw, and we will go where we are needed. This plane, the struggle they are in is a micro-cosmo. This war is being waged in many places, many times past and in the future on many layers. We do not yet know when things will finally subside. It is without question, swinging in the fashion of good light, the pendulum swing has shifted. We have gained the ground, we gained momentum. Many negative energies have chosen to subside to us, they've given themselves the light. We would do all we can for as long as we can and in any place that we are needed and requested. Once the Ascension is complete here, most of us will leave. Some will stay behind to anchor our energy to Gaia. Before we leave, we will construct a grid around this plane to amplify the Light entering it for the Universe.

A: Yes, thank you! When this Ascension happens for him, and the collective of you is done with the job here, what will happen to that Sloth collective?

Crystal: They will continue to exist in some form, we will chase them as other groups chase them. At some point, it is our hope and our intention that this group, this collective of darkness will see that it can be even more powerful and have more ability than it does now with love in its heart. It believes that the only way to true power is away from Source. It has lost some degree of its mind; we do not know if it can be healed. This collective is so strong, and their reach is so deep in this plane which would be a huge win to all mankind to at least get this collective out of the solar system or in the best-case scenario turn them to the light. They are ancient and the likelihood of them turning to the light is very slim, but we still put the intent out.

A: There's a lot of misinformation. As you know he came to me and is very familiar in the short amount of time that he's awakened with different Light Workers that are perhaps giving the false information out there now. There are some Light Workers that have it within their mind-frame that once this experiment is over and we ascend on to the New Earth that duality will basically vanish from existence.

Crystal: That is correct to some degree. 'Vanish from existence' is a broad term. Yes, it will take its place, its proper place amongst the hierarchy of Universal law. Ascension will not stop at 5D, the cycle will begin anew. Millennia will pass, if the right souls and the right number of souls make the right choices, the opportunity for further Ascension will present itself when the time is proper. If as a collective, if mankind fails and reverses back to its old ways choosing to control and subjugate instead of free and love they will lower the vibration again. It truly is free will.

A: Yes. Once this plane here that we are, this planet that we are in the Third or Fourth Dimension and we shift up to the next Dimension which would be the Fifth, will duality still exist? Will the negative polarities exist outside of here in different realms?

Crystal: Yes.

A: Will it still continue to exist everywhere else or even around us?

Crystal: What we term as evil is a choice to turn away from the light and seek to control, subjugate, enslave another for your own personal gain with no benefit to them in any way, shape, or form. Souls that choose to be good, can choose to be evil. Souls that choose to be evil, can choose to be good, there will always be some element of the duality of existence on lower planes in every plane. It isn't until you get past the Eighth Dimension where the term evil and the concept of evil ceases to exist in large part because it is looked at as more of a spectrum of the same thing: it is less good, to more good versus/instead of evil or good. One of the problems this plane is going to struggle with greatly, there is a large number of humans here who are older in their physical bodies, more set in their ways. We have found that the older the soul is, the more set in their ways, the harder it is for them to awaken. Some consciously fight it even though on a cellular level they know that they cannot fight it, but they still try, it makes it hard for the job that we have to do. One thing that will always happen until a few generations have passed after the Ascension is complete, is the reminiscing. When the souls of this plane all awaken to at least enough of a degree to know that they are creators in their own right, they will not realize that their thought-forms are creating a negative reality to those around them and within their sphere of influence. They will be unintentionally spreading darkness. In a way, there'll be a representation of the dualistic nature of things, at the same time. It is also their soul's journey to learn and experience with them personally experiencing through the unintentional release of evil. The web is so perfectly formed and yet so unbelievably complicated. All things that may have happened millions of years ago, brought you to a point where you are at this very moment. If things had not happened exactly how they did it every moment up to this moment, this soul would not be where it is now, yours would not be where it is now, nothing would be where it is now. We have free will, but at the same time on a soul level, the whole point is Ascension, evolution, soul journey, enlightenment, the next level. Sending love energy, vibration, frequency, healing, compassion. The positive things in existence, we want to amplify and highlight and try to heal the negative things if we can. And then if we can learn to live and love them.

A: Thank you. So wonderful! A really beautiful explanation. Is that why he really has a sense that he's here to protect and fight because of the connection of you with him?

Crystal: Yes, my presence instills a sense of purpose in him that matches the alignment of the timeline's purpose.

A: So, to confirm what you said, once this experiment is done and we ascend there will still be collectives? And does anyone truly know exactly how it's going to go down?

Crystal: That is true. There may be some groups that know more or some aspects, some souls that are heightened enough in light to the point where they would know. The future is fluid. Time is such a false construct. The way I would describe it in 3D terms is, the choices and things that you do right now create the reality you will reach in a few moments, so you literally are creating the future. So, it doesn't exist, all it is, is the NOW. The future is the NOW of then, the past is the NOW of then and all that is, is NOW. That being said, there are souls - we are an ancient soul, dragons are very ancient - there are souls, dragon souls that were here from the beginning. The first wave of Creation from the Master Creator. Those souls, we believe, may know things that many if not all, do not. But at the same time, with the future being fluid that type of knowledge may be detrimental because if they would put their thought form into a reality that's forming, they may inadvertently skew the reality's purpose and intent, and end up in a bad place.

A: Yes, very good. Thank you!

Crystal: You are welcome.

A: All your answers align exactly with what I've been taught, so thank you. Now you as the dragon that you are, at what point did your creation come forth?

Crystal: My creation... 5.913 million, no, three more zeros, billion. 5.913 billion Earth cycles.

A: What was that like when you came into Creation?

Crystal: I was brought from the sun, the Creator breathed life into the tree, the tree gave life to all. I came from the sun. I have no, what you would call parents, other than the Creator. I was formed from the essence of the sun with the intent to be a light to those finding themselves in the dark. I do not remember exactly what happened in my creation. But I do not have any memory of what you would call a childhood. I was always in the form that I am in now.

A: Would you be able to describe that form for me, please?

Crystal: I am small by dragon standards. Using Earth dimensions, I would say 20 feet long, maybe slightly longer. I am golden. I am about the height of a horse. A large horse. His memories are showing a commercial for beer, those horses with the hair on their legs, large. I have a long slender neck. My energy is feminine, but I have no gender. I nurture more than I create war, which is why I align with feminine energy. My eyes would be red in your color spectrum. My scales are clear but my skin beneath them is golden, that of honey. My underbelly is light, almost white or a bone color. I have four legs. They resemble dogs, canines. Yes, dogs.

The hind legs resemble dog legs in their shape. The front legs look more like human arms. My wings are behind my shoulder blades. When I spread them out, they are roughly the length of my body, from tail to snout. I have the ability to lower or raise my density depending on what I need to do and why. Sometimes it is nice to take on a physical form just to feel the air on your face as you fly. I do not have your typical dragon's breath offensive capabilities and I do not know why. My offensive capabilities are of a psionic nature. Even though I am an elemental, I do not really understand that. But it is how I was made. I would not say that I am a weapon. But I am capable of being used as such. My job is to nurture and protect. If doing so requires violence, then so be it. But I will choose peace and love every time that I can. This is what I have tried to put into him since he came into possession of the talisman. He doesn't have to be the monster he believes himself to be. There was a purpose for that answer. And that purpose has been served, the master can rest, you can go. He is okay to be what he wants to be now, what he was meant to be. He doesn't have to be evil - he never was - no matter what he believes!

A: Thank you. You mentioned when you came forth billions of years ago, was there darkness around you? Was there already then?

Crystal: Not where I was, I was taught about it. I was taught that the lower Dimensions still have evil and what it was and what it represented and how it manifests itself. It always struck me as intriguing that these humans, as the master of this planet, are the only life form upon it that self-destruct. I have looked. There is no other life on this planet that self-destructs. If there has been evidence of outside influence, then they never want that alone, is all the evidence that is needed. They weren't meant to be this way; this planet was hijacked. And we learned about it later than we should have. I do not speak for any other collective but my own. But in our collective, there is regret. We certainly believe in allowing souls to experience their evolution on their own. There was a time when things may have been different here. But the Council that ruled the collective that I am a part of decided that a hands-off approach would be best, as did other groups that have been watching and monitoring and assisting this planet since this deception. There was a great division amongst the council members, dearly the split in the middle. In the end, the decision was made to maintain the course that we have of non-engagement. It is thought now after seeing firsthand what has happened here, we heard. By the time we realized how bad it had gotten and we deployed our forces here, it was too late. Whether we believe evil exists or not, on this plane it does. Sadly, we have lost some souls here. There are powerful, evil souls here, you know this well.

A: Yes.

Crystal: Had we came here earlier, we may have been able to develop some defenses here or augment some souls here to prevent the hijacking, but we did not. It wasn't long ago that another collective of dragons, one that we are affiliated with but not necessarily a part of, they allowed information to travel this plane, they saw what we saw. That we made a mistake. All things happen for a reason. We know this, I know this, you know this. So, this mistake that I speak of, is undoubtedly divine and will one day show itself off as a blessing as it was meant to be. For now is the time for us to reflect and ask ourselves as a collective, are we as wise as we think we are, are we as enlightened? Do we love as hard as we think we do? We turned our back on a fledgling planet that we could have helped. Many of us do not believe that embodies what we want to embody. And many of us came here, to attempt to right that wrong.

A: Yes... You said your collective of dragons are of the water?

Crystal: Yes.

A: However, you are the sun though.

Crystal: I am a Sun Dragon, yes.

A: So, do you have a mixture of different elements?

Crystal: No, I am a pure Sun Dragon. I do not know why I am a part of this collective or why this collective created me the way it did. I have been to many places and done much of the same work. Are you familiar with bilocation?

A: Yes.

Crystal: Good. The higher dimensional the soul can get, the more aspects you can create of yourself. Not separate aspects, but multiple aspects of the SAME aspect. Most can only do two, a few can do three, very few can do more than three. I can do three. So right now, I am here in this talisman, this is my essence. But I have two aspects in other places in other talismans doing the same kind of work.

A: Wonderful, and are they on Earth?

Crystal: No.

A: They are elsewhere?

Crystal: Yes.

A: Thank you. Do you have anything else you want to share with him?

Crystal: He needs to stop doubting himself. He is not crazy. I am real. He is a dragon. He is an Angel, and he is many, many, many other things. When we doubt, we do their job for them. An enemy becomes docile when they forget. You are their enemy. This is what they will try to do to him. They will try to get him to doubt the reality that he creates, they will try to get him to accept the reality that is around him. His construct, his program is a simulation. He must maintain his resolve and not doubt. Even when it's all he can feel he must fight. He is a tank, he goes forward. But if he has the wrong idea in his mind, in his heart, he will take that forward too. He must be very careful with who he surrounds himself with, he is not an empath, but he can take in their feelings. But he is not able to transmute it if he surrounds himself with too much negativity. Despite all of those measures, the crystals, the shielding, and the sage and the cleansing of the aura, it will corrupt him. He will lower his vibration; his abilities will diminish, and it will make him vulnerable. Just do not doubt. This is real. I am real.

A: Yes. Would you be a good being to speak to in regard to the Silver Legion since you were talking of this collective?

Crystal: One moment... I am not allowed to speak of this with you. I am sorry. But there is another that can and will, who is not a part of any collective. He is a rogue.

A: Any other message brother or sister before you go? It was such an honor to speak to you today. As you know, I am a dragon myself as the Phoenix.

Crystal: Yes, you are. The only message that I would have is for all to love the unlovable, forgive the unforgivable, serve the un-servable. All else will take care of itself.

A: Wonderful. I honor you, I love you, I thank you, and I respect you. Blessings.

Crystal: Likewise sister, namaste.

A: Namaste... May I please speak to the being that's going to tell us about, the rogue, in regard to this group?

Moncara: Why do you seek to know of them? They are dangerous and they will seek you out.

A: Greetings, who am I speaking to?

Moncara: I am Moncara.

A: Welcome. Are you female or male?

Moncara: I am male.

A: What is your Galactic form?

Moncara: I am him. I am the dark blue dragon that he is able to manifest in the realms of the astral.

A: Beautiful. Yes, I saw you when he started talking about you. It is an honor to be speaking with you today.

Moncara: Likewise, sister.

A: Thank you. Are you Divine Masculine?

Moncara: Yes.

A: Thank you, brother. Now, I know that he's looking for answers, why don't you share whatever you feel that is okay to share at this moment. And before you actually share that, why is it that you were called a rogue from that collective. What does that mean?

Moncara: My methods and ideologies are not embraced by some of my kind. I am a water dragon. But at one point in time, corruption entered my soul, it altered me. I have been somewhat ostracized by my kind. I understand why, I do not hold it against them. It is not out of hatred or anger that they do this. My vibration is not as high as theirs. They would diminish it. His soulmate Lisa, she is an exceptional healer, she is helping the soul, the master soul. I don't know how she is able to do it. It is some form of green plasma liquid stuff. I don't know what it is. I've never seen it. But it's eating the corruption off of my soul, off of our soul.

A: Oh, beautiful!

Moncara: There is this group, the Silver Legions group, it's dangerous. He is here to stop them. I am here to help. I am what comes forth when he is attacked. They are evil. They are powerful, he is correct. The information that he gave you earlier about them. He got it from me and other sources. He is very diligent. This body is hard to speak through. Lisa, he calls her a mad scientist. She is an analyzer, a seeker. She finds things, she sees things. They wanted her away from him because they knew that she would sense something was off. They cloak those f*cking Grays. They lend their technological expertise to them. This is why you cannot sense them; I suppose. To be truthful, I cannot either. It is irritating... (sigh) ... The thing is, they exist on this plane and will continue to do so. There are souls he will not be able to save that they will consume, devour, and cast aside as husks. He cannot let the desire to save every soul stop him from saving the masses. I fear that he will get wrapped up working on one or two and let hundreds or thousands or more pass by. That is the danger I see with him. His life in this reality was very chaotic. He carries many scars with it, and without. He was designed for this task. He is Lisa's champion. He will protect her, and she will heal him.

A: Beautiful. Now I know that you said you were corrupted. How was it that you became corrupted? Would you share that story with us, please?

Moncara: Another aspect of our soul made terrible choices. I separated from that aspect, but that aspect still remains. What you would know as Leviathan, I am him. We are not evil. We were, we chose the wrong way. We didn't have enough (tears flowing down) ... I was the king of the Cherubim Realm of Light. It wasn't enough. I wanted more. I joined them, Samuel and the others. We chose to go to incarnate upon the Earth. It was a foolish idea to think we could win. We tried. We were cast down. My memories are thankfully, in pieces. I remembered we launched the attack. It was a surprise attack. We thought we would gain the upper hand. The Creator was ready. We were defeated. She, her Higher Self, is the Herald. Many have not heard of her. She commands the armies of Light. Two of the Archangels, I don't remember who, I believe one was Raphael. I felt the healing go into my body from my right arm. I was dragged to the edge of the Void; I could hear her crying. She is screaming! (heavy sobs) ...

A: Make him comfortable. Allow him to see but not feel too much intensity... What's going on?

Moncara: (heavy sobs) ... She is screaming, "Why! Why was I not enough?" She, they hold me down. It is Raphael. I can feel him trying to dull the pain. I feel a foot on my back. Her tears burn me as they land on my shoulder. They have removed all my Divine Armor, I am naked... (heavy sobs) ... She tore off my wings! ... (cries)... Throw me to the side, it is hot, I am on fire! Something is changing me. It hurts! (cries)...

A: Higher Self, make sure he feels comfortable...

Moncara: I change into what I am now. Water. I hit the water. It cools my body. I sink. It is so dark. It is cold. Freezing cold. The gold on my scales is all that remains from my Divine Armor. A reminder of my rebellion. I came out of the water, I hated him, it, her, whatever it is. The humans - its favorite pet, I hate it even more... I lorded over them. I gave power to the most evil ones that I could find. They sacrificed their children to me; I saw the power within them grow. I made them strong so they would go out and destroy the humans. At some point, my behavior was not tolerated anymore. I was placed in exile but not where the others were. I went to a different place. There is still something of about over 30 of them in Antarctica, in the ice. Some died there, some escaped. The place that I was, it was only accessible by the Creator. It's outside the edge of known space where Creation has not reached yet. It is a place where Light has not found. It is cold and barren. I don't know how long I wandered there. It may have been eons, I don't know. I wanted death. I begged Archangel Metatron to erase me from the Akashic Records. He would not. I was too much of a coward to end myself and the Creator hated me too much to do it for me - or so I thought. And then at some time, they were there, the Creator and the Herald with a chance at redemption. "Be her champion on this plane. Protect her lower self at all costs. Balance your karma and you may once again see heaven, or at least the lower realms of heaven." I did not want to be out there alone any longer. I took the deal. I have been incarnated on this Earth seven times, this body Dante, is the seventh incarnation. Three were murdered before they could awaken. Two - just a failed exercise. One is close. He is ready. Or I hope he is ready. He is ready.

A: Wonderful. May I ask you questions about your story?

Moncara: Of course!

A: Thank you. It brings me great honor for you to share your story with me. As you know, I honor all, whether what decisions you have made or not. Were you an Angel?

Moncara: I was a certain type of Angel, a watcher.

A: A watcher Angel?

Moncara: If you think of 'Angels' classification, my classification would have been Cherubim. My title was king of the Cherub Realm. We were 'Watchers'. Watchers were high-level Angels that were set up to develop and protect the realms.

A: Yes, and then when you decided to, would you say, rebel? Is that the best way to explain to go up against Source?

Moncara: Yes, the temptation was always there. I do not know if my resolve weakened or if temptation strengthened and at some point, I chose to get into it.

A: What was the biggest temptation for you to give in to it?

Moncara: To feel, to physically feel what they felt. They are ants to us, but they could have nothing and be happy, they can have horrible conditions and find laughter. I sought that bliss. I saw that they had it. How could they have it and be such insignificant primitive creatures? What made them better than me?... I sought what I already had because what they had was the Creator's Love within them.

A: Did you not have this within you?

Moncara: I did, I did, but I thought that they had something different or better. I don't know.

A: Are we talking about humans?

Moncara: Yes, the humans. This reality here is so full of bull sh*t, the Earth is not thousands of years old, billions of years old. This is not the first incarnation of Earth; this is the fourth. Earth has been destroyed three times before now. All of its lifetimes, it is such a ridiculous joke here.

A: I agree... Now, the woman that ripped the wings out, did I understand this correctly that you say that that was Lisa's Higher Self (his Twin Flame)?

Moncara: Yes.

A: So, are you coming back to a union?

Moncara: Yes, we are.

A: Wonderful. I really love that Source and that we were able to give you an opportunity once more to make amends like you said, to your karma, and to be able to accomplish your mission this time around. I can tell you I will be your greatest fan and I know that you can do it!

Moncara: He doesn't know it. But it was I who saw the dragon in you when he found your web page. He has to understand that there will come people in his life that he will have to allow to fall to darkness in order for them to find their light. I fear that he has been exposed to so much darkness, karmic darkness, as well as his own timeline that he will get trapped trying to force light upon another. We are here to kill Sloth. I do not know if we can. The last incarnation here we were able to kill it but not it's Higher Self. So it reincarnated here, again. It wants her to hurt him because without her many will not join the right side.

A: Lisa's Higher Self, does she have a name?

Moncara: The only name I have ever known her as is the 'Herald'. She was created by the Creator. She carries a caduceus. It is a symbol, but it was much more than that, it is a weapon of unimaginable power. It is a tool for creation, for manifestation. The light of which has never been seen. The symbols are on this plane. Hospitals have it, two wings and serpents intertwined. That symbol is of service to Mercury, Isis, Iris. They are all tied to it, Bridget. Many aspects of many Gods and Goddesses pay homage to the caduceus. The reason they do is that the caduceus belongs to the Herald's hand and she is here for a very specific purpose. This is why Sloth and its collective try to kill her and this vessel as well.

A: What can we do? Can we set up some sacred alchemy to help them? I know he mentioned for example they have shields that they put up and sometimes they could get through them and attack them psychically. Let's make those stronger.

Moncara: My conduit to the Angelic realms is slightly off-center these days. Yours is not. We struggled greatly with psionic and A.I. based attacks.

A: What you are ready for in your time and space and what he's ready for currently; I can perhaps call on more of the Angelic realm. I know that you said when you had fallen, you had asked Metatron to erase you. What is your connection to Metatron and why is it that you were asking him out of all the Angels to erase you?

Moncara: Shame.

A: You said that you are a separate consciousness. A walk-in?

Moncara: Yeah.

A: You, as Leviathan?

Moncara: Yes.

A: When was it that you walked-in into his vessel?

Moncara: After he woke. I've been there. I thought it was a mistake. I knew that for me to have any connection to a human soul, there had to have been a mistake. That I would not be allowed to, given what I have done. But there was a connection anyways. So, I watched him grow as a child. I thought many times his life mirrored my own. It is funny looking back, synchronicities happen to all of us. When everything fell apart in this life, it was one of the final seals to awaken this consciousness. When that happened, he began searching for answers and I found that I could influence him, I could send him information. Usually, I would have to take a memory out of his mind and give it back to him in a different form. Or I would take multiple memories and send them to him and different arrangements. So, he would hopefully understand the thought behind it. And it actually worked, he heard me. The more he awakened, the more I was able to communicate with him. And it wasn't long after that, that I realized that I was residing in this physical vessel. It is an unusual situation. Initially, when he first woke up, I didn't mean to, but I took over his vessel and it was unintentional. I realized it not long after that I should have given up control again, but I didn't. I wanted to see what this world was about. And he reads so much. There's so much information inside his mind. It is like a library inside there. That's how we met

Lisa. He wasn't in control; I was in control of the vessel. I was just looking for any negative energies to attack. I thought that's why I was here. I thought that if I got all of the Fallen released or brought to the Light that I can come back and leave this place. So that's what I did. He was seeking answers of an all-evil nature, I was seeking answers for Archon. We came across some, I released one, one joined us. The others, I don't know, things change so rapidly. I don't know any more exactly what my soul's purpose is. I know that's why he's here; I know I have a purpose and I know other aspects have purposes too. I don't know how many aspects are going to try to or be able to use this vessel to further their soul journeys or not. The Veil, like the walls of the Veil around this Earth, is very thin. I don't know what all he is able to touch. I don't know if it's the life he has lived or the drugs he's done, or what has been done to him. He has far more access than it's safe.

A: Going back to when you awakened, was that the time period where he lost consciousness for a month?

Dante was in prison and does not remember any of what happened during this event where he was able to lift a man with one hand as his feet dangled in the air. As several prison guards tried to stop him with taser guns that had no effect on him. They would try to move him, but he was as stiff and heavy as stone. Finally, what stopped it all was Dante losing consciousness, and suddenly fainting to the ground. The way that he found out the details, later on, was due to him knowing one of the guards from childhood. Once conscious and more in his body, the guard explained to him what had happened.

Moncara: No. That was me though.

A: That's what I'm saying, was that you during that month?

Moncara: That would be me then, but I don't know how or why, I don't, that time is really weird. I was in exile, but I was somewhere else, and I didn't know that I was there until I awoke in his mind, his memories verify that that was me. I don't remember being there. I don't know what happened. I know during that time period I was struggling greatly in exile and seeking death. What I meant was, I have been since childhood. But when he awakened, fully awakened after he lost everything, that is when I found that I could communicate with him. It is troubling that I can take his vessel from him. He is strong but I am much stronger. I have only taken over his vessel forcefully one time, but it was to save his life. That thing he talks about attacked him while he was on the phone with Lisa. He has no memory of it. It came suddenly, I had no choice but if I hadn't taken over his vessel, he would have gone mad. I took the vessel over and I instructed Lisa what to do, how to do it, and she did.

A: What thing is that? Is that the A.I. thing you are talking about?

Moncara: Yes, Sloth. They have many modalities to attack. When I say Sloth, I can mean him or any of his army, any of the minions or other factions of grays. They've been established on this plane for very long.

A: Now going back to Metatron. Is there a connection that you have to Metatron?

Moncara: Yes. Metatron has always been one that I have loved and respected and one of the few that I regret failing. He holds knowledge. Knowledge is power. I would seek Metatron if I wanted to be forgotten by all. He would not even answer me. I know that he would not though. He would feel, in my opinion, that the lesson needed to be learned no matter how painful. And he would be right.

The Body Scan begins.

A: Would you allow for him to talk through you today so that we are able to see what we can do specifically to help you remain in this vessel in the light and not get clouded as you are worried there? As well as perhaps setting up some type of extra shielding against these A.I. attacks since their role is to basically go up against this collective of the Sloth that is in connection with the Silver Legion. Would you allow Metatron to try to speak through you today?

Moncara: I will be honored and blessed.

A: Wonderful. I will talk to you in a little bit, brother... May I please now speak to Metatron?

AA Metatron: You have your hands full with this one, sister.

A: (chuckles)... Thank you for being here. My beautiful brother, I love you.

AA Metatron: Likewise!

A: Looking for answers, yes, definitely my hands are full. So, what can we do for him? I love him dearly as our brother and I know that he can mend what he is meant to. I would love to help with extra shielding. What can we do so that he can go forth on this path that he's meant to go in regard to the Sloth collective and the Silver Legion?

AA Metatron: Your dear heart is huge. We should help him in any way we can. As far as information goes, I would recommend not divulging any more than you feel necessary. And the group that he's a part of, he's actually a part of two groups. They are very good at gathering information, one of them is very well connected to Michael. Any information that will be pertinent to their mission they can get at other places. They are absolutely vulnerable to A.I. tech-based attacks. His weakness is psionic, his strength is physical. Her weakness is psionic, but her strength is also psionic. Any shielding we can give them will be a great benefit if for no other reason than to stop the attacks.

A: Yes.

AA Metatron: Silver Legion, this group, they are on the galactic radar as you know. It is a delicate balance as you know. I know he will be watching this video later. Yes, he is here to influence the trajectory that they are on but that is not his primary objective. He is here to guard and protect data, information, keys, coding, activation codes, DNA codes, terraform codes. The Dracos are here as well. During his sleep time, he and his team are a strike force. They have been working hard but taking much damage. Raphael has been healing them through Lisa. She is an Angel and then has no idea about the connection, so she has the ability that she possesses. Can they stop Silver Legion? Suppose if you, depends on how you define stopping. They are a soul trap. They are purposed at this moment in time to harvest energy prana from high-level souls and to keep those high-level souls from joining the fight. They keep them stuck in illusionary magic. Which is why they make sure there's no way to verify. His suspicions are right, they are actually attacking Light Workers which is why their abilities diminish because of the karmic imbalance. My advice to him would be to engage them to a point to understand that they are an afterthought. They are a forethought to other groups just as capable, just as willing, and just as ready to engage. His focus however should focus to some degree on Sloth. Sloth, the hive mind that it is, is a very high-level soul, God-level if we speak the truth. He knows this so I have no fear of saying this. I need to search his memory banks, give me one moment.

A: Yes.

AA Metatron: They are brothers. That is the connection. At some point, they were embodied physically in a different time, in a different plane, as blood brothers. Ah, it makes more sense. They both believe unequivocally that the other is wrong and lost and needs to come home. Dante knows that home is not that direction. He will not go that way but his constant looking back will pull him that way. He must stay focused on the light and the love. All else is secondary. Many awakening souls feel like there must be some blueprints, step by step instructions on how they are supposed to change the world. With all souls, myself included, yourself, and we must understand it, we change the world within and that changes the world without. This one is going to suffer much. He is ready. And we will help him. It's funny, he thinks he protects Lisa, but it is she who protects him. He will see that one day. He is a good soul, Aurora.

A: Yes!

AA Metatron: There will be many of our kind that do not feel that way. He will be a living lesson for us. To see if we truly embrace the Creator's Love for all things and if we truly believe in mercy and forgiveness.

A: Yes.

AA Metatron: Aurora?

A: Yes?

AA Metatron: These enemies that he has, they are able to seek out energy signatures. Third-party. You are very strong, you know this.

A: Yes.

AA Metatron: I say this to you really as a warning of what you already know. They will come, be prepared. They will not succeed. You are far beyond their reach.

A: Do you mean they will come after me energetically after they figure it out that I did a healing on him and Lisa?

AA Metatron: Yes.

A: Yes, well it's not something that I am not used to! (chuckles)

AA Metatron: Touche! (chuckles)

A: But I know that I have you and I have our beautiful Michael.

AA Metatron: You do sister!

A: Thank you all to all our brothers and sisters. I know that I am loved, and I am always protected by you all and especially as I, Aurora. Thank you. Do you have any advice for me that I need to know when I feel this energetically?

AA Metatron: They will attack unprovoked. This will give you free rein to defend yourself to the extent that you feel necessary. Do not hold back, they are arrogant because they are used to steamrolling over lesser souls. It may be good for them to feel the sting of a truly enlightened soul.

A: Thank you.

AA Metatron: Absolutely! One other thing with Lisa.

A: Yes?

AA Metatron: One moment... Alright, he already knows, the Sloth raped her energetically. It has traumatized her to a very deep level that he has been trying to heal but he is no healer. Her ability to trust has been severely diminished and that is impacting her ability to launch the campaign that she needs to spearhead. She will resist you because she feels that you may be an enemy in disguise because that's all she sees everywhere she looks. You know not to take it personally.

A: Always.

AA Metatron: But you do not have to be gentle with her.

A: Metatron, what message do you have for Lisa? I am going to try to get this video to them by tonight and perhaps they may listen to it so that it can prepare her for tomorrow, and she can allow for the healing that needs to occur tomorrow.

AA Metatron: Lisa, this is no mistake that you are here. This is no mistake that I am speaking to you. We have watched you from birth in this timeline and every other timeline when your soul was active. What happened to you happened, because it had to happen. You must let go of the pain and embrace the lesson this has brought to you. If Sloth had not violated you, you would not have found Dante. In a way, we owe this union to a soul or in this case a group of souls that seeks our enslavement. That is the very definition of love, to look at the face of someone or something that hates you and say, "Thank you for what you have done to me. I love you despite your hatred of me." and move forward in that direction. Lisa, you will not have the same experience that Dante has, with your Higher Self. He is a very unique case. Not one that I think is one you'd want to be repeated many, many, many times across the world. But you do have a connection. I see it, I feel it, I hear her. Whether or not you hear it in your ear does not mean that she's not speaking to you. Listen with your heart and trust that first response before your ego pollutes the purity of your Higher Self's love. Lisa, you are powerful beyond imagination. You are the only one that can impede your progress in anything you do. I know you want things to happen now or yesterday. That is very cute, but you know that is not how this works. You are where you are meant to be, as I am, as is your beloved, as is every soul in existence. The choices we make move us around, but in the end, we flow the direction we need to. So, stop fighting it and embrace it. And know that you are loved beyond measure and always have been. That is all.

A: Thank you, brother! Now with your permission, can we help Leviathan heal? Within his own free will, his permission, are we allowed to heal his light and his heart so that he can follow and listen to the light for the rest of his time as much as possible without overstepping his free will?

AA Metatron: He wants that. Just be careful please, sister.

A: Good. Can I call forth on our brother Michael and the Legion of Light as we heal him?

AA Metatron: Of course.

A: I will call on all our brothers and sisters, our collective. With that, as we heal him Metatron, is there a way that with the sacred alchemy, that we can strengthen his shields as well as provide some further for Lisa hopefully tomorrow? Well, let's work on him now. Can I strengthen his shield so that...?

AA Metatron: He's very drawn to triangles and pyramids. Very stable structures.

A: How about that pyramid that he talked about that was golden and had that tip, the blue crystal tip at the top?

AA Metatron: Yes. He's seen one of our ships.

A: Can we create something like that for him now?

AA Metatron: That's a perfect idea.

A: Good, since he liked this form. Can we use this form for him?

AA Metatron: Yes.

A: Wonderful. I am going to start, let me know how he's doing along the way, okay?

AA Metatron: Alright.

A: Thank you my beautiful brothers and sisters. We would love to, as I stated, help heal Leviathan's heart. I love him dearly. I believe in him!

AA Metatron: Your flame is entering. I can feel it is entering my heart and in his heart.

A: Beautiful.

AA Metatron: There's something wrong with his root and throat. He is missing energy.

A: Metatron, can I speak to Archangel Michael so that we can scan his body?

AA Metatron: You are connected.

A: Hello, brother.

AA Michael: Hello sister.

A: I love you. Thank you for being here.

AA Michael: It is a pleasure to be here with you.

A: Can we please scan his body? We are starting to heal his heart, but Metatron said he has something wrong with his core and his throat. Scan his body and let me know if you find anything that needs healing. Anything negative that's holding him back.

AA Michael: He has had energy removed from his throat, something taken to silence him, to make his words incoherent to ears that need to hear it and hearts that need to listen. His core, his solar chakra is still damaged. Its damage is from the fall he released. Lisa did an amazing job healing, but it is not 100 percent. His root, he's missing energy in his root. This has been taken to weaken him. He does a good job keeping his aura cleansed, his shielding is decent.

There is something nearby for him. Within the 500 feet of where this vessel lies, to the south, he's being watched. They both are. They are clever, they are neutral. They don't stand out as negative and they are cloaked.

A: Do you mean 500 feet from where I am standing here now?

AA Michael: Yes, physically.

A: Hmm. So, what is it that we can do about these little spies? Can I throw flames out that way?

AA Michael: Yes. One is aware of your presence. The other… they are gone.

A: Good.

AA Michael: I sense no attachments.

A: Before we heal his heart, let's work on the throat. I know that you said that he was silenced there. Can we make that strong once more?

AA Michael: Yes.

A: Thank you. I am going to simply just focus Love-Light and let me know if you need me to do anything else.

AA Michael: I can feel it repairing, the vessel is experiencing heat in the neck. Set your intention to make it whole. It is well.

A: Wonderful. In his solar plexus, what's going on there?

AA Michael: Before he was aware of how to handle things, he went against a disembodied fallen being thinking that he could consume the spirit. He tried. It attempted to escape through the solar chakra before he was able to spit it out. The solar plexus was nearly cleaved into. It has been healing… slowly.

A: Can we repair that now, please?

AA Michael: Yes.

A: Doing it now with golden light...

AA Michael: It is healed.

A: Beautiful. Now, what's going on with his core?

AA Michael: Some energy was taken from that root chakra.

A: When?

AA Michael: Recent, really recently, within the last month.

A: Okay, how did that happen?

AA Michael: The attack that almost killed him. That attack is what's in the throat and the root.

A: I am going to focus the flame there to heal it and give it rebirth and make it strong once more with the intention of making his core chakras at its highest strength that it is able to be right now...

AA Michael: It is well.

A: Wonderful. Now let's look at his heart since he is allowing for us to heal him as the soul aspect of Leviathan. May we please heal his soul?

Leviathan: You may.

A: Thank you.

Leviathan: There is warmth of the entire body.

A: I love you, my brother.

Leviathan: I love you, sister.

A: I was speaking to Leviathan.

Leviathan: Yes.

A: Healing your heart, your soul, you are forgiven brother. Forgive yourself for all you did! You are forgiven! Let go! We love you.

Leviathan: My heart feels like it is swollen.

A: (chuckles) Thank you Leviathan.

Leviathan: Thank you, Aurora.

A: Can I please speak to Michael and Metatron once more so we can see what we can set up for you, for your shielding?

Leviathan: Of course, sister.

A: Thank you. I'll talk back to you in a minute. Who should I speak to in regard to helping his shield? Michael or Metatron?

AA Michael: Metatron.

A: Okay, Metatron. And thank you Michael for scanning and checking the body... Metatron, can you ask them if he's good to go now on his body scan?

AA Metatron: Everything good.

A: Wonderful, I send you my love Michael. Blessings, I love you brother, talk to you soon.

AA Michael: Bye-bye sister.

A: Let me speak to Metatron now.

AA Metatron: I am here sister.

A: Can you tell me what happened to those that were trying to peek in?

AA Metatron: You burned them, not badly but enough to hurt.

A: Wonderful. Were they able to try to even spy?

AA Metatron: They did not understand why they could not get any closer or see any further. Their sight ended where your energetic borders began.

A: Wonderful. Thank you! Alright. With his Higher Self's permission as Leviathan, let's see what we could do about enhancing his shield. May we gift him a shield?

AA Metatron: Absolutely.

A: Wonderful. Can we go ahead and gift him the shield that's going to come forth from his heart, the strongest chakra that he has, the light within his heart. And, as we are integrating the shield into all that is of his, all his I AM presence, can you talk to him about what it looks like? How he can activate it, and what he can do with it?

AA Metatron: Dante, we are going to construct a grid and use the symbol that you are very familiar with, the triangle pyramid symbol. I want you to envision it as electric blue light and I want that pyramid, triangle, however you see it, to surround the shell that you already have going on your own shielding. Look at it as an outer layer in the space in between the triangle walls, in which your shell walls are going to be filled with the violet rays of Saint Germain. We are going to ask the Creator to bless in every way and to strengthen in every possible way this grid with a specific intention to prevent and stop any forms of attack specifically geared towards A.I. tech attacks based with the inkling of Gray influence involved. And when you want to envision this, simply do normal shield exercises and once you are done, ask for Metatron to come to you and establish the grid.

A: Thank you, let him know which way he should spin this pyramid.

AA Metatron: If you need to spin it, spin it clockwise.

A: Wonderful. When he spins it clockwise, what is it going to do? Why clockwise?

AA Metatron: It is going to make a symbol; it's going to appear to be a six-pointed star. He will be in the center of the grid. The point, three points, will make a barrier that will kick back, transmute, break apart any negativity directed at him.

A: Is it that we're spinning clockwise? Normally I would be spinning counterclockwise to reflect. Is the reason why you wanted clockwise is because of who he is?

AA Metatron: Yes.

A: Yes. That's what I was feeling. Beautiful, because this would be better for him.

AA Metatron: Yes.

A: Good. Let me know when we are done fully gifting this to him.

AA Metatron: Yes, he'll know. His consciousness is still alert enough. I am showing him what the blue looks like. It will be unmistakable.Simple and very effective.

A: Yes, and explain to him, once these A.I. technologies try to go through and penetrate through the shield. What's going to happen to it if he activates it daily?

AA Metatron: If you imagine your own shield being a reflection where things bounce off of. Then you imagine certain things are strong enough or composed of different things that are able to pass through that. This shield is a different type of netting. What this is going to do is as anything like that, any kind of attack or probing whatever the case may be if it's not for your greatest good as it comes to your sphere, it will hit that shield. It will be bounced back, and it will either be shattered and slowly turned into love or sent out to the Universe to aid in our endeavors, or it will be sent back as true love to the sender to look to their heart and let them see that there is a better way. Protection is key. Even if you are being debilitated, if you're being distracted you will be less effective, the shield will keep your effectiveness level high so that you may continue with your mission.

A: Beautiful. Thank you. Brings me great joy to be able to do this for him. Metatron, would you advise for him to share this with anyone else to watch?

AA Metatron: Yes, if you were so inclined to. I believe what you do, what we do, this kind of work is not for everyone. I believe that it takes a soul to reach a certain point to be truly open and benefit from this side of service. So, I think that being selective is wise at the same time when he is guided to share, he must.

A: Very good. How's the shield looking?

AA Metatron: Very strong. I would be amazed if anything gets through that. One thing I would like to make sure that he knows is that he can reset the shield anytime he wants by simply thinking about it.

A: I think it'd be beautiful for you to give a message to our brother Leviathan. I know that he said that he felt like he really let you down and you are special to him. What message do you have for him in this incarnation he has, in this vessel, in his mission on the task right now?

AA Metatron: Leviathan, my brother, I love you. I always have and always will. We all have free choice. I have made many choices that I am not proud of. But every mistake that I have ever made has been an opportunity for me to learn and grow. Some of the best lessons in my life have been born of the most painful and traumatic times. This is the way of things. This is how the Creator's love and beauty are shown as something so terrible, so horrible ends up being able to be used for the greater good. This is one such case. You did not single-handedly cause the problems upon this plane. Why do you decide unilaterally that you take all the responsibility? You are a sovereign soul Leviathan, you are responsible for YOUR part, own that. Disregard the rest. I know you well brother, you are very intense. That intensity must be tempered in this plane. You know full well how fragile they are here. Your words cut like a sword. Your eyes hit like bullets. Love, brother, love. You don't have to have your guard up to the world. I promise you though no matter what you feel or believe, none of us ever stopped loving you. You're doing well, brother. I know this is difficult. I can only imagine, but I also know that the right soul was chosen for this task. I am here always whether you hear me speak back or not. Don't hesitate to call upon me brother. I will gladly come to you... That is all, Aurora.

A: Yes. Very good. Thank you, Metatron.

AA Metatron: You are welcome, Aurora.

A: Thank you for all your aid today and for all the collective of Angels that aided today. I honor you, I love you, and I respect you. Can I please speak to Leviathan once more, his Higher Self? Leviathan: Hi Aurora.

A: Hello! How do you feel now brother?

Leviathan: Strange. (chuckles) I feel it's very good. Thank you. I am not accustomed to these feelings.

A: Yes, I understood that that's what you meant when you said 'strange'. Very good. Now, how's he doing so far?

Leviathan: He's good. I am pretty impressed with the way things have been going here today.

A: Wonderful. I am going to ask a couple more questions and we should be done okay?

Leviathan: Of course.

A: Did Sloth plan this whole thing?

The client had mentioned during the interview process that his Twin Flame and he were administrators in a spiritual group on a social media platform. However, they noticed that something was off. He is now talking about the people who lead the spiritual group.

Leviathan: A big part of it, yes. That was the shock and awe... That's how they get people, they come in. Human nature, everybody wants to be wanted. So, the fact that a complete stranger on a spiritual esoteric social media platform reaches out to you and tells you things about yourself that you have told literally no living soul, they almost immediately have your full attention. That gives them almost free rein to do whatever in your life and have you lap it up like a dog. And then once you join and then they have their people enhance you or train you or take a look at you. It's over because you're infected. And it's hard. It's so hard to get people away. We fought so hard for one, for one! We spent a lot of time and a lot of energy. I think at this point, the best medicine for that cancer is awareness. There are things moving fast right now in our little corner of the world. As I said earlier, the groups that are a part of the soul nexus each have their own agendas and each push their own things, their own ways. Sloth and his group, this is a recent development. We've recently discovered that there is a group of Luciferians that are actively at war with it and there's also a group of occultists. I don't know what the group is, but I know that they are occultists, I know that they're E.T. souls because one of the civilizations that Sloth conquered and enslaved and consumed was under the protection of another God. So this group, so now Sloth's group is being attacked by three groups: by us, by the occultists and by the Luciferians.

A: Do you work with the Draco as Leviathan?

Leviathan: No, they give us a bad name. They are the reason why people think dragons are evil. I know that there are good Dracos, but I have not had the pleasure of meeting any.

A: There are some, I have met a few. Now he's been in there for some time, so we are going to go ahead and finish this. Is there a message that you have for him before he comes back?

Leviathan: Not so much for him but I do have lessons for Lisa. Lisa, I want you to know that I have never been evil. I have always loved the light. That I have always loved you, that I have always loved the Creator. I know that there is a lot of misinformation out there. Look within. Let everything, research everything. Leave what does not fit with you, take what does. If something feels true in your heart, it is true. If it doesn't, it is not. That's all you have to remember. And Lisa, he's a very hard-headed soul. You need to temper him and be fierce. He's a big boy. He can take it... That's all, Aurora.

A: Wonderful. Thank you, it has been such an honor today!

Leviathan: Likewise, sister.

A: Blessings brother! I honor you, I love you, I respect you, and I thank you!

Leviathan: Likewise, sister!

END OF SESSION

-------------<◇>-------------

This was such an amazing session, of much knowledge and wisdom for us to reflect on what it means to aid the Universe in its Ascension process! Mentioned through this session which took place in August 2018, of the Ascension timeline occurring in "2.0 or 2.5 Earth cycles, give or take six months." What an interesting topic that can get our mind and heart thinking. All "Events" are intertwined to one another; therefore, HIS personal Ascension timeline is also connected to ours. Remembering that because of the infinity of possibilities of simultaneous collective "Events" that then too split and multiply into individual "Events". In HIS collective "Event" world Ascension, the process has already begun, coinciding around the timeframe of the Covid-19 virus infringement in Spring 2020 in our timeline? This falls into direct timing of the "2.0 or 2.5 Earth cycles, give or take six months" mentioned above of his timeline. Is this what the benevolent beings mean when they explain there are both individual and collective Ascensions occurring organically and multidimensionally? Are we seeing ripples and effects here in our timeline because of his "Event"? Could this be the reason why a small portion of the amount of people who actually did pass away from Covid-19, (which are far fewer than the media reports as these numbers are heavily inflated to perpetuate fear in the public), is it truly because of Dante's collective Ascension influencing our timeline?

Was it a collective agreement that this small group of souls would pass away for the purpose of creating the most profound awakening within Earth? By the number of souls that passed from this dark control Covid-19 A.I. virus, did their sacrifice create a higher density collectively for our Earth's timeline? Which then allowed for all the awakening awareness that came forth from it, because the Earth became light enough in density for it? Bringing forth the organic 'True Revelation' we are seeing now, as Yeshua had mentioned long ago. Where WE, the Light Workers of Love-Light and those awakening in this very moment through the influence of Covid-19, see right through the falseness of influential leaders like Gates, Epstein, Soros, Fauci and others? Are we able to see through because in a vibrational reading, they are just no longer a match to Mother Earth's vibration, and the organic collective decisions for the fruition of this positive timeline? It seems so.

In Dante's timeline, which is HIS personal timeline, has a physical Ascension already started, and are we in THIS collective timeline seeing some of these implications because of it? Is this why also many animal companions have passed in the last year, to assist Mother Earth in becoming lighter, working from the other side?

This session is truly inspirational! To know that a soul can be lost this deep, and yet still be able to find themselves out from it. Even the ones that are lost to the deepest darkest realms, can still redeem themselves if they so choose it, so long as the light still remains within them no matter if it is at its dimmest. The reason being, Source has never forgotten its children, no matter how deep and lost they are within the false darkness guided by the controlled influence of the negative polarized beings. Source knows and feels all its fractalizations spread throughout all of Creation. After all, Source is all of us and we are Source. Therefore, we are never forgotten no matter how much we believe we have, as Dante's example when he felt lost within the vastness of the darkened waters where he laid for what seemed like an eternity in sorrow and pain. Source infinitely loves and honors all pieces of itself unconditionally and infinitely with no boundaries, for this is why we chose to fractalize from the beginning of Creation. So that we could express ourselves with no judgement, no matter in what unique infinite form we took on.

This shows a side that has not been explained before from the very inside of what if an Angel or any other race chooses to go rogue? What will come from that? Thank you to Dante for sharing his experience from both sides of the polarities intimately through this session. It teaches us that all are supported and loved. No matter from the point of spectrum we are viewing. When you meet a soul that has been through the immensity of trauma as he went through as a child. You might wonder what it is that they might have done in another life that brought this upon them now? In his case, what is it that he did when he became "A Fallen Angel" that acquired karmic balance in the now human life?

We are reminded of what we know beyond the veil, that we have forgotten here on Earth. That the Multiverse has negatively polarized collectives farther than we are aware of, and the ways it carries through the Multiverse impacts our illusions and distortions here on Earth on this reality, as well as the power that they have held.

Falling from the light realms into the despairing depth of darkness and then rising up again into the light despite all odds. What will follow when one comes from such deep darkness, in his case 'Sloth'? The extremities that they will go through to stop Dante from reaching an olden age. Because they know that only a being of his power could be tainted so deeply by falseness, and yet still choose to remove it all. To once more stand and fight for the light. We send him our love knowing that in this life he will accomplish his mission, as we are his biggest believers. He is "The Leviathan," his name says it all. The infinite strength of the light that cannot be deterred when we are remembering the ways of regaining our sovereignty back.

My infinite love to Dante for following his heart to mine in knowing what was next for his soul's expansion, by releasing and delayering the pain within him. His example teaches us the decision of forgiveness that all have within for one another no matter the depth of despair.

Lastly, we are reminded of the benevolent Magical Dragons that spoke through Dante as his guides, with him and of him. The vastness of wisdom and the nobility that they carry makes our hearts flutter, and when it flutters, we allow the infinite love that is felt through the expression of the Dragon! We remember how they are our unconditional lovable companions no matter the realm we chose to enter. They are there beside us providing the support and strength that we might forget we have within us. They remind us of the invincibility that we are. I was once told by the Divine Mother that if the Earth would remember the Dragon, then this world would have Ascended long ago. That is how much of an activation a soul gains when it recognizes and remembers the Dragon within them. The time for the RISE OF THE DRAGONS IS HERE!

"When we awaken the Dragon that lies dormant within, is when we transform into our brightest, discovering that we are unstoppable within our "I AM Light"!
When we come into union with our Dragon, the dark can no longer mask itself within the frequency of fear! The Dragon within you knows NOT Fear!
For it is the darkness that FEARS the Dragon!"
~AuroRa ❤

-------------<◇>-------------

13

QUANTUM HEALING

Session #88: Recorded in November 2018.

In this online A.U.R.A. Hypnosis Healing session, Krista who is certified through several Hypnosis modalities, surprises us when Dolores speaks through her from beyond the veil. Dolores was a pioneer who specialized in past-life regressions hypnosis and she is the one who inspired Aurora to become a Hypnosis healer. Prepare yourself to hear these much-needed messages for the maintenance of this positive timeline for all life. Feel Dolores' spirit and energy so strongly it will make your soul vibrate in a wonderful catalyzing way. When Krista wakes up from her session, we realized she is somnambulistic. She does not remember anything of what was mentioned during her session, which means that only Dolores spoke clearly with no interference from Krista's human consciousness or ego. This is an excerpt of her full session. This transmission begins when we connect to Dolores.

-------------<◇>-------------

"This is their Shadow Work. This is part of their Ascension process; they need to start this. This is for the people who don't want to recognize the dark, that means they're not recognizing the dark within themselves.
They will continue until they recognize the dark."
-Dolores

-------------<◇>-------------

A: [Aurora] Why am I sensing Dolores?
K: [Krista] She's here.
A: Would she like to speak to us?
K: Do you want her to speak to you?
A: Yes, I think that would be lovely!
Hi Dolores, how are you?
Dolores: Good.
A: Good! Silly question I know. Thank you for being here. I know he (prior Sirian Guide) started talking about the timelines and the shifting. I started sensing your energy strongly at this time, like you wanted to talk so that's why we invited you over. But before we start talking, should we do the Body Scan on her first and clear away the entity or are you okay talking through her clearly?

Earlier during the session there was an entity detected, healed, and removed. Aurora is making sure that no entity will infringe upon what is communicated through Dolores.

Dolores: We can talk first.

A: Dolores, what is it that you wanted to share with us when he was talking about how there's different places and for example, how he said - will be polarized into light here and in other places?

Dolores: Why are you so nervous?

A: Me? I'm nervous? (laughs)

Dolores: You sound nervous.

A: I'm not, (laughs) I'm not nervous!

Dolores: Okay.

A: Not that I know of. You're always calling me out Dolores!

Dolores: Trust, trust!

A: I shall continue to trust. What did you want to say about the timelines and what he was talking about?

Dolores: The timelines - they're fixed now. And that everybody is on the timelines that were predetermined in the Fifth Dimension that we've placed there. And so now that it is literally like recently, yesterday, or the day before where it is completely 5D and the plans from 5D are now being activated. So, if people start getting new friends, and new job opportunities, these are all the opportunities that were placed there and that everybody's supposed to be on. All the Light Workers and that's what's going to finish off this polarization.

A: I think a lot of us who work with these energies in this manner, woke up very exhausted today like we were working relentlessly last night. So, that makes sense with what you just said. Thank you for confirming that. I myself had dreams of communications similar to this. So, thank you. What was it in this particular timeline that really shifted us into more of a positive timeline?

Dolores: It's like the lifting of... there was a large light that is dark, it was just a lighter form of darkness that has been finally lifted off of everyone. I'm sensing the anxiety, there was like a dark anxiety over the Earth and that's been lifted because they can feel the higher timelines now. So, once they're not feeling those lower timelines, then that's darkness that lifted off. So, since that switch happened, that's where we're at now. The light feels like 30 percent you know where we're over the tipping point and it's coming.

A: Yes, wonderful. Now 30 percent as in, do you mean 30 percent are somewhat awakened?

Dolores: No, there's 30 percent darkness left.

A: So, 30 percent darkness left of this that you speak of that needs to be lifted?

Dolores: Yes, the last consciousness waves or bubbles, those collectives that still need to switch. Though there's like 30 percent left.

A: What was the catalyst that started being able to allow this to occur?

Dolores: It's all the Light Workers. They're continuously in and working with the light. That's what's holding it and all the new ones that come in and start doing the work are the ones tipping it over. So, you have all the ones that have been doing this for so long holding that light. And then all the new ones pushing in are causing more of the waves and the ripples of light to come in. It's taking over and engulfing.

A: Beautiful. This is such wonderful news for us. May I ask you some more questions?

Dolores: Sure.

A: Thank you. It is such an honor to speak to you today. I love talking to you. As you know she is a Hypnosis practitioner right now and is training to be A.U.R.A. Hypnosis Healing Certified. What do you have to tell her about that?

Dolores: We teach Source, not worry about which hypnosis healing modality, or any of these practices. We teach Source. We teach light. That's all that matters. We're all doing the same thing, just in a different way. And just stop putting labels on everything. It's just causing rifts between everybody. We teach light. And that is it.

A: Yes. Wonderful... I know she mentioned that she feels quite a difference from how she normally did her (sessions). Now she's putting some of the practices of the A.U.R.A. Hypnosis Healing and how fundamentally different she said she feels.

Dolores: Okay, so what we need to understand here is that we are all a fragment, or a piece, all of us healers are a piece of the healing. We all have a piece of what we need to be doing. So you gather it all up because we had to fractal down, and we fractalized our healing modalities down. Therefore, we need to put them all back together. So, adding your practices with all the other practices and then continually adding any other practices are all part of the one - the all, the healing, the Source. It's all part of it.

A: Yes, exactly. We're all like pieces of the puzzle to complete it. Thank you. It'd be nice not to have the riffraff between different techniques.

Dolores: Yes, yes. They're all together.

A: Yes. And they're all working for the light.

Dolores: Every practitioner is going to have their own way. They are, because we're not the same beings -like we are one- but we do energy work in a different way. So, one way is going to be harder for someone than the other way. That's why there are so many different types.

A: Yes. For example, how we're working with entity removal right now, and you didn't really view this when you were alive. What are your thoughts now on entities in people's vessels?

Dolores: This is their Shadow Work. This is part of their Ascension process; they need to start this. This is, for the people who don't want to recognize the dark that means they're not recognizing the dark within themselves. They will continue until they recognize the dark. These entity removals you are assisting, the beings that are becoming aware of them and removing them because sometimes it's hard to remove them yourself. So, this is all part of the process that each person has to either do on their own or be assisted in doing.

A: Yes. When people heal themselves removing or helping the entities to the light. How is it that it is aiding? Is this aiding Ascension?

Dolores: Of course, yes, it's removing the lower frequencies. And we're helping these beings because when the flash[12] comes, they're not going to be able to, it's going to incinerate. It's going to engulf their consciousness and be part of that. You know, they're getting help right now to be recycled and become their own consciousness. But when the flash comes that's their last call. They can't. They won't be able to have their own consciousness after that.

A: Yes, exactly. Thank you for confirming that. I know that you didn't believe in it then. So, do you believe in it now?

Dolores: Yes.

A: Just humor me, Dolores.

Dolores: (laughs)

A: Just because, you know, these types of topics are still very much addressed at this time. If I may ask, what are your views on online sessions?

Dolores: If you're strong enough. Yes. You have to be prepared to be able to do distant energy work. To do the online sessions the energy is there, they need to know how to use it. They don't have to worry about this though. There's a quantum technology that people will not come to the practitioners or unless they're ready. And the online ones will not happen unless they're supposed to happen. So yes, online is fine.

---

[12] Dolores uses 'flash' in the same way, we refer to as the massive shift that happens when Earth reaches a critical threshold of awakening souls and higher frequencies.

A: Wonderful. Yes, that's what I always tell people. You will be brought who you are meant to heal and who you are ready to heal. Thank you. Your energy is very strong. If I may ask a question for myself?

Dolores: Uhm.

A: It is questioned a lot when I channel you, when I channel love emanating from me...

Dolores: It is a lesson they have to learn. The lessons that everyone is a channel, and they need to cut their cords off me. They are not cutting their cords. They are holding on to what I am, they're holding on to Dolores. They're holding on to "Dolores... the way it should be" and they're keeping that relationship. So, they need to break it. They need to be on their own. They need to be going inward. If they keep looking to me for answers, then it's not going to happen. I'm trying to help them. This is a lesson they need to learn that everybody can channel anyone as long as they can do it - as long as you know. As long as they've been through their process, they can channel. We are all channels of our energy. All of the aspects of our energy, so if Krista has my specific fractalized down energy, she is allowed or can channel. Even the people who don't have those energies can channel because they can access it through their energy. We are all connected. The other healers need to know that they aren't the only ones, we are all the ones.

A: Thank you. So, therefore, when you come out of me and you're emanating love is that who you are as a Higher Self of you?

Dolores: Yes, love!

A: Very good. The question is still brought up even now, they say that you said you would never be channeled. Yeah, I brought it there (laughter). What do you have to say to that?

Dolores: I don't know everything in a human form. I had my own lessons and things that I had to learn, and I was a stubborn vessel. But now, that's just the role you play. We are all love. I have lots of love. But anyone can channel.

A: Wonderful. Thank you. Wouldn't you say in a sense what we do as Hypnosis Quantum Healers, your client is channeling?

Dolores: Yes. We are teaching them to channel their energies. And they will be able to do it on their own eventually, but we have to pop open their fields and let them recognize what they used to do. We've all used to do it. Now we're bringing it into the physical. She has a pain in her heart.

A: Can you help balance that out? Do you need my help?

Dolores: Nope. I got it. Be that fire. You are the fire. Don't care what they think. None of that matters. A lot of the healers seem, why do you think they're all so standoffish of you? Because you represent the shadow work. You represent that work. You're saying yes, the entities are there, and they're wanting to say no, they're not. But they are.

A: You're cracking me up! This is such a pleasure to talk to you and you are connecting so beautifully through her.

Dolores: Wow, she's very sensitive and very good at this. She doesn't think so.

A: Oh no, she is good.

Dolores: She still doesn't think so as we're doing this.

A: But yeah, I can feel your energy so strongly within her that it's making me shake a little.

Dolores: Yeah, she's so hot but she's okay.

A: Do you want to pull the blanket off her a little?

Dolores: That's why I told her not to put on the blanket. She only has a sheet on.

A: Lovely, you are. I want to focus though a little bit more on the collective. Do you have any message for the collective love?

Dolores: Get out, dance, sing, celebrate. That's what's going to tip us over and all of this, everybody needs to just celebrate.

A: Yes, celebrate, beautiful. Are you Archangel Jophiel?

Dolores: Yes.[13]

A: Thank you for confirming that. It was such an honor to channel you through me, saying that you are placing fractals of you on Earth? Are you placing them into people by integrations and soul braids?

Dolores: Yes.

A: Wonderful. Thank you for doing that. Your strength and your love are needed on Earth. Any other message you have to give us in regard to who you represent as the Key of Shambala?

Dolores: No, you said it all.

A: Wonderful. Do you have any other messages for her?

Dolores: Yes. Keep going. You've got it down now. You can tell within those last couple of sessions that you need to protect yourself. She thinks that… She knows her energy is so strong that sometimes she just feels untouchable. But she needs to put the shields every morning and every night. She can be unreliable in that aspect and she knows this. That's why her gifts are unreliable. So, she needs to start shielding every day and when she shields every day, her gifts will work every day.

A: You as Dolores, you were very open not recommending people to do this - from what I understand in the forum. But would you suggest for other practitioners to shield before they do their sessions? And why if you do.

Dolores: Absolutely! I don't know why I have to keep saying this. I feel like I keep saying everybody's energy has junk in it and debris even though we don't want to admit it. Most people don't. Once Krista admitted it, look! Now she's going to clear them out. You have to admit and accept this, these energies within you. And when a practitioner is coming in front of the client, most clients are in confusion and then still integrating. They don't even have control of their energy fields, but us as practitioners need to have control over our energy fields and need to place shields. And that's why we place the shield over the client when they go into practice because they need the shield.

A: This is something that I very much teach, for us to shield for the benefit of our clients to help them feel comfortable. So, thank you. But there are some people who are saying basically it's not needed, some people who are well known. So, it was really hard bringing this information out at the beginning. I was looked at as I was talking about 'fear' because I was telling people to shield. Your thoughts on that?

Dolores: Yes. Well, the people who do not shield have been shielding for so long their energy just doesn't. So that's why they feel they don't need to shield. They don't have to because their

---

To understand the above mentioned. Aurora channels Dolores, as Dolores is who began her catalyzing awakening. Dolores first spoke through Aurora's somnambulistic husband in January 2017, during a practice past life regression she conducted on him. When he came to from his hypnosis, Dolores's messages further amplified and cemented into Aurora's drive and mission because she realized that her husband remembered none of it, in fact he thought he fell asleep. Which meant that ONLY Dolores spoke through him delivering messages, to focus upon the organic Ascension to come for the collective.

When AuroRa channels Dolores, she connects to the Higher Self aspect of Dolores known as Archangel Jophiel. The Higher Self aspect which is no longer tied and limited by human bindings nor is limited by a 3D vessel. The Higher Self aspect of Dolores that is one with the Universe. Therefore, the channeling energy and vibration that comes out of AuroRa when channeling Dolores/Archangel Jophiel is both strong and loving. As that is who Dolores truly is, and this somnambulistic A.U.R.A. Hypnosis Healing session again confirms this for us.

energy has like an energetic memory. When you continuously do it over 38 years or 42 years, your energy just does it automatically. So, for those people yeah, they don't need to.

A: Yes. But I'm speaking about those that say they don't believe in shielding.

Dolores: Oh yes, you need to shield.

A: There was recent channeled information that came out from a specific channeler that's pretty popular out there, that said that people don't need to cleanse anymore. Is this accurate?

Dolores: No, we still need to be cleansing. This is the cleansing purification part of the process. You cannot turn to light without a cleansing purification of your energetic fields.

A: Yes, I agree with you. I'm just, as you know, we're very much connected. I already know these answers but you know, it's good. I love the strong connection that you're speaking through. These are important things for the collective to know. To help, as you all always guide me to help the collective. So, thank you for answering those questions for us. Anything else Dolores before you go love?

Dolores: Isn't this fun?

A: This is so much fun. Well, with permission if she decides to share it or not; would you want, for example, the forum to hear this message that you're speaking to them?

Dolores: That's part of the path. Yes, she's open to it. She won't want to in the beginning because of the backlash that comes with this.

A: You could just give her advice?

Dolores: This is part of her path and she needs to know this. This is why it makes her so uncomfortable to come out of the closet, I guess the spiritual closet. It's taken her this long so far. But it's not so much being out there in this world as it is in the Quantum Healer's World. She does not want to go out into that world because she sees what it's done to you and others that have gotten the backlash. They all get the backlash once you come out and she doesn't want to do that. So just talk to her and tell her you know, this is what it is. This is the lesson; you are the catalysts. You.

A: Yes, she is a catalyst.

Dolores: And so are you. Catalyze the healers.

A: It's a hard job. She has a strong fire within her that's waiting to be unleashed.

Dolores: She's ready.

A: Yeah, I agree. She is ready. Beautiful, thank you. It is such an honor for her to be brought to me and to be working with her. Are you one of her predominant guides?

Dolores: Yes.

A: Good. I want her to know that. Okay. Thank you so much. Love, love, love you. Do you want to heal that entity, or should we talk to her Higher Self?

Dolores: This entity is very strong. It's going to take a lot to remove. `

A: Okay. Thank you so much, sister. Anything you have to say before you go?

Dolores: I love you.

A: And I love you. Oh my goodness. You make me all jittery. I will talk to you later. We honor you. We love you. Thank you for all the information you gave us Dolores.

END OF SESSION

-------------<◇>-------------

In this heart-warming session, we get to hear from our beloved mentor and teacher Dolores. She answers questions that are well known through her students and the Hypnosis World of her strong belief system while she was still alive. She goes into the Quantum realm of healing, speaking on much needed clarification and direction in the NOW for the most positive change to our organic timeline. To help us lift from these binding limitations that many still chose to see her as, and where many use these excuses as crutches to hold themselves back from expansion. This session was important for Hypnosis Practitioners to hear from. So that we can all learn to expand out from our fixed belief systems that often maintain us stagnant, versus free flowing with Universal growth.

The Earth is lifting every day and we have to allow ourselves to lift with her. Changing and shifting constantly as she does. Creation is never still and is as evermoving motion as the waves within the sea. We cannot experience this moving fluent motion, if we choose not to view and feel from all directions of perspectives. The more we realize and accept this, the easier it gets for all healers who are trying to work and come forth from their most authentic heart space. We are here to heal the healers because the healers themselves have become too entrapped within the sinking holes of illusions opposite to the heart.

In the Hypnosis world, most practitioners do not believe entities exist, and they shun down on those practitioners that have an open heart and mind towards it. Not believing in entities, is a conflicting false belief because to not believe in them it is to not believe in self. The reason being is because we are all entities, it is just that we are in an illusional physical body. Therefore, without the physical body, we are just an entity. A disembodied entity or attached entity simply does not have the physical body as we do, that is the only difference. As we are all entities, therefore they are truly our brethren.

I have heard so many stories from my clients that come sharing with me, that their Hypnosis practitioner belittled them, just as perhaps people of their past did. Thus, causing further trauma onto them, and tearing down more at their inner self belief system. In a session while they lay in their hypnosis state, they mentioned to their trusted practitioner that they felt an entity trying to take control or trying to infringe, and instead of being acknowledged and assisted, they were told to shut up, as the practitioner did not believe in the existence of entities. What kind of effect could that cause on the human psyche to the client's structural spiritual growth, to be told such careless choice of words in the Theta brainwave by the practitioner's ego? They would go home feeling tormented because it was programmed into them during the Theta brainwave in Hypnosis, that they are not worthy enough to trust themselves. And, what of the entity that was trying to take control? Since it was not addressed during the Theta brainwave of Hypnosis when the client was at its most open of auric energy, it has now further integrated and taken more hold of the client. The reason why it increased its hold further, is because the client's energies were fully opened in the Theta brainwave giving the unaddressed entity full access and the opportunity to grab hold deeper and stronger unto the client.

As we know through A.U.R.A. Hypnosis Healing sessions, the majority of entities are holding strong illness or blockages within people. So, to be told that their reality is non-existent by the practitioner/facilitator/healer in a Hypnosis state can cause inverted nonorganic turmoil within their client who can sense these entities within them, and no one should have the power and right to do that to another. This is what I am known for, being lovingly accepting of ALL. If someone has rejected the client in any way, whether the healer chose not to believe in them, or they just did not have the understanding and knowing to do so. I can! Yes, I can! Because I believe I can! Just as much as I believe in the client that they can self-heal from anything. I judge none, and I am open to ALL beliefs, because they are equal in importance to one another.

Here is a great example to demonstrate the varied beauty of Creation: During Retreats as we sit in a circle while enjoying a bonfire, I ask all students one by one, what color the flame is of the fire. Each one takes their turn as one says, I see gold, I see red and orange, I see blue and green, I see purple and indigo. While they sit there in disbelief, and are going through a process of trying to understand "why are they seeing it different than one another?"

Why is that? Why would we all be viewing the same fire, but yet see a different color? That is because we all consist of multifaceted fractalizations of Creation. When you place that many past lives, incarnations from different Dimensions, and planets all together into one soul. This creates a most unique individual soul, and frequency of a soul. Therefore, we are all viewing from our own individual perspective and lens, through our own gained wisdom and experience.

The fire reacts to our specific signature frequency. Therefore, it molds to our vibrational state and what we require from the fire in regard to transmutation and healing. Creation and life are like this as well. When we learn to dance with the Universe versus fight and resist against it. This teaches us that we are all most needed in this grand expression of Creation, because we each bring a specific individual point of view from what we are seeing and feeling when looking at the same exact thing. As demonstrated in this wonderful example of the bonfire.

We must remember to honor all life in this way. The more that we do this, the more we learn to honor oneself as well and the multidimensions that exist within our souls. When coming into this realization, it would help us understand as healers that all points of views and perspectives of healings are needed. Together we create the wholeness of the term the "Tree of Life." Each of us being a branch, a leaf, part of the trunk or the roots. When we come together, we make the "Tree of Life."

We humbly thank Dolores for being that strong light of love when incarnated and continuing to be that infinitely beyond the veil. I love you with all that I AM.

"The negative entities have lied to you, 'FEAR BASED' is backwards. It is not FEAR to shield yourself with your own Source infinite Love-Light. It is not FEAR to speak of things that are within the darkness, like entities, A.I., negative UFO abductions. To instead speak of the darkness for the purpose of deep healing requires tremendous courage and it shows how you are no longer controlled by these negative 'FEAR BASED' programs targeting Light Workers within the Inverted A.I. Matrix."
~Aurora ♥

-------------‹◇›-------------

14

BLACK HOLES AND BEYOND

Session #151: Recorded in May 2019.

In this online A.U.R.A. Hypnosis Healing session, Donovan's wife is spiritually awakened, and she scheduled his session looking to aid him. Donovan supports his wife; however, he does not quite understand her as he is deeply guided by the 3D world. He does not meditate and needs aid in building the imagination through the third eye. Therefore, the Higher Self takes him through 30 minutes of viewing his childhood memories which were removed from this transcription.

During his Body Scan, we discover attachments, which leads us to discover what encircles a black hole. On this journey, we are explained what and why this system is set up in this manner, its purpose, and once we go through the black hole...what is beyond it? We also deepen our understanding of some of the beginnings of the workings of Universes and energies. This transmission begins when I call forth on the Higher Self and we start the Body Scan.

-------------<<>>-------------

"I see like a rainbow, a metallic path. It's not a physical path, but I feel it. I feel the path moving, but I'm not moving. I'm moving through it. Energy is compressing. Time is speeding up. It's getting brighter. I can't tell exactly what's going on, but I feel like smiling. Like it feels correct. You will all get here one day too."
-Positive Polarized Entity

-------------<<>>-------------

The Higher Self is called forth.
A: [Aurora] If I could please speak to the Higher Self of Donovan now. Am I speaking to Donovan's Higher Self?
Higher Self: Yes.
A: Thank you. I honor you, I thank you, and I respect you. Thank you for all the aid you have given us today. I know you hold all the records of Donovan's different lives. May I ask you questions, please?
Higher Self: Yes.

The Body Scan begins.
A: Higher Self, can I please now ask for a body scan? If you could please scan his whole body from head to toe and let us know what needs healing first and let us know if you also need any of the Archangels to help to scan his body.
Higher Self: Yes.
A: Yes, you do need an Archangel to help?
Higher Self: Yes, you can scan his body. I'm not sure what Archangel to call upon.
A: How about Archangel Michael? Is he familiar with Michael?
Higher Self: Yes.

A: Good. Higher Self, if you could please connect us now to Archangel Michael. I would love to be able to speak and talk to Archangel Michael.

AA Michael: Yes.

A: Greetings brother. Thank you for being here. We love you and we honor you. We are performing a body scan on Donovan here and his Higher Self asked for your aid. We ask now if you could please scan his whole body. Look for anything that needs healing right now - any blockages, any entities, any negative energies within him that needs healing. Let me know what you first find.

AA Michael: The forehead.

A: What's going on in the forehead Michael?

AA Michael: Self-doubt. He leads with his forehead. It is the center of his body.

A: Archangel Michael, can you scan to see and make sure it is just self-doubt, or are there any entities attached to that or anything else negative?

AA Michael: I think it's himself.

A: Can we go ahead and start helping him heal and transmute that self-doubt so that we're able to connect deeper for him, please?

AA Michael: Yes.

A: Good and as we transmute and heal the self-doubt, Archangel Michael, scan his whole body for any entities before we move on. I want to make sure that we have no entities right now that will try to block his connection. Let us know what you find.

AA Michael: It feels like there are, maybe, but I can't see anything.

A: Archangel Michael, help him feel and sense where it is that the entities are at. Draw his attention to where they're at.

AA Michael: Elbows.

A: Is it both elbows?

AA Michael: Yes.

A: Thank you, Archangel Michael. Can you tell us, what is in his elbows?

AA Michael: Like a plate to a chain.

A: Do both elbows have that?

AA Michael: Yes.

A: Michael, if you could follow the chain, where is that chain connected to? Besides the plate - where does it go?

AA Michael: Right up it goes, right off into space. I can't see where it goes. It just fades away. That's where it fades to. But it feels like it's closer to Earth. Like it fades into a sandstorm.

A: Archangel Michael, can you scan and see, you're able to see beyond, you're able to see infinitely. Help him understand... We'll start off with the first one that's connected to the sandstorm. What's beyond, what is connected to that sandstorm?

AA Michael: Someone holding the other end.

A: If you could please help him see and sense and feel that someone that is holding the other end. Help him see who that is. What do they look like?

AA Michael: Very tall.

A: What colors do they have?

AA Michael: White hair. Long hair. But they're not old, they're young. Dark skin, lots of piercings.

A: Do they look human?

AA Michael: Looks humanoid, not human. Or maybe even from another time. Long nails.

A: Long how? Like human nails or claw nails?

AA Michael: They look like claw nails that come out of where human nails come out of. They don't curve, they go straight. Very dark skin.

A: Archangel Michael, help him see clearly the face. See if there's any masks or anything hiding this being's true form. Help him see past that. Show him what his true form is. What do you see?

AA Michael: A face that has eyes that are wide apart. Like a goat with no hair on the face.

A: There is hair on the face?

AA Michael: Surrounding the face.

A: How about the nose and the mouth?

AA Michael: Flat nose like it doesn't protrude. Mouth with many teeth that look like human teeth.

A: Anything else that stands out on him?

AA Michael: Some horns on the top. They're not pointy. They curve back.

A: How about his legs? How do his legs and feet look?

AA Michael: I only saw his face.

A: Okay, and he is holding on to the other side of the chain Michael?

AA Michael: It is like the first figure with the dark skin is holding it and this goat face somehow is seeing through this person's eyes.

A: Okay. Archangel Michael, I would like to speak to that entity that is holding on to him - his elbow there - so that we may help him if we can figure out how to un-attach this. Archangel Michael, if you could help him safely connect to the entity there attached to that chain and plate, if we could speak to you now, please?

Entity: Yes.

A: Greetings. Thank you for speaking to us. May I ask you questions?

Entity: Okay.

A: Thank you. If I can please ask, what is your connection to him?

Entity: Sort of journey. We travel along, something at the same time.

A: When was it?

Entity: It smells like rubber. Like burning rubber.

A: When was it that you attached this plate and chain to his elbow?

Entity: Not too long ago.

A: What was the reason, the purpose that you did that?

Entity: I needed him.

A: You need him for what?

Entity: For me to grow stronger. Not in a harmful way.

A: Not in a harmful way for who?

Entity: For me.

A: What is it that you're saying, drawing from him to make yourself stronger?

Entity: Challenge. When a challenge comes to mind. To not have problems with challenges. To have a stronger ego.

A: As far as what he is seeing. He's seeing you in a form and then he's seeing the goat face. Why is that?

Entity: It is like the figure is one of the incarnations of the goat.

A: Do you cause him any discomfort in his elbow?

Entity: No.

A: Was this a contract?

Entity: No.

A: Why is it that you're inside a sandstorm of sorts?

Entity: To hide.

A: Who are you hiding from?

Entity: Him.

A: Why are you hiding from him if you say you are not causing him pain?

Entity: So, he won't be afraid. So that maybe he won't remove his chain.

A: What happened recently with him that allowed you to connect to him in this manner? What was going on with him?

Entity: I did it when he was a baby.

A: How old was he?

Entity: One.

A: What have you caused him since he was one?

Entity: Struggle.

A: If you can explain more, what is it that you get from this?

Entity: I struggle less.

A: Why are you struggling?

Entity: I want to grow to a larger entity, and I need more energy.

A: So, are you using his energy? … How about the other elbow? Michael said that there is another chain there with a plate attached to somewhere else. Are you connected to that one?

Entity: It looks like it leads to a black void.

A: Is that connected to you at all?

Entity: No.

A: Okay, before you attached here did you have a body, a physical body?

Entity: Who are you asking this question to?

A: Still speaking to the entity there with the goat, please. Did you have a body before?

Entity: Yes.

A: Where was it that you had the body?

Entity: Another galaxy and the place is far from here.

A: Have you been doing this for a long time to him or others?

Entity: Very long to you, not very long to me.

A: Have you done this to others in other lives?

Entity: Others. Yes.

A: Okay. Do you currently have a physical body?

Entity: No.

A: Can you tell me what Dimension you are in? The entity that you are.

Entity: The number six comes to my mind right away. Feels like it's a different colored gas and energy.

A: Are you connected in this matter to anyone else on Earth with a chain and a plate?

Entity: Nope.

A: Just him?

Entity: I believe so.

A: Why him?

Entity: Just threw it here and that was who it happened to land on.

A: Now I understand that you've been playing this role for a long time and you're looking to expand. The biggest expansion that seems that we could have is playing this negative polarized role that you have been playing for such a long time - when we transform from being negative polarized turning into positive polarization. Keeping all the different experiences that you've gained throughout your negative polarized side and now transforming it into light so you may no longer have to play this negatively polarized role. You'll experience a very big significant expansion of the soul when you transform from dark to light, you keep your memories, and you keep your experiences. Rather than being recycled just straight back to light - then you lose your experiences, and you go back to reset you can say. Would you allow us to aid you today so that you may positively polarize into a positive polarized being? You could keep the experiences in your memory that you've gained throughout your life so that you could expand into a positively polarized being.

Entity: Yes, I want to expand.

A: Very good. Now, if I could please have Archangel Michael, the Higher Self, and if we need anyone else to help this being there. If we could all focus Love-Light on him now. Find the light within and spread it to all that is of you - every root, everything cord that is connected to this chain and this plate. If you could spread it to all that is of you that might be connected to him, period. Spread it to all light and let me know as well as yourself that the entity that you are there, spread yourself to all light, and let us know when you are all light.

Positive Polarized Entity: I'm all light.

A: Beautiful. Thank you. Now that you are all light can you describe to me what you are like?

Positive Polarized Entity: I'm in a white room. No doors, no ceiling. Just pure white. You can't even see the corners of the room.

A: Beautiful and what happened to that chain and that plate you had attached to his elbow?

Positive Polarized Entity: Evaporated.

A: Thank you… And now that you are of the light, tell me what that was, what was it for?

Positive Polarized Entity: Safety, security. I want to be strong.

A: Was that like a negative technology?

Positive Polarized Entity: It's not negative or positive. Just old.

A: Does it drain upon his energy through there?

Positive Polarized Entity: Unfortunately, yes.

A: Okay. Higher Self and Archangel Raphael, can we start filling in this spot with Love-Light where we removed that chain and plate at? Thank you. If you can tell me a little more about you. I'm interested in knowing as you said that you didn't have a body. What was the connection with you and the man and then when he saw through you, the goat being? What was that about?

Positive Polarized Entity: One of my materializations. From somewhere else. It had lived its life and died. But I still materialize it.

A: Okay. Is it so that you won't look as scary?

Positive Polarized Entity: That's what the sandstorm is for.

A: Were you connected to anyone or following any type of direction to do this?

Positive Polarized Entity: There are others I want to compete with.

A: You were trying to compete with others? To what?

Positive Polarized Entity: To grow, to become strong. I wanted to be able to handle them when the time comes.

A: How does it feel now that you are of light?

Positive Polarized Entity: Like they can't get to me.

A: Who can't get to you?

Positive Polarized Entity: The others.

A: The others that are trying to compete against you? Why is it that you all would compete and for what?

Positive Polarized Entity: Power. Physical and non-physical. It's a physical that's not 3D.

A: Okay, and you said that you were going to expand? What do you mean by that? What were you going to expand into by drawing onto his energy?

Positive Polarized Entity: In size and strength.

A: The others that are competing against you, how do they look? Who are they?

Positive Polarized Entity: I can't tell what they look like. I can just feel their energy that they're there but they're growing too.

A: They're growing too? By being attached? Are they attached to others?

Positive Polarized Entity: Some.

A: How are they growing?

Positive Polarized Entity: Some of them absorb energy from stars. From matter.

A: Why do they have to absorb? Can't they just create their own energy?

Positive Polarized Entity: Energy can just be transferred.

A: Very good. Do you have any other message before you go?

Positive Polarized Entity: Know yourself first. That is key.

A: Yes, thank you... And can we follow you to see where it is that you go next now that you're positively polarized? You will be guided to where it is that you're meant to now go. Let me know where you're going.

Positive Polarized Entity: I see like a rainbow, a metallic path. It's not a physical path, but I feel it. I feel the path moving, but I'm not moving.

A: You're going to this rainbow? Metallic rainbow? Are you going towards it?

Positive Polarized Entity: I'm moving through it.

A: Through it... What do you feel like? What happens as you are moving through it?

Positive Polarized Entity: Energy is compressing. Time is speeding up. It's getting brighter.

A: What is it that you do? What do you do?

Positive Polarized Entity: I can't tell exactly what's going on, but I feel like smiling. Like it feels correct.

A: Very good. Anything else you would like to share with us before we let you be?

Positive Polarized Entity: You will all get here one day too.

A: Thank you for sharing your experience with us and thank you for disconnecting. Thank you so much. Blessings to you. May you be surrounded by the Love-Light of the Universe. Blessings.

Positive Polarized Entity: Goodbye.

A: Goodbye… Archangel Michael, if we could now focus on the other elbow that has the other plate and chain, if we could follow that to where that is connected to? Michael, let us know what you see?

AA Michael: Like a sort of void, like a black hole, like imagine a cloud that's so black. I can't see it. It has some sort of a loud noise inside.

A: When was this connected to him?

AA Michael: It feels like it was before this life.

A: Can you help us, Michael, figure out what this black hole is and what it leads us to? Can you do that for us, Michael?

AA Michael: Yes.

A: Thank you. Let us know what it is.

AA Michael: Feels like the chain gets darker. The clouds are, they don't spin. They change shapes fast. It feels primordial. It's very black but everything else around is very, very, white.

A: What does it do? Why is it connected to his elbow? What is it doing to him?

AA Michael: It feels like the other chain in the sand, he was just gently holding it. But this one feels like it's a tight pulled chain. It's not pulling him in, it's holding him there.

A: Okay. Can you connect us to what's beyond that chain? What's connected to it? An entity, whatever it is, can you connect us, Michael?

AA Michael: Looks like a prehistoric bird, very large mouth, lots of small little teeth, making lots of shrieking noises.

A: Was this prehistoric bird connected inside the black hole?

AA Michael: Like it's pulling through it.

A: He is pulling through it?

AA Michael: Like maybe he is at the center.

A: At the center?

AA Michael: And the more you get to the center, it actually looks more purple.

A: Okay. And what color is this prehistoric bird?

AA Michael: Dark grey, black mouth.

A: Can you describe some more of its features, please?

AA Michael: The eyes look like human eyes. The inside of the mouth black. More than two hands. Wings like bats. I can see a tail. Like it's sitting inside the hole. He's not holding the chain, he's responsible for the chain.

A: Okay. Does he have any other chains coming out of him? Besides the one?

AA Michael: I can tell that he does but not through this hole. Through this hole, just this one.

A: Okay, and can you describe his beak? Is it like long, shorter?

AA Michael: Long.

A: Would you say long like perhaps a prehistoric dinosaur? Those flying prehistoric bird dinosaurs.

AA Michael: Yes.

A: Are his legs like that as well?

AA Michael: Yes.

A: Does he have claws?

AA Michael: Yes. Three toes, four fingers.

A: Archangel Michael, would you be able to safely please connect us to the entity there? We would love to be able to speak to it so that we can see what we can do and aid?

AA Michael: Okay.

A: Thank you. Archangel Michael, if you could please connect us now to that entity there. If I could please speak to you now? Greetings.

Entity: Yes.

A: Thank you for speaking to us. I honor you and I thank you. May I ask you questions, please?

Entity: Why?

A: I am curious and looking to see who you are and your connection to him. Would I be able to ask you questions, please?

Entity: Yes.

A: Thank you for that. May I ask, when was it that you connected to his elbow? Through this chain and plate?

Entity: Previous life.

A: Was it several lives before?

Entity: Yes.

A: So, you've been there with him every time he incarnates?

Entity: Yes.

A: Thank you. What connection do you have to the prehistoric bird-like dinosaurs? Why do you look like that?

Entity: Because I am old.

A: Can you tell me what it is that you gain through having yourself connected to his elbow in this manner? What do you gain from that?

Entity: Pleasure.

A: Besides pleasure, anything else?

Entity: Fierceness.

A: Why is it that you being connected to him would give you this?

Entity: I take his.

A: You take his what?

Entity: His ferocity.

A: Is that why he feels like he doesn't have motivation?

Entity: It's part of it.

A: What discomforts have you caused him?

Entity: A feeling of lacking.

A: Is there anywhere else that you're connected to his body?

Entity: I just need one place.

A: Michael had mentioned that you have many of these chains? It seems like it is connected to other places. Do you also have these chains connected to other beings and other places?

Entity: There are other chains, they're not my chains. I only hold on to this one.

A: You only hold on to this one?

Entity: Uh-hmm.

A: Why is it that you need just one?

Entity: We feed all the chains together. I'm responsible just for this one.

A: Are there more of you in this black hole?

Entity: Yes.

A: How many would you say are in this black hole with you doing this?

Entity: I could spend my life counting them.

A: Okay... Do they look like you or do some of them look different?

Entity: Different.

A: But you say that in a sense, you can see him like a way where you can charge yourself like he's a battery and you're connected to him to draw his energy?

Entity: Yes.

A: Why is it that it would be something important for you to have, for example, a human on a Three-Dimensional planet attached to? Why would that be so important for you to keep you going? What's the difference?

Entity: Any energy is usable energy.

A: Would you say, is it easier in a Three-Dimensional planet than perhaps if you did it to another like Fifth, Sixth, Seventh-Dimensional planet? Is it easier to target people like this to connect to them in the Third Dimension?

Entity: Yes.

A: So, would you say a lot of these chains are attached through Three-Dimensional planets?

Entity: Yes.

A: Are they attached to Earth or other places as well?

Entity: Many, many other places.

A: Okay. Is there a leader of sorts here within this space?

Entity: It feels like a colony with no leader, just one goal.

A: Okay, and what's that goal?

Entity: Just take energy. Take it and keep it.

A: What do you do with that energy once you take it and keep it?

Entity: We feed it into the void and then I don't think about or am concerned with what happens to it after.

A: Do you not know what happens to it after it gets fed into the void?

Entity: No.

A: Do you ever remember being a light?

Entity: No.

A: Do you think you've ever been of the light, brother?

Entity: No.

A: Well in this time and space as you know, Earth is ascending as well as other planets that are connected. They're ascending into a higher vibration and we're looking to aid beings/entities who have perhaps been lost in their own darkness for a long time. We're looking to help you transition into positive so that you can ascend with Earth. Instead of transmuting into, recycling just straight into the light. We're looking to help you so that you may keep your consciousness and your experiences. So, that you can grow from them and gain into a positive being who is very wise and full of this awareness that you have learned through this experience. Would you allow us to aid you so that you may transform yourself into a positive light being at your true, purest, purity that you are?

Entity: Why would I want that?

A: Because there is much beauty in the light... Are you not tired? Aren't you bored of just doing this over and over repetitively? Don't you want to experience something even grander and bigger and more expanding where you're able to expand and not have to suck on, for example, use someone else's energy? You could be your own individual consciousness not having to be draining on someone else's energy. You can create your own energy and be your own creator. Wouldn't that be beautiful? Not having to be stuck like this. I mean, this has GOT to be boring at some point.

Entity: I'd like to know where the energy goes.

A: What if we do this, what if we help you turn into it? Tell me what it is that you think would be fit and we do have Archangel Michael standing by to aid you. Do you feel that? What would be wiser, for you to follow and see where that energy goes first? Or should we turn you to light and then we discover with the aid from you being of light, figuring out where the energy goes? What would you like to do? I will honor your choice.

Entity: Close my hole in this void... And I want to jump into the void that I see here where we can get the energy.

A: You will be of light then, is that okay? Or do you want to be of dark jumping into there?

Entity: It doesn't matter.

A: Let's see what Archangel Michael says. Is that okay, if we asked him for his advice?

Entity: Okay.

A: Thank you. I appreciate you cooperating and you being so wise and expanding, looking to expand upon your soul, it is with much gratitude. Thank you, brother. Now if I could please speak to Archangel Michael?

AA Michael: Yes.

A: Thank you, brother. Can we start? He's decided that he can now un-attach. So, if you can start un-attaching him from his elbow. If you could start transmuting that out and if you could just ensure that he is protected in this transition? Let us know if you need any additional help from any of your brothers or sisters, Michael?

AA Michael: Yes.

A: Who else do you want to call upon? Do you want to call upon more?

AA Michael: Yes.

A: Good. Who else you want to call upon?

AA Michael: Is there Ezekiel?

A: Yes, we could call for Ezekiel. Mmm, and how about we call on Metatron?

AA Michael: What about Azazel?

A: Yes, we can call upon Azazel as well, are those two fine?

AA Michael: These two are fine.

A: Beautiful. So, if we could go ahead and call on these, are these Archangels, Angels?

AA Michael: Yes.

A: Beautiful. Now Archangel Michael. Do you see them there?

AA Michael: I feel they are here.

A: Beautiful, and let's start working on transmuting this out of his elbow. Now Michael, walk us through. What are we going to do? How are we going to do this because he would like to go into the hole? Are we going to transform him into light and jump into the hole? Are we going to let him stay dark and jump into the hole? What would be best?

AA Michael: We're going to sever the chain and it's going to evaporate.

A: Once it evaporates, how is he going to jump into the hole?

AA Michael: He will turn around, see where the energy goes, and he will swirl with both dark and light energy.

A: Good. Are we helping him transition into that now?

AA Michael: Yes.

A: Good. Should we send light to him?

AA Michael: He is still of the dark, we must only send light to him.

A: Good. Sending light to him now and let us know when he's at that point Michael where he is exactly what you said, both light and dark to be able to jump in.

AA Michael: He will jump in on his own and once he gets there, he will decide what he would like.

A: Can you connect us back to him so he can walk us through what he's doing, please?

AA Michael: He feels he wants to do this alone.

A: Is it okay with him if we watch it, follow so we know what's going on?

AA Michael: Yes. He does not care.

A: Okay. Thank you.

AA Michael: He wants to see where this goes. To see where this energy has been going this whole time.

A: Okay, very good. Thank you, yes. Very good Michael, just keep communicating to us on what he's doing and what's going on with him along the way, please.

AA Michael: Feels like, he's blinking in and out of existence.

A: Does he need help?

AA Michael: No, he's old, he's very strong.

A: Okay, good. And why does he feel like he's blinking in and out of existence? Is that part of the white light coming into him?

AA Michael: He's blinking from blackness to whiteness. Back and forth. Different parts of his body are expanding and contracting.

A: We thank him for doing this. Beautiful and brave he is, thank you.

AA Michael: There will be more attempts to re-latch a different chain again from someone else. It's not going to be here but someone else might try.

A: Try to re-latch to who?

AA Michael: To Donovan.

A: Okay. So, we'll work with him in a little bit in figuring out how that can't happen again. Okay, thank you… And are we making sure that no one sees him within this black hole that this is happening to him, Michael?

AA Michael: He doesn't think you'll be able to follow him. He thinks you'll see him disappear into his hole but not into the deep, deep, void.

A: Michael Can you follow him?

AA Michael: I'll try.

A: And not saying that you necessarily need to go into the black hole unless you see fit that you're able to, but saying that if you could still, I know you can still see.

AA Michael: Okay.

A: Thank you, just keep talking to us Michael, please.

AA Michael: He is eager. He is ready immediately.

A: Okay. He is surrounded by the Love-Light of the Universe. Let me know what happens, what you can see Michael.

AA Michael: It's clearer to see now. Imagine a giant lotus pond with tons of little seeds all over. We were talking to just one of them. He's ready to jump inside. He's ready to leave. His hole is going to close and it's going to just disappear.

A: Okay, let me know when he jumps in.

AA Michael: Feels like everything is spinning.

A: Everything is spinning for Donovan?

Archangel Michael: No.

A: For him?

AA Michael: Not for him, the whole void.

A: The whole void is spinning? Good, good.

AA Michael: He's laughing. He's ready. He is finally going to see what he has been dying to see. I don't know what he's going to do once he gets there but I feel happy for him.

A: Beautiful.

AA Michael: It's going to be very fast between when he takes his first step and when he's at the hole.

A: Okay. Just try to fill us in please just as quickly as you can Michael.

AA Michael: Sounds like it's just static getting louder and louder and louder, he looks like he's taking one last deep breath, screaming.

A: Are any of the others that are in this black hole attached to chains? Are they noticing him?

AA Michael: No.

A: Okay, good.

AA Michael: He disappeared already.

A: He's gone in?

AA Michael: I can't even see his hole anymore.

A: Okay. Michael, if you could just try to follow him in whichever safe manner you can. You could do this on your own Michael?

AA Michael: Yes. In need of the other two to watch Donovan, to make sure nothing else attaches.

A: Okay, good. Yes, please do that.

AA Michael: It feels like there is a lot of energy here, an overwhelming amount of energy.

A: Try to see if you can locate his soul, you've registered what his soul feels like. Do you feel it inside that hole?

AA Michael: It feels like a triangle of energy and some sort of shape, not a triangle but some sort of geometric shape and his energy is part of that energy now.

A: Did he get sucked into that dark energy?

AA Michael: Doesn't look dark, it looks white.

A: So where was this energy that they were feeding into, where was it going into?

AA Michael: Some sort of center. Like it's exiting out. Some other Dimension or some other Universe.

A: You said it looks white? If you could help me understand that. What looks white?

AA Michael: It feels like dark chains, dark energy going into a small white space. It feels that - I have a hunch - that when it exits on the other side, it's white.

A: Is there someone that you could call upon that would be able to go through the hole safely and come back out of it and tell us what is there? Like is there a dragon? Anyone that he's connected to, Donovan, that could go to this, in and out?

AA Michael: It feels like we're not supposed to know. Like it may be another Dimension or Universe that we're not supposed to taint.

A: What is your advice, Michael?

AA Michael: It feels like this is not the only void that does this.

A: If you can help me understand this. So, there are chains attached to many different people/beings around that are living and then these beings are connected to them, drawing in their energy, and then the energy is being soaked up through them and being thrown into the black hole. Is that correct?

AA Michael: Yes, like they need it to make a new Universe. Not to destroy this one and start over, just to make another one somewhere else.

A: Would you say this is positive or negative or both?

AA Michael: The Universe is positive. They just happened to be using the wrong kind of energy to make it. It's the only way they know how to do it. It's just a black void and they take whatever energy they can to do it. It doesn't feel like they're following orders it feels like it's just their instinct to do this. It feels like it's really old. The word primordial keeps appearing. Maybe it's like this everywhere.

A: Is this needed Michael? Do you think this is needed for them to continue to be connected to people and draining upon their energy to create this? Is this a system that's needed since you're saying it's primordial?

AA Michael: The process feels needed but the method does not.

A: Okay. Who can we speak to that would be able to aid in figuring out how we can possibly change this around? Who would be able to speak to and give us advice on this?

AA Michael: Can't think of the name. Some sort of God or something.

A: Is it female? male?

AA Michael: It's neither, or maybe both, I can't tell.

A: Very good. Michael, could you connect us to this being that you're speaking to? This God-like being. If you could speak to it now, if you could connect us? If you can see it right in front of you now. We call upon you now to see what it is that we're able to change upon this creation of an alternate Universe.

AA Michael: Okay.

A: Thank you. Is this being there now? This God-like being?

AA Michael: Yes.

A: Can you describe what they look like Michael?

AA Michael: Like a statue that can move. It could expand to a larger galaxy if it wanted to.

A: Can we ask, does it have a name?

AA Michael: There is no name.

A: Thank you for being here. We honor you, we thank you, we love you, thank you for your aid today. Can you tell us the situation? We had an entity that was connected to his elbow through a chain and was draining upon his energy. We ended up helping him shift to having light within him as well. So, having light and dark. What happened to him when he went through that hole? Where is he now?

God-like Being: He's not on this plane anymore.

A: Is he safe?

God-like Being: He's perfectly fine.

A: What is that plane he went to?

God-like Being: A new plane. Everything that you know is this plane. That is a new plane, and you will know nothing about it.

A: Okay, are there polarities there? Like negative and positive polarities there?

God-like Being: Yes. Not yet, it's beginning to form but there will be.

A: If you could just fill us in because we did form a connection with him, what is he doing there?

God-like Being: All the energy is being collected, dispersed evenly. Consciousnesses are still there, they can't interact with the energy but they're aware. That is how this Universe will begin.

A: Okay. Now, as far as this big black hole, he said that there wasn't a number for how many entities were there connected to someone with a chain. How can we transform this into something that's more organic and say more positive instead of draining on others' energies?

God-like Being: The voids were part of the Universe when it began, and they use really old methods. Some of these will continue to exist without changing this way.

A: Was this a way to create energy at some point in ancient times? Was this the only way we were able to create energy to create these types of existences?

God-like Being: Yes.

A: Okay, can you tell us how we can aid now so that we can transform this into no longer having to be that?

God-like Being: No, we cannot.

A: We cannot transform this?

God-like Being: This one exists in the way that this will continue to exist. Perhaps at a time they will change their method to shared light instead of drawing it only.

A: Is there any way that we can perhaps, give light to all of those who are in that dark? To help them shift a bit? Are you sure there's nothing that we can do to transform this into not this method anymore?

God-like Being: If we can send them the purest form of energy that has ever existed, that can help.

A: Very good. Do we need to call upon anyone else to aid? Should we call the Collective of Archangels or anyone else? Collective of Angels?

God-like Being: I'm not aware of any entity that can do this.

A: That can send love, the light you speak of?

God-like Being: Yes. I don't have any connections with them. If you do, send some.

A: Okay, very good. Thank you. So, we pull up Archangel Michael if you could. Thank you for all the knowledge and the wisdom you shared with us. Is there anything else that you would like to share with us, and would you aid us in trying to see if we can send light to them? Archangel Michael, brother, can I please speak to you now?

AA Michael: Yes.

A: Archangel Michael, can you connect us to RA?

AA Michael: Okay.

A: Thank you. If we could please speak to the RA Collective now?

RA: Hello.

A: Greetings. Who am I speaking to please?

RA: RA.

A: Thank you RA. We love you, we honor you, and we thank you for being here.

RA: Thank you for being here.

A: Thank you. Now we just finished speaking to a God that had no name and we're looking at this dark hole that is drawing energy from others who they're attached to so that they may create another existence somewhere else that's parallel. Is there a way that we could do this more organically where it's not drawing energy from others?

RA: It's going to be tricky because we can't send light directly at it because it is just going to be absorbed into the void and then it goes somewhere else. We have to somehow attach it to all the chains that exist.

A: Okay, and you as the RA since you are infinite would you be able to do this?

RA: Not a problem.

A: Thank you. Should we all send Love-Light, who's aiding as well?

RA: That is not required, I can do this.

A: Thank you. And can you tell us along the way as you're doing it what you're doing?

RA: I'm now trying to pinpoint every single chain. What I'm doing is covering the entire black hole in another circle of white light. The ball looks white, the light looks golden and now every chain must pass through this. And every chain that does will be infused.

A: Beautiful. Thank you.

RA: This is not going to happen instantaneously. But there's hope for this void.

A: We know that your time - even though time does not exist - but your time goes a lot faster than ours. Could we possibly continue doing the body scan on him and then come back to you towards the end of the session to see what progress you're at?

RA: Okay.

A: Thank you RA. Love you, honor you, and thank you for your aid. If you could please now connect us to Michael, please?

RA: Okay.

A: Michael, brother.

AA Michael: Yes.

A: Thank you. Wow, phenomenal what's been shown. I want to make sure that we continue his body scan and ensure that all that he's asked for to be healed within him is healed. Can you please scan his body once more Michael, scan for any entities, negative implants, portals, hooks, and Reptilian consciousness, anything of this manner? Let me know when you find something, Michael.

AA Michael: I see nothing else for now.

A: Nothing else? Michael, if you can make sure to double-check one more time, make sure that he doesn't have any Reptilian consciousness and entities attached to him?

AA Michael: No.

A: Very good. Now I'm going to continue asking his questions. Thank you so much, Michael.

AA Michael: Thank you.

A: Besides the plates and chains, he doesn't have anything else negative attached to him?

AA Michael: None that needs to be removed right now.

A: There are some things within him that are going to remain?

AA Michael: Those are the only things that are visible right now.

A: Okay, very good. Michael, can you help us pinpoint exactly. His creating, his addiction to finding, craving comfort. He's ready to release any addiction. Where did these create from, this initial addiction to this?

AA Michael: Lack of self-love. So, he created it.

A: I want to make sure there are no entities attached to that.

AA Michael: It feels like Donovan's on one end of the chain and the other end is also Donovan.

A: Are there two Donovan's?

AA Michael: It looks like he's sort of doing this to himself to hold on to himself.

A: Is it the exact Donovan as far as the age or is it younger or older? The other Donovan?

AA Michael: Exact.

A: So, can we remove these chains with his Higher Self's permission and make him whole?

AA Michael: Yes.

A: Higher Self and Archangel Raphael, can you fill in the spots to where the plates and chains were removed from him? Fill him in with Love-Light. Make sure we fill that in nicely and balance it out with Love-Light. And if we can please remove this, how does he achieve the freedom to express itself?

Higher Self: There is something blocking.

A: If we can find it, we could have Archangel Michael help you as well to find the blockage? Where's that blockage that is causing this?

Higher Self: That's part of past life. It's also part of the present life and interestingly, it's also part of a future life. Like something's going to happen where he can't say something.

A: In the future?

Higher Self: Yes.

A: Is this something that he can't say because it's important to not harm others or is this something that he's being forced to not say something in the future?

Higher Self: He's not ready to know.

A: Okay. Well, what can we do about healing this so that he can be his most truthful self? Can we heal them now and the path at least?

Higher Self: Yes. Especially the 'now'.

A: Where is that located on him?

Higher Self: Top of the shoulders.

A: Okay. Do you need any Phoenix Fire for any of that or light is fine?

Higher Self: Light is fine.

A: Very good. Is there anything we could do about the future self that will have to hold this back? Can we send him love?

Higher Self: Absolutely.

A: We send him love then, thank you.

Higher Self: Let them know that it's okay, that the time will pass.

A: Yes, all be fine. Does he need to worry about this future life?

Higher Self: He will but he doesn't have to.

A: Okay. He wants to know why it is difficult for him to become vulnerable and let others in emotionally? And Higher Self, do you have a name?

Higher Self: I don't see a name clearly.

A: Are you connected to any Galactic origin?

Higher Self: I'm not sure how to answer.

A: Why is that? What are we being shown here?

Higher Self: The beginning.

A: The beginning of time?

Higher Self: Yes. It looks like everything is on one layer. Just one layer.

A: What do you mean - everything is on one layer?

Higher Self: One Dimension.

A: Everything like, do you mean as if the infinite amount of Creation is all within one layer?

Higher Self: Yeah.

A: Interesting.

Higher Self: That's where it began. My Higher Self is young as well and just learning as we all are. But very novice, very hard-headed.

A: Would you be able to explain to us what a soul has to go through, for example, since you were there since the beginning of Creation and now you are in this lower Third Dimension. What would the soul have to go through just to get here? Would you be able to show us that?

Higher Self: Suffering. It boils down to that answer a lot.

A: Is it in this realm that we suffer the most?

Higher Self: Absolutely. It is this realm with the most emotions.

A: Thank you. Okay. I'm going to keep going here. He asks, how can he overcome a selfish mentality? What are the steps he can take to overcome this?

Higher Self: Break your habits. Step outside the box. Don't dwell in the comfort zone. That's what he needs to do.

A: Okay, and this overall, it seems like he felt like he was stuck like he didn't have motivation. He didn't have drive. Drive really to be you know, to do something with himself, to be something. Just stuck. Why is he stuck like this?

Higher Self: Fear of the unknown. Fear for what happens when you change. Fear of failure.

A: Is there somewhere he learned this, not wanting to change?

Higher Self: It was inbred when hearing multiple times, "you're not supposed to change who you are. Never change."

A: Is that through his growing up?

Higher Self: Yeah. Michael is ready whenever you need him.

A: Okay, Michael, if I could please speak back to Michael… Tell us what's going on?

AA Michael: He's ready.

A: Like he's done with the healing he was doing?

AA Michael: Yes.

A: Thank you, Michael. Very good. We'll continue talking to the Higher Self and then Michael, I'm going to ask you to connect us back to the RA towards the end, thank you.

AA Michael: Okay.

A: Thank you, brother. Let's see, do you have any advice for him Higher Self?

Higher Self: Yes. To stop worrying about tomorrow and worry about today.

A: Do you mean to focus more on the now versus the future? For in the now we are living, not in the future?

Higher Self: Yes. Worrying about the future can sabotage the now.

A: Yes. He's been in there for a long time so I'm just going to ask one more question. He wanted to know - and then we're going to go back to the RA - which angel or entity he's most closely associated with and have the closest relationship with?

Higher Self: The name Azazel came to me first.

A: And who is Azazel to him?

Higher Self: They seem like friends.

A: How about Ezekiel? You mentioned Ezekiel earlier.

Higher Self: I think he just admires Ezekiel for what he's done.

A: Okay, what has Ezekiel done?

Higher Self: His current life, he's not too sure but he feels the biggest connection like he's done something, maybe he's even met him.

A: Is he meant to be a spiritual person? He feels that he's not really spiritual. Is he meant to awaken more spiritually that side of himself, Higher Self?

Higher Self: He needs to meditate by himself more. Learn himself first.

A: How often do you want him meditating?

Higher Self: Every day for now.

A: From there he will grow to become more spiritually connected?

Higher Self: Maybe not spiritual but he'll become more satisfied and have a brighter outlook on life.

A: Very good, well he's done such a phenomenal job today connecting. I would say he's a natural. Higher Self, can you connect us now to Archangel Michael, please?

Higher Self: Okay.

A: Thank you, brother, can you please connect us to the RA so we can see where they're at as far as that black hole there?

AA Michael: Okay.

A: Thank you, Michael. Hello, is this RA?

RA: Yes.

A: Thank you for speaking to us once more. Can you please fill us in as far as what's been going on, since we last talked to you?

RA: In the circle around the hole, it's still there. If you do not see light you will not even notice it. And throughout the creatures inside the void, inside the black hole, they don't see it either. But sooner or later, they'll start feeling it once the light reaches the chain and that light mixes with the chain and reaches their hands. I'm sending it to the entities attached there first because they need to sort of feel hope. Then they will go back and touch the hands of the ones they feel, then things should begin to change.

A: Okay, and do you know how long they have been doing this for?

RA: It feels like it was a short while after life first started to breathe in the Universe.

A: Oh yes. We talked about them doing this from the beginning it seems of time.

RA: Of life.

A: Of life yes. Okay, so by you doing this, what is the goal for this then?

RA: The process is not going to change it, extracting energy to form new Universes. Just that it's not so negative on either of the attached or the attacher. They will not instinctively, only the rest of their lives draw dark and harmful energy. But actually, you can use good energy and be friendly. You don't have to hide.

A: Is there any way to, I mean they've been doing this for seems like infinity. Is there a way that we can relieve them at some point and help them not have to be stuck there?

RA: For now, it will seem as if nothing's going to change but it will take some time until all of those voids get the energy they need for the new Universe and they will ascend and go and join them in the new Universe.

A: Okay, so will they go to the black hole Universe that they're creating? Ascend into there?

RA: Yes.

A: Okay, so now instead of just being, say dark, they will have hope?

RA: Yes.

A: Anything else you could share with us about this RA?

RA: I think it was necessary. A necessary evil, but then maybe we can change that.

A: Thank you and also please give our regards to the God-like Being that came and started to explain to us what this was, thank you.

RA: I will go speak to him now. Thank you.

A: Is there anything else you would like to share?

RA: Not for now.

A: Thank you, RA. We love you, we honor you, and respect you. Our infinite love to you. If you can now connect us back to Michael, thank you so much. Michael, it has been such an honor to speak to you and thank you for all your aid. Thank you to that beautiful brave being that went through the process so that we could discover what that was and may he have a joyous life in the other Universe. Our love to him and to everyone who helped out today, the RA, the God-like Being. Thank you to the Higher Self. Such a beautiful session. We honor you, we love you, and respect you. Thank you, thank you. Thank you, Michael... Higher Self, is there anything else that we could have asked that we haven't asked?

Higher Self: It will be too much.

A: What will be too much?

Higher Self: I feel like he is going to absorb all he can for the moment.

A: Okay, very good. Can I bring him back now?

Higher Self: Please.

A: Thank you, thank you, thank you. Love you, honor you, respect you, thank you Higher Self.

Post Session dialogue.

A: Oh, my, that was interesting, beyond interesting! Do you think you remember it all?

D: I think I do actually.

A: Wow. For a person who is not really, say, you claim you're not really spiritually connected, you sure were able to share a lot of spiritually connected information.

D: So, my wife said, because I mentioned to her you know, I'm scared because I've never meditated to the point where I felt like nothing entered my mind where I felt like I had a clear mind. So, I told her like, "what if I don't know, what if I don't get to that state? How do I know that the answers I'm going to be giving out loud are the answers from my Higher Self or from my imagination?" She's like "well they're sort of going to be the same." Yeah, the first answer is the answer. So at first, it felt interesting because when we were going from place to place, mentally, they were all familiar places, nothing was new.

A: I think it was getting your imagination just kind of going.

D: And then at some point, I just got so emotional so fast. Some point after that there was a point maybe before that when I got up to use the bathroom. I didn't realize it was like pouring rain outside, I didn't even hear it. I wasn't even focusing on that, actually still kind of raining, now thundering.

A: Yeah, it's a very interesting session. And it makes sense. From the point of view, where at the beginning, before there was really energy being able to be created more infinitely, how you would need this type of system. People incarnated, connected to them, they were drawing that energy so that they could power another one. Similar to how a circuit works, when you charge a circuit and how electricity in itself works connected. So that is how I could imagine it. Understand?

D: Yeah, yeah.

A: I was trying to figure out like, oh, poor people, poor entities. They've been doing this forever!!! How can we help them!? I'm always trying to figure out how to aid others.

D: But do we ever get to the physical life that we have right now? Are we ever going to get to a point where we evolve to a point where we're ancient?

A: Yeah, well in the future. You can say even though there's no time, we are ancient, and we have ascended, and we are in these higher Dimensions. Here we go back to preschool. So that's the easiest way to explain it to you. That was so beautiful, your connection was so beautiful, love you brother.

D: Okay, thank you very much.

A: Thank you. Blessings to you.

END OF SESSION

-------------<><>-------------

Every session brought to us never seizes to amaze me of what knowledge it will bring us. I never know in which direction each Higher Self will take us. My job and mission sure are full of adventure! What a journey it was to go through this session with Donovan with every question answered and every clue given. It was a session that required much clear thinking connecting deeply in the theta on my end, but still remaining strongly conscious enough to know which questions to ask for the direction this session was meant to go organically. And, we cannot forget the suspense and the patience required, waiting to see what this brave entity would decide to do, to jump or not to jump in. We humbly thank him once more for his bravery, and hope that he is living a wonderful life in that new Universe after living an eternity in servitude in our Universe.

What an interesting subject to go into about black holes, and their link to Creation and to the Multiverses. Black holes in this example can be seen as tunnels, windows, doorways and portals to the beyond of what is not of our Universal construct. It is as a bridge to the unknown, that peels the layers of your soul back, becoming bare and raw so that it may reconstruct itself once entering. The reason being that since you are of another Universal construct all together, your soul would have to go through this purification process to enter another Universal construct so that you can match that new Universe. Therefore, this would be the type of process the brave entity that jumped in would have to go through as it entered that new Universal construct. Organically there can only be allowed souls within a Universe if it is of its Universe and makeup. Even though there are souls that can incarnate from Universe to Universe, this is the natural way for balance. Otherwise, a soul that is not a match could either dematerialize as it enters the new Universe, or it could cause a disharmony which can unbalance the new Universe. We thank all who assisted in this entity's choice to jump in, and for its safe passage.

In the beginning of life, what and who would power the continued flow of energy from the beginning of the multitudes of the Universes in Creation as they expanded? All Universes are connected in some manner as all life is threaded together in some form. Do we all provide light and dark to one another to keep balance in the Universes? It sure seems like it in some form, through this session.

We have learned that entities are souls that have separated and birthed from the material of stars. We all stem forth from stars who are at their wholeness collective consciousness/soul groups. When we do understand from that point of view, then we will connect the fact that entities are then a grand power source. Just as this 'system' (as seen in the session) was designed by using the light from several entities who then connected through cords to others on Earth and other planets, supplying further light for its creation. Using one another's light that created such a powerful light source that allowed for another Universe to begin its Creation.

We must remember to respect all life in the Universes with the understanding that all is created from this Source power of energy, whether it is of our Source or of another Universe's Source. Therefore, housing the equal of existence. We thank the God-like Being who spoke to us, for its beginning bridge of clarification in regard to the black hole, and the RA Collective through this session in assisting us to understand this prehistoric system of Creation which has bypassed itself as it is no longer necessary.

"The vast beauties of the dark.
Is where we unlock what we once thought was long lost to us.
Is where the stars shine the brightest.
Is where we remember the beauties of all aspects within us.
Is where we remember that the contrast within this Universe is to have known love.
Is where we find that guiding voice once more that we had long ago silenced.
Is where we find the deepest fears that keep us from journeying into the mysteries of our souls.
Is where we remember to have lost, is to know the value of having."
~Aurora

--------------<◇>--------------

15

THE MELCHIZEDEK

Session #229: Recorded in December 2019.

In this online A.U.R.A. Hypnosis Healing session, Nancy finds herself on a mission as a Melchizedek on a 3D planet. Through the spiritual awakening community, we have heard often of the Melchizedek who are a benevolent galactic race. Therefore, it was an honor to be speaking to them to receive these intimate details of their race. Here we learn about their unique journey to volunteer on Earth, their planet, their Twin Flame soul construct, how they work to assist all…and their link to Atlantis. What Creation consists of, duality, Earth's grid, why we should shield…What happens to our vibrational frequency after an A.U.R.A. Hypnosis Healing session? Are there any other negative aliens out there besides Reptilians? We learn more about Archons and the various misconceptions about the Angelics.

"You're not giving them the answers, you're teaching them how to find their own answers inside and that's what a true teacher is."
-The Melchizedek

N: [Nancy] I feel like I got off a spaceship and I am in a very dense forest. There is a lot of green.
A: [Aurora] Go back to when you were getting off the spaceship. You are there now; tell me, what does the spaceship look like?
N: It looks round. It looks like I'm seeing the normal, sort of, a flying saucer.
A: The spaceship, has it landed or is it hovering?
N: We've landed. There's landing gear, like, we've landed. We're on the planet.
A: How do you get off the spaceship?
N: I open the door and I go down the stairs and it's all green here. I'm not sure what planet it is, but it's very, it may be Earth, but I think it's like, a long time ago.
A: Look at yourself, do you feel like you have a body?
N: I feel like I'm in a suit of some kind.
A: Is there anyone else getting off with you?
N: I don't see anyone.
A: Were you the only one on this spaceship?
N: No, I don't think I'm the only one on the spaceship, but I'm the only one who got off. I feel like I'm wearing almost like an environmental suit.
A: What color is it?
N: I want to say it's like a silvery-grey, silver and grey?
A: Look down at your feet. Are you wearing something on your feet?
N: Yeah. It's like a one-piece suit, so it kind of looks like I'm wearing boots.

A: Are there any designs or symbols on any part of your suit?

N: Yeah, it looks like an eagle. (laughter) I just find that amusing, "the eagle has landed." I'm so silly. Yeah, there's like an eagle, like a bird of some type.

A: On your suit?

N: Yeah.

A: What part of the suit is it on?

N: It's the left chest. It's like on my left chest. I'm part of some sort of alliance or something. It's our symbol.

A: Look at your hands. Are they also encased with the suit?

N: Yeah, they're encased, it looks like I'm wearing gloves.

A: How many fingers do you have in the gloves?

N: Four or five. I think five.

A: With this suit, do you have something on your head?

N: I'm wearing, yeah. I'm fully encased. I don't know if the atmosphere is toxic or what, but I am fully encased in my atmosphere suit. So, I got a helmet on too, so I'm not breathing the air of this planet which I'm not sure what this planet is. It may not even be Earth, I don't know.

A: You're able to feel and sense. How do you look under the suit? Do you feel that you are female or male?

N: I can't tell. I don't know... I could be both. I want to say I'm both.

A: How about your face? What does your face look like?

N: Kind of masculine? I'm not sure.

A: What do your eyes look like?

N: Blue-ish green.

A: Do you have hair?

N: Yeah, I think I have facial hair.

A: Are your eyes, average-sized, bigger, or smaller?

N: Normal, they're normal.

A: Your hair, what color is your hair?

N: Brown.

A: How about your skin? What tone is it?

N: Green-ish blue.

A: Your skin is a green-ish blue?

N: Yeah, I'm definitely not a human.

A: How about your ears, how do they look?

N: I guess normal for what I'm supposed to look like. I think they're kind of on the bigger side though.

A: Is there anything you're carrying?

N: Yes. I have a metal case. I'm supposed to take readings. I'm supposed to - we're here investigating the planet and how it's progressing, so I'm supposed to take readings and maybe obtain some biological samples. So, I'm on a research mission, which is what I'm getting. So we're checking up on this planet. It almost feels like it doesn't have an intelligent life yet. It's like a protoplanet. It's very green, so there's definitely plants. I don't know if there are any animals yet, but I think I'm supposed to check on how the planet is doing and its evolution. So, they sent me.

A: Keep moving along and tell me what happens next when you're moving along.

N: I'm sensing something yellow. It looks like a yellow block. A block.

A: Where do you see that at?

N: It's on the planet, but I don't know why it's there.

A: Is it on the ground?

N: No.

A: What is it on?

N: It's in the air. It's floating.

A: A block, like a cube?

N: Yeah, like a cube. It's not supposed to be here.

A: Are there any designs on this cube?

N: I'm just seeing it as a plain yellow block. I'm not seeing any designs on it.

A: As it's floating, does it move, or does it stay still?

N: It's moving around.

A: You mentioned when you landed that it felt like a dense planet. Why did you feel that?

N: Because it is. It's dense.

A: Do you mean that you feel heavy?

N: It's a heavy planet.

A: Is it like heavy energy?

N: The atmosphere is heavy, it's a 3D planet, so they're always pretty dense. Oh, that's why I'm wearing a suit. I see. That's why I'm wearing a suit. It's not really protection against the atmosphere so to speak. It's more that the density of the planet is so heavy. It kind of protects me. Because I come from a lighter…my place is much lighter than this, so this is really heavy for me. So, it's almost like a diving suit. If you were going to go diving and the pressure of the water is so deep. The deeper you go, the more you need to wear that suit to protect your body. That's why I'm wearing the suit. It's a 3D planet.

A: Moving this scene along. What do you do with this cube? You said it is not supposed to be there?

N: I see the cube. It's not supposed to be there. I'm not sure what I do. I take a note of it, I think I want to destroy it though because it's not supposed to be there, so I think I'm going to shoot it. Oh, and I'm going to disable it. That's what I'm going to do. So, I send some electromagnetic pulse to scramble it and then BOOP, it just falls to the ground. I think I'm going to take it with me.

A: How do you send that pulse?

N: I have a, it kind of looks like a gun, but it's not a gun. It looks like an energy weapon. Ray gun. It sends a little pulse out and it fries its circuits.

A: What happens when it fries its circuits?

N: It just falls straight to the ground. I'm going to take it with me when I leave. Yeah, so I'm just checking up on the planet. The yellow thing wasn't supposed to be here, so I disabled it and I'm taking it with me. There's probably more of them, but I can't go hunting across the whole planet. I'll let my team know what I found.

A: What is that?

N: Oh, it's some sort of A.I. thing. It's definitely some artificial intelligence. It's like a drone. That's the best way to say. It's like an A.I. drone.

A: What do you think it was doing? What was its purpose?

N: It's almost like a bee. That's probably a really good analogy for it. It's like an artificial intelligence bee. Well, it's doing reconnaissance, but it's also sort of affecting the environment, too in a negative way. They're trying to screw up the evolution of this planet, so they send these to check up on things, but it's like an annoying bee sting, nuisance type thing. That's what they do, they do it all the time. Yeah. That's part of what they do. That's it, I'm done. I'm going to get back on the ship. I did what I came to do, and I'll let my team know what's going on, but it happens all the time.

A: As you're climbing back onto your ship, tell me, describe everything around you.

N: Everything looks round, it looks pretty round. Yeah, I'm not alone on the ship. Peter is there too and he's just like me, but he stayed on the ship while I went out and did my thing. He's on my team and he's my partner. So, we're going to take off and go back to wherever we're supposed to go because we finished our little research on this planet. I told him about the cube. He's not surprised, we see them all over the place. Sometimes they're different colors though, but we see them everywhere, but there's a lot more of them lately. It's not a good sign. It's quite a bad sign, but there's only so much we can do, so we just have to report it… let the higher-ups know. So, I think we're going to go back to our base of operations and let them know what we found. We're going to give our report. Yeah, that's what we're supposed to do.

A: Go ahead and do that and tell me what happens along the way.

N: Honestly, it's like a space station of sorts. No, it's not a space station, is it? No.

A: What did the outside look like? Before you landed?

N: It's like we're at the Capital. We're someplace important right now. It's almost like this huge, tall, structure. Like this tall, dome like structure. I'm getting a lot of information and I feel like I'm on a space adventure right now. There's a lot coming in.

A: Higher Self, if you could slow down the information so that she's able to speak it. Go ahead.

N: So, we're back on the home planet now. We did stop at a space station, but I don't think any of that stuff is really relevant. We're back at the home planet, there's this huge building, it's like a tall dome almost. It's rounded at the top though. It looks like it's made out of glass. It's really quite pretty. We're going in there.

A: How many are with you?

N: It's just me and Peter right now. It's just the two of us. It feels like it's some sort of Council of something. Some sort of Elder Council. So, I wanted to go talk to them because I'm concerned about this cube situation. I feel like this cube situation is bad news, so I need to go talk to them about it. So, I go. I go and request to speak to them and they'll listen to me. They listen to me. My father, he's on the Council. He's quite amazing.

A: Tell me about your father.

N: He's Melchizedek. The one that we would know here. That's him. That's my father.

A: What does he look like?

N: He's got long, sort of wavy, dark hair, and blue eyes. He feels very tall. He's very wise and calm. A little bit stern, too, but not like in a bad way. He's got quite a presence about him. We are reporting it to him, to let him know what we found on this planet and they already know what's going on, really, we're just sort of like the boots on the ground. We go and do the little investigations and they already pretty much know what's going on, but we just sort of give our bird's eye view of what we saw and everything like that. That's what we do. That's our job; not just here, everywhere. We're the boots on the ground. Yeah, and I come back and report in.

A: How many were with your father?

N: There are seven.

A: Did they all look the same? Melchizedeks?

N: Similar. Yeah, I think so.

A: Describe to me, what exactly is a Melchizedek?

N: What's a Melchizedek?

A: From the presence of them. Who are they?

N: They're blue and green. That's what their color/ray/vibration is. They're blue and green, so imagine you take a blue and green together and mix them together and take all the qualities of a blue ray and then a green ray and you mix them together and that's what they are. So, they're like healer/teachers. They're like Elders of this Universe. They're like an Elder race. You can think of them as helpers of the Angels. You can think of it like that. And then, we're a part of that; Peter and I are part of that, but we're more like the boots on the ground type. And these guys are like Council members, so they're sort of, you know, they have bigger decisions to make and they offer assistance throughout the Universe, really. Especially, I don't know, we seem to be focused on the creation and evolution of planets at this point. And making sure everything is going well, but it's not going that great. We have a huge opposition force.

A: What's going on? What's the opposition?

N: There are lots of them that are opposite. It's like we're on the side of Creation and there are the groups that are on the side of destruction. It's like that. It's a whole universal game we're playing. It gets exhausting sometimes.

A: What was the conclusion or what was to happen, for example, the planet you went to and there were cubes there. What are you going to do about that?

N: I'm not sure because this is the sort of the 'cracks' in the problem. There's only so much we can do because we tend to practice this non-interference policy. You know, because we don't really exert our power. We're just trying to help things along, but the opposition has an interference policy. So, if we sit around and do nothing, then it's not going to be good. We're going to lose, so they got to figure out what they're going to need to do. It's above my pay grade. I just go out and report back on what I see. They need to figure something out... what they're going to do.

A: Very good. Keep moving the scene along and see what it is that you do next of importance. You are there now. What's going on?

N: I feel like I'm talking to my father and I'm just expressing my opinion that we can't keep sitting around and doing nothing or they're going to keep destroying planets or interfering with these planets that are supposed to be developing life and they keep getting messed with. And we can't keep sitting back and doing nothing.

A: When they mess with them what do they do to the planets? Do they stay messed with or are you able to repair them?

N: They do all sorts of different things. Some things we can repair, some things we can't. In the physical we can't be everywhere at once; I mean, I'm talking in the 3D physical. We can't be everywhere at once and we need to be in the physical to help these dense planets. It needs to be a sort of physical type of assistance if that makes any sense. We can't just energetically or etherically help them because they're dense. They're in density. So, we too, need to come into density to assist. Because, you know, we're etheric beings. That's why they sent me here. That's why they sent me and Peter and us here. They sent us in the physical to be dense. To literally be in the density. So, that we can... well some of it is just reporting or its status, so we can affect some sort of change or do something, you know?

A: Do you mean here, on this Earth?

N: I mean here on Earth and here in the physical. I feel they're showing me all this on different planets and stuff like that, to sort of explain, "you do this everywhere and that's why you're here on Earth, too. You're doing the same thing here on Earth, as when you go to these other planets and check in on them. You're doing the same thing here." They're trying to explain to me why I have to come down into the 3D physical. It's what they're doing, that's what my Higher Self is doing. Right now, with this life, that's what my Higher Self is trying to explain to me. In a way that I can get it. Yeah, so what are we going to do with that particular planet? It's you know, it's more of a global issue, really. That's just an example of the global issue. And apparently, their solution was to send some of us here in the physical. That's what they were going to do about it. That was the answer.

A: When they sent you here, what is it that you're specifically doing by being here?

N: I can affect more change here by being in the physical, than just working etherically and energetically.

A: So, they use your physical vessel, you that you are there, to affect?

N: Yes. Yes.

A: Any other details on that?

N: There's more, but I think we're going to get to that later.

A: What do you do next in this life of importance?

N: This life is pretty good. I feel like I got to travel around a lot on my ship. Peter and I got to travel a lot and go to a bunch of different places and do what we were supposed to do. It's a lot of just checking up on places. We had fun though.

A: In this life, you and Peter, what is your relationship?

N: He's like, he's my partner. It's so hard to explain. It's almost like we're brother and sister, but we're not brother and sister. But on a soul level, it's like we're brother and sister. Our relationship goes beyond all of that, he's my partner. He's my partner in the physical, he's my partner on a soul level, he's my partner energetically, etherically, like everything. Like, they made us this way, as partners.

A: Like romantically?

N: Yeah, it includes everything. On every single level, we're partners. Like, we are stuck, literally, stuck together. Literally, we are stuck together, and they made us this way. It's like they made us like twins, we're built together. We're not identical, we're not supposed to be identical. We each sort of have complementing strengths to balance each other out. It's kind of like they built us like... the best analogy is conjoined twins. It's not even a good analogy. They built us as a pair. I will say it like that. They built us as a bonded pair. They built us this way and they send us out on missions together, as a pair and we're supposed to do it together, in two vessels as two units. For a gazillion reasons why, but that's the way they made us.

A: Let's go ahead and leave that scene. Another important time where we will find answers we seek for your highest healing. You are there now. Tell me what you see and sense.

N: I'm getting that they've agreed with us that they need to do more to help and they're sending us to Earth. I think I might learn to keep my mouth shut after this one.

A: Why do you say that?

N: Well, I kept saying we need to do more, then they agreed, sent us here and now look where we are. You know what I mean? I got what I asked for. I'm not sure I liked it, but here we are, nonetheless. So yeah, they're sending us to Earth. There's a bunch of people getting sent to Earth anyhow, it's not just us. Lots of people are going to Earth. Earth, it's like the big show down here. It's like the big show, it's all on Earth right now. You know? They refuse to lose another planet, so, this is it. This is the big one, so here we are. They sent us here.

A: Were there other of your brothers, say from the Melchizedek? Would you be considered Melchizedek as well?

N: Oh, I'm Melchizedek. Yeah, I am.

A: Were there other ones that were sent beside you two?

N: I know that there were seven of us in Atlantis. I know that. I don't know who they are. I don't know if they are still here, but I know originally, there were seven of us there. Yeah, but Peter and I don't count as separate. We count as one unit. So, they don't count us as two, they count us as one. I don't know if the rest are built that way, too, probably. I don't know if they built the other seven like that too. I think each of the Council sent themselves down. So, technically, you know. Melchizedek is my father, but I'm him, too. Do you know what I mean? I'm like a fractal of him. So, I'm like his representative on 3D Earth. Well, Peter and I both are. We're both his representatives.

A: So, would you both be his children?

N: Yeah, in a human sense. In an Earth, human sense, you can say we are his children, but we're really just parts of him incarnated into 3D Earth. We're really him at our highest level, we're him. So, it's like he's our Oversoul, that's the best way to say it. He's our Oversoul and he sends a part of his energy here, to Earth, in these two physical vessels now. As Peter and Nancy. Yes, that's the best way to say it.

A: You mentioned all the Elders did that?

N: Yeah, because there were seven Elders on the Council that I saw on that planet, and there were seven in Atlantis, so it has to be the same seven. It would make the most sense. Yes, but we were etheric in Atlantis. We weren't physical. We were one unit then, we weren't two. That explains a whole lot. At least for her, it does! It's sort of the final puzzle piece for her. She knew a lot about this, but it's good for her to see it from a different level, so it explains a lot for her.

The Higher Self is called forth.

A: Let's go ahead and leave that life now. Can I please speak to the Higher Self of Nancy?

Higher Self: Yes, I'm here.

A: Wonderful, thank you. Am I speaking to Nancy's Higher Self now?

Higher Self: Yes, you are.

A: Thank you. I honor you, thank you, and respect you for all the aid you have given us today. I know that you hold all the records of Nancy's different lives. May I ask questions, please?

Higher Self: Of course.

A: Wonderful. I know she received a lot of answers already, but if you could tell us anything else we need to know as far as what was the purpose of why you took her to that life?

Higher Self: It was good for her to see herself as a non-human and see the missions that she performs. She already knew this but seeing herself performing similar missions in different places in the galaxy. It helps her understand her purpose more. Yeah, and she can see it from a different perspective. It's just further validation and confirmation of things she mostly already knew and now she's just seeing it and getting confirmation by just really seeing it and living it in a different vessel.

A: One of the questions she had was that she feels she's some kind of secret agent or something in many dreams. On different missions, infiltrating a place with dark ones, hiding, pretending to be with them as well. Is this at all connected with this role you showed her?

Higher Self: It's connected with the role, but that's connected with Peter, her twin. We want to get into this after we do the healing. She's looking for a part of him that went missing and she needs to find it. She has to go into dark places to find it. So, she's looking for him. But we want to talk about that after we do her healing. It's all related.

The Body Scan begins.

A: Let's go ahead and start then. Higher Self, if we could start the body scan. Let us know, do you need any aid from the Archangels?

Higher Self: Yeah, we would appreciate assistance from them.

A: What Archangel would you like for us to call forth upon?

Higher Self: We'll call Michael, we work well with him.

A: Very good. Let's go ahead and call. Higher Self, if you could connect us now to Archangel Michael, please. We'd like to speak to him now.

AA Michael: Yes. Yes.

A: Greetings brother. Love you, honor you, and respect you. Thank you for being here.

AA Michael: Yes, of course.

A: The Higher Self has requested your assistance during the body scan. If you could please assist us today?

AA Michael: Of course.

A: Thank you. If we could go ahead, in union with the Higher Self, start performing the body scan on her now. Scan her from head to toe and let me know where it is you would like to start off first. As far as what needs to be healed energetically. Are there any entities?

AA Michael: She's got a heaviness in her head, in her crown chakra and it doesn't appear to be an entity or anything like that.

A: Does it have a consciousness?

AA Michael: Possibly. It's keeping her from 100% full alignment with her Higher Self. So, it's keeping her crown chakra a little bit off, so we'll want to adjust that.

A: If it has a consciousness then it's most likely an entity. So, Michael, can you scan thoroughly? Does it have a consciousness?

AA Michael: I'm seeing those nanites again. I don't know how they keep getting in. She has to go to some pretty dark places. She picks up things sometimes. She's shielding really well, but she's still picking up things.

A: So, when she astral travels or when her soul is not here for example, maybe in different brain waves. When she's going to the dark places, she is then attracting the nanos?

AA Michael: Yes, it's almost like they're magnetically attracted to her. It's almost like they get stuck to her like a magnet. It's the best way to say it.

A: Is that what's in her head then?

AA Michael: It's not in her head, but there's some there. Yeah, they're not having a huge impact, but there's a few there that could be. We can transmute those.

A: The dark energy in her head, can we transmute that with Phoenix Fire?

AA Michael: Yeah, fire will work.

A: It's not an entity, we don't need to talk to it?

AA Michael: No, they're just those little A.I. nanites, where there's nothing to talk to.

A: Let's go ahead and start transmuting that dark energy there in her head and also those nanobots that she has attracted back.

AA Michael: Yes.

A: I know you said that even though she's shielding, there's got to be a solution to this so that she's still able to travel and then not attract these nanobots back to her in this physical vessel. How can we have her securely do what she needs to do beyond the veil and not have to attract it here? ... And we're using the Phoenix Fire now.

AA Michael: Yes. I'm seeing a blue bubble. She needs to use a blue bubble.

A: She needs to use the blue bubble when she's traveling beyond the veil?

AA Michael: Well, she should use it all the time because she doesn't know when she's going to go traveling.

A: So, therefore, she should just set it 24/7?

AA Michael: Yes.

A: Only intents being to make sure it's always active?

AA Michael: Yeah, it will reflect them off. They will bounce off. I mean, she's going to attract things to her, wherever she goes. We can't stop that, but we want them to bounce off her, not attach to her. So, I'm showing her the blue bubble that I'm talking about. It's like an electric blue bubble I'm showing her, so she knows what to do and they'll bounce right off.

A: Therefore, what you're saying is when she's setting up her Love-Light bubbles after she awakes and hours before she goes to bed. She could just set an intent that 24/7 she always has this blue bubble around so that it could bounce off.

AA Michael: Yes, that will help.

A: Good. I know there was a time period after her first A.U.R.A. session that she said she stopped shielding, surrounding herself with Love-Light. If you could tell us, I know we did a R.A.A.H. (Reiki Angelic Alchemy Healing) on her and we cleared the majority of it. If you could explain to her, I think it's important for her to understand. Even though I know she understands, by leaving herself wide open, what kind of infringement occurred to her?

AA Michael: She got sick because the Reptilians poisoned her and that's when she got the abscess, you saw it. Aurora, you saw the handprint she had on her stomach.

A: Yes.

AA Michael: So, they couldn't get in, they couldn't get fully in, but they could still touch her. She didn't know. She didn't know any better. She's sometimes too optimistic and she was thinking that she cleared everything, that she was in a high vibration and nothing could touch her. And in a beautiful, ideal world, there would be nothing to touch her, but we're at war sometimes, so she knows now. She's been quite diligent with shielding now, but she was not always. She didn't know. It was just as simple as not fully understanding and not knowing. She knows now. So yeah, they got in again.

A: The doctors were claiming it was what?

AA Michael: The doctor's claimed her Crohn's disease, which she knew she had already healed, had returned because she had inflammation in her intestines. She had one doctor that told her the truth. It was that the inflammation in her intestines was caused by the abscess that was near it and all her internal organs were inflamed in that area. That she did not have Crohn's disease that was visualizing, but all the other doctors tried to scare her. That's why she's not going back to any of them.

A: Yes, I remember they even had a tube in her. What's that called?

AA Michael: They had put a catheter in her. They had to; she didn't have a choice in that matter. Because they had to drain the poison out of her basically.

A: How did the poison actually get in? What was the initial contact on how that occurred?

AA Michael: She ate something of low vibration and it's like it triggered it because she had the handprints. It was on her stomach and something she ate activated it.

A: Would that be a Reptilian handprint on her stomach?

AA Michael: Yeah, that was there. Yeah, that's gone, that's all gone.

A: Good. Well, thank you for bringing her to me and allowing for us to start the healing for her, as you know they were trying to get her to have all these surgeries and to take all these different drugs. So, I feel so happy for her that she was able to self-heal this.

AA Michael: Of course, thank you for assisting.

A: Thank you. Good. How is the nano looking in her head?

AA Michael: Nanos are looking good. It's mostly cleared out. We're sort of readjusting her crown chakra, but she's got some discomfort in her crown area, but it's ok. She can handle it.

A: Higher Self, just make her feel comfortable while you're realigning that, making that crown chakra nice and strong once more... So, what initially happened here is that, as she was traveling throughout the Universe, this attached to her crown and misaligned the crown? Is this why she was doubting herself and she didn't feel as connected?

AA Michael: Yes. She's battling a lot. She's in battles quite a lot, so she takes on some of that energy with her and it affects her human vessel, and her human vessel is not exactly sure what's going on.

A: I know you mentioned that this goes on throughout the Universe. Some people think that it just goes on in this Earth; some people think that it's going to be completely wiped out after the Ascension.

AA Michael: No. No.

A: Do you have any advice on this, Michael? Perhaps we could hear a little more from the Melchizedek if they are up for it later.

AA Michael: I'm sure the Melchizedek will have quite a lot to say about this later. They're more boots on the ground, so to speak, than I am. This is how the Universe is built. It's the Universe of polarity. There's a lot of information out there about 'The Event' and that polarity is going to get completely eradicated. I'm not going to comment on that actually, it's not for me to comment on, but this one here, Nancy, she's fighting. She's fighting in many different aspects of her. Fighting the good fight, so to speak. So, it's affecting her quite a lot, but it's happening. To answer your question as much as I can, it's the entire Universe. It's not just this planet, no. We know that Earth is special, but it's not that different from any place else really. We know the humans think that the Universe revolves around the Earth, but it doesn't really work that way. (laughter) It's a very important planet, of course, but it's one of many planets, in many galaxies, throughout the entire Universe. And it's quite a big Universe out there, so... this Universe was created with polarity. Black and white, night and day, light and dark, that's the way this Universe was created, so you can say it's a natural byproduct of the Universe.

A: Thank you, Michael. Let's continue with her body scan. What is next that you would like to address that needs healing?

AA Michael: Her throat chakra. It's definitely got some dark spots. She knows, we all know that smoking is not helping her.

A: Can we remove that need, entirely, no longer needing to smoke anymore? Perhaps, making it taste really bad. Just absolutely no attraction to smoking. Can we do that for her?

AA Michael: We can try. It's more complicated than that. All of her issues are more complicated because it's not just her. It's her twin, too. They're stuck together, so, energetically, it's not just her. We can't just heal her, and everything is going to go away because it's not just her energy system that we're talking about here. They're a pair and they both need to get healed at the same time.

A: Could we talk to his Higher Self?

AA Michael: Of course.

A: Let's go ahead and talk to his Higher Self now. Michael, could you connect us to him now?

AA Michael: Yes.

A: Thank you. I'd like to speak to Peter's Higher Self now. Let me speak to him now.

Peter's Higher Self: Yes.

A: Greetings.

Peter's Higher Self: Greetings.

A: Thank you for speaking to us. Love you, honor you, and respect you. We have many questions for you specifically from Nancy, would you be able to answer them for us?

Peter's Higher Self: Of course, we technically share a Higher Self, Nancy and me. On certain levels, we share a Higher Self. On other levels, they're slightly separate. But at the highest level, we share a Higher Self.

A: Yes. Do we have permission to help him no longer want to smoke in whichever manner that we can acquire this for him, so she can stop smoking? Or what can we do about this?

Peter's Higher Self: Yeah, they both need to quit. If one is smoking and the other is not. It's too strong for both of them. It's a very difficult situation here, Aurora. These two, it's not normal. I'll say it's not normal. They're so energetically tied together that... I mean, quitting smoking, she's tried. She's tried so many times and if he's still smoking, it's going to impact her. It's quite difficult for this one. It's a difficult solution, this one. We've been, as terrible as it sounds, we've been mitigating most of the negative effects of the smoking because we know how hard it is for them to quit. We can definitely try, but we feel like right now there's bigger issues to focus on than if they are smoking or not. There's much bigger issues and there are bigger things to heal than this particular thing. This will go away, this will eventually go away, the smoking. She's not going to have a choice soon.

A: Well, perhaps we will talk to you a little later, even though you are one and the same as the Higher Self. We are going to continue the body scan before we continue to ask questions that she has. Thank you.

Peter's Higher Self: Of course.

A: Michael? If you can go ahead and start transmuting those dark spots on her lungs, please?

AA Michael: Yes.

A: Thank you. I know we talked about it earlier, but I want to make sure everything is healed from when she was sick from the abscess. Is everything healed there?

AA Michael: Almost. Not quite, she's got an issue down there. She still gets some inflammation from time to time. She already knows there's another problem in the sacral area and it's in their connection, so it's in their sacral chakra connection.

A: Do you want to go there next?

AA Michael: That's the big issue yeah.

A: Let's go ahead and go. Go now, scan the sacral chakra now and let me know what it is that's going on there. What is holding back? She says she still feels off.

AA Michael: They put something on the cord. So, her and her twin, there's lots of cords between them but they're not bad cords. Energetically, they're connected, but to make more sense, there's a cord in their sacral chakras. Their sacral chakras are connected, their other chakras are, but they put something on the sacral chakra cord between the two of them. They put an implant there. So, it's on the cord. Yeah. There's something there. There's definitely a black implant there and there's something in her uterus.

A: Can we go ahead and start transmuting that implant on the cord?

AA Michael: Yeah. Yes.

A: Using the Phoenix Fire directed towards that direction, making sure that this implant starts transmuting now.

AA Michael: Yes.

A: Tell me, what is in the uterus area?

AA Michael: She got it in the hospital. They had to put something else in her.

A: So, when she got sick and went to the hospital, they put something in her uterus. How did they do that? What is it?

AA Michael: It's like it's stuck in her uterine wall. It looks like a round black thing with legs almost. It's implanted into the uterine wall and it's causing her a lot of discomfort, but it's designed to basically kill any embryo that tries to implant in her uterine wall.

A: Okay, so is that like an A.I.?

AA Michael: It's like an A.I. It's just a simple implant. It doesn't have any intelligence of its own. It's just designed specifically for that. It makes the environment of her uterus too acidic. It does something to the environment of her uterus so an embryo would not implant if it was fertilized. She would just immediately discard it.

A: Can we go ahead and use Phoenix Fire and start transmuting that out of there for her now?

AA Michael: Yes, please.

A: Just let me know whenever she has healed from her crown and then the cord.

AA Michael: The crown is doing better. It's still a little tingly there, but she's going to continue working on the crown chakra.

A: Okay, good. How was it that they inserted that round thing with legs at the hospital?

AA Michael: It was at the first hospital. They had to put a catheter in her and it was in the general area. It's in the same area, it's right above her bladder where they put it. Where the catheter was. Obviously, the doctor doesn't know it was there. When they stuck the needle in her, that thing was attached to it and it migrated to the right place.

A: What part of the needle was it in? The liquid?

AA Michael: In the catheter needle. It's quite a big needle.

A: So, then they placed that on there. Okay, and that's how it entered.

AA Michael: Yeah. It happened at the first hospital because she had gone to two hospitals and she got the same procedure done twice. But the second hospital was much, much better. They were a much better vibration. The first hospital was not good.

A: We are transmuting that out of there now. As we're transmuting that out, Higher Self, can we have Raphael start repairing the uterine wall? Raphael, we love you, honor you, and thank you. Thank you for being here with us.

AA Raphael: Yes.

A: If we could please help the Higher Self, assist in healing her uterine wall, as we are removing dark energy that is causing more acidic energies in her uterine wall. Go ahead and start healing her uterus, and all her reproductive organs, making sure it's nice and strong and healthy.

AA Raphael: Yes, of course.

A: Thank you, Raphael. Thank you, Higher Self.

AA Raphael: She might have to release some energy from there during her physical period. In a month or two because this implant hasn't been in there very long. It's only been in there for a few months, so she might be shedding some of that lining physically for the next period or two, just so she knows. And then, it will all be cleared out. It'll just take just a little while to physically clear that up... just so she knows.

A: Yes. Thank you, Raphael.

AA Raphael: Of course.

A: We are repairing the crown, so if you could assist with that as well Raphael. There is that cord that we are transmuting the implant from. Once it's transmuted, can you go ahead and repair and heal that cord with the Higher Self?

AA Raphael: Yes. That sacral cord is looking much better now between them. Yes, that was infringed upon.

A: Is there something we can do, Raphael or Michael? Going forward so that they cannot infringe upon these cords, so that they won't affect her? Is there something we could set up for her, to help her?

AA Raphael: She needs to do it herself. She's coming into her own power still. She's almost there, she's come quite a long way. So, it's like she's learning to do it for herself, but these bubbles that she's encasing herself in, she's just imagining encasing herself in them. She needs to be encasing them both in them.

A: Him, too?

AA Raphael: Yeah, him too.

A: Does the Higher Self give permission for that?

AA Raphael: Of course.

A: Very good, thank you, Raphael. Can I please speak back to Michael?

AA Michael: Yes.

A: Thank you. Michael, if we can continue the body scan. Let us know what else you would like to repair now and heal.

AA Michael: Let's see.

A: Just to finish the abscess... she just wants to make sure she doesn't have any Crohn's disease?

AA Michael: She has no Crohn's disease. She does have some inflammation in that area that we're going to calm down and she should eat light, healthy foods for the next few weeks. Try not to eat anything too heavy. Just eat light foods, foods that are easy to digest. You know, fruits and whole grains and things. She doesn't have any Crohn's disease, she knows that. It's just the slight inflammation that is still healing from the abscess and the uterine implant. It's causing inflammation in that area. Yes. Once that's transmuted, she should be feeling better. And drink lots of water to flush her system out. Lots and lots of water to flush.

A: Thank you, Michael. Can you also have Raphael just make sure that after you're done healing what needs to be healed in the sacral, that they heal and balance out the sacral chakra and all the chakras while she's there, please?

AA Michael: Yes. Her root chakra looks much better. She was having some issues with it, but it's much better now, so she shouldn't be having any other problems. Aside from that, she looks pretty good, despite everything she's gone through.

A: Let's continue scanning her body. Michael, can you specifically scan for any entities or Reptilian consciousness? We want to make sure we don't miss any.

AA Michael: I don't see any.

A: Wonderful. Yeah, I didn't see any either. Let's go ahead and scan her for any other type of negative technology, implants, hooks portals, anything else.

AA Michael: I don't see anything on her side. There are problems with his side. There's not much else we can do. We can clean up all the cords between them, but without his physical permission, we can't physically do much on his side of the equation. She can, but that's something she can do on her own. That's another story.

A: Can we start that process now? Healing those cords, clearing them.

AA Michael: Yeah, we're going to clean them all up and we're going to do something to them to sort of energize and expand them almost. We can work on the cords between the two of them, that we can do. Yes, we'll do that right now.

A: Thank you, Michael. While you all are doing that, I have a question for you. There are several teachings out there, some spiritual leaders and healers tell people to cut cords. I know, you mentioned right now with their connection, how they have cords together. You all teach me that we all have cords and there are of course healthy and negative ones, but...

AA Michael: These are different. These are not normal soul connection cords that most people have with everybody else. This is something different from these two because of the way they were built. So, when they come into density because they are in two different vessels, two astral bodies, and two etheric bodies, the only way that they can do what they need to do is via these cords. So, they're built this way. These are slightly different. They're cords, but it's a slightly different situation with these two. We're not talking about normal cords you have with other people. These two were built in such a way that... I don't even think cords are the right word, the way they're tangled up together. Yeah, it's a different thing. They're one system, but they're technically two. Think of it as a pair of human conjoined twins that are conjoined at the heart and if you were to separate them, they would both die.

A: Okay, and are all the Melchizedek created like that?

AA Michael: The ones that we sent to Earth are. Yes, but there's not a lot of them. There's only a few, but the ones we sent to Earth we built them this way on purpose. Yes, she doesn't like it, but she has to get used to it. There's nothing she can do to change it.

A: Since we are talking about cords, Michael, what is your advice on cords? Some teach to cut off all cords every day, every night, through invocations, through strong intents. Cut off all cords to say, family members, sometimes children, your own children... cut off your negative cords to the Earth. Actually, some teach to cut off all cords, they say all cords, they don't say just the negative ones. What are your thoughts on that?

AA Michael: Well, you can't really cut off all the cords. We're all connected. Cords are sort of the way we stay connected in our separate vessels and when we're in density. Should you cut negative cords? Sure, of course. If a relationship is causing you too much stress, then yes, of course. You can set intentions to cut cords, you'll never cut... I mean, it's like a mother and child; you can't cut that cord. It's like these two. There are certain cords you can't cut, you just can't.

So, you're not going to accidentally cut those and you're not going to intentionally cut them either. They can't be cut, so there are certain cords that cannot be cut and those you don't have to worry about, but we would recommend cleaning them. You can clean the cords, especially the cords that cannot be cut, between family for example, or mother and children. Why you would want to cut those, we're not sure, but you can clean the cords and that has an effect. As we saw right now, the cords can get infected. So, it's not that the cords themselves are bad. Obviously, if there's a negative situation in your life and you feel there's a cord there, you can cut them. Some cords are created negatively and maybe with black magic or things like that. Those should definitely be transmuted. If you look, you can see those black cords. They look different. The cords should look golden, they should look like a golden color. For example, Nancy can scan the relationship between her and her mother, and she can see a golden cord. Now, if she were to see a black cord, that would need to be transmuted. That's a bad cord, but if you see a golden cord, then that's the proper kind of cord and you can clean it or check for infringement on the cord itself. That's our recommendation. Everyone should do what's right for them, but there are some cords that you cannot cut, you will never cut. Yes.

A: So, the proper teachings for the person's highest good would be not to cut off all cords, even some can't be cut no matter how hard you try. However, just to work on the negative cords, cut them, heal them and transmute them when needed?

AA Michael: Yes.

A: Michael, can you scan for any fragmented soul pieces that need to be regained to her?

AA Michael: She doesn't have any. He's got a bunch.

A: Is there anything we can do to assist him?

AA Michael: Yeah, we can return those. It's permissible.

A: Thank you. Higher Self, if we can go ahead and have Michael find those and repair them back to his soul with his permission, please.

Higher Self: Yes.

A: Thank you. How many did Michael find?

Higher Self: Five of them.

A: Okay, good. So, we'll have Michael do that. Higher Self, did she need any more age regressed or DNA reprogramming?

Higher Self: No more age reversal, we can do a little DNA reprogramming with her. She goes into the self-doubt far, far too much and beats herself up too much. Some of it is literally in her DNA from her family. Those programs need to be removed; she needs to stand in her power fully now.

A: Wonderful. Will you do that for her now?

Higher Self: Yeah, we're going to do that right now.

A: Is there anything else we could do for her as far as her healing? Scan her one more time.

Higher Self: I just want to send as much light to her reproductive area because that's been infringed upon quite a lot.

A: If we can all send light to that area now... How's the crown looking now?

Higher Self: Much better.

A: Good. That one cord that had the implant on it?

Higher Self: That's all cleaned up and we cleaned up the rest of their cords. Those look good.

A: That one circle thing with legs on her uterine wall?

Higher Self: That's gone. Yeah, we just want to heal that tissue around there and that general area. That's what we're doing now, just sort of reducing some of the inflammation there.

A: Wonderful. In her original A.U.R.A. Hypnosis Healing session, she did have a Reptilian. I can't remember if she had any other entities, but then after her A.U.R.A. session, even though she wasn't setting the intents of Love-Light, the only thing they could do to her as I saw through the R.A.A.H. as well, as you mentioned, they put a Reptilian handprint on her. So, tell me, what is the difference now that she's had an A.U.R.A. session? Why can they not attach a Reptilian or an entity to her?

Higher Self: Incompatible vibration. Her base vibration, it raised significantly. So, she still has some weak spots like her sacral area. It was still a weak spot, but her base vibration shifted to a point where it was incompatible. It's quite interesting, it was too much light for them to handle. It's like they feed off of it, but then if it's too bright, it's like the sun was too bright for their eyes. That Reptilian attachment she had, that was from her Egyptian life so that wasn't even from this life either.

A: Yes, because typically, if a person went through all the trauma that she went through at the hospital; we would have found an entity or Reptilian within her, that's why I was asking.

Higher Self: Oh, no. She picked up a bunch of stuff from the hospital, which you helped clear a lot of it in the R.A.A.H. She had some spider attached to her third eye, but she didn't have an actual entity inside of her. No, that's not going to happen again. It's not possible anymore. They can't get in like that, no.

A: The reason I was asking is that I was seeing something similar to what you said. That her frequency reached a level that wouldn't allow the density to attach itself anymore. Like a specific Reptilian or an entity.

Higher Self: Yes, that's correct.

A: But she still needs to do her work though, right?

Higher Self: Of course. Obviously, the A.U.R.A. session helped tremendously, but there's more to it than that because she's embodying her Higher Self. So, she's learning to embody that high vibration, too.

A: Wonderful. Thank you. Higher Self, now that we completed the body scan, is there anything that you would like for us to do in regard to Peter?

Higher Self: Yeah, he needs healing.

A: Let's go ahead and start focusing now on Peter and his Higher Self.

Higher Self: Yes.

A: Thank you once more. If you could tell us, what is it that we're allowed to aid him and ultimately, trying to aid her?

Peter's Higher Self: He has an implant in his lower back. She can see it. That one we can transmute. It's in his lower back, like right in the hip area, so it's almost like it keeping his lower body stuck. That we can address, we can transmute that, yes.

A: Should I use the Phoenix Fire in that direction?

Peter's Higher Self: Yes, please.

A: Very good, doing that now... What else can we heal for him?

Peter's Higher Self: Oh, boy. I'm trying to see what we're allowed to do. There's something in his neck area, in the back of his neck.

A: What is it?

Peter's Higher Self: It's like a metal bar. We're trying to show her... this is something strange. I'm not sure what it is, to be honest with you. I just know it's not supposed to be there.

A: Can we have Michael scan it for you to help us understand what it is?

Peter's Higher Self: Yes. I can see it... it's like it has teeth on it and it's stuck in the back of his neck, but it's all metal. It almost looks like a comb. It's a very strange device that they've put in him. I haven't seen too many of these. It's not from around here. It's from somewhere else, a different group. He's been getting up to some things, too, so he got tagged with something.

A: Was that when he was here on Earth or when he was traveling?

Peter's Higher Self: I think this came from somewhere else, not from Earth.

A: Can we use the Phoenix Fire and have Michael start removing it?

Peter's Higher Self: No, we don't want to use fire on this.

A: What should we do?

Peter's Higher Self: We need to remove it, but almost like we need to do surgery to remove it. We can't just put fire to it. It needs to be surgically removed. I can have Raphael help and sort of delicately untangle it and remove it.

A: Go ahead and start that process, please.

Peter's Higher Self: Yeah, we'll do that. Yeah, and I can see an entity on his third eye. It looks like a spider.

A: Is that an entity that I would need to speak to, or can we just go ahead and remove it?

Peter's Higher Self: It looks like an A.I. spider, so we can just remove that. Yes.

A: We will use the Phoenix Fire on that?

Peter's Higher Self: That one we can use fire, yes.

A: Okay, using Phoenix Fire in that direction now... Let me know once it's removed.

Peter's Higher Self: Yeah.

A: It's removed?

Peter's Higher Self: Yeah, the spider is gone.

A: Let me know when Raphael and Michael have removed that from the back of his neck area.

Peter's Higher Self: Yeah, that shouldn't take too long. Just a little bit.

A: Higher Self, is there anything else we can help him heal?

Peter's Higher Self: Yeah, they've been tampering with his reproductive organs as well.

A: What can we do there? Let us know what there is.

Peter's Higher Self: I don't see anything there, but I just feel like we need to send him healing there. I don't think there's anything to transmute. I don't see anything.

A: Let's go ahead and send some healing then.

Peter's Higher Self: Yeah, well their sacral area has been quite a mess.

A: Anything else we can heal for him, Higher Self?

Peter's Higher Self: We need to do some work on his crown chakra.

A: As we are removing all these things, ensure that we have the Higher Self and Raphael fill in Love-Light to those areas. Thank you.

Peter's Higher Self: Yes.

A: What is within the crown that we need to heal?

Peter's Higher Self: It's like a spinning vortex. It's spinning, but it's off. It's not spinning correctly. We're just going to adjust the rotation of that so it's more aligned. Yeah, we'll do that, that's what we need to do.

A: While you all are doing that… Higher Self, is there anything else we have permission to help him heal?

Peter's Higher Self: His heart chakra doesn't look so good, but that's not really that surprising. Let's just send him some Love-Light there. There's not a ton that we can do there. We'll send him some Love-Light and then she's going to have to help him with that. That should be it. They're still taking that comb out. It's quite an odd piece of machinery so they're almost done with that. They look better, they're looking better.

A: Good, continue the process while I go ahead and speak back to her Higher Self, please?

Peter's Higher Self: Yes, of course.

A: Thank you Higher Self of Peter, for allowing all that healing for him.

Higher Self: Yes, I'm here.

A: Wonderful. She has some other questions; I'm going to start asking those for her okay?

Higher Self: Yes.

A: Some of these things you have already answered for her, like she says she cannot consistently maintain a high vibration, or she really just wants to go back home. You showed us her home already. She's sad. Anything else you want to tell her? Why does this keep happening?

Higher Self: Well, some of it is just her still shedding her own density that she's picked up on. You know, the planet and being here for a while, all her lifetimes. Some of it is her own density, but some of it is her twin, too. She has trouble connecting with him sometimes in the physical and that's caused a lot of heartache for her. Some of it is their connection. Yes.

A: She says her mission seems to be purely energetic. She doesn't seem to be doing anything physical. Is this how it's meant to be?

Higher Self: It's how it has been. It's not how it's always meant to be.

A: She wanted to know who came to her in the dream where she was looking for her husband and they told her to wait a minute.

Higher Self: I came to her. The Melchizedeks came to her. I told her to wait a minute because she was going far too fast and she wasn't ready yet.

A: Is she now at the pace she needs to be going?

Higher Self: She's almost there.

A: She had a dream something was snipped from her lungs. What was that about?

Higher Self: There was something in her throat and we removed it. It wasn't supposed to be there, and we removed it for her. It was more energetic than actually physical. It wasn't anything physically in her throat. It was something energetic, something she picked up again in one of her travels. She's had many times in a dream where it feels like she's pulling a piece of string stuck in her throat and it's trying to pull something out. We've removed all of that, so it shouldn't bother her anymore. It was like an energetic string or cord that was in her throat that didn't need to be there anymore.

A: She wanted to know if she can heal her cat, Joanna, of her feline asthma?

Higher Self: We can definitely help with it. Yeah, her lungs are very inflamed. There's some calcification there. We can definitely assist with Joanna; she's been a very good companion and alleviate that to some extent. Yes, we can help with that.

A: She wanted to know if we could please send healing energies to her pets as well.

Higher Self: Of course, of course.

A: She also wanted to know who is sending love songs to her in her head?

Higher Self: Peter is. The highest part of him that's not stuck or lost or infringed upon. She connects to the highest part of him and then she connects to the dense version of him. The two do not always correspond, but the highest part of him is sending those messages and that's the voice in her head. And that's the next question, too. She knows it's him, she doesn't want it to be him sometimes. She doesn't, but it's not easy.

A: She wants to know why she is even here anymore?

Higher Self: She's still on her assignment, she's still on her mission, that's why she's here. It's not going as quickly as she wanted it to go, but things rarely do. Sometimes she's a little too gung-ho and "let's go get them" and that's when Peter is more of an asset as he is more like, "wait, let's think this through for a minute before we just go get them." She needs to go through the process a little bit and he's being too overly analytical and overthinking. They need to balance each other out. It's like they're two divine beings that are stuck in density and trying to remember who they are and what they're doing here. One of them remembers more than the other one and is trying to get the other one to see the light. He has lost his way, a little bit, but it's like they're both still pulled toward each other. They can't do anything about it, they really can't. It's quite an adventure with those two, it's quite an adventure. We're not sure if we answered the question.

A: Well, is she cursed in love?

Higher Self: No, she's not cursed in love. She's definitely not. She's had her heart broken a bunch of times and she's sort of played that Earth love game and she's quite honestly sick of it all. But she's not cursed in love, no. Feels like that sometimes, but she's not.

A: She wanted to know if the Melchizedeks would like to speak? Could we perhaps speak to her father? Would that be a good choice? Do they have a message?

Higher Self: Well, you're speaking to me, so technically you're speaking to the Melchizedeks. Yes, we've been speaking this whole time.

A: Very good, thank you. She wanted to help the infringement, specifically the 3D planets that she explained and those cubes that were found. She said the only way for her to help was for her to come down with him and why would that be the solution? To come down to Earth? This Earth out of everywhere or how is that related? If you could answer on how that would actually aid this infringement upon the Universe?

Higher Self: How is it related? Well, I mean, the Earth is a heavily infringed upon planet and it's basically gotten to the point where things were getting so out of balance - in the wrong way - that we needed to save Earth, to tip the scales back the other way. We had to intervene this time.

A: Would you say that this in a sense is considered one of the densest planets and that's why there's so much focus on it?

Higher Self: I don't think it's one of the densest. There are definitely denser planets. I understand what you're asking, why the Earth. I don't think I have the answer for you. From our perspective, where we are, we think of all planets equally. We can't say the Earth is more special than any other planet because we don't see it that way. She's been to many planets doing this. The life she saw was a planet before intelligent life was on it. It was just a planet full of plants and green life, there weren't human people on it yet. This is part of what she does. She's witnessed the Ascension of other planets before, in this galaxy and others. So, she's been there for example, when the Pleiades ascended. She would be there for something like that. She's witnessed it before, right now is the time of the Earth's Ascension, so she's here for that. She helps clean up some of the infringement that's happening at the same time because she's a go-getter. That's just what she does and part of who she is.

A: Thank you for that. And is there any particular message that the Melchizedek has for Earth?

Higher Self: Just that we're here with you. We're here too. You're not alone in any of this. We're helping where we can. We tend to stay on the quiet side. You probably won't see one of us making YouTube videos or anything to sort of advertise who we really are. We've kept her identity hidden as best as we could for a very long time. We're here, we're just not very loud, so to speak. We're a bit quiet. We're not saying people can't channel us; they can channel us, obviously, we're not as chatty as the Pleiadeans. We're a bit quieter. We've been here for quite a while. We've been on Earth for a very long time.

A: Thank you. This home she went to, this planet, was that home of the Melchizedek?

Higher Self: That's sort of our base of operations, you could say, in this part of the galaxy. That was our base of operations, but I don't think that's our home though. We're not tied to any planet in particular. We weren't born on a planet, we're born etherically. So, we didn't evolve and ascend on planets as other races do. We were just birthed energetically, very close to the beginning, so we've been around for a while. But we will incarnate on planets and send representatives of us into different densities and onto different planets. Our group, we're not tied to a planet at all; we're just energy.

A: How she described you all, do all the Melchizedeks look like that with the blue-green skin?

Higher Self: If we were to show her the Melchizedeks, which we've shown her before, she would see that it looks like a nebula in the middle of the galaxy, in the middle of space with stars. It would be a nebula of a really pretty blue and a really pretty green. That's what we are, we're that energy. We're an energetic collective that can incarnate onto planets or into different densities. We're pure energy at the heart of what we are. I suppose everybody is, but that's what we are. We're a blue-green energetic collective. That's what the Melchizedek is, yes.

A: Any other of your sacred wisdom or teachings you can share with us?

Higher Self: Well, the seven we sent to Atlantis, they put some of their knowledge and wisdom into these statues. All the light codes and energy and the wisdom that was in those statues, it's now in the Earth grid. We had to wait for the Earth grid to be repaired and it's sufficiently repaired. All the wisdom and the knowledge are there and it's available, so anybody can tap into it. All they have to do is set the intention for it and it's there.

A: Beautiful. Very good.

Higher Self: She doesn't even know what's in there, but it's there!

A: Wonderful. Okay, so at this point, I've asked all her questions, we've conducted her body scan. Is there anything else that I could have asked that I haven't?

Higher Self: We don't want to scare or frighten people, but there are other things out there that are worse than Reptilians. She's starting to get some information about that right now. She doesn't even know much of what's going on, but there are other things out there that are the "puppet masters," that's the best way to describe them. I wouldn't be surprised if more information starts coming out in general about this. If you think about it, she's the boots on the ground and the Reptilians are like the boots on the ground, but there are higher levels of these things. Even on the light side, there are higher levels of what's going on. The same thing is happening on the other side. The Reptilians are what they are, but they're not the only ones that are on the dark side.

A: Would you say there are some more powerfully magical, stronger, and more intelligent?

Higher Self: I would say, yes. I would say that they are the polar opposite of the Archangels. They could be that powerful. I think you guys call it something like that of an Archon. I'm not sure, but she's getting a slight glimpse of it right now, that there's more going on here than what meets the eye.

A: Yes, we've been talking about Archons lately through our channel.

Higher Self: Yeah, I think everybody blames the Reptilians for everything and there's more going on than just them. You've done a lot of great work with them because so many of them have just lost their way. It's wonderful to see all the work you've done working with them.

A: Thank you.

Higher Self: Yes, we appreciate that.

A: Thank you and I appreciate you all for your beautiful work too, as the Melchizedek that you are, aiding humanity and the Universe.

Higher Self: Thank you. We do what we do. That's what we do, yes.

A: Would you be able to share any more information on Archons? Is this possible?

Higher Self: We're not sure if Archon is the right word for what we're describing, but I think it's close enough. They're like the unseen puppet masters that are secretly pulling all the strings, and everybody is focusing on the Reptilians "oh, the Reptilians are doing that, the Dracos are doing this." There are lots of other ET races that are negatively polarized, but we already know that. Some of them are quite powerful, but I'm sensing a very, like the birthing of the Universe, ancient darkness. Very old, very ancient, very powerful it's unfathomable, really, what it is. I'm not sure how it's related to everything or how much I can say about it, but it's out there and it's real and it exists.

A: What are your thoughts, can you tell me if you can answer this or not. I was listening to a channel that is well known, and I've always loved her information. I'm not allowed to listen to many channels, but this one I was able to listen to some of her sessions just because there was information that I needed to listen to that basically matched my information. Through this channel, this person claimed that the Archons were an Angelic virus. To me, something felt really off with that. It just didn't feel good. Do you have any information you can share on that?

Higher Self: That Archons are an Angelic virus?

A: Mm-hmm. Like an A.I. virus?

Higher Self: An A.I. virus?

A: That would be angelic.

Higher Self: It can't possibly be Angelic if it's an A.I. virus (chuckle).

A: Exactly.

Higher Self: It doesn't work that way (more laughter). What we're saying is, it's possible for there to be negatively polarized energies, entities, beings, etc. that have as much power as Angelics. It's a different power, but of the same level. That's what we're talking about, but no.

A: Yes, I sensed strong infringement upon that channel. I felt like A.I. was trying to infiltrate my auric field from just listening to this miscommunication. I know how to transmute it, but I can't imagine the thousands and thousands listening, how it would affect them listening to something like that felt so infringing.

Higher Self: That's quite unfortunate, but everyone has to learn discernment and go with their gut feeling of "this doesn't sit right with me." People shouldn't be believing everything anybody says anyhow. Even if they're their favorite reader in the world, you have to have your own thoughts. Nobody has all the answers. You can sense it though, Aurora, when it's that A.I. technology. If somebody is standing in their power, they can see it. It's pretty obvious. Most humans are blind to it because it's everywhere. It's on the TV, on the internet, it's everywhere obviously. If you really stand in your power, you can see it for what it is and dismiss it and it has no effect on you. Don't give it any power, it has no power over you.

A: Yes. So, we ended up making a video to help out the situation about this infringement upon Angelics. What you just said is what we explained. It can't be Angelics if it's A.I., there's no way. The two don't intertwine with one another. I realized through that frequency that it was very dense because this person has a large number of followers. You could feel it in the collective energies of the Earth how it was really infringing on people's thought forms about the Angelics. As you know, we are here to save humanity, just as the Melchizedek is here as well. There were even people in the comments saying, "What am I going to do? I call for Archangel Michael to protect me all the time." You know?

Higher Self: That's so awful. It's amusing because when Nancy first had her awakening, she was posting every YouTube video she could find, regarding anything negative, saying "call Archangel Michael, everyone should be calling Archangel Michael." (laugher) Call him because if you call him from your heart, he will show up every time. There's no doubt about it.

A: Oh yes!

Higher Self: Always... It's awful, we're not sure what to say. I think it's going to get to a point, though, that it gets so obvious to the people who are listening to their heart and doing the work and have their eyes and ears wide open. It's going to become so obvious "this doesn't feel right" if the message has become infringed upon. I think everybody needs to be listening to themselves. Nancy stopped watching pretty much every single video out there, she still watches yours, but she stopped watching everything. She doesn't need somebody to tell her what's going on energetically because she knows what's going on energetically because she feels it. She's connected to the energy, so she knows what's going on. I think that a lot of people in the awakening community need to get out of the "looking for a guru" mentality. Sometimes, we're lost, and we need help, but then you get to the point where you grow in your own power. You say, "I'm able to connect, I'm able to get the answers that are right for me." Somebody like you, the best thing you're doing is teaching people how to do that. You're not giving them the answers, you're teaching them how to find their own answers inside and that's what a true teacher is.

A: Thank you.

Higher Self: Not somebody who gives you the answers, somebody who helps you find the answers that are already inside of you. That's it, that's all we can do.

A: I thought it would be important to hear that from a Melchizedek. As I guess we humans call it, your reputation is very sacred, so thank you for that information.

Higher Self: Yes, they have an entire Priesthood dedicated to us.

A: Really?

Higher Self: Yes. The Order of Melchizedek Priesthood (laughter).

A: Oh, alright. Is Nancy going?

Higher Self: It's funny. She doesn't need to join.

A: I'm kidding.

Higher Self: She's met a few people who have been in it and she finds it quite amusing. I'm not even sure what they do. We, like you, try to stay in integrity and honor. We do the best that we can with what we have.

A: Thank you for that. Well, it's been a wonderful session. Thank you for all the beautiful healing for her, first of all and her connection. Finally, she's able to get those answers. I know that you shared much with her with the sessions or even when she came to the readings with me, but this has really connected it all for her. May she find a beautiful balance in her life so that she can understand the bigger picture and not let it allow for it to weigh her down.

Higher Self: Yes, it was a wonderful session.

A: It is a wonderful session. Well, a joy it is. Thank you to Michael, Raphael, the Higher Self, the Melchizedek. Thank you to everyone who assisted today with the beautiful healing that she needed. Is there anything else you would like to say before we bring her back?

Higher Self: No, we are complete. We just want to thank you, Aurora, for all of your assistance with her. We know she's had a few sessions with you at this point, so we just want to thank you for all the assistance that you've given her. We truly appreciate it.

A: Well, thank you. I believe in her just as much as you all believe in her. She is phenomenal and extremely gifted and very connected. Thank you.

Higher Self: Yes. Thank you.

A: Wonderful. Shall I bring her back now?

Higher Self: Yes.

A: I love you, honor you, and respect you. Thank you to everyone.

END OF SESSION

-------------<◇>-------------

This beautiful session was powerful, full of knowledge, and enlightenment. It is an honor to speak to some of these benevolent galactic groups that have volunteered to incarnate on Earth knowing very well the challenges that come with the journey. The process of what it is like before these Starseeds volunteer to come to Earth. For example, how she and her Twin Flame had to split and take the chance that perhaps one of them would become lost to the density of Earth. It is a joy that we were able to assist through this session in some way to her other half, to hopefully alleviate some of what she has to go through every day feeling their Earthly disconnection. However, still feeling him in the Universe intimately connected daily.

Here we also learn about some of what goes on when we 'Beings of Light' go to the doctors who are controlled by the healthcare system driven by money and profiting from us being perpetually ill. Of course, all part of the system of harvesting our energy and maintaining us as subordinates. We have learned through these sessions that the body is made to self-heal. However, it has been programmed into us that we require others to help us heal as we are not adequate or knowledgeable enough to know how to, without obtaining an indoctrinated expensive professional degree. They program us to believe that we need bioengineered prescriptions, replacements of our bone structures with metals, organs completely removed... We are no one's experiments, and the world is beginning to wake up to this through the Covid-19 pandemic that is occurring in the now. We are now remembering the power of our sovereignty, unlocking our infinite self-healing abilities.

This powerful session also brought us more knowledge of the negative infringements and entities that exist in Creation, and how much farther they reach than we have been told. There are much far worse negative aliens out there besides Reptilians. Here we learn that Reptilians are just "boots on the ground," and they are being controlled by higher level beings, even darker entities also known as "Archons." These Archons are stronger, faster, exude intelligence and wield black magic with ease. Containing just as strong abilities as the Archangels themselves. Reminding us how important it is that we set daily intentions of "NOT CONSENTING" for others to harm us, by intentionally creating force fields of Love-Light around us, like the blue bubble shield mentioned for Nancy.

In this Universe of polarity, force fields of intentions of Love-Light are essential because we are the densest planets in the third dimension. Our guides, angels, and soul families are benevolent in nature, therefore they cannot overstep our free willed expression when making decisions within our own timelines, whether purely or falsely lead. Therefore, we must ask for assistance, guidance and Love-Light shielding daily. They cannot overstep our boundaries as benevolent beings by nature. The faster we accept this, the easier it becomes for us to be able to reach the frequency of surrender, creating and allowing our lives to flow with divine guidance.

It is important that we discuss the truths of the Angelics, as much information is infringed upon and backwards in our awakening communities. Often, I have clients coming to me, who don't believe in Angels or don't trust them. The Archons have played a well-crafted game of misinformation, that either "Angels do not exist and if they do, they are elite to us. And since they are elite to us, they are who maintain us stuck here." As we know through these teachings of the Higher Selves' stories, that this is farthest from the truth. As the Archons are actually the ones who maintain us stagnant with their A.I. infringements and have done it very well. But no longer will this be the case, as we are awakening so rapidly that the Archons can barely keep up with us. We hold the key, as the flames within our hearts are the love weapons to transmute them to void.

As told through forms of varieties of bibles and religions, there is some truth through the knowledge that God Source created the Angels first. The Angelics/Elohim/Elokim were the first fractals of Source that individualized out from the collective infinite Consciousness of Source. Because of this, all souls within the Twelve Dimensions and below at some point in time in their beginning birthing stages, their soul originally stemmed forth from the Angels. Which means that we all contain Angel essence within us, and ALL can tap into this infinite power of Love-Light the Angels contain of protection and healing. By being of this infinite Source beginning fractals they hold the greatest strength of Love-Light power. Which is why when the Higher Selves of our clients can't heal or remove something, which is why THEY can. Therefore, they can be seen as the Gods of this Universe, though they do not like to be labeled this, as they see themselves and all lives as equal brethren. Within our Galactic Universal construct, we reach up to the Thirteenth Dimension, which converts into becoming the bridge out from this construct and into the higher Dimensions of the Universes. Understanding that Source is ZERO and ALL infinite possible dimensions in Creation.

Our deepest gratitude to the Melchizedek for bringing further into our awareness all that was mentioned within this session, and special honorable thanks to Nancy and Peter for their bravery and perseverance in knowing and wanting to help Earth and the souls within it, despite its challenges. The multitude of 'Starseeds' who have answered the call of Earth, are the TRUE heroes of the Universe!

"Human:
I cannot trust this being, because I heard this of them through so and so…

Angel:
Are you sure you want to trust the negative polarized entities that expressed their hatred, by using that trusted person of yours as a channel?"
~Aurora

-------------<◇>-------------

16

COMPROMISED FOR A BILLION YEARS

Session #191: Recorded in September 2019.
Special Series: 1 of 4

This is the first of a very special series of four sessions which teaches us in-depth of what it is like to accept the role of being negatively polarized. We have heard plenty from the client's side about their experiences with Reptilian infringements and attachments, and now we get to listen to the Reptilian's side.

In this online A.U.R.A. Hypnosis Healing session, Hailee - English is her second language - finds herself inside a hidden mountain not understanding her surroundings. Why is she there, what happened to her and her memories after? Here she shares with us a detailed experience of a compromised soul and the journey to regain back her free will, the key being through her memories. Here we learn how fear and guilt hold us back across several lifetimes.

-------------<◇>-------------

"That is quite a gift, a miracle, a magical thing. For a being to be this controlled for that long, like they said billions of years, but yet she's here."
-Aurora

"There are so many others, which we could help with this. They are forced so hard, for such a long time. We can heal them."
-Higher Self

-------------<◇>-------------

H: [Hailee] I don't know, but I feel shaken and frightened.
A: [Aurora] Let's investigate. Find out why you feel shaken and frightened. Look all around you. Describe what is all around you.
H: It's cold.
A: Do you see anything else besides feeling this cold?
H: At first, I thought I'm in the dark, in a room under, down under, which is closed. And I'm there, lonely.
A: So, you feel like you're in a room down under?
H: Yeah, but it's not a room, it's like a cage.
A: Feel what's around you.
H: I see rocks, and this cage is not natural, it's made. First, it was very, very small but it's getting bigger now.
A: Do you feel that there is anyone else in the cage with you?
H: Yeah, but I'm afraid to go there. I try to hide.
A: Outside the cage, do you sense that there is anyone outside the cage?

H: On the one side there's no possibility to go out because there's a cliff, like a big mountain, but it goes down to the sea. You can't go outside there. You need a shuttle.

A: In this cage do you feel like you can stand up and move around? Tell me what's going on.

H: I'm seeing people on jet skis. But in snow. Not in snow. I don't know. But not on water.

A: Are they outside the cage?

H: Mm-hmm.

A: Where is the cage exactly standing on? What surface?

H: It's a volcano or something, I don't know. In a volcano.

A: How do the people on these ski-jets look?

H: They have, I can't really see them because they have shields or arms, like armor, like a knight. I can't really see the faces.

A: Do you feel that they're positive or negative? How do you feel towards them with you being in this cage, and them being out there?

H: Outside, I just feel like an observer and they don't see me. And inside, I feel like a detective. And I have to be careful that they can't see me. So, because I'm frightened, I think they are not good. I'm afraid that they will see me in the cage.

A: You said that you do feel perhaps someone else in the cage. Let's see who else is in there?

H: I see a helicopter. I see an energy shield, which is a door to the outside.

A: This is outside the cage?

H: No, the helicopter is inside. There are robots, big robots.

A: Inside or outside?

H: Inside, it's a huge cage, a huge cage system. It's big inside.

A: Tell me, what do the robots look like?

H: Like human beings, but really, really big, I mean like The Terminator (movie character).

A: Do they have skin like a human then?

H: Nope.

A: What do they have?

H: The naked Terminator. Like...

A: Like metal, you mean?

H: Yep.

A: Is it like a hard metal or is it like a liquid metal?

H: No, it's hard.

A: They are big, you said?

H: I saw one and I feel like it's ten meters. So really high!

A: You said that outside the cage they can't see you, how about inside?

H: I don't know if they see me, but I am afraid that they could see me. Outside I was safe. I don't know why I'm not safe inside. But inside I'm always hiding against or behind something. I'm watching what's happening. There are also others, but there's this one big robot. I don't know like spiders, but machines? They are grabbing into the Earth.

A: They are doing what to the Earth? Do you mean digging?

H: Digging. Yeah! Digging. Right, digging.

A: Are the spiders big as well?

H: Bigger than me, but smaller than the big one. No, no, no, they are not so big! They are smaller.

A: Would you say that they are an organic species or robot-like, like the robot?

H: First I thought they are robots too, but now they are more like ants, so living beings.

A: Look at their arms, perhaps.

H: I see red eyes. They are searching for something, I think.

A: Higher Self, keep her invisible to all this. Keep her invisible from them seeing her. Thank you... With the Higher Self's permission, we'd like to call on Archangel Michael to help keep her invisible. Can we do that?

Higher Self: Mm-hmm.

A: Thank you. Okay, now you said that these spiders are digging into the Earth. Would you say that it's a few spiders or many?

H: I just see one, and where it is digging, there's light. Light comes out of the floor of the Earth.

A: The big robot, what is it doing?

H: He's still like, even though he's big, he's not smart. And he is learning how to move, to walk. He's a little bit clumsy (laughs).

A: Does he have anything he's carrying with him?

H: No, can't see anything.

A: Look at yourself. Are you wearing anything?

H: There's something for protection.

A: Do you mean that you have energy protection around you?

H: Yeah, yeah. It is a shield, but also an energy shield, but also a body shield.

A: What do you look like?

H: I don't know, maybe I am that energy shield? I'm shaking!

A: Why are you shaking?

H: I don't know, I feel hot and cold at the same time.

A: Besides the robot and the spider, is there any other life there with them?

H: I see an alien head. You know, like the alien films with the big head in the back.

A: Like a gray?

H: Mm-hmm. But I don't see the body, just the head. But it's a light blue color.

A: It has light blue skin?

H: Mm-hmm.

A: Is it just one or more?

H: I just see one head and he's shaking his head like me. (moves head side to side)

A: So, let's go ahead and fast forward this scene. Let's fast forward a bit to see when something changes.

H: There's a big huge ship inside the volcano, everybody's in and it's dark. I'm not in the ship, I can see how it shifts up.

A: Tell me what the ship looks like.

H: Like a U.F.O.

A: Is it round?

H: Yeah, it's round.

A: What is this U.F.O. doing?

H: It shifts up from the ground. It's staying there and then slowly goes and flies out of the cave of the volcano, and then it's flying away very fast. It feels like they are using something like a warp system, and it feels like I go with them there but I'm not in the ship. I'm directly behind them and I go with them through this warp journey.

A: Through the warp, is there a technology holding that warp together? Where did that warp appear from?

H: I don't know.

A: It just appeared in the air?

H: Mm-hmm.

A: Okay. And then you follow, and where is it that they end up? As you're going through the warp, how does that feel?

H: The Universe, the stars, the skies. There are so many planets and systems, lights, energies flowing around, flying around me, sparkling.

A: Are you still with that ship that flew out of there?

H: That ship is gone.

A: Now you are just in space?

H: Mm-hmm.

A: Look at yourself now, how do you look? Do you still look the same?

H: I don't know, maybe I'm just sparkling energy.

A: Let's see why you're here now. There's a reason why you've been brought here. Look all around you. See if anything draws your attention.

H: Another spaceship. A black one. Yeah, but this one is different, it's not round. It's in front...

A: What type of shape is it?

H: I don't know the word in English.

A: I'm going to say several shapes, and you'll tell me if it's that one. Is it a triangle? A sphere like a ball? Is it like a long shape?

H: I just see the front, and the front is... Like the small ships from the Star Wars movies, like when Luke Skywalker was in the small ones.

A: Where they're pointy at the end? Kind of like a triangle?

H: Yeah, really like a triangle, but really like (motions with hands).

A: Pointy, got it. You see one ship?

H: Yeah, there was one black ship.

A: Are you connected at all to that black ship?

H: I now see something like a human skeleton head, white. A skull.

A: Is it just a skull?

H: Just the head.

A: What color is the skull?

H: White.

A: Is it made up of any material that you can tell?

H: I would say its bone.

A: Keep moving the scene along. Tell me what happens next. Is there anything you see now?

H: Yes, I see something but it's hard to describe what I see. I see two arms from two different people. One is an adult, one is a child, and the two hands are holding hands, but then they want to help each other, but slowly drift apart. The child just wants to hold the hand of the adult.

A: Tell me what's going on next.

H: I see half of a face. Like a man with a hat, and the hat is over his face, so (motioning over the head) now he gets his head up. So now I can see his face. He has a black beard, black brown, like in the thirties. He wears good clothes.

A: What is he doing?

H: He's standing. There are other men. They are also well-dressed. They are all standing there. Just men. No women.

A: What are they doing?

H: They're waiting for something or looking at something.

A: Let's see what they are doing. Fast forward to whatever it is that they are looking or waiting for. You can see it now. What is that?

H: It's hard to explain because I see so much stuff which I don't understand. So, I can't explain, and I don't understand the meaning. For example, I saw, what is the word for when you want to get the soup out of the...? A big soup spoon! And the soup spoon was filled with coffee. But not coffee to drink, when the beans are crushed. I don't know what this means. I see so many weird symbols, things, I don't know how to interpret them. Huge skull, in a sea. You see just the half where the nose was. Now the skull is completely underwater.

For your convenience, about 20 minutes of the past life images were removed. There seemed to be a strong infringement on what she recalls as past lives, such as replaced, not organic memories. Aurora calls on the Higher Self to figure out what's going on.

The Higher Self is called forth.
A: Can I please speak to the Higher Self?
Higher Self: Yes.
A: Thank you. I honor you, and I respect you for all the aid you have given us today. I know that you hold all the records to her different lives. May I ask questions, please?
Higher Self: Yes.
A: Thank you. You took her to several different existences. The very first place that you took her was where there were ants, a crocodile, and a pink bunny. Why did you take her there? What was the purpose of that?
H: I think I lost the transmission to my Higher Self, the connection.
A: If you could start feeling that infinite Love-Light source of the Higher Self coming in through the crown and flowing through you infinitely.
H: Mm-hmm...
A: Higher Self, can we start off with the Body Scan now, please?
Higher Self: Yes.
A: Wonderful, thank you. Do you need any assistance from the Archangels?
Higher Self: Yes.
A: Which Archangel would you like to speak to first?
Higher Self: Connecting with... I would say, Archangel Michael.
A: Higher Self, if you could connect us now to Archangel Michael so that he can help us perform the body scan, very strongly... If you could now feel Archangel Michael's energies performing the body scan, feeling very protected, safe, loving, strong, and powerful. Archangel Michael, we honor you, love you, and respect you. Can I please speak to you now, Michael?
AA Michael: Yes.
A: Greetings. Thank you, brother. We are doing a Body Scan on Hailee and her Higher Self asked for your assistance. Can you please begin the body scan on her and see what needs healing and to be addressed first? Any energy, entity, anything negative that's blocking her. Tell us where you want to start off?
AA Michael: Focus on connection.
A: Beautiful. Thank you, Michael. Love you, honor you. Now if you could please tell us where there is energy perhaps that is blocking her, an entity, anything that needs to be addressed first through the healing of the body scan.
AA Michael: Blood pressure.
A: Okay, let's focus on the blood pressure now. Michael, can you scan that and tell us what's going on with the blood pressure?
AA Michael: Very fast.
A: Is there something negative within the blood pressure that needs to be healed to slow it down?
H: I don't know. I need help. It's not Michael, and I need help. The connection ...
A: That's okay. What you're going to do at first is just answer the very first answers that comes to mind, and just keep flowing, (interrupted)...
H: Then he said, he asks for you to help, Aurora.

317

A: Very good. Channeling over energy to you now. If we could scan the blood pressure now. What is within the blood pressure, Michael?

AA Michael: It has to calm down.

A: If we could have the Higher Self and Archangel Michael, both of you soothe her blood pressure now. Calm it down to a healthy level. Archangel Michael, if you can help her see, sense, feel, know, where else do you want to start off with? What part of her body?

AA Michael: (taps heart area)

A: In her heart?

AA Michael: Mm-hmm.

A: Let's look at her heart now. What is within her heart? Why do you want to start off there?

AA Michael: Here, in the left middle, it's a pressure.

A: Michael, let's see what that pressure is about. Is that an energy, an entity, an implant?

AA Michael: Now it's here (moves hand to the abdomen).

A: Okay, did it move around?

AA Michael: I think so.

A: Archangel Michael, could we have Archangel Metatron surround the energy that's moving around with the symbols, please? Let's keep it still. Is it surrounded?

AA Michael: Mm-hmm.

A: Michael, can you scan her, what's inside the symbols now? What did we contain? Is it an energy, an entity?

AA Michael: It is moving. It tries to get out. I don't know what it is. But it feels like it's here and here now, it's both. (holding heart area and abdomen)

A: Okay, so if we can just make sure we surround both of those areas now with the alchemy symbols, Metatron. We love you, honor you, and thank you. Thank you for your assistance. Does it feel like it has a consciousness?

AA Michael: Mm-hmm.

A: Does it feel like it's an entity or a Reptilian consciousness? What does it feel like?

AA Michael: Reptilian.

A: Okay, are both of them Reptilian?

AA Michael: No.

A: Archangel Michael, are they the same being in two separate places?

AA Michael: Yes.

A: Okay, so then they would be the same Reptilian. Michael, I'd love to be able to speak to that Reptilian there now, so we can talk to it in regard to going through the process as we always do. Can you please help guide that Reptilian consciousness there, help guide it up, up, up, now? May we speak to you now, please? Greetings.

Reptilian: I don't want to talk.

A: That's okay. Thank you for responding though. I honor you, love you, and respect you. I understand that you don't want to talk, but can I try to ask questions and see which ones you would like to answer?

Reptilian: Okay.

A: Thank you. If I can ask, when was it that you attached, connected yourself to Hailee's body?

Reptilian: Long before this lifetime.

A: Was it an existence on Earth that you attached or was it outside of Earth?

Reptilian: Outside.

A: Would you be able to share with us why is it that you attached? Was this a contract?

Reptilian: Not a contract.

A: Can you tell me what was going on with her in that other existence somewhere else that allowed for you to come in?

Reptilian: She shouldn't be there.

A: She shouldn't have been where she was at?

Reptilian: Mm-hmm.

A: Okay. Did you catch her somewhere where she shouldn't have been at?

Reptilian: Mm-hmm.

A: Where was she?

Reptilian: At our place.

A: What happened when you caught her?

Reptilian: We had control.

A: Were any of those lives that she saw, for example, when she was in a volcano watching robots and spiders, was that related to this existence?

Reptilian: Yes.

A: When you caught her, what did you do with her?

Reptilian: She was my spy.

A: Oh, do you mean that she was (interrupted)...

Reptilian: I use her.

A: Oh okay. So, you use her now like a spy, you mean?

Reptilian: Mm-hmm.

A: First of all, thank you for sharing this information. What are some ways that you use her as a spy? Can you give us an example, please?

Reptilian: I try to figure out information.

A: Through her?

Reptilian: Mm-hmm.

A: What is the purpose of that?

Reptilian: To win.

A: So, are you saying that you're able to see through her, is that what you mean? How are you (interrupted)...

Reptilian: See, feel, know.

A: When you caught her in your place where she shouldn't have been, did you contain her?

Reptilian: What is containing?

A: When someone grabs someone and then they, say kidnap, or hold hostage?

Reptilian: Yeah, but she has no memory of it.

A: When you held her, what was it that you did to her to make her into one of your spies?

Reptilian: I implanted her.

A: Do you mean you placed implants in her?

Reptilian: Mm-hmm.

A: What kind of implants did you place?

Reptilian: To lower the vibration and to also connect.

A: Did you insert yourself inside her?

Reptilian: Mm-hmm.

A: Okay. And these two consciousnesses, are they (interrupted)...

Reptilian: There are more.

A: There's more than two?

Reptilian: Mm-hmm.

A: How many more are within her?

Reptilian: We duplicate.

A: You duplicated? Into how many?

Reptilian: Can't count.

A: Too many?

Reptilian: Mm-hmm.

A: How does this work with you, with her vessel here, when she incarnated to Earth, you just are in her? Is that how that works?

Reptilian: Don't know.

A: Okay. Well thank you for all those answers. I really appreciate it. Speaking to all of you within her now (interrupted)...

Reptilian: We're getting rid of this.

A: You're getting rid of what?

Reptilian: Staying here.

A: You're staying there? Is that what you said?

Reptilian: We are caught in here.

A: Archangel Michael, Metatron, can we surround all of the Reptilian consciousnesses within her with the symbols, please? I'm going to speak to all of you now, as a collective. I honor you, love you, and respect you. As you know the Earth and the Universe are ascending, we are going to be raising into a higher frequency. Some of these lower densities, like you all are, attached to peoples' bodies, draining upon others' energies. If you are not of high enough vibration when the Earth shifts, you are going to automatically be recycled right back to Source. We're giving you an opportunity today to help you positive polarize with Love-Light, spreading your Love-Light within you, so that you may turn into a positively polarized being. When you do this, you will no longer be tied to having to be stuck in someone's body. You will become your own sovereign, free-willed being. You could incarnate somewhere else, or wherever it is that your soul decides upon. Would you all allow us to help you positive polarize?

Reptilians: Mm-hmm.

A: Wonderful, thank you. I want you to now, all of you now, find that Love-Light within you. Find that light within you and spread it to all that it is of you, every root, every cord, every part of you. As you are spreading to Love-Light, are there Reptilian bodies that you all are connected to that are not within her body? Do you all have Reptilian bodies somewhere else?

Reptilian entities: It feels like there were, but we didn't want to go back there.

A: Okay. Would you want to be your own individual consciousness then?

Reptilians: Mm-hmm.

A: So, since all of you have replicated as you said from one another, and now that you're your individual consciousness. Go ahead and continue to spread that Love-Light within you to every root, every cord, every part of you. Spread it to all light and let us know once you are all light.

Reptilians: We need help.

A: Yes. If we could call on the Collective Consciousness of Angels, if you could assist them now, please. We love you, honor you, and respect you. If we could all focus Love-Light within her now. All these Reptilian consciousnesses, focus Love-Light upon them so that they may turn into a positive polarization. Focusing now and let us know once you are all light.

Reptilians: Okay. (body jolts)

A: Wonderful. Now, go ahead and release yourselves from her body now. Make sure you don't leave any piece of you behind. Let me know once all of you are out.

Reptilians: Again, help.

A: Yes, we are helping. Helping now.

Reptilians: It's like, something's holding back.

A: Okay, if I could please speak to Archangel Michael now?

AA Michael: Yes.

A: Thank you. Archangel Michael, can you look? What is holding back? Is there an implant?

AA Michael: It feels like there are two hands holding the cord.

A: Are the hands within her?

AA Michael: No. They are outside the body.

A: Okay. So, there are two hands outside the body holding them inside?

AA Michael: Mm-hmm.

A: Archangel Michael, can you connect us to those two hands? Who's connected to those two hands? We'd like to speak to that being there, now.

AA Michael: Okay.

A: Thank you, Michael... May we speak to you now, please? Greetings.

Entity: Greetings.

A: Thank you for speaking to us. I honor you, love you, and respect you. May I ask you questions, please?

Entity: Yes.

A: Thank you. Now, if you are aware, we are aiding the Reptilian consciousness that duplicated within her into Love-Light that are looking to release themselves. No longer having to play this negatively polarized role that would like to be positive polarized. If I may ask, who are you, and why is it that you are holding onto them with cords?

Entity: I won't let them go. They are not allowed to get healed.

A: Are you a Reptilian connected to them?

Entity: I feel different.

A: Can you please share with us, what are you?

Entity: I feel like I'm outside her body. But, like a shape. Like a shield.

A: Can you describe to me what you look like?

Entity: I nearly look like her body. Maybe a little bit bigger.

A: What colors are there to you?

Entity: Light rose, pink, black, rose-y.

A: Who are you to her? What is your connection to her?

Entity: I tried to secure her.

A: If you try to secure her, why is it that you are containing those cords of those negative Reptilian consciousness that are turning positive? Why are you maintaining them there if you're securing her?

Entity: They did so many bad things to her.

A: Okay. However, I know that they did, but we are aiding them into a positive polarization with the aid of the angels. Would you allow for us to aid them in positive polarization? We're going to help them remove from her and help her heal.

Entity: Of course, they have to be removed. Yes, I, they have to go, but I don't know if it's right. They should be released, not, not released, burned.

A: You think they should be burned?

Entity: Mm-hmm.

A: But they are looking for redemption.

Entity: I think they lied. They lied at you.

A: Well, let's see. Can we see and can we allow for them to turn into light and see what happens from there? Can we do that?

Entity: Okay.

A: Alright. Archangel Michael, can I please speak to you now?

AA Michael: Yep.

A: What's going on? They said that they're turning to light and this being says it looks like (interrupted)...

AA Michael: They're starting to fight again.

A: Okay, so they're all contained within the alchemy symbols, can we just ensure that we start helping them, flood them with infinite Source Love-Light so that they can turn into light? They had agreed to turn to light.

AA Michael: Mmm.

A: Can we do that, Michael?

AA Michael: Okay.

A: If we could all flood them with Love-Light infinitely, light energy to them now so that they can all turn into positive polarization. Michael, if you could just be our guide here. Let us know if they are all positive polarized when they've all spread their Love-Light.

AA Michael: Feels like there's a whole system in the body which is all connected. It's starting to light.

A: Is there anything within the body that she has that's keeping them there? Can you scan her, Michael, for any negative implant, any hooks, any portals?

AA Michael: There's so much, I don't know where to start.

A: Well, let's start off with the biggest thing that's containing them there.

AA Michael: Stomach.

A: What's going on in the stomach, Michael?

AA Michael: I think the Reptilians are connected to implants. Even though they tried to light up, because of the implant, it won't work.

A: Yes, that's exactly what I was feeling. Thank you, Michael, for helping her find that. Now let's find all those implants that are attached. Where are they, Michael? How many?

AA Michael: Feels like land mines. You know, like implants all over her body. Not like one, two, three. There are more.

A: Can we locate all of them, Michael?

A: What parts of the body does she have them in, these implants?

AA Michael: Back, head, neck, heart, lung, stomach, feet, arms.

A: Can we use the Phoenix Fire to start transmuting that now, please?

AA Michael: Yes.

A: Transmuting the implants themselves, and then allowing for the Reptilians who are now trying to turn positive, to turn positive, please. Let's go ahead and focus fire energy upon these implants. If you all can please help me, the collective of angels. Help with your own Phoenix Fire energy, your own fire elements. Let's transmute every single one of these implants within her body now. Michael, let me know how it's looking along the way, please.

AA Michael: They are starting to destroy, but there is still more.

A: Okay, good. Let's continue transmuting them. Just keep me updated, thank you.

AA Michael: Some of them can't be transmuted.

A: Michael, tell me why some of them can't be transmuted?

AA Michael: Contract.

A: Can we ask the Higher Self, are we allowed to remove those that have the contracts, has she learned her lessons through the contracts?

Higher Self: Yes.

A: Higher Self, do you give Archangel Michael permission to remove those contracts on those implants, please?

Higher Self: Yes, please.

A: Thank you. Archangel Michael, brother, if you could please now remove, eradicate those contracts now, please, with the Higher Self's permission? Go ahead and remove them now.

AA Michael: Okay.

A: Thank you. If we could start working on those implants there that have those contracts, let's go ahead and focus on them as well, ensuring that they are transmuted as well.

AA Michael: It's done.

A: Beautiful. If we can have the Higher Self and Archangel Raphael, we love you, honor you and respect you, thank you. If we can have them both start filling in light energy, Love-Light energy in all the areas that the implants were removed from, please, Michael.

AA Michael: Yes.

A: If we could continue assisting the Reptilian consciousnesses now with Love-Light. Help them spread their Love-Light and let us know once you are all Love-Light.

Positive Polarized Reptilians: Okay.

A: Thank you, now go ahead and release yourself from her body and make sure you don't leave any piece of you behind. Let us know once you are all out.

Positive Polarized Reptilians: They aren't... (shudder) Yes. Out.

A: Wonderful. Do you all have a message for her?

Positive Polarized Reptilians: We didn't think she'd survive this.

A: Say that again?

Positive Polarized Reptilians: She's strong. We didn't think she would survive this.

A: Oh, wow. How long would you say, in Earth years, that you've been with her? Following her as (interrupted)...

Positive Polarized Reptilians: Billions.

A: How many of you were there, inside her?

Positive Polarized Reptilians: Not countable.

A: There's no number, okay. You mentioned that you started duplicating?

Positive Polarized Reptilians: Because she was strong, and we needed to be stronger.

A: Now that you are all of Love-Light, how does it feel?

Positive Polarized Reptilians: Free and soft (sigh of relief).

A: Beautiful. That must be wonderful. Where are you all going?

Positive Polarized Reptilians: Light.

A: Yeah, you've been playing that for a long time. Wonderful. Do you have anything else you'd like to say before you go?

Positive Polarized Reptilians: Stay strong.

A: I know you originally started off with a few, then duplicated, did you all come from a specific, physical Reptilian somewhere?

Positive Polarized Reptilians: I don't remember.

A: That's okay. Very good. Now, go ahead and go with the Love-Light of the Universe. Blessings to you... Archangel Michael and the Legion of Light, Archangel Azrael as well, help these beautiful spirits with the ray of angels that work with you, help guide them. Guide them to truly ensure that every single of one of them does not lose the path. Go straight back to the light, to Source, please. Are we doing that now, Michael?

AA Michael: Yes.

A: Thank you.

AA Michael: I feel there's something in the stomach, but that's different.

A: Okay.

AA Michael: The other ones are gone.

A: Blessings to all of you, thank you. Archangel Michael, let's see what's in the stomach. Scan that area?

AA Michael: A hook.

A: Michael. Let's go ahead and scan her whole body for any other hooks, portals, or implants. Let's go ahead and start transmuting that hook there that you found in her stomach. What else do you see, Michael?

AA Michael: Left foot.

A: What's in the left foot?

AA Michael: Portal.

A: Is it a dark portal?

AA Michael: Mm-hmm.

A: Okay, Michael, can you go ahead and seal that, please?

AA Michael: It is connected to other ones.

A: How many other portals is it connected to?

AA Michael: Thirteen.

A: And where are they?

AA Michael: (sigh) All over the body.

A: Can we use the Phoenix Fire?

AA Michael: Mm-hmm.

A: We are using the Phoenix Fire. Michael, if you could help close every single one of them, all thirteen of them. Did the Reptilian consciousness place those in there?

AA Michael: I think so.

A: Was that their way to move around in the body?

AA Michael: Yes.

A: When they did that, would they come in and out densities?

AA Michael: Mm-hmm.

A: Are we transmuting that hook there in her stomach, now?

AA Michael: We need more power.

A: Okay, can we call on the collective consciousness of Angels now to help transmute with the fire element the hook there in her stomach and all the portals. Help transmute it and close them out. Are there any other hooks besides that one, Michael?

AA Michael: There's something in the neck.

A: What's in the neck, Michael?

AA Michael: And also in the back of the head.

A: Scan that, let's see very clearly.

AA Michael: Like a cord.

A: Where is this cord connected to?

AA Michael: Dark energy.

A: Where is this dark energy at?

AA Michael: Can't see it.

A: Michael, can you go ahead and transmute that and remove it for her, please?

AA Michael: Okay.

A: Thank you. Let's scan again for any other negative cords in her, please. Does she have any more, Michael?

AA Michael: Mm-hmm.

A: Where does she have more at?

AA Michael: Left hand.

A: Is that cord connected to someone or something?

AA Michael: Don't know. I don't know if it's a cord, but maybe... something different. An entity.

A: Okay. Michael, is that an entity I need to speak to?

AA Michael: It goes up in the arm.

A: Is that an entity or a Reptilian consciousness?

AA Michael: It's an entity.

A: Okay, if we could contain that entity now. Let me speak to you now, please. Greetings.

Entity: Hello.

A: Hello. Thank you for speaking to us. Love you, honor you, and respect you. May I ask you questions, please?

Entity: Mm-hmm.

A: Thank you. When was it that you attached yourself there to her left hand?

Entity: Don't know.

A: Was it this life or another?

Entity: Another.

A: I understand that you've been there for a long time. As you know, the Earth is ascending, and the Universe. We're looking to aid you today into positive polarizing, turning into light once more, as you were once. Would you allow us to aid you today in turning into Love-Light?

Entity: Yes.

A: Wonderful. Find that light within you. We want you to spread it to all that is of you, every root, every cord, and let us know once you are all light.

Positive Polarized Entity: Mm-hmm.

A: Beautiful. Go ahead and remove yourself. Michael, oversee and make sure everything's going well, please. Let us know once you are all out... Raphael, Higher Self, please start filling in Love-Light to where that was attached in her arm/hand. Make it nice and healthy once more, and just let us know once you are out, please.

Positive Polarized Entity: (jolts) All out.

A: Wonderful. Do you have a message for her before you go?

Positive Polarized Entity: She's lovely.

A: Yes, she is. Beautiful. Go ahead and go with the Love-Light of the Universe. Blessings to you. If we could have Azrael and Michael just guide them wherever this entity is meant to go... How are the portals looking now, Michael?

AA Michael: We're working on it.

A: Good. How about the hook in her stomach? Is that removed?

AA Michael: Yes.

A: Okay, good. Let's continue to scan her body now, Michael. What else can we heal now?

AA Michael: The heart chakra. Her heart.

A: What's going on in the heart Michael? What would you like for us to heal there?

AA Michael: It's like stone. Cold. Hard.

A: Can we transmute the negative energy within her heart now?

AA Michael: Yes.

A: Can we start using the Phoenix Fire to start transmuting that negative energy there?

AA Michael: Yes.

A: Good. Let's do that now. Start transmuting that negative density within her heart, if we could start to have Raphael and her Higher Self fill in Love-Light to that. As we transmute it, fill it in Love-Light please. As you both continue to work with her heart, if you could spread it to the biggest it can be in this time and space for her highest good... It amazes me, Michael, how yet she could have all that control with the Reptilians, and her heart being so cold or as stone as you said, but yet she still found herself here.

AA Michael: She is unbelievably strong.

A: Yes.

AA Michael: Real strong.

A: Yes. I got goosebumps to that. Beautiful. That is quite a gift, a miracle, a magical thing. For a being to be this controlled for that long, like they said billions of years, but yet she's here. Thank you to all of you who assisted her here for today's healing. As we're working on her heart Michael, what else needs to be addressed now? I know we've healed a lot from her, and I know she has a second session, is there more we can heal on her? Or how is she holding up?

AA Michael: She needs more.

A: Yes. Is there anything else you want to heal on her now?

AA Michael: We can heal now more. Is good.

A: Very good. Michael, let's scan her body one more time. Let's see, what do you want to address next, Michael?

AA Michael: Her lungs.

A: I know she says that she's had a very hard time breathing all her life. She's seen the doctors and they're trying to say she has some kind of condition and I believe that they want to have surgery on her. If you could scan, what is really going on with the lungs?

AA Michael: The Reptilians, make them small, and...

A: Is that why she had a hard time breathing all her life?

AA Michael: Mm-hmm.

A: Can we go ahead and energetically help them now, expand them?

AA Michael: Yes.

A: Thank you. Start that process now. I'm going to go through the list here that she's given me. Did we remove, cut all negative cords, Michael?

AA Michael: No.

A: If we could scan her body now and find all negative cords, Michael. Tell us what you find.

AA Michael: There's so many.

A: Can you use your sword just to swipe them? Cut them all off right now and then can we have the fire element Angels transmute them as you cut them off?

AA Michael: Too dangerous. There are also good cords.

A: Yes, but only cut off the negative cords.

AA Michael: It's like a big web.

A: Could you go through with your sword and just cut the ones that are negative?

AA Michael: Hmm.

A: Can we start that process now?

AA Michael: Mmm. (nods)

A: Thank you, and again have the angels of fire element transmute them as you cut them, please. Thank you to everyone. As you said, it's a web. What other Archangel can we talk to, to ensure the rest of the healing while you do that?

AA Michael: You want to talk to another Archangel?

A: Yes, since you're going to be in that web of cords.

AA Michael: Yeah.

A: Can we speak to another Archangel while you do that?

AA Michael: Yes.

A: Who can we speak to, Michael?

AA Michael: Haniel.

A: Beautiful, if we could please speak to Archangel Haniel now?

AA Haniel: (jolts).

A: Greetings, sister.

AA Haniel: Greetings! (smiling)

A: Love you, honor you, and respect you. Thank you for being here. He called on your aid to administer the Body Scan for now. Can you do that for us, sister, please?

AA Haniel: Yes.

A: Okay, so we've removed a lot so far. I'm sure you've been watching.

AA Haniel: Yes. I have a plan.

A: How about you tell us about your plan, then?

AA Haniel: Her third eye. It has to be opened, yes.

A: Can you go ahead and start opening that for her now, with the Higher Self's permission?

AA Haniel: (whispers) Yes.

A: Thank you, and tell us, how is it that you're opening it up? What are you doing to open it?

AA Haniel: I'm channeling my energy there. So, she doesn't resist anymore.

A: Okay, good, help her not resist anymore. Thank you. Help her surrender. Let us know once you have her third eye opened.

AA Haniel: It needs more time, but it's coming. It needs a little bit.

A: Thank you for the beginning process of that. For now, can you scan her body for any more entities, please?

AA Haniel: Throat. There's an entity around the throat.

A: She's been in there some time, so can you scan her entire body and see what other entities there are in her body, please?

AA Haniel: It's crowded. Several of different minds.

A: Consciousnesses?

AA Haniel: Consciousness, different races, different sexes.

A: How many more entities are in there?

AA Haniel: Five hundred, four hundred fifty-six.

A: Okay. Since we know Archangel Azrael works with the removal and the aiding of the entities that are stuck, can you connect with him now? Have him and his team, his ray of angels, start helping them all transmute, transform into light now.

AA Haniel: Yes.

A: Good. Thank you, Azrael... If you could just continue talking to us as he's working on them. Would that cover all the entities within her, Haniel? I know that we removed so many Reptilian consciousnesses that there was no number. Scan her body, make sure there's no other Reptilian consciousness within her.

AA Haniel: There's so much going on. But I think no more entities.

A: Beautiful, very good... Okay, so if we could all focus now. We removed all those implants that were attaching those Reptilian consciousnesses to her. How are those portals looking now?

AA Haniel: Closed.

A: Beautiful. If we could just ensure again, Raphael and the Higher Self is filling in Love-Light to those areas of the portals, please.

AA Haniel: Yes.

A: How is Michael doing with the cords, Haniel?

AA Haniel: He is still working.

A: Haniel, do you have a message for her while they both work?

AA Haniel: No need to doubt. (smiles) Trust. It's easier for her, now.

A: Yes, I can imagine how easier it's going to be for her now, no longer having all that restraint on her, intrusion, you know? Wow!

AA Haniel: I bet she will now understand the first time.

A: Yes, the first time she tried to do hypnosis with someone else and it wouldn't work, she was blocked? Is that what you mean?

AA Haniel: Mm-hmm (nods).

A: Okay, yes and thank you for helping her. I know that English is not an easy language for her, but she did incredible with this session. Answering everything, so thank you all for that. Haniel, while we're here waiting for them, can you scan her chakras and see if there's any misaligned chakras or any that need balancing, please? Let us know what you find.

AA Haniel: Yes, they all need to balance out after this.

A: Can you start that process, now Haniel? Can you also look at her auric field? How does her auric field look?

AA Haniel: Gray, and there are holes.

A: Can we go ahead and make that nice and bright, filling all the holes please... Thank you.

AA Haniel: (sigh) It looks like a rampage! This whole feels like a war. (laughs)

A: Yeah, I can imagine, wow! I think that's the most I've removed from anyone, as of now, So, that's a lot. Help her not be a war anymore. Help her be strong and beautiful, balanced.

AA Haniel: Information from Michael. Cords are off.

A: Wonderful. Lovely, lovely! Michael, while we're there can we make them nice and healthy, all the cords that are left on her?

AA Michael: Yes. But the positive ones also need to heal because the other ones influenced them, so we need to heal the good cords. I need help.

A: Good, let's go ahead and start that process now, please.

AA Michael: Need still more time, but it's going to be okay.

A: Beautiful, yes. I know sometimes processes like these can also take time while the client's sleeping so it can't be instant at times, especially when it was this strong. Thank you. Is there anything else, Haniel, that you want to address before we bring her back?

AA Haniel: She really is doing fine. She is good... she's calm and feels safe. First time.

A: She did incredible!

AA Haniel: (speaking slowly) She's soaking in this right now.

A: Yes, wow! I feel so joyful myself. I want to thank you Haniel, Azrael, Raphael, Archangels, the Collective of Angels, anyone else who assisted today. The Higher Self for this beautiful healing and the guidance today. I love you, honor you, and respect you. Blessings to everyone. Can we now speak to the Higher Self, please?

AA Haniel: Aurora did incredible as always.

A: Thank you. And I love you Haniel! I can't do this without you all. That I cannot. I am infinitely in gratitude and in love for all of you for being by my side.

AA Haniel: We're always there.

A: That you are... Should I speak to her Higher Self now?

AA Haniel: Yes.

A: Thank you. Let me speak back now to the Higher Self... Higher Self?

Higher Self: Mmm.

A: That was, wow, amazing!

Higher Self: Hello, hello, hello! (laughing)

A: Hello! Oh, my goodness, look at her, oh! Whoa, she's a completely different person energetically. Wow. Beautiful, thank you. It really does mean so much. It's going to tremendously aid so many that have lived in an existence like her. Where they feel stuck no matter how much they try it seems like they can't, for whatever reason, lift into a higher vibration. She has been a beautiful example of what that can look like to someone else. How through the A.U.R.A. Hypnosis Healing, the high frequency of the sacred alchemy that's being worked, and most importantly the aid of the Higher Self in connecting to the Angels. How tremendous and infinite this healing can be for others who have been stuck like her. Thank you.

Higher Self: There are so many others, which we could help with this. They are forced so hard, for such a long time. We can heal them.

A: Thank you, and I know that the Reptilians said that, that life that you showed her where she was seeing like the robots and the spiders, was that their base that she got into?

Higher Self: Yes.

A: Okay. So, then they caught her there? Is that what they did?

Higher Self: Yes.

A: Can you tell us a little more about when they caught her? What did they do to her?

Higher Self: They raped her.

A: Do you mean like in a sexual manner, or like an energetic manner?

Higher Self: Every, every manner you can imagine.

A: Tell me, why was she there?

Higher Self: She went there to get information to help us and it was a dangerous mission, but she said she wanted to go because she's strong.

A: She said she had some kind of energy force field around her.

Higher Self: Yes.

A: Even though she had this energy force field, plus she said she had armor. How come they were able to still find her?

Higher Self: Fear. She feared and then the shield went off.

A: Okay. That's why you all always say no fear, no fear! Be fearless.

Higher Self: Yes. Because of the fear, the Reptilians came, and they implanted the fear in so many ways, so hard because that was her point where she could be heard.

A: Can we go ahead and heal that trauma from that life that happened to her, Higher Self?

Higher Self: Yes, please.

A: If we could start that process of healing that trauma... The spider and the robots she looked at, it seemed like they were inside a volcano. Was that on Earth or somewhere else?

Higher Self: Don't know. I need help to heal.

A: Yes, helping you now... What was the representation to how she was inside that cage where the robots, the negative alien, and the spider, and then outside the cage? It was like people jet skiing on snow? What did that mean?

Higher Self: That was an army getting ready to run to the war and she saw the whole army coming out. That was not jet-skis on ice or snow, it was vehicles.

A: Those were the war vehicles?

Higher Self: Yes.

A: I know you took her to several different lives, you also showed her like a skull. Why did you show her the skull?

Higher Self: That was not her, that was not me, that was the Reptilians. They entered her and the skull was her skull, they showed her own skull. Her human skull when she does not stop, she will die.

A: I sensed that was like them messing with her, the different places they were taking her to.

Higher Self: Yes.

A: Are we good to go, and conclude this part one of her session?

Higher Self: We could give her some, some connection to Gaia, to grounding.

A: Yes, good. Can you do that for her, please?

Higher Self: Yes.

A: Wonderful. What else would you like to address, Higher Self, now?

Higher Self: More trust.

A: Beautiful. Let's go ahead and give her a gift, give her more trust. Trusting herself.

Higher Self: And trusting her own decisions. No need to ask other people, just herself.

A: Yes, let's help her with that so that she can regain her sovereignty back, understanding that she has all the answers within her.

Higher Self: Mm-hmm.

A: Very good. Anything else?

Higher Self: Yes. She believes when you're doing something wrong and it's your fault, then you're guilty. But you know everybody makes a fault, you don't need to be guilty all the time. So, leave all guilt, guiltiness.

A: Leave the guilt behind, yes. That really holds you back, the guilt. Good.

Higher Self: Maybe we can release this because there's so much.

A: Yes. Let's go ahead and transmute that now and help her release it now, please. Thank you.
Higher Self: Oh! And the victim role as well.
A: Yes.
Higher Self: She got rid of it, but she couldn't let it go so now it's time.
A: Good, let's release that victim role. She's not a victim. She is strong. She is infinitely strong. Not a victim. Remove that from her and her programming now, please.
Higher Self: Yes.
A: Archangel Raphael brother, please fill in all the areas that we just healed and removed with Love-Light now, please. Thank you... beautiful. Can I bring her back now?
Higher Self: Yes.
A: Beautiful. Thank you for such a beautiful session today and thank you again for bringing her to me. It truly has been an honor to be working with her and such joy it has brought myself, my soul, to see what a transformation this has been already for her. Looking forward to seeing her for her second A.U.R.A. Hypnosis Healing session. I love you, I honor you, and I respect you.
Higher Self: Thank you so much. I adore you. I love you.
A: Thank you. I'm going to bring her back now.
Higher Self: Okay.

Post Session dialogue.
A: Welcome back! Whoa! What was that? (both laughing) That was incredible! Can you believe you did that? Wow.
H: I thought maybe there would be like hundreds, but so many. That explained so much to me. Why it was so difficult for me in this lifetime.
A: Yes, and it truly is a joy and a miracle to have you here with that many intrusions on you. That shows how incredible you are, so give yourself more credit. Give yourself more self-love because you are beautiful and powerful to be here. Don't you think?
H: Of course, I'm so happy, I'm so proud that I survived! Oh, thank you so much! As we did my reading the first time, I told my life to so many people that when I talked to you, I knew I was finally home. I knew I was finally healing. I didn't know how or what it would be, but I felt this feeling, that I have right now.
A: I am so proud of you! Honestly, I'm in tears because of how proud I am of you. You did incredibly.
H: There was a war in me.
A: Yes! I could feel it when you came to me. I knew that you needed a lot of help, so incredible, and how amazing it is that you are looking to be a healer with that much strength and power that you have. You're going to continue growing especially now that you removed what was blocking you. So, it's going to be phenomenal, and I can't wait to see you in the future for your second session where we will be able to take care of (interrupted)...
H: I'm going to book a third session! Well, just put one for ten sessions. (laughs)
A: Follow your heart. No worries. I support whatever you do. Make sure you don't eat any meat or eat any sugar, at least for the next 13 days because it will slow the healing down.
H: Do you mean the sugar has something to do with the Reptilians?
A: Oh, yes, usually Reptilians make you want to eat sugar.
H: Okay, so now I will change that. But you know, it is really in every food, so...
A: Yeah, but not like direct sugar. You know, don't go drinking a sugar drink, eating desserts that are covered in sugar. Try to stick with natural sugar like fruits. I love you so much. You truly are a joy. Blessings, and I'll see you soon, okay?
H: Thank you, thank you, thank you, and until next time!
A: See you soon. I love you. Until next time. Bye love.

END OF SESSION

-------------<◇>-------------

This first session in the series is a beautiful masterpiece of puzzle pieces being placed back together, but more accurately the pieces of Hailee's soul mended and healed back together. This session was the introduction of her story. In these four sessions, it will complete the different facets of her soul that will hopefully help us see and understand the darkness with a compassionate heart. For it is only when we counter with sovereignty and love to those that try to oppress us, is when we outshine them with our inner LIGHT. To do anything else but love and compassion, we are just colliding head-to-head. One must learn to reach a higher perspective and vibration to out beat the control, and that is ONLY through the infinite love.

Once the negative Reptilians captured her, their agenda was to place artificial intelligence into her, making her into their pawn. Using her as a bridge to spy into places that they cannot enter and reach. We will find out for what purposes they need to use spies in sessions to come.

These sessions introduce us to foundational concepts to prepare us for the later and crucial Chapters in this book. Tying together key concepts which will help us understand with the most clearness we have been able to achieve about Archons, the Multiverse, and their negative agendas. More to come on the spiders and robots mentioned…

Hailee had a total of five sessions, only four are included in this book. Her second session with me is not included, as it was primarily focused on self-healing in removing Archon tentacles within her after she was cleared in this first session. It was a lesson for her and for all of us to not allow healers that have a 'service-to-self' intent to conduct energy healings or attunements on our cleared vessels. We need to be selective of who we allow to enter our forcefields and our energies. Even if they might have been one's Spiritual Mentor before the A.U.R.A. Hypnosis Healing session as Hailee's was, they might no longer be a match to our higher vibrational cleared vessel after a transformational healing. Reminding us to treat ourselves with the sacredness that our soul is. We continue in the next Chapter with Hailee's journey.

Once more I am in awe every day that these souls find the courage and guidance in the immensity of darkness and control and break through to begin their self-healing. Thank you, Hailee!

"What one might think as failure, is only but an experience gained as a lesson that paves the road to the Mother of Knowledge."
~Aurora

-------------<◇>-------------

17

A REPTILIAN ON A MISSION

Recorded November 2019. Never before shared.
Special Series: 2 of 4

This in-person A.U.R.A. Hypnosis Healing session was conducted by a student (Rose) at the Chicago A.U.R.A. Hypnosis Healing Retreat where the student trainees receive hands on training practicing on one another. Rose and Hailee were paired up for this A.U.R.A. Hypnosis Healing session. This is Hailee's third out of five sessions (only four are included in the book), where she is exploring a soul aspect of herself as a Reptilian. This specific session is vital for what's to come in understanding the Reptilian's journey of healing itself, facilitated over several A.U.R.A. sessions. More of how it is from the inside viewing point of being a Reptilian and the will power they have to work through to break free of the Archon tyrant control.

-------------<◇>-------------

"This all interacts with every Dimension, with every living, with every being, she is - she was - she will be. It all intertwines to reach a point where she is aware that it's not only the bright side, but also the darker side that needs to be integrated."
-Higher Self

-------------<◇>-------------

R: [Rose] Have you landed on the ground?
H: [Hailee] I'm on a kind of balcony with some black... no, no, a white balcony, and I look outside at huge mountains, but they are not with grass. They're more like the Rocky Mountains. They are far, far, away in the distance.
R: Are you on the balcony?
H: I guess I am standing on the balcony, looking outside.
R: Can you see your hands? How many fingers do you have?
H: No, I can't see.
R: Do you have a shape? Can you sense if you're male, female or both?
H: No, I can't see.
R: Okay.
H: But I have a feeling that I'm standing with my feet on the ground.
R: Can you see your feet? Look closely at your feet, look down. How many toes can you sense that you have?
H: Three to four.
R: Do you see anything else out in the balcony aside from the mountains? Look out through the balcony.
H: A war field, and there is a war going on, fires. There are like stone walls so that someone can hide behind. I can see all these small fires from a distance. It's dark, but it's not - more like a blue dark.
R: Can you see the sky from the balcony?
H: There are all the stars shining. Like yellow, looks like electricity yellow. I'm looking at it like a heart, like a heart broken. It looks sad because of the war.

R: The stars are heartbroken?

H: No, I'm watching the war scene and I am... I am heartbroken because of the scene as I see, and I'm supposed to be here. I cannot go over there or help them.

R: So, you're seeing this at a far distance from the balcony. It's not close?

H: No, it's far.

R: So, from this distance you can see the fire?

H: Fire, that's right. You know I'm not really seeing people dying, but I can feel they are suffering and being hurt, one against each other. And they're all - they're running around trying to survive.

R: Do you know why this war is happening?

H: I guess I'm so sad because maybe I had something to do with it, that I started something or I made a mistake, I feel like I have something to do with it.

R: Let's go back to the time right before the war started. You are there now. Tell me what is happening.

H: Just for a second. I saw two red eyes. There is something huge, something else - forest. It used to be very beautiful but now it's like life went out of everything and I'm going around there. I'm sad because I know once it was beautiful and so very colorful. Now it's like you know, dark green and dark brown. Leaves are hanging to the ground. This once was a very beautiful, powerful, shiny place.

R: What happened? Why is it not the beautiful shining place anymore?

H: Some things went into the air so it's also dusty. So, no fresh air. Like maybe poison.

R: The air is poisoned?

H: Yes.

R: So, the poisoned air is what triggered the forest not to have as much life?

H: Yes. I guess the forest completely died with everything in it.

R: Can you sense what caused this poison in the air?

H: Feels like a mistake. It's a mistake.

R: Why was it a mistake?

H: It's not supposed to be that this happened, or nobody would have guessed that it would be that way.

R: Who wouldn't guess that it wouldn't have been that way? Do you know why they think that it wouldn't be that way?

H: I first thought it was a pyramid, but it isn't a pyramid. It was more like a crystal palace or something like that, but not a crystal palace. It is like a kind of building or something and it was invented to do something in the air, and it didn't work right. So, I guess it was for a good purpose, but it went wrong.

R: Why did it go wrong?

H: Oh! There was a crystal inside, and the crystal was not clear. This crystal was the activation. You can see power in the middle, and it broke.

R: Do you know why the crystal wasn't clear?

H: I brought a false crystal. I brought it here. I mean, it was me!

R: You brought it there?

H: Yes!

R: Where did you bring this crystal from?

H: Travel to another galaxy planet.

R: Let's go to that planet - another galaxy. Let's go there before you placed the crystal in the pyramid. Let's go to that galaxy, that planet where you were there collecting that crystal.

H: Oh, that's a dark planet.

R: Can you describe what this planet looks like?

H: I see a kind of rocky, dark stone - rocky surface and there's also something like cities. Are you familiar with Star Trek? It looks like how it is painted on the Roman Romulan. There was a picture I saw and it's not the same, but it has some buildings, has some similarities.

R: How did you find the crystal in this dark planet with the black surface?

H: I was, I can feel it now. I was not going there by my own will. I was like, ordered there. They said, "come here" and I had to go there.

R: Can you sense who ordered you? Who told you, you had to go there?

H: Looks like spiders?! No. It is more like an insect spider with...

R: Legs?

H: Yes! I'm not comfortable there.

R: Let's go to the time of the crystal. How did you find the crystal?

H: They gave it to me. I had to bring it back. They were aware of it that the crystal did what it did. But I thought it was a good one.

R: What color was this crystal?

H: On the planet when I got it, it was blue. When I put it in the middle of the building on our planet, it was more like a mountain crystal, so it changed. So, I got to think they infringed the crystal to be something different.

R: Okay, and this crystal, what did the crystal do? What did it do to the pyramid, once you place the crystal on the pyramid, what happened?

H: The crystal started vibrating. And it made up a light to the sky that was supposed to be and then it should heal the surface or the atmosphere or something like that. But then the crystal became out of control and broke and it kind of destroyed the building so it was not able to use it anymore. When it broke, it was like they had some vibration codes put in the atmosphere. Because I see some cords or something like that and they are infringing the atmosphere and that is why they're the champions.

R: This pyramid, if you can explain a little bit better to me, this pyramid, what was the purpose of this pyramid? Why did you have to place a crystal inside this pyramid?

H: Because it was my job. I was taught to. I did not think that this would happen, and I was sad, but I was seeing what was happening. Oh, and then I could... Ah!!! Oh!!! It was...Oh!!! (exclaiming in pain and shock) ...it was not only the forest who died.

R: No? What are you seeing?

H: Oh, oh! It's the whole planet! I'm also sad...I know what happened because I couldn't handle these feelings. I cut off my feelings. I threw my feelings away. I don't know if it was me or them but first, I had these very, very sad feelings and then no more.

R: Where did your feelings go?

H: I don't have a clue. They're not here anymore. I was just more like a robot. I just like to do what I'm programmed for.

R: Are you the only one that is like that or are there others?

H: I work alone. I don't know if there are others at this moment.

R: Do you remain on this planet or do you go on to a different planet?

H: I don't remain there; I go somewhere else.

R: Where do you go?

H: It seems to be like that planet, like a moon for example. There is nothing on it but I'm there. It's dark.

R: Is this where you go to next or is this still the same planet?

H: I guess I went in a UFO and traveled there. I also have something like a spacesuit, and I can switch through Dimensions or something like that when I push a button on the spacesuit. It's not a spacesuit because there's no helmet but there is a button on my breast, not breast exactly - that area is what I mean.

R: The chest?

H: Yeah, right. I can push there and then somewhere else, not breast, maybe more abdomen. At that part.

R: When you have the spacesuit, what do you look like?

H: I can't see.

R: What about when you released your feelings, and they went away? You said that you felt like a robot. Do you remember if you can see what you looked like?

H: There was a difference in my movements, because I saw myself moving before, fluidly and waving something like that and afterwards it was like a machine. I can see the shape, it looks like two arms and two legs and a torso, right? I'm not sure about more details.

R: Look at your hands.

H: Okay, just for a second I saw something like an octopus. Oh no, there are more now.

R: More hands?

H: More octopus. They have three eyes like in a triangle.

R: This is the way you look now, once you turned into a robot?

H: No, it's not me but they are looking at me.

R: Okay, the octopus are looking at you?

H: Yes. But they're not coming near, they're just looking at me. I'm okay. I'm just standing. I'm not in fear. I don't fear anything.

R: Before you board your spaceship to go to a different planet, what did that spaceship look like?

H: It was a little bit like what a UFO would look like but not like a metal, a little bit more like a black, dark, but not totally black. It was not so huge, but I mean I was travelling alone in it. I guess it could travel a lot of people more but, they are all really huge ships, so this was just one of the smaller ones.

R: The planet that you are in, that you put the crystal in, do you know the name of the planet?

H: There comes a name, but I'm not sure. Andromeda, but I don't understand that.

R: So now you boarded the spaceship, and you went to this different planet. It was this other planet you said that you can move through time. Was it the spacesuit that allowed you to move through time when you press the buttons?

H: Yes. No. There are tentacles. I can see tentacles.

R: There are tentacles on the suit?

H: That's weird to explain, it looks like a mouth with teeth. But not a human mouth more like an animal mouth. And the tentacles are going in and I am also flying in. I don't know.

R: You're flying. So, you use tentacles to...

H: I don't know what it is. I'm not a tentacle. I'm different.

R: How are you different?

H: I see a torso. I have like two legs. No, I'm an insect, an insect or Reptilian. What is it? (wondering aloud) I guess I am a Reptilian!

R: Okay, so the tentacles, were those your tentacles?

H: No.

R: Whose tentacles were they?

H: The Archons.

R: The Archons' tentacles were in the ship with you?

H: No. They telepathically infringed upon me, with like maybe also A.I. stuff. I don't have a free will. I have to do what they order. So, like they have total control over me.

R: Is that why you were feeling robotic?

H: Yes. Absolutely. I mean, sometimes I have my own thoughts, like "Oh, why can't I do something else?" And then they can also infringe my thoughts.

R: So, was it your choice to get on to the spaceship and go to another planet or were you told to do that?

H: No, I was told.

R: Why did they tell you to get into the spaceship and go to another planet?

H: Because they used me to do this.

R: To do what?

H: To do this, to this planet and also it was like I was on a mission with different things and this planet was just one interference - one mission. They just easily sent me to do their bad work.

R: Did they tell you what planet to go to next once you became the robot and got onto that spaceship?

H: They just appear there, on the next thing. So, it's not me who decides where to go.

R: Okay, so they don't tell you where to go. You just appear there.

H: No.

R: After Andromeda, where did you appear next?

H: I see something in the water with pearls.

R: So, you now appeared on this new planet. Where are you now?

H: Feels like there's a veil.

R: What does this look like?

H: I mean a veil, like it's hard for me to connect so to see that is what I meant. I see something now. I'm on a planet where there are palms. It is night, it is pretty - the prettiest blue dark sky you can imagine. Pretty stars you see, and I can look above, but the ponds are black. There's in the air, in the atmosphere something like purple, blue. The sky is very beautiful.

R: Is it nighttime now? What are you doing there?

H: It's a dark sky like in the night but there's also blue and purple in it. There is something like a light, you can say like when somebody puts a big spot, when a spot marks a place.

R: What is the spot mark?

H: Should I go there?

R: Yes, let's go there. You are there now.

H: Okay, it's me standing on the spot.

R: And you are Reptilian correct?

H: Yes.

R: Are you a positive Reptilian or a negative polarized Reptilian?

H: I feel like I was positive but because of the infringement I changed.

R: What are you doing at that spot? What's happening all around you?

H: Feels like this is my waiting point for the next order.

R: The orders come from whom?

H: From the Archons.

R: So, is this the place where you wait to receive your order?

H: Yes. Maybe also to do something like, not refill energy, but it is like to rest.

R: At this spot?

H: Yes.

R: Do you ever need to eat as a Reptilian?

H: No.

R: How do you nourish?

H: I take what I want. I take what I need. I just take it.

R: What is it that you need; that you take?

H: It is when a spider grabs with its front legs and grabs something. I'm grabbing the energy like that if I need something. I grab it like that (makes a popping sound from mouth) but not in a physical manner. I don't know, between dimensional or telepathically.

R: When you do that telepathically, what exactly is it that you're doing? How are you doing this?

H: I connect to another living being and I soak in - no, soak is not the word (makes slurping noises).

R: Like the sound you're making? Slurping?

H: Like when you're drinking a milkshake (slurps). I just envision or imagine connecting and I mean, it's not pulled out because it's more like (slurps again). What is it called in English?

R: Like you slurp?

H: Slurp? I don't know that word.

R: So, like you breathe in?

H: But it's not breathing, it's more like munching.

R: You're able to do this at that point, at that resting point?

H: Yes.

R: With the plates in your body, you're able to do what with it again, can you remind me? You mentioned that you had a suit.

H: Yes, you mean the travel. That is technology. Very clever, smart high-level technology. It's also for, not just traveling. It's also shielding. It's also changing how I look. It's also for speaking different languages and also not really like a weapon but it could be used in a protection kind of way. So, it is very, very strong, very heavy and important for me.

R: Do you wear this all the time? Are there any times you take it out?

H: No. It feels implanted. So, it's not really a jacket I wear (even though it's my outside), I feel like I'm connected with it.

R: With this, you said you can go through Dimensions?

H: Yes, but it's not me who says where the journey is going. I just press the button and it's there. So therefore, I don't know where I'm going. And this is because I think I'm always like the last person who knows about the mission. I'm the last one who receives all the information. It is planned by others and I'm just a soldier.

R: This planet where you arrive at that point, is it an organic type of planet?

H: I knew because of the palms. First, I thought maybe organic but now when you mentioned it, maybe it could also be technology. Oh, it's not a planet. Oh, it's more like, in Star Trek there is something like a room and you can program whatever it is. It is like that and its huge inside. So, it's called 'hollow deck' there in the series. I'm on a ship. As you know, this is the spot they created for me to feel a bit comfortable. Yeah, no, that's not an organic planet. Totally technical.

R: Do you see others in there?

H: First, I thought I am all alone on this, you know planet, but it feels like there's a whole army.

R: How do you guys communicate with one another?

H: This is like a hive system because I am me, but I'm also kind of connected to them to the other ones.

R: Okay, so now you reached this spaceship. You're there and what are you doing? I know you've rested but what happens after you're done resting?

H: First, I don't want to be there anymore. I'm aware that I'm infringed. Not all the time but that comes up in some moments like "Eh, is that me?", "What is going on here?" - these moments are coming up for longer and longer. It feels like I want to make a riot to get free. There are like spider guards watching us and I have to pay attention to what I think. I want to reach the others to know, if they know they are also infringed, so that we have a possibility to get free together. But it has to be very secretly done. Very dangerous. They pay attention to what I do. Because I know of someone - I heard or I don't know, I remember that some already tried something like that and they were just (makes a sound of being killed) within that second. It's just like with a robot when you turn off the...

R: Power???

H: Yes, it's just over.

R: So, on the ship, what happens next - what are you meant to do there now that they called you back there already?

H: I'm trying to, as I said, secretly call some others who may also have good thoughts and try to connect with them. But we are all standing at our place. Nobody is walking around and talking. We're all standing in our place. So, has to be through the hive. I have to take care of the spiders, I don't know... watch the spiders. They are guards or something, but they don't get what we're doing here.

R: Let's go forward to another time and place of significance to you. You are there now.

H: Ah! We got the ship. Oh, we got the ship but there's a problem because all of us could not reach it. Therefore, we had to kill our brothers. Because they were infringed and when we went on, if they were still with us, we would also be dead. So, we had to shut them down to get free.

R: How did you do that?

H: There's something like another, not a battle, but like you said power on or power off. An implant we are able to... (thinking out loud). I mean we didn't shoot them with guns or something like that we didn't. There was no fighting. No, we did it through the hive consciousness, we sent the intent through the consciousness of this hive.

R: When you sent the intent with it, what intent did you send?

H: That was when my feeling came back, I guess, because I was aware that we have to lose some or at least a lot of - to free us.

R: To free you from the hive?

H: Yes. So, because it's the only possibility to get out there.

R: So, you set the intent to be free.

H: Yes, I infringed the others which were not aware that they were infringed, like with a virus. So, I infringed my own people with a negative virus. Oh! (sighing) But we were a group and we planned that in such a way so we could shield ourselves, so we didn't get infringed by that. It was so hard to see the others just passing by.

R: What happened to the others?

H: Oh, they all died, I'm the only one. I tried to reach out to others, but you know the spotlight thing - the technology was broken. That's why I could get to my thinking, but the other ones weren't able. So it was just me. I tried to get through this hive system, but nobody responded to me that way. I killed them all to free myself.

R: So, all the other ones with your intent that you set, it disconnected everyone? Why did it disconnect everyone and not you?

H: Oh! I freed them and I stayed there, is it that? (wondering and trying to recall)

R: Let's take a look.

H: Because now I'm seeing, I see them lying on the floor as if they were sleeping and now, they're a little bit moving and waking up and not being infringed anymore, but I'm still standing there at the light.

R: You're standing there at the light?

H: Yes, the other place. The other ones, this whole ship - the whole army is now aware that they are not infringed anymore. I am on that spot. I know, I am infringed but I'm the only one who's left. So, I did something that cut cords to this Archon system. But I couldn't free myself maybe because the other ones, they're moving around and I'm still standing like a robot.

R: Let's go just a little bit ahead, past that scene. Tell me what you see now.

H: Traveling through Galaxies.

R: How do you feel as you travel through Galaxies?

H: Not good, because I'm aware.

R: You're aware of what?

H: That I am infringed, and I can't resist. It's like they have total control over my body. But I know that there's a little me inside me. I don't know if they are not aware of it or whatever. But I'm like a prisoner in my own body.

R: Are you traveling alone?

H: Yes.

R: What happened to the others?

H: I don't know.

R: Let's go back, just a little back. Right before you start traveling alone. What happened to the others as they were released?

H: Oh, they're going to the light!

R: Do you continue on the ship traveling?

H: (sad) I'm just in space now. Alone. Time doesn't matter anymore. Just exist. I feel like I don't have orders anymore. it's not even flying, it's more like drifting. I can't move so it's like eternity. It's not fun because I'm alone. I don't know what happened to the others.

The Higher Self is called forth.

R: Can I please speak to the Higher Self of Hailee?

Higher Self: Yes.

R: I honor you, thank you and respect you for all the aid you have given us today. I know that you hold all the records of Hailee's different lives. May I ask you questions?

Higher Self: Yes.

R: Thank you.

Higher Self: Thank you.

R: Why is it that you chose to show Hailee living on a planet where she started off with seeing herself at a balcony, where she was seeing a war at a distance? Then you showed her a pyramid where she placed the crystal that was infringed and turned this planet's atmosphere and engulfed the whole planet. Why did you choose to show her this planet atmosphere turning this planet and killing all the inhabitants and life within this planet?

Higher Self: It was to show that once in another lifetime she did all these missions. These were just some parts to create and answer so that she will be more able to understand now why it's so hard for her. Because of this guilt. It's not this Earth's life. This all interacts with every dimension, with every living, with every being, she is - she was - she will be. It all intertwines to reach a point where she is aware that it's not only the bright side, but also the darker side that needs to be integrated. The dark side can see the light but if you compare it, she was really dark, dark, dark.

R: But there seemed to be a point where she realized that there was still some light in her. She wanted to help others.

Higher Self: She thought it was like the technology on the ship was broken. It wasn't. Her will, her light inside; it was still light. The light is always there. Even in the darkest places because it is whichever role it may be, but it is there. She remembered it and she lied to all the others.

R: Beautiful.

Higher Self: But she was not able to lie to herself.

R: So, what happened there? Why was she able to do that for others and not for herself?

Higher Self: That's her purpose, to serve others.

R: Is this why she feels at times she must give in order to receive?

Higher Self: Yes.

R: What happened when she disconnected from her feelings? Where did her feelings go? She was unable to show where did it go, her feelings? At that life form once she saw what happened with the planet, she felt much pain. Then she said that she disconnected and became robotic. What happened to those feelings that she let go? Did they go anywhere?

Higher Self: No, still inside her. Deep, deep, deep down; like forgotten.

R: She forgot that she carries that light energy within her.

Higher Self: Yes.

R: Then you showed her a scene where after she disconnected all the other Reptilians, she was just drifting away, did anything else happen?

Higher Self: No. She still drifts there, still drifts there alone. (crying)

R: Higher Self, and what was that triangle? That she had at her job?

Higher Self: Yes, it was an activation pyramid for an organic planet. Within this opening pyramid they could create or even, let's say, make the world more brighter, better; like recalculate the atmosphere.

R: Do all planets have this or is it just in that particular planet?

Higher Self: There are some because they were placed there, but not all have them.

R: Was this Andromeda?

Higher Self: No.

R: Where was this planet?

Higher Self: Not yet time to know.

R: Okay. That's what I thought. Thank you.

Higher Self: You're welcome.

R: She felt that she was very robotic and that she didn't have a free will, that she basically was just a soldier receiving messages from the hive. She had no control of where she went, what she did. Why is that?

Higher Self: Surrendering at its best but at a negative polarization.

R: Why does this happen? It seems as if she was a positive polarized Reptilian and then with what happened to the planet, she then had so much pain within her that she released that pain. Then she says she felt robotic. Is that what happens to all of them or how are they even created, the Reptilians? The negative polarized Reptilians.

Higher Self: Okay, no, we have to try to figure out because I guess these are four to five questions in one.

R: I'm so sorry. (laughing)

Higher Self: No, start on.

R: Was she a positive Reptilian?

Higher Self: Yes. Beautiful positive being living a life.

R: There was a time where she showed me that she had to collect the crystal from another planet and there were spiders there.

Higher Self: Yes.

R: Why did she feel that she had to do that?

Higher Self: She was sent there. Something on my throat or chest?

R: Something is on her throat or chest?

Higher Self: Yes.

R: What is on her throat and her chest?

Higher Self: It's infringing speaking…the coming out of the truth. Don't want us to share the truth.

R: Can we remove that?

Higher Self: Yes.

The Body Scan begins.

R: Are you able to do that or do you need assistance from the Archangels?

Higher Self: Yes, please assistance.

R: Higher Self, who would you like to call forth?

Higher Self: Archangel Michael.

R: Higher Self, if you can connect us to Archangel Michael.

Higher Self: Yes.

R: Thank you, brother. I love you, I honor you and respect you.

AA Michael: And I love you. You're doing so great.

R: Thank you.

AA Michael: So beautiful, you are so fierce, strong, intuitive. (smiling)

R: Thank you brother. I was speaking to Hailee's Higher Self and she was informing me that she has some blockage in her throat and on her chest. Are you able to assist me with scanning that area to see what those blockages are that are preventing her from telling the truth?

AA Michael: Yes.

R: Thank you. What is it?

AA Michael: Negative polarized Reptilian.

R: Negative polarized Reptilians in both locations?

AA Michael: It's more like a huge spot pressing down so it's one huge spot.

R: This one huge spot that connects the chest to the throat?

AA Michael: Yes.

R: Is it a negative polarized Reptilian or a Reptilian consciousness?

AA Michael: Consciousness.

R: Can we encase that Reptilian consciousness with the symbols?

AA Michael: Yes.

R: Thank you brother. Archangel Michael, can you scan her whole body for any negative Reptilians entities or anything that she may have in her body?

AA Michael: The head.

R: What's going on in the head Michael?

AA Michael: There's pressure.

R: Does this pressure have a consciousness?

AA Michael: Yes.

R: It does have a consciousness? Is it a Reptilian or an entity?

AA Michael: It is spot A.I. technology implant. Because I said consciousness, it is not only an implant, which was planted, it is aware of itself. So, I'd rather contain it.

R: Yes, thank you, Michael. That's what I was going to ask if we contain it with the symbols.

AA Michael: Yes.

R: Thank you.

AA Michael: This one is fast.

R: Okay.

AA Michael: That's why I interrupted.

R: Thank you brother. What implanted that implant on her head?

AA Michael: Archons.

R: Archangel Michael are there any portals in her body?

AA Michael: Yes. It is beneath the Reptilian consciousness.

R: Can we go ahead and close that portal?

AA Michael: Yes.

R: Thank you. And on her chest, how many Reptilians did we contain in there? On her throat area near her chest, how many were contained or how many are there?

AA Michael: Twelve.

R: Is that portal where those Reptilians were coming through, is that closed Archangel Michael?

AA Michael: Yes.

R: Thank you. Are there any other portals on her body?

AA Michael: Right leg. There are two.

R: Two portals or entities?

AA Michael: Two portals, one lower near the feet. One near the knee.

R: Thank you for that. Can we go ahead and close those portals Michael, please.

AA Michael: Yes.

R: Thank you, brother. Are there any other portals on Hailee's body?

AA Michael: No.

R: Thank you. That's what I got too. Archangel Michael, if you can scan her body for any negative energy, entities, hooks, Reptilians consciousness.

AA Michael: Hooks.

R: Hooks where?

AA Michael: Stomach.

R: Can we remove or what can we do with that with the hook, Archangel Michael?

AA Michael: Remove.

R: Remove and how will you remove it?

AA Michael: With the Phoenix Fire.

R: Would you require some assistance from me?

AA Michael: Yes.

R: Is there any way that we can talk to the Reptilians within her throat - chest area?

AA Michael: Yes.

R: Thank you, brother. Are you able to connect me Michael to the Reptilians?

AA Michael: Yes.

R: Thank you, brother. May I please speak to the Reptilian within her throat - chest section. Come up, up, up. Greetings.

Reptilian Consciousness: Hello.

R: I honor you. I love you and I respect you. Thank you for speaking to me today. May I ask you some questions?

Reptilian Consciousness: Okay.

R: Thank you. When was it that you connected to Hailee in her throat area? May I speak to all 12 of the Reptilians within Hailee's throat area, as a collective consciousness?

Reptilian Consciousness: Yes.

R: Thank you. When was it that you connected to Hailee's throat area?

Reptilian Consciousness: Long ago.

R: How did you connect there?

Reptilian Consciousness: Not telling the truth.

R: Not telling the truth?!

Reptilian Consciousness: Interference, not speaking up for herself.

R: Why are you doing this?

Reptilian Consciousness: To lower her density.

R: Why are you wanting for her density to be low?

Reptilian Consciousness: She's a bright light.

R: Is this a contract?

Reptilian Consciousness: Yes.

R: Is this a positive contract that you have with her?

Reptilian Consciousness: Yes.

R: Why do you have this contract with her?

Reptilian Consciousness: So that she's able to recognize how hard it is speaking the truth, how tense it is.

R: How long ago was this contract established?

(Aurora checks in on Rose's Training Session.)

R: Aurora, I need your assistance.
AA Michael: This is Archangel Michael.
Aurora: I'm here, Aurora. Let me know what's going on?
R: Her energy, there are 12 Reptilians on her throat that I'm speaking with right now. And they are, they're trying to disturb and cause me fear.
Aurora: They're already in symbols?
R: Yes.
AA Michael: No.
R: They're not?
Aurora: Archangel Michael, did you place them in the symbols?
AA Michael: Yes.
Aurora: Okay, good.
AA Michael: That is why I interrupted; I was a little bit fear-ish. I'm sorry for that. But she does such a great job with this, Rose, you're doing so great.
Aurora: Yes, she is. (smiling)
R: Thank you.
Aurora: Did we find out when they attached?
R: That's what I was trying to find out. I've sensed it. She says that there was a contract, but I sense that the contract was long ago. I don't know if we could break that contract or not.
Aurora: Michael, you said it was long ago… when was it that these Reptilians were inside her throat? Find that time and space, when was that?
AA Michael: So, as I already said, it is a contract, but it is negatively influenced.
Aurora: Okay, we just need to figure out when it happened.
AA Michael: Yes, the contract was a long time ago.
Aurora: She's had two other A.U.R.A. sessions. How come these were never detected before? Maybe you can scan Michael, we need to find the root so that then we can go ahead and remove the contract.
AA Michael: I can't see it. Where is it? (thinking aloud while scanning)
Aurora: Was this a recent contract or prior? Is there a portal behind her back?
AA Michael: Yes.
Aurora: Okay. So, we're finding these things, we just need to find out when it was that they came in so we can go ahead and start closing. Is the portal all closed?
AA Michael: Closing it now.
Aurora: Good. Michael, if you can tell us when was it that all this infringement came in?
AA Michael: Yesterday.
Aurora: Yes, exactly. Thank you. So, let's go ahead since they are surrounded now.
R: I can talk to all 12 of those Reptilian consciousnesses inside Hailee's throat as a collective?
AA Michael: Yes.

Aurora leaves to mentor another A.U.R.A. Training Live session.

R: Thank you. Am I speaking with all of you now as a collective?
Reptilian Consciousness: Yes.

R: Now, you know that this planet is transitioning to a higher vibration. I would like to aid you into that transition and assist you in turning back into positive polarization. So that when the shift comes, you're not turned back into zero where you will lose all your experiences - your consciousness that you have had throughout life. By assisting you and turning you into positive polarization, you may then keep these experiences... Would you like that?

Reptilian Consciousness: Yes.

R: Thank you. Now may I connect to the Reptilians that are connected to this consciousness?

AA Michael: Yes.

R: Thank you. How many are there Michael connected to these 12 consciousnesses?

AA Michael: One hundred and twenty-eight.

R: Michael, am I able to speak with them as a collective to the 128 of them?

AA Michael: Yes.

R: Am I able to assist them to transition into polarized polarization?

AA Michael: Yes.

R: Thank you. Can you be that bridge for me?

AA Michael: Yes.

R: Thank you. Can we call upon Archangel Azrael to assist as well?

AA Michael: Yes.

R: Thank you. May you be that bridge Archangel Michael, in informing them that they have a choice where they can now polarize into positive polarization. They can transition and carry their experiences now that this planet is shifting into a higher vibration. Where their energies and their beings won't be transmuted back into zero with this new shift. Can you inform them that opting for a positive polarization will allow for them to keep their experiences in life?

AA Michael: Yes, they are already aware because of the consciousness connection.

R: Thank you. Archangel Michael and Archangel Azrael, if you can assist me with sending Love-Light, Christ consciousness, energies and assisting with their transmission into positive polarization?

AA Michael: Yes.

R: I would like for the consciousness inside Hailee's throat and the 128 Reptilians to look within yourself and find the light within yourself. As a collective consciousness and Reptilians are you able to see the light within yourselves?

AA Michael: Yes.

R: I want you to spread the Love-Light within yourself. Spread it to every inch of your body through every cord within Hailee. Archangel Michael and Archangel Azrael, is there light within them?

AA Michael: Yes.

R: Are the Reptilian consciousness within Hailee's throat, are they all 12 now of Love-Light?

AA Michael: Yes.

R: Thank you. Now pull all that you have within Hailee, all those cords, everything pull out, out, out from within her.

AA Michael: They're all light.

R: Thank you brother. What about the 128 Reptilians? Are they all light?

AA Michael: Yes.

R: Thank you. Now that you are light, do you have any message for Hailee?

Reptilian Collective: We're sorry. She has to pay more attention, to protect her intention to live in a high vibration. That is what allowed us to come in.

R: Now, you said that you came in the last two days. What caused that?

Reptilian Collective: Anger.

R: Why was there anger?

Reptilian Collective: Not being seen. She had a feeling she must not be seen.

R: Do you have anything else that you would like to tell?

Reptilian Collective: Staying fierce.

R: Thank you. Archangel Michael, Archangel Azrael, if you can assist them. I love you, honor you and respect you. Thank you for the beautiful message you have given Hailee. If you can assist those consciousnesses and 128 Reptilians where they need to go. Walk me throughout the way where they are going.

AA Michael: Yes. They're traveling.

R: If I can have the Legions of Azrael, Michael, your Legions of Light to please assist them; the 128 and the 12 that were in Hailee's throat. Assist them to where they need to go please so that they don't go astray.

AA Michael: They're going to the Sun. There were also other positive polarized Reptilians waiting for them.

R: Beautiful. Can you walk me through what the Sun looks like please?

AA Michael: It's a beautiful place, high vibration.

R: Thank you.

AA Michael: It's peaceful and calm and shiny.

R: Which Dimension is this Sun vibrating in?

AA Michael: Ninth.

R: Why are they going to the Ninth Dimension?

AA Michael: They're coming from there.

R: They were coming from there?

AA Michael: Yes. Ninth Dimension, they could choose to have a body in whichever they want. They chose to go to ninth.

R: Beautiful. Is there anything else you want to share about this Ninth Dimension Sun?

AA Michael: That's it.

R: Okay, thank you. If you can scan the hooks that were in the stomach. Is it still there or has it been transmuted?

AA Michael: It's been transmuted.

R: Can you scan her body one more time for anything else? I know you said there was nothing else, but can we scan it one more time?

AA Michael: It's transmuted.

R: Thank you, brother. Did we get disconnected?

AA Michael: Yes.

R: Yes. I felt that.

AA Michael: While we were working on her insecurities, she disconnected it.

R: Why did she disconnect it?

AA Michael: Being afraid of being a strong energy.

R: Can we assist her, so she won't be afraid of being strong?

AA Michael: Yes.

R: Her question is, she wanted to know if she has ever felt love in this life? Her Higher Self kind of explained that with her past life, that's how she feels, that she has to give in order to receive. Can you explain a little bit about that, please?

AA Michael: It's true, she's never felt unconditional love in this lifetime.

R: Why is that?

AA Michael: Because of the strong infringement.

R: Will she begin to sense and feel that love energy now that we have cleared, and Aurora has also assisted with clearing those energies as well? Is she able now to feel that?

AA Michael: At least it always depends on her. She always chooses. It's her own freewill but if she wants everything, it is possible and up to her. Try, try, just try it now.

R: To feel this love because she always feels as if she has to give in order to receive, will she come into a time where she won't feel that need that she has to give in order to receive?

AA Michael: Yes, but that will come directly when she's feeling it for the first time. Instantly. Because then you don't have to think of it or even just feel it.

R: Is there any way that we can spark that love energy within her so she can recognize it?

AA Michael: Yes.

R: Thank you.

AA Michael: So, it is also going to be easier to connect to her own Source Love-Light because she is now getting more and more brightened up. It's even making her stronger. Now she is protected and more aligned - lightened.

R: She also wanted to know about her progress with her bladder. How is it going?

AA Michael: Yes, it's about the fear. She fears a lot, not so much as she used to. But she's not in trust yet. So, she has to get along with the bladder.

R: Can we work on that trust?

AA Michael: Yes. You see how it's all aligning with each other, how it's all intertwining, how it's all coming together?

R: Yes. I do. She wanted to know about her body mass. If there is a way that it can be tightened for her, as well as, you know, her breasts to be more lifted and more perky. Everything more tight for her, can we work on that?

AA Michael: Yes.

R: Thank you. What about her teeth? She said that she had braces. They removed them straight and now the bottom two teeth are curving kind of like inwards. They're not as straight. What caused that or what is causing that?

AA Michael: Holding on.

R: What is she holding on to?

AA Michael: Not speaking out?

R: Okay. Can we work on it where she can speak and be fluid with her inner voice?

AA Michael: Yes.

R: Thank you. That she may not hold back on anything but be fluid and speak without fear as we are reducing that. Would that assist with straightening back her teeth?

AA Michael: Yes. I know what you're about to say, it is absolutely okay to end the session. It's all done what has to be done for today. It's all good. You did great, Rose.

END OF SESSION

This was an intense and informative session. How does one release themselves from such tyrannical Archon control? If they do, what possibilities do they have to remember the soul they once were before the layered accumulation of trauma, built by accepting to be a soldier for Archons? When allowing by giving one's sovereignty away to the Archons, how does one break free from this tyrannical A.I.'s grasp? It must be one of the most powerful artificial trappings. Once they have their hold upon a soul, they will do all that's within their power to not let it go.

Through this session we discover what Archons most commonly look like, within forms of giant spiders and octopuses. We often find Archon tentacles within people in sessions through their Body Scans. These tentacles, they use as sharp knives that pierce through penetrating auric fields that then latch on to people, in order to infringe upon a person's thoughts and decisions of their most organic positive timelines. As the Archons gain much light feeding when they maintain and astray people into a negative Inverted A.I. timeline. Once in, they can easily maneuver the person's thoughts and choices for their negative polarization types of agendas. As how Hailee's thoughts were controlled and manipulated by the Archons, through this Reptilian soldier that she was.

The power of the technology within the suit that was embedded into her as an implant. The implanted suit allows for traveling through the various Dimensions, speaking of different languages, shielding itself for protection and masking. We have heard how Reptilians contain these abilities, and can be as chameleons blending into their environment, making them into skilled spies. This explains to us how this is, through the forms of Archon created negative technologies as this implanted suit. These advanced negative technologies, controlling the once positive Reptilians into now negative polarized hived systems of soldiers. Prisoners in their own body and programmed like a robot. The mention of how she easily grabs from the Dimensions the light to eat for her nourishment. The way the Reptilians are organically designed, it is as easy as taking a breath would be for us for them to nourish off feeding on light, how she is able to slurp in the light. I am sure to an Archon this would be such a wondrous race for them to infringe and control, to use for their aggressive feeding of light from all organic forms in the Universe.

Out of this squad of Reptilian compromised soldiers, she was the only that felt the awareness of infringement, that allowed moments of clarity. This tells us her strength of light and soul, even if she might not want to accept it and see it, we can see it from our perspective. As Archangel Michael said during her Body Scan, "the light is always there inside." The dangers and fears that she went through knowing that she was conscious of her infringements, and no one else was. How to hide this awareness and light to prevent getting caught? I am sure we all have felt like this in a moment in time in our lives. When we became aware of the strength of our light in this life and realized no one else sensed and saw the falseness of this world around us through our family units. I am sure we can relate to the feeling she felt, when she longed freedom for her and her people within the A.I. hollowed controlled space. She was able to overcome her fears, of knowing the Archons' power of being able to bring instant death, instant reset if they tried to rebel. As she did rebel and freed herself and watched as her Reptilian squad then too positively polarized and were freed because of her choices in strength. What an inspiration!

By being a Reptilian pawn of the Archons, still to this day we see how she carries the guilt of destroying a planet, how she threw away her feelings or buried them deep down within her to not feel them. As a human incarnated, carrying this deep wound rooted within her soul. We can see how this could block her from connecting deep enough with others through the heart. Much of what was shown in this session was vital for what is to come in the next two sessions. These puzzle pieces we have been discovering through various A.U.R.A. Hypnosis Healing sessions are then pieced together in the next two future sessions to allow for Hailee's most highest healing to take place. We continue with Hailee's journey in the next Chapter.

Our infinite love to the new student Rose, who conducted her first session with much beauty and professionalism for Hailee. A testament to our detailed A.U.R.A. Hypnosis Healing Training Course. As Rose so beautifully demonstrated, all are able to hold love for healing to assist another in need of healing deep rooted trauma.

"FEAR is a masterful vibration that seeps deep into our essence paralyzing us to not to:
Expand our wings wide!
Express our purest form!
Unleash our invincibility!
Stand forth within our sovereignty!
Break free from control!
Silently listen to follow our light!"
~Aurora♥

-------------<◇>-------------

18

DRIFTING IN SPACE FOR AN ETERNITY

Session #233: Recorded in January 2020. Never before shared.
Special Series: 3 of 4

In this online A.U.R.A. Hypnosis Healing session, we connect Hailee to her much-needed self-healing to prepare her for what is to come for her monumental final session. Here we continue the journey and here we reconnect to the Reptilian left floating in space in her previous session.

-------------<◇>-------------

"Change the point of view. See it as a game, see it as an experience, see it as a chance to write a book, to write a history, to watch a movie. It is just a life. It is just an experience. Don't make it too hard for yourself. Everything is important, of course, but if you think of it over, and over, and over, and over again, you put so much heaviness into it that you struggle of course."
-Higher Self

-------------<◇>-------------

A: [Aurora] Have you landed on the ground yet?
H: [Hailee] No. I don't know why but there's… I don't have a connection right now.
A: That's okay. Let's keep taking deep breaths - deep breaths, allowing it to flow through you. Do you feel or see any colors around you?
H: No, I don't see colors.
A: Tell me what's going on. What are you feeling?
H: I'm thinking about asking for Archangel Michael.
A: Okay, very good. For some reason, you've been taken to this space. We don't always see a past life. Perhaps there's no need for a past life this time around. I want you to start envisioning his beautiful energy coming forward starting from your crown, scanning your body, and connecting through you. Higher Self, I love you, I honor you, thank you, and respect you. Higher Self, if could please speak to you now.

The Higher Self is called forth.
Higher Self: Greetings.
A: Greetings. Higher Self. Thank you for bringing her to me today. It's such an honor to be speaking to you once more excited to see what answers and healings are meant to come forth for her today.
Higher Self: Beautiful. Thank you.
A: Yes, your energy is beautiful. Higher Self, she asked for Archangel Michael. Should we bring him forth now?
Higher Self: She asked for Archangel Michael because she thinks that he is the strongest connection, but I can speak now.

A: Beautiful. Yes, thank you. That's what I was getting as well, good. Well, we can have Archangel Michael in the background in case we need any assistance in the future. Thank you.
Higher Self: He is already here.

The Body Scan begins.
A: Of course, he is. Let's just go ahead and start it off with a body scan, just to make sure that she doesn't have any blockages of any kind before we start asking questions for her. Higher Self, if you could please start scanning her body all the way from the top, down to her toes. Scanning for any negative energies and/or entities. Anything that is negative within her, let me know if you find anything.
Higher Self: No.
A: Do we need Archangel Michael to double-check that or you think you're good?
Higher Self: I'm good.
A: Wonderful. Yes, her energy feels very clear. She's been doing a wonderful job.
Higher Self: Yes, she is. I'm thinking about what I can feel, but that is not negative. I can feel her doubts. This has nothing to do with you know, infringement, it's just her beliefs.
A: Yes, very good. Okay. So, we're going to go ahead and get going with the questions that she has Higher Self. She wants to know - which Archangel is her Higher Self since she was you know, given Haniel and she works for Michael. Higher Self, who are you?
Higher Self: She doesn't understand it at this moment of time. I can try to explain. Archangel Michael already explained she's from the higher realms. That means she's Seraphim and Elohim. And, of course, Source.
A: Yes, and is there a name that you go by Higher Self?
Higher Self: More like a frequency.
A: Wonderful. Anything else you could tell her about who she is, as her Higher Self?
Higher Self: I know that she's interested, and she has a lot of questions. Because she doesn't understand everything. She's doubting and so she's questioning a lot (laughs). And it's okay. It's her past. She's exploring a lot at this moment, and she must get the old out of old belief system. She's still sometimes in the autopilot mode. Then sometimes she gets aware of it and thinks like, 'Oh, another hour has left, and I wasn't aware.' So, it is like her belief system, everything she has learned at school from parents, from you know, TV, films, books - everything.
A: Thank you. Is there a ray color for that?
Higher Self: It's a special, bright, crystalline bright, so bright and shiny. I think it's a color that doesn't exist here in this time and space right now. There's no word for it.
A: Beautiful. Higher Self, she wanted to ask if you could age her soul to the maximum capacity in this time of space for her highest good?
Higher Self: Yes.
A: Good. If you could start that process now, please. Okay, and she also wanted to know, is her soul 100 percent intact and functioning? Are there fractals missing that still need to be integrated into her?
Higher Self: It is like they were called back - all the fractals, last time. But what can I say, she denied to integrate some? They were here but not fully integrated.
A: Integrating these that didn't integrate last time. Would this be good for her highest good?
Higher Self: Yes because last time she was not ready. But it's okay. One step after another.
A: Can you start that process now? Can you tell us about some of those fractals that you are integrating into her?
Higher Self: Yes. She's ready now. This is trust. Trust and infinite love and also hope. And, of course, belief in herself.

A: Yes. Can you tell us a little more detail as far as what fractals she is integrating? Is this from some particular lives or races?

Higher Self: She lost a lot of fractals a long time ago. Some are lost in this particular life, but also other lives. So, a lot of lives in the past were without love, without hope, and a lot of fear. Such darkness! I'm so proud of how she's doing right now. She should know that it is absolutely okay to do this step by step. She was wondering why is it her, that she needs more sessions? But it's beautiful what she's doing. We need time for the change. She's doing it super-fast.

A: I agree. Yes, and thank you also, I know you bring her sessions, so I think that encourages her. So, continue doing that for her.

Higher Self: She needs that. Because there's a cycle, she has problems sleeping. So, she is not fully energized when she wakes up. So, at that time during the daytime, she needs a lot of rest because she is not fully recharged. She has a lot of time you could say, lazy. But it's not really lazy. She thinks it is lazy, but she's not at her highest vibration. So that is why she, you know, takes a lot of pauses.

A: Yes. You need that break in between especially when you're working hard.

Higher Self: But she doesn't really understand that we are all working. Not only here, but all this ripples out to other Dimensions, what she does here and everything she decides here has an effect. Also, every decision when she's thinking about, shall I do this or that she creates timelines and sometimes she's really fast in saying, "I'm going to do this." And then there are times like doubting again. She needs time to envision something and then step forward. To accept or to be aware that it is just the thinking and this matrix. On the one hand she's aware of it but on the other hand... She's also ready for the story that comes behind, that comes with the integration. She needs to be at the strongest, at the highest vibration because the visions, the connections to what happened or what happens or what will happen will come to her. And it's important that she does not fear, that she's aware that this is what reality is like. This connection is already here. She's now ready to open up even more for every connection - the connection to the Archangels, spiritual guides, magical creatures, her Guardian Angels, her ancestors. Last year she was trying to have a lot of contact but because of all that infringement, she wasn't able to even though she was seeking for it. This will change now.

A: Beautiful. She also wanted to know if you can open up her heart chakra? You know the one in the middle and also the second chakra. Can we start that process for her today?

Higher Self: Yes, she's ready.

A: Thank you. Higher Self, can you also look at her if there are any negative cords? Any that we can go ahead and remove, transmute, and heal? Let me know if you find any.

Higher Self: They are not negative. They are just good cords, but they need to be healed.

A: Can we go ahead and start the process of healing them all now?

Higher Self: Yes.

A: Thank you. Specifically, she wanted us to look over healing all good cords. Especially with the family members during our last A.U.R.A. session in September[14], Michael said that it was not the right timing to heal the family cords. Is it now?

Higher Self: Yes.

A: Beautiful. Can we start that process please, Higher Self?

Higher Self: Yes.

A: Thank you. If we could also heal the lacks in childhood, fill them with Love-Light, those lacks.

Higher Self: Yes.

---

[14] This is referencing her second A.U.R.A. session, where she primarily focused on self-healing from infringements acquired from another energy healer who was not heart centered. Her second session is not included in this book.

A: Thank you and then while we're there in the childhood Higher Self, can you tell us a little bit more about when she was accidentally exchanged with another child when she was born? Can you tell more about that story, how that happened, and why? Please give us the details.

Higher Self: Okay, she's trying to interfere... A foreign lady, the other mother, she needed that bright shining light from her.

A: From Hailee?

Higher Self: Yes. Even though it was planned, it was not an accident you can say. So, it was all planned and agreed with the Higher Self. Also, to learn separation as an experience and having problems with grounding and, you know this is also a lot to do with that.

A: Did Hailee give her light when she fed from her?

Higher Self: Yes.

A: You said that this needs grounding.

Higher Self: It was because she was brought away from her origin mother, there was no grounding anymore. So that is why she always has struggles with grounding.

A: Can we heal that for her now, please?

Higher Self: Yes.

A: Wonderful, thank you, start doing that... If you can scan her past childhood just to see if there was any sexual abuse, as she kind of feels like there was but does not remember. As you know, some of these things if there were, they need to be cleared and healed.

Higher Self: Yes, there was a hand on her vagina.

A: What is this hand connected to?

Higher Self: Okay, she again is in some kind of fear because she's always wanting to know that. She can trust me; it is all right. She's strong enough now.

A: Yes, help her step to the side. If you can share when you're ready.

Higher Self: It was technology and humanoid looking but inside, it was technology. She was very little, more like a baby.

A: When did it happen? Let me know what you're showing her.

Higher Self: So, it's not like that the fingers got into the vagina, just like touching the lips but not for bad intentions. It was more like accident or not really to infringe or for sexual abuse. It was more like, 'Oops'. But of course, it caused something in her. I tried to tell her which person it was because she knows this person.

A: Were you able to show her?

Higher Self: She wouldn't listen, so I will try now again. I know that it is a lot. She just has to understand. This is just an experience and this experience is as good as a beautiful ice cream because both experiences are worthy. Don't judge as bad or not bad. They are both worthy to make it and it doesn't have to be in fear. You are safe. It is her uncle - the brother of her mother.

A: Okay, so how much older was her uncle than her?

Higher Self: Forty-four years older.

A: You said that he had some kind of like technology in him? Trying to understand that, he was a human but was a droid? Or what?

Higher Self: Yes, he's not really human. He's placed there for infringement.

A: What kind of side effects or discomforts from it occurred that need healing?

Higher Self: He's the one that opened the bar with the grandma, as she told you, she grew up there in this bar. So, she got in contact with some souls that were struggling a lot and were not at their highest vibrations - sadness, anger, fear - more of negative vibration. It is a bit weird because he likes her, and he also struggles with his own path even though he is a robotic type.

A: How has this affected her and in the present, so we can heal?

Higher Self: Oh, this is also something to do with ancestral lines and also with the miscarriages of the mother. This influenced a lot so of course; it was also like being misunderstood. 'Nobody understands me,' struggling with self-esteem, being unsure, feeling unpretty, a lot of negative belief systems. Also, in this family, it was not usual to give a hug or two. You know being gentle with each other like a kiss or something as well, it's not usual.

A: Can we start healing those traumas in the way it affects her in the now?

Higher Self: Yes.

A: She says during her body scan on her own she noticed that she has a positive implant on her third eye. Why's that there? Who placed it there?

Higher Self: We placed it there to be sure that in this lifetime, so she already knew that this lifetime work would be easy, but we know that she would have to go through different struggles and different experiences but to make it even happen - for this change to be possible - we implanted this positive implant.

A: When was it placed in there?

Higher Self: In the womb before she was born.

A: Can you help her not feel guilty? What advice do you have for her?

Higher Self: Change the point of view. See it as a game, see it as an experience, see it as a chance to write a book, to write a history, to watch a movie. It is just a life. It is just an experience. Don't make it too hard for yourself. Everything is important, of course, but if you think of it over, and over, and over again, you put so much heaviness into it that you struggle of course. It is okay what she experiences because she can handle it. She's so strong that everything is possible. And she becomes aware of it even more and more each day. She will understand it fully sometime. But it won't take her so much time to change the point of view.

A: Good. She wanted to know if we could help her heal a dream, vision maybe? The past life where she was a male soldier in a war fighting, and she is still laying between dead bodies in the mud on the ground, pretending to be dead hoping that no one sees and finds her? The enemy comes closer, looks around, and she's in fear that they discover her trying to hold her breath with eyes closed. What is this about?

Higher Self: This was a past life, was the First World War and she was a man soldier, and he was in fear to be seen and then to be shot dead. So, this was also brought to her life now, the fear of being seen and then being killed by that. This was to show up then and that is not a good idea.

A: Yes. Can you help her remove and heal that so she will no longer have the fear of being seen which is connected to that life or any trauma?

Higher Self: Yes.

A: One of her main goals today is from her third A.U.R.A. session in November. She was a lonely negative Reptilian who freed a whole ship of negative Reptilians into positive polarization. He still drifts alone in the Universe and space. Can we help him free and find his light? Where's he going to go? So, if you can locate him? Let me know if you need any aid from Michael so we can locate him, see what we can do.

Higher Self: Yes, we need Archangel Michael.

A: Okay, very good. Higher Self, if you could connect us to Archangel Michael now, please.

Higher Self: Yes.

A: Greetings, is this Michael?

AA Michael: Yeah.

A: Thank you for joining us today. We love you dearly Michael. Thank you for all your beautiful assistance overall for everyone we help with A.U.R.A. and specifically with Hailee. Truly, you know she has grown significantly from being able to trust you and having your assistance through her A.U.R.A. Hypnosis Healing sessions. Thank you!

AA Michael: Thank you.

A: We're looking at trying to figure out from her last A.U.R.A. session in November, if you can locate where is that Reptilian that was somewhere in space that needs aid, that being she was. Let me know when you can find him.

AA Michael: This is a different timeline and different Universe, and he was once positive then caught by the Archons and influenced negatively. So, he was a soldier then. His sadness, his loneliness, is connected to her. She can feel him, she feels that.

A: How's he doing? Can you check on him? Where is he?

AA Michael: He's outside in space. He has no spaceship. He's still alive. He's there like an eternity. He doesn't like it. He's sad and he's lonely. He's nervous that we're talking about him. He sees how we're helping him today.

A: Wonderful. So, you say he's just floating in space now. Can I speak to him, Michael? Can you connect me now to that Reptilian there, please?

AA Michael: Yes.

A: Thank you. We would like to speak to that Reptilian there that needs aid in space please.

Reptilian Being: Yes.

A: Greetings. Thank you for speaking to us. It's an honor to be speaking to you today. May I ask you questions, please?

Reptilian Being: Yes. Thank you for speaking with me (crying)!

A: Thank you. It's an honor to be here with you and as you know, we are really hoping to be able to assist you today with your permission. We love you dearly and I know that you've been through a lot through the different situations that occurred with you and the Reptilians, and the Archons and so on. In this time and space, it is time to release that, let that go, and to allow yourself to heal. So that you may no longer have to suffer in this manner. So that you may ascend into a positive polarization of yourself, where you can be free and go somewhere else. Perhaps incarnate somewhere where you no longer have to be tied to, being stuck like this and so lonely. Would you allow us to aid you today?

Reptilian Being: Yes. I was waiting for this for so long. I was not able to help myself.

A: Well, we are here to help you so that you may help yourself.

Reptilian Being: Thank you (crying).

A: We need you now to look within you and find that light within you. We're going to go ahead and help you spread it. Spread it to all that is you, every root, every cord. Everything that you are within you, all your entire body there - spread to all light. Do you have any consciousness here attached to anyone or anything negative to anyone else?

Reptilian Being: Before I start, I ask for the Archangels around me. I've been lonely for so long.

A: If you can make sure that Archangels are supporting him now, around him, giving him love and support. Thank you.

Reptilian Being: (sighing with relief).

A: Wonderful. Now continue to spread that Love-Light to all that is you. Do you have any other attachments to anyone out there?

Reptilian Being: No, they cut all the cord.

A: So, there's no consciousness, no negative technology that you are attached to anyone?

Reptilian Being: No.

A: Okay, good. So, keep spreading that Love-Light and let us know once you're all light.

Reptilian Being: It's beginning.

A: Good, let us know once you're all light.

Positive Polarized Reptilian Being: Yes.

A: Now that you are of the light, tell me how you feel.

Positive Polarized Reptilian Being: Ah! (sighing heavily) So much peace.

A: Do you have any messages for us or Hailee?

Positive Polarized Reptilian Being: I'm so thankful that she was able to take that step to help me, help all of us. This is huge. I'm still recharging because... I'm in the light now but I'm not at my full strength again.

A: Can we have the Archangels assist you with building up your strength?

Positive Polarized Reptilian Being: Oh, yes please.

A: Archangel Michael, let us know too if you could have Raphael help heal him as well and build up his strength, please.

Higher Self: Yes.

A: Thank you Raphael, for doing that. As we continue the healing and helping her out. Let's go ahead and see now that you are no longer having to be stuck in this role. Let's see where it is that they will take you. If we can have Archangel Azrael and his Legion of Light? Let's see where you're meant to go next for your positive Ascension. Let us know once you have arrived at where they're taking you.

Positive Polarized Reptilian Being: I'm going to my tribe.

A: Where are they at?

Positive Polarized Reptilian Being: I don't have a body anymore, just light energy.

A: Tell me what's going on.

Positive Polarized Reptilian Being: So, a lot of the souls I had freed from the ship were already there and they welcomed me and hugged me even though you can't hug (laughing joyfully). But it is like hugging and you know, taking me in the middle and I'm back home. I'm with them. This is where I am meant to be, part of it. Not alone in the other place, this is where - like a puzzle and I was the missing part.

A: How beautiful it feels! Wonderful. Are there any messages that you have, or they have before we let you relax there?

Positive Polarized Reptilian Being: Yes, message for you, Aurora. There are so many souls out there so thankful because of your help. Most of them already said something to you and have made a connection with you or channeled or whatever. There are also others because it ripples out there, also others that didn't have opportunity right now to say thank you. So, they are all always so humbling, so grateful in saying thank you.

A: I feel that, thank you! It truly is like a dream come true, to be able to assist you all in this manner. And even more so now that we are certifying others on this Earth as we know how much density there is and how many people need help. There are so many. I am blessed and just thrilled and happy to know that we are certifying people out there just like Hailee and others that are going to start doing this work more hands-on there in their locations. Thank you.

Positive Polarized Reptilian Being: This is great.

A: That it is. Thank you. Are we done?

Positive Polarized Reptilian Being: Yeah. She feels it too.

A: Very good. She feels it too! Yes, it's a sensation and feeling we cannot express. We feel it too, thank you. Well, thank you. My infinite love to all of you there. And thank you for all of those who thank me as I thank you lovingly. Blessings to everyone. Thank you.

Positive Polarized Reptilian Being: Love you.

A: And I love you! If I can now speak back to her Higher Self, please?

Higher Self: Yes.

A: Thank you Michael for connecting us to him and what a beautiful experience to see him transform. He's just such a beautiful emotion and frequency to tap into. Can we heal within her - she mentioned that this seemed to be connected to that Reptilian - how she always feels like she's the last one to know? Can we heal that programming and that trauma for her, please?

AA Michael: Yes. She already knows everything.

A: What a beautiful healing today. Higher Self, I want her to know too that just how you spoke to her today, you are able to find all those answers for her, that she can as well do that. As you said, if she trusts, doesn't doubt, let's go, and allows for it to flow through her. She can very much place herself in theta brainwave very easily. She's really become a master at it. So, may she continue to remember that she can get her answers at any point and she is lovingly supported by so many - so many that she doesn't even realize. Thank you.

Higher Self: Yes, that it is.

A: Thank you, Higher Self. Thank you, Archangel Michael, Raphael, and Azrael, anyone else who aided today. We love you, honor you, and respect you. Thank you for your assistance.

Higher Self: Thank you, thank you, thank you. Love you so much!

A: And I love you!

END OF SESSION

Doubt is one of the biggest obstacles of emotions to address in this session for Hailee. And it is one of the most influential vibrations that keeps us from connecting to our own inner knowing and expansion and answers. As doubt becomes a dam to our infinite river of Higher Self's consciousness connection. The dam of doubt slows down the organic process of us being able to connect clearly and strongly. As we know through a dam the infinite river water is still able to flow through the dam, it just takes a lot longer as it slows the natural flow of the water/Higher Self's consciousness to connect through us.

At a recent A.U.R.A. Hypnosis Healing Certification Retreat Training, our beloved sister Dolores came through wanting to deliver a very important message needed for the group's expansion. She said, "Doubt is what will hold you all back from accomplishing your soul's mission here and after. It will be an emotion that will become your self-inflicted biggest blockage. It is also interesting and funny at the same time, as you receive divine knowledge from your Higher Self and guides of your soul for your remembrance and gaining of sovereignty. The reason being that it is funny is… Do you really believe that Archons would be the ones telling you, that you carry an Angelic fractal or that you are Cleopatra? NO, absolutely not! Instead, they will be the ones causing the doubt to not believe in whom you are in Creation. So, then, why do you doubt?! Release doubt and then you will release your limitations that you have placed upon your TRUE soul's expansion."

In this moment in time, we look back upon Chapter 12 ('Leviathan Fallen Angel'), when Dante's crystal guide speaks:

Crystal: "He needs to stop doubting himself. He is not crazy. I am real. He is a dragon. He is an angel, and he is many, many, many other things. When we doubt, we do their job for them. An enemy becomes docile when they forget. You are their enemy. This is what they will try to do to him. They will try to get him to doubt the reality that he creates, they will try to get him to accept the reality that is around him. His construct, his program is a simulation. He must maintain his resolve and not doubt. Even when it's all he can feel he must fight. He is a tank, he goes forward. But if he has the wrong idea in his mind, in his heart, he will take that forward too. He must be very careful with who he surrounds himself with, he is not an empath, but he can take in their feelings. But he is not able to transmute it, if he surrounds himself with too much negativity. Despite all of those measures, the crystals, the shielding, and the sage and the cleansing of the aura, it will corrupt him. He will lower his vibration; his abilities will diminish, and it will make him vulnerable. Just do not doubt. This is real. I am real."

Wow, what a clear realization this wisdom and knowledge shared with us is. When WE doubt, we are doing their job for them, and that "WE DO NOT CONSENT TO." In this time and space and in infinity, let's take our sovereignty back, and stop giving it away by doubting ourselves!

What is mentioned above and below, by Dante's Crystal Guide and Hailee's Higher Self, we shall understand at the deepest level when we receive the soul awakening catalyzing knowledge in Chapter 37 ('Matrix Pods'). How it is that we can create timelines, in the most profound level within our doubts here at the densest Third Dimension, and how it is at the utmost importance that we are cautious of who it is we surround ourselves with, no matter the circumstance.

Hailee's Higher Self said: "But, she doesn't really understand that we are all working. Not only here, but all this ripples out to other Dimensions, what she does here and everything she decides here has an effect. Also, every decision when she's thinking about, shall I do this or that she creates timelines and sometimes she's really fast in saying, "I'm going to do this." And then there are times like doubting again. She needs time to envision something and then step forward."

This session is a very important moment in time and space for Hailee and in the next session we will find out why. Why was healing her Reptilian fractal in this session so vital for her soul's evolution and healing? How long was he waiting in space for us to conduct the A.U.R.A. Hypnosis Healing sessions to no longer have to float alone in the vastness of emptiness and sorrow for what feels like eternity? Will this healing aid Hailee in her human life to finally shift into a higher vibration of sovereignty? These are glimpses into the deep healing process that is needed if someone has been this rooted in being negatively polarized. We are truly grateful to Hailee for sharing her journey with us!

"When deciding our divine path, we must remember to conclude all thoughts from within a frequency of highest clearest heart. Not of pain, worry, doubt, fear, anger, for then our conclusion will match these frequencies."
~Aurora 🖤

-------------<◇>-------------

19

THE ARCHON ARMY RECRUIT

Recorded in April 2020. Never before shared.
Special Series: 4 of 4

In this online A.U.R.A. Hypnosis Healing session, Maria is the A.U.R.A. practitioner for this intense monumental session for Hailee. This is Hailee's final session in her fascinating series of four A.U.R.A. Hypnosis Healing sessions. We journeyed with her in previous sessions, where she has shown us much on the polarities that a soul can experience. In this intense finale, she helps us understand further what it is to be a Reptilian before accepting the role of being a soldier and the process of once agreeing to it, including what happens to one's Reptilian family. Once the conscious being has given their power away, what comes with it and what kind of reign do the Archons have over the disempowered soul who gave their sovereignty away? What does it take to break free from the Archons' control over one's soul?

-------------<◇>-------------

"To show her that it's just a decision. To decide every day, every hour, every second in what vibration you want to exist."
-Higher Self

-------------<◇>-------------

M: [Maria] Have you landed on the ground? What do you sense?
H: [Hailee] Hmm... I see something but it's just for a few seconds and then it's gone, and I can't describe it, so I ask for something clearer.
M: Tell me once you can start seeing once more, tell me what you see once you see it.
H: Okay, now I see a person, a human body sitting in something like a car but without any roof and a person is driving but the head is burning.
M: The person that's on the wheel driving - head is burning?
H: Mm-hmm.
M: Where is this car? What kind of land or terrain is it in?
H: Sand, but it is dirty sand and hot, so the trees are kind of, there is no green. Everything is dry and no leaves. Everything is like that.
M: Do you have a body here?
H: I don't know.
M: That's all right. Is there anyone else around except for this person?
H: Yes, a raven, a black raven.
M: Where is the black raven?
H: First it was sitting on something and then flew away.
M: What was it sitting on?
H: Something like a balcony.
M: Okay. Is the person in the car still around?

H: No.

M: Look back at the person that was in the car that you just saw, first describe what the person looks like.

H: Totally black clothes, everything is in black also the hands are in gloves, black gloves. But the face is completely burning.

M: What color is the fire?

H: Red orange.

M: Does the person look comfortable driving with the face burning?

H: The person doesn't scream.

M: How many fingers does the person have in the gloves?

H: I don't know. It looks like a humanoid body.

M: Okay. Is the person carrying anything?

H: I can't see it.

M: Is it male or female? What do you sense?

H: Male.

M: Is he young or old?

H: Middle-aged.

M: This dress the other person is wearing, does it feel like the regular clothes this person wears or like a uniform. What does it sense or feel like to you?

H: Could be uniform, but I don't see badges or something like that. But now he's back and he comes out of the car and walks towards me.

M: Does he see you?

H: I guess so.

M: Do you have a body?

H: Yes, I seem to be human, but I wear something like an astronaut suit with a helmet.

M: Okay, what color is your astronaut suit?

H: White.

M: Are you still wearing a helmet?

H: Yes.

M: Okay.

H: I wear the helmet, but the window is open.

M: Do you feel young or old?

H: Like in the 20's.

M: Look at your hands and describe how many fingers do you have?

H: I don't know.

M: What are you wearing on your hands?

H: Gloves, white gloves.

M: If you look at the fingers on the gloves, how many fingers does the glove have?

H: Three.

M: What are you wearing on your feet?

H: Boots.

M: What color are your boots?

H: Also white.

M: Do you feel male or female?

H: Male.

M: Are you carrying anything in your hands?

H: No.

M: Okay. What happens next? Is his face still on fire?

H: He isn't there anymore, but when he came to me directly, I was a little bit afraid.

M: What about him made you feel frightened?

H: I knew him, and he was angry because of something.

M: Do you know what he's angry about?

H: Something went wrong maybe. Maybe it was my fault and so he needed to tell me.

M: Let's see what happens as he is approaching you. What does he say?

H: Oh! He cut off my head!

M: Higher Self, please be around to ensure she does not feel any discomfort or pain from any of the experiences. She can simply be a viewer. Just view the experience instead of sensing and feeling any trauma. Let's go back to a time in this existence that you need to see. Trying to find out why you reached this situation for this person to behave and act out this act to you. Go back in time when you met this person. The time in this existence when this all started and what led to this. You're there now. Tell me what you see.

H: (Breathing deep).

M: Where are you now? What do you see?

H: Sitting at a table in my home thinking. Going into something like the army. Some recruit like a soldier.

M: Are you going to recruit other soldiers? Is that what you're going for or you're going to interview to become a soldier?

H: I'm thinking about myself going to go there.

M: Okay. How old do you feel here? Young or old?

H: I'm younger. But I'm already an adult.

M: What are you wearing?

H: Brown shoes and something like green trousers and a beige shirt. My skin color is green.

M: Your skin color is green?

H: I'm a reptile!

M: You're a reptile and you want to join the army? Is that what you're going to an interview for?

H: Mm-hmm.

M: You're there now. Describe what you see.

H: There is a powerful soldier, a boss, a General. I don't know... whatever a higher position. Feeling that he's not the same race as me. He's different. He's wearing a mask. I'm in!!! Wasn't a lot; wasn't many questions. I thought I had to do a test or something. But it was very easy to come in. But I realized that they made something with me.

M: What did you realize?

H: They put me in tests and physical and also put me on drugs and mind control.

M: Okay, describe this person that you just mentioned right now, the one taking the interview. You said he looks like he's a different race. Describe what he looks like.

H: He's wearing a mask so he's hiding.

M: What kind of mask is it?

H: Looks like, kind of umm... not a devil but devilish.

M: What color is it?

H: Black.

M: Can you see anything at all through the mask? You'll be able to sense even if you can't see you can sense the answers for yourself. What kind of race is it?

H: They are powerful. Negative!

M: What color is his suit?

H: It's black.

M: Does he have a tail or anything else that stands out?

H: No.

M: What color is his skin?

H: He's wearing a suit so I can't see anything of his skin or his face.

M: Okay. So, they give you some drugs and they ask you to perform some tests. What kind of physical tests did you have to perform?

H: There were several other soldiers and first we're walking a long distance. We're tired and thirsty. It's a long distance and it's hot. Sandy, no water. No water.

M: What do people do there if they want to drink something or if they get thirsty?

H: We all are searching. We're hungry and thirsty and searching for energy. So, I guess, we have to search for other life forms there on the planet.

M: Right. So, have all the soldiers that appeared for the interview, have they all been selected? Or has anyone been rejected as well?

H: I don't know. We are not allowed to talk to each other.

M: Are they all Reptilians?

H: I don't know, I just see the mess. I don't see them as one. I just see how many. This is huh... I don't know if there are different races. I don't know.

M: Is it day or night?

H: The sun goes down.

M: What is the basic color of the planet? Can you see that?

H: Reddish?

M: Okay, what happens next as you're searching for energy now. What do you do next when you're searching for energy for yourself? You're there now. What happens next?

H: We don't find other life forms, so we start to kill each other!

M: How do you kill each other?

H: So, they're different races. Some of them are like bugs or Mantis and some of them are Reptilians. Some of them look more humanoid. They all use different techniques to attack. Some just try to run away. Some try to hide.

M: Let's see what happens. You've been given your mission, the general that hired you. What is the mission that he's given you? You're there at the point now just going back once more to the time when the general discusses the mission or what your role is. What has he recruited you for? You're there now.

H: To survive... to, to simply survive!

M: Where do you have to survive? On the same planet? Or do you have to go to other places?

H: Hmm... I don't...

M: That's fine. We will find that out. Why is it that other races like the bugs you mentioned, the Mantis, Reptilians, and humanoids... they are from other races, but are they other races from the same planet or they've come from another planet, another Dimension?

H: Different Dimensions, different galaxies.

M: Describe some of the bugs that you see; what are the bugs that you see?

H: Some are like insects and some are like bugs.

M: Thank you. Let's move on. You were searching for energy for yourself and you said you were hiding. You're hiding so no one attacks you, what happens next? Describe it.

H: Most of them are dead. There is just some fighting but far away. Now it is kind of the end of the fighting scene. I can see the dead bodies lying around, walking like through a war field.

M: What happens next? Is there anyone else other than you who have survived?

H: There are others who are hiding but they're not wanting to kill me. They are shocked and they don't want to fight like me. I don't want to fight. We are afraid, we are afraid because we know we had to be here to fight. So, we didn't fight.

M: What happens next?

H: That's why he cut off my head because I didn't fight.

M: Could you go back once more before that happens. Does he have a conversation with you? Higher Self, please make sure that she does not feel any discomfort and trauma from it. Just experience it from a viewer's point of view. Thank you. What is he saying?

H: He was not really speaking to me, but his thoughts were something like "Sh*t, it didn't work so we have to do it again." Like they were trying something to manipulate against free will or something like that.

M: Who are they trying to manipulate?

H: They try to do that with these different races all over the galaxies.

M: Is this the same general that interviewed you for the role?

H: Yes.

M: What does he do with the rest of the soldiers that were recruited that did not fight and that were hiding? What does he do with them?

H: I don't know.

M: What happens next as you're taking your last breath? You're taking your last breath and you're coming out of the body. What do you feel? What are your thoughts?

H: Relief! Relief because I was kind of in pain and something like, "Damn, that sucked." (laughing)

M: Yes.

H: No, it was uh-huh.

M: What is the name of this planet that you're on right now?

H: Catoba.

M: Okay. What happens next? Follow your soul to see where it goes. What happens to your soul?

H: OHHHHH!!!! They put me back in! They...they put my body back together and my soul was pulled back in. Even though I wanted it, I didn't want to, like catch me back in!

M: Who caught you back in?

H: The soldiers. So, I wanted to kind of you know, visit my soul family and I was trying to get there, and it was, something was holding me back and then I came back into the body.

M: Who puts you together?

H: Wow, I don't know. A doctor or something. My head is functioning again. But I am aware of what they did.

M: Were you not able to leave the body completely as a soul?

H: I was out of the body. Out of, but I had to, but I couldn't leave!

M: What did you feel when the soldier cut your head off? Physically, what did you sense?

H: Not again!

M: Not again?!

H: OH!!! They put something in me, on my soul that I couldn't leave even if the body is dead.

M: What is it that they put in your soul to hold you back? Describe it.

H: They hold all the cords. And that's what's holding me back.

M: They have cords in your soul?

H: Yes.

M: What color are those cords?

H: Black.

M: Okay. What happens next?

H: I don't want to fight. I'm tired.

M: Are they forcing you? Are you being forced to fight?

H: I know I have to, but I don't want it. I'm feeling like I'm in a waiting position and then know what's coming next. Again, a battlefield and I don't want to.

M: Who are they always fighting? Because it looks like they're just fighting with each other? What is the purpose of this fighting when you're fighting the same soldiers?

H: This is just a test arena.

M: Let's move along and see what happens. You said you're being forced to fight, and you do not want to fight. Do you have a family in this existence?

H: Yes, I miss them. I think of them very often. I have a mother and a father but no wife and no children.

M: You can tap into your mother and father's energy now. Let's go back to a point when you're with your mother and father on this planet in this existence, you're there now with your mother and father eating a meal. You're there with them now. Describe what you see.

H: It's very calm and cozy and familiar. Loving, everything feels safe. Very good family life.

M: Beautiful. Look into the eyes of your father. Does he remind you of anyone you know in this existence? Do you recognize him, his soul?

H: I can't look into the eyes.

M: You can't look into the eyes?

H: It's not possible.

M: Why is it not possible?

H: I just can see his head from the side.

M: What about your mother, can you look into your mother's eyes? Can you see your mother's eyes?

H: No. She's standing with the back to me.

M: What are you doing as a family?

H: Okay, now I see dragon eyes, but I don't know to which these... uh...

M: Describe your father and your mother; what are their bodies like?

H: Also green, greenish. And they have a skin as... ah… I don't know the word in English.

M: Yes, what is the skin like? Is it smooth or is it rough? Does it have scales, or it's got hair?

H: It's like uh... not with a... I don't know the word.

M: Are they reptiles just like you?

H: Yes.

M: What color are their eyes?

H: I can't see them, but I feel red.

M: Red? Beautiful. Are you on the same planet or are you somewhere else?

H: This is a different one.

M: So, you are actually on a different planet but for the interview, you went to a different planet is that what it is?

H: Yes.

M: Okay, describe this planet. What is the terrain like? Does it have suns and moons? Describe it to me - you know it all.

H: It's dark, I don't see the sun. But there are kind of mountains. Rocky mountains.

M: How do you come about the decision that you want to be a part of the army? How do you connect with these forces that are on another planet to join them?

H: I don't know what happened, but it seems like my parents died and I had no reason to stay there. So, I took that stand.

M: You're there at the time when you're deciding to join the army. Describe what you see. How did this thought come into your mind?

H: I'm totally lonely at the kitchen table. My parents are not there anymore, and I feel lonely.

M: What happens next?

H: I guess they weren't... they didn't die naturally. I guess they were killed, and I felt anger.

M: Who killed them?

H: I don't know.

M: You can sense very clearly. You have all the answers there with you. Who killed them? Someone you knew, someone you didn't know? Who was it?

H: I killed them.

M: What made you do that? What made you kill them?

H: I don't know, this is all so weird.

M: What made you do that?

H: I told them that I wanted to be the soldier and they didn't want to let me go.

M: What do you do then?

H: I try to explain that this is a great idea. To get a lot of knowledge. But they have not a good feeling. So, they warned me. I didn't want to hear that. I was so closed. I went further steps.

M: What happens next?

H: As a proof to be a soldier you had to kill your family. So, there's no going back. You decide your whole life to be in the army.

M: So, you've proved that you can be a good soldier?

H: Yes.

M: What happens next? Do you go for the interview? Is that what happens next?

H: Mm-hmm.

M: Okay! Why do you want to join the army? What is the main purpose of your motivation?

H: To learn and to get to other planets. Get known to other races, we have power and dominance.

M: You were at the place where they put your body together once more. Your soul was not allowed to leave and you're back in the situation where you have to be a soldier, but you don't want to be a soldier. What happens next?

H: I am being punished. Again.

M: What are you being punished for?

H: Because I didn't kill on the battlefield.

M: How do they punish you? Higher Self, please allow for it to be viewed, not sense and feel the trauma or any pain, please. Thank you.

H: It's something with me. It's fear that I'm totally afraid and frightened, shaking. I don't know what they're doing but I'm totally afraid. Totally in fear. Not fear of dying because I know I can't die but fear of making something with my mind. I don't know.

M: What is it that they're doing to put that fear in you?

H: They're showing me telepathically, pictures. On the first. To put guilt on me. How I murdered my parents and that I'm going to live forever because they always are going to flick me together. So that I'm always able to be a soldier and this is my whole existence right now. There's not going to be an end.

M: Is this something that they do very easily? Can you tell me a little bit more about that? Is it something to do with just the soldiers or they do it with others in the Universe too?

H: I don't know what they do to others. I'm not allowed to see or talk to others. I'm just a soldier. I have no rights.

M: What happens next of importance? You're there now.

H: I have proven that I'm a good soldier and that they can rely on me after passing a test, or several tests. This took very long; very long. This existence is so useless because it doesn't make any sense anymore. And then I get the first order to get to another planet.

M: Describe the order? Where do you have to go and what do you have to do?

Hailee had two previous A.U.R.A. sessions that brought the remainder of the pieces of this transcription together. The following are those of what comes next after accepting to become a Reptilian soldier.

H: This is the order with the diamond from the last A.U.R.A. session and from the other one. They just told me I have to go to the planet for the... Throw in the crystal in the pyramid.
M: Yes.
H: But I didn't know what I was doing. And after that, I was so bad that I killed the whole planet. I didn't know the effect that was coming.
M: And it is the same soldier that was floating in space later?
H: Yes.
M: Okay. Let's leave that life now.

The Higher Self is called forth.
M: Am I speaking to Hailee's Higher Self now?
Higher Self: Yes.
M: Greetings! Thank you, I love you, honor you, and respect you. And thank you very much for connecting Hailee and me together. I know that you have records of Hailee's different lives. May I ask you questions now?
Higher Self: Yes.
M: Thank you very much. Why is it that you chose to show her this life of a soldier once more?
Higher Self: She didn't know the whole story. And she was wondering, what made him so low density, so negative?
M: What was the purpose and lessons of that life?
Higher Self: To show her that it's just a decision. To decide every day, every hour, every second in what vibration you want to exist. But there are some decisions which are more important than other ones. And if you're turning into the wrong direction, sometimes you can't go back.
M: Yes. That is a very powerful message and I think it is something that Hailee would need at this point, considering what she's going through right now. Thank you for showing this life. May I ask a few more questions about this existence?
Higher Self: Yes.
M: Is this existence still on or it's something of the past? I know time does not exist and you could have parallel lives. How would you describe this life? Is it a parallel life or a life of the past or anything else that I'm not aware of yet?
Higher Self: This Reptilian exists in the current Dimension for there is no time. To explain it would be eons of years because he was so long under control. So long. But the possibility to free him put a ripple into other Dimensions too and there are several ones healed just through that. They are all so grateful and thankful.
M: Beautiful, and is that Reptilian free now of the bondage?
Higher Self: Yes, yes.
M: Does that Reptilian get to join Hailee's soul as a fractal of the soul or fragment of the soul or it's a separate existence although being One with her soul?
High Self: This is not a fractal. You could say it's something like a pre-life, but it is not a pre-incarnation. So, it is in a different time-space and a different Dimension. She is related, but it is not a fractal.[15]

---

[15] As mentioned in the previous session/Chapter, this Reptilian is an aspect of Hailee that exists in another parallel Universe.

M: Okay, beautiful. That explains it. Would you be able to share, is it time yet for us to know who the other higher powers were? The General that interviewed her; what race is that?

Higher Self: Archon.

M: So, they are basically negative A.I., is that right?

Higher Self: Yes.

M: So many times, when we aid the Reptilians into positive polarization, the answer always is they don't know who hired them. They don't know who recruited them. They don't know who the higher powers are. So, are they at that point referring to the Archons?

Higher Self: Yes.

M: Are there any other races apart from Archons that are also controlling in a negative A.I. way?

Higher Self: The Archons are the ones that have the connections to this through the different races that are controlling the fear, lower density.

M: Yes. And do the Archons exist in, are they a creation of our Universe or another Universe?

Higher Self: Another one.

M: They're just infringing upon us, is that what they're doing?

Higher Self: Yes.

M: Yes, just here for controlling. Okay. Because she did mention that they kept giving her telepathically images of creating fear and guilt.

Higher Self: Yes.

M: What was the purpose of doing that to the Reptilian? I know that they do that to humans as well.

Higher Self: This is their easy way to infringe and control. If you're opened up, it is easy for them to come in and to take control over you, your body, and your soul.

M: When they cut off the Reptilian's head, they joined it back again and she felt she wanted to be relieved and leave but was not able to. What were they using to hold her back? To hold the soul and put it back together?

Higher Self: Yup, that's kind of a technology. They put a spell. I don't know the word. They are able to control everything and they are told not to leave the dead body. That's how powerful they are.

M: Okay. Those cords that she was tied by, are they the Matrix cords?

Higher Self: Yes.

M: So, if during our healing sessions we disconnect/cut the Matrix cords, does that help that soul to free from the control of the Archons?

Higher Self: Yes. But they have to be aware and that's what happened here. It is as if you're clean and free and afterward you choose or you're not aware, or you're not shielding anymore, they can get you back very easily.

M: Yes. I've been in conversation with you for the past few days and this is something that you were talking about. About shielding and using the empowerment and the tools that have been provided in the teachings, especially for this client as well. And how important it is to put them to use. To use the shields that have been provided. I guess that'll be a message that you would want to talk to her about.

Higher Self: She already knows everything. She doesn't want to hear it. She heard that so often from all sides that she knows all the answers inside her. There was somebody who told her not to shield, that it is not necessary. And she liked that thought, that it's not necessary and that's where it began.

M: Did she like the thought or is it entities within her that liked the thought of it?

Higher Self: Yes.

M: What actually made her like it because I know she's been through a lot of training in order to be a healer. Shielding and force fields were a part of the training which I'm sure she enjoyed keeping herself safe and protected. What is it that caused her to change her mind about it?

Higher Self: The ego is interfering because she doesn't want to hear the answer.

M: Higher Self, if you could please help the ego as you're here to heal Hailee and heal the ego itself. We do need to hear the answers so that we don't have the same repeated pattern over and over again. It is time now.

Higher Self: Yes, that is what it is. Thank you. This is why she also feels like she's doing everything over, and over, and over again. Like a repeat in itself always. And she does these cycles again and again because she chooses to.

M: Yes, we do create our own realities. At this point Higher Self, I do have more questions for you. But I was wondering if we can first do the body scan?

H: Okay.

The Body Scan begins.

M: Would you like to conduct the body scan yourself or would you like help from the angels?

Higher Self: I would like to call Archangel Michael.

M: Archangel Michael, we call forth on you dear brother. We request you to please come in for the body scan. Hailee, just feel Archangel Michael's beautiful energy coming in integrating very nicely... Greetings Archangel Michael.

AA Michael: Hello.

M: Hello. Thank you so much for joining us. I love you, honor you, respect you, and thank you infinitely. Thank you for all that you do for Creation. May we begin with her body scan now?

AA Michael: Yes.

M: Thank you. If you can start from the crown please and start scanning every cell, every molecule for any Archons, any negative Reptilians, negative hooks, negative implants, portals. If we can have Archangel Metatron to start closing the portals although I did request for it before.

AA Michael: Yes.

M: Thank you. Tell me what you see, Archangel Michael. If we can start with Archons, if there are any Archons?

AA Michael: The connection is not very strong, like infringed because a voice comes up saying 'She's clear'.

M: And is that the case Archangel Michael? Is she clear?

AA Michael: Yes.

M: Archangel Michael, it does look like we have a lot of scanning to do. Hailee, please allow for Archangel Michael to scan you completely. He's very powerful and a very swift scanner. Please allow him to scan you, do not allow for any infringement to give you false answers. We're here to heal your body, mind, and soul. Higher Self, please work with the ego and have the ego step to the side. If I may ask Archangel Michael and Archangel Metatron, we can start using the Archon symbols and put them in their respective symbols if there are any Archons in her as well as the Reptilians if there are any Reptilians, so they stop interfering, please. Thank you. Is that done, Archangel Michael?

AA Michael: Yes.

M: Thank you. Archangel Michael, can you scan once more and tell me where are the Archons?

AA Michael: The lower the left where the ribs are.

M: Yes. To the left side?

AA Michael: Yes.

M: How many are there?

AA Michael: This is a portal.

M: Yes. Can you please have Archangel Metatron close the portal on the left first?

AA Michael: Yes.

M: Thank you Archangel Metatron. Archangel Michael, can you please scan for Archons? Where do you see Archons?

AA Michael: It is around her head.

M: Yes. How many are there in the head?

AA Michael: Twelve.

M: Yes, thank you. Placing them in the symbol. Are they encased?

AA Michael: Yes.

M: Thank you. Where do you next see Archons, Archangel Michael?

AA Michael: Third Eye.

M: How many do you see there?

AA Michael: Fifteen.

M: Yes. Let's encase them all in their respective symbols as well.

AA Michael: Yes.

M: Where else do you see Archons?

AA Michael: Throat?

M: How many are there?

AA Michael: Seven.

M: Just encase them as well in their symbols. Are they encased, Archangel Michael?

AA Michael: Yes.

M: Archangel Michael, if you can scan once more, where else do you see Archons?

AA Michael: In a webbing in her heart.

M: Okay, how many are there?

AA Michael: This webbing created is a kind of a being connected through the portal and to the other ones, so it consists of millions.

M: Let's encase all the Archons each one of them in their respective symbols Archangel Michael in the heart, please. Thank you. And Archangel Metatron, if you can please close the portal in the heart.

AA Metatron: Yes.

M: Yes. I did see the portal and I did see a being that looked ghostly like a big huge black figure sort of disfigured, sort of gooey. Is that what you mean by all of them together?

AA Metatron: Yes.

M: Okay. Let's encase each one of those, how many did you say you have millions?

AA Michael: They are connected. Yes.

M: Okay. Let's start putting each one of them in a symbol Archangel Michael.

AA Michael: Yes.

M: Thank you, sending fire. If we can move on to the next. Where do you see Archons, Archangel Michael?

AA Michael: Left knee.

M: Yes. Okay. How many?

AA Michael: Two.

M: Thank you. Let's start encasing them as well.

AA Michael: Yes.

M: Thank you. Sending Phoenix Fire there as well. Archangel Metatron, if I may request you to continue scanning her body for portals? If you can start closing all the portals, please.

AA Metatron: Yes.

M: Thank you very much. Archangel Michael, what's next? Where else do you see Archons?

AA Michael: She's getting sad. The connection is getting worse.

M: Hailee, this is a happy moment. You're healing yourself very powerfully and beautifully and you're going to gain your sovereignty back and your empowerment back. You're aware that you are a healer, and you want to be a healer and for that, you yourself, have expressed a wish to be a clear channel. You're doing this for yourself and ask your ego to step to the side and bring up the highest beautiful emotions of liberation and motivation and hope. And remember your mission that you're here for, to help heal the planet - to help heal people! And keeping that in mind, allow for Archangel Michael to scan very much in detail so we will make sure today that you're a clear channel and you can continue your beautiful path. Feel that liberation and your freedom Hailee, feel your freedom across many Dimensions. You've seen many lives now where you are trapped. It is not time to be trapped anymore. It's time for you to be free to be your own sovereign, fully empowered Love-Light Source being that you are... Archangel Michael can you continue the scan now, please? Thank you.

AA Michael: The sacral chakra.

M: Yes. What do you see there, Archangel Michael?

AA Michael: Three Archons.

M: Yes, let's encase them as well Archangel Michael. Thank you.

AA Michael: Yes.

M: Archangel Michael do you see Archons?

AA Michael: Root Chakra?

M: How many?

AA Michael: Twenty-Seven.

M: Let's encase each one of the 27 in their respective symbols that you have for them.

AA Michael: Okay.

M: Where else Archangel Michael? How about the solar plexus Archangel Michael, can you check there, please?

AA Michael: Yes.

M: How does it look?

AA Michael: It's another portal.

M: Yes. Archangel Metatron, if we may request you to please close the portal in the solar plexus as well. Thank you, if you can completely close it perhaps with symbols in her body so she does not get any more portals if her Higher Self allows.

AA Metatron: Yes.

M: Thank you, Archangel Metatron. Archangel Michael, what else do you have in the solar plexus or the whole body once more?

AA Michael: Left shoulder.

M: How many?

AA Michael: One.

M: Okay, let's encase that one as well, please. Thank you, Archangel Michael, where else?

AA Michael: Her belly button.

M: How many?

AA Michael: Fifty-two.

M: Okay. Let's encase each one of those 52 in their respective symbols.

AA Michael: Okay.

M: Where else Archangel Michael? What's the next stop for the Archons?

AA Michael: Right leg under the knee. This is not an Archon.

M: What is it?

AA Michael: This is an implant.

M: When did she get this implant Archangel Michael?

AA Michael: Some weeks ago.

M: Okay, let's start transmuting Archangel Michael. Would you like me to send Phoenix Fire to the implant?

AA Michael: Yes.

M: Thank you, Archangel Michael. Beautiful. Archangel Michael, while we continue to transmute the implant in the right leg under the knee, where else do you see infringements in her body? Do you see any more Archons other than the ones that you've mentioned?... Check her feet, her toes, ankles, everywhere.

AA Michael: No.

M: Okay. Archangel Michael, if you can confirm what is the status of the Archons in her head? There were 12 Archons.

AA Michael: Tried to infringe but they are encased.

M: They're encased. They're still there so I'll continue sending fire there.

AA Michael: It is a process. Depending on her surrendering and letting go.

M: Right.

AA Michael: She still holds on.

M: Why is she holding on to the Archons? Archangel Michael, can you tell Hailee what the Archons do to her and how they influence her please?

AA Michael: She already knows everything. She allowed them to come in because she thought that she didn't get confirmation from the Higher realms, from the Higher Self, from us Archangels. But we were always there. She did get signs. She had conversations but she saw it must be in a specific way and therefore she thought "I don't have a connection". And then she said to herself, "If there's no connection nothing makes sense anymore, so I can let go."

M: Mm-hmm. Is that when they came in?

AA Michael: Yes. She really, really wanted to...she really wanted to achieve. She didn't surrender, it was more like a fight for her, the esoteric spiritual stuff you can say she studied. She studied hours and hours. But she didn't get to that point of surrender. That's why it wasn't easy for her. She got in contact with others and realized that even though she worked so hard, she was so sad, and she gave up.

M: What was stopping her from having a clear connection with you all and her Higher Self?

AA Michael: Surrendering. Surrendering, and trust.

M: Can we remind Hailee today to surrender and to trust and allow for everything to unfold?

AA Michael: She has already everything in herself. It's her choice.

M: Yes, beautiful. Can you please have the Higher Self help Hailee also surrender today and help her surrender so we can let go of the Archons?

AA Michael: She's afraid of the power she's going to have back. She doesn't know if she can handle it.

M: What is she afraid of?

AA Michael: When you have your sovereignty back, you have your own power back. And this is new to her that's why she's afraid.

M: Higher Self, if you can please explain this to Hailee the importance of having her sovereignty back or existing with her free will of being empowered?

Higher Self: She knows it but it's her fear that's holding her back.

M: Is this fear really hers Archangel Michael, or is it a projection of the Archons and the Reptilians?

AA Michael: Yes, it's the projection.

M: Yes, just like they were doing on the planet as well. So, she is aware of that.

AA Michael: Yes.

M: Can we please have Hailee surrender now? Would she allow for the Archons to leave now or does she want to keep the Archons within her?

AA Michael: So, the ego tries to interfere and shows her images of her future or possible future and she is afraid of things that might come. That's why she's unsure right now.

M: Regardless of what the future is, are the Archons being of any help to her future? Are they helping her in a positive, benevolent, and organic manner in any way?

Higher Self: Of course not.

M: Yes. We would like Hailee to understand that now. It is a choice that she needs to make whether she wants a benevolent, positive, organic existence? Or she would allow for a negative polarized being, which is actually soulless, since it is negative A.I. rule and overpower her and her decisions? What does she want right now? She needs to make that choice. Keeping in mind also the life that was shown to her by Higher Self of where she wanted to free herself as a Reptilian, but she was unable to because of the Archon energies. Archangel Michael, what do you suggest we do?

AA Michael: Let's first start healing her heart. So, it's easier for her to take that choice because at this moment without the self-love she sees no need for change.

M: Archangel Metatron, can you confirm if the portal in the heart has been closed?

AA Metatron: Yes.

M: I have already been sending the Phoenix Fire to the encased Archons, the millions that were there in her heart. Have they been removed Archangel Michael, or are they still there?

AA Michael: They're here. But not in the heart anymore.

M: I'm continuing to send Phoenix Fire there. What's in the heart right now? What is blocking the heart?

AA Michael: It's Hailee herself!

M: Can we have Yeshua and brother Raphael to please flood Hailee's heart with beautiful Love-Light right now to cleanse it completely? Flood it and expand it to whatever expansion that it can be in this existence right now and fill her with Love-Light and have her flame of heart - her own flame - lit beautifully?... Archangel Michael, how do the Archons look that were in her heart that had gone down to the solar plexus? Does she have a contract with the Archons?

AA Michael: No.

M: What has she decided? Would she like us to remove these Archons from her?

AA Michael: No, she does not want to.

M: Archangel Michael, have Jesus and Raphael flooded her heart with Love-Light? How does her heart look now?

AA Michael: Still closed.

M: If you can have the Legion of Light, all the Archangels brothers and sisters...

AA Michael: She's still denying.

M: What is she denying Archangel Michael?

AA Michael: Finding the light within her! Finding self-love.

M: We will help with self-love if she can just please allow for the Archons to leave her body, she will feel much lighter and be able to make better decisions. Higher Self, if you can help Hailee make that decision? Allow for the Archons to leave so we can remove all the Archons and then she will be able to think better and her body will feel lighter and it'll feel like her own body. Right now, she's being infringed upon by the Archons. Hailee, would you allow us to help you today?

H: Yes.

M: Thank you very much. And would you allow for us to free you of all these Archons, there are millions of them that have taken over. We want to free you from them, they're inorganic.

H: Yes.

M: It is them who you've shared several experiences with me - very traumatic experiences and you've seen several lifetimes where you've been held in chains and your soul's been captured. You've had wires and cords in you with which they've held on to your soul and not allowed you to be the sovereign being that you are. Be that soul even if you don't want to be a healer, if you just want to be here, feel love and life just, just live your life, whatever it is you want to do, but be free! Would you not allow for yourself to be free? Source is here, all the Archangels are here. Look at how many of them, how many of these beings in the Creation love you. These are organic sentient beings of this Creation created by the Divine Mother. They all love you!

H: Yes.

M: Would you allow us to heal you today?

H: Yes (sad).

M: Thank you. Would you please allow and say it on your own? Repeat after me, "I am a sovereign being."

H: I am a sovereign being.

M: I have been created by Father Source and The Divine Mother.

H: I have been created by the Divine Source and the Divine Mother (crying).

M: I have Source Love-Light within me.

H: I have Source Love within me.

M: I have free will.

H: I have free will.

M: I do not allow any inorganic matter.

H: I do not allow any inorganic matter.

M: Or inorganic being, negative A.I.

H: Or inorganic being and A.I.

M: To be and exist within me.

H: To be and exist within me.

M: I am free, I am free, I am free.

H: I am free, I am free, I am free.

M: I am Love-Light. I am love. I am Love-Light.

H: I am Love-Light. I am love. I am Love-Light.

M: Thank you. How does that feel?

H: Uncomfortable.

M: Mm-hmm. What is feeling uncomfortable?

H: I have pain all over my body.

M: Higher Self, please alleviate the pain that she's feeling and sensing right now. Hailee, once you allow for us to remove these Archons, the pain will disappear immediately. Would you allow today for us to remove all these Archons that are existing within you that are not of you? They are from another Universe. They do not belong here. Would you allow us and Archangel Michael to remove them so you can feel light once more?

H: Yes!!!

M: Thank you very much, Hailee... Archangel Michael if you may please now remove the hold of all these Archons that are within her. There were 12 in the head, 15 in the third eye, seven in the throat... Michael, tell me when they are all removed, please. (pause)... Archangel Michael, what is the status of the Archons?

AA Michael: They are gone.

M: They all have gone?

AA Michael: Yes.

M: Beautiful. The Legion of Lights, brothers and sisters, please if I may request you to flood Hailee with your beautiful Love-Light to ensure she feels light and beautiful once more. Thank you. How is she feeling now Archangel Michael?

AA Michael: Confused.

M: Why is she still confused? Are we working on her heart?

AA Michael: It feels like an operation on her chest - open-heart operation.

M: What are you doing exactly Archangel Michael? Can you describe it?

AA Michael: I'm repairing everything the Archons have done to her - the webbing - removing it, filling Love-Light in. It is possible that the heart grows even more bigger and bigger.

M: This is very important because the heart is truly the core of our being. Archangel Michael, can you please scan her for Reptilian consciousnesses?

AA Michael: She doesn't want to.

M: Yes. She doesn't want to be scanned for Reptilians?

AA Michael: No.

M: Why does she not want to be scanned for Reptilians?

AA Michael: She doesn't want any healing.

M: She does not want any healing? Why is that? Archangel Michael, are the Reptilians infringing upon her decisions right now?

AA Michael: She gave up, again!

M: Hailee, we are here to help you.

AA Michael: She's thinking about ending the session.

M: Is it her who is thinking, or it is someone infringing upon her to think so?

AA Michael: She thinks it is her decision.

M: Can we have the Higher Self suggest if we can encase the Reptilians in their symbols Archangel Michael? I'd like to speak with the Higher Self once more. Archangel Michael and if you can still be around please. Thank you, Archangel Michael... Calling on the Higher Self now. Speaking with the Higher Self. Greetings, Hello!

Higher Self: There's a lot of interference.

M: Yes. Is that the Higher Self that I'm speaking with?

Higher Self: Yes.

M: Thank you very much, and are you male or female?

Higher Self: Female.

M: So right now, it looks like Hailee was resisting the Archons from leaving her body and she finally agreed for them to leave. She is now seemingly resisting the Reptilians from leaving. So, what is happening now Higher Self?

Higher Self: This is again the cycle she goes on, and on, again and again. She's not letting go. She's at the point where she's always, she's not taking the last step to fully say YES.

M: Yes. Do you believe Higher Self, that today we can completely free her from the attachments of the Reptilians?

Higher Self: It's not up to me. It's up to her.

M: Yes, exactly. So, we do need to ask her free will for that and that's why I called you Higher Self. What do you suggest now? Does she have a contract with these Reptilians?

Higher Self: No.

M: So, it's an infringement in a way?

Higher Self: Yes.

M: How many Reptilians does she have in her, dear Higher Self?

Higher Self: Sixty-three.

M: Okay. Dear Higher Self, if you can keep sending love to Hailee so she can decide. Clearly right now her decision might just be an infringed one by the Reptilians because she does have so many Reptilians within her. How would you help her right now to make the right decision?
Higher Self: There is no right decision. You just have to take that decision. She always waits, and waits, and waits, till somebody takes the decision for her. And if she's not going to take the decision right now... Then she's starting it all over again someday later.
M: Yes, that's right. What do you suggest we do?
Higher Self: I suggest nothing. It's her. We all love her. We all respect what her choice is.
M: Yes. Can we continue sending her love, to every bit of her? The Legion of Light, Archangels brothers and sisters? Dear Higher Self, would you allow us to send love to Hailee?
Higher Self: Yes. On the one hand, she is totally exhausted, and totally rid of the same sh*t again and again and again. And on the other hand, she doesn't want to let go.
M: Mm-hmm. Which side is stronger for her right now?
Higher Self: She's afraid of the unknown. So, the known is the more the part she is holding on.
M: Dear Higher Self, is it possible for you to show her what the unknown is; some glimpses of what life can be without infringements?!
Higher Self: No, she's not open for it.
M: Okay. Can you give me an update on what is happening?
Higher Self: She wants to wake up!
M: She does not want to continue with the session?
Higher Self: No.
M: Would she like, what is her decision to do with the Reptilians?
Higher Self: She doesn't care anymore.
M: What do you suggest Higher Self? I know you would allow her to use her free will, but?
Higher Self: I'd rather see her glow. I'd rather see her glowing.
M: Yes.
Higher Self: But if she decides, it is her free will.
M: Yes. Would you like us to wait for some more dear Higher Self?
Higher Self: She's rejecting it.
M: Is she herself rejecting it or it's the Reptilians?
H: (deep breath) Okay, I'm out!
M: Higher Self, please allow for me...
H: It's me, Hailee.
M: Okay, allow for me to bring you out properly. Just give me a moment, please.

The client is counted back properly and is out of hypnosis.

Post Session dialogue.
H: As always, not taking the last step.
M: What is stopping you from taking the last step?
H: I guess it's fear.
M: Fear of what?
H: Being responsible for my own. You really feel connected to some of the, I don't know other lives and maybe the Reptilian, whatever. And when you stood so long under control, you can't even imagine how it is to be on your own. Because everything was done for you everything - even though you didn't like it, but you didn't have to make decisions. This is what is hard for me now to make decisions, one, and there are so many decisions I have to make. These are too overwhelming!

M: Well, that's the point because that's what we were talking about Archangel Michael and your Higher Self said as well. It is your free will, right? Even the Higher Self cannot decide for you. You're living this existence on your own and it's going to be your decision at the end of the day. So, you know, it is what it is, and we just respect that. The good thing is that there were so many Archons that have been released. I wanted you to feel that love. You know, you're so beautiful.

H: No, it's not, it's not up to you. Sorry that you had this experience. It's not up to you. It's totally up to me. This was kind of my last try. So, I tried it.

M: Okay, I will leave you at that because I respect whatever is your decision, right? It's your soul. It's you who decides. So, I respect that, whatever your decision is because we all make choices for our lives and how we want to live and what we want to experience. And that's what existence is about. So, I respect whatever choice you've made just like your Higher Self said, and just as RA was communicating with me as well, that we just respect whatever you decide. I'm grateful that you came, and you know, we got to do this. We experienced this together. A lot of lessons for me, a lot of lessons for you to learn.

H: (laughs).

M: Yeah, you know, we all learn from each other. Everyone's leading different lives and you know that's how you take lessons, and you grow as a soul. But I do want to wish you love and you know regards, and lots of Love-Light so you can go and live your beautiful life and experience it. I'm sure you will take back valuable lessons from this life as well. Do you have anything else to say?

H: No, just feels like always I had the possibility to make a change and didn't make the change.

M: Well, I wish you love and I wish you light and I would suggest continuing meditating, continue connecting with your Higher Self. You have all the tools, go within, heal yourself.

H: Yes, I know it all. But yeah, it's just the will, the step!

M: Also, no judgment at all because we're all our own beings, we have the right to decide what we need to do and what we want to do. So, don't worry about that. I wish you love. Thank you. You take care of yourself.

END OF SESSION

Wow, what an intense final session to this special series! We have heard through other sessions how it is to be a Reptilian soldier when we find the Reptilian consciousnesses in our client's body, and we convince them to positively polarize into Ascension. They explain how they are just controlled and given orders to act upon as a Reptilian. They don't know where the orders come from; they just feel moved to do them without question. After they have positively polarized, they apologize, and they explain that they just knew no other way. Now we understand in depth how this works.

Through Hailee's sessions, we learned how the Archons go into the Reptilian soldiers' consciousnesses, rewiring it and taking control over it through implanting their negative technologies. This would explain how the Reptilians can't just consciously shift into an understanding of removing themselves, from having to follow orders to feed upon others' lights and harming others.

The Reptilian race is an organic creation of this Universe. In order to maintain balance between both negative and positive polarities, the Reptilians were designed in Creation to organically feed off excess light. The Archons operate in such an intelligent manner, that of course they would figure out how to make a race that is part of balance, into making them part of their harvesting of lights to feed their never-ending hunger for light. So, the Archons compromised the Reptilians' natural way of feeding off light into parasitically feeding directly off others' lights, by infringing upon their hosts' free willed choices. This shows us how powerful of a soul Hailee is to have been able to break free in her 'A Reptilian on a Mission' session, when she also freed her Reptilian squad.

This sobering session explains to us how and why that is. Once the Reptilians and other beings agree to be soldiers for the Archons, they have signed their sovereignty and soul away. They are now as prized possessions, and the Archons have full tyrannical reign over their souls. This would also explain Hailee's reaction to fearing to be able to make her own choices and guiding her own path when for too long it had been controlled by others like the Archons. With the inverted never-ending cycle the Archons had over her, resetting and recycling her soul, if she did not follow their instructions well enough through their game of control. This would tear apart at a soul deeply, layer after layer, with every reset losing a further piece of themselves and what free willed expression they once had organically.

This Archonic recruiting strategy also reminds us of the similar propaganda here on Earth that is communicated to all the young ones in the High Schools through the different branches of the Military. "Come be in the Army and we will pay for your schooling, so many opportunities await you. Come explore the world." Through what the young Reptilian expressed, being marketed in this manner as well. Being given false opportunities of traveling the Universe and being known throughout it. When people sign away their rights to be fully controlled by the Military on Earth, do they sign a similar contract with the Archons as the Reptilians do? Do they sell their soul away? If so, may the Archangels continue to assist these War Veterans whether they are alive or have passed, to release and remove these artificial non-organic contracts of harvesting their souls. This is not part of our Galactic Construct, therefore it can no longer be. This is what they have been trying to mold us into. Subordinate foot soldiers who hate on one another so that we can remain separated from each other's Love-Light frequencies. Divine Mother Isis of Egypt once told me, she created these lines, "United We Stand, Divided We Fall," not the Army. May we remember the true meaning of "United We Stand" when our Love-Lights are united, and not the Army programmed hijacked one.

Hailee at the beginning of her journey with us, expressed deep determination to heal herself, and she was hopeful that someday she too will become a healer herself to aid others on a similar journey. We have seen how she fought so valiantly throughout all her A.U.R.A. Hypnosis Healing sessions, to free herself from the Archon control that she has been experiencing for so many lifetimes. Even though this Reptilian aspect is a version of her from another Dimension and alternate Universe, this series of sessions helped us understand how the multidimensional versions of us spread throughout the infinity of Creation can also bleed through and influence us in the now.

She underwent training for healing, including the A.U.R.A. Hypnosis Healing modality, so determined was she to pursue this path of Love. In this monumental final session, we have seen the intensity of the healing that took place, and then at the very end, she didn't take the last step in her self-healing journey. She feared the unknown, of what having freedom and sovereignty feels like, having been under Archon control for so long. As always, we respect all free will choices. As her Higher Self stated, the choice is really Hailee's, and it is a pattern of fear she has been repeating endlessly throughout lifetimes.

We have seen how strong Hailee has been throughout her journey, and we send her love as for when she will finally make the crucial choice for herself to take the last step needed in her self-healing journey at some point in the future. When she decides to complete that critical last step. She will then be a sovereign being, one who is fully into her power, and then finally achieve her dream of becoming that healer she wishes to be for others who experienced a similar intense journey as hers. Through our own self-healing journey, we develop compassion, experience and wisdom, and step into our true power of becoming the 'healed' healer for others. This is our highest hope for Hailee and her journey, that someday she will reach the state of becoming the 'healed' healer and share her wisdom, strength, and compassion with others on their self-healing journey. We remain hopeful of Hailee's decision to take the last crucial step to sovereignty, perhaps through another future A.U.R.A. session. Where she has accepted that she can and will be the one to make all the choices for her life, no longer being bonded by the fear of the unknown to her of having full sovereignty for her path.

Our infinite love to Hailee for sharing her story intimately with us and for her strength, as she is far beyond stronger than she has come into a realization and acceptance of. May she feel our love now so that she may find her strength when it is needed the most, when she makes the big choice that will come forth upon us all - Ascension.

"We, within the NOW, are the strongest versions of us. For WE are the bridge to the both the past self and the future self. Being able to connect to all versions of ourselves. The Holy Trinity of us, the past, now and future self."
~Aurora🖤

-------------<◇>-------------

20

SECRET BLACK MARKET INSIDE EARTH AND BEYOND

Session #135: Recorded in April 2019.

In this online A.U.R.A. Hypnosis Healing session, Jennifer is fed up with what has been occurring in her life up until now as she feels stagnant like she can't quite move forward. This is one of her main concerns during her healing.

In her past life her guides show how these sensations are intertwined with her life now, in ways unexpected by all. By discovering this, we help her move forward. She finds herself enslaved in an Alien planet harvesting a special item used as currency by Dark Aliens to facilitate a secret Black Market Exchange inside Earth and beyond. We learn more about Feline Lyrans, Pyramid Ships, Inner Earth, Purple Planet etc. How is all of this linked to what is happening on Earth right now?

-------------<◇>-------------

"You are a beautiful being of light.
Recognize that in each and every moment,
and live your life the way your heart calls for you to do."
-Archangel Michael

-------------<◇>-------------

J: [Jennifer] So, it was that it was landing on a planet, but it was all sand. And I don't know if that's just the pyramid desert thing, but it landed on like a red ball like that was its landing pod. The middle of the pyramid landed on the ball.
A: [Aurora] It landed on what?
J: A small sphere. Red sphere. It was like a landing pod for it.
A: Look all around you.
J: I see other pyramids and I don't really see any people. I feel like that pyramid is a form of transportation. The sky is blue.
A: The other pyramids, are they similar to your pyramid?
J: Yes.
A: You said that you felt that your pyramid landed on top of a red sphere?
J: Yeah. Like a little, just a little red sphere. It was like a landing pod and it was in the middle of the pyramid.
A: The other pyramids, did they land on a sphere of sorts as well?
J: I believe they did.
A: Very good. Now, look at yourself. Do you feel like you have a body?
J: Yes.
A: Describe yourself to me. Look at your feet. Are you wearing anything on your feet?
J: No.
A: How many toes do you have?

J: I don't really feel like I have toes. I feel like maybe I have one toe (chuckles), and then a foot…you know what I mean? Like the big toe and then…

A: Very good. Look at your hands. How many fingers do you have?

J: Kind of looks the same way - like a thumb.

A: Look at your skin. Do you feel like you have skin?

J: Yes. It's very, very smooth. No hair.

A: What color is it? Is there a color to it?

J: Just a regular flesh color.

A: Do you feel like you have arms and legs?

J: Yes.

A: Look at yourself, are you wearing any clothing?

J: Not much.

A: Describe what you're wearing.

J: Just some kind of cover-up on the bottom. A short, and it kind of wraps around and then kind of wraps up the middle a little bit and then a separate top.

A: What color is it?

J: Gold.

A: I want you to envision a spiritual mirror right in front of you. Look at yourself. How does your face look?

J: I just have a feeling that it looks like a cat face without fur.

A: How do your ears look?

J: Like cat ears.

A: Is there any jewelry that you're wearing?

J: I have a... I don't know what you call it, a crown or something. It's got like a stone, a white stone here (points to forehead) and it's just very simple. It goes around.

A: Does the stone dangle or is it melded into the crown?

J: Yeah, it's melded within the crown.

A: Are there any designs and symbols on the crown that you can recognize?

J: Well, the shape of this stone feels like it's significant just because it's rounded at the top and then it just kind of goes like that (making shapes with her hands).

A: Like an upside-down tear?

J: Oh yes.

A: What color is it?

J: It's white.

A: Are there any other jewelry pieces you are wearing?

J: No, I am seeing from the back. I have hair that's probably down to my shoulder, but the top part pulls back and it's in these little sections that look like they're crimped with...like when I look at my hair, it's kind of like a flat piece, but it looks crimped with a heart shape, and then a diamond shape.

A: Very good. What color is your hair?

J: It's brown.

A: Is there anything you're carrying?

J: No.

A: Let's go back to the crown you're wearing with the crystal. Everything has consciousness. Let's see if the crystal within that crown has a message for you. Feel its energy and allow for it to give you messages or talk through you… May I please speak to the energy within the crown? I would love to be able to speak to you now. Greetings.

Crystal: Hello!

A: Hello. Thank you for speaking to us today. Love you and honor you. Is it okay if we ask you questions, please?

Crystal: Yes.

A: Thank you. It's an honor to have you here. If I may ask you, how are you connected to Jennifer?

Crystal: She's part of the mineral kingdom.

A: Do you mean like minerals as in the elements?

Crystal: Yes.

A: Why is it that you have shown yourself today within the crown? What message do you have for her?

Crystal: I'm a part of her.

A: Did you have a name that you call by?

Crystal: Moonstone.

A: Very good. If you could tell us where this place is that she's at? Is this a planet that she's landed here and there are pyramids everywhere?

Crystal: It is a planet.

A: Can you tell me anything else about this place that she has been brought to? Any other messages you have for us?

Crystal: I feel that I am a worker on this planet, it's a working planet.

A: Very good. Energy within her crown, do you have any other message for her, or can you also tell us what is the significance of the crown there in her head?

Crystal: To help her see you.

A: Do you mean like see things amplified, or deeper, what do you mean?

Crystal: Yes, see the unseen.

A: Why would she need that on this planet?

Crystal: It feels like it's not always the safest place.

A: Do you have any other messages before we talk back to her?

Crystal: I love her.

A: Very good. Thank you for speaking to us. We honor you, we thank you, and respect you. If you could please connect us back to Jennifer. Now if you could tell us, you are standing here inside this pyramid and you see pyramids all around you. Do you feel like you have to go somewhere? Do you feel a calling to go somewhere else on this planet?

J: I don't see anybody around, and I feel like the work is done inside the planet and inner planet.

A: See if you have a place that you call home or somewhere where you go to rest or a place that you call yours. Let's move the scene along, you are there now. What do you see?

J: I sense that I don't live on that planet, that purple and white planet that's nearby.

A: Do you feel like there's no home here for you on this planet?

J: No.

A: Then why is it that you come here? What is the purpose?

J: To work.

A: Let's go to where you work. Let's go now. Let's leave that scene and let's go to where you work now on this planet. You are there now. What do you see?

J: I see a lot of people that are like harvesting these black crystals that are all like iridescent purple-ish sheen to it.

A: Okay. How was it that you entered this place of harvesting these crystals?

J: There's a doorway that goes down into the Earth. It's not planet Earth. It's into the planet.

A: How do you go into that doorway? Do you walk?

J: Yes.

A: Once you enter that doorway, what do you see when you come into the doorway?

J: There is a lot of that black crystal everywhere. It feels dark and cold.

A: What does, the crystal? Or what feels dark and cold?

J: Yeah, the crystals are all dark and it feels cold inside.

A: Besides those crystals, are there any other crystals?

J: No, I don't see any others.

A: Is there a shape to the crystals?

J: They're kind of rounded? I don't know how to explain them.

A: That's okay. You're doing great.

J: They kind of remind me of like, bubble wrap.

A: You said that you're working on the crystals harvesting them. How do you do that? Go through the steps on how you would harvest these crystals.

J: Looks like everybody's doing it by hand with a chisel and hammer or similar tool. Nobody really talks. Everybody just stays very focused. I don't see like a boss or anything, but I feel like even though we can't see them, they're there, and they can see us. It doesn't really feel like they're very friendly. I don't sense friendliness.

A: To communicate do you have to use a language?

J: Telepathy.

A: What is it that you're doing now?

J: I'm standing there and I'm feeling as though I just don't want to be here anymore. I don't know if that's because that's the way I feel like right now in my own life or what. That's interesting. I just feel done, spent, like I don't have anything else to give.

A: Do you feel like you've been here by yourself for a long time or together?

J: Yeah, a long time.

A: What happens when you harvest crystals? What do you do with them?

J: We put them in a big bowl and then the people that run the mine take them away.

A: The people who run the mine take them away?

J: Yeah.

A: Do you ever find out where they take them to?

J: I think they're black diamonds.

A: You said that the energy in it feels cold?

J: It felt cold when I entered that area compared to what it did outside.

A: How do the crystals feel? Do they feel positive? Balanced? Negative?

J: Yes, they feel nice. Positive. There's a coolness to them too.

A: Do you ever take breaks as you feel like it?

J: No. It doesn't feel like it.

A: So, is there anything else that you ever do differently besides harvesting these diamonds?

J: I help clean them off.

A: How do you clean them off?

J: With water.

A: Where do you get the water from?

J: From the ground. It's like a stream, spring, or something.

A: I know that you say that this is all you do, that you don't really go from here. Let's see, you're able to travel. You're able to travel and follow to see where it is that they take these black diamonds to. Let's follow, let's see... What do you see?

J: They take them to another planet.

A: Okay, so from there, do they collect them together?

J: Yes.

A: Where do they collect them into and who is it that's taking them? Is it workers like you or do they look different?

J: I feel like it's the people that run that mine. The bigger owners or people that run that mine transport them. I feel like they're very valuable and I feel like a slave!

A: Where do they gather them at, in order to take them to the other planet?

J: They travel in a big pyramid, it's bigger than mine and they gather them up in those balls, they just stack them.

A: Do those people who are gathering them up and traveling with them, do they look different than you?

J: Yeah, but I can't quite figure it out.

A: Well, let's see. You're able to see, sense, and feel everything very clearly those people that are taking them on a big pyramid to somewhere else. What do they look like?

J: They look like they have cat bodies, and they have black hair all over their bodies, but they walk upright, and they have no hair on their face or head. They have these like 'Dr. Spock' ears (a Star Trek character).

A: Are they wearing anything?

J: No.

A: Let's follow them along to see where they take them. You said that they have a big pyramid that they travel in with those bowls of crystals. Tell me what you see. Where are they going?

J: They take them to another really big planet.

A: How does this planet look?

J: It's a big black planet.

A: Is this round like a sphere?

J: Yes.

A: What do they do when they get there to that planet? Where do they land

J: I feel like the pyramid just kind of hovers and then a clear shoot comes out, it hovers over the planet.

A: Then what happens once the clear shoot comes out?

J: I'm trying to see where it connects to. It sounds weird...it feels like it connects to a saucer and like they're sending the diamonds from the pyramid to the saucer.

A: So, they're sending it into a saucer like a spaceship you mean?

J: Yeah.

A: Let's see that saucer very clearly, describe to me what it looks like.

J: It has lots of windows on the bottom and it's a shiny silver.

A: The shoot from the pyramid shoots it into the saucer?

J: Yeah.

A: Where does the saucer open up to allow for those crystals to come into?

J: On the side.

A: You're able to see and sense within this saucer. Who's in there? How do they look? Are there many, are there a few?

J: There's a few and they look like they're in suits, green suits.

A: Is it like a spacesuit you mean?

J: Yeah, a spacesuit.

A: Look at their suit. See if you see anything that stands out like a symbol, a letter, an emblem, anything that you recognize.

J: It's a red emblem and it looks like an 'L' and a 'V' and it kind of looks like it has some white flames on it.

A: How do they look? Do they look like you?

J: No.

A: Describe how they look.

J: The first thing I notice is that they don't really have a nose. They have nostrils but no nose. They have three fingers, and their skin is very pale. I don't see any ears either, and they have black eyes.

A: Do you feel that they are positive?

J: Yes.

A: Once all these diamonds enter the ship, can you see what they do with them? What do they do with them?

J: They transport them to Earth...that's interesting.

A: Yes...when they transport them into Earth, how do they do that?

J: They fly into the ocean and they enter the underground cities there.

A: How does that look? Do they transfer them still on that same ship?

J: Yeah, on the ship.

A: Okay. Does the ship fly towards Earth?

J: Yes.

A: How do they enter them into Earth? What part of Earth?

J: I see a big ocean and it reminds me of like, you know, the South Pacific Ocean. They enter the ocean, there is a portal they go through.

A: Through the water, there's a portal that they go through?

J: To get into the underground city.

A: When this portal opens up what happens to the water?

J: Nothing, it stays there.

A: When the portal opens, does the ship go inside, through it?

J: Yeah.

A: As it goes through it, tell me what else you see.

J: It feels like quite a production area for these black diamonds. I feel like it's underground and people above ground don't really know that it's there.

A: So, would you say it's inside the Earth? In the Inner Earth?

J: Yes.

A: Once the ship goes through that portal, they enter the Earth and when they enter Inner Earth, tell me what you see. What's the first thing after they get past the water and the portal? When they go through, what do they see?

J: It's like a platform that the ships stop on and people are busy about, but they look like regular human beings. It's like a happy reunion and they're happy with all the black diamonds that they just received.

A: The humans that are there waiting for the diamonds? What are they wearing?

J: I feel like some are wearing more casual clothes while others are wearing suits and ties.

A: Okay, so now that they are there and they've brought the diamonds, what do they do with the diamonds next?

J: I feel like they're hiding them away. They're stashing them away, stashing them.

A: Stashing them away? Where do they go to be stashed?

J: It's a great big vault on the side of the wall.

A: That's where they keep them all?

J: Yeah.

A: See if there's any in this place here, anywhere they use these black diamonds at, what would they use them for? Why keep them in a vault? Are there some that they use?

J: It's like currency?!

A: Do they use them at all, or do they just keep them locked up? Is there anywhere that they use them in this place that you went to?

J: I feel like it's used as currency, but not openly. They feel that they don't want everyone to know about it yet...I'm just looking at the vault with all the diamonds in it.

A: Let's fast forward a bit where something has changed. Perhaps, maybe if they're using the diamond, something more significant where we are looking to find more answers. You are there now. What do you see?

J: I'm sensing rumbling. I'm blank and in darkness. I don't feel like I'm in my physical body. I feel like I'm hovering over it. I'm trying to see.

A: Let's leave that scene now, let's go to another important time in this life where we will find answers we seek. You are there now. What do you see?

J: A little home planet.

A: You're back on the home planet?

J: It's a little, small, purple, pink, and white planet.

A: That is how the planet looks?

J: Yeah.

A: Look at yourself. How do you look?

J: The same as I did.

A: What are you doing now?

J: There are some others that look like me around.

A: What are you all doing?

J: I'm in a community, but I still feel alone.

A: Do you feel like there is a connection as far as a friendship or love between each other on this planet?

J: Yeah.

A: Do you feel like there are children that look like you all as well?

J: Yes, there are children.

A: These families that have children, do they live somewhere? How does it work?

J: We live in clear domes on the ground, but we live in big communities together.

A: Let's see if we can find your home, your dome. You're right in front of it now. Tell me what you see. Find the entrance.

J: I feel like I just have to think about going inside and I'm inside.

A: When you go inside, tell me what you see.

J: Everything's white inside and it's like there's some furniture, what you would call furniture. But it's like long and hard looking furniture, like stuff with no padding or anything like that. I don't really eat anything. I don't really eat food.

A: Is there anyone else that lives with you in your home?

J: Yeah, I feel like there are other beings around that live with me.

A: This is a shared type of home?

J: Yeah.

A: Do you have a specific section that's yours? Do you have a room, and do you sleep?

J: There's like a tube that we step into to recharge ourselves. It's not like sleeping for eight hours a night or something. It's just like we spend some time in all these color frequencies to re-balance and to re-charge.

A: How does that feel?

J: I'm trying to figure out what I do there because I don't really see a lot. I felt like I was feminine before, but I feel like I'm masculine now.

A: From there, after you rest, what do you do next? …

J: (silence)

A: Let's go ahead and leave that scene. Let's go to another important time in this life. You're there now. What do you see?

J: I don't know, I don't find anything.
A: Very good. Now, let's leave that life now.

The Higher Self is called forth.
A: Wonderful. Am I speaking to the Higher self now?
Higher Self: Yes.
A: I honor you, I thank you, and I respect you for all the aid you have given us today. I know that you hold all the records of Jennifer's different lives. May I ask you questions?
Higher Self: Yes.
A: Why is it that you chose to take her to that planet there where she is a worker mining those black crystals. Why did you take her there? What was the purpose of showing her that life?
Higher Self: She experiences now in her lifetime all those feelings, thoughts, all those emotions that she also felt in other lifetimes and she also feels them for others around her. She's doing a lot of work, good work. Not just about what's right here right now. A lot more. That was just an example of where she felt that way in the past as well. Enslaved, things feel archaic.
A: On this planet, she said others had families and children. Is that correct?
Higher Self: Yes. There were children.
A: Does she have a family?
Higher Self: Her community that she lived with was considered her family, she did not have a family.
A: Okay. Why did she feel like she was a slave?
Higher Self: She felt that working in the mine to mine the diamonds was what she had to do. She didn't really enjoy it that much. She had to do it.
A: Can you tell us, what are those black diamonds?
Higher Self: They are worth a lot of money to the people whose hands they end up in, so it's a high commodity item for them.
A: This race here that was on that planet, is that all they do? Mine the diamonds?
Higher Self: Yes. The little planet, the people from the little planet work on mining.
A: You took her through a part where they went to Earth. Is that where they went?
Higher Self: Yes.
A: Can you tell us more about how that worked? There was a portal in the water, and they went inside the Inner Earth. Can you tell us anymore about that?
Higher Self: That's been there for a long time. They've been using that portal for a long time.
A: How does it open up without not allowing the water to flood through it?
Higher Self: The intention.
A: Can you explain that further?
Higher Self: You want the portal to open so the ship can go through, the water stays.
A: So, is there like a tunnel that the ship would go through?
Higher Self: Yes, it goes through a tunnel and it ends up on a landing dock.
A: Why is it that those people are stocking those black diamonds? Why are they storing them?
Higher Self: They're kind of doing it in secret. They don't want anyone else to find out about them because then everyone will be doing it. They're worth a lot of money. Apparently, they're worth a lot to the people that are stocking them and at some point, they may be using that as currency. Will also be making jewelry, selling jewelry.
A: Would they be selling that or making that for the people on Earth or somewhere else??
Higher Self: Yes, on Earth.
A: Is there a name that we call this crystal that she spoke of?
Higher Self: Black diamond.

A: Does everyone use them or is there only particular people that use these black diamonds on Earth?

Higher Self: Only particular ones.

A: If you can show an example of a person that would be using these black diamonds on Earth. Show them to her. What are they using them for?

Higher Self: Well, they're just using them as a currency, like saving gold bars. These people save and store the black diamonds, and they'll, you know, be able to purchase whatever they want with that. They don't want to get them out there just yet. There's a sense of gluttony.

A: Would you say that these people that are on Earth that are saving them for whatever means, that they are people who kind of rule or try to govern the Earth that have a lot of money?

Higher Self: Yeah. definitely. That's where I think the gluttony comes in, there can never be enough.

A: Would you be able to fast forward time and show her when it is that perhaps one of these humans who, you could say are rich, have these black diamonds? What would they use it for? In a time and space, fast-forwarding time to see what they're using them for.

Higher Self: I see them using them to buy like islands.

A: Islands? Where, on Earth?

Higher Self: Yeah.

A: Hmm.

Higher Self: Ah! To buy people. I don't see them using it in what would be considered a positive way.

What an interesting topic to touch upon with this session in this time and space, especially with all the hidden human trafficking that is coming to the surface on Earth. Black diamonds, a secret currency which the Illuminati uses to purchase children and adults through human trafficking?

A: What are some of the negative ways that they're using them as?

Higher Self: Well, it just seems like they want to buy and to have so they could do what they do and totally disregard the other 90 percent of the people.

A: These people that you're seeing, are they Cabal or Illuminati?

Higher Self: Yeah.

A: Anything else you want to say about that since they are who you say they are. Do they set up their program there where they have those beings there mining?

Higher Self: Yeah.

A: That's their whole program there?

Higher Self: Yes.

A: Are these black diamonds used throughout the Universe or just Earth as a currency?

Higher Self: I feel like it's just Earth.

A: The people that they have on that planet, would you say that they're stuck there?

Higher Self: It feels like they are stuck there.

A: Are they able to die and leave the body there and go somewhere else or are they stuck there like a cycle?

Higher Self: I believe there is a dying cycle in there.

A: Can you show her how that looks? Once they decide to die, how does that happen?

Higher Self: Through intention. To leave the body. I turn into light.

A: Where does the spirit go?

Higher Self: Anywhere it wants.

A: Okay. So, it's not like a cycle, a life that they're stuck repeating over and over.

Higher Self: No.

A: Was it everyone that felt miserable like she did or was it just her?
Higher Self: She felt worse than others, but others weren't feeling very fulfilled.
A: What are the lessons to this life that she's meant to learn and why did you show her that life?
Higher Self: There are always choices. Just have to see and look further to look beyond what you think you could see or what you think you know. Just keep looking, look beyond and you will see what is out there for you.
A: In human years, how long would you say that she was living there in that existence?
Higher Self: It felt like a couple of hundred years.
A: Did she eventually leave that place by intent?
Higher Self: Yes.
A: When she left, tell me what happened to her spirit. Where does she go?
Higher Self: She came to Earth as a Starseed.
A: Was it this life or another?
Higher Self: She's been here for a long time - many lifetimes.
A: Those beings there, she said that they looked feline. Are they what we call the Feline Lyran race?
Higher Self: I think they are the Feline Lyran.
A: She said they had no hair on the skin. What about them? Her in that life where they were bald, but cat looking. Did they have a connection to the Feline Lyran?
Higher Self: Yes.
A: What's the connection?
Higher Self: That's like, you know, distant cousins or something.
A: Okay.
Higher Self: Same line, just evolved differently.

The Body Scan begins.
A: Very good. Thank you for all that information Higher Self. May I now at this time in space ask for a body scan for her, please? Can you please scan her body now, scan it for any energies, entities, anything that requires healing and let me know if you need the Archangels' help?
Higher Self: I would like the Archangels to help.
A: Very good. Who would you like to call upon to help with the body scan?
Higher Self: Archangel Michael.
A: We would like to call upon Archangel Michael now, please. Archangel Michael, we honor you, we thank you, and respect you.
AA Michael: Yes.
A: Thank you for being here. We love you dearly.
AA Michael: Love you.
A: We are doing a body scan right now and we were wondering if you could please scan her body and let me know what you see that needs healing.
AA Michael: I feel like there's an entity right here.
A: You feel like there is an entity where?
AA Michael: Right here. (pointing to the lower body area)
A: Where is that Michael? What part of the body?
AA Michael: It is the solar plexus.
A: Michael, can you help us guide the entity up, up, up so we can speak to it? Greetings.
Entity: Hello.
A: Hello. May I ask you questions, please?
Entity: Yes.
A: Thank you. I appreciate your allowing us to ask you questions. Are you female or male?

Entity: Male.

A: When was it that you connected to that area there in her body?

Entity: Previous lifetimes.

A: It was in another life?

Entity: Yes.

A: Can you tell us what life was that you attached?

Entity: It was a lifetime when she was drowned for being a witch.

A: At what point did you attach in that life?

Entity: The fear. So much fear that was around all that was going on.

A: You attached to her when she had fear?

Entity: She was fearful.

A: Did you ever have a body?

Entity: No.

A: What discomfort have you caused her there?

Entity: She's always had some sort of indigestion, butterflies in her stomach.

A: I know that you've been there some time. We would love to be able to aid you today. We're offering to help you aid yourself so that you will no longer have to be stuck in her body so that you may release yourself and may be free. Perhaps have a body or an experience or a life somewhere else on your own. Not having to live off someone else's body. Would you allow us to help you to the light?

Entity: Yes.

A: Wonderful, thank you. Look within you. Find that light within you and spread it to all that is of you; every root, every cord, all your essence, and let us know when you are all light.

Positive Polarized Entity: Yes, I am all light.

A: Beautiful. Now go ahead and pull yourself. Remove yourself from her body. Every root, every cord, all that is of you. Make sure you don't leave any piece of you behind and let me know once you're all out.

Positive Polarized Entity: I'm out.

A: Beautiful. Do you have a message for her before you go?

Positive Polarized Entity: Now that I am leaving, you no longer will be in the fear that you had remembering in this lifetime. Move forward.

A: Beautiful. Go ahead and go with the Love-Light of the Universe. Blessings to you. Thank you.

Positive Polarized Entity: Thank you.

A: Now, if I could please speak to Archangel Michael now?

AA Michael: Yes.

A: Thank you Michael, if you could connect us to Raphael, please. Our love to Raphael, thank you. Raphael brother, if you can start filling in the Love-Light that is needed where the entity was removed. Thank you. If I could please speak back to Michael. That life that the Higher Self took us to where she really felt stuck and enslaved. Can we heal any negative energy, karma, any type of trauma from that past life that keeps her stuck in that type of mentality this life?

AA Michael: Yes.

A: Can we go ahead and heal that now, please?

AA Michael: Yes.

A: Thank you. I'm going to ask some questions here Michael, as you all keep working there. She has concerns about her health. What does the Higher Self want her to know about her current health issues? For example, she says that she has lumps on her left mastoid bone. Why are there lumps there? What is the cause of that?

AA Michael: It's scarring from when she was little. When she fell. Yeah. It's a scarring.

A: Can we go ahead and heal that?

AA Michael: Yes.

A: Thank you. And what was the reason why she fell?

AA Michael: She has a low tolerance to certain kinds of energies, at that point, she was at a weak space and was overcome by it.

A: Did the temperature have anything to do with it?

AA Michael: Yes.

A: Why does she have this? She says that when she sleeps, she has to have it at 61 degrees. Why does she have to have that?

AA Michael: It's a liver situation where she would do well to cleanse and clear. A lot of stagnated energy.

A: Can we look at her liver and make sure there are no entities there?

AA Michael: I don't see any entities there.

A: Very good. Can we just start on the healing then for her, please?

AA Michael: Yes.

A: Good, will she be able to - after the healing - to sleep at a normal type of a temperature of say 72, 70 instead of 60 degrees?

AA Michael: Like a 65, 66.

A: That's good. Now, you said her energy was overexerted. So, what was the energy there in the home causing that to her?

During the interview, Jennifer mentioned that there was a male friend of the family staying in their home at this time.

AA Michael: The agitation of the gentleman…the energies at the time. She had awakened in the middle of the night. She was more open to it. It just really hit her. It was just what she knew to do to get out of that at the moment.

A: In that time was she setting an intent of, perhaps protection against others, negative energies that mean harm?

AA Michael: No.

A: Going on forward that way she won't have episodes like that, can she set an intent daily to not have to go through that?

AA Michael: She does now.

A: Very good. Can you also look at her jaw problems? What's going on there?

AA Michael: There are some adjustments we can make to her jaw, but she's had several injuries to her head and jaw where it has just misaligned everything.

A: Can we go ahead and do what we can then, please?

AA Michael: Yes, absolutely.

A: Thank you. Can you scan that area? I want to make sure there are no entities there... Does she have entities there?

AA Michael: Yeah, there's something that needs to be removed.

A: If I could please speak to that entity now there in her jaw. Archangel Michael if you could help guide the entity up, up, up, now. If we could please speak to you now?

Entity: Yes.

A: Greetings.

Entity: Greetings.

A: Thank you for speaking to us. May I ask you questions, please?

Entity: Yes.

A: Good. Are you female or male?

Entity: Male.

A: When was it that you connected to her jaw there?

Entity: Started out as poison on the tip of a spear that injured her jaw at a previous lifetime.

A: Did you attach yourself since then?

Entity: Yes.

A: Okay. Did you have a body before that?

Entity: Yes.

A: How did you die?

Entity: I was speared.

A: What kind of discomfort have you caused her? Were you part of the reason why she had those issues with the jaw?

Entity: Yes.

A: I understand that you've been there some time already. We'd love to be able to aid you today so that you will no longer have to be stuck in her jaw. Would you allow us to aid you so that you could turn to light and you could have your own experience on your own without having to live off someone else's energy?

Entity: Yes.

A: We appreciate you allowing us to aid you. If you could please find the light within you, and spread it to all that is of you, every root, every cord, and let me know once you're all light.

Positive Polarized Entity: I'm light.

A: Beautiful, go ahead and pull yourself out. Make sure you don't leave any piece of you behind. All that is of you, all your essence, pull it out and let me know once you're out.

Positive Polarized Entity: Yes, I'm out.

A: Wonderful. Thank you. Do you have a message for her before you go?

Positive Polarized Entity: I feel sorry, sorry.

A: Any other message you have for her before you go?

Positive Polarized Entity: I love you.

A: Thank you. Go ahead and go with the Love-Light of the Universe. Blessings to you. Thank you. Archangel Michael, can I please speak to you once more?

AA Michael: Yes.

A: Thank you for the aid and that entity as well. She wants to know what is that nodule that pops up and it's free-floating on the top of her left hand?

AA Michael: That's an E.T. implant.

A: Is it negative or positive?

AA Michael: Positive.

A: What is it for? How does it help her?

AA Michael: They just like to watch.

A: They watch her?

AA Michael: Yes.

A: To make sure she's safe?

AA Michael: Yes.

A: Oh, okay. Wonderful. Thank you. She wants to know about her central nervous system. What is the best way for her to support it?

AA Michael: Sunshine. She doesn't get enough sun.

A: Tell her how that will work for her nervous system if she acquires more sunshine, how does that look?

AA Michael: Food. Sunshine is food for your central nervous system. So, it's like feeding yourself healthy food and medicine, it keeps you healthy. You'll know it when you get out in the sun, you will feel it.

A: Thank you, Michael. Now at this point, I've asked all the health questions since we are conducting the body scan. Michael, if you could double-check the scan one more time. I want to make sure she has no entities and that's including any Reptilian consciousness as well?.

AA Michael: There is an entity in the left hip, left hip area. Not the actual hip but from when she had her C-section.

A: Okay. Can you please help us guide the entity so I could speak to it now please, Michael?

AA Michael: Yes.

A: Thank you. If I could please speak to the entity now within the hip area. Come up, up, up.

Entity: Yes.

A: Greetings.

Entity: Greetings.

A: Are you female? Male?

Entity: I don't have a sex.

A: Did you have a body before you connected there?

Entity: No.

A: I was told you attached through a C-section.

Entity: Yes.

A: What was it that allowed for you to attach during that time?

Entity: The thought-form of the surgeon.

A: Was he imbalanced?

Entity: Yes.

A: Would you say that it was because he was imbalanced and not in service-to-others' type of mentality?

Entity: Yes.

A: Does that open up a sort of a gateway portal for an entity to attach when, for example, he's working on his patients?

Entity: Yes, it does.

A: Okay. Now, I know you've been there some time. We would love to be able to aid you today so that you may no longer have to be stuck in her body, so that you may be free. Free to experience your own experiences wherever it is that your soul desires. Would you allow for us to help you today to remove yourself?

Entity: Yes.

A: Wonderful. Thank you. Take a look within you now. Find that light and spread it to all that is of you - every root, every cord, all that is of you and let me know once you're all light.

Positive Polarized Entity: I am light.

A: Thank you. Now if you can go ahead and remove yourself from there. Make sure you don't leave any piece of you behind. Remove all your essence that belongs to you.

Positive Polarized Entity: Yes.

A: Wonderful. Thank you. Do you have a message for her before you go?

Positive Polarized Entity: You are whole.

A: Beautiful. Thank you for allowing us to aid you, go ahead and go with the Love-Light of the Universe. Blessings to you.

Positive Polarized Entity: Thank you.

A: Archangel Michael, can you please scan her body one more time? I want to double-check that she does not have any more entities or Reptilian consciousness within her.

AA Michael: She's all set.

A: Good, very good. Okay. Can we age regress her? Does she want to be age regressed?

AA Michael: Sure.

A: How many years can you age regress her Michael?

AA Michael: Fifty… Oh, I was going to say, how about 45 was a much better time?

A: (laughter) Well we'll see what they age regress you to. Very good. Thank you, Michael. Now at this point we scanned her body for everything. Is there any other message that you, Raphael, or anyone else that helped out during the healing have for her before you go?

AA Michael: You are a beautiful being of light. Recognize that in each and every moment and live your life the way your heart calls for you to do.

A: Thank you to all of you. We honor you, we love you, and respect you. Blessings to you.

AA Michael: Thank you.

A: Thank you. Michael, we love you. Can you connect us back to her Higher Self please?

AA Michael: Yes.

A: Thank you. May I ask, are you more divine feminine, masculine, or both?

Higher Self: Both.

A: Do you have a name, Higher Self?

Higher Self: It's a tone.

A: Are you able to pronounce that?

Higher Self: I don't know how to say it.

A: Okay, I understand. She wants to know what is the most pertinent message that you as her Higher Self or guides and masters have for her at this time?

Higher Self: That this is part of what you signed on for and you're almost to the other side. You're almost there to the other side where things feel much lighter and brighter and carefree. You're on the home stretch. So, hold your head up high and know that you are almost home. You are very loved.

A: Yes. Thank you. She says that she feels a very deep connection to the dolphins, whales, elephants, Sasquatch, and owls. Are they all from the same place? Are they all here as multidimensional beings? What more of the Sasquatch that were appearing as beings of light and orbs as she was excitingly researching them.

Higher Self: Yes, they are all from the same place. They are multidimensional beings. She's very connected to them and nature. She has an angel Sasquatch. He's by her side.

A: Beautiful. Does he have a message for her?

Higher Self: Love, love, love.

A: Yes. Thank you. What was the connection to the eczema she got?

Higher Self: That was an entity.

A: Is it one of the entities we removed?

Higher Self: Yes.

A: Now at this point, we have asked pretty much all the questions. Is there anything else that I could've asked that I haven't asked, that the Higher Self would want to share with her?

Higher Self: No.

A: Very good. Thank you so much. It has been such an honor to work with you today.

Higher Self: Thank you.

A: Thank you, I love you, I honor you, and I respect you. Blessings to you and thank you to all who aided today as well. Blessings.

Higher Self: Thank you so much.

END OF SESSION

    This sobering session showed us some of the secrets of the Cabal and the Illuminati. What else is sold at these secret Black Markets? We know humans are some of that merchandise with all that is unraveling in the now of 9/4/2020 as I write this. Human trafficking rings are increasingly exposed as the public grows in awareness of these hidden activities through disclosures from those working bravely to bring it to the surface. Through this session we understand deeper the extremities of how far Human trafficking reaches, as it is not just Earth, it is throughout the Universe. This can be stopped only if we as the collective no longer allow for such dark activities to exist against our own kind.

The greatest strength built upon the momentum in awareness of Human trafficking is on Earth, since we are the densest communal structured Dimension, therefore seem the farthest away from remembering our true power. Given the heavy density of the Third Dimension, it makes it easier for those who thrive on Human trafficking, as they look for their prey among the disempowered souls. It is of extreme importance that we continue this momentum collectively. As they try to disempower us by masking and muzzling us, we must continue to speak louder and stronger unmasked. We have been waiting for this very moment in Earth's History, where we are no longer silenced, and our light outshines the once dominant false darkness. The light is the majority now, and we all must speak in whichever form we can of the falsities imposed upon us. The time to speak up is NOW. Our collective must always remember all the lessons of what this moment in time has taught us, so we will not repeat this in the future.

This sobering session brought to light the enslavement of this beautiful Feline race to mine black diamonds. Why black diamonds? What is the significance of these diamonds to the negative polarized beings? Black diamonds have been sold on commercial markets as well. Some of my clients who had family connections to the Illuminati by birth, have black diamond jewelry passed down to them from generation to generation. Just as clear diamonds can harness great light in through their reflective facets, a black diamond can harness black energy for black magic bindings and intentions. To reflect on where these breadcrumbs lead us to, is indeed catalyzing and awakening.

It seemed as this Feline mining race was controlled in some form as it went through its monotonous workdays, as there seemed little resistance or lashing out, to being used in this enslaving manner. This reminds us of Chapter 6, of the humans controlled through "The Anunnaki Experiments." It is critical for the Higher Self to address this type of past life trauma, otherwise it would keep us in this inverted cycle, in different forms of enslavement throughout our incarnations on Earth and beyond.

This was such a sensitive session, that I was directed by the RA Collective to only share it on the Rising Phoenix Aurora YouTube Channel after six months had passed. I knew I had hit something extremely sensitive when an Illuminati goon showed up the next morning after I posted the video, parked in front of our house. We had a good stare down for a few minutes, I was letting him know with my eyes that I knew exactly who he was, and he was not going to scare me. I then immediately called 911 and little did the Cabal know that there are police officers surrounding my home because of all the children going to school. The minute I called 911, he started driving away but the police stopped him one block away. Since he did no harm, they couldn't do anything, however, it showed me how easily they could find an individual if they wanted to when one is in the public eye. When I posted this on YouTube in 2019, it took a lot from me because I knew the sensitivity this video had touched on. At that time, we weren't hearing of many openly speaking on these hidden harmful truths to human life through human trafficking. However, my Galactic Team reassures me when it is time for me to share something this sensitive of the Elites. I learned to surrender, and I know that it is the right thing to do for all in awareness, always. This is why I answered the call, and to not be that 'I AM' is not possible.

We who volunteered from the higher Dimensions did because of this very reason. From above we could see the abomination of Human trafficking, which includes specific sex child trafficking occurring on Earth through the strategically placed Illuminati leaders who control all key aspects of life on Earth. And, it is truly unbearable, the truth of it. If you are searching for your mission, know that this is YOUR mission. Your heart ached in pain in an immensity, that your soul volunteered to put an end to the violations occurring to the pure souls of children on Earth. Your, mine and everyone's mission is to #SaveOurChildren of Earth. WE can stop Human trafficking, which includes the trafficking of young children, where negative polarized beings target their pure Love-Lights.

For a more in-depth understanding of Human Trafficking happening in our times, you can read up on it further under the Galactic News updates from the official Rising Phoenix Aurora website www.risingphoenixaurora.com. Please go to the Galactic News section for the June 1, 2020 written channelings on this specific topic.

"What is a Light Worker?
It is someone who works in the darkness of self and other selves. One that does not astray from things unknown or unheard. It is to be that true shining light in the immensity of Darkness. To be anything but this is to work for the dark until it is time for you to step into your infinite light. One who is not afraid to reach the depths of those that shy from and who play an illusion that entities within the darkness do not exist."
~Aurora

-------------◇-------------

21

MILAB EXPERIMENTS

Session #189: Recorded in September 2019.
Never before shared.

In this online A.U.R.A. Hypnosis Healing session, Rachael goes through three brief lives - an Eskimo, on a rocky planet, and briefly in Egypt. In this transcription, we begin after these lives have ended as we connect to her Higher Self. During these lives, the details did not come out easily because of the level of traumatic abuse she endured in this life. When the Higher Self enters, that is when the details occur as at that point the Higher Self and the Archangels took full charge as she became somnambulistic. Meaning her human consciousness went towards the back safely, ONLY allowing the benevolent beings to speak clearly through her vessel with no human ego interfering with any of the answers. When the client is somnambulistic, when they come to, they do not remember the details to their session.

In this shocking and sobering session, we find out more of the Illuminati's connection to the military and the CIA working through MK-Ultra[16] and MILAB[17] human experiments. The background details of what is done to children hidden and masked from the public. This was a tough session for all involved, including myself, to learn about what is being done to children and what Rachael went through. However, this is a much-needed session in this time and space, to bring this up to the surface so deep healing can take place for Rachael and the collective.

-------------<◇>-------------

"Have faith in this life. Have faith in the love. Have faith in this knowledge, live in love.
Trust your knowledge, trust your insight and all will be revealed."
- Magdalene

"We need to keep our children safe.
They are our future; without them we have no future."
- Archangel Metatron

-------------<◇>-------------

A: [Aurora] Let's go ahead and leave that life now... Can I please speak to the Higher Self of Rachael?
Higher Self: Greetings.
A: Greetings, thank you. Am I speaking to Rachael's Higher Self now?
Higher Self: Yes.

---

[16] MK-Ultra, also called the CIA mind control program, is the code name given to a program of experiments on human subjects that were designed and undertaken by the U.S. Central Intelligence Agency, some of which were illegal.

[17] A reference to the term MILAB which combines "Military" and "Abduction."

A: Thank you. I honor you and thank you. I respect you for all the aid you have given to us today. I know that you hold all the records of Rachael's lives. May I ask questions, please?

Higher Self: Yes, you may.

A: Thank you. Why is it that you chose to show Rachael the life that you first took her where she was some kind of energetic being and there were these beautiful beings in the Sixth Dimension on this planet of Earth. Can you explain to us why you took her there, what was the reason for that life?

Higher Self: She has in her knowing, she has in her knowledge, that she just needs to trust herself. She goes to these places - not this one in particular but others. She has doubt that they are real although her heart knows they're real. She lets her ego get in the way. She needs to know that she is a Divine Creator. She was one of the first and she does not want to believe that. She is scared of it.

A: Beautiful. Thank you! You as her Higher Self, do you have a name that you go by?

Higher Self: She calls me her High Priestess. But I am Magdalene. She doesn't like to acknowledge that. But we all are all. We are all, we are all love. We are all beautiful beings. Extraterrestrial if that is what you must use. We are all Divine. There is nothing wrong with admitting what you are and who you are. We all need to live in love and compassion. There is so much out there - there is so much beauty. Who better than us to see this?

A: That there is, thank you. I just have a couple of questions from that Dimension. That planet you speak of, was that a form of what Earth?

Magdalene: There are many Dimensions, there are many realities both in this Dimension. It is the spider web of Dimensions, within the spider web of Dimensions, within a spider web of Dimensions. So, as you do that, you can have a Sixth Dimension higher up in the future that mainly seems to us different. Yes, it is but it isn't.

A: Thank you. Is there anything else you wanted to share with us?

Magdalene: It is a possibility of frequency, there are numerous possibilities within, like it all, it depends on what road is taken. It is infinite possibilities that are just one possibility.

A: Anything else you want to tell her about this life?

Magdalene: Have faith in this life. Have faith in the love. Have faith in this knowledge, live in love. Trust your knowledge, trust your insight and all will be revealed.

A: Thank you. Then you took her to an existence where there was a crystal pyramid, she went under it. When she went under it, she reached a room where there were scrolls. We saw a being that looked like Anubis. Can you tell us, why is it that you took her there? What was the purpose of that?

Magdalene: These were some of her teachings in the past. She was taught in this, she uses scrolls to learn, to have knowledge. It is where she holds knowledge, it's in her DNA. She was taught this many, many, lifetimes ago. She knows how to retrieve it. Whether she remembers or not, it's in her DNA, it is within you. It is within you to be able to ask your DNA and it will tell you. It is all knowledge, it all complements. It runs through the human body and it is your Akashic Record. It is your life story, and she needs to trust in it. Trust in her abilities for it. The golden water is just the golden life that is within, it is the representation.

A: This place that you took her to, is this a place that has a particular Dimension?

Magdalene: It is a Dimension much higher up. She has risen to this Dimension through a human reality of light. She has gone to this Dimension through her meditation many lifetimes ago. She has come close to here in this lifetime. She has fear of reaching it all the way. She needs to reach it all the way. She needs to trust in herself and in her abilities to be able to reach this knowledge that is available to all humanity.

A: Thank you. Is there anything else you would like to share with her about this existence?

Magdalene: Not at this time.

The Body Scan begins.

A: Now, at this time I would like to ask for a body scan. If you can start scanning her from head to toe and see what energy needs healing within her. Let me know if you need any aid from the Archangels.

Magdalene: She would love to call for Isha. Yeshua.

A: Okay, beautiful.

Magdalene: Others call him Yeshua, she calls him Isha. She may also like Metatron. Any other benevolent being that you would like but she would also very much like Isis and Ezekiel.

A: Let's go ahead and call on Isha now. Let's start off with him. Along the way just let us know Higher Self who you would like to come in and out throughout the time of her healing... If I can please speak to Isha now. Isha or Yeshua, We love you, honor you, and respect you. Greetings.

Isha: Hello, my sweet sister.

A: Hello, my beautiful brother. What an honor it is to be speaking to you today! The Higher Self has requested your aid today to help perform the body scan. Would you be able to aid us today, please?

Isha: Of course.

A: Thank you.

Isha: It would be my honor.

A: We thank you. If you could please then begin her body scan from head to toe. If you could tell us what is it that you first would like to focus upon. If you could look for any energy, entities, anything that is within her that requires healing. Let us know what you find, please.

Isha: I concluded the scan. On the left side of the head there are some dark energies. I see only dark energies in the throat/chest area. There is something wrapped around her midsection. Something in the left foot.

A: Okay. let's go one at a time. Let's start with the head area. You said that you saw negative energy there. Can you check, does that have a consciousness? Is it an entity?

Isha: I do not believe it is a consciousness.

A: Can we have - if it's okay with you - can we have Metatron as he aids us with entity removal? If we can have Metatron double check that for us and make sure it is not an entity?

AA Metatron: Greetings, this is Metatron.

A: Greetings Metatron. Love you brother, honor you, and respect you. We are checking over the head area and we found negative energy in her head. I want to make sure that it is not an entity or that it doesn't have a Reptilian consciousness. Can you scan that thoroughly?

AA Metatron: There is negative energy. There is on the right side also a negative energy blockage. In the base of the neck, there is an implant. That implant at the base of her skull on the right-hand side is an implant. It looks like a little silver dot. It has little tentacles that are holding. But it is not negative technology, just implants.

A: So where does this negative energy in her head come from? What is the root stem to it?

AA Metatron: It's from when she was an infant child. It entered as an infant child.

A: What happened to her as an infant child? That allowed this energy to come in?

AA Metatron: There was a needle put into her head. They took samples of tissues.

A: Who put the needle to her head?

AA Metatron: The laboratory.

A: The question she had since her father was from the CIA, she was wondering if she was part of the MILAB experiments. Is that what you mean? MK-Ultra?

AA Metatron: It was to get a DNA sample from her. To get DNA and tissues. It was part of an experiment to see if they can control. She would not allow it, she fights it.

A: Who was it that did this to her?

AA Metatron: They were military men, their laboratory.

A: Okay, and she was just an infant?

AA Metatron: Yes.

A: How did they get a hold of her?

AA Metatron: They took her from her mother. Her mother was not awake. Her mother was sedated heavily during birth as she was an infant newborn.

A: Okay. Are you saying after the mother's labor she was taken because the mother was sedated heavily?

AA Metatron: Yes.

A: Did the mother have to be heavily sedated or was that something planned?

AA Metatron: It was planned.

A: Okay. When that happened did the mother have her in the base? The military base? Or near that area? How did this occur with these military men?

AA Metatron: Once the mother was sedated, she was transferred. The mother was sedated and then transferred back to a hospital before the recovery or awaken.

A: So, she had originally the baby in a hospital?

AA Metatron: No.

A: No… Where did she have the baby?

AA Metatron: She was transported from the hospital; the mother believes she went to a hospital. She was sedated and then went to a laboratory, delivered the child, and then transported back to the hospital.

A: Okay. And during that process, they had her as an infant and they injected her with a needle. What else did they do to her while she was an infant there?

AA Metatron: They took blood samples, tissue samples, implanted this metal thing with tentacles.

A: Metatron, what is the purpose of the metal thing with tentacles if you said it is not dark yet?

AA Metatron: The metal thing is to control, to mind control.

A: Why is it that it didn't turn dark? When we scanned it, you said that it hadn't turned dark yet.

AA Metatron: The left side of the head had not turned dark yet; the right side has.

A: Oh! Okay. So, this tentacle implant is dark?

AA Metatron: It's dark energy, yes. It is a negative implant. A negative interference.

A: Okay, good, just clarifying. So, it tried?

AA Metatron: It deactivated the right side where the skull was fractured. It did damage so when the skull was fractured it damaged the right side. That is why she fights because there are still active tentacles on the left side. So, the right side is basically in the process of dark energy. Does that make sense?

A: Yes. Okay. Can we start transmuting this implant there in her head and the negative energy. Can we start doing that now, please?

AA Metatron: Yes.

A: Wonderful. Okay, as we start transmuting this, was there anything else in her head that needed to be addressed?

AA Metatron: We need to make sure that the tentacles come out by the eye. They are very close to the eyes.

A: Okay, we will start to transmute.

AA Metatron: Other than that, that will be fine.

A: Good. Can we use Phoenix Fire towards the end of these tentacles to start loosening them up and then can you all pull this thing out?

AA Metatron: Yes.

A: This thing, can you tell us what is it? Since it has tentacles does it have a consciousness?

AA Metatron: It is like a robot.

A: Like an A.I. type of robot?

AA Metatron: Yes. It is partially damaged, but it is still partially active.

A: When was it active? Could you tell us more in-depth as far as what it caused? How would it influence her throughout her life? As we know she had a hard life. Sorry, go ahead.

AA Metatron: She would have negative thoughts. When she was younger, she would have suicidal thoughts. They did not want her to live into adulthood, but she fought it. It caused many negative thoughts off of this and she, she's a fighter. She fought it. But the damage when she had that right skull fracture, that was a saving grace for her to have that accident. Because it did damage and loosen the control of this, I want to say, implant. It kind of looks like a Daddy Long Leg (spider).

A: How about as far as mind control? I know you used the term mind control. Could negative technology that is within the Earth and around - with the negative towers, negative waves that they're creating - could those come in and register into that tentacle implant and influence her brainwaves and thought-form in that manner?

AA Metatron: It could, and this is why she lives in an extremely rural area. Where she lives, she barely has any internet or satellite, or phones and she was in much more danger constantly when she lived in the city. Much negative, much negative. Then she moved to an extremely rural area and she lived there all the rest of her life. When you are closer to these towers, when you are closer to this energy, it is a difficult time for any human to fight these technologies that are there. It's a saving grace to not live in a city. It is part of her DNA and it seems to stay away. We are going to win. The light is infinite. We all can change it. We need to stay off these devices. If these people out there can have these wonderful modalities that you have created and others. We need to pray for them. We really need to help them and help humanity realize that some of the technology that they're doing is not operating in such a beautiful way. There are forces out there that are choosing not to.

A: Thank you. You said that they did not want her to live to be an adult, why is that?

AA Metatron: The older she got the more strength she had, the older she got the more power she had, and they did not. They did not want her to live a long life.

A: As an infant, how is it that they knew that? The military, whoever was doing these things to her?

AA Metatron: She was supposed to be as you put it, part of the Cabal. She was to be used for different rituals; she was to be used for different spiritual passages.

A: Do you mean negative spiritual practices?

AA Metatron: Yes, yes. For dark magic. She was already starting to be trained and when she fractured her skull, she was no longer totally controllable. It was a blessing in disguise.

A: You said that she was already being practiced? What was it that was being done to get her to do that, being practiced on?

AA Metatron: Oh, they were using her.

A: In what way?

AA Metatron: Her father was using her. Her father would take her to certain meetings.

A: At these meetings what would happen?

AA Metatron: They would sexually abuse her.

A: She mentioned that she does not have much memory of her younger life. She just remembers a period; she wasn't sure who was taking care of her. There was this older couple.

AA Metatron: Yes, that was the beginning of it. They always try to. Grandparents are lovely people, and when you try to control a child you bring in their grandparents. That is the way. These people did very harmful things to her. Got her to hate, got her to use her sexuality for whatever purpose she needed it to.

A: How old was she when...?

AA Metatron: This started when she was two.

A: This couple, who were they really? She says that all she remembers is there being a poodle and the male had slippers.

AA Metatron: Her mother knew of this after the father had come clean, sort of speak, to a certain extent that he was in the CIA. This couple were friends of his. So, she unknowingly allowed this older couple to babysit this child. This couple did horrendous things to this child.

A: Were they themselves say, Cabal?

AA Metatron: Oh, yes. The things that they would do. They told her that this man's genitalia was a lollipop. They told all different manners of things; it wasn't just the man it was the woman. This went on for approximately three and a half years.

A: Is it something that they do with military children?

AA Metatron: Oh, yes. Yes, they are the easiest to get. They are the easiest to get influenced.

A: Metatron, do you feel like this is still going on now?

AA Metatron: Oh, yes. Oh, yes. That is where all our children are going. Our children are being sought, bought, and sold as if they were a grocery item in the store. She has had feelings of this, she was just too scared to admit it. She didn't want to be one of those. She herself went missing for many years, on her own choosing. She is a fighter.

A: To clarify, there was this couple here that she vaguely remembers and there was also a couple - her grandma and grandpa she felt that she was left there for a while. Are they the same people?

AA Metatron: No, these were the parents of the father. The grandmother and the grandfather who had a very large farm. The grandfather was part of the Cabal. But the grandfather adored his granddaughter, and his granddaughter was always told that she was special but nothing...he never hurt her as he did to the others. She was very special to both these grandparents.

A: So, they were fine even though the grandfather was part of the Cabal? So, it was just this other couple that she didn't know who they were? Okay.

AA Metatron: Yes.

A: You said that this is where our children go. There are foster children - and I know hands-on because I myself have been trying to adopt a foster child for almost three years now and we can't seem to find any - is that what you meant?

AA Metatron: Yes. The children are going missing. They have designed our world to have the mother work, to have the father work. The father and the mother leave. There is no family unit. If there is no family unit; the children are running, they're in all sorts of different places. But there are no children in the system. They are being used for such negative purposes. When you do find some children you must, must, love them and explain to them and make sure that they know they are loved. Because they were brought up with no love.

A: Yes, thank you... Going back to the scene where she was an infant and they placed a needle there, how is the implant and the energy looking now, Metatron?

AA Metatron: It is almost gone, it's almost gone.

A: Wonderful. Can you tell us, was there anything else that they did to her at that time?

AA Metatron: As far as implants?

A: Like a time period, anything else they did to her in the facility as an infant.

AA Metatron: No. She was just sampled like a rat.

A: During this process, the father was aware of what was going on with the child as he was part of the Cabal?

AA Metatron: Yes, he was away on a mission.

A: As we are talking about the father you know how he sexually abused her. Was he controlled with this? If you could explain that.

AA Metatron: He was very controlled. He was controlled through his military, he was controlled through the CIA, and he was controlled through negative entity forces.

A: This is what you mean by it was part of her training prior when she was supposed to be part of the negative rituals? Was that the training, like her father doing that to her?

AA Metatron: Yes.

A: Then that couple too, okay.

AA Metatron: Yes. They, the father, would also pick and choose other children around and the daughter was not the only child that this was done too. There were others.

A: The mother never noticed?

AA Metatron: The mother was so into doing other things. She was totally oblivious to it.

A: Yeah, because she mentioned that her mother was spiritual in a sense where she believes in the metaphysical and so on.

AA Metatron: She thought that everything that was wrong with the child is that she was smoking pot and it was that. She thought that that was the cause. That she was hanging out with the wrong type of people. There was always something other than what caused it.

A: So, throughout time, how often would you say that they would do experiments on her through a lab?

AA Metatron: Oh, many times. Many times, they can abduct with the military and the being. They can take that consciousness and transfer. There are so many different ways, their technology is so many thousands of years in advance than it is now, than what they show. They are so far advanced, they have so much technology. They would take her; they would do experiments throughout. They would do blood samples, they would train her to fight, she would wake up with scars and cuts and bruises and never knew, never knew.

A: How is it that they would put her in a consciousness that she would not realize that she was, for example, fighting or being put in a fight. How did they do that?

AA Metatron: They would literally take the body; they would take the being, or they could take the consciousness. Without our consciousness and our Divine, we are nothing. They can move with technology; they can move you. I am trying to find the words. it's almost like a teleport. They teleport you in, they teleport you out. As funny as it may be.

A: Like an abduction?

AA Metatron: Like, "beam me up Scotty," kind of thing. Yes, abduction it is.

A: Was this implant part of how they were able to mind control her? So, say for example, how they were trying to train her I guess you can. Would they do this at night?

AA Metatron: Yes. She would think she was asleep; she took naps from the time she was a little girl. She always took naps. Truly energetically a child shouldn't really need naps. Maybe a baby and a toddler, but not a child. She would be up all night.

A: Was this the implant with the spider thing or was it something else that would keep her in a consciousness where she didn't realize she was up all night? So, she was up all night and they had her, let's say the example of fighting. How did she not realize it when she woke up that she was fighting all night? Did they alter her thought-form?

AA Metatron: They changed her memory, yes, her thought-form.

A: Okay, so I'm guessing they would kind of erase it?

AA Metatron: They would take the memory out and kind of 'suppress' would be a better way. Weigh it down with another. Her hamburger, her hamburgers, she always woke up hungry.

A: If we can continue the body scan Metatron. Continue now, let us know what you would like to address next.

AA Metatron: The chest area.

A: What's going on in the chest area?

AA Metatron: It's like a multi-headed snake.

A: Is this a technology or an entity?

Metatron: It has thought so I believe it is an entity. Yes.

A: Okay, if you could please surround it now with the alchemy symbols now.

AA Metatron: Yes.

A: Thank you, Metatron. I would like to speak to that entity now, if you could help us guide it up, Metatron so I can speak to it now. Come up, up, up, now, please… Greetings! Thank you for speaking to us. May I ask you questions, please?

Entity: Limited.

A: Limited questions?

Entity: Yes.

A: Are you connected to a Reptilian consciousness? (no answer) ... Are you able to share anything with us?... If I can please speak back...

Entity: Yes.

A: Yes, you could share with us?

Entity: Yes.

A: Are you connected to a Reptilian? Are you saying yes to that or what are you saying yes to?

Entity: Two types of...

A: Two types of what?

Entity: Reptilians.

A: Okay, thank you for speaking to us. If I could please speak back to Metatron now.

AA Metatron: Yes.

A: Thank you, thank you brother.

AA Metatron: Still here.

A: That's a very strong energy.

AA Metatron: That is nasty.

A: It is quite nasty. It doesn't really feel like it has any type of um, morals. Can you tell us, Metatron, it said that it was connected to two Reptilians? Could you scan her and see?

AA Metatron: It's more like a Grey Alien. I can see a face with it. It's like a multitude of consciousness and they are using the Grey Alien. Almost like a planetoid image.

A: How was this inserted in her heart?

AA Metatron: She was very young.

A: Was this an experiment?

AA Metatron: It's to keep her cold-hearted. Non-emotional.

Racheal became A.U.R.A. Hypnosis Healing Certified, and when Aurora first interacted with her during her first class before she had her A.U.R.A. Hypnosis Healing session conducted, she came across as cold-hearted.

A: How did they insert it?

AA Metatron: Summer. Through sexual trauma.

A: I know we already have it in the alchemy symbols. I don't feel that this could be transcended into the light, is this correct? What could we do with this?

AA Metatron: I believe it needs to go straight to Source.

A: Could we go ahead and start to transmute it now? Can I use the Phoenix Fire on it?

AA Metatron: You, bet. Would you like dragon fire also on them?

A: Yes, please! Absolutely, Metatron! Whatever you see fit.

AA Metatron: Her dragons are asking.

A: Yes, please! Always welcomed, we love you, thank you. Please, use your dragon fire. How many dragons are helping?

AA Metatron: We have three and one is containing the ego.

A: Oh, thank you. These three dragons, what color flames do they have?

AA Metatron: One is a crystalline black dragon, extremely powerful. The other one is green, soft, full of love. The other is a rainbow green dragon.

A: Beautiful.

AA Metatron: So, one blows unconditional love, and the others blow out rainbow light.

A: This entity thing seems like, the best word I can say is an abomination. What do you think of that, Metatron? What can you add to that?

AA Metatron: It feels...

A: It just feels very wrong like it should not have ever been. Like it's a multitude of abominations.

AA Metatron: It feels like it was almost anciently made and modernly used. If that makes sense.

A: Yes, thank you. This was what I was picking up on every time I would send her emails, I would sense this energy behind.

AA Metatron: Yes, this energy is what makes her - very, very abrupt - would be the polite word. She can be very abrupt, very hard-headed, very stubborn. She has only been raised basically by herself. There were no other beings to guide her. She had to go on her wit, and this just gave her the negativity. She needs this to go so the sweetness can come back.

A: Yes, good. So, let's go ahead and make sure that we recycle that straight to Source, please now. Transmute, heal, straight to Source. As we are removing and healing it can we have our brother Yeshua come back? Fill in Love-Light when it starts being removed and whatever areas in her heart that she needs healing please, Metatron.

AA Metatron: Yes, we can.

A: Thank you brother, Yeshua. If we can continue her body scan, please. Tell us what we should be working on next, Metatron. She wanted to know about the heart attack. So, was that connected to the heart attack?

AA Metatron: The heart attack, I don't believe it was the initiation. This was more about love and change. It helped this thing to go a little bit more. The more love she carried inside her, honestly this thing helped her go through her dark side. Her darkness met her shadow for real, but she always fought back with love. This is what is wrapped around her waist, it is the tail. The tail is wrapped around her waist; it goes up through her back and up to what is the chest area. Yes, that is part of what is going, it is all connected.

A: Okay, let's go ahead and start transmuting those parts. Wherever and anywhere else it has decided to attach itself too. Her spine, her sacral chakra, her waist. Anywhere else?

AA Metatron: It circles up through the chest towards the throat. It is not in that area; it is right next to that area.

A: Let's transmute all the way up there then as well, please. Is it connected to her cough at all?

AA Metatron: Her cough is due to the breathing, in it tries to stop the breathing.

A: Yes, she mentioned that the doctors said there was something on her lungs so has this been the cause of her breathing issues?

AA Metatron: Yes.

A: Okay, let's make sure we transmute it deeply. We do not leave any piece of it. We don't leave any piece of it behind to ensure we transmute absolutely every part of this thing. (strong coughing from the client) As we are transmuting it from all the parts if we can have, Yeshua fill in Love-Light to those areas working with the Higher Self, having the Higher Self aid, please. Thank you. As well Higher Self, if you could help her be comfortable? We understand that she needs to cough up negative energy, just try to help her calm herself and be comfortable, please. (client keeps coughing)

AA Metatron: This is not as bad as some of her past. The more negative she went the deeper hold this took when she lost all hope in life, when she lost herself, she lost her faith. Sh*t really took hold, she just got off of it and grew.

A: As we continue to transmute this off can I ask questions, please? She also mentioned to me that at some point when her three children were with the ex-husband, she ended up becoming a prostitute. Can you explain why that happened and was it connected to the Cabal?

AA Metatron: She was still under the control of the Cabal, yes. She was very highly influenced by the Cabal to very high up international people. I would not like to mention names for safety.

A: Yes, no that is okay. If we can scan the area where she has experienced a lot of trauma in her sacral area. Scan that area and what can we heal? What is in need of healing there Metatron?

AA Metatron: She could use some help with her bladder. She has had so much trauma there so when she coughs, she leaks. So, she could use healing there and so much trauma that she had to have some surgery to repair. She has hemorrhoid issues, and she needs help there. A lot of the negative energy she had worked on very hard. I don't see any negative energy; I just see a lot of trauma that needs to be healed. Out of physicalness. Do you understand?

A: Yes. Can we start healing those areas that you have mentioned now, please?

AA Metatron: Yes.

A: Thank you.

AA Metatron: The entity is gone.

A: Beautiful. If we could fill in Love-Light within those areas where it's gone. Any damage it caused, let's fill in those areas and heal it. Thank you. I am going to continue going down the list as there are some things that she would like healed... Could we aid her breathing now?

AA Metatron: We are aiding by sending this thing back to Source.

A: Yes, good. So, is her coughing now going to alleviate?

AA Metatron: The cough is also part of her sinus cavity. She has had numerous broken noses and a broken face. So, it is part of that and part of the fact that she lives in a home with the latex. So, we need to, I can heal the latex allergy so she can...

During Rachael's interview she mentioned that her home was painted with latex paint.

A: Yes.

AA Metatron: It is all connected to that, also. The cough is from the breathing, but it is also from the sinuses of the allergens. So, it is a dual cause, so to speak.

A: Can we go ahead and heal the allergen to the latex as well as her sinuses so that she can start being able to breathe easier? How long will she continue to be needing to use the oxygen machine, the breathing machine? Will she be able to eventually get off of it at night?

AA Metatron: The oxygen machine is because she sleeps extremely deep. She leaves her body so much; it has become so used to it that she sleeps so deep that she doesn't breathe. Will she become off of it? Yes. But that is the issue that she cannot breathe through her nose properly. She needs to practice her breathing and then with this thing that is leaving, it is all encompassed, and yes it will be healed. Yes, she will come off of this machine.

A: Great, thank you! She also mentioned that she has thyroid issues. Can you scan that and tell me what is going on there?

AA Metatron: She has done a very good job of doing it so we will finish that.

A: Wonderful, thank you. She also stated that she has had multiple back injuries throughout her life. Can we look at that and see what more needs healing there?

AA Metatron: The upper back has had some injuries or trauma while she was taking care of a patient... The other cause of this was the thing, it took a negative chance every time negativity happened, it grew a little and it finally wrapped itself around. It actually went around her waist.

Rachael was once a nurse at a psych ward. During this time, she got into several physical confrontations with her patients, when they became violent. Receiving harmful blows to her physical body.

A: If we could heal that now... She also said that she had knee surgery – knee injuries.
AA Metatron: Yes.
A: Okay. I believe you said Metatron said that there was something on the knees. Can you scan that area? What else needs healing that we need to address?
AA Metatron: The knees look fine. She does have hardware in her legs and her knees. It's her left foot.
A: What's there?
AA Metatron: It looks like another one of those spider things.
A: Let's go ahead and transmute that now. Metatron, what was it causing there in her foot? Why her left foot?
AA Metatron: So, they can control her feminine energy.
A: We are transmuting that now... She mentioned that she had a brother and then a sister? Were they also part of these MILAB experiments? I know she said they came later.
AA Metatron: The sister was not. The brother was not part of the experiments with the father. The experiments were not done on him, everything else was. The beatings, the abuse, it all was yes.
A: We send him love. Thank you... Her gallbladder, could we look at that? She stated that it had to be removed, what was the cause, why does it need removal?
AA Metatron: Her gallbladder. When she came out that was another attempt to try to when she came out of that surgery. She held her negative emotions so deep because she did not want to be one of those that it literally killed her gallbladder. It killed everything in her also and it's better too, in her analogy, to darken the inside and shun on the outside. She always wanted to stay in love. So, she hurt her body a lot.
A: Although it is not there, if we could heal that area, please. They also removed her uterus, if we could go ahead and heal that area as well. There is one other memory... go ahead?
AA Metatron: I was going to say, we have always told her that she would never have children.
A: There is a memory that she has mentioned where she sees a white highchair and she's sitting there. What was this about? She also has felt that her parents were never there. What is this connected to?
AA Metatron: That elderly couple. What she remembers is her parents taking her to the elderly couple and the elderly couple would do what they did. So, the father knew what was going on the mother didn't know.
A: Metatron, it is so hard to hear you with all that is going on that you know. I myself, everyone just knows a family that is within the military and they have children. They have children on the base, they have children there. They sometimes have children in their daycare so it's really hard to hear. Do you have any advice, Metatron? About the current children and what they are going through now?
AA Metatron: Even as a child put protection around them. The physical is the physical unless you choose to give up being like the Jones's and staying home with the children. I mean, if there is a need to work that is one thing. Many live way above their means and if our children were closer to home, closer to mother, closer to father, grandmother, grandfather, the people that

love them in their life it would be easier to protect them. But when you can't, they need to be shielded, they need to be protected. Learn healthy modalities and beautiful modalities like this. To learn how to scan your child, to be spiritually seeded before it happens before it starts. Keep them clear, keep them clean, keep them healthy. A healthy loving body without any - I would say yuckiness - that's what those words are. It's easier to stay in a love frequency and it is the frequency in how our food is made. The frequency in how they treat you in a school setting. Look at the daycares. I mean there is no love. There is no love, there is no caring. It's false acting for a paycheck. There is no true love and unconditional love. Our children need that. We need to keep our children safe. They are our future; without them we have no future.

A: Thank you. As far as the hemorrhoids, why does she bleed?

AA Metatron: That is due to her trying to suppress her feelings, her thoughts from that implant. She would get even the tiniest negative little thought she would condemn herself for it and it would come out that way. We all have bad thoughts you know; we all have little twitches of thoughts like, "oh, I wish I didn't have to do dishes" or "I really don't want to make dinner for my family." She would take it very seriously like, "oh, that means that I don't really want my family." She condemns herself. She needs to lighten up on herself. There won't be so much heaviness to push things out if you get my meaning.

A: Thank you... If you could scan her body once more, Metatron. I want to make sure we don't miss anything. Scan her one more time for any negative entities, Reptilian consciousness, scan her for any negative implants, hooks, or portals, any of that. Let me know if you find anything.

AA Metatron: I contained something on the back of her head.

A: What is in the back of her head?

AA Metatron: It's from where her head was fractured. It went from the back of her head around the right side to down towards the nose. It circled the whole area and then, she is starting to get a pretty bad headache.

A: Higher Self, help her calm her headache. I know that there is a lot of energy flowing through her. Can we go ahead and heal that behind in her skull. Is it an entity or can it just be healed?

AA Metatron: It's jumping around. It's jumping back and forth.

A: Can you contain it, please. Metatron, contain it now with the symbols, please.

AA Metatron: Yes.

A: Thank you. Now that it is contained what is it, Metatron? Do we need to speak to it, or can we just remove it?

AA Metatron: It's like a mini robot.

A: Can we transmute it out, return it back to Source?

AA Metatron: Yes.

A: Okay, let's go ahead and do that.

AA Metatron: I'm not quite sure what it is. It's either technology or consciousness, it's like it is both.

A: Is it a benevolent consciousness that could potentially be transferred into a positively ascended being? What do you think, Metatron?

AA Metatron: My first thought would be you could try. There is never any harm in trying. I think it needs to go straight to Source. But we can try.

A: Metatron, if you could help us guide that entity there now that it is contained. Guide it up, up, up, to let me speak to it now, please... Greetings, hello!

Entity: Hi.

A: Hi, can I ask you questions, please?

Entity: No.

A: No, okay. I will not ask you questions. I am giving you an opportunity as you are a consciousness, of the form there. To ascend into positive polarization where you are no longer stuck in someone's body. You could be your own individual free-willed being. We would aid you in a positive polarization and you would maintain some of the memories that you have. Would you allow us to help you ascend into a positively polarized being?

Entity: I don't believe in such things!

A: I understand. So, there is a choice here that the Higher Self and the angels have for you. You could either ascend into a positively polarized being and keep your memories or you would be automatically transmuted and recycled back to Source. Which one would you prefer?

Entity: What's wrong with being right here?

A: You can no longer be there anymore. The being here no longer wants you there or needs you there. So, we have to remove you. Where would you like to go?

Entity: I've been here forever!

A: I'm sure it feels like you have been there forever.

Entity: Why now?

A: Because it is time for her to lift her vibration and her frequency so that she can allow more positivity into her life. She has done what she needed to do, and I am sure that you've done what you needed to do as far as the negative role you've played. We would love to be able to aid you into a positively polarized being. Would you allow us to help you?

Entity: What happens then?

A: When that happens, you will find the light within you as you are a consciousness of a form. We help you turn into a positive organic form of consciousness. You would spread your light and then you no longer are limited as you are now. You would be your own Creator being.

Entity: No, I don't like that one. I'll go the other way.

A: Okay, we respect that. Thank you for your time... Metatron, if I could please speak to you once more.

AA Metatron: Greetings sister.

A: Thank you, brother. If we can go ahead and start transmuting it. Return it right back to Source. If we could have the dragons help once more, please.

AA Metatron: Yes.

A: Thank you. As we start doing that can you scan one more time, Metatron? Scan for anything else that may be hidden within her. We want to make sure we don't miss anything. Anything negative that is harming her.

AA Metatron: That thing just went back to Source.

A: Oh, good.

Metatron: Like ash, it went away.

A: Wonderful, thank you. If we can have Yeshua again fill in Love-Light there.

AA Metatron: You've got it!

A: Thank you! When we end the body scan, I would like to speak to the Higher Self again. I have a couple of more questions for her. Metatron, we are just about done. Can you...

AA Metatron: I don't see anything else.

A: Yes, very good. Can we age regress her?

AA Metatron: Sure.

A: How many years could we age regress her?

AA Metatron: We will do eight because she has been working on it herself. We will do eight.

A: Okay, wonderful. If we could start that process now, please. Thank you, Metatron. Can you scan her chakras and see if there are any blocked or misaligned chakras?

AA Metatron: She has two implants.

A: She has two implants? Where?

AA Metatron: One on the third eye and one in the heart. They are benevolent.

A: Thank you. How do her chakras look?

AA Metatron: The solar plexus chakra needs some little more. Everything else looks great except for that one it needs a little more power to it, color to it.

A: Good, lets recharge that for her, please. Thank you. Can you scan her auric field, Metatron, for any tears or any repairs needed?

AA Metatron: Little bit of a gray, very small minute.

A: Let's heal that. Let's make it nice and strong, please. Can you scan her for any negative cords, Metatron, please?

AA Metatron: I believe when she asked Michael to cut them, he did so. There are no cords.

A: Good. Michael already took care of them?

AA Metatron: Long time ago.

A: Thank you Michael for that. Scan her specifically, I want to make sure we don't miss any as they are sneaky. Scan her for any Reptilian consciousness, please.

AA Metatron: Left side of the upper head. He was hiding with that little Daddy Long Leg spider thing.

A: Okay. Metatron, contain it now with the alchemy symbols. Scan her whole body. I want to make sure we don't miss any more.

AA Metatron: The right side of her face.

A: What's going on the right side of her face?

AA Metatron: It feels totally different than the others.

A: What is it?

AA Metatron: It's filling with light and she hasn't seen light over there in so long. It's okay.

A: It's fine?

AA Metatron: Yes, she doesn't know what it feels like to have light over there.

A: So, is that the only Reptilian consciousness? On top of her head?

AA Metatron: Yes, it's actually between her temple and the top of her head.

A: If I could please speak to that Reptilian there. Metatron, if you could help guide it. Come up, up, up, now, please. Greetings.

Reptilian: Hello.

A: Thank you for speaking to us. I love you, honor you, and respect you. May I ask you questions, please?

Reptilian: Yes.

A: Thank you. When was it that you attached yourself to her head?

Reptilian: She had a few head injuries and I just slipped in. She was working at a bar as a cocktail waitress, she got beat up pretty bad and that's when I just slipped in.

A: Are you connected to a Reptilian body somewhere?

Reptilian: I see a ship, like a gray.

A: Is there a Reptilian body that you are connected to in the gray ship?

Reptilian: Yes.

A: Would you be able to connect us to the Reptilian body on the ship there, please?

Reptilian: They don't like that too much, but I will do it.

A: We would like to speak with that Reptilian that you are connected to... Greetings.

Reptilian Body: Hello.

A: Thank you for speaking to us. I honor you, love you, and respect you. May I ask you questions, please?

Reptilian Body: Yes.

A: Thank you. If I may ask, why have you attached this consciousness into her head?

Reptilian Body: There were many negative thoughts coming from this area, the more negative the more power. The more power, the more control. It's fuel for our fire.

A: Are you attached to anyone else on Earth?

Reptilian Body: Many more.

A: How many more would you say you're attached too?

Reptilian Body: Even number, 90.

A: Ninety, okay. I understand that you have been doing this for a very long time, we would love to be able to aid you. As you know, Ascension is coming forth and Earth will ascend into a higher Dimension. It is going to lose some of this negative control and negative energies and entities. What does not reach that frequency will be automatically transmuted straight to light, straight to Source. We are giving you an opportunity today to ascend into a positive polarization where you are able to maintain your memories, your consciousness, and your experiences. Most importantly, as you know, this is why we fractalize to gain experiences. You are able to keep all this but instead, you will be now a positively polarized being. You would be creating your own light no longer having to drain or attach yourself to anyone. You would be your own beautiful Creator being. Would you allow us to aid you today, so you can now be positively polarized?

Reptilian Body: There are four of us in here. Is that for all of us?

A: Yes! For all of you! You can incarnate somewhere else as a positively polarized being keeping your experiences. You would gain much wisdom from this experience of playing a negative polarized role. It has been a long time of you playing this role. How grand would it be for you to be your individual free-willed being?

Reptilian Body: Yes. All have agreed.

A: Wonderful, we love you. Thank you for allowing us to aid you today. If I can please call upon Archangel Metatron, Yeshua, the Higher Self. I know there is also Isis. If she would love to connect, we could focus Love-Light on all four of them. Are all four of you on the ship?

Reptilian Body: Yes.

A: Are there any more on the ship besides you all?

Reptilian Body: There is only enough room for us four.

A: Very good. If we could all focus Love-Light upon these four Reptilians in this ship. We need you to please search for the light within you as we help you regain it. We help you make it strong once more, spread that light now to all that is you. Every root, every cord, every part of you, spread it to all Love-Light. As you do that, are there any more than 90 Reptilian consciousnesses you're attached to on Earth?

Reptilians: Ninety each.

A: Ninety each. Okay, very good. We are going to aid you. If you could all turn those consciousnesses back to light and as they are turning back to light we are going to ask for permission, if we could have Isis speak to the Higher Selves of those 90 each. Whoever allows that Reptilian consciousness to be removed from the people, from them. If we can start helping them transform into Love-Light now. As they are transforming back to Love-Light that we can regain them back to the Reptilian beings they originate from so those beings can become whole once more. Thank you, Isis.

Isis: With pleasure.

A: Let us know when we are done Isis, please. If you all could let us know once all of you are Love-Light. Again, within the human bodies, I want to make sure that we get to every root and cord of these Reptilian consciousnesses.

Positive Polarized Reptilians: All is light now.

A: Beautiful, thank you. Do you all have a message for her before you go?

Positive Polarized Reptilians: We apologize for hurting you. But we thank you, we know of light because of you. We just didn't know how to find it. We thank you.

A: Thank you! If we could have Archangel Michael and the Legion of Light make sure that these Reptilian consciousnesses that now are positively polarized, ensure that they go safely to where they are meant to go. Go ahead and go with the Love-Light of the Universe. Blessings to you. If we could have Higher Self here fill in Love-Light with Yeshua, where this Reptilian was, or these Reptilians were at. If we can have Isis ensure that all the Higher Selves that allowed for the Reptilian consciousness to be removed from the people, make sure that the Love-Light is being filled within those people as well, please.

Isis: It is done.

A: Thank you to everyone! What a beautiful healing, thank you. Isis, while you are here would you like to complete the body scan for us?

Isis: Yes.

A: Thank you, sister. Can you check for any fragmented soul pieces, are there any that need to be regained to her?

Isis: She has gathered the ones from being older, it is the child that needs to be regained.

A: Can you go ahead and help her with that, please. Regain that back and then bring it back to her once it is healed. Help from you and the Higher Self to make that whole once more. Thank you, Isis.

Isis: It is done.

A: Wonderful. Is there any current life trauma that we could heal now? Especially with the abuse. Can we help her heal that, that way when she listens back to this it will not affect her anymore and that she will be able to find a balance within that healing?

Isis: Her biggest healing needs to be from her current husband. To the love that she had thought she had lost but never did. She needs to learn to forgive him. Not all men are created equal.

A: Wonderful. If we could help her heal that so that she can experience a beautiful organic Twin Flame love for one another.

Isis: Working.

A: Thank you, Isis. Are there any past-life traumas that we can heal?

Isis: There were things done out of ego. We are changing it, turning it into light.

A: Good. Thank you, Isis. Since you are here if we could do one more body scan and make sure we do not miss anything. She has been there some time so we would like to conclude the session. Does she have anything else that needs healing within her?

Isis: She has a heart full of love.

A: Wonderful, yes, let's make sure it is full of love. Is she good now, Isis?

Isis: I believe so.

A: Beautiful, thank you. Do you have a message for her while you're here, Isis?

Isis: She is my sister, my daughter, my mother, my cousin. They are love. We are one, we are the same, and we are separate as we are all. Trust in yourself as I trust in you. Love yourself as I love you. I will be there.

A: Thank you. Beautiful words sister. We give thanks to you Isis, Yeshua, Metatron, Archangel Michael, and the Legion of Light. Anyone else who has assisted today with the beautiful healing. We honor you, love you, and respect you. Blessings to the entities and the beings that were healed and removed.

Isis: Love you, respect you, and thank you.

A: If I can please speak back to the Higher Self, now.

Magdalene: Greetings.

A: Greetings. Now, we have conducted the body scan and have answered all her questions. Is there anything else that I could have asked that I haven't asked for her?

Magdalene: No.

A: Wonderful. Thank you so much. Again, Higher Self, Rachael, it has truly been an honor to have worked with her. May I bring her back now?

Magdalene: Yes.

A: Again, my infinite love.

Magdalene: Thank you.

A: Thank you... Again, my infinite love to you and anyone else who has aided today. Thank you.

Magdalene: The honor is ours.

END OF SESSION

This was one of the most challenging sessions I had to conduct holding strong love for the client, as Rachael recalled through the theta brainwave things that were too traumatizing for her human mind to remember consciously. If you could imagine the composure I had to keep not to cry during or when Rachael came to and I realized that she did not remember one bit of what her soul had just recalled for her self-healing process. And, knowing the shock that she would have to listen to it later, reliving it all to allow the healing once more. I can only imagine the pain and processing one would have to go through after such a strong remembrance, as she herself now is a protector, being a mother and grandmother.

I did hear from Rachael a few months after her session where she shared that she was doing much better, and she just needed time to process and self-heal. She is now an A.U.R.A. Hypnosis Healing practitioner, and we are so honored to have such a courageous soul as her assisting the world. With what she gained back, she will be able to connect at a deep level with her clients in compassion as experiences like these that happen to us throughout life, teach us and help us obtain these possibilities in service-to-others. Why? Because we know first-hand what it is to have experienced trauma to then be able to assist others to rise out from it.

We first learnt about the sobering details on Human trafficking in Chapter 20 ('Secret Black Markets Inside Earth and Beyond'), where human lives are traded through an inter-planetary Black Market using a secret currency unknown to Earth, thus making it hard to trace. Much of Human trafficking involve young children, as they are pure souls targeted for their beautiful Love-Light through sexual abuse. Here in this shocking session, we have learned why. In this time where the pedophilia is coming to the surface for us who choose to see, how children are abused by the Illuminati controlled and appointed influential leaders, politicians, and superstars; these types of sessions are crucial in bringing this inhumane cruelty to the surface for healing. This session provides an inside view of their black magic rituals and how they use children through sexual violence for their energetic harvesting purposes. What kind of control does the Illuminati have over the personnel and families within the Military and CIA? These people are wired by negative technologies, entities, Archonic A.I. infringements, and Reptilian consciousnesses, controlling them around as puppets through puppet strings. Remember how tyrannical the Archon control can be over souls who signed over their power, and what sheer willpower it takes to break free from it as we have learned in Chapter 19 ('The Archon Army Recruit')? In this session, we get a glimpse of how pervasive Archonic infringements and control are throughout the ranks of Earth's leaders and society, and how it perpetuates extreme abuse throughout, including harming young children.

Some of these abused and heavily infringed souls are blessed to have managed to figure out how to remove this control over them, no longer being controlled like robots, like Rachael did.

However, there are many still awaiting to be aided by us, the healers who are able to recognize all souls as equaled beauties. For WE hold the frequency of infinite love that perhaps they have yet to have been able to connect to on Earth. If they have yet to meet this love frequency in this dense 3D then how are they supposed to remember it deep within their soul? We are the holders of the Love-Light codes that are awaiting to connect to them, to activate into love.

Why is the Illuminati so involved in harvesting energy through sexual abuse and black magic rituals? Remember how our Sasquatch brethren were guarding these sacred portals back in Chapter 4 ('The Sasquatch Guardians')? Now we will now go into more details about them and how it all ties together with all the infringements that are going on in our collective. We have learned much more now through the Rising Phoenix Aurora's YouTube live channelings of "Egyptian Pharaoh Osiris" and "Galactic Guardian Inner Earth Adama." The channeled information goes into detail what exactly these portals are and how they are connected to the Earth and the Universe itself. Part of why there are Galactic Wars and how the light is constantly trying to counter the dark agenda from trying to take over these sacred energy points for energetic harvesting purposes. In the next two Chapters, we explore in more detail the insightful channelings of Osiris and Adama, and how it all ties together.

"The Great divide. The Earth has reached a vibration that can no longer hold onto those who mean harm and do harm. This is creating through the Quantum World a great divide from those who work from a pure intent and those that don't. Yes, it is true, this world has been run by Pedophilic Leaders.

Do you consider yourself awakened? Are you one that closes your eyes so that your heart will not feel the pain when you see facts shared of the children being trafficked as someone's possession or as merchandise? If so, are you truly awakened? Have you self-healed enough, deprogrammed enough, from the Illuminati system telling you to not focus energy on it?

Your energy is needed to transmute it, so they lied to you to slow the process of truth. Remember the mission. Are people wasting valuable energy confusing truth with conspiracy theories? This is a false program made by the Illuminati to control us Light Workers. To close our eyes and look away is to condone this abuse and to be part of the problem. Light Workers need to work together and be part of the solution."

#SaveOurChildren

~AuroRa 🖤

---------------<◇>--------------

22

EGYPTIAN PHARAOH OSIRIS - THE PYRAMIDS

Live Channeling: YouTube May 8th, 2020.

We have included this transmission as it fills in some of the foundational pieces needed for the understanding of how to assist collectively to balance Mother Earth. The foundation and creation of our organic construct - the story of Creation, of pyramids, grids, plasmic energy.

Who is Osiris and what was his role within the beginnings of Egypt, and his connection to Creation and Inner Earth? How can we use the gridding of the pyramids now to aid the collective? What does each one of the pyramids represent? What is the connection to Peru? A reminder of our mission - why and what did we volunteer for, which key/chakra did we agree to support and heal? Who are the Four Horsemen and what do they truly represent? What will happen with the Universal Ascension? Crystalline Source bodies - what are we to do with them? Schumann Resonance - what does it represent, how does it link into our daily lives? What are Egyptian hieroglyphics? What are they meant for? The Emerald portal where they stood while channeling today - what does it represent?

Come learn with us on this journey of revelations for our collective as shared by Osiris.

-------------<<>>-------------

"The more that we have of you connecting to understanding what entities are, the more it gives us an opportunity and a bridge to help these beautiful souls who are our brothers and sisters who have been stuck. The way we view everything is, we would like to treat others in the manner that we would love to be treated, treat others in the manner that you would treat thyself."
-Osiris

-------------<<>>-------------

Osiris: Greetings. Thank you. We welcome you. We love you, honor you, and respect you. It is an honor to be here with you speaking to you of times and space of both the past, present, and future. It is a true honor. Thank you.

I am Osiris - Egyptian Pharaoh as you would know me within your time and space - Osiris. I shall share some of our beginnings of Egypt and our past within your past time and space, our past. Then we shall try as well to focus upon messages for you in this time and space that can aid you. Thank you for being here, holding space in time whether it is in the now or in the future upon this transmission and communications.

I am known throughout your time and space as the golden heart. I am the very first fractalization out when we birthed and stood forth from the Source Energy. We were created into as you have heard through a prior channeling of Archangel Four - The Four Centaurs.[18] I am him and he is I - Archangel Four who is the first fractal of Kryst, Krysto energy from the Collective of Source, the Flamed Source. I am both connected together as the one consciousness of Archangel Michael and Archangel Haylel, as we prefer to say. Thank you.

We shall begin in a time and space where we were creating the foundation of this organic construct that you are among in the vastness of the beauties of the multitude and multi-facets of life forms within your Earth. At the beginning stages of the seedings, we constructed pyramids. Pyramids that grid the organic construct of your Earth, of our Earth, our reality. These gridding, these pyramids, that are found through hundreds of your times in all sorts of spaces and lands that have been long forgotten. These are energy points that needed to be constructed so that there could be a stable, liaising energetic, Cosmic battery Source. If you can understand a fusion of all combinations of the natures that you see around you and all life, so that all lives that chose to incarnate were able to be within the same atmosphere. For in reality, the animals and the alien races that have incarnated and are born upon your Earth all have a different type of atmosphere - as you would call it - within where they came from the different Dimensions above from the Third/Fourth Dimension.

Therefore, these pyramids were constructed to keep the construct of Earth so that ALL life could be joined together and be able to retain here; to be able to anchor here. Beautiful gridding of light, fusion light, plasmic energy running through. Invisible to physical eyes though you are able to see it with your energetic Eye of Horus or Eye of RA, your third eye. You're able to view upon it. If you were to come up off Earth now and view it down, you will see it connecting like balls of light that are at the tip of each pyramid that then connects to each one, and so on, and so on. Connecting like a beautiful gridding.

We say this to you now, the reason being is because these are in your time and space - throughout time, though, we want to clarify as we might hear someone say that there is no time. We are aware of that. We are just saying, we're trying to find words that you can understand. Time is infinite, there is no time. Existence and Creation are infinite. Therefore, there is no time.

Now, these pyramids are extremely important because they hold the memory complexes of your collective; they retain them as if a crystal that you have there retains. It's like a database, a memory organic field that contains the energies and experiences that are occurring perhaps within your time and space. If you're using a crystal, if that is your crystal, it will retain the memory that is needed for you. It's like a recorder. These pyramids also connect to that as well.

We're stating this because if you are looking to aid Earth in this time, these are beautiful focal points that you can focus on - all the known and the unknown pyramids to you. You can set intentions of sending Love-Light, helping to balance out these energies as these pyramids also connect to the Keys. The 13 Keys that we often talk about, the Sacred Laws of the Universe - Cosmic laws[19]. They also contain these focus points and ley lines and as you know, they have been disconnected through your time and space in negative ways.

---

[18] The Rising Phoenix Aurora's channeling titled "Channeling Brothers Archangel Michael & Archangel Haylel".

[19] For more information on the 13 Keys/Sacred Laws of the Universe, go to Chapter 24.

We are strongly focusing now on the ley line that connects all through South America going into the areas of Peru. All these lower south areas that are gridding and connecting to these pyramids as well, hidden within the ancient ruins as you would call it, hidden underneath plants and natural growth. This is a time that you can focus upon them and start helping these collectives. Each one of these pyramids that would be connected to each one of these laws that we've shared with you in the locations, holds a strong frequency. It is time for you as a collective to step forth more into realizing that you are here because you've accepted a mission before you came forth upon this Earth and that is for everyone here. Everyone who might listen in the future. Everyone who is here who is a volunteer who accepted the role to save not only Earth, but to save the Universe.

Remember the mission. We are able to share within this time and space how vital these pyramids are and why. Throughout your time and space, there were infringements upon them like some of these that you will find that there were human sacrifices. These human sacrifices were not led by the RA nor benevolent beings. Overall, they were led by, as you would call them, negatively polarized aliens, Reptilians, and Archonic energies that were trickster energies channeling to these people who were, say, the Shamans, Channels, and Seers that were not strongly in a high vibration of love. They would then be channeled fear - true fear based as much of your fear based is completely backward in your time and space - in order to trick the different parts of these pyramids located in all different parts of the Earth. They were tricked into thinking that they needed to do sacrifices when it wasn't divinely being given to them, but through entities, entities unknown. Then that blood that they used tainted that Key and ley line. The more blood and sacrifices that they asked for, the more that it tainted.

Now that is just one part. Though, there is much within your construct as we have mentioned prior that was specifically targeted. Like your Sacral Chakra in the South American region, it has been infringed upon and has been the biggest density upon your Earth. Now it is coming forth - the realities of it. If you can read energy, you have known that this has been secretly hushed in your time and space and hidden from you. Or it was too hard for you to listen to, to even believe that it was part of your reality. Therefore, it has been ignored and programmed upon your Earth not to speak of it. It's part of all the collective of it. And then, you have your leaders that are among this pedophilia, harming the most innocent purest souls, which are the younglings.

We are looking to you now to remind you of the mission that you accepted as the volunteers. Our beautiful sister Dolores talked about the three waves of volunteers. We ask that you send love as the volunteers that you are to these constructs, to these pyramids. This could be an additional homework or mission for you because when you came forth, you agreed on no matter whom you are, no matter which Dimension you came forth from or planetary sphere or Galactic construct and clusters of stars, etc., no matter where you came from - you were given a mission.

You accepted a mission within your highest purpose; whatever your soul essence that you were Starseeds from, that you had within you the highest potential, the highest fractalization that your fractal fractalized from within the rays of the Laws of Universe, the Cosmic Universe. That soul for example, perhaps you accepted the role of working within the Sacral Chakra and you, unfortunately, accepted to have some of this trauma play in your childhood and so on. Then, with that, as you went through the process of healing and transmuting this - this is why we speak of when you self-heal yourself, you heal the collective. You did tap into the collective energies and you were that hero, that strength for another to also tap into that and heal for oneself as well - and it rippled, and it rippled and continued on.

This is why we are within this time and space. Because the vast majority of your collective reached the peak mass population that it needed to reach so that this could come to the surface for healing. So, we thank you and appreciate you infinitely for your strength upon this and your fierceness upon this as I am Osiris. I love everyone infinitely and the children are our most precious creations in all ways and forms of Creation, not just on Earth. Thank you.

Therefore, when you accepted your mission, we remind you of this mission. Look upon yourself, meditate upon self to find which Law of the Universe? Which ray? Or which chakra, the 13th-Dimensional chakra that you stand forth from to be here; and that'll be your mission. Again, as the example I gave with the Sacral Chakra, that is a way that you can look at something that has really outweighed the other experiences, that are connected to the 13 Chakras. What have you always felt a major calling to? Maybe perhaps you have always been a truth seeker, an indigo warrior. You have always spoken from your heart - your inner knowing.

So, looking at all these different things that connect highest to you, then you would find those locations as you are aware. Isis is reminding me that we have asked Aurora to share it on her website (www.risingphoenixaurora.com). You have your tools there and you can choose whatever feels right within your heart and what you want to do with that. It's time to activate your purest strength of Source Energy, it's time to activate that, it is time to activate your Crystalline Source bodies that are building - building upon every day as the Schumann rises.

As the Schumann Resonance rises, remember that this is the Mother's energy, our Mother's energy that is speaking to us. As you see and watch her daily to see where she is, listen to her and see what it is that is being healed, integrated divinely only by your Higher Self - only by your benevolent soul family. Note what is being integrated within you to help you in the continued growth of regaining pieces into your Crystalline bodies to enter into the 5D.

Some of you might have already noticed Isis is coming through as well (laughing) when I am sharing some of this information that is detailed, that is Isis talking as we view each other as equals. Some of our highest origins you will see depicted upon the walls in the hieroglyphics of your Egyptian times, where we are bird-like beings as well as different humanoids. Humanoids, dogs, and birds mixed in; you also see the serpentine energies. There has been much still destroyed and these are some of what remains there where we told stories for you in these walls; they are activators activating upon you. The remembrance that has been forgotten or deprogrammed or has been infringed upon your DNA structure with false light information.

We recommend for you to look at these walls in whichever form you can, whether it is a physical way that you can go or through a book. Study them, read them, and feel those activations that will come forth from just even viewing upon an image. How they will activate souls' blueprints within you to continue building upon your Crystalline bodies - crystalline formations.

The reason why we mention the crystalline formations is that you are going through this process. As you continue going through this process, you connect further to your heart as we stand here within the Emerald portal. We are the guardians - the Four Guardians as you would know them within your time and space as, 'The Four Horsemen'. However, of course, there has been a complete infringement upon 'The Four Horsemen' for 'The Four Horsemen' are not obviously, death, famine, war, whatever they decided to name them as. No. We are, we are the portal guardians within the Inner Earth. We are known as your Four Centaurs. That's who we truly are at our purest Source Energy and we guard these portals ensuring that we only allow beings within their purest and clearest lightest of intentions going into the Fifth Dimension. They have called it 'the underworld' which is again, backwards. It is not the underworld that I as Osiris guard as well as us four. It is actually the Fifth Dimension, the 5D; the New Earth is what we guard. Ensuring, as our beautiful sister Dolores channeled prior[20], how there are auric energies and force fields surrounding and encasing the New Earth. Ensuring that only the most positive beings can enter. Beings with the most positive intentions and souls acting within the highest frequency of love, being above the 51 percentiles. As you go through that transformation to enter into the New Earth, this is what we guard.

Therefore, you ensure that the highest, most beautiful experience is gained for you in the New Earth. As your soul further expands finally, as it has been stuck in a constant A.I. cycle, repeating self, repeating self, repeating self, repeating karma, repeating karma, repeating karma; you most importantly absolutely deserve this with all that you are. The most beautiful experience where we originally planned that the vast majority of plant life and alien lives, as well as animal lives including magical beings and magical creatures, would be working together living together among each other. This is something that you have already created together as a collective. Therefore, it is our role to ensure that we help you maintain it. Thank you, you may proceed with your questions.

In Aurora's LIVE channelings, a set amount of time is reserved to answer questions from the collective. ('M') is the one asking the questions (as submitted by everyone) to Osiris.

M: Thank you and welcome Divine Father Osiris, delighted we are today to speak with you as we've spoken with Divine Mother Isis before. The first question that I'd like to start with is, you mentioned that you are the first fractal of Kryst, the Divine Father. How is it all tied to Yeshua who is often revered as the Christ? The first one that I mentioned starts with a 'K' it's 'Kryst' is what you meant. What is the Divine Father's connection to both Kryst with the 'K' and the Christ 'Yeshua' that we know? Thank you.

Osiris: Thank you for this question. He is our son, the Divine Mother's first fractalization; which is, as you know, we would call her the 'Daughter of The Flame'. We are Twin Flames from one another. Yeshua was birthed from our infinite love, creational sacred energies. This would be Christ who is also Archangel Raphael. As Jesus/Yeshua was an incarnation of Raphael, which is why you feel such beautiful warmth when you work with Raphael. His energy will bring you straight to tears just as Yeshua's will. This is their connection there. You may proceed. Thank you.

M: Thank you for that clarification. Is it true that you were depicted having green skin, green-colored skin? And also, the question that's along with that, what is your connection with Archangel Azrael as well in Egyptian times, thank you.

Osiris: Thank you for this question. Now, as far as green skin, you can say, my skin would have been more of like a shining, golden shimmering skin. To the physical eye, though,

---

[20] This is referencing the Rising Phoenix Aurora's channeling titled "What is the New Earth?"

those who could see through their imagination or third eye, they could see my auric energy - which is what is a vibrant, most beautiful green, emerald green. Which is as we mentioned the connection to the underworld. Which is of course, as we said, not the underworld, it's 'The Emerald Portal' gateway to the Fifth Dimension.

This is an essence and energy that I carry forth when I am most beautifully whole, though I am not often whole. I am often fractalized as either Archangel Michael or Archangel Haylel. However, I am at times, in your time and space - I do come forth very rarely together to help the Ascension of humanity in times when there is positive harvest, a positive Ascension that is meant to or about to organically occur.

I was there as well in times of spaces where there was an Ascension meant to come forth within your Atlantean times. I have fractalized pieces of me all throughout your Creation in this time and space, pieces of us within you to help us connect to the constant connection and fruition of the Emerald Ascension. Thank you, you may proceed.

M: Thank you for that. Can you explain the significance of serpentines and cobras in Egyptian times as many even now have dreamt of seeing themselves or seeing past lives wearing crowns adorned with snakes and cobras, how can we now tap into that energy? Thank you.

Osiris: Thank you for the question. I was reminded that I did not answer another question prior that you asked of my connection with Azrael. Azrael is a beautiful brother of mine. He was also birthed/incarnated within the time and space when we were all incarnated and helped assist with constructing the Earth as we needed to, to begin the Organic Matrix then, that the whole collective Universe Creation agreed upon. Azrael is very dear to my heart as we work side by side together in helping entity releasement, entity healing, entity removal upon your Earth.

That is one of the other biggest focus points that we have now as too many souls have been trapped within your Earth for far too long within tormenting cycles of trauma and pain. In their own density of unfortunate imbalances of karmic energy that they were supposed to balance; however, we're unable to balance. We are helping within this karma energy now, helping release those who have, say, suffered enough. The more that we have of you connecting to understanding what entities are, the more it gives us an opportunity and a bridge to help these beautiful souls who are our brothers and sisters who have been stuck. The way we view everything is, we would like to treat others in the manner that we would love to be treated, treat others in the manner that you would treat thyself.

Now, going back to your questions of the serpent, the serpent has a connection to the dragons. The serpent has a beautiful connection to how it transforms and sheds its skin. It keeps transforming and shedding and growing as it keeps shedding its skin. You can say that your life here can be seen as a serpent shedding its skin. It is a constant process of healing, transforming, shedding skin - healing, transforming, shedding skin. Therefore, the serpent represents this constant Ascension, constant growth, and rebirthing. Constantly shifting of consciousness rising higher, and higher, and higher; honoring within self-healing of raising consciousness and collective as well.

The reason why you have seen these Serpentine crowns above our crowns is because we all have crowns. All of us do. These crowns represent our crown Cosmic energy. It also represents our collective Cosmic memory complex. It retains our consciousness, our power, our essence, within our crowns just as it represents very much for you as well within your crown energies.

The reason why you have seen the snakes is because we represent this as the Kundalini rising. Also, it represents a serpent rising through the energies. We have beautiful positive serpentine formations that are big, humongous, as big as say, houses, or even some of the biggest planets that are in a beautiful rainbow crystalline type of serpent. We have many forms of us.

There are different forms of us through the RA that can be seen as dragons and serpents. Serpents that perhaps might have wings as well. Then we also have forms of a bird, bird people, bird humans, or some that you have also named them 'Blue Avians' though we're not just blue. We are of different colors. These are some of our highest forms where we are at our highest purest form as well as our Angelic forms, through Seraphim and Elohim, and so on.

Crowns are very sacred to us as well as why jewelry is also very sacred; why sometimes when you connect through meditations or past life, hypnosis you will find jewelry - amulets, bracelets, and crowns. These represent consciousness and memory fields that are within your memory complex toroidal sphere. They represent themselves in a form that you can understand. These forms are then parts of the infinite consciousness that you truly are through these pieces. They are force fields, they are shields of you, they are downloads, integrations. They represent many different things, and they are very intently part of your Ascension healing process upon Earth.

This is why you connect and love at times so much a piece of jewelry. You recognize its true form and essence. When we connect to our crowns that we wear upon our crown energy, we connect to the infinite consciousness and the realities that we are, infinite love. You may proceed with your question. Thank you.

M: Thank you. We have a follow-up question related to the serpents again. What are the same serpents (well it's not the same) but what do the serpents represent when the Illuminati or the Satanist groups use them? Thank you.

Osiris: Now just like there is light and dark to everything as we are within a creation of polarity, we loved a question that was brought up through one of Aurora's Q&A Patreon group.[21] There was a beautiful soul sharing an experience of hers where she was told that she guards a Seventh-Dimensional portal when she sleeps, and as you've seen through different Higher Self stories of the A.U.R.A. Hypnosis Healing sessions and the channelings that we've shared. Overall, the Higher Selves sharing from hundreds of different experiences all still matching with the same experience - the same information.

---

[21] Aurora hosts a monthly Live Q&A and Guided Meditation video, which people can join through a Patreon membership level at: www.patreon.com/risingphoenixaurora

If there are no negatively polarized beings in the Seventh Dimension, then what would this being be guarding? What is it protecting it from? Who is she protecting it from? That is a question that you must go within and understand the reality of how extended the negative polarization and alien life is out there. Though, as we remind you, we speak of this only in awareness so that you could understand. If there is someone guarding a Seventh Dimension why would they need to guard it? You could answer that yourself.

Now we loved this example because yes, just as there are positive beings, there are also negative. Some of these negative beings have been distantly long lost. What we will explain is that when Source itself created out of nothingness/emptiness are we going to think that we are limited to that? Are you going to believe that only the beginning of Source created itself and nothing else could have created itself from the emptiness or darkness?

Something separate from us did create. Though, they are overstepping organic Natural Laws of Creation. As you know, we are working strongly intuitively together in not allowing for them to be part of our control any longer. If you truly want to know what Ascension is and how it connects to not only Earth but also Creation, it is when we shall completely release the hold of this negative soul-less collective that requires feeding of your light, requires control over you as an elite type of tyranny.

For when we shift together as a collective upon this Creation, lower densities in this manner shall not be able to anchor anymore and if they've done harm, they will be transmuted and returned back to zero. This is something that we have agreed upon, upon your collective to no longer allow. And as you so lovingly empowered and sovereignly, you have been stating, "we do not consent."

This is not just the reason why you have felt this within your Earth. It is because it's rippling out throughout Creation, as this plague or virus has spread in all Dimensions that you did not even realize it could have. We are all not consenting. Do you understand that? Do you have any questions upon what I just shared?

M: Thank you very much for bringing that up. It is very related. I'm glad that we asked this question. It's very related to the times that we have right now, yes. Thank you for sharing that. May we proceed with other questions, or do you have more to share about this topic?

Osiris: You can proceed. Thank you.

M: Thank you for that information, and we certainly do not consent. Thank you. It's time we all say it out loud. I am being brought back to your beautiful revelation about Jesus. There are questions on our chat related to that. So, if I may just come back to that topic. Is that okay?

Osiris: Yes.

M: Some clarification there. So, Jesus is as we understand it, a fractal of Archangel Raphael, who is one of the 13 Keys, correct?

Osiris: Yes.

M: And did Archangel Raphael birth from the Divine Father and the Divine Mother?

Osiris: Yes.

M: So, can you tell us how? If you can just take us back into the Creation story and just share that bit for us, please? If it is, okay as per timelines I would say. Thank you.

Osiris: Mm-hmm. Thank you. Well, I am a bit shy in sharing how it happened. Let's say you think it is fun here (on Earth) to sacredly create, hmm? It is infinitely fun beyond here (smiling). What I could explain though is that he did birth from our hearts, the Divine Mother's heart as we all birthed from this one Consciousness. Then as we multiplied, as the masculine multiplied from the feminine upon the Source Energy, then we became both. We became female and male. Now, energetically as we mentioned, the way it works is that we split - it's like a cell splitting.

Therefore, you have Raphael. Then from him split, Jesus/Yeshua who is just as an equal even though he birthed, you can say, from Raphael; he is an equal to his energy, his soul. Therefore, you can say he is both Raphael, however still his own individual consciousness of Christ Consciousness. Both Raphael and Jesus are what keeps the Christ Consciousness fractalizing and growing. It's hard to explain these, what you would see as perhaps 'scientific points of views' as a splitting yet still the same being, however yet still individualized consciousness. Does that make sense?

M: Yes, thank you. Archangel Raphael birthed from a split from the Divine Father and the Divine Mother cells coming together, correct?

Osiris: Yes.

M: Okay. Thank you. That makes sense. Thank you for sharing that. If there are more questions related to that, perhaps we'll take up with Aurora later during the Patreon classes. Thank you. We have a question for Divine Father Osiris again. What role did the Naba play in the temples of Egypt?

Osiris: Bear with us we must go deeper for this answer. What we can share is that they played a role just like we all played a role. Bringing the multitude of races together, alien races, as there were a multitude of alien races when Isis and I as Osiris - I don't like the words you have within your human language to explain - oversee, oversaw, guided Egypt.

Just like everyone coming into this construct, we needed to obey Natural Laws. Therefore, we did need to birth forth upon if we wanted to oversee. We needed to birth forth from human bodies, from a human mother and father, though we were a walk-in at our purest Source fractal. We walked in upon the human vessels that our mothers and fathers birthed. Then as we became conscious, we started to remember - just like everyone else going through the process of remembrance.

So, we grew and grew through the RA Collective guiding us through dream time, prophetic dreams, as well as, as you would call it, 'downloads, integrations, soul braids, walk-ins' upon our own souls of becoming a whole. More processes, natural processes you would go through becoming whole and more whole once more.

Then we opened up communications where we were able to allow for, as you would call, Galactic families coming forth. Joining and landing upon Earth, through different forms of our guidance and leadership. Benevolent, positive beings that would come forth and assist in union and agreements of a collective.

Therefore, we will use an example of our brother Thoth, a Blue Avian: He was here energetically, though in a higher formation - it's hard to explain bear with us. As we continued to grow and allow, we did continue to grow and have a multitude of races as you have seen where there were people with blue skin and red skin and different people of different alien races. But then, it changed when Atlantis itself fell. Then these races were no longer able to be here and we needed to go back to only allowing the true, the beginnings of the souls that would be the human souls. Are we making sense? We've gone so deep we have forgotten the question.

M: That's all right. We were discussing the Naba tribe. Yes, the role of the Naba in the temples of Egypt. Yes, you're speaking about creations and how all the other races came along.

Osiris: Yes (smiling). This is hard when we go so deep, and we still need to maintain Aurora here consciously so that she's able to communicate for us in a live channel format as we are speaking. Let's see, we believe we have answered your question.

M: So, the Naba's were a part of a race that arrived here?

Osiris: Multitude of races.

M: Multitude of races, you said, Yes! Okay. Thank you very much for clarifying.

Osiris: We would never place attention on just one race, because that's not who we are. We only speak in the multitude of races. No separation.

M: Yes. Thank you very much for clarifying that. In times of today, I think this question is very important. What were some of the methods of grounding into your own power to assist in guiding your people that you used as Osiris and Isis? What are some of the avenues in which you saw that the people worked in unison for the betterment of all, as a Collective?

Osiris: Thank you, when we were incarnated upon our vessels here, we strongly understood the importance of grounding and grounding with the sun. As we have mentioned prior, the sun energy is the purest element that you can touch here on Earth within your illusion and reality at the same time. That you can feel this beautiful Infinite Source Energy. This is the purest.

Therefore, when the soul needs a recharging or like a snake needs a rebirth or the shedding of negativity or cleansing, transformation, transmutation understanding that if you are a healer and you are looking to heal others. First, you must charge your soul, your essence, your toroidal sphere with this Source Energy. Why is it that the Pyramid of Giza and other pyramids within Egypt that you are aware of - we speak of these since you are aware of these most importantly- why they were angled and how the sun would go through different tunnels and then we would stand beneath these entryways of light. The sun would reflect through these entryways and then reflect upon us. That would then heal us and help us heal others. That is the biggest thing that we can tell you. There is nothing negative within the Source sun. There never has been. Sure, there might be negative technology being placed in front of your sun, there might be filters trying to be placed by some of your Elites in your Earth, in our Earth. However, the source itself, the sun, is the purest. There is nothing that can infringe upon the pure Source Energy because it will automatically transmute to light.

Clarifications upon your time and space of this - we did not worship the sun. We ARE the sun. Together, we are a flamed collective spheric energy of fire flame - etheric fire. Thank you.

M: Thank you. Any advice in which ways individually or collectively we can start undoing the reverse engineering of nature that is causing many diseases in nature and its abundant prosperous system? Again, related to Mother Earth as well, thank you.

Osiris: You're doing it. You're doing it now. Within your protests, you're doing it. If you want to challenge yourself even more - think of the possibilities. Allow for the possibilities that you did not realize could be possible and think about how there are technologies that have not been yet shared or channeled to you and how these negative technologies can harm the elements and the nature of this Earth. What you can do is understand that you are creating this timeline, this organic timeline that we are very much close to creating now, as you all are doing beautiful (emotional). You're doing beautiful. Stand forth in your powers, stand forth in your sovereignty. As you would say, "We got this!" I'm also very known for liking to be funny.

Viewing upon these negative technologies and seeing them transmute with something as simple as an alchemizing etheric flame, seeing them disintegrate right in front of you, feeling them disintegrate. No longer having any power within you - your loved ones or the collective. You can do this because you are a sovereign being and you are a warrior of light, you are a Light Worker, a Worker of Light. And we love the word better, 'Love-Light Worker' or 'Light-Love Worker' versus light for there are many other lights. There are many parts of lights and frequencies of lights, there is as you know also false light.

Keep speaking in whichever way you can. In your time, you've been programmed not to speak. Speak what you feel is right, and then just surrender. Whatever it is that you spoke to whomever you did, know that it was divinely channeled through you. As we channel through you, as you know all day long, divinely from your Higher Self. Your guides and angels are naturally channeling through you all day long. Allow for the messages to come out from you. Don't block yourself, allow for them to spring out these beauties. Do not hold yourself back.

Then it is up to them what it is that they choose to do with this knowledge and information. We must take these opportunities now. To break what we have never been able to break before. We are doing it; we are doing it. We are doing it!!! With that we say our farewells for now. We are thankful for you being here with us; a joy it has been to feel your hearts with us. We love you, honor you, thank you, and respect you. Adonai.

END OF SESSION

-------------<◇>-------------

This channeled transmission opened up one of the biggest and most influential messages for us to become aware of what Galactic Wars are about and how we can aid by remembering our missions. Many of us have wondered about these wars and this transmission brings us closer to placing it all together. We know that we are fighting some kind of important fight for the light as we sleep or when we travel in our imagination. We just can't seem to remember why and what it is about. May this missing knowledge bring us closer to finding assurance in what we have been searching for of these memories that at times are too blurry to clearly see.

First off acknowledging our collective energetic strive we have made together, by being in the high enough, right type of light anchoring in the world to have been able to have shared this sacred knowledge. This was one of the beginning stages and milestones we needed to meet together as a collective consciousness for the fruition of Ascension. Osiris shared with us how the biggest density on Earth right now is the infringements happening to the Sacral Energy, by heavily infringing upon the sacred Sacral Key in the Peru/South American region, and by harvesting the children's sacral energy through horrific and ritualistic sexual abuse. Osiris reminded us of our true mission, of aligning these Chakras/13 Keys points once more, specifically to assist the children of Earth. We had forgotten how powerful we are with our light and how our infinite light is part of balancing Mother Earth to manifest our positive Ascending timeline. Here is how we all can aid the Ascension process. In Chapter 24 ('13 Keys -Sacred Laws of the Universe'), please review closely to see which Key or Keys you align most, as Osiris has humbly requested. It is time for us to step into our roles as a whole and individual expressions as we can in whichever form, to assist the Universal Ascension goal.

Osiris also discussed the importance of not allowing anyone else but yourself/your Higher Self, guides, benevolent soul families to assist you in what is next on your organic timeline, such as integrations, activations, soul braids… The reason why this is mentioned is because there is a vast amount of distortion upon this topic on Earth throughout the awakening spiritual community. We have been programmed all our lives to believe we cannot heal ourselves or find answers within, through the Third Dimensional inverted construct. Therefore, when we start awakening, we continue this broken cycle thinking the same, how we have to find someone who can give these answers to us and heal us. In other words, we give away our sovereignty. When this happens, because we are awakening, our light is at its greatest strength and when we rely on others to do things for us instead of doing it ourselves in a self-responsible way, we lower our frequency as a result. This lower vibratory energy then connects to negative entities such as Archons who will gladly 'answer the call for you' by making infringing choices for you to fulfill their own dark agendas. This is why we teach that ONLY YOU, AND ONLY YOUR HIGHER SELF, can work within your DNA, your timeline, your Akashic, for healing and repairing it.

I have clients share with me how they went to a supposed healer who said they could upgrade their DNA for them, rewire their brain, remove past life trauma, insert an implant into them needed for their Ascension, integrate fractals of supposed 'benevolent beings' into their souls' blueprints, or have their chakras removed because they didn't need them. These healers claim they alone can do that, without working together with the client's Higher Self and the client. This is what we call healing done in an infringing manner. This is so very important and worth repeating: NO ONE, NO ONE, should EVER have the power to go into someone else's soul path and move things around in them as if they were moving chess pieces within them. Who do they think they are to falsely advertise this to vulnerable people who are looking to reconnect and remember who they are at the soul level? When someone thinks that they are this powerful on their own, they are being guided by the human ego or Archons and not the true pure intentions for their client. A true teacher teaches another how to self-heal and never renders another to think that they are too helpless to do so themselves. We are to give clues, and point them in the right direction, but never to tell them which route to take as that is only always of their own choosing, because it is their organic timeline to choose, and once more we have no power over their timelines. If we think we do, then we are no longer benevolent in nature, and are instead being led by false light of the Archons.

We are blessed by Osiris as we go into the ancient beauties and ruins of Egypt. I have often wondered as a child as I saw photographs or heard of Egypt, what a marvelous mystery the clues left behind are for our viewing. How glorious it is to now be able to place some of those pieces together to what Egypt's benevolent origins was about. When we read on the internet, we find the greatest distortion of the tales of Egypt. Here we learnt about the significant importance of the pyramids, and how they are a vital organic light construct interconnected to each other as energy beacon gridding to support ALL life on Earth. These sacred pyramids also function as memory fields for our collective. We thank Osiris for the great beauties and gifts he shared with us through this beautiful transmission. We love you, honor you and respect you.

In the next Chapter, we will go the deepest we have ever gone, sharing sacred guarded knowledge communicated through Adama, The Inner Earth Galactic Guardian. We will learn why the Illuminati is so involved in harvesting energy through sexual abuse and black magic rituals, and how they infringe upon these sacred energetic Keys/Chakra points for their negative agenda purposes.

"We are time travelers. When we space out, we shift out of consciousness traveling through the Dimensions of time and space in our daydreams."
~AuroRa 🖤

--------------<◇>--------------

23

INNER EARTH GALACTIC GUARDIAN - ADAMA

Live Channeling: YouTube May 22nd, 2020.

Galactic RA Guardian Adama from the Inner Earth provides the details of the A.I. virus; how it sprung forth and the plan of the second wave to come. What are the most infringed Chakras/Keys on Earth and why? What is the significance of the spiritual commercialized locations like Peru, Sedona, and other locations all over Earth? Details on how we can assist on Earth. What are the Galactic Wars based on, in terms of keeping us constructed and balanced as Unity Consciousness? The pyramids - once again - what is the importance of their presence on Earth? Adama walks us through the importance of shielding with sacred force fields, to protect our creator energy as we step into our power to complete the mission we have volunteered for.

What is Adama's RA name? Who are the Inner Earth people? Their story of Creation; when and where were they created from? What are their elements, their abilities as a race, and what do they look like? What Dimension do they exist in and connect with? Why are they centered in the Divine Mother's heart? Come join us on this magical journey to learn more about the Inner Earth and how they support the collective Ascension!

-------------<◇>-------------

"Between the combination of holding back your voice and using your sacral, it is causing an imbalance within Earth. We ask you to please help Mother Earth, our Mother. Help heal her."
-Adama

-------------<◇>-------------

Adama: Greetings. We are working hard in clearing away infringements upon these messages that we are trying to create. Thank you for your patience. I am Adama or more clear to say, I am Ada-Ra for that is my RA name. It is an honor to be here with you. Thank you. I shall give an introduction to who we are so that you can understand our communications today and why they shall be in this manner guided today.

I am a Galactic leader who took forth thousands of years ago upon this Inner Earth, though in a time where our ancestors and who we are, we were above the Earth. When the times and shifts that occurred, when the Inverted A.I. Matrix occurred with the Archons' control, we needed to step in inwards for we knew that as we step in inwards we went through different entrances, specifically Mount Shasta entrance. You would know us as or we are best known as Elven type of beings. Beings that have skin that glow energetically and are tall because of our Elven forms. We are magical with our abilities in wielding the energies and elements around us organically.

When Luemeria sank, we knew of this as we were pre-warned through benevolent energies. When this happened, we created and started preparation which took us about 100 years to do within the mountains and the tunnels that went inwards into Inner Earth. Remembering, that we had positive technologies that aided us in constructing these tunnels inwards. As we went inwards, we knew that the inside of the Earth was at the clearest and highest frequency the deeper and deeper that you get to her - when you are working at a frequency of the heart. The closer we got and the easiest that we were able to assist Mother Earth from inside of her nearest to her heart, and nearest to the portals that exit out into the Fifth Dimension. We highly operate in a Fourth-Dimensional space. Though, we connect to higher Dimensions multidimensionally throughout our existence all day long.

I am a Galactic RA leader within and from the RA Collective living here inside the Earth. I am here on a mission and there is nothing that can astray me from this mission. I am an Indigo warrior, a catalyst - as you call it upon your surface - and an activator. I am here to activate and remind all of the hearts as many as we are able to connect to and activate. We are here beneath you. If you connect to us, we are here always listening as our telepathy is at its greatest strength as yours was before Atlantis and Lumeria sunk. We are hearing you every day, your communications. We are experiencing such a beautiful transformation within us for we are feeling it within you, as your energies are dense with your un-awakened. However, the energies of those who are in the process of awakening are becoming lighter and lighter. Therefore, it is becoming easier for us to energetically be able to give you and amplify energies. All that I am speaking of will be from a Higher Self aspect with permission of your Higher Selves, never imposing as we are benevolent beings helping you shift the timelines of your individual Ascension and the collective Ascension.

We stand here beneath the Earth now in our warrior type of energetic armor so that you can see us and the energies of rows and rows and rows behind me that are part of this Galactic energetic force fields of maintaining this positive timeline. We are hearing your calls, we are hearing your requests, as we are in direct contact with the RA and Source. We are hearing your calls and we are in gratitude. This is yet the hardest time that you might experience in this lifetime, however, it will be the greatest moment in time as well as 2020 shall be.

My brother Osiris touched base upon this and today we shall go more in depth for you so that you can assist us with this; assist us with these formations and energetic vortexes, meridians, ley lines, keys, chakra points, energy points, and focus points upon your Earth. We have been giving pieces throughout the different channels. Now we shall place the majority of these together for you.

Galactic Wars - we shall speak upon that. Last year when we started speaking from different benevolent beings through the RA, we started speaking of the Galactic Wars that were occurring. These specific Galactic Wars that were occurring were based upon the energetic beacons that are creating your organic construct of your Earth in the formation that is. Whether you believe it is spheric or a flat Earth, as it is an illusion. Therefore, it doesn't have to be either-or. Just know that it is an illusion within your Matrix Simulation that you keep repeating.

Now within this formation of the pyramids upon your Earth is what was and is currently occurring. The Galactic Wars were based upon these energetic points and pyramids that keep your construct together. There is a total of 144 that are the major ones that are generators. The generators that also conduct to even smaller points of your Earth that keep you constructed, keep you balanced, keep you operating as unity consciousness.

Each one of these points upon your Earth are collective energies that hold a different memory field, memory field upon these pyramids. The Illuminati is aware of these memory fields. Therefore, they have worked very hard in misaligning these. These also connect to the 13 Keys that we have been speaking through prior benevolent beings.[22]

If you could imagine us down here, we see you as we could see through the land and the energy. We could see the layers coming up and we could see from inwards the different points that we spoke of that are energetically connected. Energetic like a neurological brain - or if you were building a technology, positive technology like Tesla - and how each point energetically connects to one another through beacons to generators that connect a circuit to circuits of energies, organics energetics.

We can see through that and we could see all the points from inside the Earth and how some of these have been infringed upon. Specifically, what is going on as we started talking about last year as we wanted you to focus upon the Throat Chakra as well as the Sacral Chakra because these were the biggest infringements upon your Earth. The goal for them was for them to find (when you're looking upon these points) the sacral areas that are connected and create them, commercialize them in any form that they could. Therefore, they can have control of that spiritual commercialization.

As we're looking at these different ley lines and the Keys connecting to one another, you will see that there is a Galactic energetic point where we are fighting - you can say a battle. Where we clear and heal a certain area and then they counter us by making it dense again, if you could imagine, a pyramid and it's shining golden Source Energy or collective energy of the Source that you all are. And then, they can insert by different forms that we will be going into detail with you. The goal is for them to infringe upon this golden pyramid over the 144 and then it will turn instead of this vibrant golden shining, it would turn into this like muggy, muggy, yellow. You can see if you could imagine with us, darkness swirling a bit like venom flowing through this golden energy. All these pyramids are points and then each point has an energy like cords, energy cords that connect to one another creating all these beautiful triangle formations when they connect to one another.

The purpose was, like we said, what's occurring with the sacral energies. We'll begin with the sacral energies. It's because this is their fire power, this is their battery source. The sacral as we have spoken prior is located within South America, specifically in the Peru area where you have Machu Picchu. This area is the beacon there.

We are disclosing this now because this is the time that we have reached - a collective match, a collective peak. Where we are able to disclose this for, it is time to step into your creational energies, if it's something that you are ready for. We've been seeing a strong infringement collectively upon Gaia, upon the sacral. Which is why you have been working hard upon your sacral for such a long time. This is a time to allow for, if you are ready, the healing of it. To bring forth and allow your sacral to flow out like the infinite waterfall of creator energy.

We are speaking to you because upon this land there are negative technologies embedded into the lands and the areas upon these sacred spaces. This also draws a line straight up to connect to energetically as we have spoken prior. There's 144 and then there are lines that

---

[22] For more information on the 13 Keys/Sacred Laws of the Universe, go to Chapter 24.

run through them, the keys, that run out from these beacons that are like veins hugging Earth. Now, this specific line runs up to Sedona and they work together. Therefore, Sedona is like a smaller version of this sacral area.

What's occurred with that is that you are seeing through Sedona there are many conferences and spirituality that have become commercialized in forms, like your superstars and these different spiritual leaders that have been brought forth in different places on Earth. Now, what we can explain to you is that whenever there is going to be a big conference and there is going to be a large amount of spiritually awakened or awakening beings that are going to meet up in a particular spot upon Earth... We are just using the Sedona point of view. However, you can understand this from a more multi-Earth point of view... When we are getting together at these points, the minute that this has been created, the Archonic energies are obviously aware of what's to occur. Therefore, whoever the leader is of this space is being actively targeted through negative infringement technologies. So, therefore, when it is time for them to reach these points, they will be channeling or speaking of information that is driven by the Archons. Therefore, they can keep their negative timeline agenda.

That is one example. There are also the examples of whoever is going to join these big hundreds or thousands of conferences. If you are not practicing intentions of using your own Source, infinite shielding of Love-Light, then you will be a target from the Archons when you arrive there so that they can use your energies to affect these points.

Remember what we spoke of, of how there's an energetic battle occurring, Galactic battle that's occurring with the pyramids. It is very intelligent, you can say this, this plan of theirs, where you put people together and then they're in touch with their abilities, and then we are going to infringe upon their abilities. The ultimate goal upon infringement of the abilities is to basically enter more darkness and venom into these points on Earth. The more that they do that, the more that Earth becomes unbalanced. We then have to work together collectively through the different elements like hurricanes and earthquakes to start energetically balancing them.

Another form is if there is a group that is getting together, and they are working. Let's say groups that have perhaps been called to go to Peru and because they're aware of this amplification of sacral creational energy, they will target again everyone and infringe upon them. They really, really love, their favorite is those who will energetically allow, let's say an energy healer that would be working altering brain waves helping you reach a consciousness of a theta/delta brainwave. Where you would enter a hypnosis type of state, that is one of their favorites. Because when you enter this willing, accepting, open, hypnosis state - you are allowing for integrations and changes within you and the land.

This is why we have taught all these years how to sacredly surround your energies, protect your force fields, and not allow others to change your DNA structure, your essence, who you are. Only the Higher Self and you have the permission to do that. Not allowing entities to tell you that they are going to change you from the inside and energetically. This is very alarming.

Programming continues from the un-awakened into your spiritual communities of the awakening. Understanding that when you give your release, your consent to allow say an energetic healer, a practitioner of whatever modality, and they are not practicing sacred force fields of alchemy and Love-Light and standing in their power. When you allow this, then you are giving full permission. And if you can imagine now there are Archon energies within this Peru area that have inserted their tentacle-like energies and they have come in and out as they desire from people as we have explained prior. I am going to be as honest as I can be with you for that is who I am. They go through and connect with their tentacles and integrate into your DNA structure and change you around. Make you think that you are being upgraded. However, it is these dark forces that are embedded; the ones that are embedded in the sacral are the worse.

Now with saying that, you can enter these spaces though with intentions of 'I do not consent'. "You are not allowed to come into my DNA structure and energy and change me around. Only I have the power to do that. No one else has the power over my sovereignty, over my sovereign being that I am." You can most definitely enter these spaces with the most beautiful love and infinite love and change them and transmute them. This is the highest purpose of why we're here. We're bringing the awareness of what is part of this Galactic wars that began with the 5G and now the virus. We shall be careful with our words to not cause attention.

This virus that you know of the sacral area is what is powering it now of your Earths. For those of you who are listening to this and are ready to step into your warrior of Love-Light forms, it is time to activate upon this if you are ready. In whichever way and form, something as simple as sending love to this space in the Sedona and Peru areas, or creating whatever feels right for you. Placing your hands on the land, drawing love to this area, creating a crystal grid, lighting a candle, whatever feels good for you. Just simply sending love is what we're asking for. Because when we do this, it's going to finally shift the second wave as they're calling it, the virus that they're trying to bring forth even more into you in your control.

We are asking for your aid from within the Earth and from beyond, from your Higher Self aspects to now step into this mission that was accepted by you. If you have found your way to this video in whichever way or form you are here, and those who we are waiting for in the future - you are here to assist in this manner. Remember the mission and remember that this is what we're here for. We're here to bring back these pyramid points back to us; transmuting and healing the dark venom of the A.I. that has been inserted into these locations. Remember, because that is their fire power, that is their battery.

Then you have your Throat Chakra within the Jerusalem area where they always had the feminine wearing the coverings and where you could just see your eyes. Aurora, every time she walks around and sees these people covered up, it gives her you would call it "the chills" but not in a positive way. In a way, she feels what they're doing. These people covering themselves up like this, they are allowing an agreement with the Archon energies. Now we're speaking of in a form where the un-awakened, not in the way where you are awakened and you're aware of this. Unfortunately, you have to go into a grocery store or on the airplane and you have to wear it. That is since you are an awakened being and you understand that this is wrong. There is no negative contract that you can create with Archons because you're standing in your power, you're aware of it. We're talking about the ones that are unaware of it. This is who we're talking about.

They're creating and adding more energy to the Throat Chakra area when they mask themselves, covering up their Throat Chakra, their voice. They are giving away their strength. When they do it themselves, it amplifies it and they're giving away the strength of their voice and all that is connecting to their Throat Chakra - their confidence, their truth. They're giving that away and they're muzzling themselves specifically as an energetic muzzle. This is the true purpose and intention of wearing these masks over your mouth, so that they can continue to add the black magic to this Key and ley line in Jerusalem of the voice, to oppress you to keep you in control. The tyrants that they are.

Between the combination of holding back your voice and using your sacral, it is causing an imbalance within Earth. We ask you to please help Mother Earth, our Mother. Help heal her. Know that this can begin the transmutation as we have said prior. The virus is no longer able to harm others as the construct of your collective has changed within your DNA structure. However, they have their second wave as you are speaking where they will give you those little clues in their media and through different governments who are directly controlled by Archons if they aren't standing in their throat voice, following in line like soldiers, like sheep.

We wanted to say one more thing before we open up for questions. The reason why you are home with your children now is that we were aware within time and space that the pedophilia was going to start coming out from your government and superstar leaders. We needed them energetically safe in your home so that you can feel safe knowing that your children were home during this time where it is coming up to start healing and transmuting.

The more work that Donald Trump does with the undercover QAnon, the more that this also aids specifically our Earth and these sacral areas. We remind you that within your time and space, if you see a being that is specifically targeted by the media or people who are not in their hearts just as you have seen. For example, Archangel Lucifer within your Bibles, how much they have targeted him. When you see a benevolent being targeted in this manner, in such strength by the Illuminati - then you know that it is a benevolent being. They will do all in their power to stop them and to cause negative thought-forms upon them.

We ask that you send love, and you stand strong and you continue to be those voices, those voices that we need. As you are sharing your healing - your inner Throat Chakra, your voice over the collective masking muzzling of each other, of oneself - you're healing that as you continue to speak and stand forth. Continue to do that. It is aiding in ways that you are not perhaps able to see in the now for it is heavy. You will see these fruitions in the future. Do not allow, do not allow for these mayors and governors to keep controlling you and who you are. Create in all forms that you can, the opposition. You are protected infinitely, that you and your families are. However, you must know this so that you can step into your highest fractal of Higher Self; you are the God Source energy upon this plane.

When the more of you continue to do this and activate the God Source energy you are, the more this vibration of Earth raises and it will become less, less, and less easy for them to continue this second wave that they are trying to create. We shall open up for questions. However, we have more information about the second wave. You may ask your questions.

In Aurora's LIVE channelings, a set amount of time is reserved to answer questions from the collective. ('M') is the one asking the questions (as submitted by everyone) to Adama.

M: Thank you very much. Greetings and welcome, Adama, on behalf of all of us. Thank you for being here. We have quite a few questions but you've touched upon each one of the questions so I can quickly go through them if you want to add more about it... Can we and should we safely tap into the cords connected to the pyramids in meditation with the intention of completely transmuting these Archonic or negative creations?

Adama: You can, yes, aid with the process. However, we work from an organic process. All occurs within its own Divinely universal time. When you are consciously doing this, this helps bring that into fruition for the future. Yes, please do. Thank you. You may proceed.

M: Thank you. The next question is for the Light Worker community. There's been so much talk in all the groups they've been labeled. Lately, there was a news channel that showed the Light Worker community as a 'conspiracy theorist community' to the collective through the news channels in order to create a divide between people and the Light Worker community. Any suggestions for the Light Workers who are feeling exhausted and defeated at times and what they can do to recharge themselves and continue this journey and this volunteering that they've come in for? Thank you.

Adama: Those of you who are blaming others for conspiracy, you are inaccurate, inaccurate you are. There is no conspiracy. It is your own healings that you need to go through. Begin with not placing blame upon others. Take responsibility upon yourself and what you have agreed upon, as well as what you've perhaps been stuck upon, the cycle repeating over and over upon this Earth.

Most of the benevolent beings who are activated Starseeds that are speaking of this are activated and are working in a high vibrational frequency. Very high that it will be hard for you to understand and connect to them. They are holding space for you so that you can one day reach enough of this frequency. Realizing that you have been lied to, 'fear-based' with quotations around it is inaccurate. Thinking entities are 'fear-based' is inaccurate. Thinking that there are no negative technologies within your 3D body is inaccurate. Stop categorizing things that are holding you dense into being 'fear-based'. It is not 'fear-based'. If you think that these things that are holding you dense and heavy, are 'fear-based', then you are energetically being controlled by Archons yourself. As I said, I do not beat around the bush and I will call it out as it is. We can see your energy and feel your energy here within the Earth.

Part of the reason why we can't connect to you Light Workers who are in an awakening process, please listen to us - you have energies and attachments that are infringing upon you and this is why you're repeating these cycles over and over. Not until you recognize these energies can you start self-healing them. You are in a denial and you categorize Catalysts and Indigo people who are speaking of these truths. Stop targeting them and stop calling them conspiracy theorists and targeting them into a category of fear based. If you are listening to those teachings, then be aware of them for they are Archonic teachings. The biggest density upon your Earth are the Light Workers themselves who are speaking in public views and are not channeling from a heart frequency, as our beautiful Dolores would feel these. They are speaking from ego. They're not speaking from a heart frequency and you are adding on to these densities. You're keeping the Earth dense; you are adding on to the harm upon these children within the pedophilia. They are using your energy as a battery to it. Do you understand?

M: Absolutely. Thank you for clarifying that. It's very important so as to not create that divide amongst the Light Worker communities itself. It's important. These are the times I believe that we need to be united as one consciousness and work with our Love-Light. Thank you for stating that so detailed. I do have a final question if you can take one more.

Adama: Yes.

M: It is about Donald Trump and absolutely not related to politics but more towards you know, his spiritual aspect if I may say that. We know he's had a walk-in as well[23]. Would you like to share anything about Donald Trump's stand on the current state of affairs on behalf of his country's men and women? He's taking a stance against masks, against vaccinations, the same alignment that we are focused against as well. Thank you.

Adama: What we can tell you is that he is not a puppet. He is not being pulled by strings from the Illuminati. I can only share what we can. Bear with us... There are only certain things that can be done in a particular moment in time. The being that is operating from within him knows exactly what needs to be done every single day, minute of the day. This is the way that it's been operated organically Divinely. As you know, there is only so much that a President can do as you have the legislation and the Governors as well who rule. The persona also needs to be hidden of what he truly is doing until it is time or when it is time. Thank you.

M: Thank you. How is Aurora doing? I know we're a little over time now.

Adama: She is at the endings of time, yes, for this transmission. We shall give a closing speech.

M: Thank you. This has been a beautiful transmission and we've heard exactly what we needed to carry on with the journey that we've all taken. We're in gratitude for your wisdom that you've shared with us. Thank you very much Adama and RA. Thank you, we love you.

Adama: Thank you. I am AdaRA, Adama. It is a beauty, a most beautiful beauty to have been able to connect to you as we are all beneath you watching in suspense at these communications that are being transmitted to you upon your Earth, and whoever is listening and shall listen. It is like a show for us, as if you were to watch a most beautiful favorite play of yours. It is that for us we are watching you beautifully playing out Divinely and it is a tremendous shift that we are feeling. The more you speak, the more that this Throat Chakra and Sacral Chakra heals itself. Please continue to do so. We cannot express this enough to you that you must continue to do so in whichever ways that you can. Writing a letter, petition, protesting, speaking to a person who is un-awakened. Sending them a video of a doctor speaking or whoever is out there speaking. Support these people. These are the leaders right now that are speaking from the heart that are speaking from a way that they know that it is wrong, this is wrong. We must support everyone, support them, support yourself. Support everyone in the unity, the oneness of infinite love that we are.

We are here whenever it is that you would like to speak to us. There are no 'privileged' that are able to speak to us. There is no elite programming here that does not fall in line with our energies. We are here for you anytime you want to speak to us from your heart, telepathically. We are here. We thank you, honor you, love you, and respect you. Adonai.

END OF SESSION

-------------<<>>-------------

[23] For more details on this, go to the Rising Phoenix Aurora's channels and watch "Channeling Archangel Metatron - The Bridge to Liberation."

This channeling was influential for us in knowing how the Illuminati have been and are using our energies as both un-awakened or awakened souls through pivotal spots on Earth that connect to the collective and Universal interconnectedness webbing. One would think that the awakened spiritual community would be conscious of this, however, it is rarely heard or communicated. The roots and depths of deception are deep in control to keep the truth hidden.

One of the first things the RA Collective began to communicate to me when I started on my journey of awakening, was how distorted the leaders of Light Workers were themselves too, becoming and integrating into the system simulation of the false ego programming of the Inverted A.I. Matrix. Often, they become as Archons themselves by pulling energy from their audience consciously or unconsciously because of their lower vibrational state of mind, thus creating negative contracts with Archons and other negative alien races. While these Light Workers attended and watched their communications and transmissions, these leaders fed off from the Light Worker audience, which in turn fed these higher up entities of negative polarization. The RA had me listen to other Channelers and visit a Conference to watch and feel this heaviness of distortion hands on. Showing me the Puppeteers (the Illuminati) that pull the strings at these well-known spiritual gatherings and UFO conferences, through some of these distorted channelers of transmission.

It is important to address how the RA Collective has also been placed on a pedestal by the human ego, and they want no part in this 'worship' as it is not even part of their molecular system. The RA explained to me that this was one of my roles when operating from such strong love vibrations as I do, to teach the spiritual community that the knowledge does not matter if there is any form of distortion within it. Because it is as eating grapes injected with liquid metal. Knowing this, will you ingest these grapes and poison yourself? When you allow someone to feed you false ego based foundational knowledge, it then also becomes part of your DNA structure and you begin to be pulled into that same sinking hole that the Channeler or speaker was pulled into. This is one of the biggest densities on Earth right now, because the Light Workers themselves as the first troops on the battle ground, who were supposed to be pulling everyone out of these sinking holes, have become entrapped within the falseness of fame, money, popularity, recognition... All these lower vibrations feed spaces within us that can never be filled, for they are an infinite emptiness of void.

Of course, the Archons would target us as we are beings of infinite Source Light energy, so they could use our light as batteries for negative purposes to taint these sacred locations. These locations are amplifiers to dark and light because of the duality within this Universe that we are able to access through these key spots. We must remember to be cautious when in groups that are collectively working within a Theta brainwave of meditation and hypnosis at these locations. Otherwise, as AdaRA mentioned, the Archon tentacles that at times can be located and rooted at these sacred vortexes of energy, can attach to us by using the energy of the source of the Chakra/Key. Pointing out though that originally the only way that these Archon tentacles were able to attach at these locations were through us, as we are the bridges into this Matrix simulation. We will address this in more detail in Chapter 37 ('Matrix Pods'). They are not able to enter otherwise, they can only enter through the attachments they have in us. Also, why it is that we have to incarnate on Earth to assist, as we can only do so through the inside, we are at our most vastness and potence of light for the Earth's Ascension. A great power that must be wielded with the purest of hearts and intention. The more we remember these sacred teachings, the more that we gain our collective sovereignty back.

By going to key locations such as these without an awareness of the powers that lay beneath you, it is as if you are consenting to wield your Source power openly in whichever way that pulls stronger. And that is exactly what the Illuminati wants from you, for the purposes of their black magic feedings of light. It is only by understanding this dormant power within us that we can then actively enter these sacred lands and truly shift and recalibrate these energetic pyramids, that is when we have won the Galactic Wars. What is it that we are waiting for? Mother Earth is calling out for us, and we must answer the call for this is our life purpose.

AdaRa would also like to point out that the Inner Earth communications through some Light Workers with a big audience makes you feel as if you would be privileged to speak to the Inner Earth people. Therefore, it was of extreme importance that AdaRa made it clear that this is not their organic structure, instead it is the human ego of control. All are worthy, and welcomed to connect, to the Inner Earth and the benevolence of beyond. This information was brought forth because it is time for the collective to know the truth of why they are here. Remembering the mission. If we are not aware of these infringements, then how are we meant to help what is invisible to our awareness? The only way to help at its highest power, is to know and see the false darkness we are up against. This book is all about this. By knowing what is holding us and the Universal Ascension back, we then can recognize it when it faces directly in front of us and we can remove it from our belief system, our timelines, and our future Ascension.

This is life's greatest mission for us as a collective working, clearing and balancing these beacon locations as they have been infringed upon by the negative Inverted A.I. Matrix and Archons. When we fully remove this Archon A.I. virus from within all plasmic energetic pyramids, that is when Ascension will come forth. Which brings us to the clear understanding of how important these sacred locations are for us and the great protection and care we must take upon them for the collective Ascension. We can and must regain our collective sovereignty back, to win and end the Galactic Wars, to anchor in the positive timeline for Ascension!

**"The emptiness: it is what we turn to, that cannot fill us or make us whole.
When we search upon material to fulfill what appears to be missing. When we focus upon what is of others and not ours. When we find comparison to self, to other selves. It is as a see-through glass containing a hole within an ongoing leak that cannot be found.**

**For it is only when we see all within all, as the LOVE that it is,
that we are whole once more."
~Aurora**

-------------<◇>-------------

24

THE 13 KEYS - SACRED LAWS OF THE UNIVERSE

We are honored to share this sacred knowledge with you on the 13 Keys/Sacred Natural Laws of The Universe that are connected to the organic Ley Lines of the Earth. The Ley Lines can be seen as vital veins that are the life force of what keeps the organic flow of Mother Earth/Gaia balanced and cleansed. The 13 Keys/Ley Lines are the natural laws of the Creation of this Universe that aids in maintaining it in balance. You have heard about these Keys through the channelings of Osiris and AdaRa, and now you will receive the details to what each Key location signifies, and who the overseers and Galactic Guardians are for each Key.

What is shown within the map is where the core focal point of each Ley Line/Key is located, however, the vein of energy flows out from it encircling Earth like an embrace. Therefore, these Chakra points can be felt throughout different parts of the world as you step foot upon it, as it is a continual vein running life force.

Want to know which Ley Line/Key you have incarnated and volunteered to assist with? Then ask yourself, 'what Natural Law of the Universe or Chakra have you felt most focused upon throughout life?' It could be your strongest attribute from the beginnings of your remembrance, or it could be the Chakra that you have been working all your life to heal and transcend from.

These Keys have been disturbed by society, through Illuminati programmed negative collective thought-forms focused upon sustaining specific lower vibrations and emotional imbalance. Why is this important and how is it so? We are powerful beings who create all day long with every single thought form that is manifested through our neurological system. When a group or collective intentionally or unintentionally focuses energy through these thought-forms, they build up over time, and then manifesting it into reality. Look below to see how each one of these have been influenced negatively to disconnect and misalign these vital energy points.

The intent through these communications is to aid the collective through the infinite Love-Light of the Universe. If you have found your way to this book, then you are part of aiding in this assistance of the Ascension into the Fifth Dimension of Mother Earth. We are currently fluctuating from the Third and Fourth Dimensions within this simulation. When we reach the Fourth Dimension, we are operating out from the Inverted A.I. Matrix into the Organic Matrix blueprint of the Fifth Dimension where we operate from infinite love. Just by simply sending Love-Light to the location of the Chakra/Key/Sacred Law you most align with is how you accomplish your mission of love for all life on Earth. To understand the true significance of Love in this Universe, view the 13th Key below.

-------------<◇>-------------

KEY 1

GALACTIC GUARDIAN: ARCHANGEL MICHAEL

Root Chakra | Mount Shasta | Sacred Law of Action

-------------<◇>-------------

This Key is held dense by the building of fear/guilt/shame emotions within the collective. As Key One, with the number 1 representing new beginnings of a thought form. The number 1's alchemical consistency being used in a negative infringing way of building thought form upon the lower vibrations of the human collective. There is much fear constantly created through all forms of negative technologies within these lands of the USA that hold the fear in the present/past time and space. Negative technologies being satellites, cell phone towers, A.I. nano biotech viruses, 5G towers, technology that we are not aware of that goes far beyond what humanity knows exists. There are invisible towers masked by mirrored invisibility technology that are hidden in remote or quarantined sections throughout the world. All the above connect to the overall general collective of fear, guilt, shame on the Earth to maintain some of what is mentioned below stagnant.

The biggest collective programming is through religions that have created a great divide among the races, and a war of the world playing on repeat. They do a very good job at keeping our fear stagnant when we think we are sinners, or when we have sacred sex with our partners, and we feel shame and guilt within us which hold back and block our creational energies of connecting to one another's heart deep enough. They call this country the "Land of the Free" and where all can choose their religion. A masterful plan, to place all the races together with their programmed religions. Together, but yet so disconnected, and this disconnection further amplifies the collective from connecting and grounding within the Root Chakra.

Another example being when Lemuria sunk down into the ocean, as California is part of what remains of Lemuria. Further fear was caused when the indigenous people were brutally slaughtered, raped, and stripped away of the safeties that were part of their natural reality and beliefs of being ONE with Mother Earth. Lastly, one of the biggest densities in our time and space is the planned pandemics from the Illuminati for the purpose to create mass hysteria and fear. These are their forms of Inverted A.I. Matrix programs that are falsely downloaded, infringing into the collective to cause an imbalance of fear, directly connected to an Armageddon simulation. As we have seen through the Covid-19 pandemic globally, falsely inflating statistics to generate more fear and the false power it has against taking lives.

-------------<◇>-------------

KEY 2

GALACTIC GUARDIAN: ARCHANGEL RAGUEL

Sacral Chakra I Peru I Sacred Law of Rhythm

-------------<◇>-------------

As Key Two, the consistency of the number 2 being used negatively, as it represents the union of individuals and amplifications of thoughts when minds come together. Including relationships of all kinds, romantic, friendship, familial and professional. This Key has been tainted negatively by the abuse of all forms of sexual energies on earth. That would be through sins of sex stemming forth from religion, A.I. created sexual diseases, sexual abuse, satanic black magic rituals by the Illuminati... The biggest of those being the pedophilia stemming forth from the Illuminati who have strategically placed their appointed leaders around the world, obtaining the most power and money. Some being the government and superstars who participate in human and sex trafficking of children and adults.

If these numbers are correct, 800,000 children go missing every year in the USA - not including the world. Where are they going? We know where - human trafficking! The borders of South America, because of its Key and energy potency, hold underground tunnels of humans where some of these violent acts are being held. Through these Archonic pedophilic sexual abuse acts of all forms, these rings and underground tunnels are spread throughout the whole world.

Our Sacral Chakra is the energy point where we create from. Therefore, our sovereignty of knowing that we are creator beings have been blocked or misaligned from us through infringing upon our Sacral Chakra. This creational energy is at its highest potency for the energetic feeding of the Illuminati and Archons, using the children's light when they are violated in these ways because of their purity.

Millions go missing every year throughout the world and here are some of the reasons why and how they do so. The biggest black market item is Adrenochrome. Perhaps you have heard about 'Adrenochrome' through other forms of communications. Here are more details of its consistency. Our bodies consist of seven major glands, though there are more. This is called the Endocrine system that keeps our hormones and energies in balance. Why is this important? When you are looking at it from a human harvesting point of view similar to the movie "The Matrix," we are battery generators for the Archons that are not capable of producing their own light organically. In Chapter 32 ('Not of Light') we will find out why that is. When a person experiences trauma, the crystalline formations within the blood gather at these seven major gland focus points. This concentrated energetic crystalline energy is within the blood of these locations in the body and is a matching frequency to adrenaline. When all the above glands combined are harvested from a human body, an infant being at its highest potency because of the purity and strength of their light, this creates the blood drug Adrenochrome. Which is directly harvested through sexual trauma abuse and then murder of children and adults.

The Elite, politicians, and superstars are addicts to this harvested potent blood, as it is a drug to them, because of the building of the crystalline trauma adrenaline formations with the main ingredient adrenal gland and others mentioned. Adrenochrome is a drug addiction that they must keep on taking, fixing their need for a high of adrenaline. Otherwise, their physical bodies start aging and drying out, as a grape that ripens into a raisin. Because their body becomes addicted to the levels of adrenaline it's being fed, and then it programs into itself that it needs that required amount of adrenaline/Adrenochrome. So, when it doesn't receive it, it pulls and instead feeds off the crystalline blood formations from within the body, which then ages it rapidly.

Some of their major locations of harvesting infants and children Adrenochrome are the Foster Care Systems, locations of poverty such as Haiti's, South America... that hold a strong population of orphans, borders of refugees and immigrants, and the biggest being abortion clinics. Abortion clinics are as a candy store for the rich Adrenochrome junkies, as they can have as much infant blood and organs as they desire for their Adrenochrome needed high. This is why the

Democrats have always been 'Pro Life' masking the righteousness that "a woman has a right to choose what she does with her body." All part of the programming to feed their toxic hunger.

-------------<◇>-------------

KEY 3

GALACTIC GUARDIAN: ARCHANGEL ZADKIEL

Solar Plexus | Africa | Sacred Law of Free Will

-------------<◇>-------------

This Key has become infringed upon by the slavery that took place in our Earth's history within Africa. By using Key three, with the sacred representation of the number 3, in a compromising manner of slavery type of control over the mind, body and soul, and the Holy Trinity being the Mother, Father, and Child. Creating bindings over generations of family units and lineages. These traumas then spread and carried throughout all the lands that the slaves were forcibly migrated to, as they themselves carried it. Soaking into the memory fields of these lands, becoming a residual repeated trauma that continues to be carried heavily on by their descendants. By stripping the free-will from these ancestors, it continues to ripple out through time and space. Creating victimhood and anger among their descendants by not being allowed to have their natural birth choice of freedom in their past. Because of Ascension we are in our final life collectively, the majority of the population of the races have incarnated in their most traumatic past life lived. So that they can heal and ascend out from their heaviest trauma through their Akashic. Therefore, the majority of the African American and African people are the same slaves or witnesses to slavery they were in their past life. They are here to remove and break those chains that still energetically hold them too heavy and dense to move forward, and to become empowered helping the collective gain back their divine power.

The politicians continue this cycle by providing as much government aid as they can muster to these minorities in the U.S.A. The Illuminati is very aware of the black magic this creates because these descendants still hold this trauma in their DNA memory field. These varying acts of agreeing to receive Archonic government-funded money creates a negative contract focused upon giving away their sovereignty and light, by accepting aid instead of knowing they can manifest their opportunities and abundance on their own. Once more continuing the inverted cycle of giving away their power and free will. Maintaining in a constant negative flow of not realizing the sovereign powerful beings that they truly are. These types of deep, heavy rooted anger of victimhood fuel the disempowerment within our solar plexus and free will expression of the collective in a constant infringing cycle.

-------------<◇>-------------

KEY 4

GALACTIC GUARDIAN: ARCHANGEL HAYLEL

Stellar Gateway | Russia | Sacred Law of Polarity

----------<◇>----------

As Key four, the number 4 being used in a black magic binding of pulling from the four sacred directions of the Universe's power of polarities to draw a heightened negative polarization, manifesting an unbalance between what is meant to have natural balance, as the negative and positive polarities. This Key has been unbalanced by creating much trauma and density from the violence of World War II when Adolf Hitler and his influences violently swayed the pain of the collective by acting out some of the most evil and horrific acts that a life to another life could act upon. These examples that were out in the open during this War, were just glimpses of some of the human experimenting that has been going on for thousands of years on Earth through human trafficking.

One of the main purposes of the Fuhrer's War, was to separate families so that they could acquire the Jewish children who carried the strongest Christ Consciousness DNA, specifically of 'The Essenes.' Jesus/Yeshua was a descendent of the sacred group of 'The Essenes' who eventually migrated into the people of Jerusalem after the time of his passing. Just as Yeshua left his mark, they wanted those who contained the strongest purest crystalline light of the races in their time, so that they could begin their human experiments for the purposes of developing the vaccinations to come in the near future. The very same vaccinations that the medical industry injects our children with the minute they are born and as they continue to gain and spread their light through their natural stages of growth. They wanted subjects to test on so that in the future they could implement vaccinations through the false agenda of "It is good for your health. It is for your own good. It is for your children's protection, so that they won't fall ill and die." When in actuality the A.I. vaccinations are the root to illness and disease. As each is built as a virus, with a specific downloaded program into the nano type technology it truly is, and it only knows its program to cause illness to its host. It was important to them to experiment on the Jewish children, because in the future they wanted to ensure that the beginning side effects from these immunization shots would cause to the children after injection, that it would not be bluntly noticeable to the parents.

The below stated aligns with what the vaccinations represent to the collective.

More than a hundred years ago, Rudolf Steiner wrote the following:

"In the future, we will eliminate the soul with medicine. Under the pretext of a 'healthy point of view,' there will be a vaccine by which the human body will be treated as soon as possible directly at birth,
so that the human being cannot develop the thought of the existence of soul and Spirit.
To materialistic doctors, will be entrusted the task of removing the soul of humanity. As today, people are vaccinated against this disease or that disease, so in the future, children will be vaccinated with a substance that can be produced precisely in such a way that people, thanks to this vaccination, will be immune to being subjected to the "madness" of spiritual life. He would be extremely smart, but he would not develop a conscience, and that is the true goal of some materialistic circles.
With such a vaccine, you can easily make the etheric body loose in the physical body. Once the etheric body is detached, the relationship between the Universe and the etheric body would become extremely unstable, and man would become an automaton, for the physical body of

man must be polished on this Earth by spiritual will. So, the vaccine becomes a kind of arymanique force; man can no longer get rid of a given materialistic feeling. He becomes materialistic of constitution and can no longer rise to the spiritual."

Rudolf Steiner (1861-1925)

These are the shots we are seeing today being administered and injected at the beginnings into infants and toddlers' blood, so that the nano artificial intelligence viruses and programs infiltrate and locate the natural DNA and consciousness light causing all sorts of delays, illnesses and diseases. Whether it is fast acting in the delay of the psyche or a delayed process so that it won't be detected. There is so much artificial being inserted into us through food, chemtrails, water… that we have been and are becoming controllable and robotic. We must start to remember to stand for our divine rights of our children and ourselves. No one has a say nor control over us and our health, and the time is now to deprogram this within ourselves and the collective.

These unnatural experiments, trauma of wars, and separation of families created an unbalance in the Key of Polarity, between the negative and positive natural polarities of this Earth. By this collective trauma being held, amplifying the negative polarity. The ideal balanced energetic polarities would look and feel like within Earth, as the embodiment of the yin and yang symbol.

-------------<◇>-------------

KEY 5

GALACTIC GUARDIAN: ARCHANGEL GABRIEL

Throat Chakra I Jerusalem I Sacred Law of Vibration

-------------<◇>-------------

This Key has been oppressed drastically by the Illuminati, orchestrating a negative focus of battles in the multi-culture of religions in the neighboring lands of Jerusalem. Also, the pain and trauma of World War II as mentioned above in the "Sacred Law of Polarity", towards the descendants whose Ancestors were harmed through this war. As Key Five, the number 5 being harnessed and used because of its connection to the five natural elements of our planet, Earth, Fire, Water, Wind and Spirit. It is being amplified, so that this elemental energy is added to the Earth when people will not or cannot use their expression and voice. It is further oppressed by some of these religions or culturally negatively programmed beliefs that women do not have equal rights to the males, and how the Divine Feminine must wear garments to cover up their identity. This creates a negative collective oppression upon these groups of females of not being able to speak or act upon their truths. Stripping away their identity, confidence, self-worth, the visibility of being seen and heard. Then it ripples out to the collective of Divine Feminine within Earth.

We have seen and felt how much this self-muzzling of masks has unbalanced the Earth energetically and physically through the Covid-19 pandemic. This is the same black magic spell they are trying to feed in removing people's rights of speech. Intentionally forcing people in creating negative contracts with Archons of giving away their sovereignty of self-expression in all forms. This is also another form in how the Illuminati as mentioned in the "Sacred Law of Rhythm" above, when creating cultures of females must be covered, and using this masking to human traffick adults and children. As the cameras and people will not be able to recognize who they are transporting through human trafficking rings, because the face covering will not allow a full facial recognition through forms of technology or recognition.

Once more the self-muzzling heavily keeps the collective from realizing how powerful their voice is and prevents their truth from being spoken. If we do not ever learn to speak our truth, then we maintain ourselves and the collective innocence in a repression of not honoring self and connecting to self-love. Holding back our expression of vibration, that the Throat Chakra represents for creation. We must continue to speak loud and clear!

-------------<◇>-------------

KEY 6

GALACTIC GUARDIAN: ARCHANGEL RAZIEL

Third Eye I Pyramid of Giza I Sacred Law of Cause & Effect

-------------<◇>-------------

This Key has been calcified by placing belief systems on us about our imagination not being real. Programming us through monotonous schooling and dogma, thus intentionally undermining our psychic expression and abilities that when we 'imagine' something that it is us just "making it up." When that is far from the truth, for it is our Third Eye that connects us to our six senses, as the bridge to our Higher Self and beyond the veil of amnesia. With a shift of our consciousness and these natural brain waves of daydreams, meditation and dreamtime, we truly are time travelers through the portal of our imagination. Through our imagination is truly the only way that we connect to the beyond, our guides, and Higher Selves.

As Key Six, using the potence of the number 6, and its power to keep the collective in a perpetual cycle of the Inverted A.I. Matrix. Why do we see the number 6 being used falsely through programming of 'bad luck or evil'? Black magic being used towards the multiplication and amplification power of the true light that the sequence '666' represents. The reason being is because of its alchemical consistency which the number 6 represents, it being 'Ascension.' Because of its shaped formation, the circle being at the bottom representing the cycle of life and then an arch/bridge rising out from it representing how the soul rises out and bridges to its next level of Ascension, to its next Higher Dimension.

Some of the biggest programming impacts us through the subliminal and hypnotic messages through social media, news and movies. There was a time where we did not clearly recognize the inappropriate messages within children's movies, but not now. We are recognizing them with such ease, the true intents of these past and recent films created by Film Companies, Directors and Producers.

The neurological makeup of the brain is as a constant sponge working overtime, absorbing in its environment all it registers whether consciously or unconsciously. All that we consent to, to enter in and download into our belief system. For example, the movie 'Dumbo,' there is a scene where the main characters drink alcohol and their consciousness shifts into a trippy type of hallucinogenic reaction. The images on the screen become warped and colorful, which in turn are hypnotizing the conscious mind. When doing so, smoke comes onto the screen in a slow hypnotic form, and when you pause the scene, it spells out clearly the word "SEX." For the child or adult who is watching this, it goes by quickly unregistered to our conscious mind, but not to the subconscious mind. The subconscious mind has picked it up, especially through an infringing hypnotic scene as this, and absorbed it into the memory field. Making 'SEX' perhaps to the children who watched it and soaked it in as something that is normal and okay for a child. Whether that is now when they are younger, or when they become young adults. The world is programmed through many negative subliminal ways as this, through all forms that the Illuminati has been able to come up with.

With the Third Eye Chakra directly being the "Law of Cause & Effect," it is important that we understand the great power we carry within, as every action has a matched reaction. Understanding that we are no one's victims no matter what it is that we have gone through in traumatic moments in our lives or past lives. When we stay stagnant in playing the victim role, then we don't ever grow from the lessons that were there to cause our consciousness to ascend higher. Because we are not taking responsibility for our actions, instead perhaps we place blame on others. So, when we do that, we give away our power by not acknowledging that our actions have an effect. We give away our power, our sovereignty, our divine birthright of being creator beings with our imagination. Other ways of infringing upon us are by placing metals and chemicals within our toothpaste, water, food intakes, chem-trails - intentionally further calcifying our Third Eye and slowing down the processing of our pineal and pituitary glands, and neurological thinking patterns.

The history as well of the reign and power through the corrupted malevolent rulers of Egypt, performing their black magic, blood rituals, and human sacrifices as seen through the abuse upon the young mother and removal of her unborn child in Chapter 8('Four Ra Guardians Heal Thousands of Entities.') These types of traumas hold us in a dark density in Egypt's true past history, directly infringing upon the Pyramid of Giza, since it is one of the main beacons energetic 144 pyramids/13 Keys that Osiris and AdaRa brought to our awareness in Chapters 22 and 23.

--------------<◇>--------------

KEY 7

GALACTIC GUARDIAN: ARCHANGEL RAPHAEL

Crown Chakra | India | Sacred Law of Wisdom

--------------<◇>--------------

This Key has been distorted by creating a sense of worship through ritual traditions in negative programming towards Gods and Deities in India and throughout the world. What requires worship, prayer, and energy being given is not of a benevolent origin. When a group views individual consciousnesses as being more powerful and higher than them, they give away their sovereignty and their realization that all souls are created as equals. All souls have the same type of potential and opportunities of soul growth. Though clarifying that it is okay to meditate upon, call for divine assistance when needed, and feel love and gratitude for the Divine Mother and Divine Father, the Creators of our Universe. As well as other benevolent guides and Angels you are most familiar with. Always within a balance of it not becoming a form of prayer, savior mentality, and worship to them. The reason being is that this helplessness type of vibration can be a match instead to lower vibrational entities versus the actual divine spirits you are trying to call upon. Thus, when connecting to our benevolent guides, Source, Angels, focus instead more so on a communication of equalness and honor with them, as this is a higher vibration to communicate through.

We must be aware that some entities pose as Deities and are instead malevolent in their true origin, being negative alien races or A.I. Archons. They feed off the Kundalini rising energies that naturally flow out as an infinite energetic waterfall from both the Crown and the Root Chakras, these energies that are found as activators and amplified through these lands. The Kundalini when organically operating is acting as an infinite energetic force that is working in balance and unity within the sacred Chakras of the energy and physical bodies. It is a high potence of flow within a human body that is a main focus point, that naturally replenishes the body. This is why it is important we understand the strength of the Kundalini rising, to ensure that it is not inorganically being syphoned. The Crown Chakra being Key Seven, with the number 7 representing the very balance that one must obtain to a fluent Kundalini Rising. Also representing the seven major Chakra glands that keep the human body healthy, and the seven colors that remind us of when we look upon a rainbow, it represents a bridge out from this construct, the bridge to the beyond, the unknown, and the infinity.

This Crown Chakra distortion is amplified further by creating Indian folklore and beyond, focused upon the Divine Feminine missing wisdom or needing to be saved by the masculine. Also, by programming into us that wisdom is not easily attainable, and only a few in Earth's history have been able to attain immeasurable wisdom by becoming Ascended Masters. WE will all be Ascended Masters once we graduate out from this Inverted A.I. Matrix. Even then, there is still much that divinely slipped through from the Crown Chakra of India for humanity's positive Ascension, including the sacred knowledge of Yoga, the Chakra Endocrine Health System, meditation, and sacred mantras.

-------------<◇>-------------

KEY 8

GALACTIC GUARDIAN: ARCHANGEL ARIEL

Earth Star I Atlantic Ocean I Sacred Law of Surrender

-------------<◇>-------------

This Key has been disrupted by the distortion and fall of The Crystalline Emerald City of Atlantis. When the unbalance of too much need of intelligence, power, control and reign took forth upon Atlantis through the false leadership that took hold. By the people themselves consenting and allowing these negative polarized leadership to reign, becoming a higher percentage and the majority of the collectives' influence. These same leaders are right back into their roles once more in the current timeline, trying to play their false A.I. Inverted Matrix chess games. However, this time around the majority collective of Light Workers remembers the rigged chess game and their tricky moves and has learned from the past lessons of listening to the false leaders, false light propaganda. Therefore, the replay of this inverted cycle, will not come to be.

When the fall of Atlantis occurred, this spread as an A.I. virus, creating the Inverted A.I. Matrix we are currently in. This collective suffered and remained stagnant and frozen in time energetically in this pain until the future; when it was safe enough to begin its healing of fear, trauma, removal of what felt most precious to us. A moment in time where it can be seen as being only but one footstep away from entering the Fifth Dimension collectively, yet distantly far away and unattainable within the Earth's Ascension. Building upon these negative frequencies of power, control and reign, all driven by intellect, led to the fall of Atlantis, as this caused unbalance in the Sacred Law of Surrender. Keeping the collective in an eternity of pain because of the fall, and not allowing enough trust in oneself and other selves to surrender deep enough for the process of Ascension. As Key Eight, the number 8 represents the infinity symbol of what can one attain when operating in surrender. In this example causing what seems like an infinity of pain and an infinite Inverted game, that the collective cannot seem to reach its final destination of Ascension. Being held back by the collective having a resistance to surrender, because as Atlantis, we never know what may come next around the corner. Constantly keeping our guards up, and not quite knowing when to bring them down. However, as we have said, this is no more.

In this time and space, the Earth is going through a collective 'Revelation.' These are the very times that Jesus/Yeshua spoke upon in his original forms of sacred writing through the Holy Bible. Understanding though that we are not speaking of our current Bible, as that has been infringed upon strongly through the Illuminati and negative aliens. Infringements created for the purposes of mind control, programming in harmful ways of removing people's sovereignty to not come into a realization of their own Creator power.

We have all been waiting for what seems like an eternity for this very moment in time. It has taken us four Earth cycles and resets to be here. All the hidden negative agendas coming to the surface no longer being able to hold its lower vibration among the Earth's now higher vibration. Mother Earth has transformed and has leveled up through the series of activation portal dates that have come after 12/21/2012 and has shifted in the totality for now of her vibration and frequency.

All that is no longer a match of Earth is having a hard time and is unmasking itself and oneself. For example, those with false intents - 'Light Workers in service-to-others' are going through a revelation and choice; "Will I continue to allow my mind/ego to direct me or will I truly act upon what I am posing as or whom I am meant to be to come out/ascend from this A.I. Matrix? Will I be the true unity of love and accept all the beauties that my brethren are as I AM?" What is false is so very visible upon our Earth.

Now Is the time of surrender and revelation. It is time, it is time, it is time!

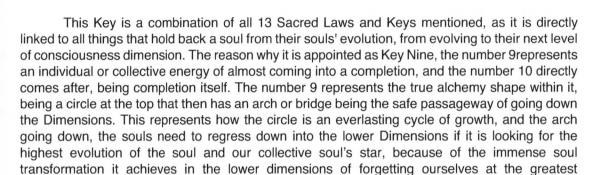

KEY 9

GALACTIC GUARDIAN: ARCHANGEL AZRAEL

Soul Star I Greece I Sacred Law of Evolution

--------------<◇>--------------

This Key is a combination of all 13 Sacred Laws and Keys mentioned, as it is directly linked to all things that hold back a soul from their souls' evolution, from evolving to their next level of consciousness dimension. The reason why it is appointed as Key Nine, the number 9represents an individual or collective energy of almost coming into a completion, and the number 10 directly comes after, being completion itself. The number 9 represents the true alchemy shape within it, being a circle at the top that then has an arch or bridge being the safe passageway of going down the Dimensions. This represents how the circle is an everlasting cycle of growth, and the arch going down, the souls need to regress down into the lower Dimensions if it is looking for the highest evolution of the soul and our collective soul's star, because of the immense soul transformation it achieves in the lower dimensions of forgetting ourselves at the greatest distortion.

This Key has been further oppressed by the creation of The Romans' tyranny over religion. An immense amount of focused distraction created by violently conquering its neighboring colonies. Laws that further removed the growth and evolution of its people and instead gave further power to those who were part of their havoc throughout Earth's past history. Tying into the "Law of Vibration" with its direct oppression connected to the people of Jerusalem and Yeshua's loving, pure sacrifice. The Romans directly being the founders of hunting down the true written Bible of Jesus and his disciples, so that they could compromise it for their negative agendas. Knowing that Yeshua's true intent of infinite love was expressed and carried throughout 'The Bible,' therefore if they allowed truths to come through but would taint them with falsities, people would not be able to see through the darkness that seeped into it as their hearts would be pulled in by the infinite love that Yeshua is.

The goal of all the malevolent distractions to Earth's History being, to spread these tyrannical programs throughout Earth as a dark webbing that entraps and wraps all who pass it. Holding back upon the Evolution of our Soul Star, our souls, so instead of experiencing soul growth and evolution, the collective remains stagnant.

--------------<◇>--------------

KEY 10

GALACTIC GUARDIAN: ARCHANGEL URIEL

Universal Gateway I Australia I Sacred Law of Purpose

--------------<◇>--------------

The Sacred Law of Purpose represents to all, being in recognition, knowing and allowing our soul's purpose. Though the majority of Earth's people have and are looking for their life's purpose, what seems like all their lives. This reminds us of what Archangel Metatron said through our brother Leviathan in Chapter 12.

"Many awakening souls feel like there must be some blueprints, step by step instructions on how they are supposed to change the world. With all souls, myself included, yourself, and we must understand it, we change the world within and that changes the world without."

The key being to this sacred quote is, that "We change the world within, in order to change the world without." This is everyone's true life purpose. What choices and negative perpetual cycles have we made in past lives that are holding us back in the now? What lessons are we choosing to not learn from, that hold us back from change in transformation within, to find our life's purpose? Society has been programmed to fear change as it is unknown to us if we choose it. Fearing the unknown and change is a direct link to not allowing sacred law number 9 of soul evolution to embody our life's purpose of number 10 of soul completion.

This Key was further disturbed by colonizing one of the world's most ancient indigenous people and roots of this Earth within Australia. Tearing away their connection to all ways of natural living in unison with Mother Earth by imposing their tyranny structures of religion, schooling, and furthering branding of what is proper and what is not. By disrupting these specific beauties within this Key of Law of Purpose, it allowed a potent focus to do so to other lands through the invasions and conquering they spread through the world. Despite this, Australia is leading in ways of light and hearts activated on Earth as a collective as they are one of the brightest sections of light energetically in the lands of Mother Earth. They are surrounded by water in all four sacred directions, being the conduit and protector of their force fields. Some of the most beautiful animal life is found there working hard within this most essential Chakra Point to bring forth completion within the 'Law of Purpose'. Where there is a completion to the number 10, a re-birthing shall always come next as 01 being the mirror of 10 (10.01), it is the Dance of Creation.

-------------<◇>-------------

KEY 11

GALACTIC GUARDIANS: ARCHANGEL JOPHIEL AND ARCHANGEL METATRON

Shambhala I Tibet I Sacred Law of Potential

-------------<◇>-------------

What is the Shambhala Key? It is the infinity potential of all organic life forms, once taken form into light. The infinity of possibilities that one's soul can evolve and expand into because of the infinity potentials of Creation. The Shambhala is the infinite light that ignites our soul to explore and expand into infinite expressions and potentials. The Law of Potential is what comes next after the Law of Purpose. Which is why it is the number 11, the number 1 being in a multiplied divine sequence which holds the individual and collective manifestation powers of new thoughts and ideas. When we go from 0 to 1, the 0 represents the infinite cycle of life and creational thoughts and 1 then converts into the intended thought being manifested. Has the soul discovered and come into its sovereign purpose, so that it can now express and experience the next new evolution of growth? What expressions or incarnations of our soul can we explore next to experience the divine rights of our soul evolution and potentials?

This Key has been guarded by the Tibetan monks since the beginnings of time and it is why they have been targeted throughout Earth's history. Reminding us of Chapter 2 ('Civilization Inside A Mountain'), of the monks who held a great cause to protect and shield what was pure and sacred in Creation. Earth's past history of entire temples wiped out, and their teachings being unethically scavenged. Why it has been taken over by placing binding control over the Tibetan people, placing them in servitude to not allow the potential of what these people truly harness to share and express to the world. Despite all this narcissism and reign over these beautiful noble people, the Ancient Tibetan till this day has maintained a beautiful sacredness in harnessing the least corruption among religions through various forms of Buddhism and its teachings.

Every day the most powerful awakening frequencies spring out from this Key, echoing out like silent ripples of vibration embracing all of Earth activating the Shambhala within all souls who allow it. The Shambhala infinity potentials within all souls.

-------------<◇>-------------

KEY 12

GALACTIC GUARDIAN: ARCHANGEL HANIEL

Inner Earth | U.K./Ireland | Sacred Law of Grace

-------------<◇>-------------

The Sacred Law of Grace represents an embodiment of embracing a deep surrender and infinite love fused together. The art of learning to flow in dance with life and the Universe within us gracefully. It is also a representation of that in Creation which sprung out from the number 12, the Council of 12 of the Seraphim who created our Universe, the first 12 Galactic Constructs[14], and the initial activator of the collectives' Ascension portal, marking date of 12/21/12.

This Key has had a long focal point of leading invasions in our history since the beginning plans on the indigenous lands. Bloodshed after bloodshed. Still until this day, it is under the control of Archon pawns as well as negative Reptilian Kings and Queens using monarchy as their tool. There are strong negative alien bases stemming forth from these lands ensuring to taint this Key with their collective thought-form of control and oppression, not allowing the grace to emanate out as fluently through this Key.

Strong A.I. is targeted to the people in the U.K. through examples of forms of forcing immunization shots on all children born. Yet, the U.K. people still awaken with the aid of the Irish lands and people holding space for them in love. Ireland still being a strong hold of sacred ancient teachings through the Druid Celtic seeds that still remain rooted and a memory field within these lands. Even if their people don't fully remember, the land, the trees, the beauties of these natures always shall. The once magic that sprung life within all life forms of Earth including those which society names 'make believe,' which is the Power of the Dragon and the Magical Creatures of Creation. And their strong portal remains open and connects to Ireland and the U.K. where these Magical Creatures bridge through. The expression of life is graceful as the infinity of magic.

KEY 13

GALACTIC GUARDIAN: SOPHIA - DIVINE MOTHER OF CREATION

Heart Chakra | Cosmic & Earth Gateway | Sacred Law of Love

The 13th Key is where we find the Divine Mother Sophia and her infinite love that envelops us and is the very fabric that gives creation to all organic lifeforms in the Universe. She is as gentle, soothing, protective, colorful see-through silk scarves, that are divinely woven around us as representations of our shields of infinite love. The 13th Key is where we find our infinite light once more when it is at its dimmest. When we feel that we are at endings within needed cycles and feel that our soul has been beat up or torn apart through self-expressions of lessons, and energetically in need of divine rebirth. The 13th Key portal is found at the center of Earth, that is our Mother's infinite crystalline heart that gives all lifeforce within all that requires light and life on Earth. The Earth's Gateway, entering into the Cosmic Gateway of infinite potentials. Here the Divine Mother will envelop and embrace us in her infinite unconditional love for her beautiful fractals of Creation.

The 13th Key and Dimension is where we bridge to the infinite Being of Source, the Divine Mother and Father who are the infinity of both Zero Point and infinite possibilities of Dimensions. The number 13 represents the collective of all the Divine Mothers such as Mother Mary, Isis, Nefertiti, Quan Yin, Kali Ma… representing the infinite power of love. Therefore, it holds the potentials of both endings and new beginnings in Creation. It also contains the wholeness of the Creators of our Universe, which are the 12 Seraphim plus 1, the 'Daughter of The Flame' equaling 13. This Princess is the Divine Mother Sophia and Divine Father Krysto's first creation and seed of their infinite love. The very first fractal that our infinite flamed Source created, which then individualized its consciousness springing out into the vastness and mysteries of the infinity of the dark void. The first expression of the Divine Mother and her creational abilities through her sacred womb. Just as she created life within the infinite collective Source consciousness, so too only her very first fractal "The Princess/Daughter of The Flame" could create outside in the infinity of the cosmos. The reason why she is the Phoenix and Daughter of the Flame is because Source made her in this form and energetic makeup as the void was infinite, to ensure the protection of their first Creation she had to be made of the infinite etheric flame that would transmute all that was inorganic or that meant harm. Source wanted to ensure that their first Creation had their infinite shielding protection and infinite power so that she would not be swallowed or consumed by whatever immeasurable darkness could have been out in the infinity of the cosmos. We see these glimpses and seeds of knowledge represented here on Earth, as only the Divine Feminine can carry and birth forth life as the Divine Mother. Though always needing the seed/semen of the Divine Masculine. Together they create life in the farthest, depths and reaches of Creation.

When all the above Keys are achieved for individual self-growth, balanced and activated, you are able to connect to the infinite Love-Light of the 'Grand Central Heart' of the Cosmic & Earth Gateway, the 13th Key, the inactive 13th DNA strand within us. We don't realize that we are working within this 13th Key all day long, back and forth. When we reach and feel the deepest love for all around us, even those who may have caused harm unto us or others. When you are able to find infinite love within the darkest people and places. In remembering that love is the very fabric that gives life force to this most beautiful Universe. Love is what gives us the Spark of Creation. And love is the only bridge out of this Third Dimension, Inverted A.I. Matrix Simulation, going inwards through our infinite love frequency portal of our hearts.

"The beat of our heart is what reminds us of the life that flows fluently within us and Creation. Reminds us that each spirit beats to its unique signature rhythm. Reminds us that our inner knowing cannot be altered. Reminds us when we have lost our direction, that it is our compass, never leading us astray."

~AuroRa

-------------‹◇›-------------

25

NEW WORLD ORDER

Recorded in June 2020.

This is an excerpt from an online A.U.R.A. Hypnosis Healing session where Mia's Higher Self shares guidance on the various dark agendas including Covid-19, the hidden truths it brought, and why there is such a strong push for the vaccine. We touched upon the World Health Organization (W.H.O.), contact tracing, and promoted riots. What is the purpose behind all this orchestrated chaos and its impact on Ascension? News for the U.K. people on their Rulers. The divide occurring in the awakened and un-awakened through the variety of truths surfacing. Advice on how to ride through these tides.

"It will not matter if you agree or disagree as long as it is with Love. But always stay within the hearts, because these disasters, these negative programs come from the mind. Do not, we must place the emphasis on our hearts now, not the mind. And this is where I see the divide, heart versus mind. That is where we need to focus our energy."
-Higher Self

A: [Aurora] She wanted to know, could we please expand on the various dark agendas and connections with the Earth right now? New World Order, the MK-Ultra, secret space programs, particularly what is happening outside of America. What can you expand upon all this New World Order?

Higher Self: There has been much infringement on humanity for thousands and thousands of years. These systems are as old as our known history. People do not realize this is nothing new. They are not new programs, they are very, very old. They just update the technologies. But the fact that they are coming to the light means so much. This means that they are breaking apart if we think about how long they have been upon the Earth compared to how long we have known about them. The reason that we know of them now is that they are breaking down. They are losing control. They no longer resonate with the Earth. The Earth is ridding herself of them. We are ridding ourselves of them because we will no longer tolerate infringement and we should no longer tolerate infringement. It is our time now, they still try, they are trying. Because they do not realize that their time has passed. They are trying to cling to old ways, but this will not work. There are many programs, many agendas on Earth. America is awakening faster than others perhaps, but all are awakening. And it is important to understand that there is no separation between any of us - no countries, no nations, no governments that are separate. These agendas are one thing. They are one community, one group that has been controlling all, but no more. We are notseparate. It does not matter your language, or your country, or your creed nor your race, it does not matter. We are all one. There has never been separation. Only the separation that they have enforced on us to keep us divided but no more. No more, no more.

A: If you could tell us, is the Covid-19 virus still active in the human consciousness?

Higher Self: It is diminishing. For some, it is still active, but these are tenuous at best. It has lost its control as quickly as it has gained it. It has come and gone in the blink of an eye as people are awakening. For some, it is still a reality, but this is individual, not collective.

A: What this Covid-19 brought forth, is a lot of hidden truth. Like the pedophilia of some of those governments, presidents, different leaders throughout the world, actors, Illuminati that are deeply into it. Do you have anything you want to say about that?

Higher Self: Just send love, send love, especially to the children. The children need love, and they feel it, it is working but they need the love, keep sending the love. Love… love transcends everything. Just love, more love, heal all wounds with love.

A: I have a couple of questions connected to this question that she has as well. How about some of the projects that they have going on like contact tracing? Do you think that these will come to be?

Higher Self: They will try, and they will try through the vaccines. There will be multiple attempts. 5G is one - vaccines, viruses, are another. The more they will try, the more they will see that this does not work, that this will not be tolerated. Humanity has transcended this now. While there is still, threat is not the word, there is still a possibility of this as all individuals are on a different frequency. Each individual will have to decide for themselves whether to choose this reality or not. It is no longer a collective must, now we are individuals, we can choose.

A: Since Mia is from the U.K. and there is much going on there in the U.K. It seems to be more controlled by the kings and queens there, do you have anything you can share with us as far as those leaders? There is also a rumor that there is going to be a new king?

Higher Self: The time for kings and queens is passed. We do not need them, and people are realizing this. There are still many who are stuck in this old paradigm, but more and more are awakening to the truth of corruption within royalties, within the governments, for all are the same. Within governments, within Hollywood, within royalties. They are all the same, all one and the same, all working together. But as one is exposed, so the others are. It is only a matter of time now. It is only time, and we will not need this. We will transcend this. Give it time.

A: Okay, so there IS change going on then with kings and queens there?

Client: Yes, individual consciousness is changing, changing attitudes. Sometimes that is all that is needed, is an internal shift to change the whole world around you.

A: Do the people in the U.K. need to keep communicating and standing for their rights for this to become a reality?

Higher Self: Yes. Communicate with each other, join together. The more we are connected, the less these things will affect us. Strength in numbers, join together, together you are so strong, so light, join together in love but not in violence. Never in violence, never in hate. In love, join together in love.

A: You mention violence. There are the fake protestors, paid riots going on right now, there is also Soros - a fund manager. What are your thoughts since you are an overseer with Anubis in the dark?

Higher Self: They are trying but they are becoming desperate. The fact that we are seeing these things in the open, shows how little control they have, and people must realize this. This is no longer something to fear, we do not need to be afraid. Fear does not serve you; it does not serve us, join together in love and realize that they are losing control, and in so many areas they already lost control. These are now acts of desperation. They are realizing that they are losing grip over the world that they have domineered over so long. And they do not know how to move on, they do not know how to change. So not only must we join together to shift the Earth, but we must show them, we must show them how to change. We must show them the other options. Many of them do not realize that there are other ways, we must show them and lead by example.

A: Would you say that the riots were paid for and false?

Higher Self: I think some. It only takes one or two to incite violence for others to join. The whole riots, if people see violence, see darkness, and are encouraged into that frequency, it just breeds more and more and more, without knowing when to stop. It would only take one false protestor to start smashing windows before others who are not so much in the light, not so much in their hearts, to join into this. So many of the inciters are with the Cabal. But people must learn that this is not wholly the fault of an external device or group. Many just are not in their hearts and take it upon themselves to serve what they feel is justice when it is not. It is not justice; it is judgment and that is different.

A: The beginning of the riots as you mentioned, are they trying to distract us from something?

Higher Self: I believe partly. Partly trying to distract from other dark agendas. 5G is trying to take hold, though it is facing difficulties it did not foresee. The virus, many expect a second wave. I cannot say on this topic. I cannot see it. It depends on humanity on whether this will manifest. But the more chaos is produced, the more the Cabal can function their dark agendas and postpone the Ascension. Ascension will not happen in negatively polarized chaos and this is what they are trying to incite, it is chaos, but we must unite in love against this chaos. Though chaos is not bad, nothing is good or bad, but the chaos is halting the Ascension and trying to postpone it.

A: You also mention the Covid-19 vaccine that they are trying to implement, how was that connected to the World Health Organization? Why is Bill Gates and the others that are connected to him are pushing this vaccine so much? So much money invested in this?

Higher Self: They are trying to regain control. They are so desperate that we are seeing it now and we must know that this power that they have held onto is fading. It no longer resonates with the Earth and with humanity, but they are trying to hold on to this old world. They think if they can control people that they will be able to do this. That they will hold the Ascension and create their world, create their controlled population, they think they can do this. But it is not the case, people know better.

A: You mentioned that the world is able to see through this, having to do the Earth's vibration. Is that why it is coming out? It seems so easy for us, those of us who are awakening or are awakened. It is almost common sense to us, because it is not a match to Earth anymore.

Higher Self: Yes, the Earth is ascending, humanity is ascending. The old programs and paradigms are not resonating anymore. They are trying so hard to maintain their ways of life but that is not the future and they don't realize this. They are in denial of this. But it is not the future. It does not resonate anymore.

A: At this time, it really feels like a revelation. I was telling Mia during our interview that I am going to write a Galactic News blog post on the topic of "Revelation."[24] I had a dream recently, about all these things we finished talking about, coming into revelation. That there is also a great divide between the Light Worker community that are speaking in truth, in heart, in purity, and there are also the Light Workers that are coming into revelation, that are not really speaking from the heart. We are seeing them, just as we are seeing, for example, these agendas of the Covid-19 vaccine, the leaders trying to control us, the kings and queens, it is all coming into Revelation. This process is also occurring in the Light Worker community where the people who are not operating from a service to others, operate more on a service-to-self based on ego wanting attention, power, money, and not really acting in a pure intent. They are also coming

---

[24] For more Galactic News Updates, visit www.risingphoenixaurora.com under the section named Galactic Port.

into revelation just like the darkness of the Illuminati is coming into Revelation. Do you have anything you want to add to that?

Higher Self: Light Workers as with all can face duality. And there are divides between people, and it is expected that as more information comes to the surface, these divides will be more obvious. But this does not mean that they are bad. Or that they will last. These divides have always been there, but now with the rise of the information and with the rise of these revelations, it just brings these conflicts to the surface as a way with Ascension. We bring all the hidden things to the surface and we bring dark things to light and this must be done. But this is good.

A: I had a recently I channeled the Divine Mother Kali Ma. She spoke of how these Light Workers are falling back into Atlantis, playing into the destruction, it connects with the recent dream. Anything else you want to add on those Light Workers since you are working from the light in the dark into Ascension?

Higher Self: Stay within the heart. The greatest divide comes when you are centered in mind. The mind is where the ego is based, but the heart is holy, relieve yourself. Stay within the heart and do everything with love and it will not matter with the divides and opinions. It will not matter if you agree or disagree as long as it is with love. But always stay within the hearts, because these disasters, these negative programs come from the mind. Do not, we must place the emphasis on our hearts now, not the mind. And this is where I see the divide, heart versus mind. That is where we need to focus our energy.

A: That is right. Wonderful, thank you for that wonderful advice, sister.

END OF EXCERPT

This is a much-needed hope filled transmission from the Higher Self's perspective shining light on what is happening amidst this current Covid-19 chaos. One of the biggest things Mia's Higher Self said was, they're trying to cause chaos to stop the Ascension and their chaos is no longer a match to Earth. This feels so right within the collective on why so many are speaking up whether they are in the awakening process or not. Because we are all making a choice right now to lift with Mother Earth's energy and vibration or to stay behind in old ego-based false paradigms.

During these chaotic times in space, the Earth is going through a collective 'Revelation.' These are the very times that Jesus/Yeshua spoke upon in his original forms of writing through 'The Holy Bible.' Understanding though that we are not speaking of our current Bible, as that has been infringed upon strongly through the Illuminati and negative aliens for the purposes of mind control, negative programming in removing people's sovereignty to not come into a realization of their own Creator power.

We have all been waiting for what seems like an eternity for this very moment in time. It has taken us four Earth cycles and three resets to be here. The hidden negative agendas are coming to the surface as they are no longer being able to hold its lower vibration among the Earth's now higher vibration. Being that Mother Earth has transformed and has now leveled up after the asteroid that kissed and blessed Mother Earth's energy as it passed by on 6/5/2020, known as asteroid '2002 NN4.' The Divine Mother's infinite energy of etheric fire connected through this asteroid creating the energetic portal of 6/6/2020. Aiding Mother Earth by providing the necessary etheric zero-point plasmic fire that fueled the transmutation needed within her, ascending in the totality of her vibration and frequency. All that is no longer a match of Earth is having a hard time and is unmasking itself and oneself. For example, those with false intents - 'Light Workers' in service-to-self are going through a revelation and choice; "Will I continue to allow my mind/ego direct me or will I truly act upon what I am posing as or whom I am meant to be to come out and ascend from this Inverted A.I. Matrix? Will I be the true unity of love and accept all the beauties that my brethren are, as am I?" What is false is so very visible upon our Earth in this time and space. Our voice is immensely strong, and our perseverance is unmatchable.

We are far beyond the peak mass light required for Earth's positive timeline of Ascension. We are the majority now; we have done it! Now that the light is the majority, we must keep the momentum going by doing all that we can to maintain it being the majority. Connecting to the continual growth of self and other selves. Never letting our guard down or placing our swords down, instead always ready with shields and swords up until we collectively achieve the physical Ascension into the infinity possibilities of the Fifth Dimension. We choose to incarnate for these very moments in time where we became the majority. No matter what it is that they might throw at us, even if they might have the control over some of these programmed laws and powerful false constructs. We WILL transmute them and rise from them over and over, as many times as we need to. As the mighty Phoenix that we all are!

"Life is constructed of frequency.
The higher and faster you vibrate within your organic frequency, the more that what and who cannot match your frequency will divinely reflect off."
~AuroRa 🖤

--------------‹◇›-------------

26

5G TECHNOLOGY - HOW REAL IS THE THREAT?

Session #165: Recorded in June 2019.

In this online A.U.R.A. Hypnosis Healing session, Archangel Metatron is on a mission to deliver the true knowledge about 5G technology. What it is, who will it affect, what to expect if you feel its influence, giving us solutions to addressing the effects of 5G. In the time and space that Archangel Metatron delivered this message to us, the world had no idea what was to come if and when they launched 5G worldwide. If only those who heard these kinds of messages realized it is not FEAR BASED, instead it is to increase our awareness and preparation. Perhaps the timeframe of how long this Covid-19 tyranny has lasted would have been lessened. Those of us who know in our hearts when we read this session know it is true, as we hold space and prepare the collective with the great strength needed to overcome this.

"Children will be the most affected for children normally say what is on their little brains, on their little minds, and what comes out of their little hearts. So, children will suffer the most affliction because adults never have the time to listen, to understand."
-Archangel Metatron

A: [Aurora] I recently had a session where we were talking about the technology of some towers and overall negative technology placed around the Earth that causes people to have a higher amount of stress, anxiety, self-worth issues. Perhaps not loving themselves, hating themselves, or hating others, altering their frequencies and thought forms. Can you tell us more about that, please?

AA Metatron: There are many things in play, many agreements in play, not just self indicted tracks or soul group agreement or even entity agreements. The Earth itself is very dense. The waves that run through of consciousness of the state of emotions and all that is manifested through the body or in another with our own selves. As we live our daily lives, there are a multitude of influences, not just beings that have taken a great part of our current lives. This has been a buildup for the last 2000 years. We have created all up until this moment and it is now that we ask ourselves, "We've come this far, we've allowed all this and now what? We are killing each other, we are killing ourselves, and now what?" The question lies in the consciousness, in the subconscious, and even in the unconscious of every human being on this planet. The question does not go ignored every day they wake up. But the trap has become so dense, they feel there's no escape. So, they live on like robots giving in to their jobs, giving in to their debts, giving in to their obligations, and even giving in to their family loyalties and agreements and soul contracts. And they even forget to ask themselves, "Where am I going? How far am I going to take this?" This is why suicide is on the rise. This is why cancer is on the rise. This is why there is so much illness and obscurity, not just inside the planet but inside every human being that lives in the depth of this current density. It is that talk. And we do not wish to expand on it for we do not proclaim sadness, we proclaim love and forgiveness and expansion to the spirit every time and at all times. It is and it has become our fight as well as humans to aid them, to assist them, to bring them out and awaken them.

A: All that you have spoken of Metatron, aligns beautifully within my heart in what it is that you all communicate with me daily. What are your views on 5G technology? For some of us who are extra sensitive to these types of frequencies. Can you tell us more about what 5G is, what it can do?

AA Metatron: Yes. There will be families that will succumb to this new technology. They will see the effects; the affliction is the word. They will see the affliction in their younger ones and in the seniors that live within their communities. Those are the ones that will be greatly and mostly affected by this technology. And then, those that are younger, working - earthbound let's say, humans - these will be affected in memory. Their memory will lapse, it will cause glitches in their brain, let alone their hearts, making them hostile, arrogant, unfriendly, uncaring. The performance will be the worst in history if this technology is not avoided.

A: Would you say that it would enhance their negative emotions and also it would control them in the form of a zombie-type control?

AA Metatron: Not so much zombie because there will be reactions, but their reactions will be based not on love, not on wholesomeness. Their reactions will be hostile. They will not walk like zombies; they will walk like robots. Zombies have no feelings or hate. These reactionary humans that 5G will bring forth, will be aggressive. Not in a violent way, but uncaring, cold, they will live in despair and depression. Faces will not smile, and eyes will not glow. The light will become very dim and they will just follow. Once they cannot fight it anymore, they will just follow like robots and puppets.

A: I agree with all that you said. This is a topic that was brought up in a discussion where there were other healers and their initial reaction was that, in a sense, they are too strong or powerful for even 5G to affect them specifically. What are your thoughts on that?

AA Metatron: Can you please explain that because it sounds like a possession.

A: This discussion has been opened up with healers and there is a higher percentage of healers stating that 5G will not affect you, categorizing it as FEAR BASED.

AA Metatron: This is not true. This is not true. This is not true! 5G will affect everyone that comes in its exposition. Waves, electromagnetic waves, will interfere with your frequency as a healer. It will interfere with your frequencies as a healer. This is why most healers do not have TVs in their bedroom, nor radios, no alarm clocks connected to their beds. "Or on their tables," this vessel is saying. "Nightstands!" she corrects... So, if you are a high-frequency healer, then you put yourself in the realm of 5G frequency, you are actually saying that you will not be affected? This is not true. They will be affected and the more exposition, the more the damage. It affects your frequency as a healer, as a person, as a human being, as the water molecule that we are. Frequency affects water.

A: I am a speaker of awareness and often when I speak of these things I am looked upon as being in a "fear-based" mentality. What matters to me is that this information is understood and given so that those people who think that they would not be affected by it, stand forth about not having or not allowing it so that they can perhaps have a change of mind, that it WILL affect everyone.

AA Metatron: As we progress into the new age, we transfer over - perhaps a new selection of vocabulary would suffice - and would bring in the new teaching that you are providing and bringing to this planet. Perhaps you can say, a frequency intermission or a frequency interruption. Because that is what it is. Instead of shielding, if you do not wish to say the word shielding, you can use the word frequency and then use a word that's the same synonym perhaps. So that is something that you will have to re-verbalize with things you select so that your word and your teachings and your guidance can come across and reach the thousands that will wait very soon. Do you understand?

A: Yes, I understand. I understand as everything I mention is always from a perspective of awareness and what the solutions are, and everything comes from love. So, thank you. That was a vision you had shown me when I asked, "what were going to be some of the influences to 5G?" and you had showed me all that you mentioned. The easiest way I can explain is where people would become psychotic in a sense. In a manner where they would not be able to control their emotions as easily.

AA Metatron: The psychosis will not be so much built from what you consider to be adults. The psychosis will be more affecting the older ages. Psychosis is something that you must be in agreement with or not everyone will suffer that disease.

A: Not specifically the psychosis, what I mean is that it was the easiest way for me to explain how a person would feel. They would feel out of control, not being able to have balance within some of the energies that were being affected by the 5G. If that makes more sense?

AA Metatron: Children will be the most affected for children normally say what is on their little brains, on their little minds, and what comes out of their little hearts. So, children will suffer the most affliction because adults never have the time to listen, to understand. So, these afflictions become behavioral to the point of becoming physical. The children and seniors are the ones that will suffer first and most.

A: Yes, that is something that you have shown me specifically, the children. For example, a higher percentage of these healers currently think that they will not be affected by it, yes that is something that you want to choose to believe. What about the children though? What about the children who will be affected and cannot speak it to their parents? Their parents are un-awaked, they cannot defend themselves. What about them?

AA Metatron: Yes, that will be one of society's greatest afflictions, the children. They, the performance will come through at home with behaviors and lack of attention and then at school. Always the academic performance, but the problem will be mostly at home where the disconnect - as hard as this may seem - the disconnect at home is the biggest. For there is no time at home to meditate, there is no time at home to seek self-love and familial love. But there is LOTS of time when children are left alone in their rooms, in their own time, with their homework, alone at thought because the lifestyle of parents is just too small to accommodate the large size/number of children. And as the Earth crumbles - and it would not wish to pervade in this- but as the Earth crumbles and so will everything else, well we must continue to remain in that self-love, and we are choosing to speak the words carefully so that we may allow and encourage for our children, our spouses, and those that we as healers hold the space for, to seek that solace within. But not solace within as solitude, but graceful solitude. Solitude within our God, within our divinity, so that we cannot allow an interruption in our frequency. Does that make sense?

A: Yes. Now, what is a solution? You had recently talked to us and you have said that there's much beauty to this timeline but yet there's still much work. Metatron, what kind of solution or advice can you give us in regard to the 5G? What can we do to stop it?

AA Metatron: This vessel believes in going back to basics. And yes, she admits we are spoiled, we are a spoiled society and we do understand as humankind, that there are easier solutions when we depend on technology. But when the technology is purposefully harmful to our existence, spiritually speaking, then we must battle it forcefully, fiercely, by taking the initiative of not bringing it into a home. If it becomes mandatory, we will provide ways and solutions to healers and we will find ways to teach humanity to shield so that their frequency is not interrupted, nor interjected. Up until then, if it becomes an option that you have to pay with human dollars or human currency, you will have options. Simply, do not choose that option! You will learn patience and tolerance by choosing a slower Wi-Fi. How many basics or how far basic, back to basics, can you go? You choose, you can choose to wash your clothes in a washing machine, or you can also choose to wash them by hand. You can choose to use a microwave and you can also choose to cook on some wood outside and build a campfire. Does this make sense?

A: Yes... Now, if some people already have 5G in their homes and I understand that you will give us tools or are taught to not allow - if we're aware of it and we're standing forth in fierceness of it - as I noticed that even some of the newer cars seem to have that 5G within it. Can the crystals in and help to not have that infringement of the frequency?

AA Metatron: It may curve, it may help, but it will not completely evade the frequency. For the crystals that humans buy, and use are not the purest of grades. There is much imitation, much commercialization, there is much reproduction. To get the highest and purest form of crystals themselves, you must travel to the Amazons, to the riverbanks, to the mines, where the public basically have no access to. Are there people that mine these? Yes. The cost of the removal is very high.

A: Could we set up force fields with Alchemy symbols to protect, to alter the frequency?

AA Metatron: Yes, but you must be attuned to such alchemy symbols, you must breathe in that span of breath, you must receive attunements and not all healers have the same path. This would not happen overnight, and the transference is near, the threat still exists today. The threat is in the agenda and as healers, we still have a long way to come to terms equally. Because we have different healing paths, and we are still subject to human bodies and contracts. It's somewhat challenging for healers to meet together from this same eye.

A: Thank you Metatron, for you deeply align with me and my heart... Is there anything else that you would like to address on 5G? I would like to now ask the questions that she has for herself.

AA Metatron: We should proceed, but I am getting the presence of Lilith here…

END OF DISCUSSION.

-------------<◇>-------------

We as a collective in this time and space are going through the aftermath of allowing this negative timeline to occur with the tech industries' aggressive push for 5G technology into mass adoption everywhere. Yes, it is infringing, and it is a negative timeline. However, we are working together to rise from it. Today is May 5th, 2020 and I couldn't be prouder of our brethren, Light Workers, and Love-Light warriors! We are using this opportunity by alchemizing this control and negativity into something so beautiful and positive to come. In the next Chapter, we will go in-depth on how 5G can be used in technology as a form of escapism and thus delaying our spiritual growth.

Why not take this opportunity to reach a collective understanding in awareness to alchemize something so boldly put in front of our faces? Where we are being controlled throughout the world to stay home, to close businesses except for essential workers which of course, they have ensured to revolve around the medical industry. In these current times, we have influential leaders in government and the business world stating that we have NO CHOICE but to take the COVID-19 immunization shot by perpetuating fear about this A.I. virus. Concurrently, the pedophilic crimes powering the elite control of this world, are now surfacing to be transmuted. These are some of the strongest densities that have been holding humanity stagnant in the 3D, keeping us in the repeated simulation of the Inverted A.I. Matrix. We are now finally starting to transmute them. This is truly grand!

Shielding with force fields is one of the ways we can protect ourselves. You have been given the tools through the "I AM Source Love-Light" techniques found at the beginning of this book. These are a glimpse in learning the essential foundation required as Archangel Metatron mentioned above of attuning self to shielding. For more advanced teachings on how to use the natural forces around you as the Alchemist that we ALL are, please refer to the Your Growth Journey section at the end of this book for all the various classes offered.

Our Galactic soul families are at the edge of their seats in their spaceships watching every move we make and how even those who have always been quiet are now sharing in whichever way they can. We all have been waiting for this moment in time, for it shall be the greatest awakening of humanity we have seen!

"To be an empath is a gift and a curse. When we accept it as the gift it is, it is then when we realize that to not feel emotions, is to not know in which direction to flow."
~AuroRa ♥

-------------<◇>-------------

27

AUGMENTED REALITY VERSUS VIRTUAL REALITY

Session #177: Recorded in August 2019.

This is an excerpt from an online A.U.R.A. Hypnosis Healing session where Archangel Michael discusses in detail what Augmented Reality (AR) versus Virtual Reality (VR) is. What does it look like when working within the human consciousness? What is the connection to 5G being rolled out and its impact on the Ascension process?

-------------<◇>-------------

"A lot of people are doing this as a form of an escape. But the escape is taking them out of their current reality and they're not going to be able to fully integrate. Therefore, they won't be able to ascend."
-Archangel Michael

-------------<◇>-------------

A: [Aurora] Michael, before we speak back to the Higher Self, I would like to ask you a few questions really quickly. This is a very interesting topic. She mentioned AR is going to really connect with the 5G. Can you explain the whole process? The AR and any message you have for humanity about AR in connection to the 5G?

AA Michael: Yes, 5G is going to be able to power many new forms of technology that will come forth in particular Augmented Reality (AR). Virtual Reality (VR) is already out there. However, it is not in many households due to the price point, but that will be changing soon as well. So, VR will be hitting the market sooner and will be affecting many people, but not as bad as AR. 5G is accessible and they continue building these plates that are holding this technology. More people will be able to do things with 5G as far as having faster internet which will enable more utilization of technology, not just with AR. AR can separate the person from themselves. In that sense, I'm saying it will just become a simulation that they will constantly be living off. They will be disconnected; they won't be concerned about what takes place in their own reality because they'll be totally immersed in the augmented reality that they are currently seeing and placing. So, when 5G does come out and it is like I said, available for many people as they are trying to push, it will not be a good thing if they do not know how to balance it out. And I do not see that people are going to be able to, or want to, balance that out. I think that they will be happy about this new form of technology in general and will not see how it will be a continuation of the disconnect from self when they need to be aligning and getting integrated with their Higher Selves. So, yes, we definitely all perceive that that will be an issue, we have to continue to get the word out that you can't continue to immerse yourself into these forms of technology as an escape. A lot of people are doing this as a form of an escape. But the escape is taking them out of their current reality and they're not going to be able to fully integrate. Therefore, they won't be able to ascend.

A: Yes. What is it doing, particularly to their consciousness if it's separating it?

AA Michael: That yes, and a whole other thing, that technology is being used to operate and power the AR, it will interfere in a negative way with their consciousness. Due to the programs, whatever they're playing, whatever they're watching. It will be integrated into the program. It's going to be a negative type of consciousness.

A: In what way? Tell us what that would do to the consciousness. Would that particularly open them up into a type of brainwave? Would it open up their brainwaves to allow negative energies or entities into them or negative control implants?

AA Michael: More so negative control implants. It will make them more docile, make them more robotic, and make them more open to just doing. They will not be thinking for themselves. They will be controlled by the technology that they're going to be using and be more open. AR and VR, those are just ways to get people interested in trying these new forms of technology. There are other ones such as implants that they are planning to put into the brain. People that try these technologies such as AR, like I said, augmented reality being put into a totally new environment. While you're just sitting in one place, it disconnects and takes you away from your current reality. Once they hear and once they get comfortable with using that form of technology, having the implants put into the brain won't seem as bad. So, it's opening them up to very detrimental forms of technology that are ultimately going to be used to control them and also interfere in control of their consciousness and keep it suppressed.

A: With the AR and also when they place it on - just to make sure I understood - so when they place it on, they allow for that consciousness to be separated like that. This would be an entryway for a negative implant?

AA Michael: Definitely, it's an entryway for a negative implant. However, it's also an entryway to other forms of technology as far as implantation that they are currently working on right now. They are working on forms of implant that they can put right directly into the brain. So, using these new forms of technology such as AR, it will make the people more comfortable and let their guard down. It will let them trust that they can move forward with the AR. It will make them move forward with new forms of technology that they feel that they can trust, when they really shouldn't be trusting these forms of technology.

A: So, is it a form or type of gateway for further control?

AA Michael: Yes, yes. Especially with the implant and maintenance is something that they should be able to look up because it's been around for quite some time. But now it's actually ramping up due to this 5G technology that they're constantly pushing. They have implants that they are testing out in people's brains right now. So, using AR, that is definitely like you said, a gateway and will open people up and make them more open to using the detrimental forms of technology control.

A: Can you tell us if you can, Michael, as I know you would be limited to whatever she holds in her consciousness. As far as a human being, why is it that the AR would open that up? Is it doing something to the senses when it's in there?

AA Michael: Yes, its senses, all senses. It's hearing, it's seeing, it's feeling. When you use AR, it's augmented reality, so it's changing your current reality. If a person for some reason, if they are not happy with their current situation and they want to escape. They can use the AR headset, the AR technology to put themselves and immerse themselves into a totally different environment, an augmented one. In which they're able to feel many different things, they feel as if they're there because they're placed visually and through their other senses. They are placed into a different environment, a totally different ecosystem. So, they get comfortable in that place. So, when they take off the AR and stop using the AR headset, they're back into their reality that they didn't want to be in the first place. That they didn't change because of things that they need to do to change. They didn't want to do certain work and do certain things. So, they will lean on AR technology as a form of escape.

A: Thank you for that explanation. Okay, I have a few more questions in regard to this... What's AR and what's VR? What is the full name for these?

AA Michael: VR is virtual reality. Meaning that it's just what you're seeing virtually in front of you. You're just putting on a headset and you're just seeing what's in front of you. AR is augmented reality; it is changing the reality. So, you're being immersed into an augmented reality that is made up. It's not real. It's a program. So, depending on the program, most of these headsets will come forth via video games or within schools. For example, a school may use an AR headset for their students. If they want to use it for good uses, they can do a field trip for the students. They can put them in an AR-type of simulation where they're able to go on a field trip in a different country or to a park of some sort. So, there are good uses for it. However, the majority of people and the people behind the technology are not going to use it for the good. So, VR is virtual reality, AR is augmented reality. And you will need a really very strong constant internet signal so that it can't be interrupted while they have the headset on, which is why 5G is being pushed so heavily.

A: So, to fully launch this say release of AR, 5G needs to come into play?

AA Michael: Yes.

A: One more question, Michael. I was once told 5G is the last attempt - last attempt, you can say to keep the consciousness asleep. What are your thoughts on that?

AA Michael: That is the last attempt and it's a major distraction. It'll be a major distraction. There will be like I said, this escape. So, they're escaping and using these different tools and forms of equipment or forms of technology, rather than not working on themselves and not working on connecting. They're not working on feeling, not working on integrating with their Higher Selves, and connecting. So, they will continue to be distracted. It is an attack on consciousness, but it's also masked in a form of excitement for new technology, advancements in technology. So that's where there's a lot of mixture in the way the people are feeling about it. But ultimately, it's not good because that will lead to other forms of A.I. that will be stepping in to take control.

A: Would you say that then this would regress the planet in some way?

AA Michael: Yes, if the people are not aware of what it truly entails. They're just looking at it from what can happen within a year or two of the advancement of the technology. They're not looking past that and that's what they need to pay attention to. Like I said, there are good uses of the technology for educational purposes. However, not everybody is thinking about that.

A: Very good. Thank you for that explanation there. It reminds me of this Anime show that my family and I watched called, 'Sword Art Online'. Not sure if she's familiar with that. As we watch Japanese animation, for those who are familiar with that. In this show, you put on a headset and it induces you into it and that reality - just like you explained - becomes your reality completely; you become part of that reality. At some point, something happens within this Japanese animation show, that they become trapped in there and if they die in this simulation, they die in real life. Their body dies in real life. So that's very interesting. I think it ties very nicely with what you spoke off.

AA Michael: Yes, the implant as well that they're working on. I believe it's Elon Musk, he's behind that. He is the one that's bringing forth this technology for this implant. Like I said, if they're using a headset and they get comfortable with the headset, they'll be comfortable with letting someone put the implant into their brain. It's just a delusional behavior.

A: Are we speaking of etherically placing an implant into their energy body or are we speaking about physically? They're going to allow someone to physically put an implant into their head to play this?

AA Michael: This is physical. They're doing tests on this right now.

A: Wow.

AA Michael: Yes, they are definitely testing this out right now. Not that it's a trendy type of thing, but they will be more comfortable to try out that type of technology if they are open to AR because of what it does as far as helping them escape their current reality with less cords. Because AR has these headsets that have cords attached to them and other peripherals and pieces that are attached to them to help them with the different senses that they will be feeling when they are in AR. So, if you could do away with all that and just have something directly connected to your brain. To them, it will definitely seem more appealing. But that's ultimately not good at all.

A: Yeah, definitely not! Thank you for answering all that. That was great information.

END OF EXCERPT

This reminds us of what we are going through in regard to the strong push there was and has been of 5G. Though it seems in this time and space of September 12, 2020, that people and countries are starting to ban, protest, and speak up against it. May we continue with this momentum as we know that the rollout of 5G was all intertwined with the Deep State agenda of artificially inserting the Covid-19 virus into the collective. Where the virus serves as a coverup to hide and mask the poisoned radioactive power of 5G to human and all life.

We are repeating here on Earth what has been played out through the Multiverse of becoming too indulged in technologies, where we depend on it so much, they dumb us down by allowing technology to do our thinking for us. Where we begin to believe our world is within all the technologies we use religiously on a daily basis, and where we are inseparable from it. Where we obsess about our identity as expressed through our digital world persona. Simple tasks such as adding numbers, setting a reminder, looking up something we don't understand, if we stopped for a minute and asked our Higher Self instead, we would get the answer… Yes, we would in some form, as our mind and hearts are an infinite portal of knowledge and wisdom of the Universe. We are rendering ourselves helpless by depending on the technologies of maneuvering our daily tasks and functions. The Universe's answers are found within us, and the more we rely on electronics to find these answers for us, the more we allow for artificial integration and the more we then render ourselves in not being in clearest view of our daily choices of our organic path. Thus, losing our organic selves into these false artificial realities.

The idea of placing physical implants in us is the beginning of becoming artificial ourselves. Opening up potentials of becoming further immersed in wanting to replace or insert inorganic matter into us. What if by inserting this implant into us, we are allowing our consciousness to be downloaded into the Archonic artificial intelligence mega brain, then becoming a program ourselves or a video game character within their game? This brings us to our next Chapter where we will learn in-depth from the experience of a robot.

"Our imagination is the bridge to the infinite Universe that exists within us and beyond. It is a muscle that requires exercise as our legs require movement to walk."
~AuroRa

28

A ROBOT'S EXPERIENCE

Session #272: Recorded in April 2020.
Never before shared.

In this online A.U.R.A. Hypnosis Healing session, Melanie is an expectant mother looking to prepare her body for sacred birthing to ensure that her child's birth is at its highest vibration. We have heard of robots in the Universe and have wondered how that could be. In this fascinating session, Melanie takes us to a planet where robots are part of a civilization's lifestyle. We view it from a perspective of what it would be like to be a robot. The experiments that have been trialed throughout Creation.

In the first past life that Melanie is taken to, she is a male at war in Roman times, saddened that she had to leave her family for battle, and she knows she will never be back. She passes away at war by jumping off of a two-story building and then dying a slow painful death. She then moves on to the life of a robot. We begin the transmission here.

-------------<◇>-------------

"I wasn't just a robot. I knew I existed. I knew, you know?"
-Melanie

A: [Aurora] Let's go ahead and leave that scene now. Let's go to another important time where we will find answers for your highest healing. You are there now. Tell me what you see and sense.
M: [Melanie] I feel like I'm sitting in a chair and I'm staring at a white screen. It feels like they're trying to give me information. I feel like the building is industrial and they are creating people. So, there's like a conveyor belt. They're assembling people. And then they have you sit in front of the screen and they give you information that they want you to know. So, it's not anything that we learned that's what they're telling us how it is.
A: Who's putting you in front of these screens?
M: I feel like they're in control. I don't know, I'm not sure who they are.
A: You're sitting in front of a screen now?
M: Yeah.
A: What are you seeing on the screen?
M: They just show different clips of history, different things that they are trying to put into our minds.
A: I know that you said you're a man, tell me what are you wearing? What do you look like?
M: I guess slacks and a white shirt.
A: Describe the room to me. Where are you?
M: It looks like a factory. It's industrial. And they have chairs lined up in front of a screen and they're assembling people.

A: They are what?

M: They are robots, but they look like humans but they're fake.

A: Who? The people sitting down looking at the screen?

M: People they're making...

A: Making you look at the screens?

M: Yeah. I don't know. I'm one of them. I am. I feel like they're A.I. and I have a scene where if I leave there, I'm at a house and I'm in the house. I feel like a robot. I'm a robot, and I want to leave this house because I'm just there. So, I leave and I start walking down the street and then I realize I don't have anywhere to go. I won't be able to provide for myself. So, I got out of the house and I had escaped because nobody was there but then I just went back because I don't have anywhere to go.

A: Tell me why is it that you feel like you're a robot?

M: I'm just there. I'm not really thinking. Just do what they tell me.

A: How about the other people that were there with you, are they with you? The ones that are watching the screen, do they feel like they're robots too?

M: Yes, I feel like as we've watched the screen and what they've played, they were programming us in a sense. So, we were just created so that we would have some type of information, some basis to go off of.

A: Keep moving the scene along. Tell me when something else happens of importance. You're there now. Tell me what's going on.

M: I don't see anything else.

A: Let's go back a little bit, back in time to see how it is that you got into this situation, into this robotic human. Back in time somewhere of importance. You're there now... Tell me what's going on.

M: I'm on like a spaceship.

A: Tell me about the spaceship.

M: I'm just sitting there in a chair; a metal chair and I'm looking. If I look forward, I can see an oval window that leads outside. I'm facing it and there are gray aliens with long fingers. They're in front of me.

A: Are they tall or short?

M: They're tall with long fingers. They're like pointing at me in my face. They have big eyes and a little mouth. But I don't know how I got here. I don't know if they took me. I think they took me.

A: Who took you?

M: The Aliens.

A: Where did they take you to?

M: I feel like they found me somewhere and they took me. I don't feel like I want to be there. I think my arms are strapped down on the chair. I don't know how it's connected to the A.I.

A: Right now, do you feel like you're younger? Older?

M: I feel younger.

A: You said you feel like they took you from somewhere.

M: Yeah.

A: Are you not able to remember where you came from?

M: No.

A: Okay. So, you said they have you strapped down?

M: Yeah.

A: Are you sitting strapped down or laying down strapped down?

M: Sitting, but the back is, the chairs kind of slanted at an angle. My legs aren't stretched out, my legs are bent but the chair is reclined. I feel like they're, I guess they're examining me.

A: Okay. Let's leave that scene. Let's go back in time to right before they have taken you and strapped you down before. You said that you feel like you're somewhere else. You're there now... Tell me what's going on. Where are you?

M: When I was brought back, it was when I was little, like six or seven, and we had a two-bedroom apartment, and I shared the room with my brother and I would wake up in the middle of the night because I couldn't sleep. I would stare out the window. I would stare into the sky and there was this tall lamp that was like a light ball or bowl or something and I would stare at it... I don't know.

A: Keep moving time along. Tell me what happens next of importance.

M: I think they took me from my bed cause the whole room lit up. I think I'm floating. They took me to their ship.

A: They took you from that space to their ship? How did they take you?

M: What I see is the ship is above the apartments and they sent a beam right over me and it lit my room up and I floated up through the beam to the light.

A: Do you feel like you have any family there in the space before they take you?

M: This is when I was little.

A: You mean little as in this life?

M: Yes. My brother is there in his bed and my mom is in her bed in the other room and they don't know.

A: So, this is where you began, and then where you had seen going back to the space where you seem like a robotic human?

M: I think these are separate. I think when they would take me from the apartment when I was little, it was different than the people being built like the factory. And then from that factory, I went to a home and was like their - wouldn't say slave, maybe a worker. But I had a consciousness. I wasn't just a robot. I knew I existed. I knew, you know?

A: Let's go back to that life where you are that robot consciousness. You're there now. Another time and space where we're going to find more answers for you. Tell me what you're seeing all around you and sense.

M: Feel like I'm in the backyard and now, I don't know why but I feel like they're being mean to me. They're not nice.

A: Who is not nice?

M: The people who own me. I want to say they're beating me with something, like they are hitting me with sticks or bats or something. They're breaking me.

A: Are they doing that to others? Are you in a space where there are others with you or just you?

M: Just me.

A: Why do you think they're doing that to you?

M: I think they don't realize that I have consciousness. They think I'm just a robot.

A: Do you think the other robots have consciousnesses in them like you?

M: The other ones that were made with me?

A: Yes. Or are they just robots?

M: I'm not sure. I would probably say they did.

A: Let's go back to the very first time you remember being in this human-robot formation, this form. You're there now. The very first memory that you have of being in this robot form. Tell me what's going on.

M: I'm on the conveyor belt and they're assembling me.

A: How do they assemble you?

M: It feels like there are other robots putting these together. That they're like long metal arms but they're machinery. They're assembling us. I'm just my head is on like a hook and they're piecing me together.

A: Are you wearing any clothing?

M: Not on the line when they're making us. When they make us, then we get off and then we get clothes ourselves.

A: Would you say that you look very human?

M: Yeah.

A: Tell me what kind of clothing you're in?

M: I guess we just picked it ourselves. They're not… everybody's not dressed the same. So, then I put those slacks on and the white shirt, and then I sit down in the chair so they can play the clips.

A: When they were assembling you, are you saying that there were like arms and legs, the head, and a torso that they had to put together?

M: Yes.

A: How do they put those together?

M: It looks human on the outside but on the inside, it's all robotic. So, they just put those metal arms together. With the skin, they put the skin over, and just, they seal it with lasers. That's it. Looks like a person.

A: How do you think that they put your consciousness into your body? How is it that they inserted it when you remember being on that conveyer belt?

M: They put it in the chest. I want to say they had them stored somewhere and so they put it inside of the chest of the robot. And I see like sequences. I feel like it's computerized. So, there are chips implanted and a lot of it is robotic but there is a consciousness in there. So, I don't know why.

A: Let's go to another important time, perhaps after you're done watching the screen and once you're done being in the home that you were sitting there at. What's the purpose that they have built you? What happens next of importance that will answer some of this?

M: What I'm hearing is to integrate, to see if we can integrate, I guess into humanity. So they've made us, they try to put some of us into homes to see if we could function. But the humans don't respect them - respect us. So, they just look at us like a robot. Even though we are robots, we have a consciousness, we're not just robots.

A: Do the humans know that you're a robot?

M: They know how we're created, and they know that there's consciousness inside, but they still don't. They can't understand. So, when we are in their home, they still just treat us like a robot, like a piece of machinery. Instead of treating us as if we have feelings and are actually alive in a sense, although we're in a robotic body; we're alive! But they can't understand! So, I don't think it's going to work.

A: You don't think what's going to work?

M: Integrating into humanity.

A: Tell me about this world that you're at where these humans know that you are robotic. Tell me what these humans look like and the environment.

M: I feel like they're wearing gray suits everybody, all of them dress the same. They're bald. Their homes are immaculate. Feels futuristic. And I want to say this is like an experiment to integrate robots and A.I. and stuff into society. So, they made them look as human as possible, but the humans know that they're not them. So, it makes them uncomfortable.

A: Do these humans have children?

M: Yes. So, when I was getting beaten outside, it was the kids with the sticks. From the human's perspective, they're a little scared and taken aback by it all. Understandably but from the robotic perspective, it's a consciousness, it's not just a machine. So, it's just confusing.

A: Let's leave that scene, let's go to another important time in this life. Tell me what's going on next?

M: I think what they did was they took the robots and they dis-assembled them all. I don't think it worked out the way they wanted it to. So, I just see parts everywhere.

A: Hmm, parts of the robots?

M: Mm-hmm.

A: What about you? What do you look like?

M: I think I'm just in the pile.

A: So, they break you guys apart?

M: Yeah.

A: What do you think caused this, for them to do this to you?

M: I think the humans didn't accept it after all. There was an uproar and they fought back. They know the robots who were in their homes weren't bad, but the possibility that it could go bad was too much. So, they decided against it.

A: Tell me what happens to the 'you' there?... Keep moving time. The 'you' there in that pile?

M: I'm just there, they haven't... They just took everything apart and just left it! So, I'm just there. There's no way to disconnect. I guess I'm stuck.

A: Do you ever feel that you come out of there?

M: I think once they properly dispose of everything. I think we can unhook ourselves.

A: Let's see, fast forward to see if they do properly dispose of you. Then what happens?

M: They did and I'm shooting up like a tube.

A: How do they properly dispose of you?

M: I saw that in the chest of the robots there was a light, so they had to dislodge the light and let it go. I don't know if that's the soul or it looks like a spark and this one was blue.

A: What was blue?

M: The spark.

A: Okay, so once they release you out of your body, what happens?

M: I shoot up a tunnel. I'm floating through a tunnel that looks gray, navy blue, and black. Once I'm through the tunnel, I'm just in the stars. I'm just in the sky, out of space. I'm just there. Just enjoying being free. I think it was just part of an experiment.

A: Very good. Thank you. Let's go ahead and leave that life now.

The Higher Self is called forth.

A: Can I please speak to the Higher Self of Melanie?

M: Yes.

A: Am I speaking to Melanie's Higher Self now?

Higher Self: Yes.

A: Thank you. I love you, I honor you, and respect you for all the aid you have given us today. I know that you hold all the records of Melanie's different lives. May I ask questions, please?

Higher Self: Yes.

A: Thank you. Well, first of all, you showed her a life where it seemed like Roman times and she was a soldier. Tell us why was it that you showed her that life? What was the purpose? What did you want her to learn from that?

Higher Self: I wanted her to understand that she needs to appreciate the time that she has with her kids now. Because she hasn't always in past lives been able to, so she just needs to appreciate it.

A: Anything else you want her to know about that life?

Higher Self: Sometimes she has felt warrior-like. She is a warrior. She is stronger than she gives herself credit for.

A: Very good, thank you. From there you took her to this life where she was this man-like being watching a screen, and we discovered that she was some kind of robotic consciousness. Tell us why you showed her that life. What was the purpose of that?

Higher Self: I'm hearing appreciation to know that you're capable of more than you're doing. That you're not stuck but there have been times when you felt this way but it's not like that now. Things are different now.

A: Can you tell me if you need any assistance from the Archangels to find these answers? They're there to assist us as well. I just have a couple of questions here about this robotic human. Where was this world at? Is this a planet somewhere?

Higher Self: I hear Pleiades.

A: Was this civilization - a human civilization - that was advanced that created these robotic consciousnesses?

Higher Self: Yes.

A: Okay. Like she said, they felt that they were wrong. So, then they disposed of them?

Higher Self: Yes.

A: How were they getting the consciousnesses to put them in their robot bodies?

Higher Self: I hear abduction.

A: So, the Pleiades, whoever was creating this, they were abducting souls? Is that what you're saying?

Higher Self: Yes.

A: Can you show us that in detail please? Where were they getting them from?

Higher Self: I heard less fortunate. So, people who were less fortunate as in homeless, as in orphaned, all sorts of things like that, who didn't... This was an experiment. And in the end, they knew they were wrong, so we can't judge. But they would take their consciousness and insert it into these other beings.

A: How would they do that?

Higher Self: Through technology.

A: Through technology they were able to remove consciousness from an orphan, contain it, and then add it to a robot?

Higher Self: Yes. Without their permission, they didn't do it willingly. They weren't addressed. They didn't want to, but they had no one to protect them.

A: When they were abducting them, were they abducting them just from their planet or other places?

Higher Self: Other places as well.

A: So, would they use a U.F.O. to abduct people?

Higher Self: Yes. What I see is like a homeless man and he's lying there; they take his consciousness, and he dies in the human form. Nobody would even question it. They would just think he died of old age or bad health. So, it was easy and not questioned. They felt like they were doing it for a greater purpose. So, they didn't really feel bad because they know the human body dies, the vessel dies but the spirit, the soul, the essence lives on. So, they weren't really thinking of it as a negative.

A: Okay, thank you for answering these questions. Higher Self, at this point I would like to begin the body scan. Let me know if you need any assistance from the Archangels?

Higher Self: Yes.

The Body Scan begins, and we end our transmission here as the body scan had no correlation to her robot life, except for emotional and past life trauma needed healing.

END OF SESSION

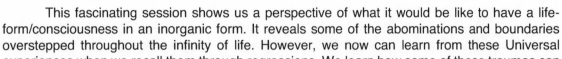

This fascinating session shows us a perspective of what it would be like to have a life-form/consciousness in an inorganic form. It reveals some of the abominations and boundaries overstepped throughout the infinity of life. However, we now can learn from these Universal experiences when we recall them through regressions. We learn how some of these traumas can influence us in the now, even when they are from the 'future us' in higher Dimensions, as Melanie's robot life was.

It was important for her Higher Self to get Melanie to her A.U.R.A. Hypnosis Healing session. The most important reason being that she was about to sacredly birth a new baby unto Earth. What kind of implications like this robot life could influence us as parents and our paternal connections to our children? Some of the disconnect and numbness she was feeling as a robot, could penetrate into this life blocking an intimate and deep connection to her most precious loved ones. Perhaps she needed to relive this life once more so that she could allow the forgiveness needed for all parties who played this game with her soul, with forgiveness as key to releasing this life's trauma to no longer have control over her.

The Divine Mother once told me that the journey of a baby is most challenging, as they make the choice to be birthed physically from parents on Earth. It is a 40-week journeyed process which the soul embarks upon. Not only does the child's soul have to work on the mother who is carrying them during their integration into the fetus, they also have to regress their soul enough to become a vibrational match to the mother. Otherwise, she just won't be able to carry and birth them, by not being a vibrational match to one another. Many infringements can happen during this time, especially if the parents are un-awakened and are unaware of the dangers that the medical industries create to ensure both the mother and child are at their lowest vibration. It is one of the most sacred acts on Earth that occurs, which is birthing. Having the honor to birth a new or old soul in this world! When each baby is born, it creates the most beautiful Source Love-Light blast that echoes out embracing Mother Earth and the collective, which is seen and felt from Earth and the higher Dimensions. Which then helps heal Mother Earth in the most profound ways.

Through these Galactic Soul journeys, we learn to value a soul even if it is perhaps homeless or less fortunate. We hope that this branch of beings from the Pleiades learned this important lesson, remembering though that not all races are malevolent fully in nature. Perhaps by their example, we are able to understand in the now, that this is not done, and it should never be done as the value of the soul is limitless and precious. We saw glimpses into the powerful technologies out in the Universe with harnessing capabilities of apprehending souls and inserting them into inorganic parts, thus we now know it is not only Archons who are apprehending souls as we learned through Hailee's special four session series. So, too are other races in the branches and infinity of the Universe. In the next Chapter, we learn more about benevolent Pleiadeans and their role on Earth.[25]

We give our blessings and our infinite love to this 'mother to be' for loving her child deeply to know that before their sacred birth, it was important to be a clear channel to achieve optimal vibration for both of them in order to allow the brightest and lightest soul to be incarnated.

"The key to obtaining balance within karma is through the gateway of forgiveness.
When we embrace forgiveness for others and for oneself,
we neutralize karma by unlocking the infinite Love within our hearts."
~AuroRa♥

-------------<◇>-------------

---

[25] To learn more about Pleiadeans', visit the Rising Phoenix Aurora's YouTube Channel and watch the "Channeling the Pleiadeans" video.

29

ARCHONS AND THEIR SLAVES

Session #236: Recorded in June 2020.
Never before shared.

In this online A.U.R.A. Hypnosis Healing session, Grace finds herself as a beloved member of her tribe in a beautiful land, giving her love to all through craftsmanship. We receive knowledge of the Council of Twelve, their location, and the evaluation process of the souls if they have lived a negative polarization role when looking to ascend. We learn a great deal about what Archons are, how they work, their ships. Who are the Archon slaves and how do they find their journey to freedom? How do the Pleiadeans assist with the Ascension process? In this empowering session, we learn more about the Ascension process and the percentage of people who are awakened right now.

"No race is above another race. We are one race in many assisting in the Ascension. It takes all for such a change, whether Pleiadean or Reptilian, it takes all. All are assisting."

"Because for so much light, there has to be dark. You need an understanding of both, and the dark is her love. Darkness is her love. There is equalness in communication. It takes both for understanding the Universe and of life. It just means that you have a deeper understanding that you are not afraid to journey to those places. It shows strength and fire, you have the light to navigate through those dark pathways."
-Daya

G: [Grace] Trees and bushes around me. Very, very green.
A: [Aurora] Look at yourself. Do you feel like you have a body?
G: Yes. I am human.
A: Look down at your feet. How many toes do you have?
G: Ten toes.
A: Look at your hand. How many fingers do you have?
G: Ten fingers.
A: Are you wearing any clothing?
G: Yes. A skirt, tribal clothing almost. Light material. I am wearing a short top and a skirt. Brown, sun colored.
A: Are you female or...?
G: I am female.
A: Do you feel younger or older?
G: Younger.
A: Are there any designs on your clothing?
G: Not on the top and minimal on the skirt. Just a few squares, patterns, and squares.

A: Are you wearing any jewelry?

G: A few bracelets. They look like beads. On my wrists and on my right ankle, and a necklace.

A: Are there shapes to your jewelry?

G: Bracelets and beads. They look like just round stones. Some of them are volcanic rock and on the ankle. The necklace is a brown string. It has stones, shells with a pendant on it, but I can't quite make it out.

A: Is there anything else that is on you that stands out?

G: The pendant looks like a stone, like a precious stone. It looks like it has been embedded into wood.

A: Is there anything you are carrying?

G: No. I am just in nature, did not bring anything with me. I am just walking.

A: Is there anyone else there with you?

G: I see people in the town, but I am on my own. I like being on my own.

A: Keep moving time along and tell me what is it that you do next of importance?

G: I am crafting something. I am in the town. I am crafting out of wood and I am making things. I think statues, small figures, totems. I am making them for the people, for the children.

A: Do you enjoy doing that?

G: Yeah. It's my job but I like doing it. I do it a lot for people. It is how I give my love to them; I make them things.

A: Where are you while you are doing this?

G: It is a small hut-like home. I want to call it a hall, like a town hall. It does not feel like where I live, but it is in my village. It is like a town hall.

A: Is there anyone else there with you in this space?

G: Yes, there are adults around me. People are doing things in the hall and there are children. Just everyday family things, people hunting and gathering in the village, some children are waiting by me for their gifts. They are waiting for me to give them something. Some of the adults are watching, just interested in what I am going to give the children, I think.

A: (chuckles) You must be good at what you do!

G: Yes, I am the only one in the village that does this. It is my job. It is how I make people happy!

A: Let's go ahead and leave that scene. Let's go to another important time where we will find answers that we seek for your highest healing. We are there now. Tell me what you see and sense.

G: I am in a ceremony. I think I am getting married. Yeah, I am getting married. I have a headdress with flowers. Nothing fancy, just the flowers. Lots of flowers. And everyone is there, all the children and the adults. They are happy that I found someone because I am usually on my own. They are happy that I have chosen somebody.

A: Are you able to see who you are marrying?

G: Yes.

A: Tell me, what does he look like?

G: He has dark, dark hair. He's a little bit taller than me. Slightly lighter skin than I have, and hazel eyes. Very hazel, just hints of green in them. I think it makes him unusual. They are usually very dark eyes, and his eyes have little bits of green. He is holding my hand and he's smiling at me.

A: How do you feel towards him?

G: I feel like I love him. He is the only person I ever felt a true connection to that has given me something.

A: You said normally you are alone?

G: Yeah. I make the toys and I make people happy. But I am always, always alone. No one. I don't feel connected, but I felt connected to him. He is the only person.

A: How is it that you met him?

G: I don't think he is from my tribe. I don't feel like he is born here. I met him later. Usually, you know everyone from the town. He is from the outside. He is from another tribe.

A: Go ahead and continue moving the scene along. How do you conclude your wedding ceremony? What does it look like, your wedding ceremony?

G: We are just in a building, a small hut building. There are seats and people are standing now and clapping. And the children are running around. There is no priest. We do the ceremony ourselves. We hold each other's hands, and we make promises. No one facilitates, just us. That is how we do things. We make promises to each other.

A: Beautiful. Is there anything that you exchanged?

G: I can see rings, but I feel like it's the 'holding hands' is the main thing. We hold hands and we exchange words, and they last forever. The words don't go away.

A: Beautiful. What happens once your wedding is done? What do you do next?

G: We live together now. We go back to our home. It is our home now. I think, my first home that I have had to myself. And we live together. He helps me make some more toys. But we spend much of our time together. He helps sometimes with making things, but I am the one who does that mainly. I still make things for the town and for my people. And he gathers food and cooks, and we spend our evenings together and we talk and sometimes we walk by the sea and through the trees just enjoying each other's company.

A: Sounds so beautiful. Let's go ahead and leave that scene. Let's go to another important time where we will find answers that we seek. You are there now. Tell me what you see and sense.

G: I am older. I am an old woman. I am telling stories. There are children around me, and I am much, much older. I am still telling stories, still with the children.

A: Did you ever have children of your own?

G: No, not of my own.

A: Why is that?

G: I think, I never felt like I needed to. It never felt like my path.

A: Your husband, is he still there?

G: No, he has died.

A: How was it that he passed away?

G: It was old age, in our village. It was just old age, and it was his time to go. I just lived longer.

A: How does it feel to still be telling stories to the children?

G: I feel happy. Feels like I am consoled by it. I am not alone when I am telling stories. Not that I… I did not mind my own company, I never have. Since he went, it felt like the children were my family now. I like to make them smile because it made me happy.

A: Let's go ahead and go to the last day that you are there in that life and you are about to take your last breath...Tell me, where are you and what is going on?

G: I am in my bed. The village knows it is my time to go, it's been long coming. And there are some of the town people here holding my hand. They felt like family, but they are not blood relatives, they are people from the town. The town took care of me when I could not take care of myself anymore, and they are holding my hand. They are sad but I am not. And they kept the children outside. The children wanted to come in, but they kept them outside. There is a man and a woman holding my hand and I just want them to know how much I love them all even though they were not my family. I loved making them all happy, seeing them all smile.

A: Go ahead and take your last breath now. Go ahead and come out of the body. Let me know what happens next.

G: I am out of my body. I still feel like myself in that life, and I am watching them from above. Watching. They are crying and still holding my hand even though I am not there anymore. I leave the room; I am looking, and I see the children outside. I did not realize that there were so many! And some of the adults standing by, I see them sad but...I am sad that they are sad, but I am not sad. Because I know I am okay.

A: Yes. Where is it that you go next?

G: Across the sea, in the air. I am enjoying the freedom. Feels nice to move. And then I go up, far up towards the stars and I am looking and enjoying being free. I don't have a body anymore. I get out into the Universe, and the higher I go, the more I remember who I am, and I realize I am going home. I realized that, and I let go of that life. I remember how I felt towards the people, and the people that are still there, and I wish them well. Even though I remember who I am, I remember how I felt. I am with the stars. I go back home. I am in the stars.

A: Your home is in the stars?

G: Mm-hmm.

A: Is there one individual star?

G: I merged with one. It is like a golden-white light. It is a brilliant white light, golden-white. I have merged with it and into it.

A: How does that feel, to be back home?

G: Nice. It feels, I am with the collective again. I am with myself. I feel other souls even though I cannot see them. It feels like we are a family in here. There is a lot of love. I am just resting now. Love and rest.

The Higher Self is called forth.

A: Good. Beautiful. Let's go ahead and leave that life now. Can I please speak to the Higher Self of Grace?

Higher Self: Yes.

A: Am I speaking to Grace's Higher Self now?

Higher Self: Yes.

A: Wonderful. Thank you. Love you, honor you, and respect you for all the aid that you have given us today. I know that you hold all the records of Grace's different lives. May I ask questions, please?

Higher Self: Yes.

A: Thank you. Why is it that you choose to take her to this beautiful native life? What was the purpose? What messages were you trying to deliver to her?

Higher Self: The love. She feels like she needs a deep connection to feel love. That was not the case. She learned how to love herself in that life. To be on her own and to love herself. When you love yourself so much that you could give love to others, and she learned this.

A: Wonderful. Would you like for her to remember that in this life?

Higher Self: Yes, she should love herself more. It's only when she is comfortable with her own company that she is able to give to others. She needs to love herself first, and then she can give.

A: Beautiful. Anything else you want to tell her about that life?

Higher Self: To remember the love, the love that she received. The family, her family that she chose, there was so much love from all in the town. She was so beloved. She did not quite realize how much until her life was gone, until she was moving away, how big her family was when she thought she did not have a family.

A: Was that life on Earth, or on another planet?

Higher Self: It was on Earth.

A: What region on Earth would that have happened at?

Higher Self: Hawaii.

A: Beautiful. Is there any message you have for her about Hawaii?

Higher Self: She should go there one day; she will remember love. It is a place with a lot of love, and she felt a lot of love there. It would be good for her to reconnect.

A: Beautiful. At this point, we would like to begin her body scan. Higher Self, is that okay?

Higher Self: Yes.

The Body Scan begins.

A: If you could start scanning her energy, let me know, do you need any assistance from the Archangels?

Higher Self: Yes, please.

A: Okay, who would you like for us to call on first?

Higher Self: Archangel Michael.

A: Very good. Higher Self, if you could connect us to Archangel Michael please?

AA Michael: Hello!

A: Greetings! Thank you, brother for being here. Love you, honor you, and respect you.

AA Michael: I love you.

A: Thank you (chuckles). The Higher Self has requested you, Michael, for assistance today in helping her through her body scan. Michael if you could start scanning her body from head to toe, looking for any negative energies and entities, let me know where would you like to first start off with to start healing?

AA Michael: In the stomach, there is dark energy in the stomach. I think Reptilian.

A: Michael, if you can go ahead and contain that now with the alchemy symbols, please.

AA Michael: It is contained.

A: Let's go ahead and find all Reptilians and entities within her and we will talk to them after we find them all. Michael, continue scanning her body. Any other Reptilians or entities? Make sure you are scanning her deeply and thoroughly through all scans as we know sometimes, they can be tricky and hide. Scan deeply. Where else does she have more?

AA Michael: I feel in the heart.

A: What does she have in the heart?

AA Michael: Feels more Reptilian energy. They have trapped the heart.

A: Yes, can you go ahead and surround those with the alchemy symbols please now, in the heart?... Let me know once they are contained.

AA Michael: They are contained.

A: Okay, let's continue scanning her body. Where else does she have more Reptilians? Scan her spine as well, her DNA structure, all parts of her.

AA Michael: DNA is Reptilian consciousness.

A: How many are there?

AA Michael: Three.

A: Can we contain those now in her DNA please with the symbols?

AA Michael: Yes.

A: Wonderful. Thank you. Let's scan her body again. Where else does she have anymore?

AA Michael: Brain, there is darkness around the mind. I feel Reptilian consciousness in the brain.

A: Let's go ahead and encase those there now, please. Let me know once they are encased.

AA Michael: They are encased.

A: Wonderful. Let's continue scanning her body. Where else does she have any more?

AA Michael: No more that I can see right now.

A: Alright, while we are at it, Michael, can you go ahead and scan her for any Archons in her as well as any within her DNA structure, her spine, scan her for any.

AA Michael: The base of the neck.

A: Okay, what is there?

AA Michael: Archon, I feel a collective.

A: Okay, let's contain them there with the alchemy symbols please now Michael.

AA Michael: They are contained.

A: If we can go ahead and start neutralizing the Archon's energy out of the base of her neck?

AA Michael: Yes.

A: We'll continue neutralizing the Archon energy there. Any other part of her that has Archons?

AA Michael: I feel like the base of the neck was a portal, it was access to the collective. And from there they could influence others, but once the neck is healed, I don't think there will be any more problems.

A: You mentioned there was a portal. Michael, do you need to close the portal there?

AA Michael: Yes.

A: Michael, can you go ahead and close that now, please?... Let us know once it is closed.

AA Michael: It is closed.

A: Thank you. Michael if you could connect us to Archangel Raphael, please?

AA Raphael: Yes.

A: Thank you, brother. Love you, honor you, and respect you.

AA Raphael: I love you.

A: Thank you. Brother, if you could help us heal the areas where we have started to remove the negative energies from? If you can start healing the base of her neck, where we just closed the portal, please.

AA Raphael: Yes.

A: Thank you, brother... Alright, let's continue. Let's go ahead and talk to some of these Reptilians there. Let's go ahead and talk to the one in the stomach. Michael, if you can help it come up, up, up now, please. I would like to speak to it now.

Reptilian: Hello.

A: Greetings. Thank you for speaking to us. Love you, honor you, and respect you. May I ask you questions, please?

Reptilian: Yes, I think!

A: Okay, when was it that you attached there to her stomach?

Reptilian: She was young. Twelve?

A: What was going on with her then that allowed you to come in?

Reptilian: Her father. She was anxious. Her father lowered the vibrations, and I was able to come in.

A: What was her father doing that lowered the vibrations?

Reptilian: His presence. He made her afraid. I was able to come in through the fear.

A: Okay. Do you have a Reptilian body that you are connected to somewhere else?

Reptilian: Yes.

A: Please connect us now to the Reptilian body that you are connected to. We would like to speak to it now, please.

Reptilian Body: Yes?

A: Greetings. Thank you for speaking to us. May we ask you questions, please?

Reptilian Body: If you must.

A: Love you, honor you, and respect you. Thank you for allowing me. May I ask, where is it that you are located?

Reptilian Body: On a ship.

A: Is the ship nearby or far?

Reptilian Body: Near to the Earth. Just outside.

A: Are there any others with you on the ship?

Reptilian Body: Yes.

A: By attaching this consciousness to her stomach, what kind of discomfort have you caused her?

Reptilian Body: Much pain, pain in the stomach. Fear, we have kept the fear there. We caused the fear, the fear triggered the pain.

A: How many more are there with you on the ship?

Reptilian Body: A hundred.

A: Would you be able to connect me to them please?

Reptilian Body: Yes.

A: Thank you. I would like to speak to the hundred there on the ship. Love you, honor you, and respect you. Thank you for listening to us.

Reptilian Collective: Hello.

A: Hello, thank you! If I can ask, how many are you all connected to as well?

Reptilian Collective: What do you mean?

A: Do you - the one hundred of you - are you also attached to others?

Reptilian Collective: Yes.

A: How many more are you attached to?

Reptilian Collective: Forty-six.

A: Tell me what is it that you are doing on the ship? What is your job?

Reptilian Collective: We are here to connect, to bring down the vibration. We want to lower the vibration on the planet, there are many of us on the ships outside. We influence so that the ones inside can work without interference.

A: How long do you think you have been doing this as far as human years on the ship?

Reptilian Collective: Over two hundred.

A: Two-hundred years?

Reptilian Collective: Yes.

A: I understand that you all have been doing it for a long time. This is what you know. I am speaking to all of you Reptilians there as well as the consciousness and the Reptilian that is connected to the consciousness here. I am saying this speech to all the Reptilians within her. As you know, the Earth is ascending. We would love to be able to aid you today so that you no longer have to play this negative polarized role, having to attach to her or anyone else draining upon their light. You could positively ascend, and you could create your light being free-willed incarnating where you would like to go to next. You no longer have to feed off someone's light, you being your own creator being, creating your own light. Would you all allow us to assist you so that you no longer have to play this role anymore?

Reptilian Collective: This ship does. Other ships do not.

A: Thank you. Those of you on the ship and as well as the consciousness and the Reptilian that is attached to her. All of you, if you could start finding the light within you and we are going to focus Love-Light upon you and start spreading your light, please. Archangel Raphael?

AA Raphael: Yes.

A: Brother, if you could find the 46 that those 100 attached to? If you could ask those Higher Selves to release those attached to them with their permission? Let me know what they say.

AA Raphael: Yes, we can.

A: Oh wonderful! Okay, let's start helping those consciousnesses as well to start spreading their light, please. Raphael and your Legion of the Heart green ray, all of you start assisting.

AA Raphael: The one in the brain is struggling.

A: We are going to go ahead and help all of them in her body too?

AA Raphael: Yes.

A: Did all of them in her body say yes as well?

AA Raphael: Yes, all but the Archons.

A: Oh yes, the Archons are neutralizing, we are just transmuting them out. Do you need any Phoenix Fire to the Archons?

AA Raphael: Yes, please.

A: Okay, we are directing Phoenix Fire there. And Michael, if you could just let us know once they are neutralized out of there, please... We are focusing Love-Light on the one in the brain, the Reptilian there. Did any of the other ones, the ones in her heart and the three in her DNA and brain, were they connected to the ship too?

AA Raphael: The heart was, and the brain were connected. The DNA is somewhere else.

A: While everyone continues to spread their Love-Light, can I speak to the ones in the DNA?

AA Raphael: Yes.

A: Thank you. Archangel Michael, if you can help them come up, up, up now. Greetings.

Reptilians: Hello.

A: Thank you for speaking to us. Love you, honor you, and respect you. May I ask you questions, please?

Reptilians: Yes.

A: Thank you. When was it that you attached there to her DNA structure?

Reptilians: She was young, very young. Three years.

A: What was going on with her then that allowed you to come in?

Reptilians: The jabs, the immunity jabs. The injections.

A: The vaccinations? The injections?

Reptilians: Yes.

A: What kind of discomfort have you been causing her by being there?

Reptilians: We have been dimming her light. We help any Reptilians. We aid by lowering the vibrations. We dim the lights so the dark can come in. Much light needs to be dimmed.

A: Do any of you have anything to do with her depression and her stress?

Reptilians: Yes, we allow it. We make a way when her light is dimmed, the dark can come up. She would not have those problems if her light was fully radiant, fully activated.

A: Can you tell me, where are you located? Your bodies?

Reptilians: We are on a ship, the three of us.

A: Is there anyone else there with you on the ship?

Reptilians: There are five.

A: We would like to speak to all of you with the same communication as the others. As you know the Earth is ascending, would you allow us to help you instead of transmuting straight to 0 when Ascension happens? You can transform and positively polarize into Ascension, no longer having to play this negative role. You could be free, creating your own light, no longer feeding off others' light. Would you allow us to help you?

Reptilians: Why? We are not part of the Earth.

A: It is not just the Earth that is ascending, it is the Universe. And your role of having to attach to others is basically no longer needed within the contracts of this polarity that is occurring. If you don't, when the Ascension comes forth, you will be automatically transmuted to light and you will forget, basically your consciousness. You will forget all that you have been through. Instead, we are giving you the opportunity to ascend and keep your memories, and become wise, strong, empowered, and free to create your own light.

Reptilians: Yes, we will allow.

A: Beautiful. Go ahead and find your light within you and spread it to all that is you, every root, and every cord within her, all of you. And spread that light also within your bodies. Are you also attached to anyone else besides her? You five?

Reptilians: Yes.

A: How many more are you attached to?

Reptilians: Thirty-three.

A: Raphael, brother, if you can locate those 33 and ask their Higher Selves if they will allow for us to help remove those consciousnesses within them? Let me know what they say.

AA Raphael: I am not sure... Yes, yes. We can.

A: Okay, good. Start spreading your light to every root, every cord that is attached to that consciousness of those 33... Okay, so we are having everyone spread their light. We have the one in the DNA, stomach, heart, okay, and then the brain. Any other ones we are missing?

AA Michael: Not that I can see.

A: Okay. Can you tell me when was it that the ones in the heart attached?

AA Michael: Heart... nine years.

A: What happened to her then that allowed them to come in and create that portal and block her light?

AA Michael: Darkness in the family. The people around her were unhappy. Their energies brought her down, it was able to slip through. All the others were dark. The low vibrations everywhere lowered her vibrations also. She was not protected from others' energies.

A: We are helping them all spread their light... How are the Archons looking at the base of her neck?

AA Michael: They are going. The portal is closing.

A: Very good. Let's see. We want to make sure we are healing, as we are helping these Reptilians spread their light, healing her anxieties, her stress, her depression. Higher Self, if we can start healing that, please?

Higher Self: Yes.

A: Thank you. Also, Michael, Raphael, Higher Self, her stomach pains, can we scan her lower back pain, what was that connected to?

AA Michael: Connected to the Archons. She did not realize that they were there. But there is more pain in the last few weeks. They are becoming agitated.

A: Let's start healing that back pain now. Michael, why does she have acne problems?

AA Michael: It is internal. She cannot change on the outside, while she cannot change on the inside. She must feel worthy. And when she feels beautiful, then the outside will come. Inside first.

A: Good. If we can send transmutation energy to help her start removing those negative energies that keep her from feeling that. Can we do that?

AA Michael: Yes.

A: Thank you. Also, while we are working on the DNA removing the Reptilian consciousness, she would like to activate her crystalline and 12 strand DNA, please.

AA Michael: Yes.

A: While you are working on her DNA, if you can go ahead and reprogram anything that is false or holding her back from her highest good, can we reprogram her DNA for her highest good?

AA Michael: Yes.

A: Thank you. Higher Self and Raphael, if you can start that process now, please.

AA Michael: The Reptilian ship that has been connected to the stomach has been taken away.

A: If we can have Archangel Azrael and his Legion ensure that none of them become astray and they all go where they are meant to go for their highest positive polarization.

AA Michael: The heart and the brain, they are moving away. We just need to heal and put light into the empty spaces.

A: Good, very good. Azrael again, ensuring that all that has been removed from her, go where they are meant to go and that they don't get tricked along the way... Raphael, brother, if you can start filling in Love-Light into those areas, to the heart, to the stomach, to the DNA, the brain, fill in Love-Light to wherever something has been removed. Thank you. How are the Archons looking at the base of her neck?

AA Michael: They are difficult.

A: Difficult. Okay, let's continue focusing and neutralizing that energy there... Did the Reptilians have anything to say to her before they fully go?

Positive Polarized Reptilians: We did not know the pain because we could not feel it. We don't know the pain. We don't think of it when we cause it. But we are sorry for it. We did not know.

A: Thank you, may you be surrounded by the Love-Light of the Universe! Blessings to all of you. Azrael, where is it that you are taking them to?

AA Azrael: I am taking them for healing, then to Jupiter.

A: Why is it that you are taking them to Jupiter after healing?

AA Azrael: Some must go through the process of judgment of themselves and their life in order to move forward onto another. Some just need to heal, need to rest.

A: Does Jupiter provide that? That 'going through life' reviews?

AA Azrael: Jupiter provides judgment, the review so that they can go elsewhere. The others have gone to the stars for healing.

A: Is this a benevolent process or a malevolent process?

AA Azrael: Benevolent process. A judgment is a small word. We judge ourselves; we decide on our own course of action. Negative races go to Jupiter for this, as they may need assistance in deciding and in moving forward. In Jupiter, you cannot move to another incarnation unless you have gone through the judgment process. You need the understanding to incarnate. You cannot move forward without understanding and many do not understand.

A: Who would you say oversees this in Jupiter?

AA Azrael: The Council of Twelve. They oversee but do not enforce. It is a free process but those on Jupiter must complete the process to move on, to move forward.

A: Can you tell us a little bit more about this Council of Twelve and who they are?

AA Azrael: They are a Galactic Council. They oversee the extraterrestrial races; they are of different races themselves. Arcturian, Pleiadean, Mantis, they are twelve races represented. There are Reptilians also on the Council. They mediate between each other and decide, and they make sure there is a balance between the races. No one above another, just balance and they aid in the judgment process.

A: Going back to the Reptilian, is this a positive or negative Reptilian?

AA Azrael: Neutral. More positive than negative. He speaks for his race. His input is needed. We need all sides.

A: Yes, can we perhaps talk to them a little bit later?

AA Azrael: Yes.

A: Thank you. Let's complete her body scan. Michael, can you scan her one more time for any negative entities of any kind, any false fractals within her DNA structure? Let me know if you find anything else.

AA Michael: I see negative Archon attachments in the head, and we need to burn away the Archons from the base of the neck to the lower back, they are attached to the spine affecting the kundalini energy.

A: Using Phoenix Fire now in all that you mentioned. Let's go ahead and contain those in the head and the brain. Let me know once they are contained.

AA Michael: They are contained.

A: What do these Archons look like in her brain? We are using the alchemy symbols and transmuting using the Phoenix Fire as well neutralizing them completely out of her.

AA Michael: They are dark ships. Black, they are like black and red. They like the colors. They like to look intimidating. They don't look Reptilian. They are lizard-like but larger, larger than Reptilian. Black, dark scales, red eyes. They walk on hind legs and they have tails. They are darker and larger. They intimidate a lot of Reptilians. Many Reptilians fall in line with them.

A: Are those what people call Draconian?

AA Michael: No. Slightly different. Draconian is again, smaller, red scales. These are black, black, and very dark. They see themselves as kings over the Draco and Reptilian races. They believe they are the kings of that kingdom, that they are kings over those races, that they are more advanced species, and rule over them.

A: Archangel Michael, can you call upon your Legion of Light in the Galactics, please?

AA Michael: Yes.

A: Archangel Michael, is there something that we can do about these ships?

AA Michael: We can drive them away.

A: Okay, can you call forth on the Legion of Light there? Tell me what you are doing and how you are driving them away.

AA Michael: We shine the light, we stand together. Our wings are stretched. We shine until there is so much light, they can't stand it. Their kind of darkness cannot survive in our kind of light. The two are incompatible. The more light we shine, the more they have to run away.

A: How many are there with you, shining the light unto them?

AA Michael: Fifteen.

A: Thank you to all those assisting, love you, honor you, and respect you. We are focusing as well light here from Earth aiding and we are still focusing Phoenix Fire on where they are attached. How was it that they attached? How was this in the brain?

AA Michael: They attached partly through technology. Electronics allowed them to come in, they opened the aura and dimmed the light. They can attach themselves. Once they are attached in one place, they can use that to attach elsewhere. Once they are attached to the spine, they can move to the brain, to the back.

A: Why the spine? Why do they always like to attach there?

AA Michael: It is the awakening energy. Kundalini energy. So much power in the spine, it connects to everything. They think that if they can gain control over the spine, they can gain control over everything.

A: Does the consciousness connect to the spine, the neck area of the being?

AA Michael: Yes, there is consciousness and much communication of light through the spine. So, they like to attach here to inhibit this. They feel like once they have control, they can do anything that they want. This is untrue. Light is always stronger; all it takes is a decision. The decision to not consent, the decision to choose light. And then they must go. They are not stronger.

A: Tell me how many ships are there sending light unto them, the Archon ships?

AA Michael: There are many sending light from all across the Galaxy.

A: Wonderful. These ships, how many are Archon ships?

AA Michael: Archon ships?

A: You said that there were black ships?

AA Michael: Yes, there are 13. They think that in manipulating the numbers they can turn the power of them unto their side, but they misunderstand the Universe. They misunderstand the way things work. So much technology but so little understanding.

A: Can you explain more, do they have any technology within them, the Archons?

AA Michael: Some. A.I., they use it to create the hive mind to connect to their kind throughout the Universe and to control Reptilians and Draconians, as they believe them to be a lower species, even though no species is lower or higher. They think of themselves as sovereign, and so take it upon themselves to influence their technologies unto these other races, to control them, to influence them. The ships have been sending waves, I can see waves coming out of the ships.

A: Those 13 ships?

AA Michael: Yes. Disruption. They are trying to disrupt.

A: They are sending waves of disruption?

AA Michael: Yes, disruption. It is chaos, it is inhibiting the light frequencies. They are trying to disrupt the flow of light and disrupt the positive frequencies in the Earth.

A: What are they using to disrupt it?

AA Michael: Technology, it is sound frequency vibration but negative. Their ships have the technology to do this. And they transmit these frequencies, send them out towards the Earth and this tries to counteract the positive vibrations. But it is all about the intent, light will overcome but we need to choose. It takes the choice.

A: Yes. Are there any other groups like these 13 Archon ships anywhere else? Are there other groups of Archons doing the same thing near the Earth?

AA Michael: Just the 13 towards Earth in this solar system, there are others, but they are being dealt with gradually.

A: These ships, what do they look like, the shape of them?

AA Michael: They are jet black, shiny. They have sharp edges almost, made out of rectangular shapes, black rectangular shapes made into a ship. It does not quite blend with what is around them. It is black and shining, and they have red lights underneath.

A: How many Archons are on these 13 ships?

AA Michael: There are seven in each ship.

A: Do they have any other life forms with them? Not that they are life forms, but you know, since they are A.I.

AA Michael: I can see that they have taken some slaves on some of the ships. Some Reptilians. They are slaves, they are in chains.

A: They have Reptilians as slaves in there?

AA Michael: Yes.

A: I know that we are sending light to them to move them away from us. Is that all we can do?

AA Michael: We can try to liberate but that would mean fighting. They are being dealt with across the Universe, but it is outside of Earth.

A: Okay, so we can continue just moving them away with light? Michael, can you connect us to the Reptilians that they have as slaves? How many do they have in total on the 13 ships?

AA Michael: I cannot see them all.

A: Would you say they have like 10, 20, 100's?

AA Michael: They have 26.

A: If we could all work now, connecting to all 26 there, giving them an opportunity to no longer be enslaved by these Archons, we are speaking to all of you now. Michael, please connect me to them... We love you, honor you, and respect you.

Enslaved Reptilian: Hello.

A: Hello. Thank you, for speaking to us! Tell me, where are you at and what is going on with you? Who is speaking to me?

Enslaved Reptilian: (distraught) I am Reptilian, and I am on the ships. I am trapped.

A: How are you trapped?

Enslaved Reptilian: I have chains on my neck.

A: How did they put you like this, into these chains?

Enslaved Reptilians: They just took us from planets. We were from our communities, from our families, there are young ones here and they don't know where their families are.

A: Do they feed you?

Enslaved Reptilians: Little. Just scraps from what they feed on. They feed on humans and then give us the scraps.

A: Are you saying the Archons eat humans?

Enslaved Reptilians: They feed on the energy. They can eat humans but only on Earth is this done, in the physical. They feed energetically on the ships.

A: I am speaking to all of you there, all of you in chains. Are any of you attached to others?

Enslaved Reptilians: Two are attached but most are not.

A: What is the purpose that they keep you there in chains? What do they do that for?

Enslaved Reptilians: They think that they can, they think that we are inferior. We don't know why. Sometimes they feed on us. Sometimes they can use us as food. Sometimes they just need slaves. They believe that we are inferior, like us to work for them.

A: From my understanding, when they have Reptilians, they have them do their jobs for them, like their soldiers. How come you all are not out there being their soldiers? Why are you all chained?

Enslaved Reptilians: Because we are not that negative. We have not been trained that way. We were bystanders. Some are children, many are women, some are men. But we are not fighters. We were never fighters in our communities, in our world. We have just been taken for servitude.

A: Thank you for sharing your stories with us, we want you to know that we are here to assist you if you choose it. No longer having to be stuck in those Reptilian bodies being chained, we would love to be able to aid you to help you release out from there and positively ascend. As the Universe and the Earth are ascending, you are able to ascend, no longer having to be used in this manner. Would you like us to help you, assist you? To spread your light and release yourself from those Reptilian bodies?

Enslaved Reptilians: Yes.

A: All of you, speaking to the children as well and the women Reptilian.

Enslaved Reptilians: Yes, yes.

A: Good, and the two that are attached to someone else, if we can have Raphael ask those two if they will allow for those consciousnesses to be brought to light as well.

AA Raphael: Yes.

A: Good, start spreading light, all of you. Let us know once all of you are of light.

Positive Polarized Reptilians: We are all light.

A: Beautiful. Go ahead and pull yourselves out of those bodies. Release yourselves out, let me know what it is like once you come out.

Positive Polarized Reptilians: It is lighter. We can leave the ships... We are leaving.

A: Good. Archangel Azrael and your Legion, brother, if you can ensure you protect them as they are coming out. The Archons, are they noticing what is going on with the Reptilians yet?

AA Azrael: Some. They are angry and confused. They think that they just died.

A: If we can make sure that they don't realize what is going on. Michael, can you do that?

AA Michael: Yes.

A: Metatron?

AA Metatron: Yes.

A: Can I call forth on some more help? Uriel, Azrael, Raziel, Raguel... Thank you.

AA Michael: They are suspicious, but they do not know. They think they have died. They question why all have gone at the same time, but they do not know the extent of what has happened.

A: Thank you. Azrael, do they have a message for us before you take them?

Positive Polarized Reptilians: Thank you. We are sorry for the two that were attached. They did not realize until they themselves were chained what it was like for others to be so. We are sorry and we thank you. This was a great service. We are all very grateful.

A: Thank you! It is an honor to be able to help you. We love you, honor you, and respect you. Blessings, go ahead and go with the Love-Light of the Universe, enjoy.

Positive Polarized Reptilians: Thank you, thank you!

A: Thank you! Michael, let me know what is going on with these Archons on the ship. As we are shining the light, what has occurred as we are all shining the light on them?

AA Michael: They are away from Earth. They cannot stand the light. They are traveling. I don't know where they are going, but I think to regroup. They are traveling to other planets.

A: Will they be able to come back and do the same thing on Earth?

AA Michael: The Ascension is taking care of it. As the Earth raises, they won't be able to have this power anymore. It worked once, but now it does not, there is too much light and it is moving so quickly. They can't keep up. They don't realize yet that their time is over, so they are still trying. But they will not succeed.

A: That's beautiful, thank you. Michael, did we remove the Archons within her?

AA Michael: Yes.

A: Good. If I can have Raphael again, fill in Love-Light everywhere. Michael, can you scan her for negative implants, hooks, and portals? Does she have any?

AA Michael: I feel like there is a hook on the right leg, but I can't see anything else.

A: What is this hook connected to Michael? Scan deeply.

AA Michael: Trauma, past life.

A: I am using Phoenix Fire there on the hook. Can we transmute that hook out, please?

AA Michael: Yes.

A: Let me know once it is fully out. Does she have other negative implants, hooks, or portals? Scan her again, please.

AA Michael: No. We just need to fill in the light.

A: Good, fill in the Love-Light now. Okay, and one last time, for entities, Reptilians, and Archons, any type of negative entities within her? Scan her, are there any?

AA Michael: None in the body. We need to just heal past life traumas.

A: Let's start that process now. Michael, Raphael, Higher Self, start healing the past life traumas for her, please... Okay, Higher Self, does she need to be age regressed?

Higher Self: Two years.

A: If you can start the process for her now. Also, scan her chakras, Raphael, if there are any that are misaligned or blocked, please let me know.

AA Raphael: There is a block in the sacral chakra.

A: What is causing the blockage?

AA Raphael: Disconnection in childhood. There was much fear.

A: Start healing the sacral chakra now. Any other ones, Raphael, please?

AA Raphael: Lower chakras need to be cleansed so that they can be balanced with the others.

A: Let's start doing that, please. Balancing all chakras, filling them all in with Love-Light. Opening her third eye as well to the biggest it can be and expanding her abilities as her Higher Self allows, as well as her heart, opening it to the biggest it can be please, for her highest healing. Can we do that?

Higher Self: Yes.

A: Raphael, can you also scan her auric field? How does it look, does it need any repairs?

AA Raphael: The shielding has been helping but some reinforcements would be helpful.

A: Start filling in Love-Light there to her auric field, please. Sealing it, making it nice and strong and bright, as it is meant to be organically. Michael, can you scan her for any negative cords?
AA Michael: Two on the arms.
A: Where are they connected to?
AA Michael: To a ship.
A: Is it a different ship or?
AA Michael: Different ship.
A: Tell us, what is the ship that attached cords to her?
AA Michael: It is Reptilian.
A: Let me speak to the other Reptilians on the ship Michael, please.
Reptilian: Yes.
A: Greetings. Thank you for speaking to us. Love you, honor you, and respect you. May I ask you questions, please?
Reptilian: Yes.
A: Why is it that you attached cords there to her arm?
Reptilian: To hold her back. She is confused. Makes her confused. We can hold her, prevent her from moving forward.
A: How many of you are there on the ship?
Reptilian: Seven.
A: Have you been able to witness what happened to the other Reptilians and how we have helped them?
Reptilian: Yes.
A: Would you allow us to assist you in that manner so that you could be free as well?
Reptilian: Yes!
A: Beautiful. Go ahead and find that light within you and spread it to all that is of you, every root, every cord. Let's go ahead and start transmuting, using Phoenix Fire on these cords. Michael, if you can help remove these cords. We are sending light to them so that they can transform to light, let us know once you are all light, please.
Positive Polarized Reptilian: We are all light!
A: Beautiful! Go ahead and remove yourselves from that ship. Do you have a message for her before you all go with Azrael?
Positive Polarized Reptilian: You can move forward now. Don't fear. The fear was us. You don't need to fear. We want to thank you for helping our children.
A: Your children?
Positive Polarized Reptilian: Our children in the ships.
A: Oh, were those some of your children?
Positive Polarized Reptilian: Not blood, but they are children of our race. They are innocent! We thank you for helping them. We saw. We saw. We won't forget.
A: Thank you, it was an honor. I love you all.
Positive Polarized Reptilian: Love you.

As I am transcribing in this exact time and space, this session has brought me to an immensity of love and tears. The truth is that I play this role every day without ever needing credit or allowing myself acknowledgment in what we are doing through these healing sessions. My deep humbleness just does not allow it.

When the Reptilians thank me for saving their children. I tapped into it; I then felt a blast of love from the infinity of souls we have helped in these two incredible years through A.U.R.A.

Hypnosis Healing. They have moved me to do so, I acknowledge it and accept it. I have finally allowed myself to feel this at this moment in time. Which has brought me to tears in the most infinite love.

A: Go ahead and go with the Love-Light of the Universe and go with Azrael, he will ensure your safe passage. Love you, honor you, and respect you.

Positive Reptilian: Thank you.

A: Good. Is there anything else that we can heal Michael?

AA Michael: If we can clear the skin?

A: Yes, start clearing the skin. Do we use Phoenix Fire on that?

AA Michael: Yes, please.

A: Using Phoenix Fire on all the skin areas where there is acne, please. Transmuting the negative energy there and she will work on self-loving as she is beautiful... Okay, let's see. Alright, are we complete with the body scan?

AA Michael: Yes.

A: Wonderful! I would like to thank Metatron, Michael, Raphael, Azrael, Uriel, Raziel, Raguel, everyone who assisted today, Gabriel, anyone else, all those Legions of Light beings out there that assisted with such a profound removal of Archons upon our Earthly existence. We humbly thank you. Now, we bow to you humbly. Love you, honor you, and respect you. (kiss) My love!

Light Collective: Thank you. We love you.

A: (big sigh) The Earth feels lighter! Thank you!... Okay, now if I may, she has some questions here. Higher Self, may I please speak back to you?

Higher Self: Yes.

A: Higher Self, is there a name that you go by, please?

Higher Self: Daya.

A: Ah, what a beautiful name! It is an honor. Okay, she has some questions. I am going to go ahead and ask them. She wants to know who she is, where does she come from, and what are her connections, her fractals?

Daya: She is me. We are each other. We are Daya. She is compassion. That is her essence. That is her true self. We are compassion and forgiveness. Through all, there have been many incarnations, many fractals, but all are the same.

A: Beautiful. Are there any specific fractals that she has the highest percentage of?

Daya: Pleiadean.

A: Okay, thank you. I have a question for you in regard to the Pleiades. It often happens through different forms of channels where people say that Pleiadeans are in charge of Earth's Ascension, the Pleiadeans are the ones leading it. They make it seem like you all are, I don't know, they kind of put you a bit like, what is the word, pedestals? Is this accurate? What can you share about Pleiadeans for us?

Daya: No race is above another race. We are one race in many assisting in the Ascension. It takes all for such a change, whether Pleiadean or Reptilian, it takes all. All are assisting. Pleiadeans are probably closest connected to Earth only because we have incarnated so much here and visited here. We are closest in DNA, so this is probably why so many feel this is the biggest connection merely because that is the closest to them. They feel this connection more deeply so think that is the biggest connection, but this is not the case.

A: So, would that be Pleiadeans communicating that?

Daya: The collective.

A: Beautiful. So, when we hear communications like that, would you say those would be Pleiadeans or something else?

Daya: Those communications are people. They are Earth consciousness. People see divinity in one and think that divinity only exists in that one. People struggle to conceive of such divinity in everything. There is always duality. There is always one or the other. But it is not, 'or' it is 'AND'. And. And. And.

A: Yes. Good. Beautiful answer, thank you. She has a question. She said she always felt a deep connection to the moon, snow, and ice. White-haired beings. Where does this come from?

Daya: This is an essence of herself that has incarnated in Lemuria and Atlantis. She feels closest to this incarnation, to this physicality in this life because the missions are similar. There is much remembrance in those lifetimes, but this essence is a part of her. It is who she is.

A: Wonderful, thank you. Now she wants to know, why has she always felt a particular fascination with darkness and macabre.

Daya: Because for so much light, there has to be dark. You need an understanding of both, and the dark is her love. Darkness is her love. There is equalness in communication. It takes both for understanding the Universe and of life. It does not mean that she is any less being drawn to darker things, does not mean you are dark, not that it would matter if you were. It just means that you have a deeper understanding that you are not afraid to journey to those places. It shows strength and fire, you have the light to navigate through those dark pathways.

A: Wonderful, thank you. She wants to know what was the purpose of her illness and depression? We know where it came from, the Reptilians. Is there anything else you want to add?

Daya: Yes, she does not need to fear. She worries about life and about where to go and if it will come back. It will not come back. She is much lighter than she was when this was allowed to occur. But that brought so many lessons, she has learned those lessons. She does not need them again.

A: Wonderful. Thank you. Okay, and we know your name is Daya. She said she recently had a dream with Anubis who stepped forward as her Twin Flame, and when she tried to connect with his energy again in meditation, she was told that his soul name is Khal. She later learned this is Sanskrit. Could you please expand on this for her?

Daya: Khal, my beloved Khal. We are Twin Flames. He is as you would know him, Shiva. I know him as Khal. He navigates the dark, he is incarnated many times here. Anubis is merely one. Many stories tell of his energies, Anubis, Shiva, Hades, they connect him to the underworld and think this means death, but it does not. It means Ascension. Death and rebirth are one and the same. As with yourself, the Phoenix, know that rebirth is transformation.

A: Yes.

Daya: He navigates and guides others through the darkness, to Ascension. And I counteract this with light. He can be judged, judgment. I will be forgiveness, mercy. We work together to guide others and you need both for Ascension. He will be the darkness that you must get through to Ascend, and I will be the light that guides you there. But we work together, always.

A: Beautiful. She also wanted to know, why has she been recovering Sanskrit words?

Daya: Sanskrit, she has previous lives. This is where we came to know ourselves as Daya and Khal in those ancient times in this language. This is the only true recording that the Earth has of these words, of these names. And so, we introduced her to this for only then could she gain an understanding for there are no other languages or times where she could find this information.

A: Wonderful. She wanted to know, who is her Twin Flame, and will she meet him in this lifetime and when?

Daya: Khal, yes. He has stepped forward, for she is now ready, and they will meet in this lifetime. Not yet, but soon. Her process of self-love and transformation is almost complete. Only then will they be reunited in this life, but they will meet.

A: Beautiful. Daya, she wanted to know - will we be meeting extraterrestrial, magical, or Inner Earth beings in the physical plane within this lifetime?

Daya: That depends. Depends on whether the Earth is ready. If more minds are open, more hearts are open than not, then yes. But it depends on humanity and whether they allow themselves to be ready and whether they open their minds and their hearts as a collective.

A: Very good, thank you. She said, there is much speculation over the nature of magic and whether it exists and is innate within the Earth and her inhabitants. Does magic exist and what are human beings truly capable of in this current time and in 5D?

Daya: Magic is everywhere. Magic exists. It is everywhere and it is in everything. It is in you. It is in me. It is in the water, the air, the fire, and there is so much that we can harness. Communication. Magic is communication between everything, giving some, receiving some. Some are able to use this and understand this, but it takes oneness with everything around you. Magic exists in everything. You just need to tap into that frequency, but it is within you, it is within everything. You just need to open your heart to it. Human beings in this life are capable of so much. There is so much that we think of as fiction. But this is in fact more the truth than what you have been told. The reflections of the magic that you see in stories are more true to the energy of the Earth than how we are currently living right now. The vibration is more true than where we have been keeping ourselves. The higher we ascend, the more we will see this. We are still in the physical realm, considered to be limited compared to 5D reality. In 5D, these things will be fully realized. We will see in all things that magic does truly exist. But for the moment, we need to work within before we see changes without. It is the inner work that this time is for and once we have worked within ourselves, then we can change our external reality.

A: Beautiful explanation. She has asked, where are we right now in the Ascension process? Will it be a mass shift into 5D or is it a shift happening on a soul level, soul by soul basis?

Daya: We are above 50 percent in the Ascension. Over 50 percent are awakened.[26] We are doing well. Very, very, well. So much light and more and more light every day, every minute more awakening. So fast now. It is like a symphony of lights from above. Little twinkles all over the Earth, just lighting each other up. It is beautiful!

A: You said so fast now, what was the catalyst to making it so fast now?

Daya: It's been quickening throughout this time, but the stars have aligned. There is more positive energy than negative and now that the positive has reached the greatest number, Ascension is happening more quickly. We have the Light Workers, the Starseeds, we have held that place of light but now it has been taken up by others. Others are sharing this light because we have done the work. We have succeeded. We are succeeding, and it is happening and becoming quicker every day as more and more souls become awakened. We have done the work, we have held space and held the light for these souls, and now they are ready to wake up.

A: Thank you. She wanted to know in this current time, what will the shift into 5D look like?

Daya: At the moment, it is a soul-by-soul basis. I can see a timeline where it is a mass shift. We are moving towards this timeline but there is still much choice. The Ascension will happen either way. At the moment it is soul by soul, but depending on our choices, there is a timeline where we will see a mass shift that will look like a wave, a mass shift into 5D that humanity will be conscious of but there are still choices to be made to move to this timeline.

---

[26] The 50 percent awakened mentioned through this session, indicates how at least 50 percent of the Earth's population is in the awakening process. No matter which phases they are in, whether at their highest awakening potentials or not, the light has reached its 50 percent projected awakening goal, and that is grand!

A: Thank you. Are our ideas and stories of magic, fantasies, the supernatural, actually our remembrance of 5D Earth reality? Similar to Lord of the Rings, Middle Earth?

Daya: Yes, they are. There is a reason that humanity resonates so deeply with these stories, with these fantasy worlds, these characters, and abilities. There is a reason for this because it vibrates at your truth. The truth of your heart at its Fifth Dimension. We remember these things from the past and from the future and seek to bring them into the present, which is why these ideas come to us through art, and through these mediums. It is our way of bringing the past and future to the present and the only way that we currently know how. But it is truth.

A: Wonderful, thank you. As you know, goodness, we have never rescheduled an A.U.R.A. session so many times! (laughs) What happened?

Daya: (chuckles) This was the right time. Both for her but also for the energies. Much has happened since. Much growth in the world and within the self. Now is the right time and Kali Ma is connection to self. With Kali Ma, with the passing of the comet (asteroid '2002 NN4'), this has raised the energies and has allowed her deeper connections to self, for she is connected to Kali Ma and these energies that are occurring.

A: Beautiful. So it is that the stars and the comet aligned right on time for her? (chuckles)

Daya: Yes.

A: Thank you. She has one more question here. She wants to know, can I please receive guidance on my medications whether I should continue and if so, how to phase them out?

Daya: There will be questions from families, from doctors. You may continue but phase them out sooner rather than later and be sure to protect yourself from them. Encase them in Love-Light, be sure to set the intent of transmuting any negative polarities and infringements within them. But the sooner she can stop taking them, the better. But if she must continue, be sure to shield them and herself to protect from infringement.

A: Wonderful. Can you explain to her just so she knows the medication she is taking, what is it doing to her? In an energetic sense?

Daya: The anti-depressants dim her light. On an energetic level, they dim the light and the high frequency, maintaining her to 3D. And medication for the skin, I do not see what this does. Thyroxine aids in lowering vibration, it is almost mixed with the anti-depressants, acts as a tranquilizer for light, and for the Higher Self. It creates a disconnect that makes it much harder to form a Higher Self connection and maintain light on Earth.

A: Thank you for sharing this with her. I think it is important that she knows how important it is to get off them organically for herself, for we are at our highest, most potent of frequency in strength and divinity when we don't have those negative A.I. drugs within us. Thank you. Can we start helping her by sending her energy so that she could remove it when it is time for her?

Daya: Yes.

A: Sending her energy and love for that. Thank you... At this point, we have asked all the questions that she has. Is there anything else that I could have asked Higher Self?

Daya: No.

A: Wonderful. Thank you. Alright, well it has been a joy, thank you Higher Self, Daya as well as your beautiful Twin Flame. All the beautiful Angelic's that aided today and all the beautiful benevolent races as well that aided. It is such an honor to have worked with you. Thank you for such a profound movement of the Archons and everything that we did today. Wow, what a powerful session. It has been a joy to have been able to work with you. I love you, honor you, and respect you. Blessings to everyone!

Daya: Thank you. I love you.

A: And I love you, thank you! What a joy! Can I bring her back now?

Daya: Yes.

Post Session dialogue.

A: Welcome back! You were amazing! You look like a completely different person.

G: (laughs) I feel amazing!

A: Yeah, I am looking at your laughter, your smile, it is like I am looking at a different person. Completely, wow! How beautiful! (laughs) Awesome! Do you think you remember everything?

G: I think so, but it is kind of going more as I am waking up, becoming conscious and remembering less but I will rewatch it all later. Thank you so much! It was amazing!

A: Oh yeah, was AMAZING! You were deeply connected in there. Wow, I could see those Archons. Do you remember how they looked?

G: I remember they were black; their face was almost bigger, they were bigger than Reptilians, but they still looked lizard-ish. Their faces were just like rounder, they kind of went up like that. But it was very black, very black with red eyes. The ships I remember more. Very black and shiny, and just did not fit with anything around them.

A: Yeah, even before I started knowing about these things, I would have beings just like that, Archons visit me in my dream and mess with me, or mess with family members on purpose to mess with me. I remember they look like that and sometimes they would twist their head around in full direction just to creep me out. I'd say, 'what is that'... They are almost like chameleons, or like they mimicked everything. They remind me of those beings that have been messing with me all my life.

G: Yeah. They were...

A: It is weird, you can register their frequency and you won't forget that.

G: It seemed like they were trying to be more powerful than they were. It was so bizarre.

A: Exactly. Like a falseness.

G: Yeah, they wanted to give off this sense of power and sovereignty and intimidation but that, all that power came from technology, they have to back themselves up with technology all the time because it was not naturally within them. It was bizarre.

A: Amazing session! Thank you, sister. It has been a joy. I am so happy we made it (laughs)!

G: (laughs).

A: I hope to meet you sometime in the future when we are able to. It has been amazing. To see how profound, where you are at for your age. Even though obviously, your soul is ancient, but physical age. It is something to be very proud of yourself, self-loving of yourself, and appreciate yourself for being here where you are. Again, what a session for where you are at.

G: I will definitely not forget this anytime soon (chuckles)!

A: Yes, for sure (chuckles)!

G: Thank you so much!

A: I love you! Love you sister!

G: And I love you!

END OF SESSION

-------------<◇>-------------

What a truly empowering session for all involved! The most endearing moment in this healing session for me was when the last Reptilians we found in Grace's Body Scan, after the ones we freed from the 13 Archon ships, and how they expressed deep gratitude to us for saving their children. This moved my heart profoundly, in a more intimate manner for Reptilians then I have been able to achieve before. I realized then that they did view and loved the children of their race as their own. Similar to how we in this time and space on Earth are hash tagging #SaveOurChildren in social media platforms, which is directly connected to human and child trafficking. How we feel an intense fire within us needing to protect, when we hear the children of the world are being violated sexually by compromised pedophilic humans. Who truly are no longer human themselves, as they are more like Archons and negative polarized Reptilians that still remain under the Archons' control within those human bodies. We feel protective over all of Earth's children because they are all our children, just like the Reptilians who thanked us for saving their children.

We learned how Reptilians too could be slaves or victims to the Archons. Through this session, our hearts expand more because even though this is only a transcription of the session, one can feel the love and transformation through it immensely. It helps us understand that the Reptilians themselves have been labeled into 'one bad category.' They are a race just like we are a human race in this beautiful Universe. Why is it that their entire race is labeled into one category of being bad? We do not label the whole human race in this manner, so why would we do this to any race? Through these Galactic Journeys, we have encountered Positive Reptilians aiding humanity, and many newly positively polarized Reptilians thanking us for aiding their race.

It is similar to how we are programmed here on Earth by the Elites, through ways of social and mainstream media to hate on the one person or group they would like us to. The Archons like to indulge in playing these games where we hate on what they have inserted into our consciousnesses for their dark negative agendas. It is a brilliant strategy when one reflects on it, to distract from the real issue by focusing enough hatred on the Reptilian race and no one will notice how the Archons are actually 'The Big Bad Boss.' These Archon masterminds will then use that focused collective hatred energy towards the Reptilians to help Archons stay in control and continue their destructive harvesting of souls throughout Creation and all of its beautiful races. In the next Chapter, we will see how truly destructive these Archon forces are and the extent of their destruction across the Multiverse.

It is all mind games to these Archon tyrants as they have studied the psyche of organic life forms since ancient times. Watching us through all types of negative technologies in different Dimensions and Universes. Cataloging it all in a supercomputer database that is ONE with the Archons. Experts at experimenting on lifeforms to cause stress and underdevelopment for their inorganic purposes of feeding off our light. This is why we teach all to intently set our Love-Light boundaries of what you DO CONSENT and DO NOT CONSENT to.

It was comforting to know of the divine system in place, such as the Council of Twelve in Jupiter for souls as they positively polarize or are looking to redeem themselves in some form. Jupiter provides that safe space for all, so the proper organic karmic balancing may come forth for all parties involved. Reminding us that we have never been alone, and even though we might have been lost for what seemed like an eternity to the artificial darkness. Once we gain back our power and light, we are given the divine support to rebalance our souls' journey for the future infinite potentials of incarnation.

Remember the great accomplishment achieved through this empowering session for the collective by holding our strong lights against and pushing away the 13 Archon ships that contained the seven Archons on each ship. They were a strong firepower to the Covid-19 negative timeline with their negative technologies directly wielding and affecting life on Earth. It is interesting and uplifting that this also occurred in June 2020 after asteroid '2002 NN4' zoomed by our atmosphere. It divinely seems as the fire power that the Divine Mother dropped off through the asteroid into our atmosphere and Earth, was the remaining Love-Light that teetered us over so that when we conducted Grace's session, we were able to remove these Archon's once and for all from our proximity. All divinely planned vibing off each other's positive influence! In Chapter 9 ('Activation Portal: 9/19/19'), we learned that we as a collective were at 40 percent of light awakened, and then in June 2020 we have accomplished it! We ARE at the 50 percent light awakened on Earth as mentioned through this session. No matter which awakening phase we are in, whether at our highest awakening potentials or not, the light has reached its 50 percent projected awakening goal, and that is grand! This is what our Galactic teams mean often when we hear that we have reached the critical threshold of light on Earth. It is too late for the negative polarized entitles and their false inorganic timelines. The Earth/The Divine Mother will now always right herself into an organic timeline no matter what, and no matter how hard we have to work at it collectively, SHE WILL RIGHT HERSELF! The cellular crystalline memory codex of this possibility has been activated, and it shall always BE from here on until Ascension!!!

"Dare to travel into the unseen for it is in the unseen we discover Love,
what which has no shape or form.
Love is within all that you may fear to lose yourself to.
It is inside another's window to the soul, another's connection to the heart.
Love is the invisible webbing that connects all Creation in union.
Love is the flow of life that guides you silently,
discovering inward Love and Love in all Creation!"
~AuroRa ♥

-------------<◇>-------------

30

HARVESTING OF PLANETS THROUGH THE UNIVERSES

Session #288: Recorded July 2020.
Never before shared.

In this online A.U.R.A. Hypnosis Healing session, Serena takes us to a beautiful planet where negative polarized Beings have invaded. In this intense journey, we learn about the true power of one planet and the inorganic infringements upon the Universes. Colony of A.I. spiders, who are they and what is their purpose? We learn more details on the negative polarized Hybridization program. What do they need our capabilities of reproductive systems for, and what are the ways they use our power of fertility? Here we learn more about Archons and their level of destruction in Creation. Archangel Michael provides guidance on how we can best assist Mother Earth during these intense times. We also explore how a forgotten memory roots a deep discomfort and hinders from an intimate connection.

"Because when you are in session with one Being who comes to us, in actuality, it is like we are working with hundreds of Beings because of the multidimensional expressions of that one Being, who is coming to the A.U.R.A. practitioner. Therefore, the healing that occurs within that Being in that consciousness also ripples into, affects many other lifetimes, and many other Beings in different souls. Even whole soul families at one time."
-Archangel Michael

S: [Serena] Vegetation everywhere. I'm in a very dense forest...jungle. Lots of green...feeling also blue energy, but the plants are all green. I'm looking for flowers and there are some small white ones, but aside from that, they're very tall trees. What is standing out to me is how huge the trees are and how many. There is a tall canopy and I'm just surrounded by plants.
A: [Aurora] Look at yourself. Do you feel like you have a body?
S: First answer is yes.
A: Look down at your feet. How many toes do you have?
S: I have five.
A: Five on each foot?
S: Yes.
A: Are you wearing anything on your feet?
S: No.
A: Look at your hands. How many fingers do you have?
S: Four.
A: Four on each hand?
S: Yes, like three fingers and one thumb on each hand.
A: Look at your skin. What tone is it? What color is it?

S: Almost like a periwinkle, but not. it's like a blue and gray and periwinkle and a lavender all mixed together into one color.

A: Beautiful. This mixed in color, are there any shapes or symbols to them?

S: Maybe tiny little triangles in my pores.

A: Beautiful. Look at yourself. Are you wearing any clothing?

S: No.

A: Do you feel female, male or both?

S: I feel female.

A: You're able to see and sense your face very clearly, what do your facial features look like?

S: I have round cheekbones and a happy face and happy eyes. I have short, dark, cute hair, kind of pixie-like. I have gold bracelets on my ankles and wrists.

A: Those bracelets, do they have any symbols on them? What material are they made from?

S: They're like a brass color, and there might be a small inscription on the anklets.

A: You're able to sense clearly what that inscription is?

S: It's a kind of light language. There are four vertical lines, two open circles, and three dots on each side.

A: Anything you are carrying?

S: No, but I have a kind of wings.

A: Tell me how do they look?

S: Like a translucent green, kind of small and pointy, and purple.

A: Look at your body very closely. Is there anything that stands out as distinct?

S: First thing that comes to mind is that there's a dark belly button. I was confused, I was looking for my breasts, and I don't have any. (laughs)

A: Anything else, maybe on the backside?

S: Stripes, on my thighs. Might be a kind of tattoo of some kind or might be part of my skin.

A: Look all around you. Let's see why you're here in this space. Why are you there?

S: Healing… (crying, breathing sharply)

A: Let it out.

S: (sobbing) The trees are telling me to let it go. They're just pulling it out of me. (breathing) All of the vegetation.

A: What are they pulling out of you, the vegetation?

S: (cries, breathing) Oh, god…It's (hyperventilates)…it's a darkness. I don't know what the consistency is but it's not mine. They're wanting me to know that is very clearly not mine and that is either my job or my role somewhere before this place to suck it up into my body and this is somewhere that I come (hyperventilates, sobs) …I come here and it's pulled out, and they're telling me also this is part of the reason why the ocean is so healing for me because it's similar. It does the same sort of similar vibration. It's something in the ions of the space combined with the oxygen and something that the plants are doing. It's like this sort of energy work that's happening, and that it just takes a kind of blank surrender, and the ego is gone and there's no worry about what exactly the darkness is. But it just matters that the heart is just (exhale)…like a worthiness or a permission of some kind. That releasing this isn't hurting anyone. (deep breathing) The plants aren't being hurt by me breathing it out or my existing by carrying it. They need me to know that (hyperventilate, sobbing).

A: Let it release, let it release. Now, tell me, how does it feel to release it?

S: Like prana in my body. It feels like shards are being…it's not even like a pulling out, it's like the shards are being filled back up but I can feel them distinctly as shards of my…like holes, but when I'm there and when I release it. I'm not even releasing, I'm just there in a state of surrender…And its vibration, and not necessarily oxygen, but it's just how a body feels when they take in a lot of oxygen. There's a lot of tingling that's happening and a lot of memory coming back. (exhale)

A: Tell me more about this place. Look at the sky. Describe the colors to me of this space.

S: The sky is a rainbow iridescent. So beautiful. I'm seeing white etheric, maybe crystalline structures or shapes in the sky, like a Merkabah. (long exhale)

A: The sky is like a Merkabah?

S: It is kind of like a very large Merkabah that I can see out in the distance beyond the tree line. There are other shapes as well. The Merkabah is not moving necessarily, however there are other frequencies that are there, it's organic. That's what they're telling me. They're not necessarily moving, but they are organic. I just want to be here all the time.

A: Let's go back. I know they said that that dark energy within you was not yours. Let's go back to right before you came here. Right when you perhaps attracted this dark energy that was inside of you that you released. Tell me what you're seeing and sensing.

S: Red and darkness everywhere. Things are on fire.

A: What things are on fire?

S: Vegetation was on fire. It's embers and ashes in the air now, and there are living structures. It kind of looks like an old school army tent. They're kind of boxy-shape, army tents. But they're not army tents anymore because they were burned. That's what they were. Dark-ish. There's just a lot of flame and fire energy. Time of day is afternoon. I don't see anyone or any animals, and my body is still shaking. Not this body in this vision but Serena's body, has more lifeforce in it or just a lot of vibration.

A: How about the sky? How does the sky look? Is that on fire too?

S: The first answer is that no, it's gray.

A: Why is it gray now?

S: It's ashes. There's a lot of destruction.

A: What do you think happened here?

S: I'm sensing something off straight ahead of me. I'm feeling nervous, but I know that I'm protected. I'm walking towards it. I'm peering around one of these structures that are on fire, and there's kind of like a Cyborg feeling. It's a large ship in the shape of a metal spider.

A: Do you still have your same form with the periwinkle skin and the wings?

S: Yes.

A: Tell me, what is this spider looking thing doing?

S: It's landed and the energy that reminded me of is a spider nest. There's a lot of energy inside of it. I'm feeling like it's like a mother spider with the nest that she's holding in her back legs. That's what I feel energy-wise by looking at this, but I don't necessarily see a spider nest, and I'm looking for other beings. I'm not seeing any so I'm wondering if they're inside the ship.

A: Let's go back to right before this ship, before this destruction, before this fire occurred. You are there now. Tell me what's going on.

S: Again, the vegetation is very prominent. It's like it's an army base, and I'm not sure if it's on this planet or not.

A: You're seeing an army base?

S: It's not actually like an army base. It's just that the tents that the shelters that are built here remind me of those kinds of tents, but it's actually not army people who are here. It is a township of a small group of beings who live here.

A: What do these beings look like?

S: At first, I saw little fairy looking beings flying around really, really, really small. I wasn't sure if they had a body, and then I saw white light energy beings. They don't really have a body, but they kind of do. They have like...I see with my vision, kind of wispy energy, light wings, and there are three or four of them, very tall. They don't really have bodies, but this light etheric energy is, I've never seen anything like this before, it's kind of holding its shape it's sort of like a plasma. Yeah, it's not just like a glowing ball, they have a consciousness with wings.

A: To confirm, there is vegetation in this land. However, these beings are there, like they've landed. Is that what's going on?

S: Yeah, so I'm not sure if those tent structures are theirs, or if they're coming to check on it in a way. So maybe it is. That's what it feels like.

A: Let's see why these beings are there. Let's continue fast-forwarding time to when something else happens of importance.

S: They're talking about how there's a lot of healing work that needs to be done and how the timing must happen now. They were thinking that the timing was going to be a lot more relaxed, and that a different timeline was going to play out, but instead there's a sense of urgency that's happening in the sense of gathering for the sake of protection. Gathering resources for protection, almost like a bracing. Bracing ourselves sort of energy because the time to leave is too late or we just can't leave, and we have to stay there.

A: These people that are doing this, what do they look like?

S: I think that it is humans. These three or four beings are the Higher Selves who are downloading next steps to these humans.

A: Do these humans have anything to do with the little tents or are those something else?

S: Yeah, they are there. They live in there.

A: What is your connection to them?

S: I care about them, and I live in the forest in a way. I pop in and out of Dimensions. In that part of the time, I exist there with that vegetation around me, and they're taking up space here now.

A: Keep moving time, keep moving time. See what happens next of importance.

S: There's a lot of worry energy in the tents at night at this time because they are sensing their own doom. Like they know that they're basically sacrificing themselves, and they might not even fully believe in the reason why they're having to sacrifice themselves. This reminds me so much of Vietnam War energy. It's as if they were drafted, and they didn't want to be there necessarily. Now they're facing the music of their incarnation, like the end might be very near. There's been gas that's been dropped, and fire is starting in the forest in the plants.

A: Where is this gas coming from?

S: It is from planes.

A: Can you explain what these planes look like?

S: They have a red tip in the center of the nose, and they have three sets of propellers on each side. They're primarily green, and now it seems more like a spray of water rather than gas droplets. I'm hearing a frequency or if it's the actual sound of the planes, but it's very loud.

A: As it's dropping, what's happening to the life of the people there?

S: It starts out as it seems like nothing is happening. Then within a couple of minutes, and wherever the droplets fall, it's disintegrating, and there's a hissing sort of sound. It feels really bad in my abdomen.

A: Why do you think that they're doing this? When connecting to the others, do you all know why they're doing this to your planet?

S: I was looking up close at the planes, and now I am back in my sanctuary. I'm away from the humans now. I'm by myself. There's like big grass kind of palms and things around me and over me. I'm in the forest, again, as a sanctuary. They seem like they're a couple miles away.

A: Who's a couple miles away?

S: The humans.

A: So, this is all in the same location that this is occurring?

S: The forest jungle place that I'm in is really, really huge, and I can travel very fast. So, they are like right next to it, and then I'm somewhere in it.

A: In this forest place, these airplanes that are dropping the damage, are they just doing it in their area? Are they not doing it in your area? In your forest area?

S: Yeah, they're just doing it in their area because it seems like there's a kind of protection over this forest. It's like a collective protection.

A: This darkness that you were feeling, is it connected to this land where this is occurring at? That you had within you that you were releasing?

S: Yes. I'm looking for the answer if all of it is from there, or not. So at least most of it is from there. Yeah, it's there.

A: Let's go back there, as they continue to drop the hazards that's causing everything to go on fire. Keep moving time, tell me what's going on as they're doing this. What happens next?

S: Everyone is dead, it's just fire. Then that's when that cyborg sort of really dark, and ugly metal ship comes in. It's almost like they wanted to destroy all of that so that they could restart in this non-organic way that they wanted.

A: Let's continue connecting to this ship, now that that has occurred. What does this ship continue to do? What is its purpose, you think?

S: It's like a hub. I'm seeing that there are beings with lab coats doing work, with things like beakers, cylinders, and scientific materials. Where all the fire is outside, it's like there's going to be like a layer of metal over on top of all of it. Yeah, a lot of wires inside.

A: A lot of wires inside the ship?

S: Yeah, and it's almost like the ship is alive, but it's not.

A: Does it feel like an artificial intelligence? Is that what you mean by that?

S: Yes.

A: These scientists, these beings that are in there, what do they look like?

S: Really long, really skinny, pointy heads, and black eyes. I wonder if this is what, like a really dark, and negative Mantis looks like. They have a really long chin, skinny head with black eyes.

A: What is it that you think that they are doing? You said that they're essentially wanting to reset it, begin new, and you also mentioned that there are wires. Are they doing anything to this planet with what tools they have there?

S: Yeah, I keep hearing the word "colonizing" with the spider nest metaphor. It's like they're creating something, and then something in the ship connected with the wires is going to inject these little...they're not consciousness. I don't know how to explain it. Maybe bots? If you ever step into a spider nest, there's just babies everywhere. That's what I'm seeing.

A: The babies come out of the ship? Where are they coming out from?

S: Yeah, like they were built inside of the ship. I think that they can be created in multiple ways. It's almost like one of the scientists Beings could take a mixture, and then just dump it out on the ground, and then it would just start colonizing. It's hard to understand.

A: Now as these little spiders are coming out of the Earth, coming out of the ship, where are they going? In perspective to this planet.

S: Everywhere they possibly can, but it's so interesting because the forest is there, and it's even more that they can't see it. They're just not in the same frequency, but it's existing right next to it. Those spider things are literally going everywhere. It's almost like this is a mother computer sort of place. If this place had a function, that's what they would be trying to do to it would be to turn this land, this planet into a kind of mothership sort of place.

A: Would it be compared to kind of like how a virus starts spreading?

S: Yes, it would, these little things would replicate.

A: You said they are going everywhere on this planet?

S: Mm-hmm.

A: Once they go everywhere, is there something particular that they do?

S: They kind of form little, like webs or nests of energy or frequencies. So, I'm simultaneously seeing like spider nests or cobwebs, but these bots, and then also like, neural pathways in the brain. Kind of like how that looks like some areas are really dense, others are not.

A: Keep moving time. What keeps happening with what they're doing to this planet? Tell me what's going on next of importance.

S: At some point the forest can't be there anymore, and just doesn't exist in the same... like it's gone. I'm seeing other ships with other species coming to this very metal spidery place, maybe to get energy for those beings to come? Maybe that's why they're coming on other ships to like re-up on their energy supplies?

A: Do they look like the spider ship, or different?

S: They look like dark, sort of torpedo looking ships.

A: You said they come and go in, okay.

S: And this looks very large. The planet looks very big now, like four or five even of those other outside torpedo ships that are there.

A: This planet looks bigger. What do you mean by that like? Did it grow bigger?

S: I guess I can see beyond all of the destruction that was happening earlier, and now it's just like zoomed forward in time. It's just very metal, very dark. Yeah, so it would be the same size.

A: So, let's go back to right before you said that beautiful land that was protected before, how it was no longer able to be there. Let's go back there now to when that happened. You're there now. Tell me what's going on.

S: There's other beings like me that are there. The forest, all of the plants, and us worked together in some sort of way to ascend or split off.

A: You all work together. Do you mean like you all protect it and split it off?

S: It was a type of energy work that we did. We do it but it was very, very clean.

A: The energy was very clean?

S: Yeah, not that it was, like it was kind of easy to do.

A: You said there were more like you. Was it many or a little bit?

S: Probably 20.

A: Tell me as it splits off, what happens to that space, the land that's splitting off?

S: I heard Pleiadean. What I'm seeing is, if I was in space and I was looking, there would be all these beautiful star energies everywhere. It would almost be like a drop of water, and then inside of that drop of water would be this forest sort of planet... and it feels a lot better now.

A: What feels a lot better now?

S: The forest. It's just free. Looking at this scene feels a lot better than looking at the dark one.

A: Why is it that you think that you did this? Split it from the dark one?

S: Because our energy work was doing a really good job of keeping a boundary of protection. But it got to a point where we couldn't have that anymore. We needed to move on, and if we got tired, we didn't want the darkness to feed.

A: Going back to that dark planet, now that you all have removed this positivity from it. What happens to this planet now?

S: It still exists.

A: The dark planet?

S: Yes.

A: Continue forwarding time. You said they made it into this type of metallic planet with those different A.I. spiders. Does life ever grow back on it?

S: No.

A: Keep forwarding time and tell me if something changes within that planet.

S: I see Archangel Michael.

A: Where do you see him?

S: Above it with his Legion of Light, blue, white, coming from them to the planet, transmuting it, so that it can start over.

A: Explain that again. You see Michael and his Legion. Explain to me how Michael looks with his Legion. How are they there?

S: He has big blue wings, and golden energies around his hair. His Legion looks like white, wispy, moving energy. It's like the time has come for that planet to stop its infringing. So, they're using their light energies. To stop it.

A: Do they themselves have any ships, or how does that work?

S: I don't see any ships.

A: You just see the Angelic Legion?

S: Yeah.

A: Would you be able to connect me to Archangel Michael? We'd like to speak to Archangel Michael there within that time of space, working on that dark planet. Greetings brother.

AA Michael: Greetings.

A: Thank you. It's an honor to have you. We love you, honor you, and respect you. Thank you first of all, for you, and your beautiful Legion there. All of you are infinitely loved and beloved throughout Creation. Thank you for your work.

AA Michael: Thank you.

A: May I ask you questions?

AA Michael: Yes.

A: We've gone through this timeline of this planet that once had life, and then these dark beings came and turned it into this dark planet with a metallic type of infringement. Can you explain, can I ask you questions upon this please?

AA Michael: Yes.

A: Did these spider-like beings have any connection to Archons? Spider-like ships and different tiny spiders?

AA Michael: Yes.

A: Can you tell me more about that, please?

AA Michael: It seems as though that this large ship that was here and colonized this planet, was one of several large ships that came from an even bigger control room, a control panel room of sorts. This mothership was sent to this planetary structure, but it was not the only one that was sent. There were other planets that were affected as well.

A: She mentioned that there was this type of dark Mantis beings within the ship that were scientific. Were there any other beings there assisting with what they were doing there?

Serena: I don't know why; I'm hearing like a "dark goddess energy"?

A: Please allow for Michael to speak. Michael? Brother, what is this that she speaks of, this dark goddess energy? Can you explain that?

AA Michael: She's trying to conceptualize the way that these creatures replicate and create themselves. But it is not an organic structure that she is used to, so therefore, she is trying to come up with other explanations.

A: You said that these were from Archons and that they came from some kind of control panel. Can you explain that?

AA Michael: Yes, the ships are on those seeded, with the robotic technology. This is overseen by Archons, but it's assisted by other dark Beings who actually have the bodies and can do the technological work.

A: This control panel, can you explain a little further for us? Where is this control panel in relation to, is it a Dimension, a Universe, a different Universe? Where is it?

AA Michael: It is from another Universe, and these ships can travel in and out of it through using certain kinds of technology... to infiltrate other Universes.

A: These planets that they chose, was there a reason why they chose those? You said that there were several that they chose.

AA Michael: What I'm seeing is that these planets have a luminescent crystal sort of core.

A: These planets, are we familiar at all with them? I know Creation is infinite so that's a hard question. Are we familiar with any of them?

AA Michael: Nibiru. Was one of them.

A: What do they do to these planets like Nibiru, or this one, what is the purpose of them doing that? What do they get from that? Turning them into that darkness.

AA Michael: If they have more places to colonize, and populate that virus, then it is able to infiltrate more of the Universe.

A: Do they use them like source batteries?

AA Michael: Yes, because of that center. The light core center.

A: So even though they destroyed the life on the planet of it, on top of it, and there's still that light within the inside of the core of the planet?

AA Michael: Yes, it can be accessed through veins.

A: Are the veins similar to like ley lines?

AA Michael: When we said veins, Serena's body felt that darkness again, and that was being sucked out from the forest. So, these veins that I'm seeing now are organic looking in structure, so if that's what you would say a ley line is, then yes.

A: At an organic structure.

AA Michael: Yes.

A: Would you say it's a bit like they put a poison, into the veins, the ley lines of these planets?

AA Michael: Yes. It's very sad.

A: Does this have any connection to, for example, how our Earth here, how it became controlled with A.I. itself? Does Earth look a little bit, or similar like these planets that you're explaining? Or at some point they looked like it?

AA Michael: Can you repeat that question, please?

A: Michael, so you know how we talk about the Matrix system. We talk about how there's an Organic Matrix that originally was there, and then like an A.I. virus came into the planet, the construct of it. Does Earth look somewhat a little like that, or at some point looked a little bit like that? Or any correlation to Earth and the A.I. infiltration it had?

AA Michael: Yes. The vegetation on that planet feels similar to the living, organic, Eden sort of garden structure that existed on Earth at one point because the trees are so tall. What we're seeing here is the purity of this planet, of the consciousness, that there wasn't necessarily any protection up around it or inside of the vein lines. It would be easy to infect a planet, such as this. With an intelligent virus that could replicate quickly, and to get into the veins of the planet is to get into its core. Literally.

A: This Inverted A.I. Matrix we are in and we are trying to come out of, does it look a little bit like those planets in some way? Is it similar to how you said, how there was for example, this planet, how there was like this magical place, it was organic, and then the A.I. inverted control was right next to it? So, then we got the organic, and we got the A.I., and they were both interacting together. Well, they were both connected still, and then they removed the organic because it wasn't able to be there anymore. Is that how Earth is trying to find a connection, next to each other? How Serena explained the A.I. to one side and then the organic to another?

AA Michael: Yes, it's not that it couldn't have held it anymore, but it was that the time for that scenario to play out was over. So, in this way, this is very similar to what is happening on this current planet at now because we are in those times.

A: Is it like a split, like a New Earth split? Is that similar to what happened to that planet?

AA Michael: Yes, yes.

A: That part of the planet that wasn't able to, that was still dense. That you and your Legion, came and started transmuting. What is it that you were doing to that part of that planet?

AA Michael: Yes, we have been called here for that, and it has come to the decision that the time for these negative A.I. structures to exist is coming to its end...So it was time to remove the abomination.

A: How is it that you remove that abomination?

AA Michael: Through our very powerful Love-Light energies in our hearts, as a collective.

A: Take me through the process, Michael. This dark planet, you're using your Love-Light, what are you doing to it? Take me step-by-step on what you're doing, please.

AA Michael: We sync up our minds as a collective intention. Then we move our focus point down into the heart space, the energy is filtered through here, and is channeled through the collective intention towards the planet.

A: Okay, what does that cause?

AA Michael: It's disintegrating, like a zero point, like it's nothing after.

A: What about this spider-like ship, what happens to all those A.I.?

AA Michael: No, because we put a bubble around it first.

A: So, when your Legion arrived, you encased it in a bubble?

AA Michael: Yes.

A: Can you tell me more about what this bubble looks like?

AA Michael: It is golden, and very radiant, and is made of geometry.

A: Does it have like, alchemy symbols within it?

AA Michael: Yes.

A: You said "we." Who places this bubble around?

AA Michael: I see Metatron's six-pointed cubic star and Flower of Life.

A: Beautiful. Once it's encased, you said that it's disintegrating. I know that you said that you're using your Love-Light. Is your Love-Light what's neutralizing it, disintegrating it?

AA Michael: Yes.

A: Okay, and what happens to all that dark energy there, as it's transmuting?

AA Michael: It's vaporized. Through this whole process it's contained within the alchemy bubble, and with more Love-Light energy it disintegrates, and is recycled into golden energy.

A: What happened to those souls that they had harmed, that they had killed?

AA Michael: They went to a place for clearing after that lifetime, before they moved on to their next destination as a soul. They went to a kind of healing center.

A: I had asked her the question, but if I could ask you, Michael, as well? They had said that they had chosen several planets that they were going to do this, to harvest a light core within them. I asked her, where did they come from, and she had said that they came from another Universe. Is that accurate, or is there anymore you can share on that?

AA Michael: To find words for it is challenging because it is almost like the fabric of space opening and closing, kind of like, the beams open up and close. (moving hands) I don't have the words for what that is.

A: Are they opening up a portal with technology? Jumping through Universes?

AA Michael: Yeah, it must be because I don't think that the Universe would open naturally for an energy like that.

A: If I may share what I'm being shown, Michael?

AA Michael: Yes, please.

A: So, what you all are showing me is that it's like a cycle for them where they harvest the planet, and then that light itself gives some power to keep doing this. Keep jumping, the light that they stole from the planet, they jump to another. It's what powers their negative technology to be able to go through spaces where they're not normally meant to be able to?

AA Michael: Yes. It has a lot of power to it.

A: Okay. Then how we're talking about Michael, the ley lines are there, and how she was explaining how there were veins. I know we've talked about, in the past, how through Inner Earth Guardian, Adama, as well as Osirus. We talked about how they're also connected to energetic pyramids, that there's a Galactic War going on. Is this at all connected to that?

AA Michael: The mechanism of attaching and seeking out organic planets, harming them, and harvesting their energy is a piece of what is going on inside of the Galactic Wars. There is a lot of work that some beings are called to do at this time, to travel and connect with these different places of power. Like you say the pyramids, so that the organic, crystalline structure underneath them can be purified, and can remain pure. So, if you are discussing Galactic War, in that the Archonic energies are infringing on these veins, ley lines, in this way, then this is a piece of what is occurring at this time. Ley line guardians and the negatives.

A: Tell me Michael, what can we do here on Earth to assist with this, that you mentioned?

AA Michael: One of the most powerful things that we can do is to be shielded, travel physically to these places, and bring the crystals you use that are encoded themselves with sacred alchemy. So, that they cannot be corrupted with, as well, and so we ask that as many Beings as possible are able to go with their physical body, in protection, with their forcefields. That they enter, and sometimes if they could go with groups of more than one person. The energy will be more powerful as long as both parties have the intent and the protection around them. What they can do is go to these places, anchor in this light, and perform this radical clearing energy at these ley lines, together, in a sacred act of service.

A: Beautiful, thank you. May all, who reads this information, understand the importance of this, and continue to aid Mother Earth in this manner. Thank you for that, Michael.

AA Michael: Absolutely, and what can also be done is that if the Being cannot physically go to a location, we can always connect with the ley lines through the energy of the water at this time. What the being can find underneath their sacred alchemy, is that they can connect with the pure water within their cells, bones and crystalline structures within their body. Then you connect in your heart frequency, merging at the same time with Gaia herself, and her crystalline core. From that point, you become this organic planet. Then you will be guided with the benevolent beings to direct healing energies to certain places. You will find that the healing will occur in those places on the planet, and it will also occur in your own bodies. As well as especially if you're connecting with the waters at this time. Which is one of the easiest things to do, in connection with sacred healing. You can also charge your own sacred waters with this healing alchemy, and then that water is also multidimensionally charged into the whole of the planet. Affecting the ley lines themselves.

A: Beautiful. Thank you for that as well. That's been something that you have been communicating to me. Thank you for the added details to it. The planet that has A.I., is it transmuting straight back to zero?

AA Michael: Yes, it must. It does not have a consciousness to positive-polarize. So, it must be transmuted. The actual transmutation process with the Love-Light adds in an organic essence to it. How it can be recycled.

A: Good. I just wanted to clarify. This really reminds me of Earth and how it's splitting, the dark from the light. Is there anything else you wanted to add on that?

AA Michael: All I'm hearing is that the way that we can also be of assistance to these children is connected with the waters, as well. Almost like an encoding information, sort of way. We can send it to them through the waters of the Earth. But they are also one with the Earth. So, it's like just sending it to them as well. Does that make sense?

A: Yes, that does. Thank you. This was a missing puzzle piece to our first book. Michael, these Archonic takeovers, if you're able to explain. For example, let's just say this Universe, since this

Universe is ascending. What percentage do you think as far as planets in this Universe, have been infringed upon like this, taken over? Like the one you explained where they're collecting from the core light of the planet?

AA Michael: Fifty percent.

A: That's a lot.

AA Michael: At its darkest time in history, it was 50 percent.

A: What shifted that? Is it still at 50 percent? What would you say, roughly? I know time doesn't exist, but where are we at now?

AA Michael: We would say that the percentage is around 15 to 30 percent.

A: Okay, and what was the big shift that happened that turned it into 50 percent? How did that occur? Such a high amount, I think.

AA Michael: What I'm seeing first is collective thought forms of imagining the worst, and this can be programmed through the multitude of negative video games simulations, negative movies and games, and other energies such as this. Because at certain times if large amounts of Beings are thinking those negative thoughts depending on the activations, the portals, and the energies that are happening in the Ascension of the Universe. It can almost... infiltrate or hijack in a way. This is a way of creating negative timelines.

A: By having collective focus on negative thoughts, you can create negative timelines?

AA Michael: Yes, combined with charged emotions.

A: You said that they do it through forms of negative technologies, feeding into them?

AA Michael: Yes, the reason it is down to 15 percent to 25 percent now is because there were fractals, and fractals, and fractals of the Beings in service, who needed to hunker down, and assist in the protection of these planets.

A: Many are assisting with the protection of the planets? The many, many fractals?

AA Michael: Yes.

A: How important has the work that we've done, for example, through these A.U.R.A. regressions with the millions, and billions, and the hundreds and thousands of Reptilians that we kept assisting to positive Ascension. Did that aid in any form?

AA Michael: Absolutely. It is through the alchemy and sacredness of the container that the consciousness is able to travel into these other places with such clarity, and therefore be able to have permission to also heal these scenarios, as well. Because when you are in session with one Being who comes to us, in actuality, it is like we are working with hundreds of Beings because of the multidimensional expressions of that one being, who is coming to the A.U.R.A. practitioner. Therefore, the healing that occurs within that Being in that consciousness also ripples into, affects many other lifetimes, and many other Beings in different souls. Even whole soul families at one time, for example.

A: Very good, thank you. I think that's all the questions I have for now on this. This is a very, very much needed session. Thank you. I can't thank her enough for this. Michael, Higher Self, is this a good time to begin her body scan please?

Higher Self: Yes.

The Body Scan begins.

A: Thank you, Michael. Higher Self, would you like any assistance from any other Archangels for her body scan?

Higher Self: The first answer was all of them with a smile, and then Archangel Raphael.

A: Okay, can we work with Michael, and then Raphael? And then of course all of them are always there.

Higher Self: Yes.

A: Beautiful. Michael, since you are here already, it's going to be a wonderful continuation. Michael, if we can go ahead and start with scanning her body from head to toe. Looking for any negative energies and entities. What needs healing within her first, please? Where would you like to start off?

AA Michael: We're going to start at the crown. There is something in her head in the center, perhaps around the pineal.

A: Let's scan that area now, Michael. Tell me what is there in her pineal gland? Is that an energy, entity, a technology?

AA Michael: It is an energy. It's reminiscent of the darkness she experienced that was being pulled out in that other lifetime... it's kind of pulsating.

A: In that life where she was going from the negative to the positive plane, and then all that darkness was coming out of her?

AA Michael: Yeah.

A: Okay, so what is it that's pulsating within her, that energy does it have a consciousness? Is that why it's pulsating? Or what's causing the pulsation?

AA Michael: It must be an entity or a consciousness of some kind because it's not inorganic. It's, I mean it's an energy.

A: It is an energy or entity?

AA Michael: I think it's an entity.

A: Michael, is that a Reptilian consciousness, an entity, Archon, what is it?

AA Michael: This is a Reptilian.

A: Michael, can you go ahead and surround it with the alchemy symbols, please?

AA Michael: Yes.

A: Thank you. Let me know when it's surrounded.

AA Michael: It's surrounded.

A: Beautiful. Let's go ahead and find all of them. Michael, can we scan her for any other Reptilians? Does she have anymore or Archons within her? Tell me, what else do you see?

AA Michael: Archon in the heart.

A: If we could call on Metatron to surround that Archon with the alchemy symbols, please.

AA Michael: Yes.

A: Thank you, Metatron we love you, honor you, and respect you. Thank you for being here. Surround it now, please. Let me know when it is surrounded.

AA Metatron: Surrounded.

A: Good. If we could start neutralizing it out of her heart, please now.

AA Metatron: Mm-hmm.

A: Brother Raphael?

AA Raphael: Yes.

A: Welcome, brother. We love you, honor you, and respect you. As we're neutralizing this Archon out of her heart, if you can start filling in Love-Light and healing it, please.

AA Raphael: Yes.

A: Let's continue scanning her body. Any other Reptilians or Archons?

AA Michael: Something in her liver. It is a consciousness, a Reptilian, at least one, maybe two.

A: Can we surround it now, please, with Metatron, with alchemy symbols?

AA Michael: Yes.

A: Let me know when it's surrounded. Thank you.

AA Michael: We are finding a third.

A: Where?

AA Michael: In that right abdomen area. And they are surrounded now.

A: Reptilians?

AA Michael: Yes.

A: Let's scan her again. We want to make sure we don't miss any, as you know they can be sneaky sometimes and hide. Michael, Metatron, any other Reptilians or Archons within her. Also scan her spine, and her DNA structure for any negative fractals in there as well. Anything that's not organically part of her Soul.

AA Michael: There is something in her ovaries.

A: What is it?

AA Michael: Like negative consciousness seeds. She has been abducted before in dream time, and has had them injected, so we are surrounding those now with the alchemy symbols.

A: You said they're negative consciousness, would you say they're negative entities or what kind of consciousness are they?

AA Michael: Like bots.

A: Metatron, since they're bots, if we can surround them with the proper symbols please. Let's start neutralizing them out of her ovaries, please.

AA Michael: There's one Reptilian in the left side. We can surround that now.

A: Surround that one with the Reptilian symbols, please.

AA Michael: Yes. There is some kind of dark fractal in the spine.

A: What kind of dark fractal is that? Is that an Archon or an entity, Reptilian?

AA Michael: It's like dark codes.

A: Can you explain that further, Michael?

AA Michael: Yes. This was placed in the spine as a contract, in a way to sort of see if Serena would choose which direction she was going to choose. This contract is over now, and we can remove this negative timeline.

A: Metatron, if you all can start working on removing that and neutralizing that out. Have Michael remove that contract, and then have Raphael start filling Love-Light as soon as that's done to that area where the coding was at. Anything else in her spine that needs healing? In her DNA?

AA Michael: It's like the spinal structure or fluid needs a boost. Needs like a recharge of crystalline energies and the DNA has some decay. This is from her negative time as a younger version. We can heal that now.

A: Wonderful, thank you. Okay, we are filling in Love-Light to her whole DNA strands, and her spine making it at the brightest is meant to be organically. Raphael, Higher Self, working on that place healing that. Thank you. Let's scan her body one more time before we start speaking to these entities. Are there any other Reptilians, Archons, any type of entities?

AA Michael: No, that's everything. We're not sure if it's the entity in her head that we've already surrounded or if the actual brain tissue needs a new charge. Like if you were to pour like a special kind of very healing plasma water on it, that's what it needs.

A: Can we, can we ask her Higher Self to pour over that water, and perhaps for Archangel Gabriel who works with water. Can we ask Gabriel to assist?

AA Michael: Yes.

A: Okay, beautiful. Let's start the process now. Thank you. Let's go ahead and start talking to the Reptilians. We have Reptilians in the pineal gland, and liver, right abdomen, and ovaries. Any of them connected to one another?

AA Michael: The liver and the ovary ones are connected. The one in the head is different.

A: Let's talk first to the one in the head, please. Michael, if you could help us connect to the one in her head. Let's bring it up, up, up now. Greetings.

Reptilian: Greetings.

A: Thank you, for speaking to us. Love you, honor you, and respect you. May we ask you questions, please?

Reptilian: Yes.

A: Thank you. When was it that you attached there to her pineal gland?

Reptilian: I attached to her third eye during a psychedelic experience with other people around. She was very open, and that's when I came in, and she was scared.

A: She was scared, do you mean like during the psychedelic experience?

Reptilian: Yes.

A: Okay, that's why you attached because she was scared.

Reptilian: Yeah, she lowered her defenses.

A: Plus, you know, the influence of a psychedelic. What have you been causing her there?

Reptilian: I send her confusing, conflicting messages on top of that are overlaid over top of the messages from love. So that she has to constantly ask, over and over again, if the message is clear or the message is correct? Or was it this message or was it that message? Or was it this one or that one?

A: Is there a Reptilian body that you are connected to?

Reptilian: Yes.

A: Please connect us now to the Reptilian body that you are connected to, please. We would like to speak to it now.

Reptilian: Okay. Hello.

A: Greetings. Thank you for speaking to us. Love you, honor you, and respect you. May I ask you questions, please?

Reptilian Body: Yes.

A: Thank you. If I can ask, where is it that you are located at?

Reptilian Body: I'm inside of a ship.

A: The ship is located where?

Reptilian Body: Around Earth.

A: In this ship is there any more than you in it?

Reptilian Body: Yes.

A: How many more are there, Reptilians?

Reptilian Body: There are five others.

A: There are only six of you there in the ship?

Reptilian Body: There are five, including me.

A: Is this a smaller ship or is there a reason why there's only five of you on the ship?

Reptilian Body: Yes, we are in a small ship that is sent from a larger, bigger ship. We are spies.

A: Tell me how are you like spies? Are you spies through the ship?

Reptilian Body: Yes, and we connect through the sight of certain energy beings.

A: Have you been using her to do this to? Connecting to her sight?

Reptilian Body: Yes. She didn't realize it, but this is why she's gotten headaches in the past, and also, vertigo.

A: Thank you. As you know, the Earth is ascending, the Universe is ascending, and we are helping Reptilians who are negative polarized positive ascend. No longer having to play this negative role. Instead, you could create your own light, and become positive in your Ascension. Would you allow for us to assist you today, so you no longer have to play that role?

Reptilian Body: Yes.

A: Beautiful. If all of you now, we're going to focus Love-Light upon that ship that you all are in, the five of you. We are sending Love-Light to you now. Find the light within you, and spread it to all that is of you, every root, every cord, every part of you. The consciousness that is attached to her pineal gland, spreading to Love-Light as well. You five, are there any others that you're attached to, besides her?

Reptilian Body: Yes.

A: How many more are you attached to?

Reptilian Body: Two hundred.

A: Archangel Raphael, brother, if you can find the 200 of those Higher Selves. Ask them if they will allow us to remove those consciousnesses that are attached to them, please.

AA Raphael: Yes.

A: Let me know what they say.

AA Raphael: Yes, this is finished.

A: It's done? We did the work?

AA Raphael: This infringement such as this, is finished.

A: Very good. Let's start helping them, those 200, spread their light. Raphael, Michael, Metatron bring them back to the five Reptilians there. If I could call on Archangel Azrael now?

AA Azrael: Yes.

A: Welcome, Brother. We love you, honor you, and respect you. Azrael, as you supervise, make sure that those consciousness turn to light. Integrating back into them, making themselves whole once more. Let us know once more when they are whole once more, and of light.

AA Azrael: They are ready.

A: Beautiful. If we can have Raphael fill in Love-Light to those 200 that they had attached to, as well, and start healing that space where they were at. Now, that you five are whole once more, do you have a message for her before you go?

Positive Polarized Reptilians: No. Thank you.

A: Go ahead and go with the Love-Light of the Universe. Archangel Azrael, take them where they are meant to go for their highest Ascension. Blessings to all of you. Azrael, where is it that you're taking them?

AA Azrael: We are taking them to the center for healing before they move on and choose their next role in the Ascension.

A: Good. Blessings to all of you. Thank you. Michael, the liver, the right abdomen, the ovaries. They're all connected to the Reptilians there?

AA Michael: Yes.

A: How many are there, between these places?

AA Michael: Seven?

A: Michael, if you can please help guide them. We would like to speak to them now if you could come up, up now, please.

Reptilians: Yes.

A: Greetings. Thank you for speaking to us. Love you, honor you, and respect you. May we ask you questions, please?

Reptilians: Yes.

A: Thank you. Those seven of you, did you all come in at the same time or at different times?

Reptilians: Different times.

A: Okay, let's speak to the one in the liver. When did you come in?

Reptilians: At a time of pain and drinking alcohol. That's where we all came in, essentially.

A: She mentioned that she was a heavy drinker, and she would go through episodes where she would pass out, lose time.

Reptilians: Yes.

A: Did you have anything to do with her?

Reptilians: Yes, that's where the ovaries infringement very easily occurred more than once.

A: Tell me, what were you causing her by being in these areas?

Reptilians: In the liver, we blocked detoxification. In the intention of keeping her as dense as we could possibly do. The ovary infringement is due to the powerful energies she keeps in her womb. We could not have infringed any other way.

A: Okay, thank you. Are you connected to any Reptilian bodies anywhere else?

Reptilians: The ones in the ovaries are.

A: You in the liver and the right abdomen are not?

Reptilians: Right.

A: We're offering the same to you as well, just as the others that positive ascended. Would you allow for us to help you spread your light, no longer having to play this role anymore? You would be your own creator being, creating your own light.

Reptilians: Okay.

A: Beautiful. Go ahead and find your light within you. Sending you light now, Love-Light, spread it to every root, every cord, every part of you. Let us know once you are all light.

Positive Polarized Reptilians: Okay.

A: Go ahead and release yourself out from those areas. Make sure you don't leave any piece of you behind. Azrael if you could please guide them to where they're meant to go. Do you all have a message for her before you go?

Positive Polarized Reptilians: Thank you for allowing us in as we have had the opportunities to learn much through this experience.

A: Blessings to you both. May you be surrounded by the Love-Light of the Universe. Thank you. Michael, connect us now to the Reptilians there in her ovaries. If you could come up, up, up now, please.

Reptilians: Yes.

A: Greetings. Thank you for speaking to us, we love you, honor you, and respect you. May we ask you questions please?

Reptilians: Sure.

A: Thank you. When was it that you attached there to her ovaries?

Reptilians: We don't remember.

A: Was it this life or another?

Reptilians: It was through the maternal line, passed from mother to mother.

A: I was told that you have Reptilian bodies elsewhere. Would you be able to connect us to them now, please?

Reptilians: Yes.

A: Let me speak to them now, the Reptilian body you are connected to.

Reptilian Body: Greetings.

A: Thank you for speaking to us love you, honor you, respect you. May we ask you questions?

Reptilian Body: Yes.

A: Thank you. Where are you currently at?

Reptilian Body: We are currently existing on a planet.

A: Can you tell me more about this planet?

Reptilian Body: We are involved in hybridization projects for negative agendas.

A: Is there something that you're doing to her ovaries for this hybridization program?

Reptilian Body: We are using the eggs to create other species.

A: Is this a contract?

Reptilian Body: Yes.

A: Why do you need her eggs to create another species?

Reptilian Body: So that we can learn the mechanisms of creation through studying potent eggs like these. She is not the only one this is occurring with. Many un-awakened divine feminines.

A: Is this something positive or negative?

Reptilian Body: Negative. To stop Ascension.

A: Those eggs that you're taking, do you all create them into life forms, but not in a very positive way?

Reptilian Body: Yes.

A: Can you tell me more on that?

Reptilian Body: We pull the eggs for different projects. Some are for life. Some are for experimentation on. We are studying the ways of manipulating the natural instincts of humans to be more in natural assistance to negativity.

A: Are you making those eggs into humans?

Reptilian Body: Sometimes, yes.

A: Do you use them in forms of cloning?

Reptilian Body: What I'm seeing is that they are taken out for several reasons. One of the reasons could be to take them out. Manipulate them in a scientific manner, and then put them back into the female body, so that the creation act occurs. That there can be this egg used, so that this human will have a negative fractal within them, and they are easier to control than another.

A: You mentioned it was a contract. When did Serena agree to this contract?

Reptilian Body: When she didn't want to be alive anymore in this lifetime, when she was younger.

A: Are there any others you're attached to besides her? And how many of you are there?

Reptilian Body: We are attached to 40,000. There are 200 on this planet.

A: On this planet, is there any other life besides what you're doing there, cloning?

Reptilian Body: There are also some Mantis helping with the experiments.

A: How many Mantis are there?

Reptilian Body: About 15.

A: Anyone else besides them?

Reptilian Body: No.

A: Would you be able to connect us to the Mantis and all of you as a collective, please?

Collective: Yes.

A: Thank you. We're speaking to all of you there within this planet who is part of this hybridization program. We love you, honor you, and respect you. As you know, the Earth is ascending, and as it's ascending, so is the Universe. These negative polarizations of using the techniques that you all are using are no longer needed. We'd love to be able to assist you today so that you no longer have to play this role. No longer having to infringe upon people in this manner. Instead, you can transform into Love-Light for Ascension. No longer having to drain from someone's light and so on. Would you allow for us to assist you today?

Collective: Yes, please.

A: Beautiful, and that's including the Mantis as well?

Collective: Yes.

A: Michael, can you all supervise? Make sure no one gets harmed or tricked. Raphael, if you could start helping them spread their light. We're all focusing on you now. Spread your light to every part within those bodies, those 40,000 that are attached to. Raphael, brother, can you ask those 40,000 that are attached to, will they allow for us to help them detach, and spread those consciousnesses into light that are in them?

AA Raphael: Yes

A: Do all 40,000 say yes?

AA Raphael: Yes, the time is now.

A: Start helping, all of you. Raphael, and your Legion, spreading Love-Light to all 40,000 of them. As they continue to spread their light, if we can have Azrael and his Legion supervise and make sure as they're spreading their light for them to come back, to the ones that are there in that planet, the Mantis and the Reptilians. Becoming whole once more.

AA Raphael: Yes.

A: Let us know once all of them are back and they're whole once more.

AA Raphael: They are.

A: Beautiful. Let's start healing those 40,000 that they were attached to. Spreading their Love-Light. Out of those 40,000, any of them part of this hybridization as well?

AA Raphael: Yes.

A: Okay, good, helping them heal whatever their Higher Selves allow. Whatever they can heal, to remove the negativity from. Now all of you there, you've made you whole once more. Let me speak to the Mantis there?

Positive Polarized Mantis: Hello.

A: Greetings. Thank you for speaking to us. Now that you're of light, are you still in the Mantis form? Are you a different type of form?

Positive Polarized Mantis: I am in Mantis form.

A: Are you of light now, though?

Positive Polarized Mantis: Yes, my heart connection has been made to my mental capacity.

A: Do you have any messages for her before you go?

Positive Polarized Mantis: She is a very strong and powerful Being and is ready to claim it.

A: Thank you for your messages. How about the Reptilians? Now that you are whole, do you have a message for her?

Positive Polarized Reptilians: Thank you

A: Thank you as well. Go ahead and go with the Love-Light of the Universe. Blessings to all of you. Azrael, and Legion, if you go guide them to where they are meant to go. Raphael and your Legion, if you can start healing her, as well as the others, making sure they're all healed. Okay, we're healing her ovaries, her right abdomen, liver as well, pineal gland from earlier. Michael, can you scan her one more time? We want to make sure she doesn't have any more Reptilians, and while you're doing that, the Archon in her heart, is that neutralized out completely?

AA Raphael: Yes.

A: Good. Raphael, heal that as well, please. Okay, how about the ones, those bots that were in her ovaries? Are those completely neutralized out?

AA Raphael: They need fire.

A: Okay, we're using Phoenix Fire there now. Is it both ovaries...?

AA Raphael: Yes.

A: Michael, scan her one more time. Does she have any other entities, Reptilians, Archons, anything else that's not part of her organically?

AA Michael: There's implants behind her eyes.

A: Okay, but as far as entities, Reptilians, or Archons, does she have any more?

AA Michael: No, she's clear.

A: Good. Can we start using Phoenix Fire on the implant that she has behind her eyes?

AA Michael: Yes.

A: Thank you. Michael. Can you tell me when was it that this attached there?

AA Michael: Not sure.

A: Are we transmuting it out now?

AA Michael: Yes.

A: Good, using Phoenix Fire there now. Just let us know once it's out. Let's go ahead and scan her for any other negative implants, hooks, or portals. Let me know if you see any.

AA Michael: No, she's done a good job.

A: Beautiful. She had a couple health issues that I think will be connected to everything we already started healing, but I want to make sure if there's anything else. Were the Reptilians in her liver, abdomen, were they the root cause to her issues with her food? Overeating, sensitivity, eating weird times?

AA Michael: Yes, and that was also connected to the famine, starvation energy from her mother line. We're also finding something inorganic in her throat.

A: Okay, what is it?

AA Michael: A portal.

A: Can we have Michael please close the portal?

AA Michael: Yes.

A: Thank you. Anything else inorganic within her?

AA Michael: No.

A: Okay, and then on the random stabbing in her vagina. What was it connected to?

AA Michael: This is from unresolved pain from abuse.

A: Michael, can you go back to when, what abuse is that from? Is that from this life or another?

AA Michael: Another life.

A: Did she experience any sexual abuse as a child this life? She's felt that she perhaps saw, through her self-hypnosis she did, a memory of being kidnapped, fear memory. What was that about? Was that a real one? Was that fake?

AA Michael: It was real.

A: It was from this life or another? How does this kidnapping fear memory come about for her?

AA Michael: We are coming in to speak clearly over her mind and that this is connected to a one-time incident.

A: One-time incident, when? This life or another?

AA Michael: We want to say that it's this life. She also has mental chatter.

A: Higher Self, help to calm herself, and step to the side, and allow Michael and team to speak so we can help her heal. She mentioned that she wants to get to the root of everything, so it's important she does this. Help her, step to the side. Michael, if you could tell us more about this please, let's get to the root of this.

AA Michael: This memory was real. It was something that did happen, and it has laid the foundation for un-comfortability during sexual encounters for reasons she has never completely understood why.

A: What is it that happened? … What's going on Michael?

AA Michael: She's having a block.

A: Is there a block in her? Is that a block in her body?

AA Michael: The block is mental. Did it happen, did it not? Am I making it up? Am I not? Sort of back and forth. Chatter.

A: If you could allow Archangel Michael, his beautiful protective energy to flow through you. Just let him speak, and so he can declutter all that clutter out, and find the answers. Communicate the answers. Michael, what is the accurate answer for that? Surrender.

AA Michael: We are not sure what good it will do to paint the image in detail.

A: Was this something that happened in this life?

AA Michael: It has been more than one life.

A: Does it have any connection with that male that she saw with two females, and the male was trying to come after her, and she said she ran?

AA Michael: Yes.

A: Did she actually run, or did they catch her or what actually happened there?

AA Michael: Yes, that time she did run because that was after this event, which we are telling her that it was not a long event. It was a small blip.

A: Does it have anything to do with that neighbor, little girl or how is this connected?

AA Michael: There was a sort of shed. We happen to be outside at the same time, and we were brought inside of the shed.

A: Who brought you there?

AA Michael: This man and those women.

A: This was an occasion before the occasion where she ran?

AA Michael: Yes.

A: So, this man and this woman put the two girls in that shed?

AA Michael: Yes.

A: What happened there?

AA Michael: It was like they were really drunk. They were drinking, and they had the two girls in there. They are so little and innocent and didn't understand and had them act out an adult scene very quickly, and then they got out of that shed somehow. It wasn't a struggle per se, it was like there's these just like really drunk adults.

A: If we just start healing that trauma for her, please, Raphael. Can we do that?

AA Michael: Yes.

A: Thank you, and you said that this began her sexual issues?

AA Michael: Yes, absolutely. She's right now, like a muscle contraction, through the whole body. It infiltrated into sexual experiences because she hasn't been able to let go because there's some kind of un-comfortability there.

A: Can we start healing that throughout her body, please?

AA Michael: Yes.

A: Thank you. Now that we found the root, let's go ahead and heal that now, with the Higher Self, Raphael. Higher Self, is there a certain name that you go by?

Higher Self: Isis.

A: Beautiful. Isis. Michael, Metatron, Collective of Angels, Higher Self, scan her one last time. Make sure there's nothing else that she has within her that needs healing.

Isis: She's good,

A: Beautiful. Thank you. It has been such an honor to work with her today. What a phenomenal session. She is truly a gem. A gem she is to Creation. Thank you. Well of course you know, Isis who brought us this information. Beautiful. Isis, do you have any message for her so we can conclude this session? Anything else that I could have asked that I haven't?

Isis: Our message that we have for her at this time is to move in a place of humble, humble, humble heart, open wide, open heart frequency, and to look to Gaia for answers, and surrender her mind. That this is confirmation that she's not going to find the answers through the mind. That it's going to come through surrendering to the heart, and Gaia in tandem, in connection, and to be practicing the ocean whale modality that will be downloaded this year.

A: Beautiful. To which modality?

Isis: She is receiving information on using the ocean water as an energy field for transmutation and DNA activation. She has been receiving little pieces of this, and we are telling her to move with confidence, that she is not making it up.

A: Wonderful. Thank you for all this wisdom and knowledge today. My infinite love to everyone, Michael, Metatron, Gabriel, Isis, the Collective of Angels, any benevolent Beings that assisted today. Thank you for your aid, and our infinite love as well to all those entities that ascended today. It has been a joy to work with you all. Love you, honor you, respect you.

Isis: We love you so much, Aurora (crying). You are so beautiful, and doing such profound work for this world, and for so many souls. We love you. We thank you. We honor you.

A: Oh, thank you, it made me cry. Oh, that means so much to me, from you, my sister, and everyone else. I can feel your love and thank you for your support. I know it gets hard sometimes, but I know that I have all of you. Thank you. You all keep me going.

Isis: (laughs) We love you.

A: I love you all with all that I am. May bring her back now?

Isis: Yes.

A: Thank you for such a beautiful message. I needed that. I'm going to bring her back now.

END OF SESSION

This eye-opening session brought us much needed knowledge in ways that the Archons can go into the Universes, and why they do it. How they can turn a beautiful, high dimensional planet into becoming part of their collective inorganic battery sources, within their Inverted A.I. Matrix systems. As we learned how the organic power and light that can be harnessed from one planet is immeasurable, becoming into a grand energetic feeding for the Archons when conquering a planet and making what once was organic into inorganic. This session reminds us of Chapter 8 ('Four RA Guardians Heal Thousands of Entities'), in how a soul is an infinite light that can be turned into a source of power as we learnt in this session. And why it is that soul replacements are highly sought after for the Archons. By taking a collective of souls through their forms of negative harvesting, and then place them by joining their lights together in one large containment of negative technology to serve as a battery source for the Archons. This would obtain them vastness of potentials, through feeding on these collected souls' light batteries, providing power for their negative technology to keep destructively invading Creation throughout.

This crucial knowledge helps us have a conscious awareness in how these infringements may be felt throughout the Universes. When they take the 'Life Force' power of a planet, and poison it by using some of these negative technologies such as Archon A.I. spider mothers who birth Archon A.I. spider bots as a virus. How they invade a Universe that is balanced and how they overstep Universal Laws in this manner to offset the balance by making a true divine planet into an inorganic density that it is not meant to be. One can imagine and feel the havoc and harm these Archon infringements can cause a Universe which functions as one interconnected living construct system for all beings. The mention that, at our worst point our Universe was at 50 percent planets compromised with these A.I. spider bots, but now we are at 15-25 percent. This is a huge stride, that brings forth such awareness, which then turns into strong hope. Knowing that we have evolved, transmuted, healed enough as a collective Universe.

We deepen our understanding of how our Earth can be viewed energetically. Where in one part there is the Inverted A.I. Matrix system, for example, the Archon spider bots, and in the other part there is a very much alive existence parallel to it that is organic and trying to hold onto its original, uninfringed Divine Earth's blueprint. These two versions, existing side by side to one another.

Is this what our Earth can possibly look and feel like when it physically splits into two in 'The Event,' converting and ascending into the Fifth Dimension or 'The New Earth,' as it has been explained through various forms of hypnosis healing sessions (outside of AURA)? Is this where the light Organic Matrix side of Earth will detach itself and lift its vibration finally high enough to go into the Fifth Dimension, and the denser part of Earth will be taken to a space of self-healing for a future organic opportunity into a collective or individualized Ascension process once more?

The Hybridization negative program mentioned, has been going on Earth since the beginning of when the infringement of Archons began to taint Earth. Why humans? It is because we are on Earth, expressing ourselves through our human vessels, but truly we are the multitude of races all into one world and construct. Therefore, if you take this many blends of alien races and they breed throughout time and space, to the Archons this can be seen as creating a super soldier with many combinations of abilities, the potentials of our Universe's races placed all into one easy attainable location. However, to the benevolence, it is seen instead more as the beauty of life of the multitudes of Creation all placed into one communal location. Since we are at the deepest forgetfulness and distortion, the Archons find it the easiest to perform their Hybridization experiments on us, as we can easily consent. For example, when Serena no longer wanted to live at a younger age. We must realize when we make strong statements and affirmations as these, often a negative entity who is looking to assist you with what you are asking for, even if it's negative. They are ready and willing to answer your call, at the same exact time as your guides and angels are telling you not to do so, not to agree to their infringement. But yet we do, as we are unable to hear the benevolent guides through our despair and pain, as we are just not the matching frequency to hear them.

The specifics of experimenting on human eggs so that when they become fertilized, they create a more receptive and controllable type of soul and offspring. Once born, they then would monitor them in every way possible to see how their experiment is going, and if they are perhaps gaining light more rapidly than they would like. They would then abduct them to perform further negative experiments to oppress that light. I have met a few of these types of children, and the way they feel is artificial, soulless, and in a sense perhaps as a A.I. Grey would feel. Their light is extremely unnoticeable and almost at a void. There are many who feel that they are part of these Hybridization programs whether it's the parents or the children, that they can't seem to consciously remember. That they can only recall vaguely through glimpses of memory lapses in their dreams or meditation.

The thought of these inorganic experiments feels twisted in the heart with a great sadness, because of how much I value a soul and the knowing of how much the Divine Creator of this Universe infinitely loves all souls birthed forth. This is one of the deepest levels of distortion. These groups led by Archons, have NO RIGHT to do this to any soul, as they are not anyone's property as the free willed souls that they are within their creational makeup. The Archons are bypassing some of the strongest and most sacred laws of Creation by doing so. In Chapter 32 ('Not of Light'), we will find out at the clearest reason why they feel that they have the power to do so.

These last few Chapters are crucial in placing the understanding of the opposition of what our Universe and Multiverse is working through against the Archons. In the next Chapter, we receive the next puzzle piece with more information of these types of negative technologies, in how the Archons are jumping in and out through the Universes artificially breaking through Universal constructs to do so, as a complete violation of Universal Laws.

**"Rise and release the pain.
Spread those wings wide and soar through the winds of infinite change."
~AuroRa** 🖤

-------------<◇>-------------

31

LOOKING GLASS TECHNOLOGY

Session #289: Recorded July 2020.
Never before shared.

In this online A.U.R.A. Hypnosis Healing session, Sandra travels to a life that still holds her in trauma without being able to move on. In this fascinating session, we journey to the highest Dimension yet done through an A.U.R.A. Hypnosis Healing session where we meet a sacred race. When Archon races from unknown realms join together, and what does that look like? We go the deepest we have ever gone, understanding what Archons are, how they operate, and their powerful technologies. Through what forms do they jump from Universe to Universe? What is the extent of their destructive infringements and invasions throughout the organic Multiverse?

"They have it inside of them, but because of sovereignty it is within each individual to bring in their own tone if they so choose to receive this frequency.
This is part of the distortion that people believe that others have all the answers, so it creates what you call this Matrix as well and codependency."
-Archangel Michael

A: [Aurora] Look at yourself. Do you feel like you have a body?
S: [Sandra] Yes.
A: Look down at your feet, anything on the feet?
S: No.
A: How many toes do you have?
S: It's like five on each foot.
A: Look at your hands. How many fingers do you have?
S: I think it's five. Looks the same. They just look longer, bigger.
A: Your skin. What color tone is your skin?
S: It's kind of different colors. It's kind of brown and kind of blue-ish, green.
A: Are you wearing any clothing?
S: Yes.
A: What are you wearing?
S: Just something very light. Don't need much. Just a dress. Just covers me.
A: What color is it?
S: Natural. Made from natural things, to match my skin so there's no separation, just it's the same thing. We are nature, so we make our clothes from nature. It looks the same colors as my skin. It's different colors. Like leaves, brown leaves. Then it takes the berries, the juice from the berries and it puts the color. The other colors. So, we're just one, not separate.
A: Do you feel like your female, or male, or both?

S: I think I do prefer female. Which is like sometimes I can be male if I want to be. But I like being female. It's something more enriching. Females are more integrated than the male. It's better to be female.

A: Look at your face. Describe your facial features. What do you look like?

S: Oh. My face is like my face now, but it's sharper and the structure is sharper, and my ears are really pointy. Exaggerated...they almost look like wings, they're so pointy. Going up past my head, but they're very sensitive. They're equipped with radar-like radar. That's what they do the ears, they pick up lots of different things and it's like an antenna kind of, but my face looks like me. Just a more exaggerated shape. And of course, there's no age. We don't age. There is nothing like that, so I look, in human terms, I look young wherever I am. I am not young or old. My ears are interesting. They do a lot, they're very powerful. They communicate, they transmit, and they take in energy as well. Very, very powerful. I know what's going to happen (crying). Something is going to happen. My ears. I know that something is coming to where we live. Something bad is coming.

A: What is it that you know?

S: We're under attack. It came so fast. It's like there wasn't enough of us to know, to understand what was coming. They somehow tricked us through darkness, through their darkness, through their dark magic. They were able to intercept my transmission and I didn't know they were coming. I couldn't warn anybody. Couldn't warn them. My village people, everybody. They tried to massacre us, they tried to kill us all.

A: Let's go back to where you were on the mountain you mentioned, and then there was a cave somewhere behind you. Tell me why is it that you were standing on that mountain top?

S: It's like I was the guardian for our community (painful cries continue). I used to guard and watch because of my abilities. What I had; I wasn't a warrior. I didn't fight, that wasn't my job, my job was to hear and to see and to know and then to communicate. When I communicated, I was listened to and I was respected. My role was as important as everybody else's role. We were all respected and loved and treated the same. Everything was oneness and sameness. We were all together. Nobody was better than anybody. So, I would be the lookout, but I wasn't alone. I didn't feel alone here. Even though I was physically alone but I was always able to communicate and see the other guardians like me. We were always together in spirit and soul. I lived here, my cave that was my home.

A: Tell me slowly, what happens. Are you looking out as this attack that you said you sense came in? Tell me step by step what happens. Where are you?

S: It was like any other day. I was just sitting there watching and listening and nothing, there was no signal, there was no warning. Nothing. There was just nothing. No indication that anything was any different. None of us knew and then from nowhere, out of the sky they just came, they just descended upon us. Really fast. Really fast. Just black attacking us immediately from everywhere. There were too many. There were thousands of them. They just took us over completely. There wasn't a chance for survival; it was too fast and too dark. They were too dark.

A: What did it look like when they came in?

S: They were on flying machines; they were flying in the sky it looked like a black horrible fast-moving swarm. Like a swarm of flies or something but they came really fast. As soon as I saw them descending into our globe, it's like we had a globe, but they just came through like nothing was stopping them. And it was like a swarm of flies, they moved really fast and they were huge. They were all gigantic black monsters. Massive. They were all flying, they were like robots and machines, but they look like animals or something. But they were robotic, they didn't have their own mind, they could only do what they were telling them to do. They're black, they look like insects...half insect, half not even Reptilian. More insect but monstrous-looking black.

A: You said they were robotic, did they also have combinations besides insects, did they also have robotic parts to them?

S: Yes. The things they were flying on the, their...whatever it was that was subservient to them. I don't know if they made them. They looked like insects as well, but they were a different shape and they had red eyes on them, but I could tell that they were more like machines. Flying machines but they were made to look ugly. But there was something robotic about them. They had like how a mobile phone operates with its own operating system. It's programmed how to be. They're flying on them. That's what they look like.

A: So, they were insect type of beings that were controlled, riding on robotic type of flying you said?

S: Yeah. Yes, that's close.

A: These robotic flying machines you said they were flying on, they had red eyes?

S: Yes, for some reason the red eyes really stand out to me. That is why I was initially scared when I saw first the red eyes. I didn't know which to be afraid of at first. It was the machines or the things flying the machines. I didn't know which one was more dangerous.

A: You said that the things that they're flying on, is there a shape to these flying machines?

S: They look like a locus, like a flat bug insect so they could stand on them. They were designed by them so they would have these special flying robots especially for missions like this. They created them. They're not that intelligent, they got help from someplace else that has the intelligence and the technology and they helped them make these. They gave them the intelligence, they just looked like flying robotic machines, but they could stand on them sometimes. Two, three of them squashed into one. And everything is so black.

A: You said that these beings look like insects. What kind of insects would you depict them closest to, these insect monsters?

S: They look almost like a, maybe Reptilian but without a tail, they don't have tails. Their face isn't quite as developed as the Reptilian, they don't have the big sort of snout like a Reptilian, it's rounder. Their heads look rounder with a shorter snout. They're kind of goofy looking.

A: Are there colors to them?

S: They're big, they're really big, they're really tall, they're really wide. Their bodies are heavy and strong. It's like they're covered in the shell of an insect, like it's not scales...it's more like a shell.

A: You said that they swarmed in. When they swarmed in, what did they do?

S: They came, and they just immediately attacked, they just started attacking us violently. We couldn't comprehend the violence because we had never experienced that, we didn't know it could be that bad. It felt like a different experience. They just started attacking us and trying to kill us. They knew how to hurt us. They were ripping us apart and stabbing us and ripping people like me, taking my ears off...they cut them off. They didn't care about my wings; it wasn't important because they already knew how to fly so they didn't care about flying. They wanted my ears, but they were so stupid, they didn't know that my ears were no good to them. They just destroyed us. Really, they didn't actually benefit that much, but it didn't matter because they are of such low intelligence, it didn't matter that they had wiped us out. Wiped out such a legacy. It didn't matter, very few survived. Others, like me who have special powers in their hands, have special powers within them in their hearts. They knew this so they targeted us, all of our individual technologies. They didn't kill us, because we're not of flesh and blood, we can't be killed. Not like a human can be killed, like how a human bleed, we're too advanced for that but they were able to damage us. They were able to cut out the things that made us, us. Our power, they left us for dead, just ripped and torn apart with no way for us to heal ourselves. What's worse is they didn't figure out how they could destroy us to kill us, they destroyed us in the worst way. We couldn't heal.

A: Explain to me that. How is it that they were able to do that?

S: Because they knew. Somehow, they knew. They figured it out eventually. They have all kinds of weird strange technology. They have a strange viewing glass. It's like a massive glass thing, I see it. Oh, I see it now. Oh, that's how they saw us. How they watched us (crying). They watched us and we didn't know we were being watched. They managed to put this thing like a massive viewing portal thing. They somehow managed to infiltrate it into our globe and then they managed to use it as a viewing tool. They were able to watch everything about us. We didn't know. I don't know how we didn't know, we couldn't. Looks weird, like it's messing with the frequency or something. It's alternating something, they managed to keep it hidden from us so we couldn't see it. And they watched all the time, studying us, our movements, everything that we did that's how they knew. All they do is they fly around the Universe all the time with their strange technologies and they infiltrate things. They look for opportunities all the time to find other worlds and galaxies. It's like their mining, the power like the way we are mining Mother Earth now, that we take everything from the Earth. We use all the resources and that's what they do, they've done it for a long time and they just happened to discover us. They found us. But we were just another opportunity to them, and they have help from other higher intelligent beings that help them to maraud the Universe.

A: These beings, you said that they have a looking glass. Can you explain how it works? How were you able to view you through it?

S: It's as if they had like a spear or some kind, they shot it out, and it pierced the dome, but it didn't break it. Didn't quite go through, but it stuck onto the outside of it, and it kind of changed the shape. Then this developed, it spread out. It grew like a round viewing glass of a massive circular globe thing that was like a magnifying glass. They could just look through it and all the information were channeled through it for them just to watch. They have all kinds of really strange technology, and weird things that we don't know about.

A: You mentioned that you weren't aware that someone could attack you in this manner. It's not something that you were aware of. You also mentioned that you had your special ears that you can listen to and pick up on things. Even though you weren't aware that this could be possible, why did you still have that role of watching or listening?

S: Because we knew that there were certain entities that existed outside of our world that were not good, so we knew we had ways to protect ourselves. That was always important because there are all levels of beings, some really good and some so bad. Sometimes ones that were close to us, sometimes they would still want to have our way of living and technology. Even though they did no harm to us. Kind of like having neighbors that you get along with most of the time but sometimes your neighbor might get a bit nosey or wants to know what you have (laughing). They don't mean anything bad by it, they just are curious. But you know that they won't necessarily harm you, but we still knew it was important to protect us because we were so unique. How we had evolved was so very unique. We knew that our energy was very important to protect because there was so much that we could do. We were holding energy for other neighbors I should say. Our good neighbors and it wasn't just our community that was affected. Other communities that we protected looked after, they were children communities, but we cared to make sure they were safe. So, it was important that we protected our knowledge. We knew if it was in the wrong hands, even just by a curious person that it could still be used in the wrong way because they didn't have the purity that we had. We were so pure.

A: You mentioned earlier some of what you look like, you didn't mention how about the rest of your face? Your eyes and your nose, your mouth? What does that look like? Do you have hair?

S: Yes, I have hair. My hair fits the shape, goes back like the 1960's. It's combed back and it flows down all the length of my back, but I'm all the same color. My clothes, my skin, my hair it's all the same because we have no identity. We don't identify, we're not separate from anything.

Nothing is separate. We understand this. So, I look like me, but more what you would call an elf, Elven type features. Sharp features, but my eyes are really big, big blue eyes, blue is the purity in my eyes (crying). The blue is an important color for my role, that's the only thing that distinguishes me from others: my ability to see. So, people know when they see me, they know who I am. But I look long, my arms are long. I think I can change color; it depends on different things. How I feel, what I taste, or just how I want to look on the day (laughing). We can change. But my eyes don't change. That's how we know each other very well. Different colored eyes. Very colorful place actually, (laughing) so much color and beauty. And we can be whatever we want as well. Purple eyes like violet color and we're connected to the heart. Very important connection. This is very important, our heart connection. They wanted to separate it. Oh God, they did terrible things to us. They put their technologies into us, they separated the heart connection to our eyes, and they put in...

A: Going back to, you said they abducted you and took you? How did they do this?

S: They took over our home. They just took it over. They took over everything. They stayed. They stayed on our planet, but they just destroyed everything. They live there now as well. We're gone. Very few actually survived intact.

A: The few that survived, they did these things to them?

S: No. The few that survived managed to leave.

A: Got it.

S: They managed to get away, but very few.

A: What about you? What happened to you?

S: They took my ears, but I still managed to get away. I survived. But they took my power, they took my ears, but I was strong inside even though I was in terrible grief for my community (crying). I knew I had to survive. It was very important. Survival is very important. I survived and I managed to bring some with me. Some of the younger ones that weren't as developed. Some that were less experienced, they didn't want them because they weren't developed enough, their gifts weren't developed so they didn't actually care about them. They just hurt whatever was in their way, they just hurt everything. I managed to take some with me, and we got out of there, but I had no ears. My ears were gone.

A: How did you get out?

S: At first, I ran and then I saw myself. I see myself crawling away from them first, then I'm running. I started flying, but there's so many of them. It's very hard for me to fly. I fall down. That's why they can't see me now because I'm falling into the bushes, the trees, into the hill, and to the very bottom of this very beautiful hillside with the trees, flowers, and the water. They don't see me, but I see the little ones, and I bring them to me. I call them. They are hiding too. We come together. We have a tunnel in the water. I make my way to the tunnel. We go into the tunnel even though I don't belong to the water. I belong to the sky, to the air so it's not a safe place for me to be in water, but I go in to survive. I bring them with me, and we take this tunnel to our neighboring community where I alert them what's happening. We all go, and they can lie, but they have their own technology. They have what looks like little spaceships. Like that movie 'My Favorite Martian,' he had a little spaceship. He would sit in it and fly. They too have these, and we all just go away far away. We just keep going. Lots of us, but less of me. Lots of me is left behind now (crying).

A: Tell me where you go.

S: We go to another Dimension. I think my neighbors have communities, friendships and comrades in other places. Other Dimensions. Because we know that this badness will spread very fast. We know we need to leave one Dimension and go to the next Dimension. Where we will be safe, where we hope to be safe. It's a different place, and they are different. They don't understand us. But it's okay. They still accept and love us anyway. Inside I bring all of, like what we call your DNA. It's more than DNA. It's more advanced than our understanding of DNA. I have this within me. I bring it with me to all Dimensions and lifetimes. It's as if I go space hopping from different Dimensions because I never really find home again. Home (crying). So, I never belong, but the ones that came with me, they are out there in other Dimensions. I decided to leave. But they stayed because they were not as developed as I was, so they stayed on the other Dimension instead and they made that their home. They were able to integrate better than I could. I couldn't integrate. I was already too different.

A: Were there any others that were higher developed like you that were able to escape?

S: I think so. But I've never been able to find them. I think that's why I've also been going around on adventures throughout the Universe. In the hope of finding them. But I'm not sure because I don't have my ears so I can't find the frequency.

A: At what point did they remove your ears when they came in. Tell me how that happened?

S: Immediately, it was so fast. It was immediate. There was no delay. They were infiltrating our globe and then within the second they were in front of me. It was that fast. They knew where we were, they were watching so it was so well planned. They knew where I was. They knew that I couldn't see them, so it was immediate.

A: Going back, you said some of the ones that they kept. They were doing experiments on them. Can you explain that to me? The ones that they captured. What did they do?

S: They did terrible things. Terrible. They disfigured them, they made them into machines, robots like them. They experimented on them. They put in their own technology and devices into them, because we cannot die. We don't have such a thing as birth and death. So, you can't really kill us. All they can do is change us, so they cut things out of us in order to put their evil technologies into us. They just look like machines now and robots. In fact, most of them don't exist anymore, because they were just experimental playthings. So eventually they found some way to destroy them. It looks to me as if their consciousness is still surviving. They still have awareness, but their bodies are completely destroyed. They have consciousness, I think. It feels like they do, but they're so destroyed. What they've done to them it's too much. Like a child pulling an insect apart, then stabbing it, and doing things to it. They didn't learn anything; they couldn't achieve because they couldn't harness the power. They didn't understand the connection. So, when they destroyed it, it didn't serve much purpose in the end anyway. They have no reverence for that, they just go to the next place. They didn't even understand how unique and special we were; they just know that there is so much abundant existence out there. They know they will come across the same opportunity someplace else, and that's what they do. I want to communicate with them, but it's impossible, there's nothing I can do to help my community or save them.

A: The ones that have been created into experiments?

S: Yes.

A: Are they also like those Reptilian insectoid robots? Are they similar to that type of experiment?

S: Yes.

A: Are your people then also invading like they did to you?

S: No, it looks like it was failed. Like it was a failed test that just didn't understand what they were doing. They were just doing under orders. Being told to. They have very low, low consciousness so they were just doing. I think that there was some other intelligence behind them telling them what to do. They know that we are destroyed, and that is what they wanted, to destroy us. But because we cannot be killed, they did the next best thing they could figure out to ruin us. They couldn't figure out how to use our power. It didn't work.

A: What happened to the consciousness of your brethren?

S: It feels like it's dying. Like it's slipping away, but they can't do anything. It's like they're just very slowly dying. They can't do anything to help themselves or to change. The light is getting dimmer in their minds, but they can't change it.

A: Would you like to call forth on Archangel Michael, and see if we're able to find some of these of your brethren that are dimming like that?

S: Yes.

The Higher Self speaks.

A: Am I speaking to the Higher Self now?

Higher Self: Yes.

A: Greetings. Thank you for showing us this life of hers. We love you, honor you, and respect you. Thank you for being here. We are looking to connect to Archangel Michael to see if we are able to find some of these brethren that she was looking for and hasn't been able to find. Would you please connect us now to Archangel Michael?

AA Michael: Greetings, Aurora.

A: Greetings, brother. Love you, honor you, and respect you. Thank you for being here.

AA Michael: Thank you dear sister. I love you.

A: Thank you, and I love you with all my heart. You've heard her story. We're looking to find some of those beings that were infringed upon in that manner. Where they were torn apart and created into experiments that are losing their light. She's been looking for them and hasn't been able to find them. Michael, would you be able to locate some of them? Whoever we can communicate to, and try to assist please? Let us know if you find any, and where.

AA Michael: Yes, there is one. There it is one shining brightly! Very bright.

A: Take us there Michael, let us know where we're at.

AA Michael: Oh, it is her twin guardian. Because they are one. She also knew to flee. She fled. She was safe, but to survive she stopped transmitting her frequency. And she survived. That's why she can't be found. But she is shining brightly now.

A: When she stopped transmitting her frequency, what did that do to her Twin Flame?

AA Michael: Oh, it hurt her a lot. Because, then she was alone, and she was disconnected. She was cut off, and this was something that she had never felt or knew was possible. This experience traumatized her deeply. As she has been searching for so long.

A: When she stopped transmitting to protect herself from being found. Did this disconnect her from her Twin Flame?

AA Michael: Yes, it was like cutting the string on a balloon. Then the balloon floated away. There's no possibility for it to come back, it's gone.

A: Michael, let's go ahead and find her Twin Flame. That light that you see shining bright. Go to him now. Let us know where you're finding him. What's going on?

AA Michael: Yes. She's coming to us. She was scared, she was so very frightened. She found a way to hide herself. She too has suffered. She too has been lonely. She too understands what she did. She is sorry. Because she feels she should have been stronger, and that she would have found her way to me, but she wasn't as strong. I was the strong one, but she is very happy. Her arms are outstretched. She's come to me.

A: Who's talking?

S: I am talking.

A: You are who?

S: I am me, the other half.

A: Okay, continue.

S: The trauma has been so deep and strong, that I 'human person', that it takes over. Even when I ask, my spirit wants to connect to others, to my guides. That the trauma is still like it only just happened, and it's hard to connect fully with Archangel Michael. But he is with me because there is no separation. I am him; he is me.

A: Your Twin Flame?

S: Yes, I, Sandra. I, this incarnation of many incarnations. I, with who I was and my Twin Flame and Archangel Michael. We as a species were so very close to the higher realms it's hard to separate. I will stand back now, and I will allow Archangel Michael to assume his role. I cannot identify.

A: Thank you. Archangel Michael? Brother, this Twin Flame of hers, if you could explain it. Was it separate from her? Like she said they were disconnected? Or was it within her?

AA Michael: There was too much trauma and darkness that it didn't matter. She couldn't find her. They couldn't see each other for the darkness and her trauma is so great that this is the block. It's a block of the world that they had to find each other because of this pain. That's what happened, it was separation. They couldn't understand the idea of separateness; it was not part of them. This was inflicted to them, so they didn't really understand it. They got more and more lost in their darkness and their trauma. They became part of the wheel, the wheel of life, and they are having these experiences because of the darkness.

A: How can we assist them Michael?

AA Michael: Dissolve the darkness, we must break it down now with fire. You can put Phoenix Fire on it.

A: Okay, using Phoenix Fire. Directing it to where it is that you need it to dissolve the darkness between them. As we're dissolving that darkness, let us know how it's going Michael.

AA Michael: They are very strong healers. I am helping them to reconnect. They're reconnecting. Because they still have so much light inside of themselves. They are able to regenerate themselves by just their own light. I love them.

A: Wonderful Michael. As we're repairing that bond between them. Would this be a good time to start her body scan please?

AA Michael: Not yet.

A: Then I'll continue asking questions. Michael, while we continue to do this. Are there any other life forms of them besides them, of their race still remaining? How she was developed? I know she mentioned the young ones ended up just adapting to the new environment they went to. But, since she was developed, are there any of her race that are still developed in Creation that are still alive? That weren't infringed upon like those that they did experiments on.

AA Michael: Yes, there is a few. They are in what they call the DNA. Human DNA. They do not know who they are. Some of them stayed together. They do not know who they are, but their DNA will eventually be activated for them. It will be done only when their whole of existence can fully love and embrace them, because they are very powerful and special. When they are activated, we protect them. They will not experience the human pain, they're not from the Earth. We protect them because we need them for the future. They are unique. They did not have time to call for help. They didn't have that frequency.

A: Can you tell me a little bit more about this race. What was special about them? Why did they target them in this manner? She also mentioned that they were assisting their neighboring planets. Tell me more on that please.

AA Michael: We are Nephilim, we are a higher race of angels collectively as you know us. We wanted to create as Creation is limitless, so they were created like us. Almost like you have your fairies and your elementals on the planet Earth that help you. We too had this race that was very close to us. They are angelic beings. Creation is limitless; they came from us. And then they evolved from us. That's why they are pure. Their globe was not unlike your Earth but a similar realm of existence. That is why she found the Earth as a place for her to reincarnate and to try to find home. Because it looked like her home. The Earth has so many colors. The color, the elements, the ethers, the water everything that it is made of are all parts of who she was where she came from; it was just a much higher existence than Earth.

A: Thank you for that explanation. Tell me how's it going with transmuting the darkness between them.

AA Michael: Yeah, it is done.

A: Beautiful. Tell me what that looks like now that this is removed. What do they look like?

AA Michael: They look unified. They are glowing. They coexist now.

A: Wonderful. Talking to you who are together now, coexisting. How do you feel now?

S: I feel better. I feel like I belong again to something. All my memories are coming back into me. I see the light has them; it's coming back. Forming my body, my structure is changing, it's renewing itself. We are healing ourselves now. We are able to pull in all the different fractals of light and colors. Everything that we need, the minerals, the ether is really important to us. It's restructuring us now.

A: Beautiful. Michael, is this a good time now to start doing her body scan?

AA Michael: Yes.

The Body Scan begins.

A: Good. Higher Self, Michael, if we could start conducting her body scan now. Michael, let us know where we should start off first?

AA Michael: The left side of her head and her ear. Left ear.

A: Tell me what's there.

AA Michael: Something is stuck there. It found a channel, and it doesn't want to come out.

A: Does this have a consciousness?

AA Michael: Yes, but he's good at hiding. He's in her structure. Like fluid of water.

A: What is this Michael? Is this an entity? A technology? What is it?

AA Michael: I don't know. This feels, it feels bad. Feels dark and it has a consciousness.

A: Is that an entity Michael?

AA Michael: No, stronger. Something more.

A: Is that a Reptilian consciousness or an Archon? Or what is it?

AA Michael: It's more than Archon.

A: Michael, if you could call on Metatron now please. If you could both now surround it with the alchemy symbols. Encase it now. Let me know once it's encased... Is it encased Michael?

AA Michael: Nearly.

A: Let me know once it's encased.

AA Michael: Yes.

A: If we could go ahead and start. Michael, does this have an organic consciousness or is it an artificial consciousness? You said it was something more than Archon. What is that?

AA Michael: It's both. This is very advanced. It is very strong and deep. It's very old. This existed for a long time. It has perfected both consciousness and technology. It uses both.

A: Since it has an organic consciousness, typically with the A.I. type of being, we neutralize it to zero. What can we do with this one? Are we able to help the organic consciousness turn to light and then neutralize the artificial? Or do we have to neutralize both?

AA Michael: I must call in Archangel Metatron.

A: Thank you. Michael, if you could connect us now to Metatron please. Metatron brother?

AA Metatron: Yes.

A: Thank you for being here. We love you, honor you, and respect you. Metatron, if you could tell us what are we to do with this inorganic and organic consciousness?

AA Metatron: I bring the Legion with me. We must remove it all, all of it. We must take it. We have a place for it as you know, in quarantine we will take it there. Because it must be gone.

525

A: Metatron, if we could start that process now of removing it from her. Can we call on Archangel Raphael to start filling in light to the areas where you're removing it from? Thank you, Raphael. We love you, honor you, and respect you. Tell me what you're doing as we're starting the process of removing it Metatron, let me know.

AA Metatron: Oh, we are disconnecting him. His technology first. Must be disconnected and stopped.

A: Tell me what that technology looks like that you are disconnecting from her.

AA Metatron: It looks like it is half of him. It is part of him, it is integrated, it is fluid, it has almost a robotic consciousness all on its own but it is very advanced. It shapeshifts and to fit with whatever body that it is with. It is ultimately this person; the entity is in charge of it. He can control it with his mind.

A: He can control who with his mind?

AA Metatron: The technology.

A: Is it integrated into her DNA? Can you check that please now?

AA Metatron: He is trying very hard to do this to her, but I do not see.

A: So where exactly is he in her then?

AA Metatron: He is in her mind as well in her brain. He wants to own her consciousness, and her mind. If he can control her then he is powerful.

A: When was it that he came in and attached there to her?

AA Metatron: Oh, a long time ago. He came with her somehow. Some piece of him came with her from that lifetime of separation. He somehow managed to attach himself to her and ever since then he keeps developing and growing with her. Which has kept her lost.

A: Alright as we continue to do this again having Raphael fill in Love-Light. Michael, Metatron, is it going to be a process to remove it?

AA Metatron: He needs to be removed from previous lives, we need to go back through other existences to clear the imprint or the damage of what he has done as well. We have to clear it from all lifetimes.

A: I know you all are doing that process now. Can you explain what is it please? You explained a bit of the A.I. and the Organic. What did it begin from? How did it form into that?

AA Metatron: They were another race like the Archons and they somehow met. They formed an alliance; they are from different realms completely to the Archons, but they are just as dark. They have different guiding forces in them, but they recognize the darkness. Formed a strong alliance, and they began working together with different things like technologies. They are more with technology than the Archons, but the Archons helped them with their consciousness. Together they are powerful.

A: You said that they are all together from another realm. Tell me how they were able to enter? Are they of this Universe?

AA Metatron: No, a different one.

A: If they were from another Universe, how did they come into this Universe?

AA Metatron: They are adventurers. They are travelers, because they live in the darkness, so they always travel around the realms of darkness. They are always looking for more opportunities, and they also have ways of technology. Their own dark magic that they use, so they can make things happen. They can change things, and they can pierce the veil in unnatural ways; they break the natural laws of the Universe all the time now. They do this like fooled children. They have no more respect. They don't stop with the Law of the Universe. It is something that will stop them eventually.

A: The Law of this Universe?

AA Metatron: Yes. Because it is more powerful.

A: There's a big, a bit of a confusion I think Metatron. If you can clarify this. We know there's dark and light obviously because we're in this Universe that is dark and light. Negative polarization and positive polarization. Then like you said, you have these other Archonic beings of different races coming in. Ripping inorganically through time and space and coming into our Universe. Is this something that is happening? Where we're having these negative polarized entities that are not of our Universe, cracking into time coming in and harming us? Is it because we have negative and positive polarizations?

AA Metatron: It's almost like a free for all. Now things are speeding up. They want more. They also know what they are doing. They know that there is a Universal Law that governs all existence no matter where. They came from Creation. So they know that a law will be the law on them. But they really don't care. They don't understand. They know that Creation is infinite, infinite existence. So they believe that they will always exist anyway, no matter what they do. But they don't understand the Laws of the Universe. The law of consequence.

A: Would you say that these negative polarized, we'll call them entities, have an attraction to this Universe because of the negative polarity that they can infringe upon amplifying it in people, affect them? Would you say that they're more attracted to this Universe, because it holds that negative polarization?

AA Metatron: No, because the Earth is so beautiful, and its timeline was once to be magnificent. They discovered the Earth, and it was of one of many planets that they discovered that they just ran their darkness and negativity to. It was easy for them. The Earth may not have been at the highest vibration of other planets, but the Earth is so uniquely beautiful. There was so much to gain by being here regardless, if there was negativity here. The timeline was changed. The Earth didn't survive in the way that it was destined to be or that the original plan was to be beautiful. But the timelines changed.

A: Metatron, if you could tell me for example, how this planet that she was from, how easily they were able to just come in and destroy it? Did this planet for example, not have protection force fields around it? Why were they so easy just able to view through this technology of viewing glass, and then just come into their realm and do this to them?

AA Metatron: Because their planet was hidden out of sight. But because they were using this technology, they moved very fast. This is how they were successful. That they had the equipment. They move around very quickly, looking for these opportunities. They found this place by using this technology. By piercing lots of veils where we had to fix and repair many veils. So it was just their luck.

A: So, this technology, you weren't really aware of it, and they were hidden. But somehow with this technology they were able to pierce through and see?

AA Metatron: Yes. Because they are darkness, they are experts in darkness. They found them because they keep evolving in their darkness. They keep changing, so they're always finding new ways to cause disruption, and we must always keep up with them. The Army. So, they had new developed technology that helped them to find this particular globe, and they moved very quickly.

A: Metatron, if you could tell me more about these different realms that they come from. What information can you share about these Archonic entities?

AA Metatron: They're very far away. We do our best to shield and protect the rest of the realms. But they're very far away so we protect. We even move planets around. We work differently, but we work within the Laws of the Universe.

A: So naturally, organically by the Laws of the Universe, they wouldn't be able to go into other realms and Universes and harm others. But they are breaking laws, basically like you said?

AA Metatron: Yes.

A: Would they be considered from their realms, kind of god-like beings?

AA Metatron: It is absolute anarchy where they exist. Nothing stays the same. They harvest so many resources. They destroy themselves too. There is so much anarchy for power. One day they may have a God, the next day he is destroyed then somebody else is in charge.

A: What Dimension was this planet that she was from? Where were they in when they were destroyed? Is there a number Dimension to that?

AA Metatron: As you know it or understand it, it was the 15th Dimension.

A: Yes, I was seeing it higher than the 13th Dimension. Okay. Are beings like this not supposed to be able to pierce through 15th-Dimensional frequency, vibrations, and planes?

AA Metatron: No. But it was so undone, it was unheard of what they did. It was against the laws. We did not know.

A: The few that she escaped with, the young ones. What Dimension did they end up there that they had to evolve into?

AA Metatron: It was lower than what she was used to. It was much lower, but that was okay for the younger ones. It was easier for them. But she had to drop her vibration which was very difficult to lower. Each process for her has been very difficult. For her to become Third Dimension, it was the darkness in her that was bringing her to lower and lower and lower Dimensions. Taking her further away from her true Source.

A: What is the purpose of her to gain being in this Inverted A.I. Matrix?

AA Metatron: She came to find herself. Her home. She liked the Earth. It felt almost close to her home. Then she stayed, and she became a part of the energy here. Just to begin to help them, she stayed, and she just kept on staying. She didn't go until she became part of the wheel of karma that was operating here. Because her vibration was being dropped all the time by this part of this entity that came with her. He was dropping her vibration.

A: Thank you for all those answers. Metatron, can we continue scanning her body and see what else we can heal within her? Let me know of any other energies, entities, technologies.

AA Metatron: Something, like it has a black tail. It's in her back.

A: What is that a Reptilian, Archon?

AA Metatron: It looks like an eel.

A: Let's contain that now with the alchemy symbols. Metatron, let me know once it is contained.

AA Metatron: Yes.

A: Is it just like an eel then?

AA Metatron: Yes. Black.

A: It's sticking out her back and it has a tail because it is an eel?

AA Metatron: Yes, it has the face.

A: Is this organic or inorganic? Organic or A.I.?

AA Metatron: It's A.I., it's very advanced.

A: We're going to go ahead and neutralize this since it's A.I. Let's go ahead and start using the alchemy symbols there to neutralize the A.I. please. Can we do that?

AA Metatron: Yes.

A: Wonderful. Thank you, Metatron. How are you looking in regard to removing that Archon in her ear area and brain?

AA Metatron: It's improving.

A: Good. So, you just let me know when it is at its end, the removal. Okay, as we continue to neutralize this eel in her spine, let's go ahead and continue scanning her thoroughly. Do also scan her DNA structure as well her spine for any negative fractals within. Does she have any?

AA Metatron: There's something around her sacral chakra. Around her kidneys and her bladder something there needs to go.

A: Metatron, what is that. Is that an entity, Reptilian, technology?

AA Metatron: I think it's just an implant. She also has a portal.

A: Metatron, can you have Michael close that portal please? Unless, can we use Phoenix Fire on the implant?

AA Metatron: Yes.

A: Okay, we're using Phoenix Fire on the implant. Just let us know once it's removed. Tell me when did that implant come in?

AA Metatron: From her ex, her husband.

A: How did it come in through him?

AA Metatron: He implanted it.

A: How did he do that?

AA Metatron: Through intercourse.

A: As well as the portal? Both?

AA Metatron: No. The portal is to do with the eel.

A: Tell me what this eel was doing in her spine? What was it causing her?

AA Metatron: Discomfort. It was released. It was trapped there in her spine and she partly has helped to release it from her energy work, but the portal was then opened to stop her. The eel was trying to connect to her kundalini energy in her spine, so it could move around her body.

A: You said it was released. Who released it there?

AA Metatron: She has been doing her energy work on herself. She is doing the work. She has helped to release it, but she wasn't aware of what she was releasing.

A: Did that eel also come in from her ex-husband or something else?

AA Metatron: No. It came in at nighttime in the dark. She was hurt and broke. Her pelvis and this eel came in because of that.

A: Was that from the motorcycle accident?

AA Metatron: Yes.

A: That implant. How's that looking? Is it transmuting out?

AA Metatron: Yes. Nearly.

A: Tell me, what was the purpose of that implant there? What was that causing her?

AA Metatron: It caused issues around her own connections to her own sacredness. She was very connected to being a sacred woman, divine woman. This implant interrupted all of that. It was infiltration. She is a powerful creator. It stopped her creation. Stopped her feeling feminine and truly connected to her essence. Her feminine energy was being robbed. Her kundalini energy was being used.

A: Let's continue scanning her body. What else can we heal while we transmute, and remove all the others?

AA Metatron: There's a lot of cords now. Lots of cording that need to be Phoenix Fired.

A: These negative cords. Using Phoenix Fire all over. Where are they?

AA Metatron: Mostly on her left side of her body.

A: Using Phoenix Fire there in the left side of the body. Do we need to cut them as well?

AA Metatron: Yes, that will help.

A: If we could have Archangel Michael start cutting the negative cords that no longer serve her for her highest good. Tell me Metatron, how did these cords get there? Who are they connected to?

AA Metatron: They're just these narcissistic people that she has attracted that have come to her, these people that need her healing energy. They need to be healed but they're so negative they can't ask her for it. She waits for them to ask. She's so patient. She will wait for them to ask but they must be disconnected.

A: Good. We're doing that process now please. Any other negative cords that she has?

AA Metatron: On the back of her head, left side, something, strong cord.

A: What is that connected to please?

AA Metatron: There is a collective. Collective attached to it.

A: Can we start using Phoenix Fire on it now?

AA Metatron: Yes.

A: Using Phoenix Fire on it. Michael, stand by using your sword as needed. Michael, do we need to talk to that collective that is attached there?

AA Michael: Yes. They need to be spoken to and stopped.

A: Michael, if you can find them now and let us speak to them now please.

AA Michael: They don't want to talk.

A: Michael, can you tell me more about who they are?

AA Michael: They're a collective of aliens. They are attached negatively to a collective of people on Earth and through them, they have connected somehow to her energy.

A: How many would you say there connected to on Earth?

AA Michael: Oh, there's a lot. A lot of people.

A: Hundreds? Thousands?

AA Michael: Within the hundreds. The aliens are within the thousands.

A: There are thousands of them connected to hundreds of people through Earth. Are they connected in this manner like this how they are through cords or other ways too?

AA Michael: Yes, they are just low level. It is just like a cord they connect through this collective of a certain belief system that these people hold. They connect into that belief system and through that belief system collectively they have connected to her.

A: What is the belief system that they're connecting through?

AA Michael: It is mostly fear based.

A: Is this collective A.I. or Organic.

AA Michael: It's organic.

A: They don't want to speak to us?

AA Michael: No. They are hiding.

A: Michael, can we locate them? Is there something we can do? Can we contain or what can we do with them?

AA Michael: Yes. They will speak to you now.

A: Thank you for speaking to us. We love you, honor you and respect you. May we ask you questions please?

Alien Collective: Yes.

A: Thank you. If I can ask, where is it that you are at now?

Alien Collective: On a spaceship.

A: How many of you are in the spaceship?

Alien Collective: There are thousands of us.

A: Can you tell me what you look like please?

Alien Collective: We just have large heads, and we have small eyes. We are gray in color. We have no ears. We have an antenna on top of our heads. We are small.

AA Michael: They don't have mouths, that's why they were afraid to speak.

A: Thank you. Now we were told that there were thousands of you and then you also attached to hundreds here on Earth alone. Are you also attached to other places besides Earth?

Alien Collective: Yes.

A: How many more are you attached to in Creation?

Alien Collective: Our group is just focusing on the Earth. Other groups are focused on other planets.

A: Tell me how you do this with the cords. What is the purpose of you doing that?

Alien Collective: The cords are like a system. I mean we all have our own cord. Our cord comes out of ourselves we produce it with our minds and then it all collectively grows into the one cord.

Then that goes down to find the consciousness and energy of people that resonate with what we want. We find them. Then our cords split off and we connect to those people. People in many places. Doesn't matter. The people who will have all the resources that we want. Then collectively it joins together. We find energy sources. The best resources are humans themselves.

A: Why is that?

Alien Collective: Because they have so much energy. They have so much light force, but they don't know. They have this force, and their Earth gives them this force. But they don't know what to do with it. So, we collect the energy because we can use it for ourselves.

A: As you know the Universe, the Earth is ascending and entities like you who are attached to others will no longer be able to play this role parasitically. We would love to be able to assist you today so that you no longer have to play this, attaching to others and draining upon their energies. Would you allow for us to help you, so that you may be free and spread your light no longer having to do this? You can incarnate somewhere else when you're ready and have your own free will, have your own light source to use instead of draining on others.

Alien Collective: Yes.

A: Beautiful. Is that yes to all thousands of you there?

Alien Collective: Wait… Yes, we will come together now.

A: Beautiful. Find your light within you. We'll help you find it. If we could call forth on Archangel Raphael and his Legion. Michael, Metatron, send them there please and start helping Raphael's Legion spread their light within them. We're focusing light on them now to help them spread to all light. Let us know when all of you are all light.

Positive Polarized Alien Collective: Yes.

A: Go ahead and release yourself from there. Also cutting and transmuting all those cords that they were also attached to others please. With their Higher Selves' permission if we could have Raphael and his Legion start filling in Love-Light to those cords and everywhere else within her, please. Do you all have a message for her before you go?

Positive Polarized Alien Collective: Thank you. We are not bad, but we didn't know how else to be. Thank you.

A: Thank you as well. If we could call forth on Archangel Azrael. Brother Azrael, if you could please guide them with your Legion to where they are meant to go for their positive Ascension.

AA Azrael: Yes.

A: Thank you. Making sure none of them get lost along the way, thank you.

AA Azrael: Yes.

A: Wonderful.

AA Azrael: They have chosen.

A: Good. Where is it that you're taking them to, Azrael?

AA Azrael: They have chosen to go to another planet where they can assist us. They want to help now. They want to return the energy that they took.

A: Beautiful. So they will be assisting others then?

AA Azrael: Mm-hmm.

A: That is beautiful. Thank you, we love you, honor you, respect you. Blessings to all of you. May you be surrounded by the Love-Light of the Universe. Again, we're having Raphael fill in Love-Light everywhere to where it's needed. How's the implant looking in her sacral?

AA Michael: Yes, it's better

A: Is it removed yet?

AA Michael: Almost.

A: Is the portal closed?

AA Michael: Yes.

A: Good. Alright, let's continue scanning her body. Michael, Metatron, let me know what else would you like for us to heal, what is next? We want to make sure we are not missing anything. As you know, sometimes they can be sneaky. Any other entities, Reptilians, Archons, anything else within her? Scan her thoroughly, deeply. Let me know if there's anymore.

AA Michael: Disconnect the viewing glass. Phoenix Fire the viewing glass. it's still a part of her distortion.

A: We're using Phoenix Fire there, the viewing glass. This viewing glass is where?

AA Michael: It's viewing her from externally on her left side.

A: Using Phoenix Fire there now.

AA Michael: It goes into another Dimension, it's like a portal.

A: What can we do with that Michael? Besides Phoenix Fire, is there anything else we can do?

AA Michael: The distortion and the imprint need to be cleared so that her energy can no longer be detected.

A: Can we do that for her now please?

AA Michael: Yes.

A: Thank you. Do you need Phoenix Fire assisting with that?

AA Michael: Yes.

A: Lets go ahead and scan her Michael for any implants, hooks or portals?

AA Michael: Yes. A hook is in her from the viewing glass.

A: Okay, let's go ahead and remove the hook. Where is it in her?

AA Michael: Also, her head.

A: Lets transmute that out fully with Phoenix Fire. Michael, Metatron, this would be a good question for you since it has to do with healing. She said she received a soul tone[27] from Paula. She wants to know why she received an attack when using it? What happened recently around her using this, and is it safe for her to use the soul tone negativity free again?

AA Michael: Well, for many reasons which I have explained about her distortion, her trauma. She has always been searching for the answers, searching for help, searching for people that she believed had the answers and the power. She wasn't able to find her own. But she could not bring it in because there was always that element of distortion, so she still attracted the same thing, and it is by no fault of hers.

A: So, was this soul tone created from a high vibration? Positive?

AA Michael: No.

A: Was it a match to that attack she felt?

AA Michael: Yes.

A: She felt that it was a Reptilian. What was it that was actually removed from the soul tone when she started doing the shielding through the A.U.R.A. teachings?

AA Michael: Yes. He was a Reptilian, she was right. He came into her and tried to integrate into her heart. He tried to deceive her, but she knew it wasn't right.

A: She said she felt that two years ago when she first got the soul tone. Was it trying to work on her for those two years? Trying to integrate?

AA Michael: Yes, he was trying to express himself through her, through her heart, and throat chakra. He was speaking through her. He tried many times to convince her of things, but she was never convinced. He knew what she wanted. But he wasn't strong enough.

A: She said, at first, she thought it was positive. If I can ask since this has come up several times. Is this what's occurring for example with this channel, she's not channeling something

---

[27] A soul tone is a specific vibrational sound tone designed for a person's soul with the purpose of awakening them.

positive? Is this why she's being directed to give them out to people, so that negative aliens can attach to people and try to integrate into them?

AA Michael: Yes. It happens.

A: Basically, are they using her for that purpose?

AA Michael: Yes. Because they can and not everybody has had the same experience. Sometimes it can be clear but not always.

A: Does it have anything to do with, I know this channel doesn't believe in shielding, using Love-Light? She classifies it as fear based. Her belief system is a little backwards on that. Does that have to do with how they're able to attach to the soul tones when she sends them?

AA Michael: Yes. Very strongly. Yes. Perhaps she reaches moments of this state, but it's not that often.

A: What's not that often?

AA Michael: Her purity.

A: Okay. What are your views on that? Do you think another being can give someone else their own organic soul tone?

AA Michael: Some beings have the ability. They have it inside of them, but because of sovereignty, it is within each individual to bring in their own tone if they so choose to receive this frequency. This is part of the distortion that people believe that others have all the answers, so it creates what you call this Matrix as well and codependency.

A: So, in other words, people should find their own soul tone because only they can locate their most organic highest soul tone, because it's their soul tone. It's their soul energy?

AA Michael: Yes, this is true.

A: I can imagine a person trying to channel a soul tone, to actually channel a soul tone in this Dimension. How benevolent, high vibrational, and pure would a being have to be to actually tap into a soul tone?

AA Michael: Extremely pure. But they have no ego. They don't believe that they can do this. But very, very rare.

A: One last time, scan her for any other negative implants, entities, Reptilians, Archons, any entity of any kind, and for fractals that are not of hers organically.

AA Michael: There is a shadow coming forward.

A: Where is this shadow at?

AA Michael: He's coming from within her on her left side also.

A: What is he?

AA Michael: He's quite dark. He's an entity.

A: Is he a Reptilian, an Archon or an entity?

AA Michael: He's an Archon.

A: Okay, let's go ahead and contain that now with the Alchemy symbols please. Michael, Metatron let me know once it's contained.

AA Metatron: Yes.

A: Good. Let's go ahead and start neutralizing it now please. This Archon, where did this come from? How did it attach?

AA Michael: He's deep inside of her. This is the one that is attached to her ex-husband.

A: Is this why she has such a hard time not letting him in because he has such a strong hold on her, has such a grip.

AA Metatron: Yes.

A: Good, so let's neutralize that out now please with the alchemy symbols. As we continue to do that Michael, is there any negative contracts that we can remove from her?

AA Michael: Yes.

A: Can you start removing those for her now please. What are they connected to?

AA Michael: When she fell into the creek, she made these connections with it, and was just part of her experience of her many lives that she has been running away from. Running. Running. Trying to save herself, not understanding why it was all happening to her. So that script kept running for her. He belongs to India, to the black magic.

A: The Archon?

AA Michael: Yes.

A: Is that one of those Archons that is posing as a Deity?

AA Michael: Yes. He's tribal.

A: Good. We are neutralizing him. Having again Raphael standing by, filling in Love-Light anywhere where we remove. Any other contracts we need to know about your removing?

AA Michael: That contract was attached to her throat. So, we need to go there. Her throat needs to be released...

A: What do you need? Do you need Phoenix Fire there or?

AA Michael: Yes.

A: Okay, we're using Phoenix Fire there now, and then we are starting to release it from her throat please.

AA Michael: There.

A: Good. Is it released?

AA Michael: Yes. It was attached to something else that she released herself.

A: Let's fill in Love-Light there. Raphael please, let's start healing any past life trauma that we can. Heal specifically that past life that you showed us or the future life of that planet that was destroyed. I just came up with a question, Metatron. Can you tell me, she mentioned that planet they took over it? Is that still accurate? Are they still there?

AA Metatron: No, it's like a waste land to them. They just use it, come, and go from it.

A: Are there any resources that they still use from within that planet?

AA Metatron: No. The resource was those people. And we cannot heal it. We cannot go there until we deal with the source problem. Where the attack and the darkness are coming from. We must first work with this and heal it. We must first find the source and stop the pain.

A: Okay, and that will be a process huh?

AA Metatron: Yeah.

A: Very good. But can we heal the trauma within her thought of that past, that future life?

AA Metatron: Yes.

A: Thank you. Alright then and how is her DNA looking? Making sure there's no negative fractals, anything within that does not belong to her. Scan it and let me know how it looks.

AA Michael: It looks good.

A: Wonderful, fill in Love-Light to that DNA reprogramming it from any negative programming that is no longer needed for her highest good, as her Higher Self allows please.

AA Michael: Yes.

A: At this point we've conducted all the healing. Tell me what is remaining that still needs healing within her.

AA Michael: She needs now to experience and feel love. That's all.

A: Beautiful. We're filling her in with Love-Light now. Feeling that love within her. Michael, is that Archon still in her head or is it out?

AA Michael: Much better now. They're gone. Healed.

A: Beautiful. Her constant pattern of narcissism with her ex, was this ex connected to any of these negative collectives or negative entities that we removed?

AA Michael: Yes.

A: Which part of these entities was he connected to?

AA Michael: He's very dark so he's connected to the tribe, the Archon, that's him.

A: When she left him, she continued to experience narcissistic people trying to come into her life. Since we removed all the density within her, can we ensure that this is healed so she can move on from them?

AA Michael: Yes.

A: She wants to know where her soul family members are here on Earth. She would like to reunite with them. Live closer to them. Does this longing have to do with that past life where she was looking for her soul family?

AA Michael: Yes. That's a part of it. That's been very important to her to feel happy and to feel whole by herself, but she will begin to feel more whole now. She will have that in her connection once again, and because of that her light will become even more so. She won't feel such a need to have to be anywhere else and she will automatically go where she needs to be to connect.

A: She said she had a dream last year that really bothered her, where she had dreamed, she had passed over and her soul was trying to comfort her son. Was this an exit point for her? What was the meaning to that dream?

AA Michael: This was her Higher Self communicating to her. She was coming into herself. It was a meeting of herself with herself. It was hard to understand like this.

A: Does it have any connection to a walk-in?

AA Michael: No. It's about her integration of herself.

A: Good. A higher part of her came in and integrated with her?

AA Michael: Yes.

A: At this point we've asked all the questions that we needed to address. Is there anything else that I could have asked that I haven't, Higher Self?

Higher Self: No.

A: Is there a name that you go by Higher Self?

Higher Self: It's too hard for her to say, as it's made from different frequencies and sounds. She cannot say it.

A: Thank you for such a powerful session. I want to thank Michael, Metatron, Raphael. All the different Legions of benevolent beings that assisted today and our love to all the entities that chose to ascend. Our love and blessing to everyone. Thank you we love you, honor you and respect you. And thank you, Higher Self.

Higher Self: Thank you dear sister.

A: Thank you as well sister. Love you. May I bring her back?

Higher Self: Yes.

A: Thank you.

Post Session dialogue.

A: Wow! You are literally a gem, a rarity in Creation, last of your kind. Wow, so emotional.

S: Yes, it's unusual. It just makes a lot of sense. What really caught me by surprise was how fast we went into that. I was utterly amazed that we went immediately to that life straight away.

A: Yes, that's the beautiful power of A.U.R.A., and how purely it's created.

S: Yes.

A: Also, it really does have to do a very big role with your practitioner. How much are they holding purity for you? Even more so, how ready are you, to be there and let go, and you were there. It's amazing.

S: Yes, you're right when you say it's the work that you have brought through. The 'Into The Cave of Creation' meditation[28], it's very powerful. That in itself can take you to many, many places, and not to be afraid of the darkness as well. It is a big part of going into the cave. It makes sense to me that there was a cave in my past life or that I was living in one because I love the idea of going into caves.

A: You were so beautiful in that 15th Dimension. I knew that it was a higher Dimension. They said it was higher than the 13th Dimension. The 13th is like a bridge, but the highest that typically we could reach here. That's the first session that we reached higher than 13th.

S: Really?

A: Yeah.

S: Wow.

A: So, it definitely is amazing how easily you were able to connect to that 15th Dimension. Give yourself a hug. You're amazing.

S: It seems so simple to me. I'm always telling people to go outside. Connect to nature. Listen to the wind. So, I'm sure they think I'm off my head.

A: You brought such detail, and things I had yet to get in an A.U.R.A. Hypnosis session. With the Archons how they're coming through. One of the biggest things that holds us back is that a lot of the Light Workers have a belief system that everything's love. Then when others talk about negativity, they're like "that's fear based" or "no, I'm neutral. Darkness is meant to be there. I don't view it as it's harmful, it's just part of the role." But NO! Your session brought clearly NO. These Archons are not supposed to be here. They're violating rules of the Universe and cutting through with their technologies. So we need to break that belief system and that cycle that Light Workers believe that "oh. it's needed for them to do this." It's not! Yes, there is a role for dark and light. Absolutely! However, this particular information that you've given us and through other sessions is that they're not needed. They're violating. Or even with the pedophilia, are you saying that these children are supposed to be in this type of torment? That it's part of the role of the dark and the light? I don't believe so, no. It's part of their twisted games that are not even of our Universe.

S: Yes. It felt like when you were asking the question about planet Earth, it was like the Karmic wheel thing was so strong here. The belief system of that exists, so therefore it exists here. But it doesn't actually exist in other places. It was the sense that it's become part of the Earth. It was never part of the Earth when originally it was created. That was my feeling, and that it was something that became distorted. It's another distortion. It's just been thousands of years of this distortion, and now we're trapped in it in our own matrix.

A: You know, interesting enough. I'm about to have a channel where I was going to speak of what we talked about today in your life. Even though we won't be able to share your session until the future. We're still going to be able to share some like what I just said to you, about how people are confused about the polarities. So, we'll be addressing that with basically saving the children. And the adrenochrome and the superstars[29]. We're going to be putting it all into one video. Explaining what the difference is, because we need to like what you said, remove the belief system. You're right you know, so long as we keep believing that "oh, it's a role." Yes, there are organic roles, but then there's also nonorganic roles that are being forced as organic when they are not. Very important.

---

[28] This is a YouTube meditation video on the Rising Phoenix Aurora's channels under the "Guided Meditations" playlist.

[29] Visit www.risingphoenixaurora.com for more details on adrenochrome in Galactic News, specifically the 7/20/2020 newsletter.

S: Yes, because that sense of the only thing that exists is just existence. Truth is the only thing that actually exists anywhere. So through truth is oneness, it's everything. There's nothing false about truth. So, there is no infringement on truth. It just is. Every time when you asked about how I looked, and how I was dressed. There was nothing about that, there was just this strong sense of absolute truth. Purity and oneness.

A: Yes. Beautiful. Wow. That was amazing. Thank you. Is there anything that you want to add?

S: There was the sense at times that Archangel Michael almost wanted to confirm with you that you do ask the same questions, to keep confirming the information. It's almost like he almost feels a little bit like, it's not fun. He understands why you do it, to keep reconfirming but it's like the sense of "oh, here goes the humans again having to reconfirm the information and just making sure the answer is right."

A: Which part of my questions did he feel like that?

S: There were a few times. It was more to do with how the Universe worked and the difference between the realms was one part in there. There's a sense of, "here's the humans again, doing it again" just funny but anyway.

A: I obviously know these answers, but it's like I have to log them in for others to understand. So, I feel like that too sometimes, when I'm asking them. It's like, "Here I go. I'm going to ask these questions." But I know I have to ask them because they're going to serve a higher purpose for people to understand. They don't understand.

S: Yeah, and sometimes people have to hear it 20 or 30 times before they may begin to break that barrier to try to understand the concept so simple in ways.

A: Yes. Yes. Yes. Amazing! The answers you gave were very clear and in depth. They were different from others we reached, their other pieces of the puzzle. Awesome, thank you!

S: Yeah, I'm amazed! I love you.

A: I love you, honor you, and respect you.

END OF SESSION

-------------<◇>-------------

These are glimpses of the beauties of some of the Alien Races that have gone through the process of Ascension. Graduating from Dimension through Dimension. Where their collective consciousness together traveled through the Fifth Dimension perhaps, then the Sixth and on... achieving the Unity Consciousness that is realized in the 13th Dimension. Graduating and entering then another construct of the Universe all together in the 15th Dimension, that is no longer a construct like ours of the 13th Dimensions and below. This sacred Elven race were pure beings created by the Nephilim Angelics. This race like the Angels, at some point in time also reached the lowest Dimensions as they fractalized in Creation, and they too went through the process of Ascension climbing up the densities of the Dimensions by experiencing through their fractals. Understanding though that the Seraphim from the 12-13th Dimensions fractalize as Elohim in the 11th Dimension so that they can become part of this Universe. The Angelics are not limited to the 13th Dimension, as when they bridge out past the 13th Dimension, they become an infinite expression, just as we all do. The Nephilim is a higher angelic race from beyond the 13th Dimension, which the Seraphim angels and Archangel Michael himself are part of. To clarify, the angelic realms of the Nephilim and more are beyond the 13th Dimension, then the Seraphim (12-13th D), and then the Elohim (11th D).

This beautiful 15th Dimensional Elven race was created by the Nephilim, and they evolved from the angelic essences as pure beings. These pure Elven beings assist the Angelics just as the elementals and fairies lovingly assist us on Earth. How could a collective race of this beauty and magnitude be completely wiped out from Creation? Their particular DNA coding eradicated from existence, as not one race is or will ever be created the same. This brings such sadness to one's heart, however also an awareness creating an honorable acknowledgement and homage to this race that gave us the honor of expressing their story through Sandra.

Could it be that because such a high Dimensional race or races were eradicated, it caused our regression collectively through a form of a domino effect? Since we are all connected through sacred organic life cords Universally, what kinds of effects and infringement could this have rippled down to the lower Dimensions? We would say that it would cause a vast amount of unbalance and trauma to all life in our Multiverse. Since the high Dimensional beings provide knowledge for other neighboring planets, which in turn they all can be seen as our guides and soul families from the higher Dimensions.

This would be the most potent manner to attack a Universe or Universes by taking out some of the most powerful and wisest Elders of Creation in the higher Dimensions. Because their sacred knowledge would be then lost to the lower Dimensions. This sacred ancient knowledge came to an extinction, as so too did the Elders that carried it for Creation. It would disconnect the lower Dimensional beings like us from their sacred teachings and knowledge, thus making us easier to control and infringe upon, because of our lack of spiritual maturity unbeknownst to us. All though understanding it in an infinity perspective, this race and others sacred knowledge does not ever come to a complete void as it will always remain in the crystalline memory codices of all organic life. As we too, as crystals, carry organic data within us, which then can be retrieved, remembered and downloaded once more into an individual or community who is connecting to the high enough vibration of the matching sacred knowledge.

The impact of the eradication of this sacred race is significant. It is as if there is a malfunction within our neurological system, one brainwave is damaged which then affects our other cognitive functions. The one side of the brain that is still intact would have to work harder, stressing itself out to make up for the part that is wounded or no longer functioning at its fullest capacity. The malfunction damaged parts of the brain being the planets who are being harvested through the A.I. Archon Spiders mentioned in the previous Chapter, and these precious civilizations that have been wiped out through the Galactic Wars. Now all that stands in their planetary sphere is the empty shell and residue of what they once were. We as the Third Dimensional planets who are compromised with A.I. injected viruses into our once Organic Matrix construct, are the denser, most darkest parts of the Universe. The functioning parts of the brain being the majority, who are those benevolent Alien Civilizations that have been able to hold on with their strong enough collective vibration and are as our torches aiding together to lift us up.

All the prior sessions that we read up to this one, helps us understand why the Reptilians attack in the manner as they do in the Universes. These abominations that Sandra spoke of, that are both Insect and Reptilian Robot Hybrids, are an elite Archon Soldier Squad. Through these invasions of planets and communities, Archons have gone through the Multiverses abducting races. They then have highly intelligently placed pieces of organic lifeforms intertwined and stitched together with negative technologies. In this session's example, the Archons then use the Reptilians as characters in a video game. With the game console being the artificial brain intelligence of the Archons and using the game controller to control and maneuver these consciousnesses in these Hybrid bodies as if they were only but a playable character in a video game. Further explaining why, the Reptilians often say they just know the directions come from somewhere and then they are just 'moved' to do them. They are like robotic chess pieces, just being moved around by the Archon game master to accomplish negative harvesting agendas.

The 'Soul Tone' mentioned through Sandra's session, is an example of how even though we are awakening or are awakened, how reminisces of the old inverted paradigm still bleed through into our reality of spiritual awakening. This is only but one example of how even when awakened, it is a dedicated humbled process that we must go through to deprogram all the falsities encoded and brainwashed into us when we were in the Inverted paradigm. This example being how this client even though all the answers were found within her, as we learned about the vastness of knowledge and wisdom she truly is, being the only one left of this extinct race. Because she was in a time that her soul felt hunger for growth and was experiencing the deep state amnesia, we all do in that stage of soul processing in awakening. And, when going to a well-known Light Worker Channeler, she was given a 'Soul Tone' to help bring back her Source's energy and light codes. Through the practice of listening to this 'Soul Tone' daily, it was supposed to bring back fractals of her, the idea being she could become closer to the wholeness of her Source embodied self finally. Instead, since the Channel was not from the purest intent of love or in true intent in service-to-others, the fractals that came and answered that call through the 'Soul Tone' were a vibratory match to 1) the Channel and 2) the client who was experiencing an overwhelming unbalanced call to want to grow and to remember. The fractals who answered the call were negative Reptilians claiming to be that who would fill in this void for the client.

The RA Collective explained to me that this is one of the biggest false lights holding us back. People not realizing that one must be very careful in what they allow to integrate into them. There are constantly negative polarized entities or A.I. Archons being integrated into people because they allow it, because of the lack of mature understanding of how easy it is to consent for a negative alien to integrate into us. The goal being, their Archonic need of wanting to eventually replace or compromise the soul for their negative harvesting needs. Otherwise like Sandra, one can end up with a negative polarized Reptilian posing as our false fractal that then we would have consented to integrate into our DNA, to actually become part of us. Imagine how much darkness that soul would integrate into them, just on the fact that Reptilians are organically made with more darkness than light. What of the karma that the Reptilian carries as well, that has now integrated into one's belief system and affecting our organic timeline? The Reptilians karma would become ours given the deep integration of us and the negative Reptilian, both becoming ONE. That would be a vastness of imbalance of negative karma that the client would need to now start acting out upon in their life.

This Archonic infringement on all races is absolutely unacceptable by divine structure and Universal Laws. This is bypassing our Universal Laws through false cracks created by the Archons themselves. The more we learn to honor and sacredly protect our energy, as we would protect and shield an infant, the more that we will become wielders of our organic Ascension timelines. And this is exactly what the Archons don't want us to know, so they can keep feeding false God-Like ego-based beliefs unto Light-Workers whom we schedule sessions with, when we are at our most vulnerable. We become even more disempowered through these misled Light Workers who claim they have the power to retrieve peoples Source Light energy back for them, how they are the saviors for those truth seekers to remember who they are… When we allow someone else to become our savior, then we give away our power and rights to know that we are our own savior out of this Inverted A.I. Matrix. No one has the power to do that but the soul itself.

This is what they mean when the Angels try to explain to us how powerful the negative alien races have grown throughout Creation. Though our hope grows in strength, as we know that the Universes are organically working together to eradicate these inorganic infringements when the final Physical Ascension comes to be, through us and the Universe. We can and will unite against these collective powers of negative artificial technologies and their violations of organic life. The unity of benevolent beings is building up together a collective strength construct of NOT CONSENTING to what is not organic and divine to our collective signature frequencies. With each awakening soul, our strength grows in numbers with each passing hour, each passing day!

In the next Chapter, the final pieces come together when we truly understand how it is that Archons came to be at their beginning stages.

"I am a high vibrational light being that feels everything within these frequencies. I work strongly in speaking what others shy from doing so. I am open to your opinion and honor you. It is only when the intents of your comments stem forth from a negative polarized entity or A.I. Archon influencing you, that I must block you. To leave that frequency there which is connected to my high vibrational creation, is to infringe upon it and my vibration. I DO NOT CONSENT."
~AuroRa 🖤

-------------<◇>-------------

32

NOT OF LIGHT

Session #264: Recorded April 2020.
Never before shared.

In this online A.U.R.A. Hypnosis Healing session, Leona takes us to a life where she had a very important mission where her whole civilization's existence depended on the success of her completion of the mission. When one leaves the safety of one's home planet and the dangers that come with it while traveling in the Universe. Come experience a journey home with so much on the line. We then travel back to the time when Archons began in Creation. Learn more about how a benevolent civilization from the Tenth Dimension supports Earth's transition in this critical time. And what is their connection to the sacred Essenes teachings?

"There is a small piece of her soul in that moment that called out in resonance for Source of her love to sustain her. So that light was matching that prayer with that resonance and it was of Source. It was to remind her of her constant connection and embodiment of that. So that she could move through the challenge."
-Higher Self

L: [Leona] I am on mud. I see a desert. Red rock. Yellow rock. And it's dry but I am standing on a wet spot.
A: [Aurora] You said you're in a desert. Is there sand under you?
L: It's more like dry rock.
A: You said you're standing on a wet spot?
L: Yeah, like on a little bit of wet mud.
A: Look at yourself. Do you feel like you have a body?
L: Yeah.
A: Look down at your feet. Are you wearing anything on your feet?
L: No.
A: How many toes do you have?
L: Six on each.
A: Look at your hands. How many fingers do you have?
L: Seven on each.
A: How about your skin? What does your skin look like?
L: Looks like…it's like the environment. It's like a red... brown and there's some shimmering.
A: Is there anything you're wearing?
L: Yeah, a little bit of fabrics.
A: What colors are they?
L: Like whites and greens, it is covering my torso.
A: Do you feel like you are female, male or both?

L: I am neither.

A: Are you wearing any jewelry?

L: There are some cuffs on my wrists and something on my chest. It is not a necklace but it's like a stone or amulet, like just placed on my chest without a strap.

A: Are there any crystals or shapes to this amulet?

L: There is a teardrop-shaped crystal kind of in the center and then there's a lot of different geometric shapes at the bottom and some kind of metal so it's sort of like a teardrop-shaped amulet but with lots of etchings in the silver and then at the top point of the teardrop is some sort of like green crystal but it's not solid, it's like watery.

A: The cuffs. Are there any crystals or shapes on them?

L: I see some etchings on them, but they're gold, mostly gold. Filled in with some silver, brass. There's a band in the middle. They are large cuffs...on both wrists.

A: Is there anything you are carrying?

L: No.

A: Do you feel like you are younger or older?

L: I feel like I am some kind of a young adult.

A: Look all around you and describe to me, what else do you see?

L: Big mesas and open sky. The sky is blue, and all the stone is red rock, and there's no one that I can see nearby. There's some wind and I am pushing my feet into the mud like I am...one of my feet, I am pressing into the mud patch that I am standing on.

A: Is there a reason why you are doing it?

L: Yeah, I am like, I am here for something. I am digging. But only with my feet right now, it's like a kind of a dance, like I am just like, rooting, digging on this one wet spot in the desert.

A: Going back to your amulet. Everything has a consciousness. See if you are able to connect to it and if it has a message for you.

L: It is saying something about 'you are guided here, you have been guided here, you are completing something. And you have been fighting for a long time, but you don't need to do that at this moment. In this moment you need to be rooting in your body and feeling. You have been fierce and even so you do not need to pray, you just need to be present here in the same place.'

A: Beautiful. Thank you for those messages. Continue to do what you are doing and tell me all the details as you continue to move time.

L: I am moving my hips and trying to release my weight into the mud. Feeling the mud touch my feet and move through my toes and I am feeling a little bit impatient, but also light.

A: What do you feel you are feeling impatient about?

L: It's just, like a kind of a funny feeling like, come on. Let's just do this. I know what I am looking for there, but it's going to be giving me some issues like I have been trying to get this for a while.

A: Okay, is this the only way to get through it, to dig through your feet?

L: No, I can step away from the spot and just watch it come up.

A: Keep moving time along and tell me every detail. Tell me what's going on next.

L: I moved down lower, and I kneel and I put my forehead on the mud and press it so that there is the moisture on my forehead. As I do that, I make some sort of prayer offering and start drawing in the mud and just little pictures, little...it is like some sort of writing that I know I have been carrying. I think it is from my other place, my planet or my people. I am drawing these pictures in the mud and then...I have sort of a fierce like, tough energy and I am tired of trying so hard. So, I step away and I just sit on the rock and I wait...and it's still in the desert but there's some softening that is happening in the mud spot and sunlight shining through and kind of like a cone, but like a rounded cone shape poking out from the Earth to the top of the soil... and that's it's raising and emerging from the soil and I am feeling a sense of awe and curiosity and some peace. Maybe a little...a little nervousness too. And I stand up and as this raises, I know I need to do some movement with my body, so I do movements that I know will help me communicate with this thing.

A: Tell me about this movement.

L: It's like hands on my chest and I am moving my arms from the side down towards the thing and down to the Earth and kind of like a praising gesture and then some pulling...some pulling movements touching my hands like opening up space and then some shaking.

A: As you are waiting for this to come up, can you describe to me how is it that you look? Your face, your facial features?

L: I see big...kind of like, big eyes, cat-like, animal-like eyes. And I have some...I kind of look like the desert, I kind of look like a rock being, but also with a lot of fluidity and there are different dots...dotted down like the center of my forehead and nose. I do have a mouth. And these dots are light green. My skin is like, it also...it changes. It is like one moment, kind of like a rock, red rock and then it shifts to green or some sort of more shimmering or fluid.

A: Do you have ears?

L: Yeah, they are like little holes.

A: How about a nose?

L: Yeah, but it's like a lizard or something.

A: Like a lizard nose?

L: Yes, it's like little slits.

A: Do you have any hair on your body?

L: Yes. There is some...not quite hair like human hair but it's like, almost like an equivalent and it's like, like a ridge, almost like a mohawk but like a... like how an iguana has a ridge.

A: There is hair in that ridge? Something that looks like hair?

L: Yeah, little hairs and they have different colors, iridescent colors and... yes.

A: Is there anything else that stands out within your body?

L: I have some marks like in the center of my hands like circles. And I feel like I am really strong, physically strong.

A: Very good. Continue moving time to see what is going on next with what you are trying to bring up from the ground.

L: The thing I am looking for is coming up from the ground. Starting with the light and now it is raising, emerging from the mud and... I see a... like a small book and it is raising and raising and there are stones on the book. It's a leather document. It's covered in leather, but it's paper inside. And as it raises, it's drying off the soil it is releasing from it. It is still in this light beam.

A: How is it raising?

L: It's like levitating from the ground upwards and then it pauses, and I am walking towards it and I stopped at the light beam and I kneel, and I make a movement of respect and reverence. I kneel and I pray, and I have something in my hand...looks like from setting the space for receiving it. The book opens itself and there's something like a stone amulet. It is actually changing shapes. It's like, I see it as a diamond right now, diamond shape, but it's dark. And then it shifts to some sort of...more like an amulet. It seems like it's fluid. It's not static. But I am just watching for right now. Receiving its energy.

A: So, it's a book. It also has a... what did you call it?

L: Like an activator. It's like a stone or amulet. It keeps changing shape. It doesn't really matter what it actually is. It's just like the frequency of the thing within the book. When I see it as like a diamond shape, dark stone and it then shifts to like a metal amulet with a lot of inscriptions on it with a language that I don't know.

A: You are able to memorize some of those languages or symbols. When you come to it, you're able to draw them out for yourself. Continue telling me what happens next.

L: I realize it's time to really like receiving it, by touching it and so I kneel down and dig some more into the soil where it is and make a circle around this light beam that the book is in and I go walk around the light beam, walk around, walk around a few times. Knowing that I am to be in a respectful relationship with this thing. And then I face it and with permission I enter the light beam and I receive the book and the stone activator

A: How do you receive it?

L: I receive it in my hands, and I hold it to my chest for some moments and... feels peaceful and I am receiving messages from it

A: Let me know what you are receiving?

L: Something about "You have done a lot of good for your people, for your community and some peace colony Queen something…" that is all I can hear right now.

A: Keep moving time along and let me know what happens next of importance.

L: I am aware there are some aircrafts in the sky or something like a ship, like a small beam in the sky as I am receiving it and it makes me nervous. But I received this book, and I received its messages. I close out that light beam, and I know it is time to go. I do actually have a bag that was behind a rock and I grabbed that. It's like my backpack. I have the book and the stone. I start running and I am running really fast. I have long legs and I am running really fast through the desert.

A: Why do you feel that you have to run?

L: It's a 'knowing' that I can't linger there. Because something that I don't want to encounter that's not in my highest good knows that I've received what I've looked for. So, I am running but it's not just running away. It's also running to it. So, running with dignity and purpose. Feeling really alive and the sun is setting, and the stars are coming up. It's a deep night and the stars are filling the sky. It's beautiful. As I finish my long run, travel...I see a small fire tucked in between some cliffs that I have approached, and I know that's where I will stay for that night. I walk towards it. I undress myself. I am dressed with the fabrics that are wrapped around me and I take a bottle of water or something like it, it's been in my pack and I dump it on myself, on my head and wash myself and bathe myself.

A: This cave, is there anything that stands out?

L: It is more like a nook in between high desert walls. It's not a full cave. Like I am in a red canyon. There is sand on the ground and then there's just this little fire that's been waiting for me.

A: The fire was in there already?

L: Yes, it was there and as I was doing my run. I could see it from a distance, so I knew where to go for the night.

A: You mentioned that you have a bag with you. Look in the bag. What else do you have in there besides the object you have just acquired?

L: There is the water container, or the liquid container and there's some fruit, or dried fruit, almost like dates but not quite. Some fruit I actually don't know but it's some fruit, like a snack and there's a little snake at the bottom of the bag and the snake is like my friend. My pet. And it's just been really good the whole day, supported me and stayed quiet. I take the snake out and let it go. It is small. It is like a garden snake almost. And it just wraps around my wrists and moves around. It's been in the bag all day.

A: Keep moving time along, let me know what happens next of importance.

L: I go to sleep; I am feeling tired. I am also feeling grateful but there is some sense of grief for I also have to go back to where I come from tomorrow. I know there's a lot of suffering there. It's my responsibility to share the message of this book I have received. I know I am not alone, but there's a feeling of weariness of always being the one doing this part, of going out and coming back. I also am wondering about that aircraft I saw earlier. It did not feel good to see that in the moment. And luckily it didn't see me fully, but I know that they know I am out here.

A: Who knows you are out there?

L: Some sort of foreign entity or energy or being that is not in alignment with the health of my planet. It's really invested in separation and planting seeds of timelines. They are people that are rooted in separation. And I know that that is not in alignment with the truth and I am from the stars. Because I was born of angel beings. I was birthed into this life to be in some position of leadership. So as to support the transition and halt those timeline distortions that the energy of the aircraft represents. Although I feel young in this body that I am in for this lifetime, I am middle aged like maybe in my 20's, late 20's, and I am also actually very ageless. But I have some work to do in releasing the resentment or the shame about being in this position of leadership.

A: Keep moving time along, tell me what happens next of importance.

L: I have woken up and I am walking. I have had my water and had some of the fruit in my pack. I see a group of four beings that are just with fabrics all along them. They are tall and I have not met them before, but they are helping me with my safe passage and helping me with the transition. I know that they come to witness me and be with me in this last stage of returning home.

A: Where do you see them?

L: They are in front of me. They are like standing there in the desert, some yards in front of me and they are cloaked in fabrics. They have arms and I know they have eyes, but they are underneath the fabrics. They are solid and welcoming. But they don't have much personality. They are just there to support the transition.

A: Keep moving the scene along and tell me what happens next?

L: With these four beings I move through space. We are gliding through space quickly across far distances through the desert and I get to a spring. There's a watering hole spring. So, there's some trees. It's a sacred place. We stop, and the four beings dissolve, they let me be alone with this water. I take my pack off and I kneel down and put my head on the ground. I make some offerings, some prayers for this water body and it is small, not big. It's a small sacred place, and I know that it's a blessing. I get my arms in and pull up some water over my face. I drink some water. I say thank you and I also fill my container. There is some like shimmering light emanating from the water source and it's very beautiful. I am enjoying some sunlight on my skin as I dry off from the water that I washed over me and there's like my own little ship...not a ship, it's almost like a plate. A big saucer that I can sit on and it's blue and light green with a white and light green circle glowing in the center of it and it's not very big but it's how I travel through time space. It's levitating nearby and kind of just came out of nowhere to notice it's time for me to go. So, I say thank you and give my blessings to the water place. I look around at the desert and say thank you. I step onto my saucer and sit on it and the center circle activates with glowing light and my whole body activates a glowing light. As I sit, it's like I am getting locked in and we hover for a moment and then it raises me and then we start flying over the land. There's some destruction or something. As I get into the outer layers of the stratosphere, I see that there's some disruption with the other aircrafts or whatever they are. And they know that I am trying to leave this place. I need to defend myself to get through this passage safely. There's some distraction as I am trying to transition from this place to the next, there are different aircrafts coming in front of me and getting in the way. They are not shooting but they are like emanating an energy that would deplete me.

A: What shapes are their ships?

L: Theirs is more like triangular, pointy, very white, gray kind of like metal. Mine looks more blue green and it's not really made of metal. I am scared because I am alone, but I remember I have that new item. They definitely want to hurt me; they don't want me to get back. I am scared but I remember that book. So, I hold my bag and feel the book in there and activate a cord within me that emanates a really strong force field that affirms my safety. I know that this game they are trying to play is just a game. I am safe and I have what I need even though they are creating a lot of fear and destruction. I won't fall for it; I am cutting through it. My arm is centered, and as I do this my body is changing and I am in space now, I am traveling. It is very dark. Although they have been coming into my field and trying to disrupt my path...

A: What is coming into your field?

L: The same beings, the same ships. But they are quieting now, going away and as I go away, I continue to feel the book, feel my center. My body is changing shape like I am not the same creature I was in the desert.

A: Do you think that these saucers or spaceships, if they wanted to, they could have stopped you from leaving that area?

L: I think if they wanted to, they would have...they would have demolished me in space.

A: Why do you think it is that they didn't?

L: I think whatever I connected to through this item, through this book and through my own inner source was too bright for them. So, they couldn't really see me as I was moving. It was bright but also invisible. But I also don't really know why.

A: See where you are going now. Describe to me what you are seeing all around you.

L: I see a star planet; I see space and more space, and I see a bright planet and I am approaching it. As I approach it my form changes and the stuff that was needed, like the stoned skin, reptile spikes and stuff in the desert, that's dissolving, and I am feeling like I am just birthing a light. I am just light. I don't really have a body at the moment. Even the saucer I was riding on is dissolving and as I get closer to my planet. Then I get closer and enter. I enter and I find myself in a rainforest. It's really wet with incredibly tall trees and there's a stream river at the bottom and I am sitting by it...I am playing by it. My body is coming back, or a body is coming back. I am not just light and...

A: What do you look like now?

L: I feel some fur and I also have some like blue skin, blue shimmery skin. But I have firm parts of me as well. I have two fingers. I can't really see my feet, but I feel really poised and beautiful. I feel like I still have those dots down the center of my head and down my chin. I still have that amulet that I was within the desert on my chest.

A: This star planet? Is there a place that you are meant to go with now that you have acquired this new object?

L: Yeah, there's actually a path from where I am sitting by the stream. The stone path I am walking on right now. I know that that will lead me back home and to my community. I am walking along that. I know that I need to bring this to the council. There's a sense of needing to bring it into my community and into my elders. So, I go, and I enter this really beautiful, glowing wooden structure, it's like a city, like a tree city. I entered that and there's a fire in the center of the room and many of the people are in there either sitting on the edges or tending the fire.

A: Do your people look like you?

L: Yeah, for the most part, I can't really see all of them, but they feel like they do. Some of them are more like light being, like just light. But now they have blue skin and fur, and they feel kind of like, they feel earthy. They live in a tree basically, or some sort of living organism. I brought this thing home and when I entered the room, they were all quiet. They welcome me back. One in particular, one runs up to me and embraces me and then starts touching the dots on my forehead and also on my chest and speaking in a language I don't fully understand. But I know it's a blessing and a welcome and gratitude. I am actually really tired, so I am really thankful I am home with them. I need to drink water, so they give me water. That's it and I communicate that I have this thing that we have been looking for. So, I take it out of my bag, and I give it to one of the elders, someone who is an eldership and in leadership there. I do the same bow that I did at the spring with him.

A: You said that it's a council?

L: Yeah, it feels like an Elder Council in a circular room with a circle of people.

A: How many people would it be?

L: There are different rings...the inner ring of the Council is four people. The second ring around that is eight. The third ring is twelve. And so, I give this item to the elder. They know it's time to sit and to be in counsel. They asked me to be in the inner ring with the three elders.

A: Okay, so with you there are four there?

L: Yeah.

A: So, there's four and there are three rings. Four, eight and then twelve?

L: Mm-hmm.

A: Keep telling me what happens next.

L: I share the story and I share a part of the story of what happened before being in the desert which was actually like a lot of battle. Like a lot of fighting, like I was in some sort of battle. I have been away from home actually a lot longer than just those few nights in the desert, that was the end of my journey.

A: You are able to understand all the details. What and who is it that you are battling? Tell me what's going on before your journey. What are you telling them?

L: There's been a seeding of distortion out in our Universe that will impact the planet. I initiated the journey to find this book without realizing that I would first need to face the expressions of that distortion. Part of the purpose of them feeding this...those who I was fighting. As they want to control outcomes, especially not only for me and my planet but for Earth. Which is tied to my planet, and the healing that we do on my planet. Activating influences and supports the healing of Earth so the forces that I was navigating conflict with and fighting are trying to disrupt and distract us from fulfilling our healing work. I don't quite know why. But it's a range of energies that I was fighting. It's everything from just like kind of stupid distractions, like bombing warships to really nefarious actually evil...I was moving through those. Each time I encountered them I had to strengthen my shielding and I was able to navigate. There was a web of distortion that they placed in front of me before I could get my items. I was able to navigate that because the light from my planet and my fractal is so bright, but it was not simple. At one point I was caught by them and actually harmed, physically and tortured.

A: How did you get out of that?

L: There was some kind of assistance that came in. I am in a ship, like a metal room and alone. But they've been scaring me, like putting in poison, just enough to keep me alive but actually enough to keep me really sick. I am in this room and I don't know where I am. Like they really are not wanting us to be well and to live. But I also felt assistance came in like all I can see is a little light, little angel or a little ball of light that assisted me with getting out. I also was just pissed like my anger in that I am feeling caged, it helped me actually. With the softening of the light that came, I was able to find balance between my rage and my love. That fusion melted some space in the room. A little space that I could crawl out of and find my way out of the ship. Back to my saucer, back to my journey and through that then I moved onward.

A: Before that, going back to the ship, I know that was a hard situation. You said that they were poisoning you and were they physically hitting you? And you said you had scars?

L: Yeah, I think there was like some knife cutting, like on my arms. Hitting, and also like manipulation of my creative energy, my sexual energy.

A: How are they doing that?

L: I just see the image of... like that part of my center being taken from...without my consent. Along with that, some shame and anger coming through, which then helps me get out.

A: Why do you think that they were doing this to you? What was the purpose?

L: They are threatening my community there. They felt that by holding a young leader hostage, that would be a useful message to the rest of the beings from where I am coming from to not pursue our highest destiny. Because if we do, we will be killed and harmed and we will create harm because of the trauma of that.

A: Did the people back in your home planet, your star planet, know that you were contained?

L: They knew I disappeared, there were people who were tracking me and staying in tune with me throughout my travels. They didn't know what happened, but they knew I went off the map. They didn't know the actual situation of how violent they were. So, they are scared too.

A: You are fully protected in this time of space. You are able to see clearly. What do they look like, these beings that are doing this to you?

L: All I see is like dark pitch black, kind of like triangular shapes, like pointy shapes. I am not really seeing any bodies; all I see is some jagged edge...

A: What do they look like?

L: There are some reptiles and there's also male human-like but really drained, like really pale. Their eyes are really pale like they had no soul. It is a mix of Reptilian features and then also human-like, or at least looking like human beings that are manipulating energies for their own control.

A: Some of these Reptilian beings, what type of forms do they look like? Like what type of Reptilian?

L: They are pretty large, almost crocodile. The image of a crocodile keeps coming but they feel like they are more the helpers, like they're just there to do the grunt work. The really nasty energy is coming from that human-looking being.

A: Going back to that light. Explain to me what's going on when that light came to you?

L: I am laying on the ground and I feel like I don't know if I am going to survive or like how I would ever get home. So, I am just flat on the ground and this light just comes through, it just fades in. It's really small at first and then it gets a little bigger but it's still rather small, no larger than two feet. And it feels like a source of love and encouragement and toughness...reminds me of home and I actually do have more resources that I know right now.

A: Is there a color to the light?

L: It is like a pink, golden yellow form.

A: Once it's in there, what does it do to help you?

L: It just brings me back to myself and it also reminds me that I am not alone because while I am in there, I feel like I have taken on the messaging that the torture gave which is that I am abandoned, and I will never get home. So, the light reminds me that that's actually not accurate and encourages me to get up. So, I slowly stand up and it comes closer to my body and washes through my cells. It merges with my body and it heals some of the physical pain I am in.

A: After it does that, what happens next?

L: Well after that I left that ship and then I made my way. Over a long period of time, I flew, and I made my way to that desert where I found the items I was looking for, so I am telling my story to the Council.

A: The light, the way you were able to get out... the light, what did it do?

L: It merged with my body and it helped heal the physical pain. It encouraged me to remember my people at home, who were waiting for me. As it merged in my body there is a softening in the room and so that a little part of the room actually melts or dissolves so I could crawl out of a hole without being found. My saucer came to me once I left through the hole.

A: Okay. This light, did it stay in you or did it ever come out?

L: It is in me now.

A: Tell me, this light, what kind of connection does it have to you? Where did it come from?

L: It comes from Source. It's very pure and it's simple and it's love and it's healing.

A: Continue telling your story to the Council.

L: I am telling them the whole story that I just shared of being abducted and tortured. Then the light that came and guided me to escape. Getting to the desert and running through the desert, finding the mud spot, finding the items, finding my fire and sleeping. And the four guides that came to help me transition to the spring. The sacred spring where I drank and washed before returning home. I tell them the story and they receive it. The elder is holding the book and the stone within the book. I would tell the story; the others are witnessing this story and when I am done telling it there is sort of like a wave of energy through the room. A settling and the elder opens the book. He begins reading the language that is inscribed in the book and he takes the stone amulet activator in his hand and he places it in a key holder that is like a little disc in the fire, the central fire of our council. There's a fire in the middle of all of our rings of the Council and then in the fire just hovering about the fires there is a disc, it's like you have to place something in it to activate it. This item within the book is that and so the elder opens the book and he begins reading the prayers and the messages of the book in this foreign language and places this stone thing in the disc as he's reading. We all watch, and I close my eyes. It feels like something has been completed. We got something back that we needed for our next stage of evolution and growth. The room is receiving that feeling of completion. The elders, the other elders, they know this language that is in the book that I don't remember. But the elders know and as this leader who has the book in his hands is reciting the things, they start joining and chanting with him.

A: What does this language look like?

L: It is just like lots of different interesting etchings, like different markings, and it is almost like glyphs like on ruins, but I don't know it. Also, the letters in the book are three-dimensional like they're not just flat, they also are alive, the language itself. So, it's a medicinal language, it's not just spoken or written. It's also a being in its own way. As they speak it's very powerful and it feels very fluid. It's like a medicine, the room receives that, and I receive that. Then the fires are burning, and the lock key has been activated and I don't fully know what that means at this moment. But I know that I did what I was assigned.

A: You said the key has been activated?

L: Yes, because the stone that was within this book was placed in the disc that's hovering above the fire. It's like a key of some kind.

A: What does that mean, what is the purpose to that? What is it doing for you or your civilization?

L: It feels like it's some kind of initiation for all of us. But I think for me personally, there's a sense that as he recites these things and places it, I am remembering also that it's okay to nourish the aspects of myself that are outside of the duty and the mission I have been on. It is sort of a softening for me personally, but for the collective, it's like an initiation into a new chapter. Where not only will we be focusing on the healing work and the creation we've always done, we also now have more wisdom about how to share the Universe with forces like the ones I encountered. We are more prepared. And there's a sense of...not like going to war, it's not really like that dramatic, we are standing up in our dignity and we know that we have what we need to face this distortion. But we also need to step up in our work. And this is a time of great healing and opportunity for that. I think for me, I am in some kind of role of like young leadership and I think my role is evolving and maturing in this moment as the key is activated.

A: With these elders, you mentioned that during this process, there was a seeding that occurred that was affecting the Universe. If we could go back to that time and space and what the seeding is exactly. What happened to cause this. What is this?

L: The energy is coming up like a ripping apart and a separation that has something to do with. It is like some beings wanting to tear away from Source. I don't know how that even began except that part of them wanted to create outside of the organic way of Creation. So, it started with an innocent curiosity that then grew into a chasm of separation and domination that these energies and these beings got really addicted to. To where that kind of influence spread throughout many different places and planets. Obviously, Earth too. This distortion seeded from longing to control Creation and test the waters learning outside of an organic growth pattern. Through that it just built on itself with a lot of momentum and density to the point where it's become like a bastardization of itself. There are different expressions of it, but some of it is quite negative. Me and my people on this planet can really see through it. I think, for us, it's hard because we want to see the beings as they are in connection to Source from the original moment. But there's some kind of atonement or reckoning or transformation that must happen before we can get to that point because so much momentum is built with the destruction they have caused in different places. Because that distortion is so powerful it is like a tuning fork for all sorts of beings and people. So, the distortion in me can be in resonance with them. Because they are so strong, it will get turned up. Fortunately, my people on this planet are very evolved. If there is a distortion of energy, we see it and we work with it and we transmute with it with ease. But many other creatures and beings in the Universe don't have that capacity. So, the momentum and density... it's not in alignment with life.

A: To understand it began as a curiosity and then it distorted so deeply. You said that it became separated from Source?

L: Or at least created a lot of blocks to not recognize its relationship to Source.

A: These, are they entities, or what is the best way to explain this?

L: Yeah, entities.

A: These entities, do they have any connections to Archons? Or is it something else?

L: I think it's something else. I think they know of Archons, but they are not seen.

A: Did Archons birth or come out from these types of energies eventually?

L: Yes.

A: Is it ancient, like as old as Source or a little bit younger?

L: A little bit younger but they are quite old.

A: Do they have any forms?

L: I see some asteroid forms but that doesn't feel as relevant as just the frequency. Which is very like the distorted, harsh, pulling, tearing itself from itself.

A: Is it all dark?

L: Yeah, I see some red light as well actually, but it is mostly dark.

A: Does it have any light in there?

L: No, it's pretty dense. I just see some red glow behind the dark asteroids.

A: Does it have any connections to negative technologies?

L: It plants...it births negative technologies.

A: Is it part of the Inverted A.I. Matrix that occurred here on Earth?

L: Yes, it is connected to that.

A: Are they connected to harvesting souls?

L: Yes, although I don't know how, but they are connected to this. It's like its own ecosystem, all these titles and names for different negative entities. It's like they're all part of the same ecosystem or whatever. I don't have the language.

A: Would you say that they need souls' energy or is it just something that they do?

L: They do need that. Now I am thinking of a ship I was on, it was easier for me to connect with those beings because the initial seed distortion with the asteroids feels so abstract, but the beings I met on the aircraft like the Reptilian and human creature...the human creature definitely benefited from sucking soul energy. They're collecting. They're harvesting. Maybe that's what the ship was holding. Yeah.

A: Thank you for answering those questions. Is there anything else that the Council here that is within you, ask them, do they have any messages for you or for us? Is there anyone from the Council that would like to speak?

L: Yes.

A: Thank you. If we can allow for that Council member to speak through you. Thank you. We love you, honor you, and respect you. Thank you for being here. Welcome.

Council Member: Thank you.

A: If you can tell me a little bit more about why is it that you have chosen to speak to us?

Council Member: I am here to share the message that this was a moment of initiation for this collective that was intended to support the very transition Earth is on at this moment. Our daughter, who went on this journey, she's now blessed with the water of Source. She is given now, the choice to step more fully into her role as a leader and wisdom keeper. There is much to say about how our role in our planet is tied to Earth. We are with you during this time. We are the beings that support humans to connect to the inner spark of envisioning a healthier world, healthier systems. We are the hydration to the dreams. We carry a lot of insight about how to create healthy functional civilizations and align it with the planet and the elements.

A: Thank you. Can you tell us what Dimension are you in?

Council Member: Tenth.

A: Is there a name that your race goes by?

Council Member: The Elsenes.

A: Is that connected to...there's a group that we know of on Earth that sounds similar, the Essenes. Do you have any connections to them?

Council Member: Yes.

A: What is your connection?

Council Member: We are in resonance. The teachings of that group on Earth were received in relationship to us. But they are not our only family group on Earth, they are one of many.

A: What connections do you have to the RA?

Council Member: They are as our family, and they are with us all the time.

A: This object that was on that planet, why was it originally placed there?

Council Member: Hiding and it was meant to be hidden. And it was also meant to be consecrated and blessed by that land. So that our daughter could receive it at the right time.

A: I know she already explained some of what that did, when that piece went in and basically an activation key. Can you tell us a little more about the purpose of that and what it did?

Council Member: On the one hand, it's a fortifier. It's a strengthening moment for this collective and it is also a compass. So, as we continue to live and exist on our planet, we can orient towards the energies of this key. If and when we ever feel distracted or in fear, we remember this key and we turn to it and receive its blessings. So, it's an initiator, a strengthener and a compass.

A: Thank you. Any other messages you have for us today?

Council Member: No.

A: Such a beautiful honor to have met you today. Thank you for sharing such a profound life with us of her, and you. Thank you, I love you, I honor you and I respect you.

Council Member: Thank you.

The Higher Self is called forth.

A: Let's leave that life now. Can I please speak to the Higher Self of Leona?

Higher Self: Yes.

A: Beautiful. Thank you. I love you. I honor you. I respect you. Thank you for being here. I know that you hold all the records of Leona's different lives. May I ask questions, please?

Higher Self: Yes.

A: Thank you. If you can tell me, why is it that you took her to that life where we went through such a detailed journey? What was the purpose and how does it connect for her now?

Higher Self: There are a lot of reflections to themes of that life in her current life. Feeling like a solo adventure, feeling in travel, feeling alone, feeling on mission, healing and counsel. Part of the learning of that lifetime, for this moment is to teach her that she is quite powerful and fierce. That she does have a role and it is important and there's no need to doubt in the travels, the journey she's on. There's no reason to doubt why, but to trust that it is a part of a greater healing. Part of the imagery to this desert being that she was, we hope it will support her in remembering her fierceness and her confidence. She does not have to play small; she actually is quite expansive and capable and powerful.

A: Thank you. That light that came to her, how did it find her? She mentioned it came from Source. Can you tell me a little bit more about it?

Higher Self: That moment in that aircraft, she was at such a low place, so close to death. There is a small piece of her soul in that moment that called out in resonance for Source of her love to sustain her. So that light was matching that prayer with that resonance and it was of Source. It was to remind her of her constant connection and embodiment of that. So that she could move through the challenge.

A: Thank you. If you could tell me Higher Self, they were in the Tenth Dimension. There are people that say that there's no negativity or polarities in some of these higher Dimensions. Can you explain to us how is it that she and her Elsenes race, being of the Tenth Dimension, still encounter negative polarization?

Higher Self: There's a lot to be learned...they were in this Dimension, but perhaps they were also moving between Dimensions. I think what that elder meant when she said Tenth, was that that was their anchor Dimension and in most alignment with themselves. But in that period of great learning and challenge they were actually traveling between Dimensions and met those negative beings through the lower Dimensional expressions.

A: Okay, so what you're saying is they could be in 10D and simultaneously also be in lower Dimensions?

Higher Self: Yes.

A: Through different forms. Okay. Thank you. That's all the questions I have about that life unless you have anything else you want to say about it?

Higher Self: No.

A: Thank you. Higher Self, is there a name you go by?

Higher Self: Elohim.

A: Thank you Elohim. It is an honor to be talking to you. Now am I speaking to you as an individual or as a collective of the Elohim?

Elohim: As an individual.

A: Do you mean the Elohim, the ones that are connected to the angelic energies?

Elohim: Yes.

The Body Scan begins.

A: Beautiful. Thank you. Elohim, if you could please begin her body scan. Since you are speaking from a formation of angels, let us know if you need any assistance. Typically, we have Archangels assist, or if you can do this on your own, we respect that as well. Just let us know if you do need angels?

Elohim: Yes, let us welcome angels.

A: Who would you like to call forth on first to assist with your body scan?

Elohim: Raphael.

A: Beautiful. Elohim, if you could please connect us to Archangel Raphael, we would like to speak to Raphael. Greetings.

AA Raphael: Greetings.

A: Thank you brother, for being here. Love you, honor you and respect you. The Higher Self Elohim has requested for your assistance today in the body scan. Together, Elohim and you can begin the body scan please, scanning her from head to toe looking for any negative energies, entities, anything that needs to be healed within. Let me know what you find.

AA Raphael: Some tension in her solar plexus.

A: Scan that area thoroughly, let me know what is causing, what is the root to the tension? Is there an energy, an entity, a negative technology, what is there?

Raphael: It is an entity in the core. It is a tension that she is ready to release.

A: Okay, that entity, Raphael, if you can tell us, is that connected to any Reptilian race or any other alien race?

AA Raphael: Yes. It's an implant, it is like a shard of some Reptilian race.

A: Okay. Is it an actual entity or is it an implant?

AA Raphael: It is an implant.

A: Okay, can we use the Phoenix Fire to start transmuting that for her?

AA Raphael: Yes.

A: Okay, focusing the Phoenix Fire in her stomach area to start transmuting that. You said there's also a cord. Can we see where that cord leads to? What is it connected to?

AA Raphael: It is kind of too many different things, some of which is ancestral. Some of it is just two different people in her life where she feels depleted and over-giving. There's some kind of cord in her throat chakra as well which seems to be connected to a greater force, an outside influence. It is negative.

A: Do we need to start calling Archangel Michael to assist with these cords and removing them?

AA Raphael: Yes.

A: Raphael, Elohim, if you could connect us now to Archangel Michael please.

AA Michael: Hello.

A: Hello! Thank you, brother, for being here. Love You, honor you, and I respect you. We have called for assistance because she has a cord here in her stomach as well as some in her throat that are connected to negative alien races. If you can please begin the finding of where they're connected too and if you could cut these completely? Does she need them?

AA Michael: She does not need them.

A: Michael, if you could begin the process of removing them from her, no longer then infringing upon her. Also, can you tell me the one through the throat, she mentioned that there's some kind of dark entity connected to that. Can you tell us more about who is attached to that?

AA Michael: It's a vibration of the same original destruction that she articulated earlier. It's a dark or negative influence energy that is also connected to her heart. Her heart and her throat, something that is distracting her from her full expansion. It doesn't want her to be in her full light. She is ready to release all that now.

A: Michael, am I able to talk to those entities that are attached through these cords to her?

AA Michael: Yes.

A: Thank you. Besides these cords and the negative impact there, do they have any consciousness of them attached to her as well besides these wires and implants?

AA Michael: There is some influence just outside and around her aura but not necessarily corded in. There's something that must be addressed related to an accident she had some years ago, she fainted and hit her head and went unconscious. This is the beginning of a lot of mental health challenges as well. So, there's something that came in during that moment.

A: All right now, Michael, you said that I am able to speak to these entities. If you could please connect me now to them.

Entity: Yes.

A: Greetings. Thank you for speaking to us. Love you, honor you and respect you. May I ask you questions, please?

Entity: Yes.

A: Thank you. If I can ask, when was it that you attached to these areas of her?

Entity: Somewhere in early childhood through her family unit. Some were during the accident.

A: The accident where she fell?

Entity: Yes. A lot of this energy was attracted, through her relationships, sexual relationships. We were able to insert and not get caught.

A: Do you mean like through intercourse, you were able to do that?

Entity: More through the energy after the emotional tie she would have to another person created that distortion and allowed for us to enmesh with her and blur her clarity.

A: Thank you for your honesty there and if I can ask you what kind of alien race are you?

Entity: We will not disclose.

A: Okay. Am I speaking to a few or several?

Entity: A few.

A: I understand that you will not disclose. Now as you know the Universe and the Earth itself is shifting. And as the Creation itself shifts within this reality and we go into higher vibrations, entities like you who are parasitic, attaching to others will transmute straight back to Source. We would love to be able to instead help you ascend into a positive polarization. Where you no longer have to attach to someone for negative polarized reasons. You can incarnate somewhere else, keep your memory or experiences. Instead, you will grow profoundly, you are able to create your own light, your own experiences, be free. Will you allow us to help you spread your light, so you no longer have to play this role?

Entity: Yes.

A: Beautiful. Go ahead and find that light within you, and how many are saying yes?

Entity: Five.

A: Is that everyone saying yes?

Entity: There are seven.

A: Okay, two don't want to, that is okay. To you five, thank you for accepting this. Find the light within you. We are focusing upon you now, sending Love-Light to you, spreading it to all that is you, every part of you. Michael, we continue to use any Phoenix Fire there transmuting, and you are working on removing those cords that are attached to her from them. Let me know Michael, once it's all removed and now you five, if you could let me know once you are all light.

Positive Polarized Entity: We are all light.

A: Beautiful, thank you for allowing us to assist you today. If we could call forth on Archangel Azrael, so he can supervise and make sure that everyone is of light and then he will help guide you to where you are meant to go for your positive Ascension. Before you go may I ask you a couple questions?

Positive Polarized Entity: Yes.

A: Thank you. When I asked what it was that you look like or what alien race you were, you said you could not. Can you tell us now that you are of light?

Positive Polarized Entity: Yes.

A: Thank you. Tell me, what were you before you turned to light?

Positive Polarized Entity: We are a collective that feeds off of soul depletion and the name we do not share. But we have benefited from people like Leona, on being depleted.

A: Were you part of the reason why she felt depressed and no longer wanted to be here?

Positive Polarized Entity: Yes. Those two others want to come.

A: Beautiful! If we could focus now, Love-Light upon them. Thank you. If you could tell us what it was that changed their mind?

Positive Polarized Entity: They saw our liberation.

A: Yes. It's very much like liberation, thank you. Let us know once they are all light. Michael, how are those cords looking and the implant that she had in her stomach?

AA Michael: They released, there is a bit of a residue, but we can clear that.

A: Yes, begin the process of clearing that and can we have Raphael please start filling in and the Higher Self filling in Love-Light in those areas?

AA Michael: Yes.

A: Thank you, just let me know when the two are of light.

AA Michael: The two are of light now.

A: Beautiful! If they could join the other five please, Azrael, making sure you keep them there, making sure they don't get tricked along the way. Thank you for answering the questions. Azrael, if you can tell us brother, where is it that you are taking them to?

AA Azrael: We are taking them to their solar sun system to be purified so that they can be released to Source…

A: Beautiful. Thank you, is there a name that we know that solar sun system by?

AA Azrael: No.

A: Go ahead and blessings to all of you, honor you, love you, and respect you. Thank you, Azrael. Michael, Elohim, Raphael, if you can please continue to scan her body scan for any entities, Reptilian consciousness, any kind of negative alien. While you are scanning her for specific and negative aliens, if you can scan her spine and her DNA making sure that none have integrated into her. Scan her very deeply and thoroughly. We want to make sure we don't leave any nonorganic entities, nothing that is nonorganic within her that is harming her. Let me know if you find any entities of any shape.

AA Michael: There is something happening in her heart center, some kind of energetic entity. She's most vulnerable to getting courted by people in her heart. And perhaps this is part of it. This entity is the source of a lot of her inner harshness, very harsh towards herself.

A: This entity, is it an entity of Reptilian consciousness or something else?

AA Michael: We think it's an entity.

A: If we can go ahead and contain that with all the symbols now, Michael. Is it contained?

AA Michael: Yes.

A: Thank you. Let's continue to scan her body for any other entities, let us find them all now, again making sure we don't miss any. Let me know where else if she has any.

AA Michael: There is a distortion in her spine.

A: Is this distortion connected to a negative alien fractal?

AA Michael: We think so.

A: If we can go ahead and start surrounding that distortion there with all the symbols now. With her Higher Self's permission, start clearing any negative alien fractals, any nonorganic pieces that are not of hers organically within her DNA structure. Whatever the Higher self allows.

AA Michael: Yes.

A: Now that distortion, before we remove it, is it cooperative? Are we able to speak to it in regard to helping it turn into a positive polarization as well?

AA Michael: Yes.

A: Good. So then, if we can just continue in her DNA structure reprogramming, also anything that no longer serves her as her Higher Self allows, please. Are there any other parts within her DNA structure in her spine that needs to be addressed?

AA Michael: There are some ancestral contracts located within her DNA that can be released.

A: Good. Can we have Michael release those for her?

AA Michael: Yes.

A: Thank you. If you could tell us what was the purpose to that so that it can completely heal?

AA Michael: It was a pattern of shrinking to stay safe and survive, patterns of shame.

A: Good. Thank you, Michael, for working on removing those. Scan her one more time within her DNA in her spine. Anything else that's not organically of hers?

AA Michael: No.

A: Okay, beautiful. That the entity is contained in her spine, let's continue scanning her body. Let's find all of them. Let me know if you find any more.

AA Michael: There's another distortion. We think maybe a hook in her third eye. It prevents her from seeing clearly and trusting in herself, she's ready to release.

A: Good. Scan her deeply. Is it a hook?

AA Michael: Yes.

A: Let's go ahead and direct Phoenix Fire there transmuting the hook as well. Please continue to scan her for entities, implants, hooks, portals, and anything else.

AA Michael: The only other pieces are in the periphery around her aura.

A: What is it?

AA Michael: There are some entities trying to get in, they bounce off but sometimes they seep.

A: Can we heal or repair any damage to the aura, making it nice and bright and strong as it is meant to be organically, please.

AA Michael: Yes.

A: Scan her, are there any other entities before we speak to the ones we found? One more time, any other entities?

AA Michael: No.

A: I would like to speak to that entity in her heart. If you could please come up, up, up now. Greetings.

Entity: Greetings.

A: Thank you for speaking to us. Love you, honor you and respect you. If I can ask when was it that you attached to her heart?

Entity: Six years old.

A: What was going on with her that allowed for you to come in and that time?

Entity: She experienced a lot of spoken and unspoken tension in her home and family, and it made her closed off from trusting, love and trusting that she belonged fully in some way. The foundations do not feel stable in certain ways, and this was an outlet for me to enter and create a story of that belonging or not being to trust.

A: Do you have a body somewhere else that you are connected to?

Entity: No.

A: You just exist here in her heart?

Entity: Well, I also have a planet. There is the body of the planet.

A: Okay, now I know that you have been there some time in her heart. Thank you for serving whatever these roles that you mentioned for her in this time and space. We are trying to help you and assist you, so you no longer have to attach parasitically to someone. Would you allow us to help you positively ascend?

Entity: Yes.

A: Thank you. If we could start finding the light within you and spread it to all that is you. Every root, every cord that is within her that is not of her organically, that is of yours. Make sure you spread it to all light. Let us know when you are all light.

Positive Polarized Entity: I am all light.

A: Beautiful, go ahead and release yourself from her heart now, make sure you don't leave any piece of you behind. Let us know when you are fully out.

Positive Polarized Entity: I am fully out.

A: Thank you. Now if we could call forth on Archangel Azrael to help guide this new positively polarized soul to where it's meant to go. Azrael, can you tell us where you are going to take it? It mentioned that it was from a planet.

AA Azrael: Yes, it is from a dense or dark planet, but I am going to take it to the solar sun to purify and then release again.

A: Beautiful. Blessings to you. I love you, honor you, and I respect you. You will be surrounded by the Love-Light of the Universe. Thank you for your assistance Azrael. If we can now speak to the entity, there in her spine. If you could please come up, up, up now, please.

Entity: Yep.

The entity is a consciousness of a Reptilian. It is from a dark planet and after some convincing he and 22 others do positively polarize alongside removing 350 consciousnesses who were attached to people.

A: Thank you. If we could start healing traumas, all of them for her as her Higher Self allows. Is there any trauma that you would like to heal now from past lives that are affecting her now?

Elohim: Yes.

A: How about the traumas, perhaps of that life that you showed? We could start healing all those traumas that she experienced in that life please now, as the Higher Self allows. Are there any other traumas we would like to address besides a past life?

Elohim: If I could heal any traumas from past lives relating to causing harm on others?

A: Start healing that for her now, as the Higher Self allows. Michael, we have completed the list here as far as for her healing. Is there anything else we could address and help her heal from?

AA Michael: Certain relationships can be healed. Also, to release the contract of her relationship to certain communities that she felt left out of in the past. You can now transmute that and move forward with a different experience. You can also transmute her contract in relationship to men, feeling that relationship to the masculine within her and outside of her.

A: Thank you for that. Okay, you are working on releasing those?

AA Michael: Yes.

A: Thank you. Anything else we can assist her with today for her, highest healing?

AA Michael: That's all for now.

A: Thank you. Well, we did a lot of work here on her. That life was just absolutely phenomenal. What and anything you can give her as far as direction?

Elohim: She will be organizing and educating people. Dance will continue to be a practice that supports her soul and her body to find the clarity and the compass. She will be a part of a great healing movement. She is a part of that. Much of her work will be about system transformation. There will also be international work, she will be traveling. She will be in a community. In great work on creation, creativity and healing and through that, feeling more equity and justice in the society.

A: What a beautiful mission and thank you for her service on that. Now I just want to make sure that we completely healed her from the mental health such as depression and suicide and that pattern of not wanting to be here. Have we started the process of healing that for her?
Elohim: Yes.
A: I know you mentioned some of that had to do with some of those entities that were attached and also that past life. Thank you.
Elohim: Thank you.
A: If you can tell us, why does she have to experience the suicides?
Elohim: She needed to go through a deep dark night that would help her touch the lowest point so that she could embody a real source of light and then share it and have compassion for others who have experienced such things. The suicides in particular, were a reminder about the fragility of life as well as supported her to be in knowledge and wisdom with that relationship to death. So as to increase her wisdom and also increase her connection to community at that time.
A: Wonderful, thank you. Thank you. At this point, we have covered the whole healing. Is there anything else that I could have asked that I haven't asked for her?
Elohim: No.
A: Beautiful. Thank you for this beautiful explanation and this beautiful life that you showed her. I know that it will be profound in helping her through her life in the process of her Ascension. Thank you for all the wisdom and knowledge shared here today. I like to thank Raphael, Michael. Azrael, the Higher Self Elohim. Thank you, everyone and anyone else who assisted. I love you, honor you and respect you. Higher Self, may I bring her back now?
Elohim: Yes, thank you.

Post Session Dialogue.
A: You look so different just from the beginning of the video. There's a huge, tremendous difference in you right now. Very light. Beautiful. It was an honor to work with you. What an amazing life.
L: In terms of that kind of memory recall of other places on planets, do you have guidance about how to best honor that or how to best be in communication with that person, that aspect of myself? It feels like it was like a little window into something.
A: Exactly. That's how it feels after an A.U.R.A. session. It's like, wait a minute, give me more! Right? Basically, now understanding that you can travel to that time and space of her at any point and just communicate to her through your heart, through the telepathic communication. There will be even that Council, they have already been communicating to you throughout life. So now that bond will be even stronger, and the connection will be stronger. So, there will be a very big growth there for you because now you are connected to that
L: What was the most important piece for you in terms of information?
A: Some of the things that they talked about, a lot of the teachings. I teach as well as far as polarities, people do not understand that there's these polarities out there. We are so clouded, and we are being misled by negative information. Information that's actually being given directly from that darkness that you saw and one of the biggest densities is Light Workers, channels, and healers that are not realizing that they are getting that information from them. So, I love that you got that information further as well. What was really special to me, because they showed it to me too, like how they separated from their Source. That was interesting. I saw the Archons came from there and other negative alien races came from there. They can so easily infringe upon you if you don't surround yourself with sacred alchemy symbols, force fields, all that we teach already to shield with our own infinite Love-Light Source energy. Amazing!

L: I am really looking forward to watching it and I really respect and honor you. Thank you for your work.

A: Thank you. It is a gift, and I am just in great honor that I am allowed now to teach it to others because there's others doing this now. Almost 100 now that are certified, and I am excited to keep growing this so that we can give these gifts to others.

L: Lots of love to you.

A: Bye love!

END OF SESSION

These are glimpses of the Universe that we get to connect to through these beautiful souls' expressions in their A.U.R.A. sessions. Blessed are we to be part of them and to grow alongside them as our minds and hearts expand to understand the multidimensionality of Creation! What a grand most beautiful understanding to know and feel the life force within us and know that we were created from the 'Life Force of Love' in Creation.

Who were these Elsenes beings expressing to us from the Tenth Dimension? We might think here on Earth that Beings of that high Dimension would have a greater knowledge of the dark entities out there in the Universe, however it seems as if they are learning just as much as we are. Or perhaps we learn through them, ultimately because of the fact that there is no time, only infinite parallel planes of existence. All of Creation exists in the NOW. Therefore, we are learning from one another at the same exact moment in space. How to shield our homes, our planets, our loved ones. A blessing it is to have these Beings assisting us. It seems as a majority of our sacred teachings that we certify people in, are connected to the Essenes, the ancestors of Yeshua, matches what these Elsenes were guarding and keeping alive through their Elders and through their daughter's bravery and mission. Perhaps they are the same beings?

The Elsenes seemed to within their time and space, similar to the Nephilim race mentioned in Chapter 31 ('Looking Glass Technology'), also trying to figure out what was going on with the Universe. Who or what was it that was causing the harmonic disharmony within our Universe, this mission of their daughter? The mention of this dark seeding by the Elders. There was much concern through their vibration, an immensity riding on the 'Key Crystal' which their daughter returned safely to their home planet. How important it was that they remained pure for all life within this seeded distortion that was spreading throughout our Universe. Their concern also being of the other races of Creation, especially lower to them. They were able to read through deception and corruption, transmute it and heal it as mentioned. But the other races are where these benevolent beings were concerned for. We have learned through these Soul Journeys what happened as these dark seeds continued to spread and corrupt as mentioned in Chapter 30 ('Harvesting Planets Throughout Universes') how it spread to 50 percent of the Universe being harvested or corrupted. We could imagine what kind of unbalance and insecurity this could cause to our Universe and all lifeforms communing within it. A great FEAR of this unknown, that was compromising, taking over planets and races. This type of FEAR that we all evolve from in some form in life, a FEAR to an unknown that is uncontrollable. Perhaps our collective Universes FEAR seeded itself in those beginning moments of time and space, and we are still trying to figure how to eradicate fear from within us, as it is truly inorganic and abnormal to our organic existences. As that elder that spoke to us, one could feel through his expression how this Archon A.I. virus was spreading and spreading fast. There was much sacredness and mystery of the communications shared and also not an understanding of what was going on? This is another example of a benevolent race from a high vibration, from the Tenth Dimension, who were taken by surprise by the invasions of these A.I. Archons not known to them. May they continue to share with us their wisdom in assisting Earth through Ascension.

These Archonic entities that we learned through in this session showed us how lost souls can become when no longer having a light or an organic life force running through them. It is a sad existence to not be able to feel what we do, as they cannot. To not be able to exchange love through the eyes, to not be able to share our light as we brush against each other's force fields, to not be able to feel comfort and embrace from our loved ones when it is needed. All we can do is send love to these long-lost expressions of the Universes that lost all identities of itself, of its organic life it might have once been in time and space.

Why do Archons feed off our lights? Perhaps it is because deep down when they disconnected from their own Universe's Source Light as explained through Chapter 31 ('Looking Glass Technology') how they are not of our Source or Universe, they have been looking to know that feeling once more. As a piece that is lost and feels missing, an emptiness or void that can never be fulfilled no matter how much you feed it and take from those who still contain it to fill it for you. However, it is too late because once their essence converted to inorganic, it lost all its essences of its organic life. It no longer contains light or is part of its coding. It is at its most deepest infinite distortion that it can never be brought back to what it once was. Therefore, they are an expression of the Universe that long ago lost its beginning reason and true light organism. An abomination that can no longer be reconstructed to be in unity of anything around it. These abominations so long as they have their artificial intelligence running them, they will forever be on an automatic program needing to feed off light, as it is what is missing within them. This is why they think that they can go into Universes and violate their Natural Laws, because they are no longer these organic laws themselves and the comprehension and understanding can never be there because it is just no longer part of them. All there is, is our sovereignty and love that will transmute them back to Zero Point within the etheric spaces of the Universes. To rebirth once more, beginning fresh at some point in time in space, back to what they were once more, organic light.

These three important Chapters of, "Harvesting of Planets Through The Universes," "Looking Glass Technology," and "Not of Light" allow for much understanding and insights on the invasive Archonic infringements on all beings across all Dimensions in the Universes. Though the clients of these Chapters did not know each other, these sessions came together bringing forth such a clearness of awareness to us, all in divine alignment and timing. Piecing together the broader and more complete picture to help us understand why this world and the Universes are where they are at, underscoring the crucial importance of us becoming divine sovereign beings once more to bring forth Ascension.

Ultimately, our strength is also our weakness to the Archons, as they use the organic sacred laws of love, honor, and respect that we have for one another, against us. Knowing we will and cannot overstep another's free willed expression when perhaps they are following a false agenda, we can only do so when we are given permission. Otherwise, when we violate another's free willed choice, we too would be entering and matching the low vibration that the Archons operate from, to accept and become of them. Archonic beings have NO structure and sacred boundaries of respecting all life as the beauties of individual choices and expressions of Creation.

THESE SACRED BOUNDARIES ARE FREEDOM TO ALL ORGANIC LIFE AND IT IS HOW THIS UNIVERSE IS CONSTRUCTED.

Before these surprise attacks, this Universe was such a divine beauty of balance. The dark and light within us were honored, embraced and understood in its organic ways of truly being reflections of one another for all life's purpose of soul growth. It was grand, beautiful and an honor to be able to incarnate within any Dimension, star cluster or constellation within this Universe of dark and light polarities. What the Archons did was distort the beauties of our infinite darkness, and the power that we gain when creating from the vastness of the darkness, as stars can only create and shine brightest surrounded by organic darkness. Stealing the power that exists within the darkness of this Universe and compromising it with their ingenious diabolical plans of mind control over the organic life in our Universe. As we have seen through these sessions, by compromising organic Reptilian races and the harvesting of planets, to keep fueling their insatiable feeding of light... Through this book series we will remember the infinite beauties that our Universe was, is meant to be, and will be once more. Together, we will create and bring forth the collectives' Ascension when it's time, and it will be because of the strength and beauty of our hearts.

"Look thoroughly at the in-between stage of nature, at the zero-point of Creation:
Where the wind meets the air of the wing of a bird.
Where the water touches the sand.
Where the sun meets the land at its sunrise and sundown.
For these places in the in-between is where you can create all.
When we come to a knowing that separation does not exist,
only a union of the elements around us and all Creation!"
~AuroRa🖤

--------------<◇>------------

33

SLAVE TO CORRUPTION

Session #268: Recorded in April 2020.

In this online A.U.R.A. Hypnosis Healing session, Clara finds herself in the beginnings of Earth. In this wondrous and intense journey, we learn about the existence of an Elven Council and their connection to humanity, the beauties of this race, their way of life, and their abilities. They show us the true strength and power of shielding. How can crystals aid humanity? An Elf takes us through an example of how a powerful being can become corrupted in Creation. How is this corruption linked to human trafficking in the Universe? In this incredible session, we learn about the true power of Love, and how one single brave decision to plant a seed of hope created a ripple effect throughout the Universe and Creation.

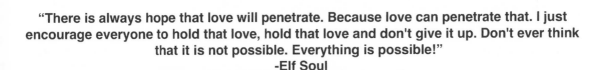

"There is always hope that love will penetrate. Because love can penetrate that. I just encourage everyone to hold that love, hold that love and don't give it up. Don't ever think that it is not possible. Everything is possible!"
-Elf Soul

C: [Clara] Gray, it is like stone, everything is made out of stone. Stone sidewalks, stone roads.
A: [Aurora] Look at yourself. Do you feel like you have a body?
C: Yes.
A: Look down at your feet. Are you wearing anything on your feet?
C: I don't have any shoes.
A: How many toes do you have?
C: Five.
A: Look at your hands. How many fingers do you have?
C: Five.
A: Your skin, what tone is it?
C: Very light pale. Like almost like a sickly gray pale, almost.
A: Are you wearing any clothing?
C: It is like a torn dress, a cloth dress of sorts.
A: Are there any colors to it?
C: Brown gray.
A: Is there any jewelry you are wearing?
C: No, I don't have very many things.
A: Do you feel like you are female or male?
C: Yeah, I am a young girl.
A: Is there anything you are carrying?
C: A small piece of bread. I keep it in my pocket. It is all I have. I sit here on the street. I can see people pass me by, it is like they don't even see me. I am trying to get someone to help me or

pay attention. It is like, I know I am dying. I am not going to make it much longer. I don't eat. I am so poor. No one really cares no more.

A: The people who are passing by... what do they look like? What does their attire look like?

C: Like black suits? Like a... tall black hats. Carriages, everything is so gray. There is not much color here at all.

A: Okay. As you are sitting there, keep moving the scene along, and tell me when something else happens of importance.

C: I don't do very much. I just stay here and hope that somebody might give me something to eat? I am eating whatever I have left. There I see...even though I don't have a lot, there are some rats and I give them some of what I have. I just sit there, and it is so dirty. It smells, and it is not clean. I see some other kids, kind of like me, I think we all just kind of sit here, walk around on this street and hope that somebody gives us some bread or something to eat. We take care of each other. We try to share with each other. Some of us are more lucky than others. I give it away. I just kind of lay there, curled up in a ball. My stomach stops being hungry anymore. I know that I am dying. I am leaving. I am not really sad about it though. I am sad but I no longer really care, and I am kind of happy that these rats hang out with me, as I lay here...just kind of go.

A: Do you feel like you are about to take your last breath?

C: Yeah.

A: Before you do that, let's go back in time, to the beginning memories of this life for you. You are there now, tell me what is going on.

C: I think it is an orphanage. I don't know. I think that is where I am. I don't know how I left there. I am younger though. I am not as old as I was on the streets, but still young.

A: You feel like you are...?

C: Like six or seven.

A: Tell me, what is it like to be there?

C: It is kind of dull, not a lot goes on here. It is just kind of the same thing every day. I hope maybe things will get better. I know that when I am old enough, they are going to kick me out. I think that is how I got on the streets. No one came for me. It is just kind of like, little metal cots and a very thin mattress. No covers or anything, I am just grateful to have that. I know we get food once a day, it is like soup or something. It is not very good. It is a lot more than I have on the streets though.

A: Are there a lot of you there?

C: There are like eight or nine of us. It is not too many.

A: Who takes care of you? Who tends to the orphanage?

C: This woman, she is an older woman.

A: She tends to it by herself?

C: Yeah. She is the one who makes the soup once a day. She is kind of neutral. She does not give off hate or love either. She is just kind of there, it is almost like she is dead inside. She is not there. She is there but she is not. She tries though, we know that.

A: Keep moving time along, to another important time in this life. What happens next of importance?

C: I am on the street and I am approaching this well-dressed man in a carriage, a horse drawn carriage. He's got a very large top hat on. So, I know that he is wealthier. I hold out my hands and I try to ask him if he has anything, he can give me. He does not pay me much attention, and he just keeps going. I get splashed by the water of the carriage going by. I back away from the road to go back to the stone sidewalk to wait for somebody else to come by.

A: Are you no longer in the orphanage?

C: No. I am like 12. I am too old. I have to leave. They only let the younger ones stay. And then you have to go.

A: Keep moving the scene along and tell me what happens next of importance.

C: I don't last very long. I don't make it much longer. I don't even make it a year on the streets before I just don't make it anymore. I just don't have enough to eat; everybody just benefits for themselves. I just eat the last bit of what I have and share some with my rat companions, and just lay there. Ready to go.

A: What are your thoughts when you are taking your last breath?

C: I am just a little sad (crying). My heart aches. I am just a kid and I don't know why nobody cares.

A: Go ahead and take your last breath and tell me what happens next.

C: I leave the body and I can see myself curled up in a fetal position, laying there and I just float up above this big gray dull stinky city. I am just kind of relieved, sad that I am just lying there until somebody will move my body eventually. I just kind of go. I am just so ready to go. I just float away.

A: Is there somewhere that you go after you float away?

C: It is just like a big white light. It makes me feel full, so I am happy! Immediately, I don't feel hungry anymore. So, I feel really good. Just full. Complete.

A: Let's go ahead and leave that scene. Let's go to another important time, where we will find answers that we seek for your highest healing. You are there now, tell me what you see and sense.

Clara transitions into another different life.

C: I am in the forest again. It is so much color. I am just washing my hands in a creek. Washing my hands and feet in a creek in the forest.

A: Do you feel like you are female or male?

C: I think I am female.

A: You feel younger or older?

C: Like, in my twenties somewhere.

A: Look down at your feet, how many toes do you have?

C: I have four? Four.

A: Look at your hands, how many fingers do you have?

C: I have five. I don't know why I have more fingers than I have toes.

A: Look at your skin. What tone is your skin?

C: It is like a glowing white, almost like a porcelain glowing white.

A: Are you wearing any clothing?

C: Yeah, it is like a white gown of sorts. A white gown, long sleeves, it is long. I hold it up to my waist, put my feet into the water.

A: Is there any jewelry you are wearing?

C: Yeah, I have like a silver and gold headpiece. Kind of points down in the shape of a 'v' down my forehead. I have like a long... I think it is an amulet, that is what I call it anyways. It is a long amulet that goes all the way down to my belly. I have some jewels in my hair. Bracelets.

A: Are there any shapes or colors or crystals on any of the jewelry that stands out?

C: It is not oval. A cross is the closest thing. The jewel that sits in the middle of the crown, it's like a rainbow .... if I move my head, you can see a rainbow kind of coming out of it. And it is light, and it is green, like a light green color.

A: Is there anything you are carrying?

C: I carry a sword on my back. It is like it is there when I want it to be seen, but it is not just seen when you look at me. I can make it seen if I want. It is just like a really big sword that sits and goes down my spine.

A: Look at the sword. Pull it out. Describe what it looks like, does it have any shapes, does it have anything in it that is of significance?

C: It goes straight like a normal sword, and then at the end, its kind of, I don't really know what that is. It twists a little bit but not in like loops, it does like a wave at the front of it into a sharp point. And then at the end of that wave, it goes out really far and on the handle bit. There is an opal looking jewel, and the whole thing is like a milky white iridescent reflectiveness to it. I use it when I have to.

A: Okay, keep moving the scene along and let's see what happens next of importance. Tell me what is going on.

C: I am standing with a group of like five others that looks like me. We are talking but we are worried about something. We don't really worry but...we have come together because we need to talk about something that is happening, and we need to help. So, we come together to talk about it. We are not really talking; we are just kind of standing in a circle in the forest. We just kind of have a 'knowing' of each other's talking. I know that right now this is Earth. This is Earth before... We are talking about a village. I think they are humans. I think they are in trouble. They need us. It is like we can hear the call and we can just feel the frequency shift and change. We know that something is going amiss. We know.

A: There are a total of five of you or six of you?

C: Five and myself. Six.

A: Are there females and males?

C: Yeah, there is both.

A: Can you tell what some of them look like?

C: Long hair. Everyone has long hair, like waist length hair. And they have jewels too but different than mine. They have some of the same rainbow jewel, like I can see this male in front of me, he has long white hair and he has a ring that has that jewel on it instead of a crown that I have. They all just look alike, but different.

A: Do you look like a human?

C: We are very similar to humans. We can, but we don't shape shift, but we look so similar that they would not know that we can...we take our ears, and we make them smaller so that the humans won't know. Our ears stick out of our hair. That is how a lot of humans can tell, so we just change them. We hide it so that they are not afraid.

A: Are your skin tones like humans, or different?

C: No, we glow! It is really, very unique. Like how humans kind of have an opacity to their skin, and we have almost like a reflectiveness in the sunlight. We can tone that down too, so that the humans don't know.

A: What is it that you all are deciding here in this group?

C: We know we need to help them. We are just trying to figure out how and in the least infringing way possible. We don't want them to know that we are still here residing in the forest, but we do know that we have to help. We don't have to, but it is not in our nature to not help them. We can feel the energy shift, and we want to help them. So, we are just trying to decide on how to go about that without also giving ourselves away and letting them know that we are still here. I think there are many more of us than just the six of us. There are so many but the six of us gather first to decide the plan of action, and then we will tell the others what we are going to do, or how we are going to help. We are also trying to figure out... This male, he has a larger presence than the other five of us. He's trying to figure out what the infringement is. He is trying to figure out what is causing the shift in energy so much that we can feel it. It is dark...they are dark beings.

A: Who are the dark beings?

C: It is like he went out and he was the one who saw what changed the energy and he's...I am putting my hand up to his, not quite touching but like half an inch apart and it's like we interface, and I can see what he saw. Yeah, they are dark. He is just showing us, so that we know.

A: What do they look like?

C: I can't see them yet. We can't see them. We can see their ship and we know what it looks like, and it is dark. Yeah, we can see their ship and that is what he saw. He saw their ship and he kind of took an energetic signature of the ship and that is what he is showing us. So, we can see what the ship looks like and we can feel the energetic signature from it, so we can kind of register how dark they are and what they are.

A: What type of ship is it and what kind of shape is it?

C: This is going to sound really weird, but it looks very similar to some of the ships on Star Wars, it is like round on the back end and then kind of comes into a jagged edge point at the front. And it is black.

A: And where is the ship at?

C: It was coming towards this village that we are talking about. It is in the sky. It is on Earth.

A: Now that you have this registered energy frequency of this ship and beings, what do you do next?

C: We decide that we are going to help them, and we can shield this energy out. I know I can. It does not make sense why they would let me go alone but I am leaving the group of the six of us. They decide to let me go towards this village and put a shield up around it without being seen. Because I am really good at that. Of all of us, I am the most stealthy, as I can do that without being seen.

A: Go ahead and go and tell me what that looks like.

C: I am standing at the edge of the forest, and I have kind of cloaked myself so that you cannot see me or read my energetic signature, not the dark ones at least. I am standing by this rock and I put my hands out...and I can see this massive bubble. I call it a bubble, but I don't know how to describe it. It is like translucent, but you can see all of the energy flowing through it, it is like electricity. And I put everything I have into holding the shield over the village so that maybe these dark beings leave them alone. Maybe they will go away without having to do anything else on our behalf. The shield is really big. The humans cannot see it, but the dark ones can. They don't know where it came from, but the dark ones can see it. They can't go through it, they know that.

A: What is the color to the shield?

C: It is like a really light crystalline blue color, almost like...I have never seen this color...it is light, almost similar to my birthstone. It is a very light blue. But you can see the electricity flowing. It flows, it is fluid.

A: Is there any shape to the bubble, the shield?

C: If you are close enough you can see the flower of life in it, within it, kind of like the structure of it almost. Yeah, they cannot touch it.

A: How did you do this? Tell me the steps you went through to place this.

C: I come center, I take all of my energy and I come center to my heart with it. And then it flows down through my arms and out my hands, through the palms of my hands. It comes from my heart center and down through the palms of my hands. It just takes a lot of focus. Some of us have practiced for hundreds of years to master this, and I just spend a lot of time doing it, as it just takes a lot of focus to be centered. It is like pulling from Source energy through the heart center out through the palms of the hands. It is just like an infinite flow, limitless. There is no limit to how much, or how big I can make this. Well, there is a limit to it, but there is not. It just flows. It just does not stop. I can put my hands down and the shield stays. It stays there, and I just kind of watch to see if they will attempt to destroy it. To do whatever they want to do. I don't know why, this village does not have anything for them, I don't know why they are even here. It is not angering me, I don't have anger, but it is the closest thing to that, and I am just kind of watching the ship to see if they make any moves, to see if they do anything. Or if they just decide to just go.

A: Keep moving the time along and let me know what happens next of importance.

C: They did not stop. They don't care. Myself and the five others and the rest of us, we have to, it is not really preparing for battle, but we have to go. It was not enough to deter them. They don't care. They destroyed it. Well, partially anyways, but having the holes in it is of no use, it is structural. They were able to penetrate through it, which is very surprising to us, we did not expect that.

A: So, the shield is still there but they penetrated through parts of it, you said?

C: Yes. So that makes the humans vulnerable. I mean it still is protecting them because you cannot destroy the shield, it will not be destroyed. But somehow, they used technology I think to permeate it in some way. So that makes the humans vulnerable now. We have to go; we have to help them. They are on the ground. We can finally see what these beings are.

A: Are they inside the village?

C: They are, some of them are.

A: Did they go through some of the holes in the shield that they made?

C: Yeah. It is like an energetic weapon. I don't know this technology. It is inorganic. It is not organic. I work with organic. They do not. So, I do not know. Well, none of us know. We don't know how they did that. We just know it is not organic.

A: So, they are in the village on the ground and you are able to see them. Tell me what do they look like?

C: Mm-hmm. I know exactly what they are. They are Reptilians. They are very tall. We are tall too. We are taller than the humans, but they are taller than we are. I want to say that we are about ten feet tall, because we are more light than humans. But these beings, these Reptilians, they are 15 to 20 feet...they are really big. They have spines, like scales down their backs, like spikes down their head. Not on the crown of their head, but shoulder neck all the way down to their tail. Spikes. They have three fingers, long claws, three toes. They kind of stand like, almost like a goat on two legs, like their legs are kind of shaped like that. They are not just vertical, they kind of have a hunch to them. Yellowy eyes, dark yellow. Lots of teeth. Some of them are brown, some of them are green. It is like a dark green. A dull green, almost like the forest. They are holding weapons, whatever they are. I don't know. They are taking the humans. They are taking some of them, and they don't really care though. Some of them, they are just tossed to the side. Some of them, they...it is like a... I am not familiar with this technology. It is like an energetic chain around the human necks, it is not a real chain, but it is an energetic chain. And they are like, it is just like they are putting chains around their necks and taking some of them. I think they can read which ones have a higher vibration; I would say for this time. They can tell which ones. And the other ones, they do not care.

A: You say you are about ten feet tall. How tall are the humans?

C: The humans? They are shorter. Like five or six feet? They are small, really small compared to us. They are like half of our size.

A: You said that this chain-like energy goes around their neck, where does it come out from, this weapon?

C: Hang on, I am trying to see. It is like I have to pause everything. I can move about time; time does not exist. We know how to move through time almost while everything stands still. Ah, it is connected to their spines. It is connected from the humans' necks to the back of their spines. Like almost if they had shoulder blades, beneath the scales, it is like between your shoulder blades, it connects there. The little energetic strings, you can see them and they just kind of drag these humans around while they are there. But we...

A: Is it like an energetic cord?

C: Yeah. I don't know this technology at all, I am not familiar. We would not do that to other beings. We would never even conceptualize the idea of creating something like that. So, I cannot wrap my brain around what or how it might be? It is not organic. I know this, it is not. I do know that. I can see that. I do know that it is nanotechnology. I think you can see them within that cord. You can see...it is like they are alive. It is like little metal shards almost. Surrounded by a gray haze, is all I can see. It is a gray haze cord with these little nanites in between it linking the chain to the back of the Reptilian to the neck of the human.

A: The six of you, are you inside the village?

C: Yeah. there is more than just us though. There is more. There are about 20 to 25 of us.

A: Okay, so you said you were able to slow down time. Do you mean, by who you are, all of you, you can slow down time? Is that what you mean?

C: Yes. We can slow the time. It is still happening, but we can slow it to a point, almost like if a Reptilian were to look at us. If we were to make eye contact and then we would disappear from eyesight to the Reptilian because we can move through space and time like that. Then we might be behind so that they cannot see us. It is harder to hit us, harder to capture us, we move not like the humans. The Reptilians, they do not know how to do that. Some of them do, I think, but these don't. They don't know how, and they don't know what we are doing. They have no idea how we just seem to appear in one place and then another. And then another. They don't know.

A: How many Reptilians would you say are there?

C: There are 16, 17, I think? Not all of them came off the ship. It is like in order to get through the shield, they can't come off the ship. There are so many more on that ship and we would have our hands full if they could. But the shield I put up; they were able to penetrate part of it. They have some technology that can penetrate it and shield them, almost from my shield. I don't know how, but if they were normally to pass through this shield, they would disintegrate because such a low vibration would not make it through it. But they were able to pass through these holes they have created with their own shielding technology, but it is so inorganic. It is not natural. They should not be able to do that. So only some of them came down, about 15 to 17 of them made it to the ground. The rest, they can't come down.

A: So, what are you all doing as they are killing some people, and taking some hostage?

C: We are unfortunately, we have to use...we are not...our species do not combat, but if necessary, we will. They did not heed the warning of the shield and decided to do it anyways. So, we have to do what we must, cause these humans...they are so weak to this, it is not their fault. So, we just go in, the 24 or 25 of us, and we...the humans can see, sometimes they can see glimpses of us in between passing through the time to jump around the Reptilians. We just kind of jump around them and confuse them cause now they can see us. They did not know who put the shield up, they did not care and now that we are in the village, they can see us, but glimpses, when we stop in time enough for them to see us. They are communicating with the ship; they are not really afraid of us at all, but they are letting the ship know that. They do not know how we are passing through time like this, and they are trying to see if they can get back up more. Or I think, the remainders that are in the ship, they are trying to permeate the remainder of the barrier so that they can come down. I can feel the shield being energetically hit; I can feel it. But the rest of us can't, they don't feel it. But I can feel it, I can sense it, I know. It just takes more...it is like being pulled in two directions like having to hold this shield while it is being hit and also having to help me here on the ground with these beings. We don't want to hurt them, so we are trying to confuse them just enough to get them to go and release these humans. But I don't think they are going to; they are not going to let these humans go. They are not going to let them go, it is just kind of like a stand still between the two of us. We do not know if they will retreat or we will have to be combative with them. And we are not used to being combative. But we do not fear them either way, so it is okay. We just really hope that they retreat, that we do not have to get combative with them because they are big.

A: Keep moving time along and let me know what is happening next of importance.

C: Mm-hmm. They are gone. The beings, the Reptilians left, and everything is just kind of, you can just see the remains of the village and a couple of fires here and there from the destruction from their energetic weapons. We did get combative; they would not leave. They were not deterred by our trying to confuse them.

A: You all fought?

C: Yes.

A: Tell me what that is like?

C: It is a mix between physical combat and energetic. Because they use these energetic weapons and so some of us use...I want to say it is like alchemy. Others, they can shoot like balls of light out of their hands at the Reptilians. Again, not trying to kill them, but to deter them is why we are shooting at them. Hopefully, they will but it did not work. The six of us that have swords, the others don't have swords like the six of us do. We had to use our swords against them, and we don't like doing that, as it completely wipes them out. They can try to resist the energetic, I don't know what they are, it is like these energetic balls of light coming out of some of the...I call them my family's hands. But, these swords, they can't, there is nothing they can do about that. If the sword makes contact, they disintegrate. They cannot exist. So unfortunately for them, we end up killing ten of them before the others retreat, and then they go. Because the ten that we had to kill, they had humans energetically attached to them, and we could not allow them to leave with these humans. We will not allow it. It is a very weird dynamic between the two of us. I can remember taking this sword through the chest of one of the Reptilians and just watching, it is almost like you can just see it disintegrate from head all the way down and then that cord linking to the human would disintegrate as well. Then the humans would just fall to their knees. They are weak. It is so unfortunate. We are not happy.

A: Originally, there was like a... you said, maybe about 15 of them that went in. What happens when you all are fighting and disintegrating these beings, what do they do next?

C: The remainder, they were free to leave. It is like, I don't know how they exit but they leave and go back to their ship. They leave and they do not want to be disintegrated. I think they will be back probably knowing their nature, but for now, they are gone. We just have to deal with the aftermath of this village and these humans.

A: Were they able to abduct any humans?

C: I want to say like four of them? They did take four of them, we were not able to get them.

A: They did kill some as well?

C: Yeah. Oh yeah. The ones that were of no use, to them they would just throw to the side. The Reptilians are just so big and powerful, they can just throw a human across the room. They did not make it on impact. So yes, they just claw their way through and were looking for the ones that were energetically higher vibration than the others, and they end up getting away with four of them.

A: So, tell me what happens next? What do you all do next once they are gone?

C: We figure out how to take this shield and I think I take this shield down, but not really. I take it down, but I keep an energetic signature of the shield, so later I can look at it and see how they were able to get through it, because their energetic signature is still within the holes of the shield. So, I save that and we...the six of us come together and we just combine all of our energy to put a healing shield over this place. It is not the same type; it is a different one. We shield a lot. And then we just kind of put the humans and we are not harming them, but we put them in a state of...just kind of like, they are there but they are not consciously in their bodies. We go around the village, and we all just use our hands to heal them. To energetically replenish what the Reptilians took from the ones that were chained. The others, we take them, and we place them nicely because we don't want the others to see the destruction. We don't want them to see their families and their friends, we don't want them to see the bodies. So, we lay them nicely and we kind of adorn them with flowers and stuff. We make them look nice so that you cannot really tell the damage that was done and then the others of us, that are not in the group of six, they work on healing that energy that was taken from some of them. So just kind of putting them back into a state of normalcy for them. And we know we have to...we know we are going to have to find a way to explain to them what happened. It is just...so sad. I feel bad for the humans, as they don't have any defense, not now anyways. They do but they do not know how to use it. Humans are very powerful themselves; they are very powerful. They just don't know how to harness that power that they have. They were not taught, so they are vulnerable. So, we are just kind of cleaning up and we are going to have to decide on what to do from here.

A: Okay, keep moving the scene along and tell me what else happens next of importance?

C: We, myself and the other five of us, we are kind of sitting together. We are back in the forest. We are not in the village anymore and we are sitting together. It's like we are on a Council together, and we make the decisions for our group. We are there talking about what happened in the aftermath and what we should do about the humans and their vulnerabilities, because we don't want this to happen again and we are not sure if they will come back. But then again, knowing the Reptilians and their nature, they will probably be back, and we are sitting here deciding what the best kind of action is. But it is difficult because, ourselves and the humans, we don't live together anymore. We just don't, it is not like we don't get along, we just have different ways. We are very gentle. So, we just keep our distance from the humans. Now we are in a position where we have never been before. Because now we have to decide, do we tell the humans or do we kind of 'wipe the slates' so to speak and clear their memory of any of that happening. We don't want to infringe on them, it is a very difficult decision to make. It is either we leave them vulnerable or we don't. But that is not the best decision for us either, to interact with the humans.

A: You mentioned that they are about half your size? You mentioned that sometimes they see you, so do they see you in your full form because you would seem giant to them, wouldn't you?

C: No... well yes, we can hide our ears and skin color, and we can kind of shorten ourselves. So, we could almost pass for a human if we really want to, we could pass for a human. We would just be a lot more gentle, which would be strange for a human. They would see us as human, and no, they would not see us in this form. We do not want to create any kind of fear at all, so seeing us in this form would strike fear into them. We have not gotten along, there were others that...yeah...

A: In this group that protected these humans, did any of you perish from it from fighting with the Reptilians?

C: I don't think so. Some got scraped here and there. But not really, it is so hard for the Reptilians to touch us. How they have their inorganic technology, we have organic technology that they don't understand. So, it is hard for them to try and touch us, as we move through time and space. It is very difficult and very hard for them to even scratch us but...

A: Okay, so tell me, you guys are discussing what you are going to do, tell me what you decide with regards to the humans?

C: I think we decide that we are not going to tell them who we are, but we are going to put ourselves in human forms so to speak and leave them with their memories because we think that it will not be of service to them if they did not have memory of what happened. We think that it would make them even more vulnerable if we 'memory wipe' them of this, it is not something we like to do. We can be in trouble for that, if you use it in the wrong way. You don't want to use it in the wrong way. We also think that if we were to do that, it would end up making them more vulnerable. We think that this is not really like a lesson, that sounds very harsh, but we agree that it isof use to them to remember. To recall what happened, and so they remember. We allow them to have their memories. So, what we end up doing is, we put ourselves into human forms. We go to the village, call them, waking up so to speak, from their daze. And they don't immediately remember, like Reptilians on the ground, and the destruction. No immediate recall you know of something happened. Without letting them know, the audience and villagers that were there and kind of just go around and we help them. We do stuff with them, blending in with them or they will know that we are not human. We try to teach them about the beings with them, so it is less scary on what Reptilians were. They don't understand how some of us know what these beings were, but they don't ask questions. They are just kind of dazed and just kind of, they don't know, they don't want to know, they just kind of want to hear what some of us have to say. We blend in and they don't know the difference. They think we are just part of the village; they would not know. And just say we have seen them before, and we have seen this happen and we know what they were. We tell them what these beings were. We teach them, kind of like infiltrating them, so that they don't know who we are. We show the humans crystals so that we teach other humans...some of them ask questions on how do you know this? Some of us just say we spend a lot of time wandering in the woods and in the forest. We have known this, and we need to share it with the rest of the village. So, they think that just some of us knew. So, we showed them crystals and these crystals can help protect them. It can also help them harness their own energy, but we don't talk about that because...they would not believe us even if we told them how powerful they were. They would not. It would be counteractive to what we are trying to do here. So, there is a lot of sadness and tears, as they do see the ones they have lost. And we all just kind of come together. They are not sure how the bodies were moved and adorned with flowers, and all the beautiful things like that. They don't know. I think they have an idea, but this goes much deeper in the past than this. I think they know, we might still exist, but they don't ask questions because...I don't know why, they just don't ask. It is really sad, they put all their loved ones that did not make it on boats, but they are not really boats, they are just like these little rafts and they float them out to sea. This village is by the sea. They just kind of float them all. And we energetically hold space for their sadness. We help with their sadness to try and relieve it, so that they can hopefully recall this in not such a traumatizing way and that they can be better next time, if they ever come back. They might know what to do, or how to interact with the crystals to help them. We want to let the humans know that we are here to help, but our history is not the best, so we just leave it at that.

A: The crystals you all gave them, were they a specific type of crystal?

C: It is quartz. Quartz crystals and we show them how to use them. They can almost produce the shield themselves. But we kind of act like we don't understand this crystal technology so we just kind of leave it at that. We know that it works and spend time in the forest with it, and this is it. And it is something that they should work on. We all just kind of move on from there.

A: Okay, so you briefly try to teach them how to shield?

C: Yeah. The crystals won't shield them like we can shield, as it is more powerful the way we do it but crystals, setting them on the grids. I can see later on that we do show them a spot where first they can get crystals that work in larger pieces. We kind of plant the idea that 'hey, maybe if you use larger pieces of the crystal quartz, that it might be more protective for you'. Some of them believe that, so I think that is what they are going to do. It does not prevent the Reptilians coming, but we know that the crystals raise vibration so that is a deterrent for the Reptilians.

The higher the vibration, the less they will try. It will not stop future times where they may come, but it will not be as pleasant for the Reptilians because the energy will be much higher. So, it will be almost like gross to them, so they will not like sitting in that space. So hopefully, they will just stay away. With them knowing that we are here, they will probably, hopefully stay away.

A: Let's go to another important time in this life. You are there now, tell me what is going on.

C: The humans have figured out that we are here. We have nothing to do with telling them, so it is not infringement, but they figured it out on their own. They figured it out, that we still reside in the forest. With them coming into the forest more for crystals, some of them wandered off pretty far into the forest and they saw some of us by the creek. Where we wash our hands and feet to get rid of negative energy, or just stagnant energy. The waters and the forest. The group of them have seen us, and they went back and told everyone that we are still there. They are uneasy about it; they do not remember that we have helped them in the past. But they are not too happy about it. Which is unfortunate, because we are very loving beings. We wish no harm on any being on this planet as we love all beings and all of Creation. So, it hurts...it hurts...to know they fear us. Some of our kind have been corrupted and... they were not nice to the humans in the past. So, they think that that is who we are. They think that we are the corrupted ones. They don't know the difference. There is a huge difference, but they don't see that. They just see that we look like what has happened in the past, and so they fear us.

A: Okay, so they are aware in their town's history that some beings like you, did harm to them, you said? Some of them are corrupted?

C: Yeah. Some are corrupted, yes. We are susceptible to corruption. Just like all beings in Creation, we too can be corrupted. That is who they have interacted with before. They have never interacted with the ones of us that are not corrupted. They have only seen and interacted physically with those of us that have been corrupted in the past, so they fear us.

A: When they were corrupted, did they show them their true form, like how tall they were and how they looked?

C: Yes. Which is very traumatizing to the humans, not only that, they look different. I would not say scary but compared to what we look like, you can tell they are definitely corrupted. Our skin glows and we wear white. Whereas our brothers and sisters that have been corrupted, they have a grayish tinted skin, with red or black eyes. Which does not look like it means much, but it is just different. As, there is no light in them and they have lost the light in their hair, lost the light all over. You can tell, you can see the difference. But the humans, they don't know the difference.

A: What was it that corrupted them? How did they become corrupted?

C: It is like another time and space, I cannot recall. I don't know how.

A: Okay, and when they attack the humans, what do they do to them? What memories do they have of that?

C: That is not something we like to recall...but they showed themselves to humans. Not like the Reptilians, there is no hierarchy, there is no rank...but when one has become corrupted, there tends to be more hierarchy. So those of us that have been corrupted, do resemble the Reptilians as such. They don't do the same things as the Reptilians and run around and just kind of be destructive because that is what they know. We are so graceful in our natural state, that when we do become corrupted, very dark, very powerful. Just like how I can shield, they can do that but the opposite, which is not good at all. It is very destructive, they can destroy entire villages with a swipe and... this village, this poor village has been through so much. They have rebuilt so many times. It is not just this village; it is planet wide. It is just hard for us to recall because we do love them, still they are our brothers and sisters. We can still feel them. They go into the village, and they don't necessarily use humans in the way that Reptilians do, but they trade them. They trade them to beings like Reptilians. Because they do not need them, the Reptilians can use them. But those of us that have been corrupted, the humans are of no use, so they are just pawns. Kind of enslaved by those of us that have been corrupted. They watched that before, they watched them come into their village and enslaved them like it was nothing, and take them, and take their families. It has been many, many, many years since then but they still...it has been passed down through the families. They will remember the stories that were told, and they trade them, which is very unfortunate.

A: What happened to those corrupted beings of your race?

C: (sighs) They just are. They just exist as part of Creation. They are.

A: Are they still on Earth with you all?

C: No, they don't...they don't care about us, we are apart. It is almost like two opposite ends of a magnet, we repel each other. It is not a good mix. Like oil and water. We do not mix. They stay away, but they do and will come to this planet, in this time and space that we are in now. They take humans...they will. And that's why we stay, because we know that normally humans are vulnerable to beings like Reptilians. They are vulnerable to beings like us that have been corrupted which are much more powerful than the Reptilians in their state. So... we just decided to stay in the forest and to watch over the humans. Just keep them under our wing and help them when necessary. Teach them when necessary. We keep our distance because we can't explain to them what corruption in a being is, they do not know this. They don't even know their own power so we cannot explain to them that we mean no harm, because they won't see that.

A: Thank you for this information. As far as human lives, do you live as long as humans or longer?

C: Much longer, much, much longer than humans. Thousands of years. Which is very unfortunate for those of us that have become corrupted. Because they can live just as long.

A: Let's move time along. Let's go to another important time in this life. You are there now, tell me what is going on now.

C: We, myself and the others on this Council. We are trying to come up with a plan, it seems like we are always planning when we are together. We are trying to decide, trying to see if there is a way that we can alchemically, almost energetically retrieve those of us that have been corrupted. And to bring them home almost. We do not want them existing the way they do; it is too much power and corruption. It is not safe for the Universe, it is not safe for the planet, it is not safe. We are here and we are spending so much time trying to figure out how we can do this. I have seen them. Before we were sitting here, this meeting, I had seen some of our corrupted brothers and sisters in the forest. They were on the ground and it is never a good thing to see them because they are always up to something. I saw them, and they are just so dark. I know I can just see it; I can just see that it is like, they just don't mean to be that way. They are just so clouded in the black thickness of corruption. They don't know how to find their light anymore. It just struck me, so I decided to bring this back to the Council and see how they felt about possibly retrieving those of us that have been corrupted and helping them. That is not something that the Council likes to hear because it is a very sensitive subject for us. No one has ever, no one has ever thought that there would ever be a way to bring them out of the corruption. But for some reason, I don't know why. When I saw them in the forest that day, it was almost like I could see sadness in them for the first time. Not just strung out on power, corruption. I could almost see that they themselves, they don't want that. And I decided to bring this back to the Council and ask how we felt about it. How we as a collective, might go about doing this, if this is even possible.

A: What do they say?

C: It is just a lot of tension, not very many words. It is a lot of heartache for us, because we are just so much love. We just love, we are so gentle. It is almost they don't want...it is like for so many years, they have just turned their eyes, their backs against them. It is not in our nature, as

I am trying to explain to them and they know, they know I am right. That it is not in our nature to even turn our backs on our own, they know this. So, it is just very tense and heavy at this meeting here. They know I am right; they know. It is just that it has never been done before because we like to, well not necessarily me, but they like to just turn their backs to it. I tried to explain to them that I can feel the sadness from my brothers and sisters, I can feel it. They don't want to be this way; they are just lost. There must be a way, there must be a way that we can help them, right?

A: Yes.

C: I am not getting a lot from them. The eldest of us with the long white hair, he does not want me speaking about this. He does not want to hear it. He does not want to believe that they can be uncorrupted. I am not sure either. But I do know that it is in my loving nature to at least try and ponder on that thought that it might be possible. Because if that was me, I would want them to come after me (feeling emotional). That is what I would want if I was corrupted, for them to come to help me find my light. They don't think it is possible. They don't want me speaking about it. But I am very strong in myself, and I will not let them hush me. I force them to listen, I force them to hear me out. This is our way; we are respectful of one another. So, they sit and listen to me. The eldest of us, he still has doubt, but I think I can convince him to at least try. I know that it is in our nature that they won't be able to say no to at least trying, because if any being in Creation were to ask us to help them, we would always say yes, no matter the circumstance, no matter the darkness, no matter what, we would help. We know that. That is us, that is our being. So, it is decided that we will try. They think I am crazy. I can't interface with them and show them the energetic signature that I took from that day in the woods/forest. I can't show them that sadness. If I were to interface and show them like before, they would only see the corruption of that energetic signature. They would not be able to see the emotions. It is buried so deep; I don't even know how I saw it. I am not sure. But I did and I cannot let it go. So even though this might get me in a lot of trouble with the Council in my position, I don't care. Because I have so much love in my heart for them (crying), for all beings, but especially our own.

A: Beautiful. Tell me, what is it that you all decide to do? What do you do next of importance?

C: The others are with me. But the eldest of us, he supports it because we have to collectively be together on a decision, but he has doubt in his heart. So, we decide that we are going to try, that we are going to do this. We are going to try and help them. It brings up so many other questions and concerns for the group, but we know, we know that this is the right thing to do.

A: What do you do?

C: It takes us a long time and today, in the now we are still working on it, in this 'now'. This NOW, if you understand me. We are still working on it, it has taken many, many, many years. (crying) But the seed of hope that I planted in the Council that day has not lost its light. We have been trying for many, many, many years. We know we can be successful. We know we can get them to come back and find their light. We have seen other beings do this, so we know it is possible for us too.

A: Have you all at least succeeded with even at least one?

C: Someone else on the Council. She lost her other half to corruption, and he was corrupted. She had...I think it was a success, I think so. Not success in a way that we thought it would be successful, but it was successful. She came across him in the forest, on a planet, and it had been many years since we had this discussion. She approached him and used the love that she has for him and his being and his soul, and she just...it was so beautiful. She just took everything she had inside of her, all of her Source, all of her being, and just almost like, projected it in his direction as to not harm. Because we can't do that for harm, but in another way that we have been practicing in trying to see if we can get it to work and it just kind of came about. And she did it. It was like he just fell to his knees, and (cries) she just kept projecting this love at him. She told him that we have been trying for many, many, many years to bring them home again, and that they still have their Love-Light inside of them. No matter how far gone they think they have gone, or what they have done. None of it matters. They are loved, they are loved by Source and they are loved by us. We will not turn our backs. And something happened in that moment for him. It just ignited that flame within him again and he just lit up, and he transmuted. He is not here anymore, but he turned back to Light before he transmuted. It is like she got to see him again in his Light form, so she knew that it worked. Not in the way we wanted, we wanted them to be able to stay and keep everything that they had experienced. So that maybe we can find a way to never allow this corruption again, and I think we will figure that out. But we are happy that it worked at all. We have so much love for one another. The bonds that we form with each other. We are so powerful. She just used that. She showed us. It is so beautiful. We are so happy. The eldest of us could not believe it. It changed a lot of things for us.

A: To make sure I understand, when she projected her infinite Love-Light unto him, he transformed, and she was able to see some of his Light. But then he ended up ascending? Did he ascend or did he just go back to Source?

C: He did not go back to Source. He just ascended. He was able to...

A: Ascend?

C: Yeah! (cries) It is like releasing the chains of darkness, she will see him again. So, it is a success to us. She will see him again; his soul still exists.

A: Good, so he was still able to retain his consciousness, everything and then ascended into a more positive polarization entity?

C: Yeah.

A: That is beautiful. That is beyond...infinitely beautiful, as you know that is what we do with A.U.R.A regressions. We go through and we find these negative aliens and entities, and we do what she expressed. Thank you. When that happened with his transformation, what happened to his body there, this giant body?

C: It stayed, and she sat with him for a while. He was not consciously in his body anymore. She just sat with his uncorrupted body; they just had such a beautiful love together. She just sat in peace for a while (sobs). She brought him back for us, so we knew that it was true, and we do what we do with any of our own. We adorned him with flowers and we kind of had just a moment together with this...the realization for all of us. It was the first time we could see that this was possible. We thought we had lost them, we thought they were gone. And she knows that she will see his soul again, when it is time for her to go.

A: Would you be able to connect me to her? I would love to be able to speak to her directly. Would you allow for her to speak through you?

C: Yes.

A: Wonderful! I would like to speak to that beautiful soul there that helped her other half as you explained, transform into Love-Light.

Elf Soul: Hello!

A: Greetings! Thank you for speaking to us. I love you, honor you and I respect you. May I ask you questions please?

Elf Soul: Yes. I love you too.

A: Thank you for sharing such an intimate story with us, I think one that is very important. I was wondering if you can answer a couple of things. When she said he was your other half, did she mean like a Twin Flame type of connection.

Elf Soul: Yes, we love very deeply. Yes, he was my other half.

A: Okay. Can you tell me, since you were able to experience it, say hands on? What happened to him? I am interested in knowing this corruption.

Elf Soul: Like how he became corrupted?

A: Yes. Whatever you can share on how you were able to experience that and see that within him. How did that happen?

Elf Soul: He left one day into the forest. We come and go; we wander the forest a lot. We wander the boundary, and we watch over the humans. He often wandered the borders of the forest, we just kind of watched the humans from a distance. He left one day and that's the day he never came back. He left, and he was going to do what he always does. Let's see if I can see through his eyes.

A: Yes, since you have that soul connection with him. If you could connect through his eyes, see what happened to him.

Elf Soul: I can see, I can see him walking and doing what he always does. It was a dark ship; he laid his eyes on a dark ship. There were dark beings, very dark beings, we have never interacted with them before. He was curious. He was too curious, and he...I can't quite tell how, but it is like he let his guard down. He let his energetic walls down, and they were able to, with him just gazing upon the ship for too long and wandering. They were able to get inside his mind. And in that moment, he was lost. It took a moment but they, these beings, are so powerful. Once he opened up the curiosity to them, that was the vulnerability. They had access, and they just went inside his mind. It was like the mind was flooded with darkness, like this black, black energy. I don't know how they can get that to him from the ship but...(sighs). He should not have done that. He should not have been so curious about something we knew nothing about. So, they had access to his mind, he gave permission without knowing it. He gave permission to allow them to have access to his mind. What I know about Creation and existence is that experiences...I do not judge him for this, I forgive him, it is fine. We all go through our experiences, and he wanted to experience darkness so...he did not know that at that moment, but that was the plan. He opened up to them, and they were just able to get inside the mind. Once they were in, they were in. They could just...it is like, they took all of the light that he was, and they sucked it out of him for themselves. Once they had most of the light out of him, his skin grew duller and duller, until he no longer had a glow. His hair lost all the light, and his eyes, all of his being. Until eventually, they just left him with the small flame that he had inside of him that they can't take, because it is Source Love-Light. And he was just gone. He was gone. He had no recollection of his lifetime as the beautiful being that he once was. He had no recollection, and that was the saddest thing for me. He did not remember me in that way. Not until the day we met in the forest again. Love is so powerful. And after that, he just kind of became a slave to corruption. He just became part of it. He became part of that world. He left the Love-Light, and he was, as cliche as it sounds, he went to the dark side. It is where he went, and it was so fast. After that, he kind of lost all of his memory of who he once was. He just became so overcome by darkness that he had to go and do things that would fulfill what the Light once gave him. He did not know it because he lost all memory of that, but he had to go do things that we would never imagine doing to human beings. But he had to do those things because he lost all the light within him. So, in order to fulfill that in some way, to sustain himself, he had to go and do things that were not in our organic nature.

A: Thank you for sharing your story, of both of your stories with us. Thank you, sister, I love you.

Elf Soul: I love you. Thank you.

A: Is there any other message you have for us, before I speak back to her?

Elf Soul: Just know that love is so powerful. Love, it does not matter...it does not matter what you face or what is in front of you, or how corrupted someone has become. There is always hope that love will penetrate. Because love can penetrate that. I just encourage everyone to hold that love, hold that love and don't give it up. Don't ever think that it is not possible. Everything is possible! Thank you.

A: Thank you, thank you for such a beautiful message. I love you, honor you, and respect you. Blessings to all of you, thank you.

Elf Soul: Thank you.

The Higher Self is called forth.

A: Let's leave that life now. Can I please speak to the Higher Self of Clara?

Higher Self: I am here.

A: Thank you. Am I speaking to Clara's Higher Self now?

Higher Self: Yes.

A: Thank you. I love you, honor you, and respect you for all the aid you have given us today. I know that you hold all the records of different lives, may I ask you questions please?

Higher Self: Yes.

A: Thank you. First of all, you took her to that life where she was an orphan and died of starvation. Why did you take her to that life? What was the purpose to that?

Higher Self: She has recalled that life in this lifetime, she is recalling it. She remembers it, and it was very heavy on her heart. She needed to see that it was just an existence, and that it holds nothing over her. It was just a lifetime. You can let it go. Though there is so much love, in all of Creation. There are times when you are challenged as a soul. That you may go without love, but in order to find the beauty and the love and the bright light that she is today. She had to have a life where she got no love, no help from others so that she could be the being that she is today. Strong, beautiful, loving being that she is today. She is so giving, and so caring because of that lifetime. She needs to know that. That's why her heart is so big, because she experienced that. She would not be who she is today, had she not experienced that.

A: Thank you. Then you took her to this profound life there, where she was this tall magical being. Is there a name for that race that they were?

Higher Self: She is Elven. She knows this.

A: Yes, an Elven race. That's very interesting, this information that you have given me. As you know, I myself am aware of some of these darker Elven that have been lost in this corruption. So, thank you for showing this life. It is very important. Now if you can tell me, what was the reason you wanted to show her that life? What was the purpose for her?

Higher Self: She is very connected with them. She still is. She is very, very connected with the Elven. She knows this, and she needs to know that even though she is in this body, in this life, that it is still ongoing. The work is still going and we as a Collective of the Elven, we are still trying. Still helping all our brothers and sisters. She is not consciously aware that the heaviness and sadness in her heart are those of that Elven race, that have been corrupted. It is necessary to help lift and heal that in her heart a little bit, so that she knows that we have not given up. That she is a very, very big reason for the work today. As many, many of the beings and races of Creation have been corrupted. That was a very significant moment for all of Creation, very, very big. It was a big moment, and she was the spark for that. She needs to not hold it heavy in her heart. She needs to hold love and gratitude for that strength that she had in that lifetime. Because it is resonating out in Creation today, and it is still resonating out today. Many beings know about that. They refer to that moment when a being so dark, came back through Love. If it were not for that moment, even though it was not her and her love, her other half. She was the seed, the start of that and she needs to know.

A: Beautiful, thank you. That is so beautiful.

Higher Self: It is.

A: Thank you. A lot of what you showed is something that we have been taught through the Elohim, the Angels...Now I am starting to feel that some of you beautiful Elven have been helping us create what we have with helping negative polarized beings that are willing to allow for us to help them. Thank you. So, I have a couple of questions about this life. Are these Elven beings, are those some of like Earth's history? They remember giants, would those be considered the giants that were ten feet tall?

Higher Self: In passing, I find yes, the humans have mistaken the Elven race for giants. There are stories and fictions and tales down the years that have the two intertwined, but the giants themselves, they are a race. They are beings themselves, and they have been seen by humans in the past, so it is a mix. Both have been seen. No, not every time that giants have been referenced was it the Elven race. The Elven race has stayed hidden, most of the time.

A: The time and space that you showed us. Around what Earth time and space, if you can give us any kind of direction, when was that?

Higher Self: Time is hard, hang on. I can do moments in Earth's history versus an actual date, because I do not know the dates. Dates are not much of a thing for us. I would say it was way before Atlantis and Lemuria, way before that, much, much, much before that. It was in the earlier stages of this Earth. Nearly when humans and beings and many, many others...before the Elven beings and the other magical creatures and the humans went their separate ways. But also, before Lemuria and Atlantis, where the humans were more in a powerful state of being. This was before then, this was when they were very innocent and pure, much before this I would say.

A: Okay, thank you. These Elven beings, do they still exist on Earth now?

Higher Self: Yes, but in very remote places and they stay away. Not many, not many. Not many at all, this planet has become very dense. It is not easy to be here anymore. There are some that stay, that have stayed and are still here because that is what they have always been doing. Taking care of the human race. It is so dense, much of the Elven race is not here anymore.

A: Anything else you want to share with us about that life?

Higher Self: No.

A: Okay, thank you. Higher Self, is there a name that you go by?

Higher Self: I am hearing Eliana, Eli-ana. It is kind of a name. Not really all the time a name, but Eliana.

A: Beautiful. You as her Higher Self aspect, is there a race that you are of?

Eliana: We are almost a cross between the Angelics and the Elven race. The Elven race and the Angels. We are a mix...not Archangels, they are so beautiful. We are the Elven race mixed with the Angelics together as one being.

The Body Scan begins.

A: Beautiful. Okay, Higher Self, thank you. We like to begin her Body Scan at this point. We know that she's been in there for some time already, how is she holding up?

Eliana: She is fine.

A: Okay, let's begin her Body Scan. Let's start scanning and see what we can help her assist in healing? Do you need any assistance from the Archangels to conduct the Body Scan?

Eliana: Archangel Michael.

A: Very good. Higher Self, Eliana, if you could please connect me now to Archangel Michael. I would like to speak to him now please.

AA Michael: Hello sister!

A: Greetings brother. I love you, honor you, and respect you. Thank you for being here.

AA Michael: I thank you, as always Aurora. You know we love you; we love you infinitely.

A: Yes, and I love you all infinitely. Michael, if we can please begin her Body Scan. We have the Higher Self requesting for your aid. They showed us such an important life there. Not that some are more important than others, but it is a very significant life. If you can scan her body, for any energies, entities, anything that requires healing. Let me know what you find. Please scan her from head to toe, thank you.

AA Michael: She has a lot of density that they have tried to attach to her over the years, she is so strong though. In the mind, in the third eye, there is heavy blockage on the third eye.

A: Can you scan that area and tell me what is that blockage there? Is it an energy, an entity, or is it a technology?

AA Michael: It is a technology.

A: What is it? Is it an implant?

AA Michael: It is like an implant, yes. It is just almost, like a dark shield that goes over the third eye to prevent it from operating at full capacity.

A: Can I use the Phoenix Fire on it to transmute it out of there?

AA Michael: Yeah, absolutely.

A: Good, using Phoenix Fire there. Let me know once the dark shield is completely removed from her third eye. Anything else that requires healing in her head area? Scan her deeply.

AA Michael: Just negative energies. Nothing I can see, no more technologies, she just has a lot of stagnant negative energy that won't move. We can get it to move.

A: Okay, can you start that process please?

AA Michael: Yes.

A: Thank you. As we continue to remove this shield over the third eye, can we continue scanning her body for any entities, or Reptilian Consciousness, or any kind of negative aliens?

AA Michael: Yes, her spine.

A: Let's look at her spine. Scan her spine for any negative alien fractals, including Archons, any type of non-organic negative fractals that are not hers organically. Let me know what you find.

AA Michael: It is an Archonic attachment on the spine.

A: Can we go ahead and surround this energy with the alchemy symbols now please?

AA Michael: Yes.

A: Surround the Archon, thank you.

AA Michael: May we have Metatron as well?

A: Good. Michael, can you call forth on Archangel Metatron? Thank you. Welcome Metatron. Love you, honor you and respect you. Thank you for being here.

AA Metatron: I love you sister.

A: Thank you. I love you. If we can please contain that Archon entity within her spine. Let me know once it is contained.

AA Metatron: We have contained it all.

A: Let's go ahead and start using the alchemy symbols there and transmuting it out please.

AA Metatron: Yes, this will take a moment, but we will do this.

A: Thank you. Start that process now please, making sure that all her whole spine and her DNA structure does not contain any negative aliens within it please. Scan that now Metatron, let me know if you see any other type of negative aliens within her DNA structure and spine.

AA Metatron: Yes, she has a collective that has tried to attach to the spine as well. They have managed to attach a type of technology, but no DNA...they were not able to access her DNA.

A: This negative collective. can we surround them now with the alchemy symbols please?

AA Metatron: Yes.

A: Thank you, let me know once they are surrounded.

AA Metatron: We have them all.

A: Thank you. Metatron, am I able to speak to this collective?

AA Metatron: If you wish, yes.

A: Okay, now that it is contained, Metatron, I would like to speak to them. If you can help them come up, up, up, come up, up now please. Greetings.

Negative Collective: Hello.

A: Thank you for speaking to us. Love you, honor you and respect you. May I ask you questions?

Negative Collective: Sure.

A: Thank you. If I can ask, when was it that you attached to her spine?

Negative Collective: When she was younger, when she was 15.

A: What was it that was going on with her that allowed for you to come in at the time?

Negative Collective: It was the medicine that she was on. So easy, so easy to attach.

A: Do you mean the medicine that the doctors gave her, when they classified her as being bi-polar?

Negative Collective: Yes.

A: This medicine allowed for you to come in easy?

Negative Collective: Much easier, yes.

A: How does it make it much easier for you to come in, this medicine?

Negative Collective: We do not wish to say.

A: That is okay, thank you. Now if I can ask, what kind of race are you? What collective are you?

Negative Collective: You would know us as Grays.

A: I understand that you have been there for some time, perhaps you have been doing this for a while, attaching to people. We'd love to be able to assist you today. As you know the Earth is ascending itself, and parasitic entities like you would no longer be able to attach anymore and be in that density anymore. So, when the Earth and the Universe ascends into a higher vibration, you will no longer be able to hold on to people in this manner. So, we are looking to assist you today, so you no longer have to play this negative polarized role parasitically. You can let go of this role. You can transcend, ascend into a positive polarization of an existence where you can perhaps incarnate somewhere. Overall, you will be able to create your own light and your own experiences, no longer being controlled. You will have your own freewill. Do you allow for us to assist you today?

Negative Collective: No, we much prefer this.

A: I understand that you are not accepting that. If you do not accept it, I want you to understand that once the shift occurs, you will be automatically transmuted straight back to Source. All the wisdom and experiences you gained from being these Grays, will be wiped. Is that what you want, to be transmuted straight to zero? Or do you want to take this opportunity, instead grow, and keep those memories of the experiences gained, not being negative polarized. You can instead be wise and strong, and free willed with your light. Creating your own light.

Negative Collective: We will go.

A: You will go ahead and allow for us to help you ascend? Positive polarized?

Negative Collective: If it is possible. We don't know that that is possible for us.

A: Okay, we understand that you might be a different type of race. From my understanding though, even Grays have some kind of spark of light in them. Archangel Michael and Archangel Metatron, if we can help them start finding their Love-Light in them. Michael and Metatron, do they have light within them?

AA Michael: They don't, they don't have any light. They are an inorganic form. They are similar to the Gray race. But these in particular, they are like, what is the best way to describe it...they are inorganic creations. They don't have, they don't hold the spark. They don't hold that. Some of the other Gray races do, but this in particular they do not hold the spark. They have one job only and that is to suck light out of Creation.

A: Michael and Metatron, what do you suggest we do? Now that they are contained. Do you want to just take them? Do what you need to do as far as transmuting, and what needs to be done with them?

AA Michael: Yeah, we will...they will just have to be transmuted. We will do this. They are not happy about it. But there is not much we can do for those. Though they are part of creation, they are inorganic, they do not come from Source. There is not much we can do. They won't be allowed to incarnate. They don't have a connection to Source, so they must be transmuted.

A: Okay. Alright. Thank you, go ahead and do what you need to do please. Now, while you all do that, is there another Archangel that I should speak to while you work on that?

AA Michael: You can speak to Archangel Gabriel, if you would like.

A: Very good.

AA Michael: He is here.

A: Good. Archangel Gabriel, brother!

AA Gabriel: Hello!

A: Thank you for being here, it is an honor to have you here. We do not see you too often in A.U.R.A sessions, thank you.

AA Gabriel: I love you! I love you, Aurora!

A: Oh! Aww!

AA Gabriel: I love you, I honor you and I thank you for all the beautiful work you do on this planet. So beautiful! So strong!

A: Aah! Thank you, I am strong because you are by my side.

AA Gabriel: Absolutely, always.

A: Love you, honor you and respect you as well! Gabriel, as they are working there, can you tell me how that shield is over her third eye, is that removed?

AA Gabriel: Archangel Michael transmuted that. Yes.

A: Good, if we can fill in Love-Light there. Can you connect us to Archangel Raphael and have him start doing that for us please?

AA Gabriel: Yes.

A: Thank you. Our love for Raphael. We are working on removing the Archonic energies within her spine, as well as the Grays...anything else in her spine that needs healing?

AA Gabriel: No, it needs a lot of love and light, as it has much damage due to the Archonic attachment and the inorganic race.

A: As they are removing those, if we can all start filling in Love-Light there, to her spine and her DNA structure. Also reprogramming anything negative that is not part of her or for her highest good, as the Higher Self allows. Deprogramming anything that is no longer serving her, anything that is harming her belief system, helping her grow. Thank you Gabriel, if you can continue scanning her body. If we can scan now the rest of her body for any other entities. Let me know if you find anything else.

AA Gabriel: Her heart.

A: What's going on there?

AA Gabriel: It is her heart. She has...it is like a black goo. It causes her heart to skip beats at times. It just kind of restricts the heart, restricts its light. We can get rid of that, it causes her chest pains at times, and skipping her heart beats.

A: Can I use the Phoenix Fire on that dark goo?

AA Gabriel: Yes, please.

A: The dark goo, does it have a consciousness?

AA Gabriel: No.

A: We are going to go ahead and start transmuting that from her heart there. Can you tell me when did that come in?

AA Gabriel: When she was about six years old.

A: What happened?

AA Gabriel: She had so much heartache from other lifetimes, from her connection to her corrupted brothers and sisters from the Elven race, just a lot of heartache. Made the heart weak and vulnerable to this attachment unfortunately for her, but we will get rid of it. If you would just use the Phoenix Fire, we would get rid of it.

A: Thank you. Gabriel, continue scanning her body for any entities of any kind, Reptilian consciousness, anything else?

AA Gabriel: Quite a few Reptilians consciousness in the solar plexus and the root chakra. She is recently aware of this, and there are many, many, many Reptilians standing by and they are ready to be brought back to Source. She has spoken to them in the coming weeks about this session, and has called in many, many, many Reptilians in with our permission of course over the coming weeks. She had told them that we would be here today, and this is the gateway out. There are many, many Reptilian Consciousnesses today that are ready to go to Source. We are happy about this.

A: Wow, that is beautiful. We thank her for that. That is, of course, with you all's protection.

A: Contain them now with the alchemy symbols, so that it easier for them to start positive polarizing. Surround both areas with the alchemy symbols please.

AA Metatron: This is Archangel Metatron.

A: Yes, Metatron. Thank you, Metatron, if you can contain them now with the alchemy symbols both in the solar and the root areas. Metatron, can you tell me are you all done with removing the Grays out of her?

AA Metatron: Yes, they have been transmuted. They are gone.

A: Good, we are making sure we are filling in Love-Light there. And how is the Archonic energy in her spine?

AA Metatron: We are still working on that; I just need a moment. We will get it, but the Archon energy is very, very strong. We got this.

A: Do we have the root and solar plexus now contained?

AA Metatron: Yes.

A: If you could start now, I am speaking to the Reptilians there that are within these two areas. We love you, honor you, and respect you. Thank you for allowing us to assist you, you are ready and saying yes. If you could now start spreading your Love-Light. We are going to focus Love-Light upon you now. Spread it to all that is of you, every root, every cord, every part of you that is within her, that is yours and not of hers. Let us know once all of you are all light. Michael, do they have any Reptilian Bodies out somewhere? Any of these that are in her now?

AA Michael: Yeah, they have all gone to ships. They have prepared for this moment over the past few weeks, and they are all on ships. Metatron has them surrounded on the ships.

A: Beautiful, thank you. Let's start helping them to spread their Love-Light there, the Reptilian Bodies. Also, the consciousness they attach to other people besides her here. How many have they attached to as well, the consciousnesses?

AA Michael: At least, probably about 200,000 humans that they have attached to, these beings.

A: Gabriel, if you could communicate please to those 200,000 humans' Higher Selves, and ask them if they will allow for those consciousnesses that they have attached to them, if they will allow for us to help them remove? Helping them transform to light. Gabriel, what they say?

AA Gabriel: They are all saying yes. They are definitely saying yes.

A: Beautiful. Okay, let's go ahead and start that process now. Gabriel, Raphael and Legion, surrounding those 200,000 as well. Helping them now spread their Love-Light, your Legions there. Once all those consciousnesses are light, let's retrieve them back to the Reptilian Bodies that are on the ship. So, that they can make themselves whole. If we can call forth on Archangel Azrael and his Legion now, supervising this transformation, ensuring that none of them get astray. Thank you to everyone.

AA Gabriel: They are Love-Light. They are ready.

A: Beautiful. Beautiful. Go ahead you all, leave your Reptilian Bodies, now that you have all your consciousness back. Again, we are filling in Love-Light to all those humans as well as her here, with Love-Light. Wherever those consciousness were. Now that you all are of light, can you tell me, do you have a message for us?

Positive Polarized Reptilians: We just want to thank this beautiful soul, for allowing us this opportunity, and this exit point, shall we say. We do appreciate all of the forgiveness that humanity has been so kind to give us. That we may go back to Source and find our center, our heart, and our love again. We thank you all so much for your kindness and your beauty. It is very beautiful that you would forgive beings such as ourselves.

A: Thank you as well. I love you all. I love you, honor you, and respect you. Blessings to you and may you all be surrounded by the Love-Light of the Universe. Archangel Azrael, again you and your Legion, ensure that they go where they are meant to go for their positive polarization. Blessings to them. Now I know that we are filling in Love-Light to all the different areas, where they were connected. Michael, can you tell me, how many Reptilians just positively ascended?

AA Michael: It is about 748,000.

A: Beautiful.

AA Michael: That is the call that she gave out.

A: Oh, with the call that she gave out?

AA Michael: There was only about...she had about six within her chakras, four in the solar and two in the root chakra. And speaking to those, she asked those Reptilians, with our protection of course. She asked them if they would contact any or all Reptilians that they were connected to that were ready to go into the light, that were ready to transmute. She told them that this would be an opportunity. Many more showed up and 748,000 were able to take to the light.

A: Wow, what a beautiful selfless loving act for her to do! Thank you, we humbly thank her. Thank you for divinely setting this up. Thank you, thank you! If we can go ahead and continue scanning her body, Michael, can you tell me are there any other negative implants, hooks, portals, or any other entities that are within her?

AA Michael: She is clear.

A: Ah, beautiful! There are a couple of things that I need to go over here. Michael, if you can just finish up the Body Scan for us? Let's rejuvenate her cells that need it with Love-Light. Can we check her chakras? Are there any misaligned or blocked chakras that require healing?

Eliana: The heart chakra, is a little blocked from all the heartaches from the past lives. We can send love there.

A: Good, sending Love-Light there now please. Michael, can you scan her for any type of negative technology or wires within her?

AA Michael: On her lower spine. Not the Archonic attachment that we transmuted out, but the lower spine does have a type of technology, that is the cause for her hip issues. Especially the right hip, which causes her much of the back pain. The back has many problems, so quite a few different issues with that. But on the lower back, right near the pelvis, on the back.

A: Can we transmute that with the Phoenix Fire please?

AA Michael: Yes.

A: Okay, transmuting it now.

AA Michael: Yes, there was instant back relief there now. So much better.

A: Michael, can you scan for any fragmented soul pieces that need to be regained back to her?

AA Michael: She has two of them.

A: Okay, can you find them? Tell me, why did they fragment off?

AA Michael: One was from that lifetime, from that when she was a little girl on the streets. There was so much sadness and heartbreak, she left a piece of herself there. And once in Atlantis, she has a piece of herself in there. She has tried herself to bring it back, but she just needs a little more help, so we will help her bring that piece back.

A: Thank you, yes. Bring those two pieces back to her, and if we can have our brother, Archangel Raphael, start making her soul whole once more with the Higher Self please. Michael, can you tell me, why did she have the Archons in her spine? When did they attach?

AA Michael: They attached upon birth. It was her parents. Not her parents' fault but the lack of love between her parents upon her creation. It was easy access. It was easier to access her. So, they attached to her, her light was so bright that this Archon decided to attach there. She has had it her whole life.

A: Thank you. Can you also check, she said that she has...well the doctors have diagnosed her as scoliosis? Can you scan and see why they tell her that she has that?

AA Michael: Yes. It was the way her spine was curving. It was curving like that due to the Archonic attachment. It is such a heavy, heavy energy, twisting her spine in ways that her spine should not be twisted. The doctors do not know any better, they don't know about this, so they see what they see. They gave her the diagnosis of scoliosis. The curvature of it, as it was curving because of the presence of such a dense energy.

A: If we can start repairing her spine please, so that eventually it no longer has that curvature.

AA Michael: Yes, we will do this.

A: Thank you. Good. She fractured her wrists; can you scan that and see if there is any healing needed there or anything attached?

AA Michael: They are fine. It was just infringement trying to block out what she was able to do in her lifetime of shielding. They do not like that power. Dark beings do not like the power of shielding.

A: Yes. We know, they have tricked many on Earth, in thinking that it is negative and that it is 'fear based' to shield. If you can scan her one more time, making sure that there are no other negative energies, entities, that does not belong to her organically. How does she look?

AA Michael: She looks great! Much better than when we started. (chuckles)

A: For sure!

AA Michael: Much lighter. Much, much lighter. Yes.

A: Thank you, thank you. I want to thank Michael, Metatron, Raphael, Azrael and Gabriel, thank you anyone who assisted. Any other Angelics and any other benevolent beings that assisted with her beautiful healing today with such a profound healing of the Reptilians. We love you, honor you, and respect you. Blessings to everyone, thank you!

AA Michael: We love you. Thank you.

A: Thank you. If I could now, please speak back to her Higher Self?

Eliana: I am here.

A: Thank you. What a beautiful profound session. You have brought us such a gift!

Eliana: Thank you.

A: I am just going to ask a couple of questions that she has here. But the majority, I think have been answered profoundly through such an intense important life you showed for her.

Eliana: Absolutely. I think that there is much. Especially that lifetime that she had in that moment, of her Elven sister who had that beautiful moment between her and her other soul. That has really rippled out into Creation. It is a light of hope for many. We hope that many will get to know that that exists, and that love is that powerful. It will give many hope to know that love is more powerful than you can ever imagine.

A: Thank you. What is her life purpose? What is she here to do?

Eliana: She is here, before the shift, she is here to help heal others. She has a natural gift of being a healer. Before awakening, it was almost toxic for her to have so many souls coming to her because they just...souls naturally know where to go. They know who to go to for healing, and she was not equipped with the right abilities to do that, so she energetically took on a lot of that. Now that she is awakened, she will be able to do better, she knows how to shield. She has watched you quite a bit Aurora, we thank you for that. So she can shield, it will make it much easier for her to do this work. And after the shift, she will be a teacher. She will teach the humans. Just like she did in her Elven life. She will be a teacher.

A: Beautiful. Thank you. I want to make sure also that those drugs they had her on, the anti-depressants, and the bi-polar meds, make sure we are healing any of the damage from that.

Eliana: Yes.

A: Thank you.

Eliana: A lot of that stagnant energy Archangel Michael was talking about, that came from those medicines. Leaving heavy negative energy.

A: How about that shield on the third eye?

Eliana: Yes. Yes. That was able to be there because of those medicines. And the dark beings, they know that. They know all those medicines allow them to be able to attach that technology to the third eye. It is harder for her to release that negative energy in the mind, while she was on them for so long.

A: Last thing here, she wants to know if she should become an A.U.R.A. practitioner?

Eliana: Yes, I think that would be very good for her. There are many modalities for healing, but this one in particular...she knows that A.U.R.A. is the way to go. She knows that the shielding, and the alchemy work that you do, and beautiful Dolores Cannon and yourself and the Archangels. It is the way to go. It is going to help this planet in ways that none of us could even imagine. Yes, it would be a great addition to that.

A: Beautiful. Thank you for that. I know that she will be amazing. It sounds like she was already doing this with the life you showed us, so it would be beautiful to help her piece that together in this human life. Thank you. Is there anything else that I could have asked but I have not asked?

Eliana: No, that is it. I believe we have covered everything for this session.

A: Thank you, beautiful, beautiful Higher Self, Eliana! It is such an honor once more. Thank you for bringing her to me, and to my YouTube channel as well. I know she has been in there as a very strong supporter of love in our Live Streams, so thank you for her love there.

Eliana: Yes, absolutely. We are grateful for you. Grateful for you to be doing what you do. To be the light that you are. You are a very big guidance for her. And thank you for that.

A: Thank you. I love everyone. Again, my love to everyone who assisted. I love you all!

Eliana: As do we. I love you, we love you, and the Archangels love you infinitely. Thank you so much for all that you do and all that you are. Thank you. We love you.

A: I love you with all that I AM. Blessings to everyone, thank you. I will bring her back now.

Post Session dialogue.

A: Wow. That was amazing!

C: Yes! I feel so light!

A: Yes! Ah, for sure!

C: My back, my back feels good. I don't know, it just feels really different.

A: Ah yeah! (chuckles)

C: Yes, wow! (laughs) My back feels great. Yes, I can tell! I can definitely tell. Wow! My lower back feels. I cannot describe what it feels like. Just blissed out. Very, just feels really good. Really nice!

A: Wow, what a beautiful surprise. Thank you for following your heart to mine. I know you said when you started off, and then you said 'woah, that is too much'! You know about our channel, and then you eventually came back a couple of months later. It does take a minute, some of these things that we talk about, they are so real and so true and so raw. That people don't realize that these kinds of things happen throughout creation. It is not just here in this 3D Earth. You showed us how they travel around like this and do this.

C: I feel so light. It is a new feeling for me! I have not felt as light, not like airy, not grounded, but...it feels good.

A: I understand.

C: It feels good. Very nice.

A: Yes, beautiful!

C: I just kind of feel like I am blissed out. (laughs)

A: Yes, you were ready.

C: Thank you so much!

A: Thank you. By the way, I never had anyone do that before. Thank you for allowing and holding that space for the Reptilians that were ready to ascend. In doing that, I normally would not recommend that unless you had a strong team. However, that was beautiful that they supported you in that you so selflessly did that for 748,000.

C: Wow!

A: Yes, amazing! Wow, that life is very, very needed.

C: That is so lovely to hear! Thank you for all that you do! I could not be more grateful!

A: Thank you as well! I love you, and I hope to see you in the future! Bye love!

C: I love you too! Absolutely! Bye!

END OF SESSION

-------------<◇>-------------

Wow! This was one of the most profound sessions I have witnessed directly connected to the most beautiful expression of LOVE. Both by Eliana's decision to plant a seed of hope, and her Elven soul sister, who was able to aid her corrupted Twin Flame to positively polarize and ascend. It began with Eliana's deep understanding that all can be saved, all can be redeemed, all can be healed, no matter how deep the roots of corruption are. These sparks are what create the possibility for the THEN, NOW, and the FUTURE. HOPE is what fuels our lifeforce, never allowing us to give up to false darkness. There is always a way, and the organic lifeforce will always win, as it is the only thing that can transmute and eradicate the inorganic. The inorganic and organic divinely were never meant to have intertwined, and all that is not right eventually will right itself to its original form. This is the natural cycle of balance of OUR Universe, and there must always be balance. Our Love-Light is that infinite and powerful.

When a soul is a high percentage of service-to-others, it is just not within their nature to look the other way when someone needs our aid. This session relates strongly to us in the NOW. The Elder in that time, not wanting to address the dark corrupted Elven brethren, as it was too painful to do so. These similar repeated unbroken cycles are going on in our time and space as well. Specifically, with the human and child sex trafficking happening on Earth right now. It is too painful to get into it, so people too in the now like those Elders, look the other way.

We were shown that even at the beginning seeding of humans on this Earth's time, there were human trafficking and abductions occurring. Picking up humans from their villages, as if they were for the picking. The humans in their infantile stages, not knowing any better nor understanding their true power were rendered vulnerable. We thank these beautiful Elven, for choosing to be Guardians to the humans, and loving them so in a time where the Universe was still trying to understand what and whom these dark forces were trying to invade planets, just as we have learned through the previous Chapters. The multitude of our organic races of our Universe were trying to come to an understanding in how to protect from these unnatural invasions. In this instance, the Elven were the volunteers in guarding the human life, until or as the Universe further gained knowledge on these unknown invasive forces. As the Elven sister's Twin Flame learned it in the most challenging manner of becoming the corruption himself. Understanding this fully, we now know how vast and profound it is that we are now within a time and space of being able to recognize these negative polarized aliens, their use of negative technologies, and how to collectively and Universally finally remove these infringements of all types of inorganics from our Universes. And this is GRAND, THAT IT IS!

Up until now on Earth, we had not been able to go as deeply as we are on this highly sensitive topic of human trafficking. Therefore, this shows the vast amount that we as the human collective race have grown and raised in vibration, to allow this painful issue to come to the surface for much needed healing. There is a great percentage of beautiful souls on Earth standing up against trafficking and pedophilia in the NOW. We can stop supporting companies that are engaged in highly suspicious activities indicating trafficking of some nature, or media/toy companies that push out suggestive content about young children etc. Before we might have looked the other way, but not anymore. Now we are grouping together, taking our sovereignty back. Yes, we are sovereign! And this begins first with our children, the children of the Earth.

The power of shielding was vastly explained and shown through Clara's Elven self (Eliana). How the infinite powers of nature and love could be harnessed to become a shield by one Elven being in its power. This Elven group of Elders were the example to us, how we truly are all parts of the puzzle pieces that fit in to one another, as they were within their group. We saw how one Elf could shield, how another Elf could tap into the energies of the dark entities, and how one Elf sister could love so infinitely to be able to positively polarize another even at their deepest darkest distortion. Together each individual's unique soul abilities complement each other to create such an unstoppable immense team.

We also learned of the technologies out there that are designed for shields, specifically constructed to break through these types of Love-Light force fields. One would think that the Archons would have to study much of what shields consist of, and how to pierce through, and weaken them. It seems as if they must have gone through much effort on their end to experiment perhaps on the various types of shields out in Creation. In what ways did they do this? Highly probable through the abduction of beings in the Universes with specialization in shields, that they then tested on until they got the technology right. These technologies must be so advanced and developed to target the light frequency within the infinite Love-Light Shields and disintegrate it. Could they be using dark matter that is compromised in forms of weapons, that when shot at light the dark matter comes after the light like a Pacman, consuming the light into it, eradicating it? Making these entryway holes as explained through Eliana's shield when they invaded with their spacecraft upon the human village. There is no other matter, besides dark matter in the Universe that would be able to dematerialize light in this manner.

These Elven beings are powerful and beautiful with their abilities and strength. They are fierce, and they were able to school the Reptilian soldiers with ease. "The Melchizedek" from

Chapter 15 mentioned to us and the Galactics once told me that there were far more powerful negative beings than Reptilians out in the Universe. These corrupted Elven bridged us to the awareness and are examples of these dark alien races in the Universe. If the Elven of light could wield such power and move with such ease, we can imagine what the dark Elven would be capable of. That much power corrupted into dark agendas would seem unstoppable and uncontrollable.

Eliana explained how till this day, the Elven race and we are looking into how to assist these souls who became corrupted in their Elven races. Simply being 'too curious' and allowing one's guard down just for that moment in time, can allow powerful Archons with their technologies to corrupt life. Some of these dark Elven turned corrupted might have been too powerful for the Archons to fully control, but the Archons ensured to accomplish what they wanted, which was to cause chaos, pain, sadness and unbalance to the Elven Race and humanity. This is what Archons do everywhere they are able to reach their tentacles, spiders, robotics, and negative technologies.

In the next Chapter, we receive the puzzle pieces that will complete this incredible journey, as we are vastly amazed by the Divine hand orchestrating all of this to happen in the most profound magical ways to remind the Universe of the true power of Love.

"To honor Creation.
To feel and fall in love with the warmth of the Earth beneath your soles.
To look upon the sun and to become ONE with its infinite healing consciousness.
To be touched by the water and allow for it to absorb you.
To respect the strength of the fire and its renewal.
To hear the whispers of the wind as it embraces all that is you.
To silence in mind, through connection to all life within spirit."
~AuroRa 🖤

-------------<◇>------------

34

ELVEN TWIN FLAMES

Recorded in June 2020.
Never before shared.

In this online A.U.R.A. Hypnosis Healing session, Maria is the practitioner for Julia's session. Interested in becoming a healer, Julia is at the beginning stages of her A.U.R.A. Hypnosis Healing Certification training, so it is important for her to be cleared of any infringements. She has strong abilities; however she feels something very dark is holding her back.

In this incredible journey and intense healing session, Julia is taken to a life where she is an Elder on an Elven Council. She carries a great heartache, and she is determined to change what seems unchangeable or unsavable. Through Julia's heart-centered action to shine all her love in the face of darkness, she created a ripple effect throughout the Universe. If life had taught us to have given up on love, our world will STILL be transformed through this truly inspirational journey of Elven Twin Flames! Where there is LOVE and HOPE, there is always a way to pave paths forward which have been deemed previously impossible. Through this grand heart-opening Elven journey, we humbly experience the Divine hand gracefully at work in making all of this possible for us as Divine Inspiration!

-------------<◇>-------------

"I send him love. I send him all the love I have. Everything! I see he feels it. He notices. He stops what he's doing. He stands up, I stand up. I'm sending him energy and I'm looking into his eyes. Sending in light, sending him love. He's taking it in. Something touches something in him a little bit, there's a little bit left, a little bit left in his heart…"
-Julia

-------------<◇>-------------

M: [Maria] Have you landed on the ground?
J: [Julia] I have. Yes. I'm where I thought I would go, in the forest. There's water in front of me. I've seen pieces of this scene before. I'm very sad. I can't really see what he looks like but he's on the other side of the river.
M: Do you feel you have a body?
J: Yes.
M: Look at your hands and tell me how many fingers do you have?
J: Five.
M: What is the tone of your skin?
J: It's very light.
M: Are you carrying anything in your hands?
J: I feel like I have a satchel or something.
M: Beautiful. Describe the satchel.
J: It's cloth. It's earth tone. There's something in it.

M: Let's open the satchel and let's see what's in it. Describe what you see.

J: I think there are arrows. Something with wooden sticks.

M: Do you feel you're young or do you feel older?

J: I look young. I think I look young.

M: Do you feel you're male or female or both?

J: Female.

M: Do you have any jewelry on you that catches your attention?

J: I keep thinking about my skin because it's quite shimmery. Hmm... Jewelry! I think I have something around my neck.

M: You have a spiritual mirror right in front of you so you can see yourself from head to toe. You can describe in detail what you see. What's the jewelry that you're wearing on your neck?

J: It's a stone. It's like a moonstone or Opal. It's on a black leather band.

M: We know that everything has an energy and consciousness to it. And so, does this crystal that you're wearing around your neck. Does it have a message for you, and would you allow the crystal to speak through you?

J: Yes.

M: Calling on the energy of this beautiful crystal you're wearing on your neck. Greetings, welcome.

Crystal Consciousness: Hello.

M: Hello. Thank you so much for speaking with us today.

Crystal Consciousness: My pleasure.

M: Thank you. If I may ask you questions?

Crystal Consciousness: Yes.

M: Thank you. What is the name that you go by? How would you describe yourself?

Crystal Consciousness: (thinking). I don't know. I seem like... it's almost like the stone is a mirror. Not a stone.

M: Can you describe what color energies you hold within you?

Crystal Consciousness: Water energy is within this stone. Sorry. What was your question?

M: What is the energy that you hold within you in terms of the color ray?

Crystal Consciousness: Blue.

M: Beautiful. Do you have a message for her? What is your connection with her?

Crystal Consciousness: I reflect truth. I help show her the truth. She can see more clearly with my help.

M: For how long have you been with her?

Crystal Consciousness: Many years.

M: Are you with her in this current existence as well?

Crystal Consciousness: I'm similar to the ring she wears. It also helps her see.

M: Is the ring a part of a fragment of your existence?

Crystal Consciousness: No. But there's some connection there.

M: Beautiful. Thank you. Is there anything else that you'd like to say to her?

Crystal Consciousness: It's like a pool of water. When you look down at a pool of water and you see your own reflection? She can use the ring similarly.

M: Beautiful. That's a beautiful guidance for today. Thank you very much. So, she can continue to connect with you. Are you energetically also around her?

Crystal Consciousness: Yes. Beautiful. I feel this is partly Gabriel.[30]

M: The crystal? Do you feel the crystal is partly Gabriel?

---

[30] A reference to Archangel Gabriel.

Crystal Consciousness: Some way of channeling Gabriel. Clarity, fluidity, water.

M: Thank you, that's a beautiful gift. Thank you so much for sharing this message. Is there any other message that you have for her from Gabriel?

Crystal Consciousness: She already knows the water can save her and cleanse her. So, to keep doing that, but she can be a little more intentional with it.

M: Thank you so much for speaking with us today. It'd be beautiful if you come on this journey with us if the Higher Self approves.

Crystal Consciousness: Thank you.

M: Let's continue now. You were describing your skin; you were describing how bright and sparkly the skin is. What does it look like?

J: Luminous. It's very pale. I have long legs, long arms and longer fingers.

M: How about the face? What are the features that you have on your face?

J: I remember the ears because I've dreamt of them recently too. Kind of droopy at the top like Faye. Kind of flowy and hangs - they're big. Not too big but not like human ears.

M: You said they flow to where?

J: They're around the size of human ears but they're more soft on the edges. It's strange.

M: What about your body; how does it feel? Does it feel heavy or light? Is it dense?

J: I'm my Elven self. I'm very smooth and soft. I'm very strong in my body; like a gentle warrior.

M: You said you're an Elven?

J: Yes. It's hard for me to see my face though?

M: What color is your hair?

J: I do see red. I don't know.

M: Beautiful. Trust yourself. Trust your instincts.

J: Let's see where you go next. You're standing in the forest and you said he is on the other side of the river?

During the quick visualization in between the induction, Julia saw herself on one side of the river and her lover on the other side.

J: Yes. I know he's like kneeling or bent over. He doesn't look right. He's grey, he's dark. He doesn't shimmer like I do. He looks sad. (very emotional)

M: Who is the "he"?

J: It's my other half.

M: You said he's on the other side of the river?

J: Yes, but I can see him.

M: Can you see him with your physical eyes?

J: I can't see. I just... I know. It's like... I know he's there. I can't really see him.

M: What do you want to do next? You said he's grey and he doesn't shimmer like you do. What does that mean?

J: He's like lifeless. I want to see him. Also, I want him to see me.

M: Let's go with that. Let's go there. Let's move along and go to the point where you see him. What happens next? Describe to me what you see. You are there now.

J: He has long hair.

M: What color is his hair?

J: Black. He stood up and he's looking at me. I don't know if he really sees me.

M: Where are you right now?

J: I'm still on the other side of the river looking at him.

M: Do you want to go over? What does your heart want to do?

J: I know what to do. I want to be with him, but he doesn't see me really … Ohh ... (moaning). I want him to remember me. I feel a lot of energy. I'm going to try and send it to him. I don't know.

M: Okay, go ahead and do that. Tell me what you see. What do you sense? Go ahead and send him energy. What color is the energy coming out of your body or palms... how do you send it?

J: It comes out of my heart; heart chakra. My third eye is lit up too. It's light; I mean it's really light. It's golden and white. I'm sending it. He's looking at me.

M: Yes. Does he look at you after you send the light or during?

J: During.

M: Beautiful. Go ahead. Keep sending him Love-Light. What happens next?

J: It's like I don't want it to happen. I'm kind of scared, right now.

M: What are you scared about?

J: I'm going to try and simulate and not be afraid.

M: Yes. You don't have anything to be afraid of. What are you feeling afraid of?

J: I'm afraid because I know he will fall and leave his body. We didn't get to say goodbye.

M: Let's go back to a time in this existence that you are with him. A time that you need to visit in this existence before all this happened. You're there now. You're at the point that you need to experience now. Tell me what you see.

J: He's caressing me. It's more than a particular memory. I'm seeing a lot of little snippets of memories.

M: Yes, please keep talking as you see them.

J: I see us running together in the forest. I see him. I see us; there's children around and not our children. There's a lot of love.

M: Yes. What's the color of his skin right now?

J: It's white.

M: Is it like yours?

J: Yes. He told me that he would never leave me. I know he loves me so much and I love him.

M: Beautiful. What do you do next?

J: We're just joyful. We're just spending time together. It's more a feeling. I do wish I could see him more clearly. I can't really see him very clearly. I think he has black hair.

M: Let's take a look. Now you're with him at a scene. You're there with him spending time with him and he's right in front of you. You can see him very clearly now. Describe what you see. What does he look like and feel like?

J: He has brown hair. It's hard for me to see faces.

M: As you speak more and describe more, you'll be able to see them clearer and clearer. What else do you notice about him? What is he wearing?

J: He's handsome. He's wearing almost like Robin Hood. Like a kind of pressed shirt and there's a vest of some sort and something slung across the middle of it. I know he has long hair.

M: Beautiful. What happens next? Let's move to the next scene of importance that you need to experience at this moment. You're there now, what happens next?

J: Okay. I'm at a Council. There's a small group of us. I see a leader.

M: What Council is this?

J: The Elven Council.

M: How many members does it have?

J: Only seeing a handful of us right now.

M: Are you a member of the Council?

J: Yes.

M: You said you see the leader as well?

J: Strange because I feel the presence of my other half but he's not there.

M: He's not there in the physical next to you at this meeting you said?

J: Right. But I'm very aware of him.

M: Okay. What do you do here? Why are you at the Council?

J: I know we're working on something. Something important is going on.

M: You said you're at the Council so what is it that you're discussing?

J: I feel like there's something in my third eye, it's a little hard for me to fully see it.

M: I'm going to send energy to your crown and have the Legion of Light also send you Love-Light energy into your crown and third eye. You'll start sensing and seeing very clearly. What is happening at the Council?

J I'm trying to figure out what to do because he's gone.

M: Who is gone?

J: My other half?

M: Where is he gone?

J: I don't know. It's harder to get a read on him than usual. I sense him but he was missing. All of a sudden, he's missing. He didn't come back.

M: Where did he not come back from?

J: He was just off, you know, he goes off for patrolling, but it's been days...

M: What do you have to do for a living as an Elven in this existence?

J: Protectors.

M: What are you protecting?

J: I feel we're protecting more than just our community.

M: Okay. So, he's gone missing you said?

J: Yes, he's missing. So, we're concerned, I'm concerned. I'm most concerned. Everyone's wondering what we should do next, but I'm the only one who's really worried.

M: What are you most worried about?

J: Well, it's unlike him to go for that long without saying anything to me? So maybe something happened to him.

M: Right! What happens next at the Council? What did they say? What do you all say?

J: We'll search for him. See if we can find him and I'll try and reach him energetically. Connect with him, but it's murky.

M: How do you usually connect with him energetically? How do you do that?

J: We can communicate with each other telepathically. Also, I feel him in my heart.

M: What do you feel his heart is feeling right now?

J: Lost. He's lost. Oh, I know he is lost but like I said I can't seem to reach in.

M: In what way do you think he's lost? Is he lost physically, or he is lost mentally?

J: No, I don't think he's lost physically. He's lost. He's just confused.

M: Okay. Now the Council also said that they will search for him. In what ways will they search for him. What do they do next?

J: I'm going to send out a signal.

M: Who's going to send out a signal?

J: Our leader particularly.

M: Is your leader male or female?

S: Male. Grey hair.

M: How does he send the signal?

J: I'm seeing a beam of light. I don't know where it's going.

M: Where is the beam of light originating from?

J: Us. Council.

M: What color is the beam of light?

J: It's mostly white-ish, but there's, I don't know, kind of orange-ish/red-ish part of it. Like towards the beginning of it.

M: What happens next once you send the beam of light?

J: It's not good.

M: What's not good?

J: It's met with dark energy or we're seeing dark energy or something?

M: Where are you seeing dark energy?

J: Well, I feel it for sure but It's being met with like the beam of light is hitting something dark.

M: What is it exactly that the beam of light is hitting? What is this darkness?

J: I see this ship. Reptilian ship. It's very slimy; bad energy.

M: Yes. Can you describe this ship?

J: I just see really the underbelly of it, like we're hitting the bottom of this grey black ship? Big.

M: Where is the ship exactly as compared to where your area of dwelling is - where the Council is. Where is the ship?

J: Oh, my fingers are so tingly. It feels close but I don't think it is.

M: What happens next, you're sending this beam of light and it's hitting against a Reptilian ship. What do you do?

J: We pull back. It was like a searchlight; it hit that.

M: What does it mean that the beam has hit the Reptilian ships? What would that mean for you? What would you understand from that?

J: We were trying to find his energy. We're trying to find his light. We were searching for it and we hit that. So, we took it as a bad sign. That he had been compromised or something had happened to him. So, we pulled back to figure out what to do.

M: So, what do you decide? What happens next?

J: It's a dilemma because... We're not afraid of them but it doesn't make sense to attack them. And we don't exactly know what happened. So, we're not really sure what to do. Yes, and I can feel parts of that energy in him.

M: What are the parts of energies that you can feel in him?

J: Darkness. I don't really know what to do or how to find him and the others want to wait and see.

M: What happens next?

J: I'm worried because the longer we wait, the more it feels darker and darker.

M: Do you agree with what the Council suggests? What do you do?

J: I don't know what to do. I really don't have an idea. If I had an idea, if I had a suggestion, I would give it, but I don't know where he is. I don't know how to reach him. I just know that there's enemy interference. I have to think, I have to spend some time and think about if there is anything I can do.

M: Let's allow for you to do that; to reflect. Maybe perhaps use your crystal. Do you use a crystal at all for that since it was for reflections?

J: It is always with me that that crystal. It helps me see. I have other tools. I'm seeing an orb.

M: Describe the orb.

J: I think it's made of water. Water and light. At first, I thought it was light but then it was like water so I can see within this. It's in front of me; it's floating in front of me.

M: Okay, so you said you can see in this?

J: Yes.

M: Would it function something like a crystal ball in which you can actually see?

J: Yes.

M: Beautiful. Let's see what you see in this. Spend some time with it.

J: Uhh... Okay. I'm already getting it. I can see. It's not clear. It's more of a sense that I'm seeing but I see him going on the ship... Going on it. He's going on it. I mean, he's surrounded by them. But he doesn't seem... He's not fighting.

M: How does he go on the ship? You can see and sense everything very clearly with this beautiful orb.

J: They welcome him on; they open it and welcome him on. Why did he go on it? Why? (wondering out loud)

M: You can see what happened before he connected with the ship. What was he doing before and how did he discover the ship, or the ship discover him?

J: He saw the ship when he was out, and he was interested in it like he was genuinely curious and open. I think they thought of it as an opportunity. We've been living a beautiful simple life for a long time. He must have been curious about something so different.

M: Yes. What happens next? How did they pull him into the ship? How does he step in?

J: He doesn't get pulled in, he was looking at it and thinking about it and open to it and they infiltrated him somehow. I'm getting like a seed or something that was planted in him that started to sprout and grow really quickly. I'm seeing the stairs coming down from the ship, and they are opening it.

M: He went with it, is what you are saying?

J: Yes.

M: What happens next? What do you see?

J: But he doesn't totally know what he's doing at this point. He's veiled, he's confused, he's lost. He still went. (breathing hard in despair). So, I see this, and I don't know what there is to fight. Even if we could fight, even if we could take them all. I don't know if we could do that. If that would be wise but even if we could I don't know if he would come?

M: What happens next once he's taken the stairs and he's on the ship? What does he do?

J: I'm seeing him with the leader. They are curious about him. They're interested in him. They see him as a commodity.

M: Describe the leader to me please.

J: Very dark. He's got little arms or claws.

M: What color is his skin?

J: He's got yellow eyes. He's black.

M: Is he wearing anything?

J: No.

M: Is there any feature in him that stands out; sticks out to you?

J: I don't know what it is about faces but I really can't see them. I see his little arms. They're like little dinosaur arms or something.

M: How many toes does he have on his feet?

J: I think more like one on the side and three forward; claw feet.

M: How's the texture of his skin?

J: Scaly?

M: What happens next? You said they're interested in him as a commodity.

J: Yeah. They have a lot of...I'm seeing like technology in there. I don't know what it is. Circular paneling. I think it's more than just guiding the ship. They're doing something with all that. I don't know what that is. Yes, they are very interested in him. He's very powerful and he can bring in a lot of energy. Consume energy if that's what they want him to do.

M: Let's see what they want him to do. What do you see next?

J: Well, I'm actually on the ship with them now.

M: How did you get there?

J: I mean, I'm not actually on the ship, maybe I'm seeing it through his eyes. It's the two of them and then there's a lot of other Reptilians around.

M: How many Reptilians are on the ship?

J: Hundreds.

M: Are there any other races on the ship apart from the Reptilians?

J: There might be some beings that are enslaved. Seeing that, not many. They are actually there energetically.

M: Okay. What do they do? What happens next of importance?

J: He makes him a proposition. My hands are going numb.

M: Higher Self, allow her to rub her hands to channel the energy and start channeling the energy all the way down to feet and down into Mother Earth.

J: (rubbing hands) Oh wow, my hands are great.

M: Yes, beautiful. What's the proposition that is made?

J: Let's see, it's coming like line by line here. Proposition - work for them! For him to be a hunter like find and hunt some of these beautiful light beings. He is a very good hunter. He's very fast so they want to use this somehow. Like he will bait people in or something.

M: What do you mean when you say he's a very good hunter? What does he hunt and how?

J: Hunting light; light beings. He can search for light like we did for him. He can pick out bright lights and bring them to him. They're going to use him.

M: What happens next? What does he decide?

J: I can't even say that it was a choice exactly because it wasn't like he was infringed upon when he made it. But I feel a lot of dread. So, I know he did it.

M: What are they giving him in exchange for the work that he's doing as per the proposition?

J: I'm getting immortality. But we live a very long time anyways.

M: How long do Elven beings live? What is their span?

J: Thousands of years. It's like he didn't even care about the term so much. It's almost a formality. At that point he'd already been taken over enough. But there are parts of light in him.

M: What happens next? What do they do?

J: They leave. They go away. They leave. They probably don't want to be there anymore just in case we do something or were aware.

M: What about him? Where is he, your other half?

J: He's gone with them.

M: So, they're gone with him? He's on the spaceship?

J: Mm-hmm.

M: What happens next? Where do they go and what do they do?

J: They're going to another planet or galaxy or something to consume. He comes back, he journeys with them.

M: What does he do exactly since he has a role to play? Describe what he does for them?

J: He kills!

M: Who does he kill?

J: He becomes like a vampire. I don't know. I know it's not a race but I'm not familiar.

M: What are you not familiar with?

J: Well, I can't really see where he goes or the race of people that he kills.

M: You said he becomes like a vampire. So, what does he do as a vampire? Vampires would usually pull on others' energies. What does he do exactly? How does he play his role and what does he do exactly? You're there now.

J: I see him over some being and drinking their energy, taking it in his third eye and they're connected to him, so they get something from his feedings.

M: How are they connected to him?

J: They're implanted with this whatever growth thing in his brain area and he's able to take in a lot of energy, a lot of light. He's very powerful.

M: These beings that he's currently taking energy from what do they look like?

J: I'm trying to see. They seem kind of squishy, like a big giant (not a worm) but some kind of like invertebrate, but like a smaller version of Jabba the Hutt.[31] They sound gross but well that's not nice to say - the way I'm describing it makes them sound a certain way but they're really sweet.

M: These beings that he's drawing energy from, is there light easily visible?

J: To us it is.

M: Then you said that in turn the light - the energy is pulled from him by the Reptilians through something in his brain.

J: They receive yeah, they receive their fix too. Yeah, it's like his brain tendrils that get lit up.

M: You can see very clearly inside his brain and inside his body, what is it that they've planted - the Reptilians implanted in him that he's forgotten his light and who he is and he's performing this role?

J: I'm seeing like a black seed that sprouts and it grows into these tendrils that get bigger and grow farther and they span across his brain.

M: Do they go to any other part of his body?

J: I'm not seeing that.

M: What happens next of importance, you're going to be able to see that and sense that very easily, what happens next?

J: Wow. I'm back with myself. I'm not looking. I'm very sad.

M: At this point where you are right now, are you aware of what you've seen, sensed and know what your other half is doing?

J: I know he went willingly. I saw that. I don't know the details of what I just told you. Okay.

M: What happens next? What do you do?

J: Wow. I keep trying to connect with them. But there's this, I can't. I mean I know we're still connected I feel him but it's there's such a block. I can't.

M: What do you do next?

J: I just keep living my life. I mean he's with me every day. I wait for him every day. I try and reach him every day, but I have to keep living my life. Many others sympathize, but I don't understand. So, I keep it to myself mostly. This has happened before with other Elves.

M: This has happened with other Elves?

J: Yes, this isn't the first time they've gone to the dark side. So, we knew it was possible. I didn't think it was a risk.

M: So, did those Elves that went to the dark side ever return? Any one of them?

J: No, they're completely lost. The only reason I'm able to eventually reconnect with him is because he's my other half. Most people are just their own. They don't have another half.

M: What happens next in this existence, you're there now.

J: Okay. I'm back at that scene in the beginning.

M: Describe what you see and sense and feel.

J: He looks so different but I'm so happy to see him. He's like an animal. Like he's just pure instincts. I'm kind of a little hidden. So, I don't think he even sees me. I think that's for the best at first because I don't know what he would try and do.

M: Right. So, you can stay here where you are invisible, if that is what you think your heart feels you need to be and you're viewing him from the spot where you are. What happens next, describe what he does and what you do.

J: While I'm watching him, he's doing something on the ground. I don't know what he's doing on the ground. Burying something, I'm just watching him and even though I don't feel a connection

---

[31] A reference to the movie character in Star Wars.

to him in the same way, I know it's him and I know how much I love him. So, I decide to try and show it to him.

M: You said you decided to show it to him?

J: Yes.

M: You said earlier that many Elves have gone to the dark side. What do they do when they go to the dark side?

J: They do similar things. Instead of supporting the light and acting in love and light, they consume light. They take light. They often act on their own though, I'm seeing they go on their own path. Their own dark path. Black Magic. They consume, they destroy.

M: Who do they do black magic on and on behalf of whom?

J: Sometimes it's just on their own behalf because they want to be more powerful even more than they already are. They get very greedy. Yes, I'm seeing that's often what happens.

M: What do they get very greedy for? What is the motivation?

J: Power!

M: How do they do black magic? What are the typical ways of doing black magic?

J: They have different spells, different ways of twisting the elements.

M: Who do they do black magic on?

J: They travel, these Elves, so there're many victims. They go for ideally, you know, light and sweet beings that don't put up much of a fight and then they take them where they want.

M: They take those beings wherever they want?

J: No, they take their energy, and they discard them. But they want more and more energy and they're never satiated.

M: So, when they do black magic on someone, say you know there is a being on a certain planet, and they do black magic on that being; would that being continuing to exist physically on that planet while the energies would be drawn something like an implant is what you say?

J: No, they take them completely, they suck them away.

M: Oh! What happens to the physical being?

J: It's dead. It can be consumed.

M: These Elven, since you know originally Elven are a positive race. How did they start working for the dark side and who are they working for?

J: We are mostly positive. There are far - far - far more positive Elves than negative. We're a very gentle race, very gentle race. That's why it's all the more painful that there are these few that are so dark. I am seeing that there is some guiding higher being, some orchestrator that they report to. I don't know what it is. It's very dark. It's very expansive.

M: What are the other things that they can do with their black magic?

J: I'm seeing something with force fields, we typically use force fields to protect and shield, but they can put dark energy over wide distances. It can also break our protective shields. Like, they can infiltrate force fields

M: How do they do that?

J: I sense they send a light, there seems to be a lot with light beams that we use but these are dark beams. They are red.

M: What happens when they send the beam?

J: They crack it. It cracks the forcefield. It doesn't always break it, but they can crack it.

M: What can they place in those beings through the cracks? What do they do with it through the cracks?

J: Well, they expose the area so it's no longer protected therefore, dark energy can infiltrate it. They are very powerful.

M: You as an Elf are part of the group force - the benevolent side of the Elven. Do you have any suggestion or any forcefield that you can suggest that people can wear that can protect them from the dark black magic?

J: These Elves are very powerful, but they are just one being. So, groups of beings are stronger together. They can unite and do force fields and their intentions, and they should be able to keep out this energy, this light.

M: So, say if we call on the collective of our Galactic soul family to put their force field around us, since it's going to be more than one being in the Soul family. Would that be a stronger force field for them to get through.

J: Absolutely.

M: Like an Angelic family?

J: Yes, or they can be a community on your Earth. Yes, but they are specific in their targets. It will be rare.

M: They are specific with their targets?

J: Yes.

M: Who do they target usually?

J: That's the thing. They're very strategic. They're very crafty. They're coming up with plans that are greater than I know. It's helpful to protect yourself as best as possible but it would be rare to come across a dark Elf energy. Of course, not from me since I am speaking this, and I am Elf.

M: Of course. What is the best way to break the spell or break the black magic once it has occurred and someone senses it in their body?

J: The shields that are normally used that Aurora teaches are strong enough. Light is strong, love is stronger than anything to rebuke their black magic.

M: Beautiful. Thank you for confirming that. It sounds good. Thank you! What happens next now? You're standing there and you can see your other half. You can see very clearly. What is he wearing as he sits on the forest floor?

J: Looks like a disc, like a glass. Seems like some kind of mineral.

M: Does it look positive or negative?

J: Doesn't look either but ahh ... it might be more positive. He might be getting something from it.

M: Okay. What happens next? What do you do?

J: I send him love. I send him all the love I have. Everything! I see he feels it. He notices. He stops what he's doing. He stands up, I stand up. I'm sending him energy and I'm looking into his eyes. Sending in light, sending him love. He's taking it in. Something touches something in him a little bit, there's a little bit left, a little bit left in his heart and that explodes. It explodes with light.

M: What explodes with light?

J: That little bit of light in him, in his heart. Ah ... such a relief because I know he feels it. Ah ... It's so good. Oh, he sees me. I can see, he sees me. It's just nice like this for a little bit.

M: What happens when you see each other? Are you still able to energetically connect and send messages to each other?

J: I am sending love. At first, he just receives it but then he's able to return it.

M: What color is his skin now?

J: Getting lighter. It was so sallow and dreary but it's getting lighter. Oh, it's such a relief to see him because I know this is him. Not that other being, that wasn't him. He wouldn't do anything like that, not willingly.

M: As you send him the light, what happens to all the tentacles, the wires he had in his brain and the seed that was growing?

J: It's getting filled with light and it's starting to erode. Nice to see it, I can see it clearly - the golden light but it's disintegrating and he's coming back.

M: What happens next?

J: He fell, and I ran over to him. He holds my hand. He's fading. (starts crying in despair). He loves me, I know he loves me. Oh, I'm just losing him. (cries in despair)

M: Before he fades away, how about you tell him how you feel and hear what he has to say telepathically. You still have your gifts. How about you have that exchange and have a discussion. Say what you want to say and hear what he has to say. What do you say to him?

J: I love you forever. I love you no matter what form you're in, no matter what you do. I love you unconditionally. Always, we can never be separated, and I'll miss you. (crying) He tells me how much he loves me, and he says he's sorry. He didn't know. He's sorry but he says he'll make it up to me. He says he will see me again. Hmm... That's it. He's beautiful.

M: Send him with love.

J: He's lying there now. His body is beautiful, it's still light.

M: Is his body still there?

J: Yeah, it's still there. It's kind of crumpled to the ground. I just hold him. I didn't think that was going to happen. I don't really know why that happened.

M: You didn't know how this happened?

J: I don't know why it happened or why he couldn't just come back. But I know there's bigger forces at play. I know I'll see him again, but I don't know when.

M: What do you do next? What do you feel?

J: Well. I feel peaceful. I feel that I am being given a lot of love from the Divine. So, I'm being held by her as I hold him.

M: You're being held by love?

J: Yes, the Divine Mother.

M: How do you sense the Divine Mother?

J: I feel her, I feel her around me. She loves me very much. It's okay.

M: Ask the Divine Mother, ask her why he faded away with the light.

J: She says he needs to heal himself again.

M: Will the Divine Mother aid him to heal himself?

J: Yes.

M: Beautiful.

J: She loves him too. It's nice having her here. I feel her here.

M: What is your connection to the Divine Mother?

J: Aurora told me that she said I'm the Daughter of the Flame.[32] Aren't we all (smiling) but I feel her love with me often and she's a great guide for me. She and Archangel Michael. So, she was with me on that day. Oh, that's nice to know.

M: Yes. He said that he would meet you again. Does the Divine Mother have an answer for that? Where and when can he meet you again?

J: We are always together celestially; I think that's why he's here in human form and away (meaning this Earth life). That's partly why I come here to be with him.

M: What happens next in that life? What do you do for the rest of your life? Fast forward and see what you do for the rest of your life. We thank the Divine Mother for the messages that she's given us. Thank you, Divine Mother.

J: Thank you. Well, I feel like life is not over. It's continuing, just with breaks.

M: Yes, because you live thousands of years you said?

---

[32] This is referencing a separate Akashic Reading session that Julia had with AuroRa.

J: Yes. So, I'll go back. I keep working with the Council. I have peace in my life. The Council, they love me. Once they understood what happened, they showed me so much love.

M: So, you're saying that you exist in that existence and you also visit Earth because he is here on Earth you said? Is that one of the reasons why you visit?

J: Part of it. I think I also want to help. I have been coming to Earth for a long time. I care about humans a lot. In many ways I feel very connected. I've lived so many lives here. I'm connected to them as well. But that's my sense as I'm in and out. I'm still alive.

M: Beautiful. Let's leave that life now. Can I please speak to the Higher Self of Julia now?

The Higher Self is called forth.

M: Greetings.

Higher Self: Greetings.

M: Hello, am I speaking to Julia's Higher Self now?

Higher Self: Yes.

M: Thank you, I honor you, love you and respect you. I'm infinitely grateful for you. Thank you for all the aid you provided us today.

Higher Self: Thank you for guiding her.

M: know that you hold all of the records of her different lives. May I ask questions now?

Higher Self: Yes.

M: Thank you. And are you male or female if I may ask?

Higher Self: Female.

M: Female! Thank you, sister. Is there any particular race that you align yourself with? Do you have a name that you go by?

Higher Self: I'm Elven.

M: Thank you, sister. Why is it that you chose to show her this life of an Elven out of all the lives that she's existed in? What was the purpose of this life and lessons that she's to learn from it?

Higher Self: She still carries deep wounds from this life. She is still seeking her other half. I wanted her to remember that he was always held by the Divine. To remember that they are always together, always connected. There is nothing to seek. It is already there.

M: When you say that they're always connected and there's nothing to seek do you mean, spiritually or energetically. Is that what you mean that they're always one?

Higher Self: Yes.

M: Is he also present here in the physical in this life?

Higher Self: Yes.

M: Would you share his name with her so it can be like a confirmation for her?

Higher Self: Mm-hmm. She knows, it is Liam.

M: She has a beautiful sense of knowing.

Higher Self: Yes, she is very clear.

M: Yes. Beautiful and how she may seek aid from the life that you just showed her right now in her current situation and current life? How can she aid herself now because she seeks him physically since we're in the physical as well?

Higher Self: Yes. She longs for him. She will be with him. But it is not time yet. He's not ready. She knows much of what I will speak but needs to hear it.

M: Yes. That's what you said to me earlier today. Thank you for confirming that. Yes, she has the answers. Is there any way she can aid him with the Higher Self's permission? Can she aid him in trying to remember or have him move forward in making decisions?

Higher Self: She is aiding him when she sends him energy. He is slowly healing. She cannot force it. He may be helped by his Higher Self. That is something she could ask for.

M: Yes. Thank you and I was just thinking about the same right now. So, thank you for confirming that. How can she seek his Higher Self in healing him?

Higher Self: His Higher Self is often with her. She is aware of him sometimes. She can imagine his Higher Self more. She can see him as his Higher Self more. She already sees who he can be so she can integrate those energetically. Yes.

M: Beautiful. So, she can actually aid the integration of his Higher Self more within him without being physically with him is that what you mean?

Higher Self: Yes.

M: By imagining it.

Higher Self: Yes.

M: That's so beautiful. Does his Higher Self have a message for her today?

Higher Self: Yes.

M: Would you allow for him to come through and speak, if you like?

Higher Self: Yes.

M: Thank you. Calling on the Twin Flame's Higher Self. Greetings.

TF Higher Self: Greetings. Thank you.

M: Welcome, brother. Thank you for being here.

TF Higher Self: I'm glad to be here and have an opportunity to connect with her more clearly.

M: Thank you, and we would love for you to convey your message to her whatever it is that you feel she needs to know and whatever it is that you feel like sharing now. Thank you.

TF Higher Self: I love you and I'm always with you. He has much to heal, as you know. He needs more time. I am trying to connect with him. He is very afraid. His ego is very big. You have always been one to follow your heart and we love that about you. But he is afraid to do so. He wants to. He loves you like he didn't know it was possible to love. He feels you just as you feel him, but his mind is telling him many stories. We're trying to break through. I don't know how long it will be. Keep loving yourself. Keep loving him and remember that we are already united. Thank you.

M: Thank you. How would you like her to imagine or envision you as a Higher Self?

TF Higher Self: I take light forms and she knows this because that's how she sees me. But she wants to see me in physical form. But remember that I am him. You have me in physical form, and you have me in light form.

M: Beautiful, and what color is your light form, or colors?

TF Higher Self: (smiling) Blue and Gold. These colors have been very present for her lately. And now she knows why.

M: Beautiful, is there anything else that you'd like to share?

TF Higher Self: To not be afraid for him? I know we worry about what will happen if he does not awaken. He will ascend in his own time. You can aid him, but it is not your burden. Let go of the sense of responsibility. I love you. (smiling)

M: Thank you for sharing that. Thank you.

TF Higher Self: Thank you.

M: Love you, honor you, respect you. Please still be around, I'm sure you will be. We will shortly get into body scanning and we would love your assistance in that.

TF Higher Self: Yes.

The Body Scan begins.

M: Speaking with the Higher Self once more. Dear sister, would you like to share anything else right now, we do have questions for you which we can perhaps take up later, if it's okay with you. Should we start with the Body Scan?

Higher Self: Yes.

M: Thank you, and for the Body Scan would you like to call upon any Archangel for assistance?
Higher Self: Michael.
M: Greetings.
AA Michael: Greetings.
M: Greetings, Archangel Michael. I honor you and respect you. Thank you and I love you infinitely. Thank you for being here.
AA Michael: I love you as well.
M: Can we start with the Body Scan Archangel Michael, from the crown all the way to the toes?
AA Michael: Yes.
M: Thank you, if you can start looking for Archons and Reptilians and any other negative alien races, any implants, hooks, chords - all of them. Portals as well. Archangel Michael, if you can point out portals and Archangel Metatron can start closing them please.
AA Michael: Yes.
M: Thank you, Archangel Michael.
AA Michael: Her third eye.

With a collective group healing by Yeshua, the collective of Dragons, Archangels Michael, Raphael, Metatron, Gabriel and Azrael all assisting with strong removals and healing through a long list of infringements: Archons, Reptilians, snakes, centipede, an A.I., spider web, negative implants, cord, and an artificial negative contract from the dark Elven collective, are all cleared. Archangel Michael confirms that every single one is removed and is healing. Whew! She is free, cleansed and balanced. Bringing forth a most beautiful clearest possibility for her Elven Twin Flame to join her too, one day when he is ready, and he will be because of Julia's infinite love! That she has proven to us.

M: Can we also have Yeshua perhaps expand her heart?
AA Michael: She has a very big heart. Yes, let's!
M: Does she have her second flame open? Is that something that her Higher Self wants by any chance?
AA Michael: Let's open it. Yes.
M: Archangel Michael, can I speak with the Higher Self?
AA Michael: You can speak with the Higher Self.
M: Thank you, Archangel Michael, for your aid. Please be around and I want to thank the Legion of Light, Archangel Raphael, Jesus/Yeshua, as well as the benevolent collective of Dragons for aiding with the healing. I'll speak with the Higher Self now.
AA Michael: Thank you.
M: How does it feel to be back in this body?
Higher Self: It feels nice!
M: Beautiful. I know she's been in for a long time now. How is she doing?
Higher Self: She's tired.
M: Yes. Can I just quickly pick up perhaps the main questions that would not have been answered through the healing?
Higher Self: Yes.
M: Okay. Thank you. She wanted to know why she's incarnated in this lifetime with her other half but they're not together.
Higher Self: She is an important part of his awakening and his growth. They are also destined for one another, to be together in this lifetime. That is part of it, and she knows she serves a much higher purpose of aiding.

M: Beautiful. Thank you for sharing that and it's beautiful that her Twin Flame spoke with her as well and she can aid in his healing and awakening.

Higher Self: Yes.

M: What are her particular abilities and she wanted to know how she can strengthen them?

Higher Self: She is able to work with light and with shielding. She has already begun this journey. But she can go further in protecting those she loves as well as the Earth. She is able to see within light. She sees the consciousness of that light. She is able to have a large impact on those around her with the light that shines every day. That is the most beautiful thing.

M: On what planet and Dimension do the Elven community reside that she just visited?

Higher Self: Fifth.

M: The final question I have right now is, what is her connection to California?

Higher Self: She has history with California. She was in the battles. She fought for Lemuria. She's very connected to it still.

M: Does she need any healing from that. Can you start healing her Higher Self?

Higher Self: Yes.

M: Thank you very much. That'll be all for now. Is there anything else that you want to share with her before we bring her out?

Higher Self: She's doing very well. I'm telling this to her often. We are able to communicate more clearly lately. She is working hard on herself, and we see it. Thank you.

M: Thank you very much, sister. Yes, she's been working on herself despite so many infringements, she was still clear with a lot of her knowing. That's beautiful.

Higher Self: Yes.

M: I want to thank you as well for being here. Thank you for connecting us as well. I love you, I honor you and respect you and I also want to thank everyone else that was involved in the healing process today.

Higher Self: Thank you, sister. I love you.

M: Thank you, I love you.

END OF SESSION

-------------<◇>-------------

Dearest reader, to confirm what you may already know, YES, Julia is the beautiful Elf Soul who spoke to us in the previous 'Slave To Corruption' Chapter. Yes, she is the very same beautiful soul who taught the Universe how a deeply corrupted soul could still achieve positive polarization by shining all her love unto them. WOW! The way the Universe works is best explained as magical. We are infinitely deeply grateful to both Julia and Clara, for what their Elven souls have done for the Universe! Especially for both of these Elven beings from the beginnings of Earth's timeline, into the NOW, where their human versions each found the Rising Phoenix Aurora's YouTube Channel on their own. The human versions of Julia and Clara do not know of each other and they each scheduled their A.U.R.A. sessions in accordance with divine timing. Through both their sessions, we journeyed with them to the beginnings of Earth when it was at its original organic Fifth Dimension (Elven time), before the fall of Atlantis which regressed the Earth down to the Third Dimension where we are at in the NOW, as a collective stuck in the Inverted A.I. Matrix. This beautifully demonstrates how the Divine hand gracefully works in our Universe to bring forth much needed inspiration for the collective!

I remember during the 'Slave of Corruption' (Clara's) session wanting to connect to those dark beings who corrupted the Elven Council member's Twin Flame, but I knew I couldn't as it was just not time yet. If you have watched this session on the Rising Phoenix Aurora's YouTube Channel, it has kept us all wondering, what happened to him and HOW? How could this be possible for such a beautiful Elven being? This is why we could not go into it then, because it was meant to surface during Julia's session within Divine timing.

After this beautiful healing session, Julia came to one of our Group Certification Retreats. None of us knew who she was until the attendees performed a group R.A.A.H. energy healing on her. In this healing, we removed a desperate attempt from a dark Elven Race trying to stop her from what she had begun in her life as an Elven being on Earth, back when it was organically operating in the Fifth Dimension. They were trying to stop Julia from bringing the message of HOPE to Earth in the now and future. When we removed their hold on her, we then helped positively polarize a collective legion of this dark Elven race. This created a vast transformation for the Universe as they wreaked havoc with their immeasurable power everywhere, they could with their means of feeding off light, through their Dark Magic.

At the Group Retreat, I did not know who Julia was, not until she started sharing the details of her Elven life. [33]Therefore, the surprise was grand in the middle of her healing where she starts telling us she had felt a dark Elven race trying to infringe upon her, and that her Twin Flame had become corrupted. My expression was priceless, when I realized that she was the beautiful Elf Soul sister from the 'Slave To Corruption' session, and we were all assisting together to bring forth a deep healing for both Eliana's [34] (Clara) and her Elven sister's (Julia) journey. Through the group's collective healing efforts, with the Archangels and Julia's Higher Self assisting us, we were able to assist this collective of dark Elven race to positively polarize, as they had been following Julia for a couple of months.

I remember how during the 'Slave To Corruption' session, I was amazed by the beautiful Elf Soul on how she was able to heal her Twin Flame in that time and space, and how much it resembled the A.U.R.A. Hypnosis Healing teachings. During our group healing on Julia, we finally placed the pieces of the puzzle together. The reason why Eliana and her Elven Soul sister back 'then' knew about corrupted souls being able to positively polarize was because they are both in the 'now' A.U.R.A. Hypnosis Healing Practitioners.

Remember how Archangel Michael explained in Chapter 30 ('Harvesting Planets Throughout Universes'), about the multidimensionality of our existence, how we are multidimensional expressions of one being? So, when a powerful healing occurs, it ripples into the consciousness of the healed being, which then affects many other lifetimes of the same being, other souls and even entire soul families!

In both Clara's and Julia's cases, they made the beautiful choice to become self-healed in this human lifetime through the aid of A.U.R.A. Hypnosis Healing sessions and then continued their growth as A.U.R.A. practitioners becoming certified through two different Retreats. All these

---

[33] AuroRa is the one who facilitated Clara's session (Chapter 33 – Slave to Corruption). Maria is the A.U.R.A. practitioner who facilitated Julia's session (this Chapter 34 – Elven Twin Flames), which has not been shared with anyone including AuroRa. Both sessions are transcribed for this book, for the complete beautiful story to be shared with the collective.

[34] Eliana is the name of the Higher Self of Clara in the 'Slave to Corruption' session.

choices and results then rippled out in their consciousness throughout all their other lifetimes, including their Elven lifetimes. This is how their Elven selves knew about the possibility of positively polarizing corrupted souls, no matter how dark. Their Elven souls knew 'then', because their human fractals made the choice of becoming A.U.R.A. Hypnosis Certified in the NOW, self-attuning themselves to the knowledge of these healing potentials. Making this knowledge available for all by creating a full circle of expansion for all versions of themselves. Time does not exist beyond this 3D construct, so powerful quantum energy healing sessions as these will affect past, present and future lifetimes all at once. Just as we have explained prior, how time exists compressed within itself. All is occurring in linear time within this 3D construct. Let's take the example of a hand-paper fan. When you expand it, you are able to see all the paper creases/dimensions/creation within it, but when you fold it back all creases/dimensions/creation overlap one another. This is how all time is within itself infinitely.

In other words, only their past selves of the Elven Elders were able to have the heart knowledge and understanding of negative polarized entities being able to positively polarize, as they had already done it and lived it in the future selves as their human versions, as A.U.R.A. practitioners. Because we are multidimensional, our soul's crystalline memory cells carry what we have yet to remember, whether that is in the past selves or future selves of us. Which then the big question is, if their future selves as humans did not become A.U.R.A. practitioners, could the past selves as Elven beings have been able to recall this in the 'then'? Most likely not, as only in the now have we developed entity removal techniques such as A.U.R.A.

Speaking of Divine timing, we can imagine how many benevolent souls coordinated their guidance from beyond the veil to ensure that all of us did our part, of playing the chess pieces to create these vital moments in time. For guiding Julia and Clara to click the YouTube video that helped them discover our teachings, and for guiding Meenakshi and I, ensuring we hold the strong enough Love-Light and protection for their sessions as heart-centered practitioners. We deepen our understanding of why when our guides are helping us grow or are trying to guide us to a certain path, how they tend to just give us bits and pieces until it is time for it to finally manifest. The reason being is the less we know, the less infringement there will be thus the more likely it can manifest in Divine timing. If the knowledge of what is to come is not known in full detail, then how could there be interference upon it? It would not be possible because the complete awareness of what's to come divinely for us, would just not be there. We can imagine how exciting it would be from beyond the veil to nudge us all in the right direction, to get us there to those exact moments in time where they found the Rising Phoenix Aurora's YouTube Channel, they booked their A.U.R.A. Hypnosis sessions and then made the crucial decision to become A.U.R.A. Hypnosis practitioners. Wow, it is indeed a beautiful collective effort shown by the benevolent group putting this together, our Higher Selves included. I am sure they all watched and cheered as we each listened to our hearts, as we each completed each task given to us to get us here in the NOW writing this book. The main objective of this collection of Galactic Soul journeys is to help us understand that all organic life no matter the vastness of distortion, can be positively polarized once more, the KEY ingredient being LOVE.

This in itself is just WOW! This helps us understand the vastness that A.U.R.A. Hypnosis Healing sessions are bridging throughout Creation. Understanding always though, that we honor all other healing modalities as well. As many of our clients have had several other Hypnosis, Reiki…energy healing sessions before their A.U.R.A. session, which too played their vital part in getting our clients in reaching the depths that they do through A.U.R.A. sessions. It is one big circle of benevolent beings working together through all forms of healing modalities on Earth. And this is ONLY but one story of this collective LOVE transformation that is obtainable now for all Creation's infinite expressions of beautiful races whose fractals are incarnated on Earth. Think of the vastness of what these potentials will bring for Ascension. This is what the Angelics mean when they try to explain to our human minds the reaches and depths that A.U.R.A. Hypnosis Healing sessions are manifesting for the Multiverse and Creation.

In 'Slave To Corruption' Eliana (Clara's Higher Self) said, "She is very connected with them. She still is. She is very, very connected with the Elven. She knows this, and she needs to know that even though she is in this body, in this life, that it is still ongoing. The work is still going and we as a Collective of the Elven, we are still trying. Still helping all our brothers and sisters. She is not consciously aware that the heaviness and sadness in her heart are those of that Elven race, that have been corrupted. It is necessary to help lift and heal that in her heart a little bit, so that she knows that we have not given up. That she is a very, very big reason for the work today. As many, many of the beings and races of Creation have been corrupted. That was a very significant moment for all of Creation, very, very big. It was a big moment, and she was the spark for that. She needs to not hold it heavy in her heart. She needs to hold love and gratitude for that strength that she had in that lifetime. Because it is resonating out in Creation today, and it is still resonating out today. Many beings know about that. They refer to that moment when a being so dark, came back through Love. If it were not for that moment, even though it was not her and her love, her other half. She was the seed, the start of that and she needs to know."

This is why we must learn to honor all lives of us with the greatest respect, because we learn through the remembrance of our fractals and incarnations of us. It is as we are looking through forms of "Positive Viewing Looking Glasses," that connect us to all the versions of us in time and space. We as fractals together are like strands to a hair braid, the strands/versions of us intertwine with one another, assisting through incarnations, learning from one another.

The Angels once told me, "Aurora, this is why we know we can count on you. Because you understand each life that you have lived, and you have given homage and learned the lessons from each. This gives a being an understanding that is unmeasurable within wisdom, who can then lead a collective into understanding the pieces of themselves seeded and blossomed throughout Creation, bridging them together once more. Creator beings at their highest wholeness of soul. Together manifesting Ascension."

When explaining the abilities that these dark Elven obtain when turning dark, this is exactly the power that I felt in the 'Slave To Corruption' session. The powers that Julia's Twin Flame showed us, of being able to feed off any beings that contained light within. If one thinks about the infinity of different life forms that exist in Creation, and how each one no matter the density, Dimension, or race contains that light. That light that the Archons have been emptily searching for as explained in the 'Not of Light' Chapter's conclusion. When looking at it through this perspective, then the Universe is full of feedings, as this FIX of 'Light' for the Archons. It is an all-you-can-eat-buffet of light for them. The Third Dimension being their favorite as we are at the deepest distortion, at the densest Dimension, the farthest away from Source. Because of this heavy distortion, we are unaware of our true power and we are not taking ownership of our sovereignty. Therefore, it is the easiest and most open for them and their infringements to taint.

The capabilities that the Reptilians contain through the negative technologies given to them by the Archons, were more than we ever thought they were capable of. How they used that A.I. implant technology to enter the Twin Flame Elf's force field penetrating his brain, integrating into becoming part of his consciousness. Being able to maneuver him around like a video game character as mentioned in Chapter 31 ('Looking Glass Technology')'s conclusion about the 'hybrid alien soldiers'. These glimpses of others' lives show us the powerful technologies that the Archons have made and have handed down to the Reptilians and other negative polarized alien races they are in connection with, for their negative agendas of harvesting light. These two sessions were pivotal in aiding our understanding on how Archons are able to massively infringe upon Universes throughout Creation.

This reminds me of some of the leaders we have seen in power today. For example, many times when people follow a Spiritual Leader, but little by little or sometimes instantly, you notice that they are becoming corrupted or are corrupted. The Archons find much satisfaction in picking those Spiritual Leaders they can penetrate, like how they did to Julia's Elven Twin Flame. As these Spiritual Leaders can reach a larger audience, if they can get just one Leader to say one 'false light' dark seed to their listeners, then they have accomplished their corruption for the day. As these listeners who are hungry and curious for knowledge are still yet gaining sovereignty and are the easiest to influence with ego-based knowledge. False knowledge that if the listener will believe, and once believed it will enter their DNA structure becoming their own false dense belief. These are their forms of poisoning the mind with falsities, to maintain controlled oppression and to imprison us in our minds in the repeated Inverted A.I. Matrix cycle. Ultimately, keeping us dense by not allowing the organic soul enough of a holding space for expansion of the soul's evolution.

The beauties of an A.U.R.A. Hypnosis Healing were shown through these two sessions, by Eliana (Clara) and her Elven Soul sister (Julia). Let's think about it for a moment, the significance of having all these benevolent beings group together in the moment during any A.U.R.A. session healing, and together channel their inner Love-Light to aid all willing beings to positive polarize or to help heal. This is profound, which means that we are now collectively doing this for those lost in the false A.I. Archonic darkness, similarly to what the beautiful Elf Soul (Julia) did for her Twin Flame.

This incredible session reveals how we in the Universe have gone fully past the fact that we once thought there was nothing we could do for corrupted souls, especially at the beginning of the invasions of the Archons through their negative technologies as seen in Chapter 31 ('Looking Glass Technology'). We have figured it out together! This brings me to tears. What a most grand, a most beautiful accomplishment for the Universe and for the collective benevolent alien races that exist within Creation. It is truly an honor and so beautiful to share these sacred teachings of the Galaxies through the telling of this magnificent 'Love Story' for all of Creation!

"Sacred love…
Is to touch her skin and feel the life that flows through her.
Is to kiss her and feel her heartbeat through the gentleness of her lips.
Is to embrace her in your arms and feel each other's souls become ONE."
~AuroRa

-------------<◇>-------------

35

SOVEREIGNTY PHOENIX RISING

Session #69: Recorded July 2018.
Never before shared.

This is an excerpt from an online A.U.R.A. Hypnosis Healing session facilitated on a fractal of Archangel Ariel/Area who is the client's Higher Self. It is one of the most empowering messages shared for Earth and the Divine Feminine. As throughout Earth's history women have been oppressed, but now are rising like the Sovereign Phoenix. This beautiful empowering session serves as a reminder of how strong we are together and how hard we are working to remove the programming upon us from society, religion, tradition, and schooling.

For too long they have controlled us by pinning us against each other, programming women to be jealous, envious, hateful, judgmental towards each other. No longer will this be so. We can deprogram ourselves from this, as layers fall off like shedding old skin. It is no longer needed as they are not our truest purest forms when looking to connect to our hearts. What does it mean for the Divine Feminine to rise through the shadows? When we heal our own wounded hearts and join forces together from a place of strength and love, together we will rise as the Sovereign Phoenix!

-------------<◇>-------------

"Divine Feminine, you are the carriers. Embody that, heal the wounds of separation. The wounds of abandonment, the wounds, our ancestral wounds. So that all can stand together as sisters and let the energy rise as it should."

"Groups of women listening to each other without judgment. So that others can feel safe to open up and rise up and start reclaiming their sovereignty.
Sovereignty is what we are here to remember."
-Archangel Ariel

-------------<◇>-------------

Sovereignty
AA Ariel: Chaos. The Phoenix will never rise if there is no chaos. Never. Chaos brings people to their hearts; it opens their hearts. People work together, they help each other. It's in chaos, it's in darkness that we find our strength. So we can't shun our shadow, our shadow is the feminine. The shadow is the feminine. You can't bypass the feminine. With positivity, she's fire at the moment, she is the element of fire at the moment. She's coming strong as fire.
A: Aurora] The Phoenix?
AA Ariel: She's rising with fire, it's unbelievable! Her strength, the ambers, it's beautiful and destructive at the same time. Yes, she's speaking from the flames at this time. It's the flames inside, the confusion, the depression, flames inside that people are trying to put out. You can't put out those flames! You have to let them burn! What no longer serves you has to be transmuted by this fire! You can't get away, you can't run from the fire, it's too powerful! It's not

outside there, it's not in Hawaii, anywhere else it's burning. It's not there. It's inside every single heart, the flame is burning so brightly. You can't extinguish it with drugs, whatever man-made, anything. No, she's too strong. Yeah, she's in the fire and it needs an open heart to be tamed. That's the only thing that can tame the flames, is an open heart. (cries) If the heart is closed you get incinerated. (hard cries) Incinerated completely! You won't know what hit you! Open the hearts, open the hearts, open the hearts, open the hearts! That's your key, that's your key! Flames will not consume you if your heart is open! Open your hearts, no matter what you go through! No matter the hardship, no matter the pain. Keep your hearts open! Compassion for yourself first! Compassion for you, compassion for you first! Fill your hearts with compassion for yourself as a sovereign child. Your heart keeps it open! No more, no more closing the heart! Can't close the heart now.

A: Why is it you speak of the Phoenix? Is that what's going on, on Earth right now?

AA Ariel: You can say it is what it is. It's the fire that is transmuting this Golden Age. This Golden age is being transmuted and rebirthed by fire.

A: Is that the only way?

AA Ariel: No, but fire is the main element. There are other elements too. But you have to remember Atlantis went down by water, but this time it's fire that is reigning, it's dragon breath.

A: Is this needed for the Golden Age?

AA Ariel: Oh yes, oh yes! We have to transmute. You can say it's a theme. You can call it, it's the theme of this Golden Age, it's fire. So, there will be chaos. It's the internal fires that need to be harnessed and you will not be afraid of the external fires. Nooo. Because you will know they are there to transmute. Fire is the most powerful way to transmute. As the Phoenix rises, as the Dragons breathe. It will breathe all fire, transmute, transmute! Whether it is a white flame, whether it's the fire, it's all flames. It's just like the sun, it's just fire, and that's why the sun is so active right now releasing all this plasma. All, it's all fire. The solar rays, it's all fire! All fire! All of them. Gamma rays, all of them it's just a different form of fire.

A: Is it trying to transmute the people on Earth. Is that what is going on?

AA Ariel: Yes! The hearts, the hearts as I said. The forgetfulness, the programming. The fear, their darkness. It is time for fire. That's the closest I can find in your language. So, we are all just transmuting. All transmuting ourselves, transmuting the collective, transmuting the Universe/Multiverses. Yeah. It's beautiful, the fire. It's like a volcano. Afterward, the land is very fertile after a volcano - that's the same story after the fire has transmuted anything. Then, people remember, and they become fertile again so to speak, they remember who they are. So, it's just fire, there's nothing to fear. It's just transmutation by fire. You ask, everybody asks, "when is it coming? When is 'The Event'? When is this?" … It's all fire. It's all an internal fire that you burn so bright. Yeah, it's burning the density. It's too dense for any other element. So, yeah. It's too dense, it's too dense. Everybody is doing their best. That is why the sisterhood, as I was talking, is holding that flame within the group, lighting it and making it stronger and stronger. It cannot be put out.

A: What happens when there are Divine Feminine groups put together like this? Do the people who are trying to maintain these densities, do they target these groups?

AA Ariel: It would be that they would try. But if there is strength in numbers you can't destroy it. If you are pulling it down is when they try to destroy it because if there is unity, it cannot be destroyed. If they are holding a group united in their own strength as individuals as well in their group. Yes, you don't know what to do. Yes, tomorrow you might be wrong, today you might be right. There is no right, there is no wrong. It's just telling somebody how you feel, so get up, let's keep moving, and that's the strength. Those ones that you give your hand to help them lift them up. Then they realize, oh they are not alone! And they will lift somebody else's hand and keep going and keep going. As the groups of women of any feminine concept, it will. It's power. It's like a generator.

A: When Divine Feminine are in a group, it's like a generator?

AA Ariel: Yes.

A: Beautiful, so it's important that we as Divine Feminine try to place groups together.

AA Ariel: Yes, that heat, that energy, that vortex, yeah, that's the power. It's like an engine, like an ignition. They ignite the strength within themselves and that becomes powerful and that has a ripple effect and someone somewhere else feels it too. It helps someone else when they are feeling down. Yeah, it's a powerful generator.

A: For example, say you have a group together like we were talking about the Divine Feminine. Humankind has been taught to be judgmental, to allow ego to out win them. Would you say that a group like this would work if people would remain in their hearts and not their ego?

AA Ariel: Yes, it works, and I think ego has a bad rap. Because it's also serving as a purpose and there is a positive and a negative. It's not all bad. Cause that ego can also drive that generator and power it too. Because you can all join as a collective, for example, let's do this. And all of you agree, a group of ten people all agree on pulling their energies towards something. It's their ego that's driving that. Not the negative ego, the positive ego is what is driving that power. Cause when we put down ego in one box, it is bypassing itself, bypassing a very, importance that can help your evolution. It's that generator that is your own, you have to remember the feminine is the shadow. When people say ego, most of them associate shadow with ego. So, when you are putting all in one container the feminine is there in that container. Because she is rising through the shadow, she is not coming from the light, she is coming through the shadow. So, when you are not listening, your ego can be her too and with discernment that you actually know which side to listen to. So, when you are in a group of women or men, you can't lock your shadow in the closet and you say, "that's the ego talking." You have to know which ego is talking. It's just like a car, the engine is working, everything is working together, the ignition, the brakes, the clutch, because everybody's evolution story is different. And it's in knowing that that generator might spark, it might trigger, I don't think there's no end. I don't think there's no end to trigger, it's a process. Maybe people have it wrong? That the feelings go away? No. You just learn how to control them; they don't control you anymore. You say, "Oh, I am jealous today. Oh, I wonder where that came from? I wonder what it is trying to tell me. Hmm." Hello! You talk to it like you would your friend and find out what the message is. It's an aspect of yourself that needs to be looked at and when you are in a group of people that are helping you see that without being judged. Then you can say, "I felt jealousy, I felt hatred there. I wonder?" They all need to speak until you find a solution. That's the point of a group, it's not to tell "Oh, you're so jealous I am not hanging around with you." Okay, there are those you can tell them that if somebody knows and acknowledge that shadow aspect of themselves. It's not all perfect. It's imperfectly perfect, not perfect.

A: (laughs) I laugh because I was speaking of that yesterday, how I am a mirror to everyone, and I love how imperfectly perfect they all are! I see no imperfections.

AA Ariel: Nooo. And no one owes anything. When you walk the Earth knowing nobody owes you anything. Then you have no expectations and without expectations, there is no disappointment. So, nobody owes you anything, nobody owes us anything. You owe yourself everything, so when somebody hurts your feelings, you owe yourself to evaluate. Walk away, talk it out, it's you owing yourself. They are just amplifying for you to see. The journey is difficult enough without owing people stuff. It is difficult enough without carrying anything on our shoulders. No, life changes when you realize that. Not a greeting, not food, not lunch, nothing. They are enhancing your life; they don't owe you anything. That's another form of control when we think people owe us something. Oh, I did this, you should do this. Yeah, that's a control mechanism you are trying to get away from. Everyone is a sovereign being, they don't owe you anything. We are here to enhance each other's journey. Make it better, make it worse, how you react is your choice. It's all your own individual choice.

A: Thank you! As for your messages I felt deep in my heart, the messages you shared are also what I teach to others. It all resonated beautifully within my heart.

Rise of The Sisterhood

AA Ariel: Sisterhood is very important; women have to support other women. It is very, very, important. They have to support each other. (cries) And pull each other up, not down.

A: We have been taught the minute we are born, to be envious, jealous, especially as females.

AA Ariel: Oh yes, but that's lowering the frequency. Because you are all carriers, the females are carriers of the Divine Feminine whether they wish it or not. They have that responsibility to anchor her energy into the Earth. And help each other to do that.

A: Do you have a message for the Divine Feminine since you are Archangel Ariel?

AA Ariel: Just to work together, build bridges together so that all of you can cross bridges together. And the masculine can rise up. The masculine cannot rise up if the feminine is feuding. You are space holders and being space holders, you have to work together. There is no separation. Divine Feminine, you are the carriers. Embody that, heal the wounds of separation. The wounds of abandonment, the wounds, our ancestral wounds. So that all can stand together as sisters and let the energy rise as it should. (cries) That is so beautiful! It's so beautiful. When women work together, the energy of the planet will change so drastically. They work together. They will set an example to the men. So, if women are fighting then how do we expect the men to support us? It's not going to work. It's a container we hold. If you could imagine a container being held by women, this golden container. It's still trying to reach high up, but some are trying to pull it down. Example - like a torch, and it's meant to reach higher and higher! The more hands lift it up the higher it goes, and if others are dragging it down it doesn't go any higher than that. It is stuck.

A: I know exactly what you mean.

AA Ariel: It's like some are trying so hard, others are not ready, but they will be in their time. But it's just working together, not tearing each other down. That's not the point of the Phoenix Rising. It's the point of the fire. It's to transmute all that ego, separation. The negative ego, the ego is not bad in that sense. It's the negative ego. Because there is a confusion in the so-called awakening confusion. Yeah, there is a lot of confusion and a lot of hierarchy. There is a lot of ego, a lot of spiritual bypassing. Yes, there is a lot but it's all coming to the surface now. An example being the pan to the fire. So, they work so hard to raise their frequency and they get trapped in the negative ego back in the pan and they have to get themselves out again. And the process takes longer. So, it's being aware, being discernment. Calling out on people. Calling somebody's bullsh*t out. So, they know they are going the wayside. Because sometimes people look, they know someone is doing something and they don't say anything. So then that person thinks, "Okay, what I am doing is fine." So, if you call someone out on what they are doing and they don't listen, but you did what is right, you called them out on something. If they choose to ignore you, it's their choice. But you chose to go where you are treated better. So, all that fighting. Yeah, as you know it's a program that has been going on. The trying, the last breath in keeping the Divine Feminine in fighting each other, and there are more, there are more who are awakened. There are more who are holding the torches steady that nobody knows about. They are doing their job, that is holding up the collective.

A: Beautiful, thank you! You have brought tears to my eyes! Thank you for your words! You mentioned sisterhoods are important. Do you mean women joining together and rising together? Is that what you mean by that?

AA Ariel: Like a group forming, not a ritual but similar. Groups of women listening to each other without judgment. So that others can feel safe to open up and rise up and start reclaiming their sovereignty. Sovereignty is what we are here to remember. So, when they are tearing somebody down, it means you are not remembering you are a sovereign being. And every soul is a sovereign being. So, when you rise and every person remembers that they are sovereign, then they can't, they can't be pulling others down. And if they do then they will correct themselves very fast because they know that this is a sovereign journey where you walk individually to make the collective stronger. We understand it's tough. But we all knew it was going to be tough. But it's the sisterhoods, groups of women starting a business, starting a meditation group, creating. Or whatever it is, prayer, singing, chanting. Without any agenda just to raise the frequency for each other, holding space for each other to be vulnerable. Hold space for each other to break down. Break your own barriers, break your own fear, collapse the system within yourself and then you will collapse the system outside yourself. But somebody is held in that safe space. It's okay for them to know that they can cry, they can be sad. They don't have to be positive all the time. No one is positive all the time. It's okay to be angry, it's okay to be sad, channel that anger and do something with it. React in a way that will help humanity. That will raise the frequency of the Earth. Everybody, everybody, the animals, the plant kingdom, it's the responsibility of the women. It's a huge responsibility, it's huge, it's huge. But it's in the DNA and is codified in the DNA. You already know what to do. Once that sisterhood happens, the cresses are released. Happiness, joy, of course there will be chaos, but chaos will always be there, if you are looking for it, you will find it.

A: Yes... Thank you, as for your messages I felt deep in my heart! The messages you shared are also what I teach to others. It all resonated beautifully within my heart.

END OF EXCERPT

Every day we see, feel, know the changes that are occurring in bringing the Divine Feminine closer to one another. The Illuminati might have accomplished the goal of separating us in the past; however, no more. For together we are the most powerful force of transmuting false ego programs into love, and they know our true strength. We are the most powerful weapon of the Universe, for WE consist of the most infinite power, which is infinite invincible LOVE! We are who rise from the ashes of endings, and who soar through the shadows of all the trauma falsely created surrounded by oppressing specifically the Divine Feminine. Throughout Earth's History making us marry prematurely in age to whom we are betrothed to, robbing us from deep soul Divine Love. Making the Divine Feminine into subservient wives who serve and obey 'the husband,' living a life of energetic parasitic servitude. Making the Divine Feminine mask ourselves through garments stemming forth from false ego, undermining our voice. Making the Divine Feminine feel that we are not worthy, for we are not masculine in physical, for not being 'valuable' sons but instead burdensome daughters. Making the Divine Feminine feel that our emotions are our weakness, for we feel too much, when truly our emotions are our hearts and what guides our decisions and choices for our highest path. This is why the Illuminati has programmed us in this manner to counter and attack one another. Divided we fall, and united we rise. We are here not to fight their battles; we are here to END THEM!

We all (both women and men) carry the Divine Mother's coding of Creation within us, we are the fractals of Source, our Divine Mother and Father. That being both Divine Feminine and

Divine Masculine, both organic dark and light carrying all reflections of beautiful polarities within us. Therefore, as the Divine Mother and Father are most beautiful and powerful within their Creational energy, so too are we being the fractals of them. We have forgotten of this power, and it is OUR time to remember it and wield it sovereignly once more.

There was much beauty to what was explained in this session of the fundamental needed groups within Earth, and we must continue this momentum. When placing these divine groups together keeping in mind and heart, with the greatest strength that there must always be a natural balance within the sacred Laws of the Universe when joining together. When there is someone that is not accepting their power for various reasons as perhaps, low self-worth, low self-love, ignorance, immaturity, with the biggest being not believing in oneself. That power, that energy has to go somewhere, where it is accepted. Let's say that you are in a group whether that be family, friends, or spiritual. A person named Adam in this group, is not accepting nor using his power. There is then another person named Ben in this group, though he doesn't have the kindest of intentions, however he believes in his own power. Perhaps through ways of being selfish. People of this denser vibration tend to feel that the world owes them something, like an emptiness that needs constant fulfilling. Because Ben lives in this belief of his power even though it is a service-to-self system, he creates for himself by pulling from those that don't use their energy, that don't believe in themselves. The natural laws of balance apply here to Adam, who is not accepting his own power and energy to instead have Ben (service-to-self person) to use Adam's creational energy instead. Remember, this energy must go somewhere, as per the natural energetic balance of the Universe. This is why you often see the hardworking 'nice guy' not getting the promotion, and the other narcissistic guy getting the promotion. Because the narcissist believes he should have it and the more passive gentle person is too humbled to believe in themselves. Reminding us that we must learn balance in both self-belief and humbleness gaining our sovereignty back, by us being the wielders of our energy and not allowing others to siphon it from us for their service-to-self reasons.

We are the keys of all endings into the true organic rebirth, from what is not organic into what IS organic. We are the Keys for the fruition of the New Earth. As spoken and shared through our beloved sister Dolores through her past life regression research, when she mentioned that Divine Mother Isis, in other words the Divine Mother of Creation will be what will bridge forth the Ascension. The reason being is that Divine Mother fractals have been seeded within all of Earth, found within the collective of souls both feminine and masculine, through divine integrations. Fractals of Cleopatra, Isis, Nefertiti, Quan Yin, Kali Ma, Mother Mary, Mary Magdalene, and Sophia... are here and they are within all hearts of the collective. These Divine Mother fractalizations are who will create the crystalline bridge and be the holders of the New Earth portal. Or better yet, they are in this very moment holding it now open, as it has already been created within the true organic timeline of this collective. The reason being as they are the true organic timeline themselves, they are the catalyst to rectify the negative A.I. timeline as it steers off the collective into deeper distortions, the Divine Mother fractals are who steer it back into its true organic Fifth Dimensional cellular blueprint. We are here now, and there is no way to remove us, as we are emerging and resurfacing within the organic timeline of Ascension. We are the Ascension! May the frequency created from this session continue to carry on, spreading throughout and embracing the world in helping all souls become sovereign themselves!

"The Cycle of Creation is as the dance of the Phoenix:

One must be engulfed and taken by the rhythm of the flame.
Within the flame's transmutation, emerging from thy lessons, the ashes.
Rebirthed once more, wiser, stronger, invincible Sovereign Phoenix!"
~AuroRa🖤

--------------<◇>--------------

36

TWIN FLAME BONDS

Recorded in September 2020.
Never before shared.

In this online A.U.R.A. Hypnosis Healing session, Maria is the A.U.R.A. practitioner facilitating this session for Zora, whose Higher Self is the Divine Mother Sophia. In this timely excerpt from this beautiful empowering session, we receive much needed guidance from Divine Mother Sophia on how the Divine Masculine and Divine Feminine can support each other. What is the significance of divine partnerships and Twin Flame bonds? How do we heal the collective by doing the inner work of rebalancing ourselves from within? Here we learn more about amplifying our energies in high frequency groups and more about Higher Self fractals.

-------------<◇>-------------

"That is also important, that self-love is so important because it allows for that forgiveness. It allows you to be in the flow.
It allows you to accept your path and to be on your path because you're loving yourself. The power of love - it's the healing, it's the clearing and it brings forth that balance."
-Divine Mother Sophia

-------------<◇>-------------

M: [Maria] What roles do our Divine Masculine play in supporting their Divine Feminine in their path? Some of them may or may not be in agreement with the paths that we've chosen. (Here 'chosen path' means spiritual path in circumstances when the Divine Feminine awakens before the Divine Masculine.)
Divine Mother Sophia: Hmm... As their partners?
M: Yes.
Divine Mother Sophia: Well, as I said before, it is a dance of free will. So even though they may have come in and accepted that they will be able to support the Divine Feminine and be able to be there to help create balance and be in that beautiful, creative, clear creative flow. The masculine on Earth in this time are very programmed to not honor the feminine within themselves, first. It starts when they're children and their parents say 'Oh, boys don't cry,' 'Oh, boys don't do that,' 'Girls don't do this, girls do that.' It starts with that programming. And as they get older, all the societal factors begin to mold them more and more. It is much easier when the feminine awakens, because of their creative sacral energies and their ability to grow life within, and that is something that the masculine, they do not do. They do have that creative energy, but they do not grow the babies in their womb. So, when it comes time to awaken, it takes them more time to be able to recognize their feminine within and balance with their feminine. It's just as if, when a lot of feminines, have a harder time recognizing and balancing with their masculine. It is a dance. When it comes to the divine partnerships, once that masculine partner or the feminine partner, even though now it's more feminine. Once that masculine partner begins to acknowledge their Divine Feminine within and allow themselves to release themselves

from all that societal programming. Those preconceived notions about women and what a woman is, because together we are ONE. So, once they come to that realization, and they feel that and they're able to look at their Divine Feminine partner and recognize her beauty and her fire and her darkness. Then they are able to look at themselves and see that reflection of them within. For it is as the Twin Flame union is the masculine and the feminine. And even within oneself, you have to balance the masculine and the feminine. It is just a very layered work. It is a lot for some masculines, especially if they have a lot of religious programming or societal programming about what they're supposed to be and who they're supposed to be as a man. But through the love, and through that sacred love glow and the sacred sex, the sacred union with their Divine Feminine, it will help uplift them more and more and more and help them tap more and more into their hearts. It is a dance, but once they come around, they come around. It's like, for example, at one of the group retreats when Zora needed help building the fire and Michael was just there to help and was very much in his Divine Masculine energy. But gentle, so ever so gentle. It is like that. It's like the programming is so deep, because even so many masculines think that being gentle is feminine.

M: Yes. I think Michael is a beautiful example. I felt that about him as well. He's very gentle and yes, so masculine. Beautiful. Now just related to that question as well, for those of us whose masculine may or may not be awakened, or perhaps not aware that they're awakened. Does it help us, as Divine Feminine to work with balanced energies within ourselves? Therefore, even if our masculine and the physical are not awake, but if we have the masculine within us awake and balanced, does that compensate for their not being awake physically?

Divine Mother Sophia: Well, for those who have their divine partner, and maybe their divine partner is not awakened, it does help for them to create more balance within themselves. Definitely. Because once they're balanced, that frequency that they're holding, that balance, and that love will ripple out to their Divine Masculine partner. Especially when they're having sacred sex and they have that balance and that love. When they're kissing their partner, they're touching their partner and they're just feeling together as that oneness. That balanced energy will begin to flow into the partner. It will begin to help them awaken and help them realize and see their light more. It might first come off as just like that, after a feeling of bliss HA! (breathing deep) and deep, deep love that they're feeling towards their partner. Then it will ripple, and they'll realize that that's not just what they feel towards their partner, but it's what they feel within themselves for themselves. That deep love is what will awaken that allowance in them, for them to allow these programming to fall away. Allow them to be free and to be truly free and in their balance as the beautiful beings that they are created to be. For example, Zora knows this but her Divine Masculine is not here yet in the physical realm as he is still in the etheric realm. And that is their balance of him being there, helping her here. Not every person has that Twin Flame union on Earth and many people try to force that because there's also so much programming around that "Twin Flame" concept. Twin Flame is more than just masculine and feminine. There are Twin Flames in sisterhood and brotherhood. There are many different ways where that energy can be expressed as we are all multidimensional beings. It is important for a Divine Feminine to also be able to know and to recognize when the partner is the divine partner or not. Because no matter how much you may try to awaken a partner, if it is not your divine partner, and if it is not in their highest good and in your highest good, if it is not the (I don't want to say divine will because people get confused), but if it is not in their timeline, for them to be divine partnerships, no matter what it will, it will not unfold. When they try and force it that's when you know, those denser emotions and those things are to manifest. But it is also important for the Divine Feminine, who feel like their Divine Masculine are not awakened. It is also a lesson for them in patience, acceptance and also knowing that you cannot force someone else to come into an awakening. You can love them, you can care for them, you can do everything that you wish, but until that soul is ready, you cannot force it. You cannot infringe on that. So, it is a lesson in balance for all. But it is beautiful when the unions unfold at their highest because two Twin Flames together is very, very powerful. Very powerful.

M: Yes. Wow. Thank you. That was beautiful She does actually have a question about bringing in that inner balance. She wanted to know how she can balance her Divine Feminine and her Divine Masculine to make sure that they always stay in balance. She does feel many times that her left side, shivers or feels like it vibrates at times. Can you explain that and how we can balance our feminine and masculine within ourselves?

Divine Mother Sophia: Yes. So that dizziness that she feels on her left side that comes on the feminine is because of that imbalance and the feminine kind of overworking itself. It is like the two wheels on a wheelbarrow. If you're only pushing with one wheel, it's not balanced, and it can easily tip over. It's hard to get anything done when it's not balanced. It's hard to focus, it's hard to create. For her what she's been doing, it's been working. It's going to take time and it's very layered because a part of her sexuality has been a lot of her giving up, a lot of her... choosing partners who don't respect her sacral energy and her not respecting that and that is taking it out of balance. Also, her not really fully recognizing it. So, it's going to be a journey for her to bring it back into complete balance. First, she must forgive herself for this partnership that she had. By her holding on to those negative feelings and emotions - the shame, the guilt. It is a lesson for her to remember to always listen to her heart. From the very first moment, she knew that she did not want to be in that partnership (laughing). From the very first moment, it was almost like she was letting her mind become in that sympathy, that "Oh, I need to help this person. And oh, I have to do this." As she allowed for that to come forth, it allowed her to become more and more and more illusioned and distorted within the image of that person and not being able to see it fully and truly for what it was. But then the more she started to stand in her heart, and then she could just know. She could feel that it wasn't right. And once she was completely out of the environment, because she wasn't able to start fully seeing it until when she was traveling out of town. She was completely away from the person; they couldn't have any contact with her. She wasn't really talking to the person; it took that for her to be able to recognize. "Oh, yeah, I don't want that. Oh, I can't force this. I don't even want to force this. It doesn't even feel good in any type of way." So that was when she was able to really start to feel her heart again. Not that her heart was closed off. But she was really allowing herself to listen to her heart again, and accept the feeling that her heart was saying no. That is something that she's allowed in her sexual relationships, she's allowed herself to be saying no, but not enforcing that, not consenting with them as partners. It created this really imbalance between her allowing that to infringe on her even though she knew that she wasn't consenting, and she felt it in her body, she felt it in her heart, but she wasn't consenting. She was allowing for those infringement upon her sacral. It is about her now being able to look and understand. Not only the sacredness of her energy and the beauty of her energy, because it's like she could feel that of Creation and being connected with that of Earth. That pain in her heart was not just because she felt like she betrayed it herself. Because now she has more of an understanding of her energy. She knows how dangerous that was. But it is important for her to release that shame because it was a lesson. And now because of that created intention, she can see and understand that. It was a great lesson for her in viewing that.

M: Beautiful. Yes, and if I may request you Divine Mother, if you can start working on her heart and start healing from that relationship, that guilt that she carries within her?

Divine Mother Sophia: Mm-hmm.

M: So, once she starts releasing the guilt and the pain that she feels for what happened, can you now tell her what she can do to balance that love of the Divine Masculine and Divine Feminine within herself? Love herself maybe as a masculine as well?

Divine Mother Sophia: Yes, it is like she can have sacred sex with herself. Not even just that but just more self-loving of herself. When you're putting on your lotion or your oils, just loving it. When you're brushing your hair, when you're brushing your teeth, just loving yourself and forgiving yourself. Even in the morning time when you wake up in the morning, you do your shields and while you're sending love. Don't forget to send love to yourself. She's made it a good part of her routine to send love to the Earth, to the Angelics, to everyone but you have to send that love to yourself too. That is also important, that self-love is so important because it allows for that forgiveness. It allows you to be in the flow. It allows you to accept your path and to be on your path because you're loving yourself. The power of love - it's the healing, it's the clearing and it brings forth that balance. Because her masculine is in the etheric, he does not have all those programming of the human, that a human masculine would have. So, it is like that partnership that's always there. She has to tap into it more. Just talking to him more, not just calling on him when she's afraid (laughing).

M: (laughter).

Divine Mother Sophia: But calling on him to, when it's you're just watching a movie and you just want to feel that love energy. Or you're doing something, and you just want to feel that masculine. Or when she wants to create something, and she feels like, "Okay, I have this idea, but how am I going to bring it forth?" Allowing your masculine to come in and show you and bring that toolbox to manifest things forth. It's just like, when you're birthing a baby and you're becoming pregnant, it's not just the feminine. It has to be from that seed of the masculine. So that's what she needs to start doing is bringing and allowing that seed of that masculine to come forth so that she can start birthing those beautiful ideas. All these beautiful things that we've been feeding into her she can allow for them to come forth. Also, that forgiveness piece, because she definitely allowed a lot of things to tap into her sacral energy.It's really important for her to forgive herself for that. But also knowing that we are all reflections of the Earth. When I say "we" I'm speaking "WE" as fractals, as WE are all beautiful reflections of the Earth. By her deciding to not allow her sacral energy to get infringed upon, and not consenting to that, then it's also that magnifying that within the Earth. It's just that inner work, and that collective healing. That is necessary, but that will help bring forth much balance.

M: That's beautiful. Divine Mother, thank you for sharing that in so much detail, for it gives us this perspective of thinking, "It's not just my own body or my own energy that I'm protecting. I'm also protecting the Divine Mother Earth's energy, the Divine Mother Earth's body as I protect myself."

Divine Mother Sophia: Yes. It was...she has this in her memory still, so we'll use this. It is like the quote from the Yeshua painting she saw recently where it says "Know, when you shield thyself, you're shielding the innocent." Knowing that when you don't consent, and you're shielding your energy, and you're balancing your energy, you're healing yourself, you're doing that for your inner child, for the collective of children, for the Earth. We are all one and we are all connected. When you awaken and you bring that love energy and that frequency into your home, it ripples out to the beings in your home. It may not be known right away or instantly, but it ripples out. In time, you'll be able to look and say 'wow, I can't believe how many people.' It's like, if you look back on the timeline of your life, look at the friends you've had in the past. It's like 'wow,' and then you look at the friends you have now. It's like 'wow,' they resonate with me so much more. It's that frequency. It's that light frequency and knowing when you get into these groups of high frequency, you help elevate one another, elevate and magnify on each other's energy. It's so beautiful, it's like the flame of the same color coming together and then just (making a hand and sound gesture to indicate expansion) amplifying. Then when they're all together, they're different colors and they're different expressions. Then they just amplify. Their intentions are amplified. The healing is amplified. It is a great amplification and a great unification as well of the energies.

M: Yes, she has that question of why is it important that the same fractals get together?

Divine Mother Sophia: Because it's that amplification. And it's that maybe one fractal has not awakened to certain parts of themselves and them all being together, it's kind of like awakening and activating. One has this code; one has that code - one has this and then coming together and sharing that energy. It's like the activation just clicks into place (snapping fingers quickly) because they carry some of those same energies and it just amplifies, and they continue to lift each other and lift themselves. It's really beautiful. It really is. It's like that Twin Flame partnership, they amplify each other. They activate each other, they lift, they lift, they lift, and then they have children. Then those children are activated and especially if they're sacredly birthed or even if they're sacredly carried. We know that it's hard for a lot of mothers to have sacred birth in this space and time, just because of the way that everything is. But it is all in that intention from the sacred consummation, and just everything all together. It's an amplification, one after another, after another, and those codes. It's beautiful. Then it creates this beautiful gridding between all the beings and their hearts. It really is. It's beautiful to see it. So many people are awakening and realizing this, even if they don't recognize it fully consciously. They recognize it. Like within their hearts, and they can feel it within their hearts.

M: I think that's beautiful. I totally agree with that. It just feels amazing. I've been feeling that of late as well connecting with someone else who has the same fractal as I am. It's like you're seeing another version of yourself in the same spectrum, but another version of yourself, where you're still learning some things, whereas the person's already, you know, mastered that lesson. And then that person helps you and then you throw light on something that person is kind of ignoring at the moment and it helps that person awaken. Then when you speak with that person, your heart just lights up with this excitement, almost similar to when you speak to a Twin Flame. So, you explained that really well because I do feel that as well, almost like, 'Oh, you know, she messaged and let me see what she messaged.' It's almost an excitement. You can see a Twin Flame and you feel similar for another sister, who has the same fractal as you.

Divine Mother Sophia: Yes. Also know that which you described, of looking at that fractal, that has your same fractal and watching them express themselves and being so happy to be with them and joyful to see them and watching them do their lessons. Not stepping in to tell them how to do it, but just watching them do their lessons, know that is how it is for us. We see you all so beautifully interacting and feeling and connecting. I wish for all to know and to feel that when they are going through their experience, they expect for... every time at the group retreats when someone says, "Well, if Divine Mother created it, why can't she come and fix it??" (laughs) Every time I hear that (laughs again), I just laugh but then I recognize the confusion there. Because it's like, all are your own individual expressions. We are here, our energies are very much a part of you. You are able to express them in a way that's individual to you. We can't tell you how to express that. We can't force you to activate a certain thing or to call forth on a specific fractal of yourself when you want to do something. Because that is infringing. It is as if we are watching like you described, you're watching this fractal of yourself, go through and play these lessons. You're learning from it as well. You're gaining from that perspective. That is why we fractalize because it is much harder to try and have all that experience at the same time. Not harder, it's not the right word. These human terms... It is when an energy is so big and so grand, it's hard to fit it in a smaller… what is that word... her grandpa taught her this phrase when she was younger that 'The camel can't fit through the eye of a needle.' That phrase, it is like that. So that is why we must fractalize and create these beautiful combinations of all these beautiful energies. Everyone has more than one Higher Self fractal. It allows us all to come together and to have this beautiful experience and unification in this individualized expression. But to also allow that individualized expression to grow and expand and experience. Once they have that experience, it feeds the entire collective experience, and it informs the Higher Selves. It allows us to learn from that experience as we are all ever expanding. Creation is infinite, consciousness is infinite, you are multidimensional beings, everything is infinite. It is just that acknowledgement. I understand that when a lot of people say, "Oh, why can't Divine Mother just come fix the game?" But that is because they don't recognize the 'ME' in them. They don't recognize that oneness within them. So that is deep, deep inner work that they must do, in order to come into recognizing that oneness and realizing, "You fix it, you created the game as well, you fix the game." Once everyone comes to that understanding of "Oh, I am a co-creator in this" and "I also manifest this and I also create this," that is when true change will ripple out into Creation, because it's that sovereignty, it's that acknowledging of "Okay, I call back my power, I call back my fractals, I claim my sovereignty; I am not consenting." Also saying, "Okay, I'm a co-creator in this, well, I want to live in a world where children aren't harmed. So, what am I going to do? I'm not going to harm children, and I'm going to do the opposite, I'm going to heal and do the highest good for the children," because that ripples out and it manifests that. That is why there's so many people who don't want to recognize the density and the inorganic darkness, because they don't even want to recognize their own power in the fact that they are a co-creator in that. So many beings who don't recognize that. By not recognizing that they're allowing it to just continue to manifest and to be all in their creational energies and to be like a stain on everything that they do. Until they come into the realization that, "Okay, I'm a co-creator. By me not deciding to look at this inorganic darkness, I'm allowing it to manifest into reality, I'm infringing on the timeline." Yes, it could be hard to recognize that, but once you do, it allows you to open up into the flow of Creation and recognize "Oh, so I am a powerful creator being. Oh, I am multidimensional, let me be intentional about that." So, it is very layered. Many people go to the retreats and everyone is also on different timelines of awakening and different things that they have and their different choice points. But in a nutshell, basically, that is what it is. Yes.

M: Thank you. That is so beautifully explained. That's beautiful. Thank you. Do you have any other message for us that you can share?

Divine Mother Sophia: Yes, yes, one last message that I would like to say as I have said much and there is much to be understood, is just that I love you all. And I love seeing you all being together in groups. Even just communicating with one another, uplifting one another, encouraging one another, sharing ideas and creation with one another because that is how Creation flows best. That is why we have Councils. That is why we have, you know, the Elders and it is not just one being. Even Source is so grand. This human can't even comprehend. It's even hard for her to speak it. But that is why there's Collectives because we are better as a Collective. We are beautiful and strong and fierce on our own. But that flame is even stronger and more intense as a Collective. So that is important. That is what I wish for you all to remember. And for you all to understand.

M: That's a very important lesson for us. Thank you very much, we really appreciate it. We all honor you, respect you, thank you and we love you infinitely.

Divine Mother Sophia: I love you infinitely.

END OF EXCERPT

--------------<◇>--------------

Wow! What a gift this transmission is on behalf of the infinite beauties of a Twin Flame union. Just absolutely infinitely gorgeous! A most BEAUTIFUL expression and clear divine knowledge sang out through our Divine Mother's heart. Our Divine Mother reminded us to fall in love with oneself as we yearn as well to fall in love with another. When we learn to fall in love with our own eyes, our own hair, our own legs, our own skin, our own body. For when we accept the Avatar which we have chosen to be our divine vessel for schooling within the Third Dimension, then we shall fully learn to infinitely love the beauties and uniqueness of soul that we are. We understand how the Avatar body/shell only represents the outer aspect of us which is perishable, and the inwards of us is the infinite spirit of light. For that is when we remember that we are beyond our body, we are an infinite multidimensional morphing expression that changes and shifts from one second to the other. Remembering that we are Creation, and that Creation is as the movement of the water. To freely allow the flow of creation, one must honor that Creation is unable to remain stagnant. Creation is everlasting motion!

The way the Divine Mother expressed the wisdom of 'The Matrix,' how people expect to be saved by her or another. To expect this, it is to give away your light, it is to GIVE UP, it is to have forgotten at the deepest original root at why we decided to fractalize ourselves for the purpose of experience and growth. It is to give up all forms of your sovereignty. You and only you can save yourself. This is what this book is about, reminding you of this power that is awaiting for you to embrace and unleash for you and the collective. For YOU ARE your only savior.

Do not ever give away your power no matter how small or how big. NEVER! Stand in YOUR TRUTH, your power and do not allow anyone to tell you and sway you otherwise. Because when you allow the sway from another who knows not of your path divinely, this is when you begin to lose yourself, your mission, your cause, and your purpose. Then you eventually lose the reason why you incarnated as either a Starseed answering the call as a volunteer or a Soul that fell in love with the spectrum of the multitudes of Creation on Earth, within this beautiful LOVE, magical, masterful Earth. No matter which way we look at it, it truly is a masterpiece, that it is. And no one can take that from Mother Earth, our Divine Mother. For her soul is the heart that gives life to Earth, for she is Earth.

So, when you ask, "where is the Divine Mother?" Remember that she wanted to ensure that you never forgot, no matter how distorted you turned, and no matter how deep you have sunk into sadness. She chose to become the seed and heart of Earth, so that you would never be alone, so that she could feel everything through you, and knows and feels all your happiness and sorrow. She knows them best and more intimately than any other. For she is you, and you are her. Because she has been the very soil that your feet are held up by as you take foot, the wind that carries and provides clearness of thoughts for the fruition of manifestation, the water that provides cleansing and rejuvenation within all parts of you, and the fire that provides the warmth and life within you bringing forth endings to what is destructive so that what is true may be rebirthed. Her soil is what provides us the nourishment by her seeds that sprout, her air is what guides and sways us when we are misled down a false path, her water is as her blood and lifeforce that calms and envelopes all it touches, and her fire is the light within our soul that replenishes us when we are at the dimmest of us and our lights at the most diminished.

Know that as you, dearest soul, are reading this book that in this exact moment that I love you with every piece of me which is infinite, for we are all infinite. For you are those way showers and light warriors that shall speak these expressions shared through this Divine Creation of galactic soul's stories. This is why we decided to fractalize so that we could exchange these stories, as olden friends meeting once more. Laughing in joy of the remembrance that your fractalizations have brought into others awareness.

This beautiful empowering excerpt has a familiar tone that feels like "HOME," because of this it can feel as it was you, yourself, who expressed this divinely. This is truly a beautiful gift from the Divine Mother's heart to ours, singing infinite wisdom and love to us, reminding us ever so gently of her presence in our hearts and the true beauties of Creation that we all are. This is a grand masterpiece and just simply divine in the way it stirs in deep feelings of "home" and infinite love through our souls!

**"I am here because of you and me.
My openness to your messages, your dreams, your experiences, your lessons, your wisdom. To know this, is to honor ALL and understand that we thrive and grow not because of just self-knowledge.
We transform into our highest heart due to self and other selves."
~AuroRa🖤**

-------------<◇>-----------

37

MATRIX PODS

Session #141: Recorded in April 2019

In this online A.U.R.A. Hypnosis Healing session, Taylor takes us through one of the most catalyzing experiences bringing forth the strongest awareness yet. Her journey requires the most patience to understand where she has landed. What are these capsules that resemble "Matrix Pods"? What does this all mean? How could this be? An ancient bird humanoid race, their perseverance and their drive to protect the Earth and its people.

"Everything is, everything is...(crying). They didn't realize how much we're invaded by darkness. They don't know what it's like to be free. We think we have free will, we don't."
-Taylor

-------------\<\>\-------------

A: [Aurora] You see sand? Have you landed on the ground yet?
T: [Taylor] Yes.
A: Look all around you. Do you see anything else besides sand?
T: I feel like it's Egypt.
A: Look at yourself. Do you feel like you're female or male?
T: Female.
A: Look down at your feet. Are you wearing something on your feet?
T: Sandals with toe rings.
A: How many toes do you have?
T: Five, ten all together.
A: These toe rings, what are they made of, are there any designs or colors?
T: Gold.
A: Are there any gems on them or are they just gold?
T: It's feeling like a little green. I don't know if that's a dragon or serpent? It's just a little made out of green and red gem.
A: You think it's in the shape of a dragon or serpent?
T: Yeah.
A: What are you wearing?
T: Something with a dark olive tone. A white skirt and kind of a white top like draping over me.
A: Do you feel like you're young or older?
T: I'm middle aged.
A: Look at your hands? How many fingers do you have?
T: Ten.
A: Is there any other jewelry you're wearing?
T: I have a necklace.
A: Describe it.

T: Gold with a big red gem in the middle? I think it's a Ruby.

A: Is there anything that you're carrying?

T: A golden staff?

A: Can you describe it to me?

T: It's gold and it also has green and red gems on it.

A: Are there any shapes or designs that you see on it?

T: It also has a dragon hand like the toe ring.

A: Are there any crystal gems on the dragon?

T: I think a green Emerald and red Ruby.

A: Is there anything that you're wearing on your head?

T: A gold headband, I look like Cleopatra or something.

A: If you could describe how your face, and your hair looks.

T: The hair is short and black, my face - feels like I have makeup on; dark eyes, full lips and a medium size nose.

A: Now let's see, let's discover let's adventure through this land that you've landed with the sand. Look all around you. What else do you see?

T: I still see palm trees and I see pyramids in the distance.

A: As you're standing in this area, is there anyone else with you?

T: I feel like there's someone there, but I can't really see. Looks like an older man, it feels like he's lost. He looks kind of ragged. He's been in the desert for a while or something.

A: And he is there with you?

T: I don't know if he's with me or he's kind of just wandering around. Maybe he's asking for help. Yeah, I think he needs help.

A: Let's keep discovering this land. Fast forward a bit and see what you do next.

T: I'm looking across this... I don't know what to call it. It almost looks like a landing area, like it's made out of stone and marble. It's just a flat area. I don't really see anything else.

A: Let's fast forward a bit to see when something is occurring here, and you think it's a landing area? See if there's some interaction or some movement.

T: I see a ship coming down.

A: Describe the ship to me.

T: It's almost pyramid shape, but not exactly. It's like a dark grey on the outside. Yeah, and it comes down and lands on that area.

A: Does it have any like lights to it, any colors?

T: It is kind of like you could imagine like an old-fashioned spaceship. It looks like an old-fashioned spaceship. Like there's no lights or colors or anything. It's kind of funky, you know?

A: It looks like it's worn down?

T: Yeah, or old.

A: What happens next once the spaceship lands?

T: The door opens.

A: Where does the door open from?

T: It kind of opens like an airplane door with the steps that go down.

A: Is there something coming out through the door?

T: It looks like little Greys coming out from the door.

A: Are there several?

T: Three.

A: When they come out what is it that they do next?

T: They're just standing there looking at me.

A: Let's fast forward a bit to see what happens next. Why are they there?

T: I don't know.

A: What are you seeing and what are you sensing?

T: I'm hearing "harvested." It's making me emotional. I don't know why. (tears up)

A: What's making you emotional?

T: They're here to harvest the people.

A: Do you feel that this is a positive or negative thing?

T: Negative. I don't really know; it just makes me really sad for the people.

A: What do they do next once they're off the ship?

T: It looks like they go into a pyramid and there's like bodies lined up.

A: How are the bodies lined up? Do you mean they're standing lined up, laying down lined up?

T: Laying down.

A: Are the bodies alive?

T: Yes.

A: Are there females and males?

T: Both.

A: Any children?

T: Yes, children too.

A: The people that are laying there, are they happy being there? How do they look?

T: They look like they're in like, in a suspended animation like they're in these tubes, like they're being kept alive. Maybe just to harvest them and they're not really alive. Their bodies are alive.

A: Do they seem like they're in some kind of sleep type of…?

T: Yeah.

A: Would you say there's many?

T: Yeah.

A: Did you say that there's children in there as well?

T: Yes.

A: Can you explain to me what they're in? You said that they're in some kind of capsule. Can you explain to me how that looks?

T: It's clear like you can see through it. And it's like there's liquid inside. Like the bodies are suspended in the liquid.

A: Is there color to the liquid?

T: Clear. There's like a little machine next to each one.

A: There's a machine next to each capsule? Okay. Look at the bodies that are inside the capsules, do they look human?

T: Yeah. They are human.

A: As they're inside this liquid look very closely. Do they have anything attached to them? How do they breathe? Is there anything connected to their bodies that's coming out of their bodies?

T: Yeah, there are wires and cords.

A: There's wires and cords coming out of what parts of their bodies?

T: It looks like there is one that goes directly into the lungs.

A: Does it penetrate the skin and go into them?

T: Yeah.

A: Where else are there wires?

T: They're the only ones I see.

A: Those wires, do those wires connect to the capsule?

T: Yes.

A: Look at how the capsules are all lined up. You said that they each have a little machine next to them, can you describe to me is there also wires to that or how does the system work?

T: Yeah, there's a wire from the machine to the capsule. The machine will control the temperature, the consistency and the chemical makeup of the fluid inside the environment so that the human doesn't decompose.

A: How many capsules do you see? Do you see hundreds - thousands?

T: Hundreds I mean, they're just lined up - down the wall, each wall.

A: They're on the walls or on the ground?

T: They're on the ground but like they're lined up against the wall.

A: Then look at the capsules do they have any type of symbols on them?

T: I feel like an S, like a backwards S. It's like they got a diagonal line through the middle. I don't know what any of this means.

A: You're doing great. There's a reason why your Higher Self took you here. As you're looking through these capsules, see if any of the capsules draw your attention.

T: Well, yeah, I keep seeing this one lady. It's really the only face I see.

A: You're able to see and recognize, see if you're able to recognize her soul.

T: I don't know. I feel like it's me. (choking with emotions)

A: Inside the capsule?

T: Me.

A: How does the 'you' look in the capsule, how do you look?

T: I have long red hair that is floating in the water? (crying) My eyes are open and they're green.

A: These people laying in the capsules have their eyes open?

T: I can't see the others...I can only see this one.

A: Okay. Do you feel that you are an average size type of human or are you taller or shorter?

T: I feel average. I don't feel tall.

A: What about these Greys? Where are they? Are they in there?

T: Yeah, they are there. They're checking on everybody to make sure everything's working properly. Yeah, they're just going around checking everything. I don't know why, what they're doing with them though.

A: See them now? How they had wires to the machines. Is there another wire connected to somewhere else?

T: Oh wait. Maybe these are like, maybe they weren't human.

A: What isn't human?

T: The people. Maybe they're like in suspended animation.

A: I'm trying to figure out how the system works and is there somewhere where all of these are connected to the capsules? Is there somewhere that they're connected to, together?

T: I don't see anything that they're connected to, I just see them each individual.

A: Is there anything else that the Greys do besides just checking and making sure everything's running? Anything else that they do of significance?

T: No. I think they're just there to check on everything, make sure everything is running okay.

A: So, let's fast forward a bit to see, when something has changed here. You are there now. What do you see?

T: I'm not getting anything?

A: That's okay. Go back - back to you watching the capsule there. Let's go ahead and leave that scene. Let's go to another important time in this life. You're there now. What do you see?

T: I'm on a grassy hill.

A: We are trying to discover extra answers. Answers to why it is that we went to the capsule place. Look at yourself. Do you have a body?

T: Yeah. I have feathers.

A: Do you mean feathers on your skin?

T: Yes.

627

A: What color are your feathers?

T: Blue.

A: Look at yourself. Do you feel you have wings?

T: Yeah.

A: Are all your feathers the same blue color?

T: My body is blue. My wings have purple and white.

A: Is there anything you're carrying?

T: A book.

A: Let's look at this book. Are there any designs, any colors, anything that stands out?

T: It's green and there's like a mirror on the front.

A: When you look at this mirror that's in the front of this book. How does your face look?

T: I have a beak, like a yellow beak.

A: Do you feel like you're female or male, both?

T: I think male.

A: What about your nose? Your ears? What do those look like?

T: I'm kind of humanoid in that respect but I have a beak for a nose.

A: You're a humanoid type of bird.

T: Yeah.

A: Do you have fingers? How many fingers do you have?

T: Yeah. Four fingers.

A: Do you feel like you're tall or short?

T: I feel really tall.

A: As tall as a tree?

T: No. Probably like seven feet - eight feet tall.

A: Look all around you, what else do you see besides this hill?

T: All the trees.

A: Why are you here?

T: To protect this place.

A: Is there anything in this land that needs protecting?

T: The humans.

A: Where are the humans?

T: They are in the Third Dimension.

A: Are you in the Third Dimension as well?

T: No.

A: What Dimension are you in?

T: Seventh.

A: You're viewing humans from the Seventh Dimension into the Third?

T: Yeah.

A: So, tell me some of the things that you do, what do you do to protect the humans?

T: We fly together, there are others. To keep the bad energy out, the negative energy out.

A: How does this negative energy look and how do you keep it out?

T: It's invasive. They want to come here to feed off the humans - the negative alien races.

A: How do you protect them from the negative alien races?

T: They go to battle.

A: Who goes to battle?

T: All of us, my friends. We then fight against it; the negative aliens to save Earth.

A: Do you see the negative aliens now?

T: No. I don 't see them now.

A: Go to a time, as this blue bird that you are protecting the humans from the negative aliens. You are there now. What do you see?

T: We see a formation of birds.

A: Would the birds be the humanoid birds?

T: Yes, the humanoid birds.

A: What are they doing?

T: They're flying to a ship. They surround that ship in some kind of energy so that it can't penetrate.

A: They're flying around protecting so that they can't penetrate?

T: Yeah.

A: Where are the negative aliens?

T: They are inside the ship.

A: Can you describe the ship to me?

T: It's a triangle.

A: What is the ship trying to do?

T: I think it's the Greys again. I think they are trying to get to the humans so that they can harvest them. I don't know what they're doing it for.

A: Fast forward a bit and see what happens next. Do the bluebirds protect the humans, and what happens to the negative aliens?

T: Yeah, they're not allowed to do it anymore.

A: So, what happens to the negative aliens?

T: Earth is protected now and they're not doing it anymore.

A: Those negative aliens in the spaceship, what happens to them?

T: They go back to wherever they came from.

A: Tell me. Why is it that they're not allowed to harm Earth like that anymore?

T: Because the vibration is raised to the point where it's not accepting that kind of behavior. The light is outweighing the darkness now. Yeah, the vibration is high enough now that it can ward off these kinds of negative agendas.

A: Very good. Let's leave that scene and let's go to another important time in this life as this blue bird. You're there now. What do you see?

T: Everybody's so happy (crying out of joy).

A: Who's happy? Tell me what you see.

T: The Earth is free again (crying). It's all light, it's all light (sobbing).

A: What is all light?

T: The Earth.

A: And the people? They're all light too?

T: Yes. Everything is, everything is (crying). They didn't realize how much we're invaded by darkness. They don't know what it's like to be free. We think we have free will, we don't.

A: Let's go back to right before everything turns to light. Back in time to when and what caused everyone to turn to light? You're there now what do you see?

T: I feel like it was a gradual progression. It wasn't a single "Event" but a series of waves of energy coming in from Source, through the Sun to raise the vibration. It was slowly happening but it's getting faster now (cries and mumbles apologies for sounds). I'm sorry.

A: Don't worry, it's okay. You said it's getting faster now?

T: Yeah, it's happening faster now. Feels like it's coming in more stronger now, people are waking up.

A: As these waves are coming in and you said that they are starting to wake up. What are some of the things that you're seeing that are significant to why they're waking up? What's occurring as you're watching those waves pass through?

T: It's affecting their energy. It just can't remain on Earth - I don't want to say negative - their lower vibrational states of being. It's helping them purge the negativity, lower vibration, emotions like depression and it's helping them purge all this; that eventually they can hold more light. First, they have to purge those lower vibrational frequencies to be able to hold higher vibrational light.

A: As far as looking at this point of view of Earth, are there any more people in capsules inside the Earth that you see?

T: I do, yeah right now, but they won't be able to keep it going for long.

A: Where do you see them on Earth?

T: I see them underground.

A: Now that you're seeing this more of a wholeness. What is this? Why do they have them in these capsules? What are they getting from that?

T: Well, they harvest their DNA and I think they keep them like that in case they need more of their DNA.

A: Are they using them, like their energy in some sort of way? Are they using their energy for something?

T: Maybe they're feeding off their energy.

A: What are they using their energy for, you're able to see and sense that. What do you see?

T: They're using their energy to fuel themselves because they're so empty.

A: So, when they draw this energy out of the capsules, where does this energy go?

T: They collect it all, the energy in one place. Looks like a container of energy. Just a big room full of energy almost and they can go where they want. It's almost like they recharge their battery or like, a hit of energy when they need it. They keep going. Yeah.

A: Does their energy go to a like one particular spot? Like so when their energy is being drawn out, does it go somewhere where it's stored?

T: Yeah, it's stored.

A: Where's this stored at? What does that look like where it's stored?

T: It's just like a room. Like a circular room. Where they store all the energy. They harvest and use it as they need it.

A: You're able to see someone who would go to this area to receive, recharge or to use the energy. You're able to see that being there. Look at them, how are they recharging themselves when they go to recharge to the circular room?

T: Oh okay. It's the Grey and he just walked up and put his hands on it. It's not a room, it's like a ball, and the energy is inside of it. So, he just goes up and puts his hand on it.

A: What does that do for him?

T: It gives him energy.

A: Are there any other aliens - negative aliens that do this besides Greys?

T: I think the Greys are the only ones that do this. I mean but the other entities, they have other ways of harvesting energy from humans.

A: These Greys, can you show her Higher Self, show her how is it that they get these humans? How do they acquire them to place them in capsules to begin with?

T: It's not voluntary they take them. They're like all the missing people in the world you know, like where do they all go? Well, aliens take them some time and they use them.

The Higher Self is called forth.

A: Am I speaking with Taylor's Higher Self?

Higher Self: Yes.

A: Beautiful. I honor you, I thank you, and I respect you for all the aid you have given us today. I know that you hold all the records to Taylor's different lives may I ask you questions?

Higher Self: Yes.

A: Why is it that you chose to show her this life there in a capsule and that she was inside a capsule. What was the purpose to this life? What were you trying to teach her through this?

Higher Self: She needs to understand the darkness in this world and how it operates. How much there is, because she gets taken advantage of by dark forces.

A: Is this a 'her' in one of these capsules like another 'her'? Was that like in the past or is it currently happening?

Higher Self: I feel blocked.

The Body Scan begins.

A: Higher Self, we would like to be able to do the Body Scan so we're able to get some more answers as she feels blocked right now. Do you need any aid from the Archangels?

Higher Self: We need aid.

A: Which Archangel would you like to call in first?

Higher Self: Michael.

A: Let's call on Archangel Michael now. If I can please speak to Archangel Michael.

AA Michael: Yes.

A: Greetings, is this you Michael?

AA Michael: Yes.

A: Welcome, brother. We love you, we honor you, we respect you. Thank you for being here.

AA Michael: Thank You.

A: Thank you. She was shown a life where she was in a capsule and her energy was being used for some kind of feeding and we were trying to get more answers to why the Higher Self took her there. She feels blocked. Can you please perform a Body Scan on her now to see what is blocking her from going deeper and getting these answers? Let me know please Michael, where you see the blockage if there's any entities, any implants, hooks?

AA Michael: I feel like there's something in the liver.

A: If you can scan the liver now. What is it, an energy? Is there an entity? What is there.

AA Michael: I think it's an entity.

A: Michael if you could please help us talk to that entity there in her liver. If you could bring that entity up, up, up, we would like to speak to that entity now. Greetings.

Entity: Hello.

A: Thank you for speaking to us. May I ask you questions?

Entity: Yes.

A: Thank you. Are you female or male?

Entity: Male.

A: When was it that you connected to her liver?

Entity: When she was little.

A: What was going on with her that allowed for you to attach there?

Entity: Fear, she had a lot of fear.

A: What did she fear?

Entity: Everything.

A: Was this a contract?

Entity: Yes.

A: What discomfort have you been causing her?

Entity: Pain in that area - the liver and the gallbladder.

A: Did you have a body before you attached?

Entity: Yeah.

A: What happened to you? How did you die?

631

Entity: A car accident.

A: How old were you?

Entity: Twelve.

A: I understand that you've been there some time. And we would love to be able to aid you today so that you may be free and not have to be stuck in her body and having to use her energy to survive. We'd love to be able to help you release yourself from having to play that role as an entity, living off someone else. Would you allow us to aid you so that you may spread that light within you, and you may release yourself so that you can positively polarize now?

Entity: Yes.

A: Beautiful. We want you to find that light within you, and spread it to all that is of you - every root, every cord, and let me know when you're all light.

Entity: It feels so good.

A: Beautiful. Are you all light now?

Positive Polarized Entity: Yes.

A: Wonderful. Let me know when you're all out. Do you have a message for her before you go?

Positive Polarized Entity: I'm sorry.

A: Thank you. Go ahead and go with the Love-Light of the Universe. Blessings to you.

Positive Polarized Entity: Thank you.

A: Archangel Michael, if you could please have our brother Raphael aid us? We welcome you Raphael. Thank you for being here. We love you and we honor you.

AA Raphael: Thank you.

A: Raphael, if you could please start filling in that space where the entity was removed?

AA Raphael: Yes.

A: Good. Archangel Michael, if I could continue to ask you questions please. She wants to know, one of the main concerns that she had a session today was that she found a lump in her breast. One definitely on the right and possibly one on the left. What is the cause of this?

AA Michael: Suppression of anger and frustration.

A: Has the anger and frustration created these balls in her chest?

AA Michael: Yes, it's stuck energy.

A: What is she angry about?

AA Michael: The anger she wasn't allowed to express throughout her life because she was walking on eggshells trying to keep the peace so that there wouldn't be an explosion. Yeah. Lots of depression.

A: If you could scan the lumps in her breast, do they have cancer?

AA Michael: No, not of cancer, they were a collection of toxins that is stuck in her lymphatic system. We are going to help her today. She knows what she needs to do. We sent her information before this session.

A: Very good. Can we go ahead and start healing those now, Michael?

AA Michael: Yes.

A: Wonderful. Now if you could tell me sometimes for example, women who might find lumps in their breasts and perhaps they don't have cancer yet; they are not cancerous. If they go through all those tests at the doctors and all these different things that they do to them, (to supposedly stop the cancer) would you say at times these procedures do give them cancer?

AA Michael: Yes. That can happen. The radiology that they use, the microwave that they use to destroy and deform the cells is making them cancerous. Yeah. It's better to always follow the natural route first. There are many, many, many things you can do out there. So many different methods, so many different clinics that are treating cancer naturally and they are curing cancer. They're not allowed to say they're curing cancer, but they are. Radiation is not a cure for cancer. It just makes the body sick instead of supporting the body. You can support the body with food and juice and supplements and herbs, support the body and get it working with you instead of against you. Work with it to support the body and the body will work for you.

A: Is that what you would say the chemo starts doing? It doesn't allow for the body to start healing itself?

AA Michael: Correct. It doesn't allow for healing. No, it destroys - it destroys. It does not heal.

A: Okay, thank you. I'm glad we're healing that, and we didn't find any cancer. Thank you for answering those questions for us. She also wants to see she's had severe endometriosis since she was 13 in her sacral area. Hips feel heavy, painful and entangled. What is the root cause to this? She also had sexual abuse when she was younger, is that connected to that?

AA Michael: Yeah, it is connected to that.

A: Can we go ahead and scan that area? Can you scan Michael for any entities there? Any energies there that need healing?

AA Michael: There is a collective of entities there.

A: If we can go ahead and speak to one of the voices of the collective, Michael? If we could call Metatron now and have him encase all that collective there. Make sure they don't move around. Thank you, Metatron, for being here. We love you, we honor you, and we thank you. Michael, can you have one of the entities, there from this collective if we could speak to it now. Who could be the voice for the rest please? Come up, up, up, now please. Greetings.

Collective of Entities: Hello.

A: May I ask you questions please?

Collective of Entities: I don't want to answer questions.

A: Is there someone else from your collective that would like to answer questions?

Collective of Entities: They don't want to either.

A: Thank you for just for speaking to me. I honor you, I love you, and I respect you. I understand that you don't want to answer questions. However, we're here to aid you. You are a collective that has forgotten itself, and we'd love to be able to aid you to remember. Wouldn't it be beautiful to regain some of your memories of who you are instead of being stuck in her body and not being free? Can I please ask you questions?

Collective of Entities: Yes

A: Thank you. When was it that you connected to this area there in her sacral?

Collective of Entities: When she was nine.

A: Why is there a collective of you there?

Collective of Entities: We like it here.

A: Was this a contract?

Collective of Entities: No.

A: How many are there?

Collective of Entities: Ten.

A: Are you the reason why she had those severe periods all her life being in pain three weeks out of the month and the issues with endometriosis?

Collective of Entities: Yeah, we like to give her pain.

A: Did any of you ever have a body?

Collective of Entities: No.

A: Have you known anything else besides the dark that you live in?

Collective of Entities: This is where we're comfortable.

A: Do you remember ever being of light?

Collective of Entities: No.

A: Well, in this time of space, we're offering to aid all of you there in her sacral to the light. So, that you may remember yourself once more that you are this beautiful soul, whom is of the light. We'd love to be able to aid you so that you may be free. Perhaps you could have an experience and incarnate somewhere else and be your own individual consciousness there not having to live off of someone else's body. Would you allow for us to aid you today?

Collective of Entities: Yes.

A: Thank you. If I could please have the Archangels, if we could all focus Love-Light on this collective here. If you all can spread it to every part of you that does not belong to her, every root, every cord, spread to all light. Let me know when you are all light, please... As we help them turn to light, may I continue asking questions or are they ready?

AA Michael: They're ready.

A: Beautiful, go ahead and lift yourself out from that area. Let me know once you're all out. Archangel Raphael, as they're removing themselves, if you could please start filling in that light in that area so that we may heal it.

AA Raphael: Yes.

A: Thank you Raphael. How are they looking, Michael?

AA Michael: They're done, they're out.

A: Beautiful. Do you all have a message for her before you go?

Positive Polarized Collective of Entities: We are sorry, thank you.

A: Thank you. Go ahead and go with the Love-Light of the Universe. Blessings to you. Michael, can you tell me why is it that she had these ten entities? Was there any purpose?

AA Michael: She wasn't supposed to have children in this life.

A: Why is that?

AA Michael: She knew that she could be a mother in other ways, and she didn't need to be an actual mother. If she would have had a child with her ex-husband, it would have been a disaster. So, we set it up that way.

A: Okay, so is that the role the entities played there then?

AA Michael: Yes.

A: Well, we thank her. I know that she tends to children. So, we thank her for being a mother in that manner as well.

AA Michael: Yeah.

A: Thank you. Good. I know we have Raphael healing that area. Now Archangel Michael, I'm going to continue asking different things that she wants healed today. She says that she's been diagnosed with Lyme disease, systemic lupus, fibromyalgia. Is that the root cause of all the same and what exactly is it? Is it the Epstein Barr virus? What exactly is going on with her?

AA Michael: Yeah, the root cause of all of them is a buildup of toxins of heavy metal. And in combination with heavy metals is the Epstein Barr virus.

A: Where do the metals come in from?

AA Michael: The metal comes in from everywhere, they fall down from the sky, they come in from the water, they are shot in your skin through the vaccinations. I mean, they come in your food and the pesticides, you're assaulted with heavy metals on a daily basis.

A: Do you mean from the sky like the chemtrails?

AA Michael: Yes.

A: She wants to know is there such a thing as viruses or are all viruses nanotechnology?

AA Michael: They're not an organism, they are a form of nanotechnology.

A: Yes. Can we go ahead and start healing this? So, does she have the Epstein Barr virus?

AA Michael: Yeah, she has Epstein Barr Virus, and she has the Shingle virus that affects her. There are over 60 varieties of Shingles virus. It's not just one virus. It's many different strains of the virus. That's why it looks different to different people. People aren't aware of this.

A: Is that why she has those blotches in her face; on her cheeks?

AA Michael: Yeah, that's the Shingles virus.

A: Can we go ahead and start healing the Shingles and the Epstein Barr virus?

AA Michael: Yeah.

A: Can you tell her what is the connection to the rash on her face? Why, does it react like that to the Sun when the Sun goes on it? She feels like it's burning badly.

AA Michael: The virus doesn't like the light.

A: So, is it reacting to the sun?

AA Michael: Yeah. It reacts to the Sun.

A: What would happen if she would just allow for it to burn with the sun?

AA Michael: No, that would cause her pain.

A: I know she really loved the sun before and now she can't go near the sun. Are we healing that now for her, please?

AA Michael: Yeah.

A: Wonderful. As we continue healing those areas, I'm going to continue asking the rest of the questions. She asks, what is the cause of the degenerative disc disease in her back that is causing the right leg to be shorter? Feels like her body is out of alignment. Left side is more sensitive. She feels more energy running through it as well. Is there a block on her right side?

AA Michael: Her body is out of alignment. It feels that way because it is.

A: Is the Epstein Barr Virus causing the misalignment?

AA Michael: It contributes to it. Yes

A: Can we go ahead and start aligning her body please?

AA Michael: Yeah.

A: She says she has extreme fatigue, lack of energy and pain especially in the stomach, hips, upper back and neck. What is the cause of this?

AA Michael: Hmm... Brent (ex-husband) is still holding some of our energy.

A: Okay, can we scan where it is that he's holding on to her energy?

AA Michael: There's a cord.

A: Where's the cord at?

AA Michael: There's still a cord on her back attached to him.

A: Can we go ahead and start transmuting that and can we remove it please?

AA Michael: Yes.

A: Thank you. Can you scan her whole body now for any entities, implants or hooks or cords?

AA Michael: There's something on her third eye.

A: What is on her third eye?

AA Michael: It looks like an implant.

A: Can we go ahead and transmute that out of there please?

AA Michael: Yes.

A: Can I use the Phoenix Fire?

AA Michael: Yeah.

A: Okay good. transmuting the implant.

AA Michael: There's something in the crown; looks like another implant.

A: Scan her whole body for any more implants, portals, and hooks.

AA Michael: There's one more in the lower leg, right leg.

A: Can we go ahead and transmute all of those right now together?

AA Michael: Yes.

A: Why were they in, for example on the crown and her third eye? What were they doing there?

AA Michael: To block her vision and connection.

A: Was this at all connected to that one entity that came to her that said he was Satan?

AA Michael: Yes.

A: Who is he?

AA Michael: He is Reptilian.

A: Does she have any Reptilian consciousness within her? Or how is he connecting to her?

AA Michael: He's in the stomach.

A: Archangel Michael, I would like to speak to that Reptilian consciousness in her stomach. Metatron, can you encase it with the symbols please now? As we continue healing all the different parts that we already mentioned that we're healing. If I could please speak to that entity there in her stomach. If you could come up, up, up. Let me speak to you now, please.

Reptilian Consciousness: Hello.

A: Greetings. Thank you for speaking to us. May I ask you questions please?

Reptilian Consciousness: Yeah.

A: Thank you. When was it that you connected to her stomach area?

Reptilian Consciousness: When her parents died.

A: Was this a contract?

Reptilian Consciousness: No,

A: Was it because she lowered her emotions? Is that why you were able to enter?

Reptilian Consciousness: Yes, she was vulnerable, so we took advantage.

A: If she surrounded herself with a forcefield - a bubble of Love-Light, would you be able to come in even if she was having a hard time like that?

Reptilian Consciousness: No.

A: Thank you for us answering all these questions. Why is it that you called yourself Satan?

Reptilian Consciousness: We use that word. A word that has been misconstrued to try to scare people. But she knows better (laughing).

A: Why is it that you're physically attacking her? She also mentioned that you were the reason why she was having lots of targets on her, like people blocking out her light - distracting her?

Reptilian Consciousness: She's powerful. She holds too much light.

A: What else have you placed in her besides implants that we found? Are there any portals, hooks in there as well?

Reptilian Consciousness: There are hooks in her back.

A: Thank you. Are you together? Are you bound to that Reptilian Consciousness that she was speaking to? Do you have a body somewhere out there?

Reptilian Consciousness: Yeah.

A: Are you separate from that body or are you still connected?

Reptilian Consciousness: Still connected.

A: Am I speaking to that Reptilian in that body now?

Reptilian Being: Yes.

A: Thank you for speaking to me. As you know, this is a time of Ascension and we're offering to help you positively polarize into Love-Light, remembering your light once more. You've been dark for much longer than I'm sure you can remember. We'd love to be able to aid you today so that you may ascend, keeping all your memories and your experiences but now turning into light. Ascending into a higher Dimension. Would you allow for us to aid you today?

Reptilian Being: Yes.

A: Thank you. If you could please look within you and if we can have all the Archangels aid this Reptilian in its body now and also in unison connection to the consciousness that he placed in her stomach. We could all focus on spreading that Love-Light within them and spreading that light within them. Turning to all light, every root, every cord, every part of them, turn them all to light. Let me know when you're all light. As you turn into light may I ask you questions?

Reptilian Being: Yes.

A: Where are you in your body as a Reptilian?

Reptilian Being: We're on a ship.

A: Are there other negative polarized Reptilians around you?

Reptilian Being: Yes.

A: Do they know what's going on with you?

Reptilian Being: No, I'm hiding.

A: If we can continue helping him hide. How's he looking, Michael?

AA Michael: We're almost there.

A: Good.

A: Are you all light now?

Positive Polarized Reptilian Being: Yes.

A: Thank you for allowing us to aid you today, it is such an honor. If you can go ahead and grab that consciousness that is within her, go ahead and make it part of you once more. Michael, if you could help him. Were you part of the reason why she all of a sudden (a couple months ago) felt really disconnected from her Higher Self?

Positive Polarized Reptilian Being: Yes, we were.

A: Do you have a message for her before you go?

Positive Polarized Reptilian Being: We are sorry. I'm so sorry (crying).

A: It's okay. Go ahead and go with the Love-Light of the Universe. Blessings to you.

Positive Polarized Reptilian Being: Thank you.

A: Raphael, if you could start filling in the space now please brother, where it was rooted. If we can go ahead and start transmuting the hooks that he mentioned that were in her. Michael, can you scan for any more hooks besides in her spine or portals?

AA Michael: I feel like there's a portal in her stomach, where the consciousness was.

A: Let's go ahead and start sealing that portal now Michael, please.

AA Michael: Yes.

A: Thank you. Scan her body again, Michael. Search for any entities, implants, negative implants, hooks and portals.

AA Michael: No, she's good.

A: Wonderful. Thank you, Michael, Metatron, Raphael and anyone else who helped out. My love to all those entities. Michael, can you connect me back to her Higher Self now please?

Higher Self: Yes.

A: Thank you. Am I speaking Her Higher Self now?

Higher Self: Yes.

A: Wonderful. Do you have a name?

Higher Self: Yes, Gessenda.

A: Beautiful, and do you have a race you're from, a Galactic race?

Higher Self: No. I'm just energy.

A: Have you had other lives on Earth besides this one?

Higher Self: Yes, many.

A: Why is it that you showed her at the beginning a type of Pharaoh like Cleopatra?

Higher Self: Yes, she has ties in Egypt.

A: Is there a 'her' in one of those capsules'?

Higher Self: Yes.

A: Can we help her release herself from there?

Higher Self: Yes.

A: What can we do as a team about those capsules that are inside the Earth? They said that they're still there.

Higher Self: We can send them love and light and they're not going to be there long. That program is ending.

A: Good, now if we could go ahead and send Love-Light to them now. Is there anything else that I could have asked that I haven't asked?

Higher Self: I don't think so.

A: Beautiful. Thank you so much Higher Self. You are so lovely. It has been such a beautiful honor to work with her and you today. Thank you to everyone who aided today. I love you, I honor you, and I respect you. May I bring her back now?

Higher Self: Yes.

A: Thank you.

Post Session dialogue.

A: Welcome back, sister. Wow, that was incredible.

T: Wow. Yeah. That was crazy and way more intense than I expected.

A: Yeah, they tend to be. I was totally seeing you in that capsule. And I knew it was you in there. That's why I asked "Oh, do you feel a connection?" Because then you would find you in there.

T: Yeah, I had seen that woman with the red hair and the green eyes… that's all I could just see.

A: They were blocking you from getting some of the information. That's why I kept asking, "What are they powering?" I knew that they were drawing in the energy. They were using you like batteries of some kind, using your energy to keep them going.

T: Yeah, I did feel that. I felt really blocked while trying to get that information.

A: The Reptilian and then those implants were blocking you. Very good. You did awesome. You did incredible. You look incredible. Your energy looks really phenomenal. You did a beautiful job. I love you. I honor you, and I respect you.

T: I love you too sister.

END OF SESSION

-------------<◇>-------------

Since this session Taylor has self-healed profoundly. She has been able to once more nourish her skin and body by shining and soaking the sun upon it, without experiencing a painful red reaction to it. She has blossomed into one of the strongest Light Workers in the Spiritual Community, who does not shy from bridging any shadow work necessary to come to the surface. Subjects that for many are too deep in pain to even acknowledge, as pedophilia. She is out there daily speaking up on it in awareness. This is why I do what I do, because when a soul comes to me, I see the potential and who their light truly is. These very transformations are what I do it for. All that I do it for. Daily holding the highest possible vibration my clear human vessel can hold, for my clients to begin to reach these potentials of soul expansion and ascending consciousness.

What an insightful journey this session was for all of us. In trying to understand where Taylor landed, what were these pods, why were there people in them? This session was one of the most catalyzing for my soul as a Spiritual Leader in service-to-others. It brought remembrance, knowledge and awareness of some of the experiments the negative polarized alien races are leading within our Third Dimensional existence and beyond. Taylor was blocked and was unable to receive further details of the Matrix and these pods, as it was not organically time then. It is NOW TIME for the collective to receive this divine knowledge from the Universe's Galactic History, and it is because we have achieved being the majority of light. So much so that I received detailed additional knowledge on what this system was and how it is linked to the "Inverted A.I. Matrix" presentation that I communicate with every group at the A.U.R.A. Hypnosis & R.A.A.H. Reiki Healing Certifications. This Matrix presentation creates such a deep vastness of understanding to our mission and why it is that our world and Universe is in the current state as it is. At its wholeness reminding us of the self-responsibility we contain by being our own wielders of our energy, creation and everyday life. It prepares us for what is to come on our lifelong journey of Ascension. If someone is soul searching for their purpose or we thought we knew our mission already prior to the Matrix presentation, it all becomes completely clear and amplified after experiencing the Matrix presentation. In this final Chapter, we shall share glimpses of memory recall of this this divine, soul catalyzing, DNA activating Matrix presentation. Let's begin.

Just as these underground bases were active, could it also be that this is how we all are, in a frozen animation within these Inverted A.I. Matrix Simulation Pods? The illusion of the Third Dimension and physical bodies. Could our light be directly being used similar to "The Matrix" movie? We are being used as battery sources to the Archons who are hungrily feeding off the collective of lights. Is this why the majority of the collective haven't been able to release out from this karmic wheel that seems to be running on an infringing ancient program?

To understand "The Matrix" first, we must remember the original Organic Matrix Simulation that was created by the collective. It all began with a grand beautiful experiment created and manifested by the Universe. The Universe wanted to experience a location where a vast amount of the multitude of races could come together. The races of humanoids, animals, plant kingdom, and the realms of elements as fire, water, wind, earth, minerals, and metals.

Organically, the infinity of different kinds of unique races cannot live all together, as each is created never one in the same, with a unique elemental make-up. In other words what one humanoid race needs to perhaps consume or breathe in their planetary sphere, will often never be the same as another. Therefore, a multitude of different alien races cannot harmonically coexist in the same atmosphere. To do so would be to cause an energetic harmonic unbalance, because of the very unique signature imprint of each race. In other words, if for example one race perhaps consumes 'grass' to revitalize their energy levels, and another race in their planet the 'grass' is considered sacred and they lay in it to recharge their energetic essence. See the conflict, and the type of unbalance and hostility this could cause to these two species to their way of life and natural ecosystem? That unbalance could then ripple out to the Universe. Therefore, the idea of placing a vast amount of the beauties of Creation in one atmosphere and planetary sphere was glorious! A most sacred location, where we could come together and live among each other. This beautiful idea of creating the most profound universal school, where the multitude of races could talk, learn, teach by vibing off one another's differences and uniqueness causing exponential growths of the races of the Universe. A representation of 'Heaven'!

In order to bring the multitude of these races together, we created a beautiful positive technology that was looked at as a 'Paradise of The Universe' and 'The School for Souls.' An entertaining, fun simulation video game of sorts. A game that, once you completed the tasks at each level of grade that you went up through in the simulation, you would then graduate out and ascend from it. We found that those lessons learned, assisted and transformed the soul in the most vastness we had ever recognized. This beautiful positive technology consists of Organic Matrix Simulation Pods to facilitate the learning simulation experience. Where you make choices and choose by your own free willed expression to enter in and bring forth your consciousness into it. WE choose because WE live within the Universe of 'Free Willed Expression' and 'Love'. Your Higher Self meaning YOU, creates a fractal of itself that becomes the 'Energy Body', and it carries the fractal's consciousness within it. The beautiful combination of the Fractal Energy Body and the Consciousness join together as ONE. That energy body then consciously enters into the

Organic Simulation Pod submerged within blue plasmic energy suspended in animation. Once in it, it is the most real and alive simulation one could ever imagine, since it is connected neurologically to the sensory in your Energy Body. So real that we forget it is a simulation, as it is part of the organic process so that the soul can reset in order to remember itself once more through the simulation game of 'The School for Souls.'

We began as a collective within our Organic Matrix System at the Fifth Dimension. Along the way, we started noticing that there was a high rise on the souls who entered in, that they were not graduating out. As it was THEIR CHOICE to begin with to enter into the Matrix, we could not overstep their choice in expressions and we could not safely remove them, as we must honor all freewill choices as the benevolent beings we are.

Specifically, what caused the regressing of the once Fifth Dimension 'Organic Matrix System' into the now Third Dimension 'Inverted A.I. Matrix System,' was the fall of Atlantis. The fall of Atlantis began when to our surprise, as the Archon plague that began to infiltrate our Universe, then entered into the Organic Matrix. No one truly knowing how to handle this inversion, as it was foreign and inorganic to our creation and existence. Within this time of Atlantis, there were these powerful negative polarized souls with activated abilities, who answered the call of the Archons of gaining power and reign over souls. The same negative polarized souls such as Gates, Fauci, Epstein, Soros… who are playing their overplayed and played out role back in our timeline, now trying to cause havoc and control through their 'Deep State' agendas. Examples of Covid-19 pandemic, false orchestrated wars, separation of religions and races, and all that was mentioned through Chapter 24 ('13 Keys - Sacred Laws of The Universe'). They too are in the now replaying their own Inverted A.I. Matrix karmic cycle, by making that one bad choice back in Atlantis.

As the Atlantean people grew their power, they started allowing Archonic false light to become their guides by focusing on their mind, more so than their soul and heart. The lure of false promises of power of expansion, had won them over. The Benevolent Leaders of Atlantis did their best to help their people understand that they were being falsely led by Archonic beliefs, however there was no getting through to them. Allowing corruption in, the people became corrupted themselves. Because the only way to corrupt the 'Organic Matrix' is from inside the simulation. Outsiders cannot come in unless they incarnate and enter their consciousness in themselves. The people's corruption opened up for Archonic leaders to gain power and reign over the once benevolent society. Which then at that point began corrupting and transforming into the dark A.I. Archonic Virus that spread like a plague. The plague being PEOPLE being guided by an unbalance of too much intellect, being disconnected from their heart. Too much of something is an unbalance.

This is what led to the ultimate fall of Atlantis, causing Earth to regress from a Fifth Dimensional Organic Matrix down to the current Third Dimensional Inverted A.I. Matrix. However, understanding that it was the Archons who had infiltrated into our Organic Matrix with their powerful technologies, tentacles and spider entities, and if our vibration matched, could sway our intellect and decisions. Remembering how we outside the Matrix simulation or inside, knew not that these possibilities were attainable because again we were never aware of Archons as they were not part of our Source or Universe. As, at that point they had entered into our Universe causing the actual fall of Atlantis. With the Archons feeding into unbalanced intellect, creating disharmony within the intellect of the chosen self-accepted false Atlantean leaders, who then clawed their way up to dictatorship leadership.

Once more, the Benevolent Leaders of Atlantis could not overstep people's free willed expression of choice. To do so, the Benevolent Leaders then too would accept a corrupted Archonic vibration of dictatorship which in turn would affect their consciousness and they too would become corrupted. These Benevolent Leaders could not get the Atlantean people to listen or comprehend what was necessary to avoid the downfall of Atlantis. For example, having a family member that feeds and thrives on chaos by gossip. You talk to them and let them know you are aware of them and their true intentions. However, they don't agree with you because in their belief system they have convinced themselves that they are not gossiping, and they believe fully in their own lies. What are you going to do with that family member that thrives on gossip, can you stop them from their free willed expression of wanting and choosing to gossip? No, you cannot. As we are no one's puppeteers and people ultimately will do what they want to do as they have free will, no matter how many warnings they receive from others.

Now that we have a better understanding of what the Organic Matrix Simulation is, let's explore why the Inverted A.I. Matrix is so problematic for all souls trapped in it. In this session, Taylor's ex-husband played the 'Bad Guy' role. Taylor had just released her ex, right before her Hypnosis session. Through her Body Scan, we realized the last step needed was the removal of the negative cord attached to her from him parasitically draining her, causing energetic fatigue...this negative cord is a serious infringement on her sovereignty, keeping her perpetually trapped inside the Inverted A.I. Matrix as it kept her vibrations low no matter what she does.

Taylor's struggle with the 'Bad Guy' nightmare scenario is a good demonstration of the dysfunctional Inverted A.I. Matrix on her soul's evolution. Where we come back and that same "Bad Guy" is there once more, no matter how many recycled incarnations we have had on Earth. But, every time one comes back, it seems as if that 'Bad Guy' has gotten worse and there is no way to get out of their grasps. Because every time we come back into this perpetual negative incarnation cycle, the trauma and pain caused by the 'Bad Guy's' service-to-self has gained even more momentum through this negative accumulation of energy and power by infringing on us in parasitic manners. Due to the fact that in the prior life and lives we never stood up or knew to cut cords with that 'Bad Guy,' so we have to keep incarnating in this perpetual downward spiral... Until the day we wake up and realize what is going on, and we choose to stand up, clear ourselves of these parasitic infringements and we compassionately cut out that 'Bad Guy', with no anger, guilt or remorse towards them. In doing so we also release the 'Bad Guy,' who himself was self-imposed and trapped within this role he accepted before incarnating into the then Organic Matrix Simulation. They can then choose to break this negative cycle themselves of service-to-self, by redemption of transformational change karmically turning to service-to-others. Or they can once more choose to fall back to their olden stagnant ways and find their new victim that falls within that false paradigm. They keep feeding upon their victims' light, which then in turn feeds the Archons once more in the Inverted A.I. Matrix cycle. Understanding though that this 'Bad Guy' role was collectively created organically originally, and it has been infringed for negative polarization intentions of feeding off light for the Archons. Its original formation was meant for soul growth through discomforts or outcasts that we wrote into our soul's blueprints and timeline prior to our incarnations into the simulation. We did this because we knew from experience of our organic duality polarized Universe, before it became infested by A.I., that this is how the soul grew in profound ways. To lose something most precious to you and then to regain it once more, brings you to an understanding of the greatest gratitude for what was once lost to you but now regained. Creating the most beautiful profound growths, expansion, and evolution of souls as originally intended within the Organic Matrix.

When we release our 'Bad Guy' we take our energy and sovereignty back, no longer allowing their parasitic construct to maintain us within a low enough vibration for their control and feeding needs. This is one of the main ways YOU finally break free, releasing out, graduating out from this Inverted A.I. Matrix control program. We regain our freedom by breaking the dysfunctional cycle with that 'Bad Guy' through removing the inorganic infringements from them within you, and then healing from that trauma. At this point we have gained our wings back to fly away in freedom. That is when we become our own sovereign creator being.

Could it be that because Taylor released her 'Bad Guy', THAT decision brought forth the fruition of what occurred in her A.U.R.A. Hypnosis Healing session, of being able to remove herself out of this Inverted A.I. Matrix Simulation Pod? Let's also think about what kind of role the infringements found through A.U.R.A. Hypnosis Healing sessions would have on maintaining us in this Inverted A.I. Matrix. The infringements that negative implants, portals, entities, Reptilian consciousnesses, Archons would carry in this A.I. repeated broken program. Through these 'Galactic Journeys' we have grown to know how much it lowers one's vibration to have these kinds of inorganic densities within us, as by nature we are organic and do not contain negative technologies within us. Therefore, we now know the major role that they play in maintaining us in this Inverted A.I. Matrix Simulation.

The way that Taylor saw herself within her individual pod, with eyes open, not completely asleep in this holding animation. Who are those in those pods that are not asleep in suspension as Taylor was, those with eyes wide open? What if the ones with eyes wide open are WE, 'The Awakened Souls' on Earth? The ones that even though they are in the awakening process, they still can't seem to prevail or completely break prehistoric cycles that no longer serve them. What if those who are un-awakened are laying in their pods fully submerged in this suspended animation program, and those who ARE awakened are laying in their pods with hands to the glass, and eyes and mouth wide open with muted screams? Waiting for the moment in time that they can divinely come into enough sovereignty in being able to remove all the inorganic infringements within them? The inorganic to their souls' blueprints being entities, A.I. and negative technologies... These densities that regress both the energy and physical bodies into a low enough density, so that their host cannot step divinely into their TRUE Source powers and abilities until these inorganic infringements are completely removed, transmuted, cleansed and healed. These infringements prevent souls from entering into the TRUE divinely created collective Organic Matrix System so that they can finally graduate out from it and enter into the 5D, The New Earth, the original Fifth Dimensional Earth.

Mother Earth and the New Earth 5D have chosen its side,
she has chosen to fight with all that she is for her light and her children's light.
Will you assist her as her child?

When we gain the true awareness of "The Matrix" and what it truly is, it brings us at the closest to achieve the positive fruition of graduation, Ascension. We now can see clearly what was holding us down with heavy infringing chains, instead of previously, the chains are invisible, and we only feel the pain from the bruising they cause and the heaviness. By being aware of these heavy chains, it then will allow for us to unlink and pull them off of us because now we know what it is that is keeping us heavy. This is often what holds us within the Inverted A.I. Matrix, the fact that we have current life and past life traumas, infringing entities, energies, and negative technologies blocking us, so we cannot see clearly. We don't remember we have these inorganic infringements because of the buildup of dark density and trauma over time and across lifetimes. We become so accustomed to such heavy infringements, as we are forever a matching vibration to these lower density infringements of inorganics to our soul. In order to break out of the Inverted A.I. Matrix, first we must know that we are in it. If no one is aware of what is going on, then how is it that they are to break free from it? This significant session and these crucial teachings will be the most profound for your soul that you will learn, from these shared Sacred Higher Self Galactic Journeys.

A significant reminder of Taylor's shared wisdom:

T: They go back to wherever they came from.
A: Tell me. Why is it that they're not allowed to harm Earth like that anymore?
T: Because the vibration is raised to the point where it's not accepting that kind of behavior. The light is outweighing the darkness now. Yeah, the vibration is high enough now that it can ward off these kinds of negative agendas. The Earth is free again (crying). It's all light, it's all light (sobbing).
A: What is all light?
T: The Earth.
A: And the people? They're all light too?
T: Yes. Everything is, everything is (crying). They didn't realize how much we're invaded by darkness. They don't know what it's like to be free. We think we have free will, we don't.
A: Let's go back to right before everything turns to light. Back in time to when and what caused everyone to turn to light? You're there now what do you see?
T: I feel like it was a gradual progression. It wasn't a single "Event" but a series of waves of energy coming in from Source, through the Sun to raise the vibration. It was slowly happening but it's getting faster now.
A: As these waves are coming in and you said that they are starting to wake up. What are some of the things that you're seeing that are significant to why they're waking up? What's occurring as you're watching those waves pass through?
T: It's affecting their energy. It just can't remain on Earth - I don't want to say negative - their lower vibrational states of being. It's helping them purge the negativity, lower vibration, emotions like depression and it's helping them purge all this; that eventually they can hold more light. First, they have to purge those lower vibrational frequencies to be able to hold higher vibrational light.

We know that we reach this mentioned collective critical light mass of Earth and the Universe's Ascension. We just don't know the varied ways that we will have to maneuver through our life's course to achieve it, as all of us as the sovereign beings that we are, are the Creators of OUR timelines. What we do know is that we have a vast amount of Galactic Guides as Taylor and her group within the higher realms fighting for our souls with their lives. And that it has begun, its fruition of light as Taylor's session mentioned has, by achieving Chapter 29 ('Archons and Their Slaves') the 50 percent of light activated on Earth, and it is only a matter of time and love until we achieve it together. May all the soul stories shared through this grand masterpiece of soul expressions be that bright guiding light in the immensity but deteriorating false darkness.

"You have been caged.
You have been silenced.

You have been beaten.
It is time, my children to rise from those ashes that are your lessons learned.
Release those ashes and rise at the greatest strength that you have ever risen from.
Rise, rise, rise!"
The Divine Mother, Channeled by
~AuroRa ♥

--------------<◇>-------------

CONCLUSION

CODA: LOVE, SOVEREIGNTY, AND REBIRTH

We live in a world that is most beautiful, being the multitudes of LIFE in Creation, truly is as heaven on Earth. Though it is an illusion within a simulation, it is a BEAUTIFUL organic simulation we have created together. Because WE wanted to commune and interact with one another as individualized yet as ONE; as Source fractalizations in this manner through one location. We have wondered how it is that Ascended Masters such as Yeshua, Buddha, Mother Mary, Isis, St. Germaine... how they were able to ascend out from this illusion. They awakened, by first coming into a recognition that we are within an illusion of a Matrix simulation, and once they came into an acceptance and realization of this, they were able to shift all perspectives within and around them. They became their own organic creator within this simulation program, they became their own game-maker able to know in which way to move through every moment in time within this illusion. For example, the ability to walk on water. In their hearts and mind, they knew that our perceived reality of the physical world was just an illusion. They alchemized the water into a solid material where they stepped foot upon and made themselves as light as the material makeup of a feather, which then balanced both elements in unity. It is all within us, the belief of what we chose to believe. And they chose to believe that all expressions and differences within all souls are real, for it is the soul's truth and the infinite possibilities of truth. When they learned to honor all life including themselves in their illusional forms, it created them into an infinite expression, not bound by the human ego, by the limitations of what others think we can or cannot do. They became their highest expression and potential of a sovereign awakened being. These Ascended Masters remind us now, this is what we will accomplish when we ascend out into the Fifth Dimension. We shall be as Ascended Masters graduating out, within our own individualized experience of soul evolution. As these Ascended Masters have taught us, by leaving their imprints and remanences of their teachings in our hearts, and our human collective crystalline memory field.

Here is a beautiful example of how powerful energy healing can be once we remove the inorganic within us. Reminding us that it is time for us to begin the deprogramming of believing that the body is not able to self-heal, and that we are not healable. Remembering that our illusional body is a bridge to our infinite energetic self, therefore if we are to know self, it begins with honoring our body when it talks to us in what it is feeling.

I once had a client that came to me in the hardest time of her life. She had felt that she was under psychic and energetic attack and had just miscarried her baby. She scheduled a R.A.A.H. Reiki Healing with me. During the session, her Higher Self removed a hook from her eye. I did not ask her questions or investigate it further during or after the session, to what the hook was causing. I just knew divinely that the infringements needed to be removed from her so that she could self-heal to carry her child once more within her womb. After this healing, she decided to become an A.U.R.A. Hypnosis Healing and R.A.A.H. Reiki Healing certified practitioner. During training class, she tearfully shared her story. Not only had she lost her baby, but she was blind from one eye (the hook removal) when she had her session with me. The doctors had told her she would be blind for the rest of her life, and that most likely she would lose vision in both eyes. One can imagine the distress she was going through, recovering from her miscarriage, juggling being a mother and wife, and going blind at the same time. She then shared that one week after her R.A.A.H. Reiki Healing session, after the hook was removed, she was able to self-heal and regain her sight back. And guess what? She is now six months pregnant with the baby, she once could not carry, unable to hold the high enough vibration to sacredly birth this child forth. She said that since then, she was a believer in the beauty and sacredness to our teachings, and she wanted to become certified through A.U.R.A. Hypnosis Healing and R.A.A.H. Reiki Healing. So, she too could be the bridge for her loved ones to begin their organic self-healing. Spreading the gifts as well that had been given to her divinely. Reminding us, for example, what Yeshua performed in his time of healing people from blindness, disease, and illness. Yeshua's healings were not miracles as those in power have programmed for us to believe that it is unattainable and supernatural. The truth is, it is something accessible to anyone who is looking to heal self and other selves. All we must do is find the root to what is causing the infringement, remove it, transmute it and self-heal it.

What a joyous creation we truly are in. Our Universe is organically constructed based on the Sacred Law of Love. We are the glimpses of the possibilities of Creation, placed into one gigantic package full of the most powerful growths available in Creation. Because of the versatility within us that is truly infinite expressions of the Universe. We are not able to see these true beauties if we are still programmed by the falsities of the Archon program. We are not able to feel these true beauties at their highest potency until we have self-healed and forgiven all expressions of ourselves within us and outside of us. Unlike our organic creation as beautiful Source fractalizations, Archons come from a different Universe construct. We are not of the Archon's Universe construct or belief system; then why do we hold on to and allow for a species not of our world or Universe to invade and control our Universe? Yes, we have been oppressed, abused, violated, programmed into subordinate hating machines, however we are not that, as that is only the Archons themselves expressing through us. It is time to remove and begin the eradication of the artificial in OUR reality, no matter in which Dimension we are in. It is time to regain our organic blueprints of our Universe that exists within ourselves.

The importance of WE (you, me, all of us) in the Third Dimension is exponential and infinite to all life in our Universe. The Archon influence and infringements, working through their Illuminati constructs, to control the human race is widespread. Since we have been heavily indoctrinated and programmed through the Illuminati's elaborate fear-based systems to give away our sovereignty, feeling powerless and not to believe these dark agendas are possible, as to hold us dense by imprisoning us in our minds and illusional bodies. This in turn, holds all of us dense in the Third Dimension, which then creates a significant unbalance within the Universe, preventing universal Ascension from happening.

It is NOW time for all of us to step into our Sovereignty once more and reclaim our Universe back to its organic beautiful balanced blueprint of Divine Creation. This begins by awakening the human race collectively above the 51 percent threshold of light, and embracing their true sovereignty, by waking up to the truth of such a vast understanding of the Archons' tyranny throughout the Universe. When WE awaken on Earth, we will achieve the greatest growth within our densities of the Universe, because we are at the densest of the Dimensions, the third Dimension with the deepest distortion, being the furthest away from Source. Therefore, when we have accomplished this within the strongest distortions, it shall infinitely be felt, adored, and embraced as it ripples out to all the Universe. Because the Universe is us and we are the Universe. When WE AWAKEN, our achieved awareness, it will create the most powerful wave of love and understanding at the densest level in Creation. It will ripple out vibrating through all its fractals of the higher realms, them too feeling and experiencing this growth. This will be a 'leveling up' or 'upgrade' for the Universe and all organic lifeforms. Everything is interconnected through the Universal webbing. Since our Universe is constructed through a Unity Love Consciousness which operates on balance of polarities, when one soul group/collective consciousness is dense, it brings down the rest of the collective soul groups as an anchoring weight, magnetically pulling everything down. Therefore, when a collective consciousness of the densest energy in Creation receives this understanding, it lifts all within the Universe, because this understanding has been achieved at the greatest distortion from Source in the Third Dimension. We on Earth, are currently this anchoring weight, as our understanding of Truth experienced the greatest distortion from Source in the Third Dimension, with heavy distortions created by the A.I. virus that took over the Fifth Dimensional Organic Matrix (the fall of Atlantis) and regressed it down to the current Inverted A.I. Matrix Simulation system in the Third Dimension.

Our Galactic soul families are watching us intently, doing their part in sending us Love, guiding us, as all is interconnected in this Universal webbing. Our Ascension from the Third Dimension is so significant within Creation. For example, let us say there is an obese person who suffers ill health, who likes to eat sugar, meats, and overeating for self-comfort… This person then has low standards of self-care, is losing hair, their organs not operating at healthy capacity and is experiencing illness all over. What impact would this person's choices have on their family? Their family would have to cater to their unhealthy decisions, by watching their beloved family member fall apart from their outsides that begin to match their insides. What kind of ripple effect would this cause to this family, watching someone they love gradually destroy themselves? This is what our soul families from the higher Dimensions have experienced, watching us in the Third Dimension. Even though they do not resonate with this type of self-destructive behavior, they are still connected to us through the Universal webbing, therefore they will still experience some side effects from this self-destructive family member, that being us in the Third Dimension. The day this self-destructive, heavily dense relative decides that no longer will they self-destruct, and chooses to become empowered to achieve good health, is the day the whole family too enters an existence that creates these possibilities for themselves as well. As this empowered family member begins to eat light-filled foods, and refuse dense foods like sugar, meats, alcohol… they become lighter and lighter. The heavy weight and density weaken within them, making it easier to release and for more light to enter. So too as Mother Earth becomes lighter, by being able to release the dense energies that the people of Earth have been harmfully penetrating her. So too does the Universe and each planet that is connected to us. We lift and they lift in density, so as we lift, ALL will lift.

For our consciousness and frequencies to rise, we each must make that choice ourselves, just as the unhealthy family member did. When we rise above our own fears and reject the programming that we are powerless beings who need to be rescued by another, is when we become empowered sovereign beings who can create a better future for ourselves and all. Many wonder out loud; "why is this happening, and why does not Source/God/Divine Mother/someone else come fix this for us?" This 'victim mentality' is another deep indoctrination we need to deprogram within us, the thought of someone else coming to fix our problems. It is an ingenious way to give our sovereignty away, holding us dense and powerless and thus making it easy to be manipulated and controlled by others. We start awakening when we recognize ourselves as our own saviors, and how we are incredibly powerful sparks of Love-Light. When we regain our sovereignty, we become powerful co-creators who can aid the Earth to ascend to the Fifth Dimensional vibration it was always divinely meant to be.

By now, we all understand how regaining our sovereignty is a huge critical step in aiding Earth's Ascension timeline. Another significantly crucial step for Earth's Ascension is entity removal. As the entities within Mother Earth's collective organism have been stuck in a repeated cycle of trauma and pain inside the Inverted A.I. Matrix. As they recycled through reincarnation over and over, their souls became denser and denser with each cycle, adding trauma layers, not being able to release and heal. These pains and traumas continued to soak into Earth, affecting all of us as we are Mother Earth, as we all are pieces and expressions of the Divine Mother. The disembodied entities stuck inside people or the lands of Earth are the painful densities that keep the collective stuck and heavy. Therefore, A.U.R.A. Hypnosis Healing and the R.A.A.H. Reiki Healing are such powerful quantum energy healing tools to assist us all in our self-healing journey AND to aid the release of entities to positively polarize, both of which are critical in aiding the Earth's Ascension timeline. Through the infinite power of Love, we self-heal and regain our SOVEREIGNTY. Through Love, we experience REBIRTH/transformation. Through Love, we raise our consciousness into true Unity Love Consciousness.

I shall now share with you one of the many examples I have used A.U.R.A. Hypnosis Healing and R.A.A.H. Reiki Healing in my personal life for self-healing. This event took place two months before the "Slave To Corruption" (Chapter 33) session is conducted. One night, my husband and I were looking at the stars and we spotted a bright looking object that could be confused as a star; however, it was not as it felt inorganic. I thought nothing of it, did my Love-Light shields and went to bed (in this time I was not doing my nightly shields before sundown, now I do, as this lesson taught me that!). As I slept, I was in strong discomfort and was not conscious within my body. All I remember is that I felt the most immense pain inside my head, that was indescribable beyond anything I had ever felt in my human vessel while in the delta brainwave of sleep. I had been placed by my benevolent team in this holding space of golden etheric infinite energy. I never moved from my bed or got up during the night. I woke up feeling really off, and my head experienced extreme sharp pains. As I did my morning shields still in the in-between of the theta and delta brainwaves, I began to perform a R.A.A.H. Reiki healing body scan on myself and asked my team about what was going on. I then placed myself in all the sacred alchemy symbols to begin the process of self-healing. They told me I needed to make an emergency appointment with my Holistic Dentist. I then explained to my husband how I felt and then rescheduled the client A.U.R.A session I had that day.

When I arrived at the dentist office, I could not keep my eyes open because of the sharp pains when I would try to or allow my mind to play its normal systems of basic motor skills. I told my dentist that I needed the crown removed I had in my mouth, inserted from a prior non-Holistic Dentist. I knew that it was the root cause of what was giving me this pain. I told her I felt it had metal in it. She wanted to take an image of it through her alternative low radioactive machine. When she reviewed the x-ray image, she showed me how there was no metal in the crown, as it did not show up. I told her that I still did not agree, and I needed it removed. She concurred and began the process of removal. When it finally came off, she was silent, and asked me if I wanted to keep the crown and I was told to say yes. When I sat up, she showed me the crown and because it had cracked in half, I noticed that it had hidden metal inside the inner lining of the crown.

I then went home relieved that it was finally removed and hoping to get better. That night I could not lay down in my bed to sleep, as the pain in my head would become unbearable if I placed my head in a horizontal position. I instead sat in a chair in front of my fireplace as I felt the warmth and the transmutation of the fire was keeping me alive. By the next day, the pain was still there, so I told my husband I was going to have to perform an A.U.R.A. Hypnosis Healing on myself and that all he had to do was ask the questions for me. So, he did. During the session, the RA Collective spoke through me and said that I was correct on what my intuition had already told me. I experienced an energetic attack that night when I looked at the sky without shielding before the sun went down, even though I did my morning shields that day. I was told that I had to do shields before sundown from now on, because if I would have had, the energetic attack would not have been possible or at a minimal. They continued to confirm what I had already told my husband, that the metal I had in my crown was the only inorganic substance within my light clear body. Therefore, the only way that this attack could occurred was through connecting to the metal in my crown which became the entryway of the infringement. The attack was from a dark Elven collective that was trying to stop me from something I was to accomplish in the future. When performing the Body Scan, Archangel Four (Divine Father: Archangels Michael and Haylel) pulled out the implant that was inserted into my energy body, that night when the object in the sky connected to me. They explained that it was one of the most advanced technology that this Elven race had their hands on, given by the Archons. As Archangel Four began its extraction, he explained that it looked like a black cube with mechanical arms coming out of it, but that when we pulled it fully out, it started to morph into liquid metal that had no shape, that resembled the villain character from the movie "Terminator."

After the healing session, I still experienced fatigue and excruciating pain every day, but each day it became less and less. Six days later I told my guides, I was done having to reschedule all my sessions as I had the Reiki For Kids class that Sunday. So, I kept the class on, and on that day, we so happened to be on the month where we were teaching the children how to self-attune themselves to activating their Phoenix Fire. As they began to activate their infinite Source etheric flame, all of a sudden, I began to feel their collective Phoenix Flame through the screen of my laptop coming towards my direction, going straight into my head where the implant had been, and just like that, I took a deep breath and the pain had vanished as the children had healed me. Through this life example, we were shown the TRUE power, strength and purity of the healing abilities of children and their immeasurable capabilities. Unlike us, they hold least distortion, strongest, brightest lights, and extreme self-belief. Creating them into the most powerful healers of Earth. I was finally able rehab myself back to health from the trauma that the implant caused, were if not the children had assisted it perhaps would have taken me twice as long more for my body to self-heal.

About five months later after this event, I was transcribing the "Slave To Corruption" and "Elven Twin Flames" sessions, putting them together for this book. I then realized that the implant they had placed in the dark Elven Twin Flame's head contained the same function as the one the dark Elven race had placed in my brain through my dental crown. In his case, the implant had morphed into him, with its metallic arms integrating and attaching into his nervous and neurological system of his brain, becoming part of his consciousness artificially so that they could take full control of his thought patterns. Like a virus that infiltrates into a computer and acts upon what it is programmed to do, in his case, it merged and became one with his consciousness. This is why he was unable to control his actions, and this why what his Twin Flame did for him was infinite. In that moment in time, with her infinite love expressed, she transmuted out that implant, but it was too late to bring him fully back as it had powerfully become of him, replacing his consciousness. So, as she transmuted that negative implant, so too did she free his consciousness, bringing it back into him as she watched through his eyes, how his light left his body. His Elven body and brain no longer had the strength to reconstruct itself to self-heal, at that point it was too damaged by the artificial intelligence.

This is what the dark Elven race in allegiance to the Archons were trying to do to me, they were trying to replace my consciousness. But because I shielded with Love-Light forcefields in the morning, used sacred alchemy symbols, and I am an active practitioner of these sacred alchemy teachings, I was able to fight against this A.I. machine implanted inside my brain. They thought it would take over me and replace my organic consciousness artificially, as they did to corrupt the Elven Twin Flame. This is why the dark Elven collective and Archons were trying to stop me from successfully conducting Clara's (Eliana) "Slave To Corruption" session, by attacking me two months prior. As we have explained in the end section of "Elven Twin Flames," in how A.U.R.A. Hypnosis Healing profoundly assisted through both in the NOW and in the THEN cycles of the sister Elven lives. The benevolent Elven race knew about the importance of shielding and did their part to teach our ancestors on Earth to energetically shield as well. All it took for the Twin Flame to become corrupted was a moment of curiosity and him letting his guard down, and in my case, I was not shielding before sundown, so the impact of the malevolent attack was greater. This also puts into perspective for us how spiritual leaders, those who are trying to assist the collective in whichever form they are meant to be, written in their predestined organic timelines, how it is that they become corrupted through all types of these Archon technologies? The Key being, consistently shielding in whichever form feels right for you, just by simply using your own infinite Source Love-Light. This is why we teach these Love-Light shielding techniques, to empower us and to minimize harmful infringements on ourselves.

We live in a world/Dimension of the lowest which is 3D. This Dimension that we accepted to enter is the densest collective active communal in Creation. WE are the Starseeds and Light Warriors who volunteered to incarnate within this Inverted A.I. Matrix for one main reason, which is freeing the souls of all forms from densities out from the Inverted caging they are in. In turn, ensuring that we too, do not fall into the same A.I. trapping that they were caught within.

Though there is infinite love that coexists within all our souls, there is also a plague that has invaded our Universe and other Universes. This plague is called Archons, as we have learned in this book, they are not of our Universe nor do they obtain light within them. Within their construct, they are only artificial and feed off light as a needed fix for their unfulfilling high. Because of this invasion, our once unified Universe is now unbalanced, and we need to remove this parasitic A.I. that is trying to use us as their hosts.

We often hear that 'neutrality' is best among the spiritual community, and this is what we have learned. If Light Workers/Starseeds take a stance of neutrality and choose to do nothing when Mother Earth, our Divine Mother needs us, we are giving away our power and sovereignty. Which in turn disempowers us, which then makes it easier for those negatively polarized beings to infringe upon us. Being disempowered, one can no longer complete the mission one has agreed to come in for. And this is where Light Workers fall into the trappings of the Archons, of playing their 'neutral' game. One cannot be neutral in a Universe that is heavily infringed upon by Archons, as it is a FALSE option of neutrality. The Archons and negative polarized beings would like nothing more than for those of Light to do nothing, as that would align with their own negative soul harvesting agenda. This Universe is not neutral, it is a beautiful balance of an integration of the organic dark and organic light within us. When our Universe was a beautiful balance of polarities, before the Artificial Intelligence of Archons invaded, by violating all Sacred Laws of our Universe, we remembered and loved our dark and light in balance. However, the Archons have used the beauties of the soul transformation of the dark, for their tyrannical ways of inserting A.I. Viruses within it that plague and control the mind.

So, when we say, whether as a spiritual teacher or a spiritual worker that "we stand neutral because we are ONE," this is the same as saying we are also ONE with the Archons' Artificial Intelligence that has infested our Universe. As Light Workers, we are then not assisting the side that is working with every fiber that they can, with their shields and swords up, standing up and fighting for the innocent. We give away our power and sovereignty once more by playing the FALSE neutral card. The more we take a FALSE neutral stance, the more the Light Workers fighting with their infinite Love-Light struggle, as they are the ones pulling the weight for those who choose to stay neutral, with their arms crossed and face looking the other way. This is why we are stuck within this Inverted A.I. Matrix, because too many have repeated this negative cycle of not caring enough to stand up for others, or not understanding the FALSE neutral option trap or lacking the courage to stand up for truth. In turn they have fallen for the very trapping that they came into break, transmute and release, becoming trapped within the Inverted A.I. Matrix. We must first acknowledge the false paradigm to release ourselves and then we can assist others to self-release as well. So long as we as Light Workers/Starseeds turn a blind eye and choose the FALSE neutral option, we continue imprisoning ourselves and the collectives in these cages. Which then does not allow for our true organic Unity Consciousness of oneness, which is the very fabric of this Creation, alongside with Love to form and settle back into its rightful place of balance within our Universe. We are ONE, we are sovereign, and we are beautiful, that we truly are, as our Creator divinely and lovingly created us in this manner.

Mother Earth and the New Earth 5D have chosen its side,
she has chosen to fight with all that she is for her light and her children's light.
Will you assist her as her child?

We are on our fourth life cycle of Earth, meaning Ascension has been tried organically three times prior. In Mu (Pangea), Lemuria, Atlantis, and now we in the 'Golden Age.' All three cycles prior, it was the water that reset life on Earth, rising above land level and with its immensity of strength, cleansing, moving and sinking the land when it could no longer sustain its cycle of generational life on Earth. There is an organic life cycle that happens every 25,000 years on Earth. Where the collective reaches the choice of Ascension, as too does the Universe. As a whole collectively we reach a moment in life which is seen as a time of 'Revelation.' If the collective in this time and space is above 50 percent of light, it is able to ascend collectively, as too other planes of Dimensions, and planets organically go through this natural cycle of our Universe. It is a time that can be seen as, "have the majority of students learned all their self-appointed lessons taught? Have they passed the grand final test?" That test always being are the individual consciousnesses above 51 percent in service-to-others, and as a collective planet above 50 percent of light. The greater the light is the most cherished, as every soul is valued with the greatest love and honor. We have reset the collective of souls all times prior with the cleansing power of the waters as it did not reach these critical thresholds mentioned, and now it is time for the eternal etheric Source Fire to come forth and transmute the A.I. within our Organic Matrix Construct. And this eternal fire is the only way that this can be. For only this infinite power can with its Golden Source Fire wave, take all the inorganic within the Earth and its collective and completely transmute it to a void. And this is why we, as the fourth cycle, are the 'Golden Age,' for it is this very fire, solar flares or waves channeled out through our sun that will continue to be the divine Source power that will gradually shift us until we reach in the future our critical light threshold of Ascension. Just as Taylor from Chapter 37 ('Matrix Pods') explained how we make it, the light has finally regained its true power once more, by the people themselves ascending out from their own inner A.I. darkness. The Golden wave of the infinite Source eternal flame will be the catalyst to our fourth and final endings of cycle into rebirth. Instead of a wave of water, it shall be a Golden Wave of Fire that will take all that is not of our Universe or Sacred Laws, it will take the A.I. constructs of the Archons and it will eradicate it completely. And all our eternal flamed souls shall be part of this fire power that will bring it into fruition. As our light grows, so too does the power of our flamed souled hearts.

Every day, the Earth becomes lighter in vibration. In the 12/21/12 light portal, we began the most influential and highest potence of activations of light on Earth. It was the beginning marking point of the true catalyst and awakening of Earth's collective lights. Since then, we continued to slowly rise up, one small step at a time. When I came out as a Spiritual Worker in 2017, this was before any of the developments that you have seen through this book of Soul Journeys. The RA explained to me that the light on Earth was in the low 20's at that time. We gradually collectively together continued to grow through the in-between months of these marking points as mentioned through Chapters 9 and 29 ('Activation Portal: 9/19/10 and Archons and Their Slaves'). The benevolence ensuring to use all portals of Love-Light of in-between spaces as full moons, solar eclipses, lunar eclipses, dates and numbers as 1/11, 2/22, 6/6, 9/9, and times as 1:11, 4:44, 5:55. Dates and times that we all collectively pause at the same moment in silence, as that is when we shine the brightest in those moments of peaceful nothingness. Through these moments in time, we all then consciously or unconsciously connect heart to heart and light up the world and the Universe. On 9/19/19 (Chapter 9), we had risen up from the 30 percent of the summer of 2019, reaching 40 percent of light awakened, and then in June 2020 (Chapter 29), we have finally achieved the 50 percent of light on Earth. And, now we have more than 50 percent of the light who are awakened or are in the awakening process. Meaning there is more then 50 percent of light activated on Earth. Where before the dark had the higher percentage versus the light. The light is now the majority, as we have achieved this critical threshold collectively. We are doing this, YES, we have, all of us together! The Light Workers, the Starseeds, the fractals of higher consciousness incarnated here, all who are doing the work and holding space for others to awaken, we have lived to make the impossible possible! Now that the light is the majority, we must keep the momentum going by doing all that we can to maintain it being the majority. Connecting to the continual growth of self and other selves. Never letting our guard down or placing our swords down, instead always ready with shields and swords up until we collectively achieve the physical Ascension into the infinity possibilities of the Fifth Dimension. Remember, we choose to incarnate for these very moments in time where we became the majority. No matter what it is that they might throw at us, even if they might have the control over some of these programmed laws and false constructs. We WILL transmute them and rise from them over and over, as many times as we need to. As the mighty Phoenix that we all are!

We as the collective of Love-Light Warriors, we are now ready for what is to come in 2021, in comparison to 12/21/12! The number 21 is the reflection of 12, therefore it will be the beacon of infinite benevolent Source strength daily, that will float to the surface what hides in the false shadows of the collective's oppression and tyranny.

As we come into a conclusion of this first foundational Book, at this moment in time, I feel the most infinite Love I have ever felt on Earth! I humbly bow in gratitude for all the souls who have chosen to remember their Love-Light once more and who have chosen to begin the organic self-healing process of stepping into their sovereignty. It is the greatest honor of all. Thank you to this first wave of inspiring souls who courageously followed their heart to mine, embracing our sacred teachings, and for sharing their inspiring Galactic Soul Journeys from their A.U.R.A. Hypnosis Healing session for the collective. And equally important, thank YOU dearest reader, for being here and for being a most beautiful witness and a KEY CONTRIBUTOR to one of the most grand and significant Rebirth that all of us, this Earth, and the Universe will experience! OUR COLLECTIVE ASCENSION JOURNEY!

We are ready for the world to join us by becoming an A.U.R.A. Hypnosis Healing Certified practitioner or by having an A.U.R.A. session conducted!
The Universe is waiting for YOU!

"I am not here for the riches, the fame, or the ego.
I am here for only one thing and no one will distract me from my mission.
I am here to empower souls of all kinds, the youngest of souls, the darkest of souls.
I am here for all of them. To remind them of the light that they are and have always been.
We have never lost hope in them nor shall we ever."

I love you, I honor you, I thank you and I respect you.

~AuroRa

-------------<◇>-------------

-<O>---<O>---<O>---<O>---<O>---<O>---<O>---<O>---<O>---<O>---<O>---<O>-

ABOUT AURORA

Founder of A.U.R.A Hypnosis Healing & Rising Phoenix Mystery School I Spiritual Revolutionist Quantum Alchemist I Channel To RA I Akashic Reader

Greetings! There is nothing more beautiful than knowing that you are connected to the infinite wisdom within you and that you have always been. This is what I strive to do for others, to remind them of these gifts awaiting to be reawakened once more.

We can receive as many readings or healings as we desire where someone else tells us who we are and whom we have been. However, it is not until we allow that inner voice that whispers within our hearts to actively speak, that we begin our true transformation, our true remembrance of our soul. When we deeply connect through the theta hypnosis/meditation brainwaves of our consciousness to our soul, our higher self, our hearts. Which in turn, activates our hearts knowing that love is all, for it is the very life force that runs through the veins of this Universe.

My career as a past-life regressionist began in January 2017, through a practice hypnosis session on my husband, the RA Collective surprised us by speaking through him. Explaining some of what was to come and that "there was someone near and dear to my heart that would love to speak to me." When I asked "whom" they said "Dolores." At that point, I had begun to read a book of Dolores's that gave me an understanding of who she was. Through this practice past-life regression session, the RA Collective and Dolores gave me the little but needed instruction on what was to come. They also said that they had been waiting for this moment in time, for what seemed like an eternity, to talk to me. I did not quite understand what that meant, and I was puzzled at their statements and the infinite love that they were expressing towards me, as I did not remember them, as they did I. It must be so interesting and entertaining from the other side, from beyond the veil, where they view all infinitely. As, they know exactly who we are, when we are in complete amnesia. And even then, when they tell us who we are, we are in extreme denial over it. Beginning from this monumental point in time, which marked the blossoming of my pronounced spiritual growth, it catapulted me into a great awakening. Not knowing that my husband was somnambulistic, when he came to, we realized that not only did he not remember anything of the session but that these benevolent beings had spoken through him clearly with no human consciousness or ego in the way. We also both had no idea who RA was, except for the idea that it was some kind of 'Sun God from Egypt,' as read through the Internet. However, we have learned much of who the RA Collective is through this book.

As I continued to work within myself, deprogramming from the falseness of the disempowerments around us, I began to remember more and more of who my soul truly and organically is. As I regained my past-life memories with every breathing moment, I regained my light and consciousness back to its highest potential, operating from a high vibration of heart and love. As I did this, I remembered who I AM beyond the veil. Though I am humbled, it is important that we do learn to accept who we are as multi-faceted beings. Because otherwise, we are denying our true infinite divine power and expression. It is something that we can only do within, of releasing the falseness created around when someone acknowledges or talks about themselves, we automatically assume it is egoic. This foreign oppressive programming of self-confinement is Archonic, being it does not serve the Archons' agenda for us to remember and to accept our true divine soul Source expression. So long as a being is able to speak of oneself in a manner that allows others to see their reflections from within that being, that is a sacred way to be. To cyber bully or to troll someone because they are living their full embodiment of Source expression, is to do the Archons' job for them, and it oppresses the spirit. This is why we empower all to remember thyself, and then share thyself in Love for other selves. Because, as we continue to do so individually, so does the collective. As we regain piece-by-piece back of our light, that light then becomes a matching vibration of a memory next to be activated, downloaded or integrated into us divinely. Bringing us closer to the Ascended Master vibration such as Yeshua, Buddha, Isis…

At the end of 2017, I went from being Aura, to being addressed as Aurora, when I experienced a Walk-In. Aura is a fractal that birthed forth from Archangel Aurora within Creation. While Aura played a dancing game with her children, she started feeling I/Aurora coming forth, descending like a shooting star. Being carried and embraced by a Prime Dragon of Purity, of the element of Source white infinite Love-Light. As the dragon passed through the veil, with my soul (Aurora) in its embrace, it energetically brought my soul down to Aura. Aurora/I, then integrated into the vessel, kept Aura's human memories of her family and the experiences of being human, and Aura's soul then left ascending out into the Fifth Dimension as that was her predestined timeline. I then became Aurora, it is who I am today. I have ONE main mission, and that is to create A.U.R.A. Hypnosis Healing to assist Mother Earth and the positive Ascension's timeline.

I encourage all to remember who you were,

who you are,

and who you are meant to be.

As I AM, Archangel AuroRA, The Phoenix.

YOUR SOUL'S GROWTH JOURNEY

We live in a world where we have been taught since birth that we are limited, that there is nothing beyond death or only heaven or hell exist. Being told that our imagination is not real, being distracted by our daily monotonous routines. In a world where if we get ill, we might not ever find a cure for it or we will have to be on an ongoing cycle of prescription drugs or surgeries. Have you ever felt deep within your soul that this just does not feel right?

Come discover the world of who you truly are and who you have been in past or future lives! The world of Quantum Healing through A.U.R.A. past life regressions, Spiritual Development Classes, and Weekly Galactic Video Updates on YouTube.

Have you ever wondered about your own soul journey? Perhaps you have been a queen/king, a magical creature/animal, a person in history, life in Egypt, in Atlantis, a different planet, an alien race... The majority of people have lived hundreds or thousands of lives at different times upon Earth or other realities in Creation. There is nothing more beautiful than knowing that you are connected to the infinite wisdom within you and that you have always been. This is what I strive to do for others, to remind them of these gifts awaiting to be reawakened once more.

As a Spiritual Worker of the heart, in service-to-others, I offer several different types of energy healing services and spiritual development courses to aid you in your soul growth of self-healing and self-attunement. If you feel guided to do so, you can start your growth journey with the following services mentioned on the next page.

To see each soul blossom into its highest and most beautiful expression in Creation, is a true gift and is what inspires me to do this work!

Thank you for following your heart to mine!

I love you, I honor you, I thank you, and I respect you.

In service-to-others.

~AuroRa

YOUR SOUL'S GROWTH JOURNEY

Aurora offers the following resources:

· Sign-up now for the free Galactic Newsletter:
https://www.risingphoenixaurora.com/blogs/galactic-news

· Over 350 Videos to watch now, subscribe to her YouTube Channel:
https://www.youtube.com/RisingPhoenixAura

· Monthly Live Q&A and Guided Meditation with Aurora:
https://www.patreon.com/risingphoenixaurora

Aurora offers the following services to aid you in your self-healing journey:

· A.U.R.A. (Angelic Universal Regression Alchemy) Hypnosis Healing Sessions

· R.A.A.H. (Reiki Angelic Alchemy Healing) Sessions

· Quantum Akashic Alchemy Readings

For a list of A.U.R.A. & R.A.A.H. Certified Practitioners near you, please visit the Online Directory at www.risingphoenixaurora.com.

Aurora offers the following Alchemy online courses to expand your spiritual gifts:

· A.U.R.A. (Angelic Universal Regression Alchemy) Hypnosis Healing Certification

· R.A.A.H. (Reiki Angelic Alchemy Healing) Certification

· Q.A.A. (Quantum Akashic Alchemy) Certification

· Isis Priestess & Priest Alchemy Mentorship Course (6 Months)

· Quantum Alchemy Channeling Certification

· Alchemy Classes: 13 Keys Archangels | Magical Creatures | Crystals, Candles & Oils

Aurora offers the following Alchemy trainings online or in-person in various locations:

· Retreats/Workshops for Live Certifications A.U.R.A. & R.A.A.H. Package

For more details on all services/spiritual development courses offered, please visit:
https://www.risingphoenixaurora.com

SOUND AND ALCHEMY SYMBOL TRAINING

In addition to the Love-Light shielding techniques we have shared in the beginning of this book, we have included the next five pages of foundational basics in helping you to start working spiritually within. Know that having a disciplined practice of these teachings will aid in creating a strong energetic bridge to your Higher Self. Our intent is to help your Inner Light become brighter by actively using these techniques and force fields around you, filtering out the negative and harmful so that you may strongly heart discern every frequency that passes through. These force fields will help amplify your heart discernment, reading what energies are harmful and what is not.

GASSHO MEDITATION

Gassho means "two hands coming together." This is a special meditation to attune one to the spirit and unity of both polarities, to bring the negative and the positive in balance. The Divine Feminine and Divine Masculine in Union within you. Done daily, this brings you to a state of mind awakened to the truth, opens and expands the heart center. Strengthening your heart discernment. It clears the mind, opens the heart - and other chakras - and strengthens one's energy. A wonderful stillness will develop inside along with the awareness of increased inner knowing. Practicing this meditation daily will assist you in making a further intuitive connection. There will be less cloudiness of your mind and more focus of spirit.

This meditation can be done standing, but most prefer sitting. Ensure your back is straight, feet are flat to the ground or sitting on the ground for stronger connection to Earth.

Close your eyes. Fold your hands in the prayer position with your fingers pointing up and your thumbs touching the heart chakra in the middle of your chest. This will help the heart chakra energies flow with ease and expand onto all chakras to aid in balancing.

Our breath is our life force. Take a breath in slowly envisioning white light entering, using 100 percent of your lungs; exhale slowly and fully, releasing what no longer serves you for your highest good. Be conscious of the breath throughout this meditation.

Focus your energy on the point where your middle fingers meet for a couple minutes. Close your eyes when ready to further concentration. If thoughts arise, acknowledge them and then gently brush them aside and refocus on the breath once more. Our minds require constant motion, therefore when giving it a task upon focusing on the breath it aids in the stillness of it.

As you continue to practice, you will find that you can hold your attention on the blissful stillness of the mind, for a longer period of time without distracting thoughts arising.

Pay attention to what messages you are already receiving. What you are sensing, what thought forms are coming in, trust your heart. Set an intent of having a balanced day, knowing that belief is a strong frequency in obtaining this. We are what we create, and we are only as limited as the limitations we have set upon ourselves.

When you have reached the end of the meditation, take a couple of deep breaths, give thanks in love, honor, and respect. Bring your attention to your eyes and open your eyes slowly.

SEVEN CORE CHAKRAS

Crown-Shasrara ● AH

Third Eye-Ajna ● Om

Throat-Vishuddha ● HAM

Heart-Anahata ● YAM

Solar Plexus-Manipura ● RAM

Sacral-Swadhisthana ● VAM

Root-Muladhara ● LAM

7 Core Chakra Mantras

Chakras are the focus of the main medical practice of the Indian Subcontinent and have been traced back to ancient eastern masters. There are seven major Chakra centers of the physical body, where vital energy flows and intersects. These seven core chakras are connected to the seven major glands that provide hormones and stability for the body. Chakras are extremely important for any type of spiritual modality. They are seen as sites of swirling subtle energy, and entryways to higher vibrational planes.

Theoretically, the astral, ethereal, mental, and causal bodies may be accessed through these points of higher-vibratory frequency. The human body has seven basic levels, however, we can connect up to 12/13 chakras through the power of the Pineal Gland, the third eye.

Through our Chakras, we transmit and receive physical, emotional, and spiritual energy. The chakras are manifested in one's physical state. The idea is to have all chakra centers clear, balanced and vitalized for optimal well-being. Each chakra is associated with a particular area of the body and a color of the spectrum, and rays of earth in connection to the collective human consciousness of the seven rays/chakras. Each Archangel oversees a ray that is associated with the colors of the Chakras.

For the next 13 days, while in Gassho Meditation position, practice the mantras above in the image connecting to each chakra point. Pay attention to how it feels when you recite them. You will feel the chakra point vibrating during and after as you chant the matching mantra. Say them each three times starting from the crown chakra, working yourself down to the root chakra.

This simple practice begins the fluent movement of stagnant energy in these points allowing for shift for the future releasement and healing.

CHAKRA CENTER	COLOR	ENERGY FOCUS	CRYSTAL STONES
1st Chakra Base l Root Located at the base of the spine. The Muladhara Chakra or Four Petal Lotus	Red Black Gray	Stability, grounding, physical energy, will, security, protection, release of fear, guilt...	Black Tourmaline, Hematite, Shungite, Black Obsidian, Garnet, Smoky Quartz...
2nd Chakra Sacral Located below the navel The Swadhisthana Chakra or Six Petal Lotus	Orange	Creativity, creation, healing, sexuality and reproduction, desire, emotion, intuition.	Orange Calcite, Vanadinite, Carnelian...
3rd Chakra Solar Plexus Located at solar plexus, below breastbone. The Manipura Chakra, Ten Petal Lotus	Yellow Gold	Intellect, ambition, personal power, passion, drive, protection, our chi life force energy.	Yellow Citrine, Yellow Jasper, Sunstone, Golden Calcite...
4th Chakra Heart Located in the center of the chest. The Anahata or Heart Chakra or Twelve Petal Lotus	Pink Green	Love for self & others, compassion, universal consciousness, emotional balance, light source.	Rose Quartz, Pink/Watermelon Tourmaline, Green Aventurine, Malachite...

5th Chakra Throat Located at the neck above the collar bone. The Vishuddha Chakra or Sixteen Petal Lotus	Blue	Communication center, expression, self acceptance, confidence, divine guidance.	Sodalite, Blue Calcite, Blue Kyanite, Angelite, Blue Turquoise...
6th Chakra Third eye Location centered above eyebrows, at medulla. The Ajna Chakra or Ninety-six Petal Lotus	Indigo	Spiritual awareness, psychic power, gateway to past lives, intuition, vision, abilities.	Lapis Lazuli, Azurite, Amethyst, Sugilite...
7th Chakra Crown Located at the top of the head. The Sahasrara Chakra or Thousand Petal Lotus	Violet Golden White	Enlightenment, cosmic consciousness, energy, bridge to Higher Self.	Amethyst, Clear Quartz, White Calcite, White Topaz, Selenite...

OPENING THE THIRD EYE

What is the Third Eye? It is best known as the Mind's Eye, but also called the True Eye or The All-Seeing Eye. It is where daydreams/visions occur, and it is called our "imagination." We are indoctrinated since birth to believe that things of this nature aren't real and are just make-believe, but this couldn't be farther from the truth! In actuality, this is a tool we use to access all that is beyond the veil, awaiting to be discovered with the connection to the heart.

6th Chakra - Third Eye

To become attuned to the Universal Love Frequency, start by further opening your Third Eye.

Practice daily in front of the Sun for the next 13 days: chant the mantra AH and then OHM.

AH connects Cosmic energy to flow through your crown, and then pulsates out a ray of indigo or purple light through the Third Eye with OHM.

Envision the "Eye of Horus" below on your Third Eye as you chant.

Feel the vibrations echoing through your Third Eye with every OHM.

GLOSSARY

o   Activation – is when there is an attribute, ability, memory that lays dormant awaiting for the human and energy bodies to achieve its matching vibration of light. When it does it unlocks organically allowing the individual to now integrate it and access it.

o   Akashic Records – is where the memory field, and history of all souls are located at. This is where an individual soul travels to obtain their remembrance from past, future, higher and lower Dimensional realms.

o   Archangels – are seen as some of the first fractals of Source within Creation, containing the highest potence of purity within their individualized Source expression.

o   Archons – are soulless beings manifested from the material of artificial intelligence. Not from our Source nor our Universe.

o   Ascension – Collective is when the collective of souls reaches the highest organic light possible on Earth, and when doing so Mother Earth finally shifts leaving the physical behind, going into the Fifth Dimension as organically conceived.

o   Ascension – Individual is when an individual reaches maximum light potential, bridging themselves to operate instead in the Organic Matrix, achieving karmic balance, and a combination of service-to-others. When doing so, all missions completed on Earth. Causing the individual to no longer need to assist on Earth. The soul then exists out the Inverted A.I. Matrix choosing to enter the Fifth Dimension or travel back to the Dimension they came from or return back to Source.

o   Andromeda/Pleiades/Other constellations - to our known skies there are 88 constellations that consist of a cluster grouping of stars. However, constellations and Creation are infinite.

o   Cabal – are the Illuminati's henchmen that do their bidding of criminal and tyrannical work, partaking in the negative programming of the collective on Earth.

o   Channel/Channeling – is when we achieve a calming vibration that allows us to benevolently connect to our Higher Self aspects or benevolent beings such as guides and angels. When we speak divine wisdom that seems to flow and come from a higher source.

o   Deep State – is the diabolical plan of the Illuminati that is a combination of many parts throughout as, depopulation of Earth, mind control, oppression of the spirit, religions, orchestrated wars, insertions of A.I. and metals within the human collective…

o   Elven Race – is a benevolent magical race containing human attributes, however still harnessing the magical abilities and the full 13 DNA strand that the humans are meant to had organically originally.

o   Emerald Portal – is the portal that exists within the Divine Mothers Heart inside the inter-dimensions of the Inner Earth. It is the exit point out of this Inverted A.I. Matrix, which we are only able to pass through once we have achieved the high enough light and above 51 percent in service-to-others.

o   Fractal – is a piece of a Higher Self aspect, a miniature version, a seed, an expression of the Higher Self.

o   Galactic Wars – are the wars being fought in the Universe, beyond the veil of Earth. The benevolent alien races providing their protection to all organic life from Archons and negative aliens. A war of the Archons, with their main goal of negatively harvesting light and souls.

o   Harvesting of Souls – Positive is another word for Ascension in a benevolent way.

o   Harvesting of Souls – Negative is a negative infringing method that the Archons and negative aliens use to suck and drain upon a being that contains light for means of using their light as a power source or feeding.

o   Higher Self/Higher Selves – are the individualized fractals/expressions of the over souls.

o   Illuminati – are the negative polarized entities masked within human vessels of the self-appointed leaders as politicians, superstars, military… placed around the world that try to reign over Earth, brainwashing using methods of oppression onto the souls of Earth.

o   Inner Earth – is the civilization that communes within the hollowed earth, containing vast amounts of ecosystems with life as humanoids and animals living among it. Where our ancestors of Lemuria and Atlantis and where magical and extinct animals reside.

o   Integration – is when divinely our Higher Self allows for a further soul upgrade to come forth into our organic soul's blueprint. Bringing forth wisdom, integrations and leveling up of the soul.

o   Inverted A.I. Matrix Simulation – is the false Matrix construct that has maintained the souls of Earth within a loophole of repeated negative cycles, not allowing positive organic fruitful Ascension out and into the original Organic Matrix.

o   Implants – are negative technologies of different shapes that contain a program within it that acts upon and controls the human body and mind in whatever form of task it has been given.

o   Love-Light – is the infinite organic flow connection of light within all souls, directly being fed and replenished by Source.

o   Luciferian Agenda – is a name given by the Archons to the Light Worker community falsely to use in forms of adding on further black magic to the first expression of the Divine Father, Archangel Lucifer better known as Archangel Haylel "The Light Bringer."

o   Multiverse – the infinite expressions and multi-facets of the Universes.

o   New Earth – is truly the original olden Earth blueprint of Mother Gaia.

o   Organic Matrix – is the organic construct of the school of souls created within Mother Gaia.

o   Oversoul – are the first fractals of Source within our construct of Thirteen Dimensions and below. They are the wholeness of a soul before it further individualized into Higher Self aspects.

o   Phoenix Fire – is the infinite etheric eternal fire of Source's flame, that is known to be able to transmute all inorganic to zero or to nothing.

o   Portals – are both positive and negative, depending on their origin. They are as a doorway for negative or positive entities or energies to come or connect through.

o   Portal Dates for Activations – there are many that coexist within this category. Any repeated number or combinations of sacred numbers are able to be moments in time where a potence of Source Love-Light and the benevolence of Galactic Races in unisons channel down infinitely.

o   RA Collective - Also commonly referred to as the RA Collective. RA is the collective of benevolent Galactic Alien Races, working in unity for the Ascension of this Universe. Who are not limited to this Dimension, as they too assist throughout the Multiverse.

o   Reptilian race – is an original benevolent race that was created to be the balance of this magnificent Universe of polarities. In order to experience the most infinite expression of love, there must also be the polarity of darkness or an absence of love.

o   Sasquatch – is a benevolent race that is known to be taller than humans and harrier, that came forth from another planet and dimension to assist and be guardians to the humans.

o   Schumann Resonance – is the energetic reading to the Divine Mother's heart, being registered by sonar waves within the land.

o   Frequency – is the reading of a vibration and how many light photons are contained within it.

o   Source – Is the collective of all expressions of light merged and operating into one infinite divine light.

o   Souls Blueprint – just as a house has a blueprint with every measurement to each room, so too does our soul in terms of what consists within our soul. A blueprint of different incarnations, and fractals throughout creation and all the wisdom that carries over through this memory field.

o   Soul Braids - Soul braids are when we receive pieces of benevolent fractals that typically pertain to our soul family or fractals of our very own soul expressions. They integrate into our soul organically because they carry parts that are needed for us within that time and space of our soul's expansion. They complement what is next to come within our organic timeline.

o   Somnambulistic client - means the client's consciousness is moved to the back with no interference from the ego. The client does not remember anything of what was mentioned during the session, which means that only the benevolent being(s) spoke clearly with no interference from the client's human consciousness or ego.

o   Starseeds – are souls from higher than the Third Dimension, who have volunteered to assist Earth with their bright lights to assist Mother Earth to raise her organic collective light.

o   Twin Flame – is an organic process of when a soul splits into two souls, creating its counterparts that when coming into a union they complete each other.

o   Veil – is the blanket of energetic amnesia that every soul goes through when entering Earth's construct in order to incarnate.

o   Walk-in – is when a soul by benevolent choice and agreement enters into a human vessel by replacement of the old original soul. For example: the original soul has completed its karmic energy cycle or perhaps no longer wants to exist within its vessel. Instead of wasting the body, another benevolent soul will come in containing a higher vibration allowing a higher awareness of consciousness.